Essays on the History of Mora.

Essays on the History of Moral Philosophy

J. B. Schneewind

OXFORD
UNIVERSITY PRESS

OXFORD
UNIVERSITY PRESS

Great Clarendon Street,
Oxford OX2 6DP

Oxford University Press is a department of the University of Oxford.
It furthers the University's objective of excellence in research, scholarship,
and education by publishing worldwide in

Oxford New York

Auckland Cape Town Dar es Salaam Hong Kong Karachi
Kuala Lumpur Madrid Melbourne Mexico City Nairobi
New Delhi Shanghai Taipei Toronto

With offices in

Argentina Austria Brazil Chile Czech Republic France Greece
Guatemala Hungary Italy Japan Poland Portugal Singapore
South Korea Switzerland Thailand Turkey Ukraine Vietnam

Oxford is a registered trade mark of Oxford University Press
in the UK and in certain other countries

Published in the United States
by Oxford University Press Inc., New York

British Library Cataloguing in Publication Data

Data available

Library of Congress Cataloging in Publication Data

Library of Congress Control Number 2009938547

Typeset by SPI Publisher Services, Pondicherry, India
Printed in Great Britain
on acid-free paper by
CPI Antony Rowe, Chippenham, Wiltshire

ISBN 978–0–19–956301–2 (Hbk.)
      978–0–19–957667–8 (Pbk.)

1 3 5 7 9 10 8 6 4 2

For the Rortys and the Coopers

Contents

Foreword   ix
Acknowledgments   xvi

Part I Theory

  1. Moral Knowledge and Moral Principles   3

Part II Victorian Matters

  2. First Principles and Common-Sense Morality
     in Sidgwick's Ethics   21
  3. Moral Problems and Moral Philosophy
     in the Victorian Period   42

Part III On the Historiography of Moral Philosophy

  4. Moral Crisis and the History of Ethics   65
  5. Modern Moral Philosophy: From Beginning to End?   84
  6. No Discipline, No History: The Case of Moral Philosophy   107
  7. Teaching the History of Moral Philosophy   127

Part IV Seventeenth- and Eighteenth-Century
          Moral Philosophy

  8. The Divine Corporation and the History of Ethics   149
  9. Natural Law   170
 10. The Misfortunes of Virtue   176
 11. Voluntarism and the Foundations of Ethics   202
 12. Hume and the Religious Significance of Moral Rationalism   222

Part V On Kant

13. Why Study Kant's *Groundwork*?   239

14. Autonomy, Obligation, and Virtue: An Overview of
    Kant's Moral Philosophy   248

15. Kant and Stoic Ethics   277

16. Toward Enlightenment: Kant and the Sources of Darkness   296

17. Kantian Unsocial Sociability: Good Out of Evil   319

Part VI Moral Psychology

18. The Active Powers   343

Part VII Afterword

19. Sixty Years of Philosophy in a Life   405

J. B. Schneewind: Bibliography   425
Name Index   433
Subject Index   438

Foreword

The essays assembled in this volume were published between 1963 and 2009. Except for the first essay and the last, they are about the history of moral philosophy and moral psychology.

The last essay is autobiographical. It was written in response to an invitation from the Eastern Division of the American Philosophical Association to give a Dewey Lecture. In it, I say a little about how I approach the history of moral philosophy and why I go about it as I do. I also suggest how I came to have these views. In accordance with the terms of the invitation, the lecture is as much about changes in professional philosophy during my career as it is about my opinions on history and historiography. Still, it gives the contexts in which I wrote the other essays included here.

In the first essay, I criticize what I take to be, or to have been, a widely accepted model of reasoning about moral issues. We can give reasons, on this kind of view, only by showing that a particular judgment is warranted by a general moral principle; and that principle must itself be justifiable. Two questions arise: First, how can an infinite regress of justifying principles be avoided? The standard answer is that there must be at least one general principle that is justified without being dependent for its warrant on any other principle. It must be self-evident. Second, what features must this self-evident principle have? Plainly it must be general in a strong sense: applicable to any particular case where moral guidance is needed. And when it is applied to specific circumstances it must be capable of giving *conclusive* reason for the particular judgment that purports to give the needed guidance. This means that the principle must either specify all its own limits and exceptions, or else have no limits or exceptions. Otherwise there would remain a doubt: the particular judgment might be an exception. On this view, then, a self-evident exceptionless universal principle must be at the foundation of all moral reasoning.

During my first years of teaching, I read Charles Peirce's early essays "Questions concerning certain faculties claimed for man" and "Some further consequences of four incapacities."[1] I found Peirce's attack on intuitional foundations for any sort of knowledge quite convincing. In the work of J. L. Austin and of John Dewey, I found further reasons for rejecting the search for foundational principles. The essay that opens this volume is the result.

Intuitionism was on my mind because I had done a substantial amount of work on Sidgwick. In the second essay reprinted here, I argue that his *Methods of Ethics* presents a classical instance of foundationalist ethics. Rejecting earlier efforts by Gay, Paley, Bentham, and John Stuart Mill to support utilitarianism, Sidgwick offers an orignal two-step argument. First he tries to show that rules or principles less general than the utilitarian principle all have exceptions or limits. The rules accepted by common-sense morality are of this character. The gaps in common-sense principles cannot be fully specified. Hence no common-sense principle can give a conclusive reason for any particular judgment. Any such judgment might be one of the unspecified exceptions. If we are to have conclusive reasons for particular judgments, there must be some wholly universal, exceptionless principle. Less general principles will depend on this principle, Sidgwick says, for their validity. But the most general principle cannot in the same way depend on anything. It must be self-evident. I call this the dependence argument.

Sidgwick then argues that the utilitarian principle serves to systematize our common-sense principles. It shows how they fit together and it gives us a method for answering questions they leave open. I call this the systematization argument. If there must be a universal self-evident principle, as the dependence argument claims, then the systematization argument shows the utilitarian principle to be capable of doing what is needed. Unfortunately, the principle of moral egoism is like the utilitarian principle in these respects. It is self-evident, Sidgwick thinks, and can also systematize common-sense morality. Sidgwick concludes in some despair that common-sense morality is incoherent unless there is a deity who can make self-interest and concern for the common good coincide; but he sees no way of proving such a premiss. This essay sketches the major argumentative points in *The Methods of Ethics*. It therefore gives an outline

---

[1] Available in Peirce's *Collected Papers*, vol. 5 and in *The Essential Peirce*, ed. Nathan Houser and Christian Kloesel (Indiana, IN: Indiana University Press, 1992), vol. I.

of the part of my *Sidgwick's Ethics and Victorian Moral Philosophy* commenting on that book.

In trying to understand Sidgwick I came to ask about the relations between moral philosophy and the societies or cultures in which it is created. This in turn led me to study Victorian intellectual, social, and religious history. Literature, particularly novels, seemed to be a rich source of insights into cultural tensions and problems. The more I read of Victorian fiction the more it seemed to me that some of it was being used to express general moral outlooks. Of course fiction did this in different ways from those used in moral philosophy. But I thought that certain themes in Victorian fiction could helpfully be discussed in terms of the controversies between intuitionism and utilitarianism to which Sidgwick gave so much attention. Histories of literature, however, paid no attention to such philosophical debates. In the third essay, I try to show how some patterns of intuitional ethics are displayed in the lives and actions of characters in novels by Charlotte Yonge, Mrs Gaskell, William Hale White, and George Eliot. I am not attributing influence nor am I "reducing" the novels to philosophy. I argue that both philosophers and novelists are articulating aspects of our common moral life and that the philosophers provide a useful approach to the fiction. We enrich our understanding of the novels' protagonists and what they do when we see them in the light of the major controversy in Victorian moral philosophy.

When I had done what I could with nineteenth-century British moral philosophy, I considered—briefly—turning to continental work on the subject from the nineteenth and early twentieth centuries. But I found the post-Kantian idealists dauntingly difficult. And I was put off by the thought of needing to plough through the many lengthy texts on ethics turned out by German professors like Herbart, Lotze, and Nicolai Hartmann. I looked at some of them and decided, perhaps mistakenly, that they were not likely to be as interesting as some of the similarly neglected British texts I had resurrected in the historical part of the book on Sidgwick. I decided instead to back up, and to try to find out what had led to the philosophical situation from which nineteenth-century moral philosophy began: the dominance of Bentham, Reid, and Kant. As I say in my autobiographical essay, I was decisively spurred on to this venture when I chanced upon Josef Schmucker's work on the origins of Kant's moral philosophy.

I first met Alasdair MacIntyre in the Fall of 1963. His remarkable *Short History of Ethics* was published in 1966; I reviewed it a couple of years later. We have been arguing back and forth since then, and much of my thinking about how to study the history of moral philosophy results from the invaluable stimulation our controversies have given me. In the fourth essay included here, I take on MacIntyre at some length, discussing his *After Virtue* and other work that came out after the *Short History*. In it I make use of ideas I developed as I worked on the history of pre-Kantian moral philosophy.

The fifth essay incorporates some of the new material I was learning about moral philosophy in the seventeenth and eighteenth centuries. MacIntyre was present at the conference at which this essay was presented, and we had some sharp and enjoyable exchanges. But the essay is not attempting specifically to controvert him. If any contemporary is a target, it is G. E. M. Anscombe, whose important essay "Modern Moral Philosophy" I discuss in more detail in the tenth essay.[2]

From 1988 until 2000 I served as President of the Board of Editors of the *Journal of the History of Ideas*. The sixth essay, published in 1997, responded to an invitation from the Editor, Donald Kelley, to contribute to a volume on writing the histories of various disciplines. In it I included some material I had just worked out for my *Invention of Autonomy*, which was published the following year.

These essays all, in one way or another, give overviews of early modern moral philosophy. The ideas proposed in them were often tried out for the first time in courses I was teaching, undergraduate as well as graduate, on the history of modern moral philosophy. When I began teaching the subject there were no available collections of original sources for classroom use. To remedy this lack I prepared an anthology, *Moral Philosophy from Montaigne to Kant*, published in 1990.

My interest in developing ways of teaching the history of modern moral philosophy came to a head in 2002–03, when I had the honor of being the Laurance S. Rockefeller Visiting Professor for Distinguished Teaching at Princeton University's Center for Human Values. One of the expectations for this professorship was that the incumbent would devote some time to

---

[2] First published in *Philosophy*, 33 (1958); reprinted in G. E. M. Anscombe, *Collected Philosophical Papers*, III, (Minnesota, MN: University of Minnesota Press, 1981), 26–42.

developing ideas about teaching. At my suggestion the Center supported a conference which brought together philosophers and historians who shared interests in developing new histories of modern philosophy. The participants all spoke about ways to teach histories of our subjects that would incorporate recent and ongoing innovative work. The Center published the papers from the conference, and sent the volume free of charge to all Philosophy Departments in the United States, and to anyone else who requested it. I cannot recall another conference devoted so intensively to teaching the history of philosophy; and I remain grateful to the Center and to Princeton University for their support of the venture.

The seventh essay here is my contribution to the conference. I note that the standard "history of modern philosophy" course is almost universally a history of metaphysics and epistemology. Students tend to take this course early in their college career. Its one-sided bias skews the way they understand the rest of philosophy. Some correction is much needed. I suggest ways of constructing a one-semester course on the history of modern moral philosophy that will be at least as adequate to the real complexities of that history as the usual "Descartes to Kant" course is to the development of its topics. An introductory history course that covered both ethics and metaphysics/epistemology would be ideal. But lacking that, I suggest that a history of ethics course could be used to satisfy the normal modern history requirement for philosophy majors.

The next set of essays represent some of the work I did as I explored early modern moral philosophy. Much of what I wrote during these ventures found its way more or less unaltered into *The Invention of Autonomy*, so I have omitted it. In the eighth piece I set out some ideas about the conceptual structure of natural-law theories of morality. Here Aquinas was the main source of my idea about natural law; I wrote the essay before I had studied Grotius and Pufendorf. In fact, it was my attempt to see whether my ideas were borne out by their work that led me to read them. I learned—not surprisingly—that my more or less Thomistic, and rather *a priori*, construal of natural-law theory was in many ways inadequate to the actual history of thought on the topic. But my scheme served to guide the beginnings of the research that led eventually to *The Invention of Autonomy*. And the structure I presented there still seems to me to be interesting in its own right.

Pufendorf, I learned, though unnoticed by Anglophone moral philosophers in the nineteenth and twentieth centuries, was a major figure in early modern moral philosophy. I published a long essay on him in 1987 and incorporated it into *Invention*. In its place I have included the ninth item here, a brief essay, "Natural Law", which sketches some of his main claims.

The tenth essay, "The Misfortunes of Virtue", was stimulated by remarks made frequently by philosophers who were actively resuscitating ethical theories centered on virtue. It seems to have been a commonplace of the revivalists—here in accordance with Anscombe—that the topic of virtue was quite neglected after Aristotle. I set out to show that this view was seriously mistaken. In the course of doing so I raise some questions for virtue's revivers.

In the eleventh article I outlined an understanding, new to me, of the importance for the development of modern moral philosophy of theories holding that God's will is the source of morality. The divine command theory, often labelled voluntarism, was forcefully propounded by Pufendorf, among others. It aroused fierce opposition, on religious as well as political and moral grounds. I argue that the major theories distinctive of modern moral philosophy arose out of this opposition. Voluntarism is thus a key to the history I trace in *Invention*.

The twelfth essay is a kind of afterword to the eleventh. It shows how Hume uses orthodox fear of voluntarism to force a dilemma on Christian moralists. They could resist voluntarism by accepting a rationalist view of morality. But then they could not easily show what need there is for revelation, or for ministers to explain it. If they reject rationalism to safeguard revelation and its expounders, they have no readily available ground for opposing voluntarism. Hume's criticisms of rationalist ethics thus reach beyond moral philosophy. They are part of his long-term critique of religious belief.

The next five essays reprinted here all concern Kant. I have never thought of myself as a Kant scholar. I do not know Kant's *Gesammelte Schriften* from beginning to end and inside out, as a Kant scholar does, nor have I read extensively in the vast body of Kant scholarship. But Kant's moral philosophy perplexed me at my first introduction to it and continues to do so even now. In the thirteenth essay I try to explain, as simply as I can, why the *Groundwork of the Metaphysics of Morals* is worth study despite its difficulty. One reason I give is that Kant's view is genuinely new in important ways; and I try to spell out what some of those ways are. In the next essay I offer the best understanding of Kant's ethics that I could arrive at. Some readers of *Invention* complained that I did not include something like it in that volume. The book, however, was overly long even without it; and it was not my aim there to defend, or even to offer, a synoptic interpretation of Kant's ethics.

In the fourteenth essay, "Kant and Stoic Ethics" I try to controvert some readings of Kant's moral philosophy that diminish its uniqueness. I argue that Kant does not ground his moral principle by showing that it brings about something of value. I resist the suggestion that his ethics is not a "deontology"—if that later term is useful at all. And I point out several important ways in which Kant's view differs importantly from Stoic ethics and moral psychology. Toward the end of the essay I make some methodological remarks. But I have generally avoided discussion of method. Discussion of it seems to me to be useful mainly when joined to historical work exemplifying one's favored way of proceeding.

Essays 16 and 17 are explorations of two specific Kantian views, which are only indirectly connected to his moral philosophy. Working on both of them led me, rather to my surprise, to a neglected aspect of Kant's moral psychology: his theory of the radical evil of human nature. In "Toward Enlightenment" I argue that radical evil is for Kant the source of our resistance to thinking for ourselves. It is thus the cause of the darkness which the enlighteners all worked so hard to dispel. Examining his famous thesis of unsocial sociability I came to the conclusion that radical evil, again, is for Kant the explanation of why it is that humans find it so difficult to get along with one another. A fuller look at radical evil in Kant's thought would, I suspect, reveal other places where it plays a role.

The eighteenth essay is a broad survey of a major set of issues in the moral psychology of early modern philosophy. Here Kant is only one of several important contributors to the discussion. The essay supplements similar material touched on much less fully in *Invention*. And I found it interesting to come back to Kant by a route other than that going through the development of modern moral philosophy.

Some of these essays provide good introductions to my two long books. I hope all of them are of sufficient interest to stand on their own.

Acknowledgments

I am grateful to Peter Momtchiloff of Oxford University Press for his warm welcome of my proposal for this volume and his guidance during its preparation. My thanks also to Mary Rorty for advice and encouragement concerning the project.

All the essays collected here have been previously published. I have not changed them, except for typographical corrections. I thank the original publishers and editors for their permission to reprint the essays, which appeared in the following publications:

"Moral Knowledge and Moral Principles", in *Knowledge and Necessity*, Royal Institute of Philosophy Lectures 1968–69, ed. G. N. A. Vesey (London: MacMillan 1970,) 249–62, reproduced with permission of Palgrave Macmillan.

"First Principles and Common Sense Morality in Sidgwick's Ethics", in *Archiv für Geschichte der Philosophie* (Berlin: Verlag Walter de Gruyter GmbH & Co. KG, 1963), 137–56.

"Moral Problems and Moral Philosophy in the Victorian Period", in *Victorian Studies*, Suppl. vol. 9, Sept. 1965, 29–46.

"Moral Crisis and the History of Ethics", in *Midwest Studies in Philosophy*, vol. VIII, eds. Peter E. French, Theodore E. Uehling, Jr, and Howard K. Wettstein, (Minneapolis: University of Minnesota Press, 1983), 525–39.

"Modern Moral Philosophy: from Beginning to End?" From *Philosophical Imagination and Cultural Memory*, ed., P. Cook, 83–103, (Durham, NC: Duke University Press, 1993). All rights reserved. Used by permission of the publisher.

"No Discipline, No History: the Case of Moral Philosophy", in *History and the Disciplines*, ed. Donald Kelley (Rochester, NY: University of Rochester Press, 1997), 127–42.

"Teaching the History of Moral Philosophy", in *Teaching New Histories of Philosophy*, ed. J. B. Schneewind, University Center for Human Values, (Princeton, NJ: Princeton University, 2004), 177–97.

"The Divine Corporation and the History of Ethics", in *Philosophy in History*, ed. Richard Rorty, J. B. Schneewind, Quentin Skinner (New York: Cambridge University Press, 1984), 175–91.

"Natural Law" by J. B. Schneewind, reprinted by permission of the publisher from *A New History of German Literature*, ed. David E. Wellbery, pp.325–9, (Cambridge, MA.: The Belknap Press of Harvard University Press, 2004), copyright © 2004, by the President and Fellows of Harvard College.

"The Misfortunes of Virtue", in *Ethics*, vol. 101. 1 (Oct. 1990), 42–63.

"Voluntarism and the Foundations of Ethics", in *Proceedings and Addresses of the American Philosophical Association*, vol. 70. 2, Nov. 1996, 25–41.

"Hume and the Religious Significance of Moral Rationalism", in *Hume Studies*, XXVI.2, Nov. 2000, 211–23.

"Why Study Kant's *Groundwork*?", in *Groundwork for the Metaphysics of Morals*, ed. and trans. Allen W. Wood. (New Haven, CT: Yale University Press, 2002), 83–91.

"Autonomy, Obligation and Virtue", in *Cambridge Companion to Kant*, ed. Paul Guyer (Cambridge: Cambridge University Press, 1992), 309–41.

"Kant and Stoic Ethics", in *Aristotle, Kant, and the Stoics*, ed. Stephen Engstrom and Jennifer Whiting (Cambridge: Cambridge University Press, 1996), 285–301.

"Toward Enlightenment", in *Cambridge Companion to Early Modern Philosophy*, ed. Donald Rutherford (Cambridge: Cambridge University Press, 2006), 328–51.

"Kant on Unsocial Sociability", in *Essays on Kant's 'Idea for a Universal History'*, ed. Amelie Rorty and James Schmidt (Cambridge: Cambridge University Press, 2008).

"The Active Powers", in *Cambridge History of Eighteenth Century Philosophy*. ed. Knud Haakonssen (Cambridge: Cambridge University Press, 2006), 2 vols, 557–607.

"Sixty Years of Philosophy in a Life", in *Proceedings and Addresses of the American Philosophical Association*, vol. 83 (2009).

PART I
Theory

1

Moral Knowledge and Moral Principles

What is the function of moral principles within the body of moral know-ledge? And what must be the nature of moral principles in order for them to carry out this function? A specific set of answers to these questions is widely accepted among moral philosophers—so widely accepted as almost to constitute a sort of orthodoxy. The answers embody a view of the place of principles within the body of morality, which crosses the lines between cognitivism and non-cognitivism. Though I have put the question in cognitivist terms and shall discuss it in those terms, I think a similar question and a more or less parallel discussion could be given in non-cognitivist terms. Perhaps the time-honored debate between the two positions can be suspended, at least temporarily, while we examine, not the nature of morality, but its structure.

The generally accepted view of moral principles consists of four main points. First, moral principles must possess a high degree of substantial generality. Generality of logical form is not sufficient; moral rules have this type of generality, but principles must in addition be applicable to a wide variety of cases and circumstances. They must, I shall say, be relatively context-free; unlike "One ought to help old ladies crossing busy streets," which is relevant only to a fairly limited set of situations, "One ought to help people in need" is applicable to an indefinitely large number of kinds of case, and can, so far, be a principle. Second, these moral principles must allow of no exceptions, nor can they rightly be overridden. Unlike moral rules, such as the one telling us to keep our promises, which may rightly be broken or suspended in certain circumstances, the principles of morality must always hold and always be binding. Third, moral principles must be substantive and not merely formal. It must, that is, be possible to derive answers to specific and detailed moral questions from a moral principle by applying it to the facts giving rise to the questions. This is the feature which critics of Kant's ethics have frequently said is missing in his formulation of the moral law; its absence is fatal to its claims to be the principle of morality. These three features mark what, for convenience, I shall call a classical moral principle. When we add a fourth feature to these three—relative context-freedom, unexceptionability, substantiality—we have what I shall call a classical first principle. The fourth feature is that the principle must be foundational or basic. Other principles, rules, or particular judgments may derive their validity from a first principle, but it must be an originating source of the authority of lower-order parts of morality and must not in turn depend on other moral judgments or principles for its own binding power. It must possess prior basic validity or authority or truth, not derived or dependent power.

This view of moral principles rests—at least in part—on the claim that if there is to be such a thing as genuine moral knowledge, then there must be at least some true classical first principles. It is this claim which I propose to examine. There are a number of interrelated arguments in its favor. The first, which is tied to the three features making a principle a classical moral principle, is that there must be such principles if any reasons for or against particular moral judgments, or less context-free rules, are to be sound. There must be classical moral principles, that is, according to the first argument, if it is to be possible to reason about moral problems. Building on this position, two further arguments are used to show that these principles must be first principles. One is an attempt to show that first principles must exist if morality is to constitute a rational and coherent system; the other is an attempt to show that first principles must exist if morality is to be more than a merely hypothetical or possible system—if it is to be genuine knowledge, then, the argument goes, we must know the truth of at least one classical first principle. I shall sketch these arguments briefly and indicate why they seem to me to be unsuccessful in establishing their conclusions.

The attempt to show that there must be classical moral principles if reasoning is to be possible about moral matters proceeds on the assumption that the reasoning needed in morality is purely deductive. Now if the only generalities available as premisses for such reasoning were rules to which exceptions could be made, or which could be overridden, then one could never be certain that a particular case to which a rule applies is not one of the anomalous ones. Then it would always be possible to assert the general premiss—the rule—and the fact-stating minor premisses, and yet deny the conclusion. But then no reason at all would have been given, on this view, for the particular moral judgment asserted in the conclusion. Hence, if it is to be possible to give reasons for moral judgments, there must be some exceptionless principles.

An explanation can of course be given along these lines of the reasoning involved in applying rules or practical principles to the cases where they are relevant, and similar explanations can be given of the many other ways in which we actually think about moral problems—drawing comparisons with similar cases, using analogies, considering what some ideal or admired person would do. Our procedures may, however, be given another interpretation, according to which to adduce a principle may be to give a good reason for doing a certain act, and to apply a principle may be to subsume a case under it in deductive fashion, even if the principle allows of exceptions. For in morality, it may be argued, as frequently in law, we have to do with rebuttable subsumptions. When a relevant and acceptable principle has been adduced, a reason has been given for doing the act it dictates in the circumstances. The burden of proof has thereby been shifted to anyone who thinks that the act ought not to be done. It is open to an objector to give reasons for thinking the case in question to be exceptional; but if no such reasons are given, then the act dictated by the principle remains the act that ought to be done, since it is the act for doing which the best reason has been given. In the absence of definite grounds for thinking the particular case exceptional it would be foolish to take the logical possibility of its being exceptional as a serious reason for doubting that it ought to be done. Similarly it would be foolish to take the bare logical possibility that I might be hallucinating now as a serious reason for thinking that I am not now perceiving my surroundings correctly. We are, therefore, not compelled to interpret the procedures we use in thinking about moral problems as aiming at the production of logically conclusive reasons for or against moral assertions; and so the argument to show that there must be classical moral principles if there is to be reasoning on moral matters collapses.

The next step in the argument is an attempt to show that there must be classical *first* principles if morality is to be rational and coherent (and rationality and coherence are clearly necessary if morality is to be essentially a body of knowledge). The line of thought I shall consider is in fact used to prove an even stronger claim: it is used to prove that there must be one and only one first principle. It is a simple argument. No rational, coherent system can contain contradictions. But if there are a multiplicity of rules and principles, they are liable to become involved in conflicts over particular cases. These conflicts are the equivalents of contradictions among assertions, and it cannot, therefore, be admitted that they are the final truth about morality. It follows that there must be a method of resolving them. There must, then, be a principle in terms of which any conflicts arising between or among relatively context-bound principles can be resolved. There can be only one such principle, for if there were more than one the same sort of conflict could arise again. This principle must be completely context-free, since it must be capable of being applied to any kind of situation. And, finally, it must be supreme in authority, for it may be called upon to adjudicate disputes involving any other principles within the morality over which it reigns. Hence, it must be able to override any other principle and no other principle must be able to override it. And this being so, the authority of other principles must depend on their being allowed to dictate by what is plainly the first principle.

This line of thought—if I may make an historical comment—is of great importance in classical utilitarianism. It enabled Bentham and J. S. Mill to give reasoned support to the utilitarian principle as the one candidate that could fill the requirements for being the classical first principle, without relying on any premises drawn from the content of the accepted morality. The line of argument they invoked is epistemological, yet, if sound, it establishes a principle which can be used to override any common-sense rule or principle, even if no conflict of principles has arisen. For the argument establishes the total supremacy of the conflict-resolving principle and therefore justifies its use in any context.

Yet I think the argument is not sound, for two reasons. First, to say that there are conflicts of rules and principles in specific cases is not to say that there are contradictions in morality which destroy its coherence. Just as there may be good reasons for believing each of two incompatible factual assertions, so there may be good reasons for doing each of two incompatible actions. We may be in a position in which we are unable to tell which of the two assertions—if either of them—is really true, and we may similarly be unable to tell for which of the two actions—if either—there are ultimately better reasons. It might in such cases be *morally* desirable to have a principle which would always resolve such conflicts, but even if it were this would not show that the existence of such a principle is a necessity for the cognitive status of morality. Second, even if there were some conflict-resolving principle (or perhaps I should say, even if there is one), it would not follow that such a principle must be the first principle of morals, in the desired sense. From the fact that a given principle is supreme in resolving conflicts it does not follow that it must be supreme in every context. To suppose that it does follow would be like supposing that every decision and rule agreed upon by a happily married couple depends on the authority of the divorce court, since that court has the final word in settling all their affairs if they cannot settle them by themselves. An authority to settle difficulties may conceivably be restricted to doing just that, and its interference in normal cases, where no other conflict of principles or rules is involved, may be totally unwarranted. Any principle established with the help of this argument might simply be as it were a moral ambulance, not for everyday use, having the right of precedence only in emergencies and not in the ordinary run of events. I do not say that this is the correct view: I mention it only as an alternative possibility, which militates against this particular argument.

The last set of considerations to be examined leads to the conclusion that there must be some classical first principles, but does not allow the conclusion that there can be only one. It embodies an argument that frequently leads to intuitionism or "Cartesianism" in ethics, and though it is extremely old it has a perennial appeal, appearing even in the thought of those who do not intend to draw intuitionist conclusions from it. Thus Professor D. H. Monro, a defender of naturalism, writes that "we settle moral questions by appealing implicitly to some general principle," and this principle serves as a major premiss to enable us to deduce from a minor, factual, premiss a particular moral judgment. "There does not seem to be any way of testing this [major premiss]," he continues, "except by an appeal to some further principle about what is right or what ought to be the case."[1] This is the way the argument usually begins. It continues with the threat of an infinite, and vicious, regress of moral principles, each one used to support the one to which we have just appealed. The conclusion is that there must be some

---

[1] D. H. Monro, *Empiricism and Ethics* (Cambridge, 1967), 8.

principle which can be known to be authoritative or true without needing further moral support, and which can give support to the lower-order principles, which have been adduced to prove the particular judgment. But such a principle answers to the description of a classical first principle.

This argument presupposes the strict deductive model of giving reasons, which we have already touched on. More interestingly, it presupposes that there is a context-free order of dependence among moral propositions, so that if a particular judgment or a rule or principle ever depends on another then it always does. Since it seems undeniable that we frequently settle particular moral questions by appeal to general principles, and support these by showing that they follow from still more general principles, the conclusion of the argument follows quite obviously. Yet the assumption that there is a context-free order of dependence, though rarely discussed by moral philosophers, is to say the least doubtful. It has been attacked, in rather different ways, by C. S. Peirce and other pragmatists, and more recently by J. L. Austin. They have argued that the distinction between knowledge which depends on being inferred, and knowledge which is independent of inference is not one which can be drawn simply in terms of the content or the degree of generality of the knowledge. It is a context-bound distinction. What is for me dependent on some other information need not be so for you: that your name is Jones may be known by me through a complicated inference, and if so my knowledge depends on the premises of the inference, but presumably the knowledge of your name is not thus dependent for you. Similarly, time can make a difference: presumably after years of friendship my knowledge of your name is not dependent on the premises from which I first inferred it. In fact I might now adduce my knowledge of your name as evidence that those premises themselves were true. This point applies as well to moral as to factual knowledge. What is a matter of moral perplexity for one person need not be so for another, and hence a moral assertion, which is in need of support and is dependent for its authority on a further principle, need not be in this position for everyone alike. I may change my mind about a particular class of cases under the influence of a principle I have always accepted; but I may later come to see that this class of cases also falls under a different principle which I have not previously accepted, and may come to accept the principle as showing more clearly the justification for my judgment of the class of cases. Moral philosophers, whatever their theoretical programs, have in practice always recognized that allegedly basic moral principles depend no less on fairly specific moral propositions than on the other sorts of grounds that have been offered for them; a principle that led to the conclusion that truth-telling was usually wrong, and torturing children normally permissible, would be rejected, no matter what kind of proof it might have. But if general principles may sometimes depend on particular moral judgments, and particular judgements sometimes on general principles, then there is no impersonal, necessary order of dependence within the realm of moral knowledge, and we are not compelled to conclude that there must be classical first principles.

So far we have discussed arguments to show that there *must* be classical first principles. Could it simply be that there just *are* such principles? There seem to be two difficulties with this. One is the problem of finding any candidates which fit the requirements for being a classical moral principle. The principles that operate in daily life seem generally to allow of exceptions or of being overridden, and the candidates proposed by philosophers fail, either—like Bentham's version of the utilitarian principle—for the same reason, or—like Kant's formulation of the moral law—because they are only formal. But even if some such principle were to be found, there would remain the problem of whether it would be a *first* principle in the required sense. And here the difficulty seems to be insurmountable. For it is a defining characteristic of moral directives, as contrasted with those of law, tradition, custom, or manners, that none of them can be always relieved of the need to be justified. If particular moral assertions need at times to be justified, so too do moral principles. The facts seem to be that we give reasons for particular judgments in terms of principles, and also that we justify principles in terms of particular judgments. If in different types of situation and in response to different problems we use both procedures to justify moral directives, then it cannot be claimed that in fact there just are principles which never receive support and always give it. To say that there must be some acceptable classical first principles is to insist on forcing the facts to fit a theoretical model.

The epistemological arguments we have considered do not force us, then, to adopt the view that there must be classical first principles if there is to be moral knowledge. There may well be other important arguments to show that there must be principles of this sort if a given morality is to be viable, and it would be interesting to discuss the question of the extent to which, and the ways in which, the above arguments could be rephrased to fit a non-cognitivist view of morality (how can moral attitudes guide conduct if they are not coherent, and how can they be coherent if they are not ultimately based on one fundamental attitude?). Yet as one of the considerations leading to the belief in classical first principles is that there is no other model for understanding moral knowledge than the one which involves commitment to them, I should like to devote the remainder of this essay to a very rough sketch of a different way of viewing it—one which does not involve this commitment.

The model of knowledge which I shall use for discussing morality is the scientific model. It is almost inevitable that a cognitivist view of morality should stress the resemblances between science and ethics; yet to do so is not necessarily to escape from a demand for classical first principles. The ideal of reasoning, and the correlated ideal of knowledge, behind the belief in classical first principles, is a geometric and deductive ideal, and frequently leads to intuitionistic positions. But it can also lead to certain varieties of "scientific" morality. Thus, Herbert Spencer's moral theory is essentially a deductive system based on a single classical first principle. What is supposed to be distinctively "scientific" about it is that the principle is allegedly derived wholly from the discoveries of the positive sciences. J. S. Mill's version of utilitarianism is less wholeheartedly scientific than Spencer's view: Mill does not think that the single basic principle of morality can be scientifically proven. But every moral problem and every other rule of morality can, under the supervision of the utilitarian principle, be given purely scientific treatment (or will be susceptible of it, when the social sciences have matured). Still, one need not fall back on classical first principles when one attempts to show that morality can be understood along the lines of a science. There is at least one other way in which science can serve as a model, a way pointed out in certain of its aspects by John Dewey. It may be argued that what is scientific about morality is neither some basic principle or principles on which it rests, nor its reliance on special sciences for most of the premises on which moral reasoning proceeds, but the general structure of its contents and its methods. Moral beliefs show the same kind of susceptibility to systematisation, criticism, revision, and resystematisation that factual beliefs show. There are analogs to theory and data among our moral beliefs, and these can be understood as related in ways like those in which theory and data are related in the sciences. If we can show that this way of understanding morality is feasible, we shall have undercut the argument claiming that the model which commits us to classical first principles is the only possible one.

Principles of morality function in some ways like the formulations of laws which scientists propose. There are, at any given time, a number of specific judgments, rules and ideals, the correctness of which we have no hesitation in affirming. Formulations of moral principles serve to systematise and generalise these beliefs, and in doing so they articulate what may be called the spirit of our morality. They pick out the aspects of our less general beliefs, which are not tied to specific circumstances and which would remain constant in a variety of situations. This enables them to express the point or rationale of specific moral convictions. And this in turn enables us to carry out a critical and explicit projection of our moral beliefs to new kinds of problem and new combinations of circumstances. The formulation of a principle to cover classes of cases where we know the rights and wrongs, and the application of the principle thus formed to the solution of difficulties which arise where we have no firm convictions, are analogous, in a rough but fairly clear way, to the formulation of a law to cover a set of well-established data and its use to predict results of new combinations of causal factors.

We must avoid taking too simple a view of this procedure, either in science or in morality. Recent work in the philosophy of science shows that it is misleading to think of each formulation of a scientific law as operating in isolation from every other formulation. Laws are expressed in the context of general theories, and they, as well as many of the concepts involved in assembling the data of the science, must be understood within that context. Similar points hold of morality. I do not mean to suggest that philosophical theories of ethics occupy the position of general theories in the sciences. What occupies the analogous position is rather the general world outlook— typically a religious outlook, or a non-religious world-view still conscious of its non-religiousness—in which a morality is embedded. A large part of the terms and beliefs of these general metaphysical views of life and the world are inseparably intertwined with what we tend to think of as distinctively moral beliefs. The very concepts by which we pick out subjects for moral predication may be rooted in religious or metaphysical propositions, and these in turn may be unintelligible without their evaluative and moral implications. Thus it will take a whole set of moral principles, understood against a metaphysical background, to articulate our moral beliefs adequately and to provide an intelligible and applicable projection of them to new problems. These complex interconnections give rise in morality to a phenomenon comparable to the use in scientific practice of "theory-laden" observation terms. Many terms employed in the description of particular things and events carry strong theoretical implications, so that in using them we are committed to accepting certain scientific laws. Similarly, many of the terms used for describing our commonest actions and social relations have moral implications built into them. Those who use them are by that fact committed to at least the *prima facie* acceptance of certain moral directives: to say, for example, that I am "married to" so-and-so is to imply my acceptance of a directive against having sexual relations with anyone else. The moral implications of terms like this have been called "practice-defining rules," and contrasted with "summary rules." It is not necessary that a comparison of moral principles with scientific laws should force us to accept the view that all moral principles are of the latter type. But it must equally be borne in mind that the vocabulary embodying practice-defining rules is itself open to alteration and in this respect like the theory-laden terms used in scientific observation.

If the relations between fact and theory in science are complex, so is the way in which the acceptability of a theory depends on the data it organises and the predictions it warrants. Laws that unify a large body of well-established facts and empirical generalisations, that enable us to make successful predictions over a wide range, and that suggest numerous points for further fruitful experiment and theory-construction, are not easily abandoned. A well-founded theory cannot be overthrown by the negative results of a single "crucial experiment." Logically speaking, it is always possible to defend a formulation of law from a counter-instance by explaining the instance in terms of an *ad hoc* hypothesis, or by treating it as due to faulty instruments, bad observation, freakish accident, and so on. In terms of the economy and strategy of research this is not always a bad move to make. It is only when the amount of evidence that must be avoided instead of absorbed grows fairly large, when the original theory becomes cumbrous and difficult to use because of the qualifications and adjustments needed to make it fit the evidence, that serious exploration of alternative theories takes place; and the existence of some viable alternative theory is needed before an accepted view will be abandoned. A new theory, if it is of the most attractive kind, will explain the evidence which told in favor of the older view—perhaps recasting it in a new terminology—and it will explain as well what was anomalous or required special hypotheses from the older standpoint. It will enable new areas of investigation to be developed and new types of prediction to be successfully made. It will, in short, perform the same functions as the replaced theory, but better.

If the study of the history of science is still at a comparatively early stage of development, the study of the history of moral systems has hardly even begun. At this point it can only be proposing a hypothesis to say that the pattern of thought revealed in studies of "scientific revolutions" may be useful as a guide in investigating the development of norms and values. Still, even a rudimentary knowledge of history may allow us to see how this pattern could be relevant. Moral systems are used, not to predict, but to direct and evaluate conduct. They can fail to operate in any number of ways, as scientific theories can fail. Yet accepted systems have a definite value in virtue of the fact that they are widely accepted: they give shape and coherence and predictability to large segments of life, and they are therefore not lightly to be abandoned. Hence no single failure is likely to suffice to overthrow an accepted morality. As in the case of reasonably good theories, it is likely to take an accumulation of difficulties before serious investigation of alternatives occurs. These difficulties may arise from a number of causes. There can, for instance, be failure of relevance to prevalent problems. A morality developed within one type of social or economic situation may be carried over while technological or financial changes occur which effectively alter the nature of the society in which people accept it; and in the new situation the old directives may simply fail to cover recurring problems generally felt to be important. In such circumstances a morality also may fail by giving guidance which is not specific enough, or which it is not feasible to expect people to follow. R. H. Tawney's well-known discussion of the failure of the medieval church to provide an adequate set of precepts for action in a developing capitalist economy gives illustrations of these points. Either the types of monetary transaction vital to a capitalist economy were not covered by any of the standard directives or else they were covered by directives involved in concepts like that of usury and just price which it was no longer feasible to apply. People simply could not live in accordance with the dictates implied by those terms, and were forced to find new ways of organising their actions. Another kind of difficulty with a moral code arises when a change of circumstances transforms a once coherent set of practical demands into directives that repeatedly require incompatible or self-defeating actions. This is the sort of situation involved in what R. K. Merton calls "anomie," where (roughly) socially acceptable goals can only be reached by breaking socially acceptable rules; and there are other types as well. Still another kind of difficulty with a moral system arises when the religious or metaphysical outlook with which it is involved ceases to be widely accepted: its categories may then cease to seem relevant to the daily problems people face, and therefore its judgments may be increasingly wide of the mark.

Complaints of these kinds about an accepted morality have often been answered by its defenders with the claim that the fault lies not in the moral code but in the social system which is changing in immoral directions, or in the weakness of men, which makes them less willing than usual to expend the effort needed to live up to moral demands, or in the faithlessness of men, which leads them to abandon the revealed truth, or in any of an innumerable variety of factors which allow one to admit the failure of the system to give useful guidance but to cling to the system nonetheless. As in similar cases where counter-evidence to a well-based scientific law is presented, this procedure has a definite justification. But in morality, as in science, it is not always used. There are times when abandoning a moral principle seems more reasonable than continuing to claim that it is true despite the numerous exceptions and qualifications it requires. And the abandonment of one principle is likely to involve repercussions in other parts of the system: the controversy over the morality of birth control may be mentioned in illustration, touching as it does on the nature of the family, the function of sexual relations and the permissibility of pleasure, the place of women, the authority of various institutions, and so on. In this connection it would be interesting to investigate the part played, in basic moral change, by the availability of some alternative system of morality, which would incorporate what is still held to be true in the old view while advancing to new insights on the points of difficulty in that view.

These brief comments may indicate some of the ways in which the structure of morality is like the structure of science, and may point towards an interpretation of moral principles and moral knowledge which does not force us to a belief in what I have called classical first principles. It may help to clarify the hypothesis being suggested if I add one or two further remarks.

The claim that morality is "cognitive" and that we now have some moral knowledge is not the claim that all our moral convictions as they now stand are true or justifiable. We do not think any such implication to be involved in the claim that we have knowledge of geology or physics or mathematics. We are aware that many of the particular opinions and theories we now hold in these disciplines will eventually be discarded as mistaken, but we have no hesitation in claiming knowledge within these fields nonetheless. The situation is the same as regards morality. I have suggested that moral principles can be supported by showing that they provide adequate articu- lation of less general moral beliefs which are at a given time held without doubt. I do not mean to imply, however, that the beliefs to which we are at this moment committed are beyond criticism—far from it. Our morality has been derived from many sources and shaped by many influences. It is moreover deeply involved with our factual and religious or metaphysical beliefs. There is no guarantee that it is free from inconsistency, error, or superstition, either on the purely moral plane or in its non-moral involve- ments. Though it is bound to be our main starting-point in thinking about practical matters, we must assume that progress and improvement in moral knowledge are possible. This is no more, and no less, than we must assume in every area of thought where truth is an aim. Most moral philosophers, however, have thought of moral progress chiefly as the progressive improvement of the human race—as a slow growth in the degree to which men live up to the demands of morality. Few have considered the possibility that moral progress may consist primarily in the growth of moral knowledge. One reason for this may have been their acceptance of the presuppositions that lead to a demand for classical first principles. For on that view, if we do not now know at least the first principles of morality, we cannot really know anything of morality (though of course our opinions may be true). But if we already know the first principles of morality then whatever progress is to be made in our knowledge of the subject (discount- ing that which will result solely from the improvement of scientific know- ledge) must be comparatively minor. The view being put forward here in opposition to this places no such block in the way of contemplating the improvement of even our most general or most cherished principles.

Does this view leave open the possibility that moral knowledge might be, or become, esoteric, the possession of a small group of experts? This did happen to scientific knowledge, yet we do not wish to grant that it could occur with respect to morality. Nor, indeed, are we required to grant it. Any claim to know something must be open to assessment by the relevant group of those qualified to judge. In the case of morality this group consists of those who are able and willing to live their lives—to the usual extent—under the guidance of moral directives understood as such, and not taken simply as customs or taboos or religious commands or positive laws. It is a necessary, if not a sufficient, condition of the justifiability of any claim to knowledge that those who are competent to judge should come to agree with the claim when they investigate it in the proper manner. Moral claims are no exception, and the disagreement of informed and thoughtful moral agents with our own moral assertions gives us a reason for being less confident of them. Still, disagreement, even when the reasons for it are given, is not refutation, and one defense of controversial opinions which must be admitted does leave an opening for the charge of esotericism. It must, I think, be granted that some people really are more insightful and sensitive, morally speaking, than others, and that these people may possibly be ahead of the majority in their grasp of the morality of a particular kind of action. But the distinction between insight and delusion—between wisdom and charlatanry—is no less real than that between science and quackery, and it involves the same basic point: eventually the community of competent judges will come to accept the one and reject the other, if it looks into the matter with sufficient care.

Our moral principles, then, must articulate our unshakable convictions and provide us with adequate guidance for future decisions. In addition they must be capable of calling forth agreement in a potentially unlimited community of moral agents. How can we be sure enough of any principles, under such stringent conditions, to claim that we know they are correct? Well, of course, our scientific theories and hypotheses must survive similar tests, and we manage to make this claim about some of them. And after all the quest for moral knowledge did not begin yesterday. The moral principles most of us accept have had to survive a fair amount of testing and sifting in the course of time. There is therefore a fair amount of evidence to show that they can give acceptable guidance and can form the nucleus of a moral community. To say that we *know* some of them to be correct is to express our reasoned confidence that they, or something very close to them, will, of those available for consideration, come out best in relation to all the evidence, future as well as past. It is also to express our decision, at least for the present, to hold to these principles despite any objections to or difficulties with them. This decision need be no more irrational than similar decisions made by scientists. The principles that we decide, in this fashion, to maintain are the ones we consider basic. The theory of classical first principles involves mistaking this kind of decision for a discovery that certain principles are basic because of their own inherent nature.

PART II
Victorian Matters

2

First Principles and Common-Sense Morality in Sidgwick's Ethics

1. A large part of Sidgwick's *Methods of Ethics*[1] is devoted to an examination of common-sense morality. The outcome of the examination is twofold. First, Sidgwick claims to have shown that the principles of common-sense morality are not independently valid and binding. They need to be supplemented by some further, fundamental principle or principles. Second, he holds nonetheless that common-sense morality is not to be rejected. Properly understood it provides sound guidance for action. Moreover we must use common-sense morality in order to discover the needed first principle or principles and—paradoxically—in order to give reasons for accepting it or them. In this paper I shall try to explain what Sidgwick means by an "independently valid" first principle and to trace the complex arguments by which he moves to such a principle from the principles of common-sense morality. Although these arguments are general in nature, and are not necessarily tied to the defense of any specific first principle, Sidgwick uses them to establish the utilitarian principle. I shall therefore discuss his argument primarily with reference to utilitarianism.

I

2. The problem Sidgwick faces in trying to establish the utilitarian principle as the first principle of morality can be brought out by comparing

---

[1] References to this work will be given in the text, following the letters *ME*. All references given in this way are to the 6th edn., (London 1901).

briefly two earlier views as to the status and function of the principle. For John Gay and for Paley[2] the utilitarian principle is not the first principle or foundation of morality. The will of God is the foundation of morality: what makes an act obligatory is, ultimately, that God wills us to do it. But the principle of utility is still of great importance to us. By applying it in specific cases we can find out what is obligatory. For God, being benevolent, wills what is good for his creatures, and what is good for men is happiness. Gay thus calls the principle of utility "the criterion of virtue, but once removed", since it is a "criterion of the will of God" which itself is the "criterion of virtue immediately"[3]. By similar reasoning Paley establishes that "the method of coming at the will of God concerning any action . . . is to inquire into the tendency of that action to promote or diminish the general happiness"[4]. Thus for Gay and for Paley the utilitarian principle gives us a method for discovering what acts are obligatory, but it does not tell us what makes an act obligatory. For Bentham and J. S. Mill, on the other hand, the principle of utility does tell us what makes acts obligatory, and it is precisely because it does so that it can give us a method for discovering what particular acts are obligatory. Bentham's views need not be repeated. It is enough to recall his quite explicit definitions of "ought" and "right" in terms of "utility"[5]. And we need not settle the question of whether Mill did or did not commit the "naturalistic fallacy" to find that he disagrees with the Gay–Paley interpretation of utilitarianism. Speaking of the "faults in Paley's conception of the philosophy of morals", Mill says:[6]

In the first place, he does not consider utility as itself the source of moral obligation, but as a mere index to the will of God, which he regards as the ultimate groundwork of all morality, and the origin of its binding force. This doctrine (not that utility is an index, but that it is an index and nothing else) we consider as highly exceptionable . . .

The only view of the connexion between religion and morality which does not annihilate the very idea of the latter, is that which considers the Deity as not making, but recognising and sanctioning, moral obligation.

---

[2] For Gay, cf. *Concerning the Fundamental Principle of Virtue or Morality*, 1731, reprinted in E. A. Burtt, *The English Philosophers from Bacon to Mill* (New York 1939), pp. 769–85, esp. sects. I and II. For Paley, cf. *The Principles of Moral and Political Philosophy*, 1789, esp. Bk. II, chs. 1–6.

[3] John Gay, *op. cit.* sect. II.   [4] Paley, *op. cit.* Bk. II, ch. 5.

[5] Bentham, *Introduction to the Principles of Morals and Legislation*, ch. I, sec. 10.

[6] J. S. Mill, *Prof. Sedgwick's Discourse on the Studies of the University of Cambridge*, in *Dissertations and Discussions* (London 1867), vol. I, 125.

The utilitarian principle must do more than give us a method of discovering whether an act is right or wrong. It must itself determine the rightness or wrongness of acts. If it does not we are left with an incomplete moral philosophy.

Sidgwick's problem in attempting to give reasoned support to the principle of utility can be seen as emerging from criticism of these two views of the principle. He sees a problem in making the principle true by definition, as Bentham and Mill apparently do. It is not merely that the particular definition of "ought" or "right" offered by Bentham is mistaken. No such definition is possible:

What definition can we give of "ought", "right", and other terms expressing the same fundamental notion? To this I should answer that the notion which these terms have in common is too elementary to admit of any formal definition.

(*ME* 32; cf. *ME* 26, n. l.)

He also explicitly rejects the solution of theological utilitarianism (*ME* 31; cf. *ME* 79–80). His refusal to be satisfied with a criterion once removed or an index is clearly indicated by a remark about the motive for the search for a "philosophical intuitionism" which will go beyond both perceptional and dogmatic intuitionism: "Without being disposed to deny that conduct commonly judged to be right is so", he says, "we may yet require some deeper explanation *why* it is so" (*ME* 102). Insofar as Sidgwick wants to establish an ethical first principle, he wants to establish a principle which is more than just a method for discovering obligations which are logically independent of it. His problem is to find a way of doing this without falling into the Benthamite error of making the principle true by definition.

3. Sidgwick is well aware of the logical difficulty involved in any attempt to prove a first principle. He holds, in fact, that it is impossible to prove a first principle if we only allow the term "proof" to mean "a process which exhibits the principle in question as an inference from premisses upon which it remains dependent for its certainty". In a proof of that sort the premisses rather than the conclusion would be the real first principles. Hence

if utilitarianism is to be *proved* . . . it would seem that the process must be one which establishes a conclusion actually *superior* in validity to the premisses from which it starts.   (*ME* 419)

Sidgwick attemps to give an argument answering to this description. The argument falls into two parts or sub-arguments. The first, developed at length in Book III of the *Methods*, Sidgwick describes briefly by saying that "the utilitarian must, in the first place, endeavor to show to the intuitionist"—who is the philosophical representative of common-sense morality—"that the principles of Truth, Justice, etc., have only a dependent and subordinate validity" (*ME* 421). I shall call this the Dependence argument. In the second sub-argument, which I shall call the Systematisation argument, it is to be shown

how utilitarianism sustains the general validity of the current moral judgments . . . and at the same time affords a principle of synthesis and a method for binding the unconnected and occasionally conflicting principles of common moral reasoning into a complete and harmonious system. (*ME* 422)

This argument is developed mainly in Book IV of the *Methods*.

Both the Dependence argument and the Systematisation argument rest on the assumption that there are some valid or binding moral judgments. Sidgwick does not try to defend this assumption. He argues against various interpretations of the concept of moral obligation which would make moral jugdments relative or subjective or "non-cognitive" (*ME* 25–35), but he does not try to refute the complete moral sceptic, who denies that he has any such concept of obligation as Sidgwick is discussing. "I, at least", Sidgwick says, "do not know how to impart the notion of moral obligation to any one who is entirely devoid of it" (*ME* 35. But cf. *ME* 213). His arguments are addressed, moreover, to those who take the morality of common sense to be valid and binding, at least to some extent. He is trying to show that if a set of moral principles like that constituting common-sense morality is to be fully acceptable, then a first principle of the *kind* that utilitarianism proposes must also be valid and binding. The main point of the Dependence argument is to show this. He is also trying to bring out the way in which the content of common-sense morality points rather to the utilitarian principle than to any other first principle. This is one of the points of the Systematisation argument. The whole argument is thus a regressive argument—an attempt to show the conditions under which alone our acceptance of common-sense morality can be justified.

4. Sidgwick's view of the nature of moral judgments has a central role to play in this argument. The logical nature of the moral judgments of

common sense gives rise to the conditions that the utilitarian principle can best satisfy. The first central point here is the objectivity of moral judgments.

It is well known that Sidgwick defends the objectivity of moral judgments, but what he means by "objectivity" is not obvious. The claim that moral judgments are objective entails, for him, that it be possible to speak of truth and error in connection with judgments of obligation or rightness; that if two people disagree on a moral matter one or both may be mistaken; that conflicting answers to a moral question cannot both be accepted; and that moral judgments are primarily matters of cognition, not of feeling or sense: "the term Sense suggests a capacity for feeling which may vary from A to B without either being in error, rather than a faculty of cognition: and it appears to me fundamentally important to avoid this suggestion" (*ME* 34). Now Sidgwick might hold these views and hold also that rightness or obligatoriness or "what is common to these" (cf. *ME* 32, quoted above) is a quality of particular actions, and that it is this which makes possible the objectivity of judgments of obligation or rightness. Occasionally his language suggests such an interpretation. Thus he remarks (*ME* 105) that "we have hitherto spoken of the quality of conduct discerned by our moral faculty as 'rightness' ", and he says that certain questions arise because of "differences arising from a variation of view as to the precise quality immediately apprehended in the moral intuition"[7] (*ME* 103). But I do not think that Sidgwick actually does hold the sort of view about objectivity which this language suggests. His way of accounting for the objectivity of moral judgments is different and more interesting. The important point is brought out in a passage in which Sidgwick explains the difference between the kind of objectivity belonging to judgments of fact and the kind belonging to moral judgments.

There seems, however, to be this difference between our conceptions of ethical and physical objectivity respectively: that we commonly refuse to admit in the case

---

[7] In the earlier editions of the *Methods* his language is even more clearly suggestive of a view similar to the view of Prichard or Ross. Thus he introduces ch. VIII of Book I in the second edition in this way: "We have used the term 'intuitional' to denote the method which recognises rightness as a quality belonging to actions independently of their conduciveness to any ulterior end. The term implies that the presence of the quality is ascertained by simply 'looking at' the actions themselves, without considering their consequences" (*Methods of Ethics*, 2nd edn., (London 1877), 85). This passage was altered in the third edition to what is substantially its final form, in which no mention of a quality of rightness is made.

of the former—what experience compels us to admit as regards the latter—variations for which we can discover no rational explanation. In the variety of coexistent physical facts we find an accidental or arbitrary element in which we have to acquiesce, as we cannot conceive it to be excluded by any extension of our knowledge of physical causation. . . . But within the range of our cognitions of right and wrong it will be generally agreed that we cannot admit a similar unexplained variation. We cannot judge an action to be right for *A* and wrong for *B* unless we can find in the natures or circumstances of the two some difference which we can regard as a reasonable ground for difference in their duties.   (*ME* 208–9)

The suggestion here is that the objectivity of judgments of obligation or rightness is essentially bound up with the existence of reasons for and against them. It is not a matter of their reporting the presence of a quality in an act. What makes a judgment of obligation or rightness objective is the possibility of giving reasons in support of the judgment. If no reasons can be given to support the judgment then it is what Sidgwick calls an expression of "quasi-moral sentiment" (*ME* 27–8). He is not suggesting that at the time of passing a moral judgment one must have reasons consciously before one's mind. His view is simply that a judgment of obligation or rightness for which no reasons can be given is justifiably treated as being merely an expression of personal feeling.

That moral judgments are objective, in the sense that reasons can be given for them, is thus on Sidgwick's view an analytic proposition. But it follows from this that there is a condition that must be satisfied if moral judgments are to be possible: it must be possible to give reasons for and against judgments that a certain act is right or ought to be done. It is this condition that lies at the base of the Dependence argument.

The objectivity of moral judgments involves the possibility of disagreement on moral matters, and there is no need to adduce evidence to show that such disagreement exists. The problem in fact lies in the other direction. There seems to be so much disagreement on moral issues that it is hard to believe that moral judgments are matters of rational cognition at all—or if they are made so by definition, it is hard to believe that there are many moral judgments to be found. Hence if we are to maintain the rationality and thus the objectivity of moral judgments (or if we are to maintain that many judgments of obligation and rightness *are* moral judgments) we must be able somehow to show that in spite of all the disagreement that exists on moral matters, rationality is at work in common-sense morality. It will thus be a condition of the acceptability of a proposed first moral principle that it enable us to do this. There is a second way in which the existence of moral disagreement gives rise to a condition of the acceptability of a first moral principle. Sidgwick holds that the knowledge or belief that an act ought to be done gives a motive for doing it, but not a motive so strong as automatically to override any and every other motive or impulse. Questions and judgments of obligation only arise, he thinks, where there is at least a possible conflict of motives and where, as a result, we need to know which of several possible acts to do (*ME* 34–5; cf. *ME* 41). Sidgwick puts this at one point by saying that "the question of duty is never raised except when we are conscious of a conflict of impulses, and wish to know which to follow" (*ME* 81). Since the function of moral judgments is to resolve such problems, and since there must be correct, reasoned solutions in such cases, it is a condition of the acceptability of a first moral principle that it make possible the rational settlement of disagreements and difficulties concerning moral matters.

Two requirements, then, result from the existence of moral disagreement. It must be possible to show that common-sense morality is not as completely non-rational as it seems, and it must be possible to settle moral disagreements rationally. These two requirements underlie the Systematisation argument.

II

5. Sidgwick does not state the entire Dependence argument in any one place. The statement of it which follows is a construction designed to bring out the principle at work in the examination of common-sense morality in Book III of the *Methods*.

(i) In many cases where questions of the rightness or obligatoriness of actions arise, the answer seems clear and certain and is known without any conscious reasoning about the matter. But people are not always sure about what ought to be done in a particular case, nor are they always in agreement with others even when each is sure of his own opinion. In such cases people ask for reasons for or against the moral judgments involved in the difficulty. In giving reasons appeal is often made, not to further particular moral judgments, but to more general moral rules or principles.

(ii) When a general principle is offered as a reason it often settles the particular difficulty at issue. But sometimes it fails to do so, because common-sense moral principles are not precise or exact. Everyone admits that some cases which seem to fall under a rule or principle are really exceptions to it, but there is no clear agreement as to what the exceptions are; everyone admits that some principles are relevant in some cases, others in other cases, yet there is frequent lack of agreement about which principles are relevant; cases arise in which no established principle of common-sense morality seems relevant; and in other cases two principles, both relevant, come into conflict, and there is no agreement about which of them should be followed.

(iii) When the principle first appealed to does not settle the issue, appeal is made to some other general moral principle. The principle appealed to as finally decisive takes various verbal forms, but in substance it is always the same. It is the principle that one ought to do the act which, of all those open to one at the time, will produce the greatest amount of good. It is, in other words, a form of the utilitarian principle which limits, regulates, and overrules common-sense principles and which settles cases that they cannot settle.

(iv) Now the plain man, like the intuitionist, considers that the principles to which he appeals are valid and binding.

(v) He thinks, moreover, that they are independently valid and binding. But if any principle A has the limits of its applicability set by another principle B and can be overruled by B, then its validity is conditional. A will depend for its validity in any case on what B dictates. Since the utilitarian principle can limit and overrule common-sense principles, they cannot be independently valid and binding.

(vi) Common-sense principles never limit or overrule the utilitarian principle. Hence that principle *can* be independently valid.

(vii) Now it is agreed that the principles of common sense are valid and binding. But it is absurd to suppose that valid and binding principles might be limited and overruled by a principle which was not valid. Hence the utilitarian principle must be valid. And since it can overrule common-sense principles, it must be *superior* in validity to them.

Step (v) contains the central point in the argument. It introduces the concepts of dependence and independence and shows what Sidgwick requires of an independent principle. This requirement is most clearly stated in the course of the discussion of the customs regulating acts of benevolence. It cannot, Sidgwick says, be an absolute duty always to obey these customs, or any others, for there is no settled way of changing or abolishing customs. The only way we can get rid of customs which become pernicious is through the refusal of some people to follow them. But when are customs to be obeyed and when not? There does not seem to be any clear answer to this question in common-sense morality, except insofar as we can appeal to a judgment as to the expediency or inexpediency of following the customs. "And if we say that customs should generally be obeyed, but that they may be disobeyed when they reach a certain degree of inexpediency, our method seems to resolve itself into utilitarianism", and is no longer intuitional. Sidgwick then makes the following statement:

> We cannot reasonably rest the general obligation upon one principle and determine its limits and exceptions by another. If the duties above enumerated can be referred to independent and self-evident principles, the limits of each must be implicitly given in the intuition that reveals the principle.   (*ME* 247)

An independent principle, it is here suggested, must include a statement of all its limitations and exceptions. Sidgwick returns again and again to this point in examining common-sense moral principles. Repeatedly he shows that they are not precise enough, not clear enough about their limits, not exact enough in specifying exceptions, to stand as independent principles. In showing that the Dependence argument is involved in Sidgwick's examination of common sense, or intuitional, morality I shall note a number of passages in which this point is made.

6. I have now to show that Sidgwick does use the Dependence argument. That he takes the first two steps is quite clear. Introducing the discussion of intuitionism, he says that "reflective persons" naturally appeal to "general rules or formulae" in order to "settle the doubts arising from the uncertainties and discrepancies that are found when we compare our judgments on particular cases" (*ME* 214; cf. *ME* 100–1). These rules, however, are "often deficient in clearness and precision": Sidgwick gives two brief examples. If they are "really to serve as scientific axioms" they must be raised "to a higher degree of precision than attaches to them in the common thought and discourse of mankind in general" (*ME* 215; cf. *ME* 229). The fourth step is simply an explicit statement of the premiss of the whole argument: that common-sense morality is by and large acceptable

(cf. sec. 3. above and *ME* 215). That Sidgwick takes steps (iii) and (v) should become plain from noting the following passages, in which he is commenting on the adequacy of the ordinary rules governing classes of obligations.

Intuitionists commonly claim that the duty of gratitude is a "truly universal intuition". Sidgwick admits this but adds that "though the general force of the obligation is not open to doubt . . . its nature and extent are by no means clear" (*ME* 259–60). Are we to be grateful for every well-meant but blundering attempt to help us? Are we to repay in proportion to the good done, or in proportion to the effort made? Either of these rules alone would lead to actions that would be thought extreme. "Something between the two seems to suit our moral taste; but I can find no clearly accepted principle upon which the amount can be decided" (*ME* 261). With regard to benevolence in general, there are "a number of broad and more or less indefinite rules" but no "clear and precise principles for determining the extent of the duty in any case" (*ME* 262). A similar point is made as respects Justice. It is of no avail to appeal to "what Justice demands" when faced with conflicting calls for our service. The principle of Justice gives us no way of determining the relative weights of various claims, unless it is a way that is "either implicitly utilitarian or arbitrarily dogmatic" (*ME* 271; cf. 272). Sidgwick's definition of "arbitrary" is worth noting. "By 'arbitrary' I mean", he says, "such definitions and limitations as destroy the self-evidence of the principle; and when closely examined, lead us to regard it as subordinate"—as dependent (*ME* 293, n. 1.). A similar set of problems arises with regard to the principle that men have a right to freedom from interference. This is generally admitted; yet we think that children and idiots do not have this right because they will be better off if they are cared for and directed, and some would say that people in a low state of civilization do not have this right either, for the same reason. But if we admit these exceptions, what rule can we give for determining cases in which the principle is to be applied? We might say that it is to be applied only when people can take care of themselves better than others can take care of them: and then "the principle would present itself not as absolute [as independent], but merely a subordinate application of the wider principle of aiming at the general happiness or well-being of mankind" (*ME* 275). Much the same sort of thing must be said, Sidwick argues, of the generally admitted principle that we ought to obey the laws. Laws are rules of actions laid down by a rightful authority: a rightful authority (however we may determine who that is) may command acts which would otherwise be clearly immoral. Are we to do them? There is no clear answer forthcoming from common-sense morality (*ME* 301). And there are other similar difficulties about the duty of obedience or, as it is sometimes called, the virtue of Order.

> Since, then, on all these points there is found to be so much difference of opinion, it seems idle to maintain that there is any clear and precise axiom or first principle of Order, intuitively seen to be true by the common reason and conscience of mankind. There is no doubt a vague general habit of obedience to laws as such (even bad laws), which may fairly claim the general *consensus* of civilised society; but when we try to state any explicit principle corresponding to this general habit, the *consensus* seems to abandon us, and we are inevitably drawn into controversies which seem to admit of no solution except that offered by the utilitarian method. (*ME* 302–3)

The obligations that fall under the head of promise-keeping involve many perplexing problems to which "Common Sense seems to give no clear answer" (*ME* 308). Even the exemplary duty of Veracity cannot be "elevated into a definite moral axiom": we agree that sometimes the truth need not, or perhaps ought not, to be told, but "we yet find no self-evident secondary principle, clearly defining when it is not to be exacted" (*ME* 316–19). Sidgwick's review of his examination of common-sense morality contains repeated remarks to the effect that concerning some difficulty or other "we do not seem to be able to obtain any clear and generally accepted principle for deciding this point, unless the utilitarian formula be admitted as such" (*ME* 348), or that certain rules are to be criticised for not carrying with them "any intuitively ascertainable definitions of their mutual boundaries and relations" (*ME* 350), or that the exceptions and limitations to certain principles are "commonly determined by utilitarian reasonings, implicit or explicit" (*ME* 355).

These references should suffice—though many more could be given—to show that Sidgwick does take steps (iii) and (v) of the Dependence argument. The necessity of step (vi), which asserts that common-sense principles never limit or overrule the utilitarian principle, is obvious. Unless this is correct the utilitarian principle is itself a dependent principle. It seems unnecessary to offer evidence to show that Sidgwick accepts step (vi), and

I shall not discuss the ways in which he tries to defend it against the classic objections, though the first part of the Systematisation argument is relevant here. The final premiss needed in step (vii) to complete the argument—that an overruling principle must be superior in validity to an overruled principle—is not, so far as I know, explicitly asserted by Sidgwick. But it is involved in the whole attempt to find a type of argument which can establish "a conclusion actually *superior* in validity to the premisses from which it starts" (*ME* 419), and I think it may safely be assumed that Sidgwick would accept it.

7.   Having stated the Dependence argument and given evidence to show that it is actually used by Sidgwick, I shall now try to bring out the way in which it is related to the requirement, arising from the nature of moral judgments, that it be possible to give reasons for and against judgments of obligation or rightness. The link between the two is Sidgwick's view of what makes a statement a reason for a judgment of obligation or rightness. His view on this point is simple. Reasons are premisses, particular moral judgments are conclusions, and the essential relation between them is that of deductive entailment. The principles or rules or maxims or formulae of common-sense morality are viewed as major premisses, statements of the facts of a particular case are minor premisses, and to give reasons for a moral judgment is to subsume a particular case under a general principle. Sidgwick simply takes this for granted. But the belief that deductive reasoning, as exemplified in the syllogism, is the proper model for ethical reasoning, enables us to understand why Sidgwick holds that there must be an independent first principle; that is, a principle that holds unconditionally, with no limitations or exceptions.

If the principles of common sense morality which must serve as major premisses (cf. *ME* 215) were strictly universal in form there would be no particular problem, and the claims of Intuitionists like Whewell and McCosh could be sustained. Unfortunately those principles are not strictly universal. They are at best general. They tell us that acts of a certain kind ought to be done *except* where . . . and the list of exceptions cannot be completely specified in detail. Consequently if there were no other principle beside the one first appealed to, we would not have managed to give *any reason at all* for a judgment of obligation. For it would be possible to accept the statement of the facts and the statement of the principle and still consistently deny the conclusion. The premisses would not entail the judgment of obligation because they would leave open the possibility that the case at hand might be one of the exceptions. Now the detailed examination of common-sense morality has shown that *every* specific common-sense principle gives rise to this problem, and therefore if these were the only valid principles we would never be able to give reasons for judgments of obligation. There would then simply be no moral judgments at all, that is, no objective, rationally supported judgments about what we ought to do. But this is a conclusion which we cannot accept. There seem, then, to be two alternatives. We can try to specify all the exceptions, limitations, and conditions in the statement of each principle. This would enable us to give deductively conclusive reasons for judgments of obliga- tion, though not in any simple syllogistic way. We would have to see if the case at hand fell under the principle and then check to see that it did not fall into any of the classes of exceptions. But Sidgwick has argued that this way of stating moral principles robs them of any claim to self-evidence. The point is that there is no such *consensus* about the exceptions as there is about the principle, that we simply are not prepared to assert that this, that, and the other type of case and no more will be exceptions. To adopt this alternative, then, would be to give up intuitionism and to go beyond common sense. One might argue, more strongly, that it would be impossible (or perhaps undesirable) to work out all the exceptions and limits to a principle in advance, but Sidgwick does not use this argument, nor does he need to. The remaining alternative seems to be this. We must find a principle which has no exceptions or limits, which holds unconditionally in absolutely every case. It must be a principle which we—the plain man, the intuitionist—are prepared to accept as the principle that governs the limitations and excep- tions involved in common-sense principles. It must, that is, be the principle that determines whether or not a given case is an exception to a rule or principle. Given a principle that answers to this description, we can get a relation of entailment between our premisses and our judgment of obliga- tion, thereby making our premisses into reason for a moral judgment. For after seeing whether or not a case falls under a common-sense principle we can check it against the independent and absolute principle to see whether or not it is an exception. If it falls under the one and is not declared an exception by the other, we have a conclusive demonstration of a moral judgment.

We can now view the Dependence argument as involving two stages. It establishes the general point that there must be a first principle which is absolute, unconditioned, and independent. In doing this the argument relies essentially on the analysis of moral judgments which shows that it must be possible to give reasons in support of them. It also shows that in the light of the actual content of common-sense morality the utilitarian principle is the strongest candidate for the position of independent first principle. For the examination of common-sense morality has shown that in fact the utilitarian principle settles hard cases, overrules other principles, and justifies making exceptions, and that it is in fact accepted as valid with no limitations or exceptions. Granting the general validity of common-sense morality, we must grant the superior validity of the utilitarian principle.

8. This, then, is the main line of argument by which Sidgwick solves the difficulties of giving rational support to a first principle. In giving an argument which "establishes a conclusion actually superior in validity to the premises from which it starts" (*ME* 419) Sidgwick has also solved the problem posed by Mill's criticism of Paley's theological utilitarianism and his own criticism of Bentham's "definitional" utilitarianism. The utilitarian principle is not a mere index to morality. Conformity to the dictates of the principle is what makes right acts right, as is shown by the fact that the principle overrules any other principle when there is a conflict with what it dictates. But the utilitarian principle is not valid by definition. It is valid because it is demanded by our actual moral principles (cf. *ME* 420). In a world that was very different from ours, in which very different moral principles were commonly accepted, some other principle might be the independent first principle.

III

9. Sidgwick points out that the argument as so far developed has shown at most that the utilitarian principle can be *one* "moral axiom" or independent principle. It has not shown—what the intuitionist denies—that "it is *sole* or *supreme*" (*ME* 421). To show this a further argument is required, and it is this argument that I have called the Systematisation argument. There are fore-shadowings of it in the early sections of the *Methods* (cf.e.g. *ME* 12, 77, 102–3),

but it is developed at length in Book IV. There are two aspects to the argument.

10. One point to be made by the Systematisation argument may be put in familiar terms by saying that it is to show that the utilitarian principle enables us to construct an adequate explication or rational reconstruction of common-sense morality. utilitarianism

> supports broadly the current moral rules ... sustains their generally received limitations and qualifications ... explains anomalies in the Morality of Common Sense that from any other point of view must seem unsatisfactory to the reflective intellect ... supports the generally received view of the relative importance of different duties ... where we meet with marked diversity of moral opinion on any point, in the same age and country, we commonly find manifest and impressive utilitarian reasons on both sides: ... finally the remarkable discrepancies found in comparing the moral codes of different ages and countries are for the most part strikingly correlated to differences in the effects of actions on happiness, or on men's foresight of, or concern for, such effects.   (*ME* 425–6)

Sidgwick supports these contentions by reviewing once again the morality of common sense and showing in detail that it can be viewed as an attempt, sometimes successful, sometimes not, to provide a set of rules which embody the utilitarian principle in its application to various specific types of action. His position here recalls J. S. Mill's view that the rules of common-sense morality may be viewed as providing a sort of "moral almanac"[8], containing the results of the experience of generations of men in applying the utilitarian principle and making this experience readily available to us, so that we can use the principle without having to go through inordinately complex calculations each time we must act. The point is not that common-sense morality is already perfect from a utilitarian point of view: far from it. The point is rather that in its weaknesses as in its strengths it can be grasped and understood as *striving to be* perfect from a utilitarian point of view. If this is so then common-sense morality can be viewed as already implicitly accepting the utilitarian principle. One effect of this part of the Systematisation argument is thus to supplement the Dependence argument by showing how complete and profound is the dependence of common-sense morality on a *specifically utilitarian* principle. But there is a second and more essential

---

[8] J. S. Mill, *Utilitarianism*, ch. 2, second paragraph from the end.

point involved here. Sidgwick has argued, in his analysis of moral judgments, that morality is a function of reason. How, it might be objected, can this be so, when there is so much disagreement and dispute, so much conflict of moral opinion, so much change in ideals and standards and norms, so much variation in accepted principles, among people whom one can hardly deny to be reasonable? Is this rational morality merely something that ought to be, not something that is? And if so, what is the point of arguing from the demands of "common-sense morality"? The function of the Systematisation argument here is to show that behind all the apparent confusion and disagreement on morality there is far less basic disagreement than there seems to be. If we look at common-sense morality in this light—as implicitly accepting utilitarianism and striving, through blunder and error and partiality and ignorance, to apply the utilitarian principle—then we can see it as being even now actually rational. We thereby satisfy a requirement imposed by the analysis of moral judgments and in so doing offer some justification for taking the demands of common-sense morality so seriously.

11. The second point made in the Systematisation argument is that utilitarianism provides a consistent method of reaching decisions in cases which are not clearly settled by appeal to more specific common-sense principles. When ordinary formulae are not "sufficiently precise for the guidance of conduct" or when "rules commonly regarded as co-ordinate come into conflict" the utilitarian principle gives us a standard method for solving the problem. The method gives results "in general accordance with the vague instincts of Common Sense, and is naturally appealed to for such solution in ordinary moral discussions" (*ME* 425–6). It is worth emphasising Sidgwick's use of this argument[9]. He returns to it frequently in the course of his discussion of the relations between utilitarianism and common-sense morality.

---

[9] It is also worth noting that this is one of the lines of argument used by both Bentham and Mill in support of utilitarianism. It can be seen at work in the first two chapters of Bentham's *Introduction to the Principles of Morals and Legislation*, and it is clearly brought out by Mill in a number of places in *Utilitarianism*: at the end of the third paragraph of ch. I, for example, and in several passages in ch. II. His remarks in the concluding paragraph of that chapter are particularly pertinent: "There exists no moral system under which there do not arise unequivocal cases of conflicting obligation. These are the real difficulties . . . If utility is the ultimate source of moral obligations, utility may be invoked to decide between them when their demands are incompatible. Though the application of the standard may be difficult, it is better than none at all; while in other systems, the moral laws all claiming independent authority, there is no common umpire entitled to interefere between them . . .".

Utilitarianism furnishes us with a common standard to which the different elements included in the notion of Justice may be reduced. Such a standard is imperatively required: as these different elements are continually liable to conflict with each other.   (*ME* 447)

(In regard to the morality of personal relationships) the difficulties which we found in the way of determining by the intuitional method the limits and relative importance of these duties are reduced in the utilitarian system to difficulties of hedonistic comparison.   (*ME* 439)

(In utilitarianism) we have a principle of decision between conflicting political arguments.   (*ME* 441)

(Thus we have seen) several illustrations of the manner in which utilitarianism is normally introduced as a method for deciding between different conflicting claims, in cases where common sense leaves their relative importances obscure.   (*ME* 453)

The fact that the utilitarian principle enables us to reach decisions on hard cases[10] differentiates it from other principles which, like it, have no exceptions or limitations. Sidgwick calls some of these "sham axioms"— "principles which appear certain and self-evident because they are substantially tautological" (*ME* 374–5; cf. *ME* 343–5). Principles which tell us to act rationally, to govern the lower parts of our nature by the higher, or to live according to Nature, have the characteristics required for independence. But they are totally incapable, by themselves, of giving us any guidance whatsoever, since they give us no way of identifying rational action, or higher parts of our nature, or natural action, which does not appeal to some other, more substantial, moral principle (*ME* 375–9; cf. *ME* 79–83). Sidgwick's treatment of the principle of impartiality also depends on this point. The principle that "Whatever action any of us judges to be right for himself, he implicitly judges to be right for all similar persons in similar circumstances" (*ME* 379) is recognised by and essentially involved in common-sense morality. It can be derived "by merely reflecting on the general notion of rightness, as commonly conceived" (*ME* 208). It has no exceptions or limitations and is therefore independent. It is, moreover, needed by the utilitarian as a starting point for deciding questions of the

---

[10] In the course of arguing that the hedonistic view of the ultimate good, as universal happiness, is the most acceptable view, Sidgwick adduces a similar consideration. If we accept that view of the ultimate good, we are able to make comparisons of alternative actions and reach decisions on important points. On other views we are not able to do so. "If we are not to systematise human activities by taking Universal Happiness as their common end, on what other principles are we to systematise them?" (*ME* 406; *ME* 391–3).

right distribution of good (cf. *ME* 416–17). Why, then, is it not as good a possibility for the position of sole or supreme first principle of morality as the utilitarian principle? The answer is that it is at best a negative principle (cf. *ME* 380), and at worst empty or purely formal. In any moral disagreement it can be adduced on either side equally well. It can even be used by a careful Egoist (cf. *ME* 420–1). It is therefore incapable of settling such disagreements. Discussing what he takes to be Kant's attempt to deduce all the rules of duty from the categorical imperative, Sidgwick says that thoroughly conscientious disagreement is possible, and that we cannot say that both parties are objectively right, for to say this would be to say that, aside from factual error,

whatever any one thinks right is so . . . But such an affirmation is in flagrant conflict with common sense; and would render the construction of a scientific code of morality futile: as the very object of such a code is to supply a standard for rectifying men's divergent opinions.   (*ME* 210)

That the utilitarian principle gives us a consistent method for making specific moral decisions is not a merely adventitious benefit. Sidgwick's analysis of moral judgments puts him, as I suggested earlier, in a position to argue that a consistent method for making decisions is necessary for common-sense morality. Sidgwick has emphasised the point that questions of what we ought to do arise when there are conflicting impulses to action. When we ask for a *moral* judgment as to what in such a case we ought to do, we are asking for a rational decision among the alternatives to which we are prompted. A rational answer to this sort of question is one which must be at least implicitly general. It must be one which will hold for anyone in the same sort of situation. But the only way in which we can reasonably hope to find such answers to practical problems is by appeal to a consistent and methodical procedure for solving them. If we do not use such a procedure we may well come to one conclusion in one case and to another conclusion in another case which is for practical purposes the same as the first. A coin-flipping method will not suffice: we must have a rational procedure for reaching decisions if we are to get objective answers to our questions about what we ought to do. And since in asking moral questions we are asking for objective answers, the availability of a rational method for solving practical problems is presupposed by the very questions we ask as well as by the moral judgments we pass.

12. In both its aspects, then, the Systematisation argument extends support to the claim of the utilitarian principle to be the sole valid and binding first principle of morality. It shows how that principle brings out the rationality of common-sense morality which the analysis of moral judgments would lead us to expect. It shows how the principle enables us to keep on being rational in our moral judgments, in a way that we have seen to be necessary. The argument thus provides the necessary supplement to the Dependence argument. For it shows that the utilitarian principle alone, of the principles which can be independently valid and binding in the way the Dependence argument has shown is required, answers to all the further requirements imposed by the nature of ordinary moral judgments and by the contents of common-sense morality.

IV

13. This conclusion must unfortunately receive a serious qualification. I have so far said nothing about the third method of ethics which Sidgwick considers: the method of rational egoism. And something must be said about what Sidgwick regards as "the profoundest problem of Ethics"— the problem of "the relation of Rational Egoism to Rational Benevolence" (*ME* 386, n. 4.). The problem here is *not* what Broad[11] says it is. It is not simply that both the principle of rational benevolence, or utilitarianism, and the principle of rational egoism seemed to Sidgwick "self-evident when he inspected each separately. And yet they are plainly inconsistent . . . ". Sidgwick does not say that the principle of rational egoism is self-evident. It is rather the principle of prudence—that "Hereafter *as such* is to be regarded neither less nor more than Now"—which is self-evident (*ME* 381), and this principle is only "implied in Rational Egoism as commonly accepted" (*ME* 386). The problem arises because, to begin with, it is widely held that "it is reasonable for a man to act in the manner most conducive to his own happiness" (*ME* 119).

Indeed, it is hardly going too far to say that common sense assumes that 'interested' actions . . . are *prima facie* reasonable: and that the *onus probandi* lies with those who maintain that disinterested conduct, as such, is reasonable.   (*ME* 120)

[11] C. D. Broad, *Five Types of Ethical Theory* (London 1930), 245.

The principle of rational egoism can, moreover, be an independent prin-ciple: it can be held to have no exceptions or limitations. It can further allow the validity of the principle of impartiality or justice. The egoist can hold that every man ought to pursue his own happiness. Even as so held it can to a large extent satisfy the requirements of systematisation. Careful examin-ation shows that "the performance of duties toward others and the exercise of social virtue seem to be *generally* the best means to the attainment of the individual's happiness" (*ME* 175), so that we could give a fairly adequate explication of common-sense morality from this point of view. Although "it is improbable that this coincidence is complete and universal" (*ME* 175), the coincidence between utilitarianism and the present morality of common sense is not complete either. And the philosopher "is expected to transcend Common Sense in his premises, and is allowed a certain divergence from Common Sense in his conclusions" (*ME* 373). Finally, rational egoism gives us a reasonably workable method for making consistent decisions, though perhaps not a completely reliable method (*ME* 131–50; cf. *ME* 158, *ME* 195). Consequently none of the arguments which show that other principles are dependent on the utilitarian principle can be used against the rational egoist. It is for these reasons that rational egoism is such a formidable theoretical rival to rational benevolence.

Sidgwick can see no rational way of proving one of these principles to the exclusion of the other. But the fact that he feels this to be an insoluble problem is significant. It shows how heavily he relies on the arguments I have here presented, and how little weight he is prepared to put on intuition unsupported by such arguments. He does not say what in essence is said by Bishop Butler and by Dr. Whewell, who follows Butler here: that we can simply see conscience, or moral principles, to be superior in authority to self-love or prudence[12]. They think of conscience or intuition as ultimately being the voice of God speaking within us; and they think that ultimately, because of God's moral governance of the world, virtue and self-interest lead us to the same actions. Sidgwick's hope is that without appeal to any

[12] Bishop Butler, *Fifteen Sermons*, 1726, Sermon II, esp. paragraphs 9–14; Sermon III, esp. paragraphs 1–5. William Whewell, *Elements of Morality, Including Polity*, 4th edn. (Cambridge 1864), Pref. p. 10: Butler "maintains that, by merely comparing appetite and reflection or conscience, as springs of action, we see that the latter is superior in its nature, and ought to rule. This truth, I, with him, conceive to be self-evident; and I endeavor to express it by stating, as a fundamental Moral Principle, that *the Lower Parts of our Nature are to be governed by the Higher*". Compare Sidgwick's remarks on Butler in his *Outlines of the History of Ethics*, 4th edn. (London 1896), 195–8.

beliefs of this sort we will be able to "frame a complete synthesis of practical maxims and to act in a perfectly consistent manner" (*ME* 12). But his conclusion[13] is that "the whole system of our beliefs as to the intrinsic reasonableness of conduct must fall" without some such belief.

If we reject this belief, we may perhaps still find in the non-moral universe an adequate object for the Speculative Reason, capable of being in some sense ultimately understood. But the Cosmos of Duty is thus really reduced to a Chaos: and the prolonged effort of the human intellect to frame a perfect ideal of rational conduct is seen to have been foredoomed to inevitable failure.

---

[13] From the final paragraph of *The Methods of Ethics*, 1st edn., (London 1874), 473.

3

Moral Problems and Moral Philosophy in the Victorian Period*

In the present essay an attempt is made to bring out some ways in which the understanding of a literary work may be assisted by an understanding of philosophical issues. The literary works here discussed are novels by a variety of nineteenth-century authors—Charlotte Yonge, Mrs. Gaskell, William Hale White, and George Eliot. The philosophical issues related to the novels are those involved in the controversy over ethics between the utilitarians and the intuitionists, a controversy which was at the center of English moral philosophy for more than a century following the writing of Jeremy Bentham's *Introduction to the Principles of Morals and Legislation*.[1] I do not mean to suggest that interest in this philosophical issue was confined to the nineteenth century—far from it. But philosophers shift their emphases

*The author wishes to express his gratitude to the University of Pittsburgh for its award of a Mellon Post-doctoral Fellowship, during the tenure of which (1963–64) much of the research on which this paper is based was done.

[1] The *Introduction* was printed but not published in 1781. It was not until the publication of Henry Sidgwick's *Methods of Ethics* (London, 1874; 1907) and F. H. Bradley's *Ethical Studies* (Oxford, 1876) that the basic terms of the controversy began to shift; and even these books, while marking important changes in methods of argument, are concerned to reconcile the intuitionist and utilitarian views. Bystanders and contenders see the controversy in the same way. Thus W. E. H. Lecky begins his *History of European Morals* (London, 1869; 1897) with a reference to "the great controversy, springing from the rival claims of intuition and utility to be regarded as the supreme regulator of moral distinctions"; and he goes on to give the epithets used to distinguish the schools: "One of them is generally described as the stoical, the intuitive, the independent or the sentimental; the other as the epicurean, the inductive, the utilitarian, or the selfish" (1: 1, 2–3). See also M. J. Guyau, *La Morale Anglaise Contemporaine* (Paris, 1879), 190–1. Where two dates are given for a work, the second date is that of a later edition which I have used.

from time to time, and nineteenth-century English philosophers were concerned about the utilitarian–intuitionist debate in a way that differentiates them fairly clearly from both their predecessors and their successors.[2] William Whewell, H. L. Mansel, James Martineau, John Grote, J. S. Mill, and Henry Sidgwick, who, among others, carried on the debate, were all Victorian philosophers: this fact suggests that their work in moral philosophy may be used to explore the work of Victorian novelists concerned with moral problems. Thanks to J. S. Mill everyone is familiar with the utilitarian position on the issues, but the intuitionist standpoint is, quite surprisingly considering its importance for the thought of the period, almost completely neglected in histories of philosophy no less than in surveys of literature.[3] I begin, therefore, with a brief, and somewhat idealized, statement of the two views.

On the purely conceptual side of the debate, the differences between the two schools are as follows. (1) Methodologically the utilitarians hold that to justify particular moral judgments is to show that there is *inductive evidence* for them, while for the intuitionist no evidence is either necessary or possible for particular moral judgments: they must be known immediately, non-inferentially, by direct awareness, or—at most—by simple deduction

---

[2] The break in interest can be dated fairly sharply at both ends. Bentham is the starting point for the nineteenth-century controversies, G. E. Moore for those of the twentieth. Bentham (like William Paley a few years later) lumps together as "principles adverse to that of utility" almost all of the schools of thought of the eighteenth century. He dismisses the moral sense, the common sense, the understanding, right reason, the fitness of things, and laws of nature, under this heading *(Introduction*, ch. 2); while Paley, in his *Principles of Moral and Political Philosophy* (London, 1786), with equal scorn sweeps aside honor, custom, and scripture as rules of life, and the moral sense, innate maxims, natural conscience, instinctive love of virtue, and "perception of right and wrong intuition" as foundations of morality (1, chs. 4–5). The Benthamite simplification of the issues was taken as the relevant starting point for discussion during most of the nineteenth century, just as Moore's statement of issues in *Principia Ethica* (London, 1903) has been taken as the relevant starting point in recent discussion. But of course these were those in the years following the 1780s and in the years following 1903 who carried on the older modes of thought.

In this light it seems absurd to classify Bentham as "typically eighteenth century" because of his appeal to reason and his simplified view of human nature, just as it would be absurd to think of Moore as "typically nineteenth century" because of his appeal to intuition. So far as I know no one has said such a thing of Moore, but remarks of the type indicated are frequently made about Bentham.

[3] For Mill's views see especially the *Autobiography*, ch. 7. Harald Höffding and John Passmore have nothing to say about intuitionist ethics. Oliver Elton and Samuel Chew do not discuss the intuitionists at all, while Sherard Vines and Hugh Walker touch only on James Martineau. Neither Basil Willey nor Walter Houghton discusses the intuitionist ethic, although each gives much space to the utilitarians. Even in specialized studies, where it would be relevant, the intuitionist view is not mentioned: thus Humphry House in *The Dickens World* makes no reference to it, despite his frequent mention of utilitarianism as something Dickens sometimes opposed.

from a rule that is intuitively known.[4] Thus for the intuitionist the paradigm cases of moral judgment are those in which we know straight off what we ought to do, while for the utilitarian they are those in which we must figure out what to do. (2) Connected with this is the fact that for the utilitarian the paradigm moral problems are those in which we do not know what we ought to do, and in which the solution comes as soon as we do know; while for the intuitionist the central sort of problem is that in which the agent knows what he ought to do but finds it difficult to bring himself to do it. His problem is one of will or feeling.[5]

(3) Perhaps the best-known point of dispute is the disagreement over the relative value or importance of motives and consequences, or of intentions and results. It is easy to get lost here. No utilitarian ever denied that motives and intentions may have value, nor did the intuitionists ever say that consequences are totally unimportant. They agree in separating the evaluation of an agent from the evaluation of an act, in distinguishing human acts and agents from other events and causes, and in holding that distinctively *moral* evaluation is only pertinent where human acts or agents are in question. The conceptual point of disagreement is brought out clearly by John Grote. Utilitarianism, he says, "considers actions to be of value in the universe, in the last resort, solely in respect of their usefulness. . . . Unless

---

[4] William Whewell in his *Elements of Morality, Including Polity* (Cambridge, 1845; 1864) thinks in terms of intuitively known rules or principles: see pp. 10–12. For a strong statement of the view that we intuit the moral quality of particular instances, see H. L. Mansel, *Letters, Lectures, and Reviews*, ed. Henry W. Chandler (London, 1873), 126–9, 135 (an essay of 1854); 372–3 (an essay of 1866); and also James M'Cosh, *An Examination of Mr. J. S. Mill's Philosophy* (New York, 1866), p. 391: "Our intuitions are perceptions of individual objects or individual truths; and in order to reach an axiom or 'principle of morals,' there is need of a discursive process of generalization."

[5] John Grote, for example, in his *Examination of the Utilitarian Philosophy* (Cambridge, 1870) draws attention to this distinction, in his usual cautious way, when he remarks that "what is needed in respect of philanthropy, though to some extent *knowledge*, is still more *will* . . . such philosophies as by their principles are likely to strengthen the will are more valuable, and therefore perhaps likely to be more true, than such as go rather only to add to the knowledge" (p. 235). See also ch. 16, esp. p. 248: "utilitarianism is far from providing a complete remedy for the helplessness or igorance which [is] one of the chief obstacles to the promotion of the general happiness. . . . The other obstacle . . . indisposition or want of kindly feeling, it will scarcely remedy at all: it is the other kinds of ethical philosophy, which utilitarianism despises, that really are occupied with the causes of this."

Utilitarians from Bentham through Sidgwick claim that one major superiority of their view over intuitionism is that they provide a means for discovering in every case what one ought to do while the intuitionist cannot give such a means. For strong criticism of this claim and of the general view of philosophy which it presupposes, see F. H. Bradley, *Ethical Studies* (London, 1876; Oxford: Oxford University Press, 1927), 193; and also Bradley's *Principles of Logic* (London, 1883; Oxford: Oxford University Press. 1922), 1: 269–71.

there is produced by them something which independently of them may be described as good or desirable, the universe, it is said, is no better for them."[6] But this is a gross oversimplification, for "there are two kinds of value ... the value of usefulness or result, and the value of worthiness of feeling ... which has gone towards the result," or, as he later puts it, "there are two separate and independent good qualities in regard of action, its generosity ... and its usefulness." In the happiest cases these work together, but even if no good results are produced still "generous and self-forgetting action would be worth having in the universe" (pp. 72, 76–7). Since the utilitarians think of the kind of value that results can have as the only kind of value there is, they are forced to evaluate motives or feelings solely in terms of their tendency to produce goodness of this kind. But for the intuitionist this sort of value is "something in a manner pre-moral, something with the consideration of which morality is not as yet properly begun."[7] The kind of value which only human willing or human motives can have is, for the intuitionist, the distinctively moral, and therefore supremely authoritative, kind of value.

(4) The utilitarians are all determinists, while their opponents take a strongly libertarian view. Martineau is stating a commonplace of the Intuitional position when he says that "either free-will is a fact, or moral judgment a delusion."[8] The utilitarian's denial of this sort of freedom forces

[6] John Grote, *Treatise on the Moral Ideals* (Cambridge, 1876), 69–70.

[7] Grote, p. 74. James Martineau, in his *The Seat of Authority in Religion* (London, 1890), says that what calculations of utility supply "is not really *Moral* at all, distinguishing right from wrong; but simply *Rational*, distinguishing wise from foolish" (p. 81). The second and third chapters of Book I of this volume provide a useful short summary of Martineau's ethical views, the detailed exposition of which is given in *Types of Ethical Theory* (Oxford, 1885; 1891). Martineau's views were worked out, in substance, by 1845, and were first published in a review of William Whewell's *Elements* in the *Prospective Review* for 1845–46. He holds that what we intuit is always the relative value of two (or more) competing motives to action. Conscience tells us which of the motives present in us is higher, and thereby indicates the one from which we ought to act. Similar points are made by Mansel, pp. 365, 369–71, who argues that the consistent utilitarian must deny the existence of morality altogether; and by Whewell, pp. 2, 12, 65–7.

[8] 2, 41. His defense of free will is to be found primarily in *A Study of Religion* (Oxford, 1887), 3, ch. ii. See also James M'Cosh, *The Intuitions of the Mind Inductively Investigated* (London, 1860; New York, 1869), pp. 266 ff.: "We have seen that conscience pronounces its decisions on acts of the will.... its judgments proceed on the supposition that ... the will is free.... The possession of a free will is thus one of the elements which go to constitute man a moral and responsible agent." Mansel says that if there is no such thing as free will, then "no amount of special pleading will enable us to escape the inevitable conclusion that there is no such thing as morality.... there may be pleasure and pain ... but other good or evil there can be none.... an utilitarian morality—that is to say, the denial of any morality at all—is the necessary consequence of a determinist theory of the will—that is, of the denial of any will at all' (pp. 375–6).

him to reinterpret key concepts of morality—duty, responsibility, personal merit—in Hobbesian terms, as referring ultimately to various ways of exerting social pressure to control individual actions. But to do this, the intuitionist believes, is to pervert the terms from their central, and ordinary, sense.[9] The utilitarian reply is that such an interpretation is the only way to preserve morality without committing oneself to a concept of freedom that entails denying the law of causation, and that is therefore either inapplicable or nonsensical. (5) Finally, the utilitarian holds that moral knowledge as such carries with it no motivating force. One may know what one ought to do and still have no motive to do it. Hence sanctions—that is, reasons beyond the fact that something is a duty—must be attached to duties if men are to be led to act rightly. The intuitionist typically denies this. On his view, simply knowing what we ought to do gives us a motive for doing it, although, of course, that motive will not always be the one from which we act. No special sanctions or desires are needed to explain why a man does what he thinks he ought to do: the fact that he thinks he ought is a sufficient explanation.[10]

[9] Martineau would have said of the view of J. S. Mill just what he said of those of Hutcheson, who, like Mill, was a determinist: "To his prepossession upon this question must be attributed the loose and unsatisfactory account which he gives of the central group of words in the Vocabulary of Morals; for example, 'Duty,' 'Ought,' 'Right,' 'Merit,' 'Approbation,' 'Reward,' and their opposites: a set of terms with which, it is plain, he feels himself ill at ease, and can hold no pleasant intercourse, till he has made converts of them, and baptised them into a non-natural sense. For him, perhaps, they may emerge regenerate; to the unconverted, they appear bereft of their wits" (2, 565). The position is a powerful one. Sidgwick admits not only that "the common retributive view of punishment, and the ordinary notions of 'merit,' 'demerit,' and 'responsibility' ... involve the assumption of Free Will" (p. 71) but also that I cannot at the moment of decision think of my act as determined "without at the same time conceiving my whole conception of what I now call 'my' action fundamentally altered" (p. 66). Compare J. L. Austin, "Ifs and Cans" (1956), *Philosophical Papers* (Oxford, 1962): "Determinism, whatever it may be, may yet be the case, but at least it appears not consistent with what we ordinarily say and presumably think", (179).

[10] For Martineau, in knowing what we ought to do, insofar as this is purely *moral* knowledge, we have a motive to do it because what we know is the relatively greater worth of a motive already present and active. See Grote, *Examination of the Utilitarian Philosophy*, ch. viii; and *Treatise:* "I think that conscientiousness or deliberate reason is itself an original source of action" (p. 457 ff.). M'Cosh argues that Mill is wrong in representing intuitionists as holding that the sanction of morality is a feeling. "It cannot be said to consist in 'feeling,' except we use the phrase in so wide and loose a sense as to include all mental operations, and the native principles of action from which they spring. ... it points to and implies an objective reality, a real good and evil in the voluntary acts of intelligent beings," etc. (*Examination of Mr. J. S. Mill's Philosophy*, 392).

The fact that moral knowledge by itself is thought to have power to move us to act (or, to put it another way, that it is thought to be a sufficient explanation of why a man did something to say that he believed he ought to) is responsible both for certain confusions of the part of the intuitionists and (in part) for the Benthamite insistence on treating the rationalist and the sentimentalist—in contemporary terms, the cognitivist and the emotivist—forms of intuitional doctrine as being equivalent. If it is held that

This brief sketch of the major conceptual disagreements between typical utilitarian and intuitionist positions may show up the close unity of the different points on each side. The utilitarian, not seeing anything onto-logically special in human action, sees no special moral kind of value. He is thus forced to look to natural value for the differentia of action, and natural value can only be determined by calculation. Individual agents are no more moved internally to create the greatest possible amount of natural value than physical objects are moved internally to create the greatest possible amount of natural beauty, so that externally imposed adjustments are needed to bring about the desirable result. The intuitionist sees human agency as being of a unique non-mechanical kind, and he sees it therefore also as bearer of a unique kind of value which is of higher authority than natural value. In this aspect man is by nature a moral agent and therefore necessarily moved by moral knowledge, and since moral value attaches to what man knows most directly—his own active powers—there is no need of calculation or infer-ence to obtain such knowledge. There is rather need of the strength of will to overcome that aspect of man which is moved only by desire for the non-moral natural values.[11]

The logical and conceptual portrayal of a controversy like that between utilitarians and intuitionists makes the philosophical debates seem far removed from the moral problems and moral attitudes of actual people in

reason or knowledge cannot alone move men to action, then either moral beliefs are not matters of reason or knowledge (since they move to action) or else a sanction is needed, in addition to the knowledge, to move one to do what reason tells one that one ought to do. Benthamites take the second alternative. It is possible to take the first view, and hold that what looks like moral *knowledge* is strictly speaking moral *feeling*. For there is no problem as to whether feeling can move men to action. The Benthamites see that their opponents do not happily take this alternative; and so they accuse them, often correctly, of being muddled, and of using sometimes a sentimentalist and sometimes a rationalist interpretation of morality. Hence it does not really matter to the Benthamite which view the intuitionist takes, since from the Benthamite standpoint the intuitionist really wants to have it both ways—and this does not strike the Benthamite as a possible position. For a recent restatement of the view that moral knowledge includes in its nature a motive to action, see W. D. Falk, "'*Ought' and Motivation*" in Wilfrid Sellars and John Hospers, *Readings in Ethical Theory* (New York, 1952), 492–510.

[11] I have said nothing about the utilitarian hedonism and the opposition to it on the part of intuitionists, because this issue, insofar as it is not misunderstood, is the same as the issue over the existence or non-existence of a distinctively moral kind of value. The utilitarian use of the terms "pleasure" and "pain" is extremely broad. They are meant to cover all the possible satisfactions and dissatisfactions or repulsions which enter into human experience, and not just those of which paradigm cases are the enjoyableness of having one's back scratched or the hurt of having a pin stuck into a finger. Whatever someone is *for* counts as a pleasure to him; whatever he is *against* counts as a pain. Anti-utilitarians often misunderstand this, but the utilitarians themselves are fairly clear about it.

real situations. Yet each of the positions I have outlined articulates a definite moral attitude and can be viewed as a response to a certain kind of moral problem.

Our morality has two directions of concern. We must live in large groups and get along with people whom we do not know or with whom we have contact only in the course of business or in the accidental meetings of daily life. This is a pervasive feature of life, but so is the fact that a part of our lives involves extremely close contact with a very small number of people whom we know intimately. Morality may be involved in each sort of relationship, and consequently it is possible for the moral philosopher to take either sort as paradigmatic of human relations. In a variety of ways utilitarianism presents a morality which is primarily impersonal, appropriate to the life of the large society or city and to the relations between strangers, while intuitionism speaks more clearly for a personal morality, drawn from the life of the small group or the family, from the relations between old acquaintances or close friends.[12]

(1) Strangers are people whom one does not know, and among strangers one must either figure out what to do in each case or else act according to fairly definite rules which make little allowance for personal variations among individuals. To know people well, to feel at home in a group, is on the other hand to know straight off what the others will do and what to do in response, and to be able, consequently, to act in ways closely fitted to distinct personalities. Calculations and rules come in only as personal relations resting on sympathetic understanding break down.

(2) Among strangers one may make mistakes because of miscalculation or because one does not know the rules, but the problems that arise in families or other intimate groups are not likely to be due simply to ignorance or intellectual error. They tend to be problems of adjusting the feelings and desires of the various members of the group, where these are all fairly well known to the members.

(3) John Stuart Mill's "estimate of what a philosophy like Bentham's can do" is suggestive. "It can teach," he says, "the means of organizing and

---

[12] This theme is in some respects a well-known one, and references to it in Victorian literature itself could be multiplied endlessly: see, for example, the discussion, and references, in Walter E. Houghton, *The Victorian Frame of Mind* (New Haven, 1957), 77–80.

regulating the merely *business* part of the social arrangements."[13] When I am engaged in a business transaction with someone, his motive for carrying out his part of the bargain is of no intrinsic concern to me: that he does what he agreed to do is the main point; and whether he does it from a sense of honor, a desire for profit, or a fear of punishment, does not matter. Still, in considering him for possible future transactions, I shall take his character into account: his reliability, his honesty, his firmness of purpose, are all relevant to an estimate of the way he will carry out his future commitments. Similarly, in one's relations with strangers one is concerned primarily with *what* they do, and only secondarily with *why* they do it. By contrast to this, in a closely knit family or among a group of good friends, one will not stand on one's rights or call in authorities to enforce promises. Resolutions of disagreements among divergent desires will be felt by everyone to be satisfactory only to the extent that they do not leave anyone feeling thwarted or hurt or angrily unwilling to accept the settlement. In contexts like these, then, it will matter relatively little what is actually done, but the motives and feelings of the persons involved will matter enormously.

(4) We cannot avoid predicting the actions of other people, but the basis for prediction varies greatly from context to context. Where we do not know people well, we can, obviously, use as the basis for our predictions only facts that are likely to be true of all people and that do not involve highly individual characteristics. We cannot easily then see the acts of others as being much more than expected responses to standard sorts of situations, and we consequently tend to think even of our own acts in this way. But where we have intimate and detailed knowledge of other people, we can see their actions as natural expressions of their whole personalities, and our sense of the individuality of our own actions will consequently be heightened.[14] The contrast may be seen in a different light by noting that where impersonal social life is predominant, one tends to think of one's own

---

[13] J. S. Mill, "Bentham," *Dissertations and Discussions* (London, 1868), 1, 366. Mill goes on immediately to say that Bentham "committed the mistake of supposing that the business part of human affairs was the whole of them; all at least that the legislator and the moralist had to do with."

[14] Both Bentham and Martineau speak of motives as "springs of action." In Bentham one has always the image of steel springs, triggered off by the releasing mechanism of some combination of circumstances. But in Martineau the association is with springs of water, so that one's actions flow from one as a stream. Cf. *The Seat of Authority in Religion*, 358.

actions as one thinks of those of others, in the third person, so that prediction is central and decision exceptional; while where there is a predominance of close and sympathetic contact with others, one tends to think of other people's actions as one thinks of one's own, so that decision is central and prediction secondary. The determinist, we might say, is impressed with the fact that we predict the actions of all but one person in the world; while the libertarian is struck with the importance of the fact that one's own actions result from one's decisions.[15]

(5) In a large society or among strangers each man must look out mainly for himself. Insofar as there are socially sanctioned rules they will seem essentially external to the individual—reasonable enough, perhaps, as making the existence of the society possible, but to be obeyed only because of the social benefits and penalties involved. This is a consequence of the feeling that one's connections with a society of this sort are more or less accidental, that they do not contain what really pertains to oneself. It is what someone likes and wants that shows who he is: his duties are simply forced upon him by the world. Where, on the other hand, one lives in a small and stable group, one tends much more to think of oneself in terms of one's membership in the group. One is consequently more likely to think of moral demands as issuing from oneself, or from a part of oneself. The social and personal claims that one feels one ought to satisfy are at least as much made by oneself for others as they are by others for themselves. Difficulty in fulfilling such demands is not taken to suggest that they are unjust or too severe: it shows rather that the lower or worse part of oneself needs to be subdued by the higher and better part. Not one's merely natural wants and likes show one's character, but the duties one has and the way one carries them out. It is where the individual feels himself identified with a "station

---

[15]   See, for example, Sidgwick's *Methods of Ethics*, Bk. 1, ch. v, which gives a careful discussion of the reasons for accepting determinism, all involving the regularity and consequent predictability of events and actions, and then continues: "Against the formidable array of cumulative evidence offered for Determinism there is to be set the immediate affirmation of consciousness in the moment of deliberate action. Certainly when I have a distinct consciousness of choosing between alternatives of conduct, one of which I conceive as right or reasonable, I find it impossible not to think that I can now choose to do what I so conceive,—supposing that there is no obstacle to my doing it other than the condition of my desires and voluntary habits,—however strong may be my inclination to act unreasonably, and however uniformly I may have yielded to such inclinations in the past" (p. 65). It is mainly because of the strength of this point—the existence of decisions—that Sidgwick feels unable to settle the issue one way or the other. For a discussion of different kinds of bases for prediction and their consequences for our moral attitudes see F. H. Bradley, *Ethical Studies*, ch. i.

and its duties" that he will most clearly feel the call of duty as one which he is moved to obey simply because he hears it; and it is where this holds least that moral demands will be most apt to present themselves as external and as needing external sanctions.[16]

One more point needs to be added. In a small and stable society it is possible to make the kind of moral use of exemplary persons which has traditionally been made of the main figures in the Bible and of fictional characters like Bunyan's Christian. Models or patterns like these have an important social function. In educating children into morality and in carrying on the deliberations of mature morality, these models provide a unifying center both for the instruction of activity and for the encouragement of effort. When moral goodness is held to consist in resemblance to the model, moral rules dictating specific kinds of act will matter mainly because of the shape they can give to character: the primary task will be to become a person like the pattern person. His knowledge of what to do cannot be put into any set of explicit formulae, just as the know-how of the skilled craftsman or artist cannot be summed up verbally.[17] Consequently, to understand and to follow the model, sympathy and intuition are necessary—the one enabling us to grasp his hidden motives, the other showing us the rightness of his practice. Since the model person responds to the uniqueness of each individual with the uniquely right action, he is beyond rules; and an appeal to what he would think or do can therefore serve as support for the criticism or modification of a rule that has become rigid and lifeless. The pattern person represents the culmination of that emphasis on the personal which I have suggested is central to one aspect of our morality and to its articulation

---

[16] Alexander Bain, *The Emotions and the Will* (London, 1859), ch. xv, gives the utilitarian theory of conscience. In his view it is "an imitation within ourselves of the government without us ... conscience ... reproduces, in the maturity of the mind a facsimile of the system of government as practiced around us" (p. 313). "External authority" is thus "the genuine type and original of moral authority within" (p. 318). For the intuitionist view see Martineau, *Types of Ethical Theory*, 2, 27 ff., and 401 ff., where the involvement of one's identity with one's social relations is stressed.

[17] See J. A. Froude's comments in "Representative Men": "In life, as in art, and as in mechanics, the only profitable teaching is the teaching by example. Your mathematician, or your man of science, may discourse excellently on the steam-engine, yet he cannot make one. ... The master workman in the engine room does not teach his apprentice the theory of expansion, or of atmospheric pressure; he guides his hand upon the turncock, he practices his eye upon the index, and *he leaves the science to follow when the practice has become mechanical.* So it is with everything which man learns to do; and yet for the art of arts, the trade of *life*, we content ourselves with teaching our children the catechism and the commandments" (*Short Studies on Great Subjects*, 1 [London, 1867; New York, n.d.], 471–2; first italics are mine).

in the intuitionist philosophy.[18] In a world where paid change and easy social movement predominate, however, and where traditional moral teaching is no longer widely maintained, it is much less feasible to center morality on pattern persons. More stress falls necessarily on action in accordance with moral rules, and an impersonal principle which can be applied by some impersonal technique takes the place of the embodiment of the spirit of morality as the source of justifiable reform of the rules. The utilitarian may make a passing bow in the direction of the personal influence of a great moral figure, but he is not basically very interested in him.

"To imagine a language," Ludwig Wittgenstein says, "is to imagine a form of life."[19] Moral attitudes and orientations of the sort I have outlined are inseparable from concepts, and these in turn from the words—"person," "act," "decision," "responsibility," "right," "wicked"—which we use to express them. To analyze the key concepts embodied in a language is therefore to work toward one kind of understanding of the form of life which is lived in terms of that language. What Bradley says of metaphysics— that it is "the finding of bad reasons for what we believe upon instinct"— may be true of all philosophy; but it is equally true, as he adds, that "to find these reasons is no less than instinct."[20] Our desire for understanding moves us naturally toward the sort of abstract perspicuity which philosophy can give, and is not fully satisfied until it has attained it. And, consequently, where material of the sort that a philosopher attempts to understand is present, we will find ourselves trying to grasp it in a philosophical manner. When we do so it is frequently, though not always, helpful to avail ourselves of categories and concepts which have already been developed in purely philosophical contexts. We need not attempt to reduce a literary work to a message or convert it into a proof in order to find philosophical classifications useful in describing and analyzing it. True enough, the use of such terms will relate the work to something outside the realm of literature; and this relation need not be considered of importance for the description of the

[18] James Martineau pays particular attention to the pattern or model person and to the importance of the kind of influence such persons have. His sermon on "Christ the Divine Word," in *Hours of Thoughts on Sacred Things*, 2 (London, 1896), is especially relevant. Though he there emphasizes the person of Christ as pattern, he uses principles derived from his whole philosophy. See, for example, *The Seat of Authority in Religion*, 53–5.

[19] Ludwig Wittgenstein, *Philosophical Investigations* (Oxford, 1953), 80, par. 19.

[20] F. H. Bradley, *Appearance and Reality* (Oxford, 1893), xii.

work as literature, whatever its interest may be for the historian or the student of culture. But if the work portrays human life, it cannot but portray it as existing in some form or other; and, consequently, it must embody at least some of the data from which moral philosophers start. A writer primarily concerned with politics, or with the surface manners of his time, or with thrilling or frightening or extraordinary happenings, may not tell us enough about his characters and their world for a determination of their moral outlook to be possible at any level beyond that of the commonplace. But many writers do give us enough to go beyond this point, either because of their selective focusing on relevant material or because of the total richness and complexity of the world they construct. To describe a work of this sort in philosophical terms is to point up something in the work, and something essential to its being the work it is. And if the work presents or reflects problems which have analogs among the conceptual difficulties of philosophy, it can only add a level to our understanding of what is in the work if we see the moral problems in the light of the conceptual ones. To say that in giving this kind of description of a literary work we must often go beyond the range of the writer's knowledge or conscious intention is to say only what holds of most literary criticism.[21]

In discussing the intuitionist and the utilitarian I have tried to show that each of them presents a picture of morality which simplifies the reality even when it claims only to clarify it, and which offers a justification of one morality in the name of the truth about morality as such. There may perhaps be some realm of abstraction in which we can have that complete moral neutrality which philosophers occasionally profess—after all, in some sense we all speak the same moral language—but the two schools of the nineteenth century were working on a different level. Their theories each articulate a definite and limited attitude toward life. And the fact that this is so makes their philosophical positions all the more relevant to literature. For it is not simply in presenting morally relevant aspects of human life that a writer gives us occasion for discussing his work in philosophical terms. There is to be considered in addition his general attitude toward life or what Wallace Stevens calls his "sense of the world"[22] as this is shown not only in his explicit statements but in his style and vocabulary, his selection of

[21] See Northrop Frye, *Anatomy of Criticism* (Princeton, 1957), 100.
[22] See Stevens's essay, "Effects of Analogy," in *The Necessary Angel* (London, 1960), esp. 118 ff.

material, his handling of images and themes, as well. The writer does not stand aloof and neutral, presenting without addition or modification a report on some segment of the world. Like the philosopher, he presents the world as justifying a certain attitude or outlook; and this attitude, much more than the details of the contents of the work as such, will determine what philosophy, if any, is likely to provide a useful set of concepts for the discussion of the work.

Charlotte Yonge's *The Heir of Redclyffe* (1853) is a clear and simple example of the way in which a morality can be presented and endorsed in a novel with a minimum of explicit statement. The world she shows is that of the intuitionist, a world of close-knit families living in a peaceful countryside. The problems with which her people cope are all personal; and they all arise from personal failings or weaknesses, and not from any complexity in the situations of the agents. The imitation of a pattern person is the source of such intellectual structure as the book possesses. Every major character is either a pattern or a follower; and the character and actions of each follower are shown to be deeply influenced by his pattern, for good or, as in the case of Laura and Philip, for evil. Central, of course, is the tormented Heir, Guy de Morville, whose life is one long battle between his higher and his lower self. He is a model for Charles and for Ben Robinson, both of whom improve strikingly as a result of his presence.[23] Amy is Charles's pupil as Laura was Philip's, and Philip has a follower—his "young man"—to match Charles.

For these lesser figures the function of the pattern is as much to instruct the mind as to encourage the will, but for Guy himself there is no problem of knowledge. His difficulty is always depicted as being that of bringing himself to do what his better self tells him he ought. In the key scene in

---

[23] See ch. xxix, where Charles himself says to Guy, "You must not think I have not felt all you have done for me. You have made a new man of me." See also ch. xliv: " 'As if you wanted a hero model,' whispered Charlotte.... 'I've had one!,' returned Charles, also aside." For Ben, see ch. xxiii, where Guy's courage in the face of great danger is the inspiration. Guy attributes Ben's reform, noted by the clergyman, to the night's adventure. But the clergyman knows better: " 'Yes,' thought Mr. Ashford, 'such a night, under such a leader! The sight of so much courage based on that foundation is what may best touch and save that man.' " In ch. xxiv Charles contrasts Laura as Philip's pupil with Amy who is his. It is interesting that Miss Yonge, like George Eliot, slips in an occasional remark on the educational value of novels. See ch. xxxii, where Amy, discussing Laura's concealment of her love from Mamma, says: "You know he [Philip] never would let her read novels; and I do believe that was the reason she did not understand what it meant." This of course is in perfect keeping with the emphasis on models and patterns for moral teaching.

which he fights the temptation to yield to his fierce anger against Philip, he has no doubt that he ought to forgive him, but he finds it very hard. He repeats over and over the relevant supplicatory words from the Lord's Prayer: "Coldly and hardly were they spoken at first; again he pronounced them, again, again,—each time the tone was softer, each time they came more from the heart. At last, the remembrance of greater wrongs, and worse revilings, came upon him; his eyes filled with tears, the most subduing and healing of all thoughts—part of the great Example—became present to him; the foe was driven back" (ch. xvi). The concentration on problems like this, as well as the tone in which they are portrayed, make it plain where Miss Yonge's sympathies are: her own attitude, corresponding as it does to an intuitionist morality, is perfectly suited to the only world she sees. It is in part this too easy harmony which makes her work so insipid.

Mrs. Gaskell shows us another intuitionist conscience without qualms in *North and South* (1855), but she shows us at the same time a world full of problems for it. When Margaret hears that other people would think the lie she told to save her brother quite justifiable, she replies, "What other people may think of the rightness or wrongness is nothing in comparison to my own deep knowledge, my innate conviction that it is wrong" (ch. xlvi). But Margaret must come to terms with Darkshire and with Mr. Thornton, whose life and views incarnate the utilitarianism of the industrial North. To his belief in the sufficiency of the cash nexus between man and man is opposed her insistence on a closer personal relationship, and it is in conjunction with the growth of his personal feelings for her that his morality undergoes a change.[24] Thornton, after investigating the reasons Higgins gave for wanting a job, "was convinced that all that Higgins had said was true. And then the conviction went in, as if by some spell, and touched the latent tenderness of his heart; the patience of the man, the simple generosity of the motive . . . made him forget entirely the mere reasoning of justice, and overleap them by a diviner instinct" (ch. xxxix). Mrs. Gaskell sees a wider world than Miss Yonge; and her confidence in the older morality is more hardly won, and more interesting, as a result.

The novels of William Hale White show neither the untroubled vision of Miss Yonge nor the hopeful firmness of Mrs. Gaskell. He presents

---

[24] For Mr. Thornton's opinions see ch. x and ch. xv. The relation between Thornton and Margaret may be compared, with roles reversed, to that between Felix Holt and Esther Lyon.

repeatedly a world in which the intuitionist view is beginning to be irrelevant; and his hero, Mark Rutherford, might be described briefly as an intuitionist whose moral vision is failing or gone. For the agent who has not yet developed moral insight there is nothing to do but to follow rules and maxims derived from the practice of those who have. The same will hold for the man who has had insight and lost it; but where the one may follow such rules with confidence, the other will always feel them to be inadequate and will never have the direct sense of the rightness of an act which once he had. "I have at my command," says Mark Rutherford, "any number of maxims, all of them good, but I am powerless to select the one which ought to be applied."[25] This is a constant theme in Hale White's novels.[26] It appears again, for example, in *Mark Rutherford's Deliverance* (1885), when Rutherford contemplates marrying the girl whom he originally rejected because of Miss Arbour's advice. "How true that counsel of Miss Arbour's was!," he muses, "and yet it had the defect of most counsel. It was but a principle; whether it suited this particular case was the one important point on which Miss Arbour was no authority" (ch. vii). Miss Arbour shows us the sort of confidence Rutherford lacks. "The voice of God hardly ever comes in thunder," she says, "we can lay down no law by which infallibly to recognise the messenger from God. But . . . when the moment comes it is perfectly easy for us to recognise him" (*Autobiography*, ch. v). The conflict between insight and rule appears again in *Clara Hopgood* (1896), where it is made explicit in the dialogue in which Madge refuses to "give up my instinct for the sake of a rule" while Clara replies that she cannot "profess to know, without the rule, what is right and what is not" (ch. v). And the balance of the tale does not force us to decide between the two.

Mr. Cardew, in *Catherine Furze* (1893) preaches a sermon in which he shows us one form of what Mark Rutherford wanted:

. . . it is absolutely necessary that you should have one and one only supreme guide. To say nothing of eternal salvation, we must, in the conduct of life, shape

[25] *The Autobiography of Mark Rutherford* (1881), ch. v. He continues: "A general principle, a fine saying, is nothing but a tool, and the wit of man is shown not in his possession of a well-furnished tool-chest but in the ability to pick out the proper instrument and use it." Cf. Froude's use of the concept of the skilled craftsman, n. 18 above.

[26] His essay on "principles" discusses the problem quite explicitly and ends with remarks on the importance of the incarnation of principles in a man. The essay is printed at the end of some editions of *The Deliverance*, such as that published by Jonathan Cape (London, 1929).

our behavior by some one standard, or the result is chaos. We must have some one method or principle which is to settle beforehand how we are to do this or that, and the method or principle should be Christ. Leaving out of sight altogether His divinity, there is no temper, no manner so effectual, so happy as His for handling all human experience. Oh, what a privilege it is to meet with anybody who is controlled into unity, whose actions are all directed by one consistent force![27]

But Rutherford cannot accept the old form of life, and he will not accept the impersonal substitute that the utilitarian rule offers.[28] In the end he finds some sort of resting place in helping a few people, in the personal relations finally attained with a wife, and in a temporary revision of traditional faith. It is the best he can do to reconstruct a world in which intuition can survive, and significantly enough it is the rejected part of his life, the coldly impersonal business office to which he goes daily to do work he cannot think of as truly part of himself, that kills him.

If in the novels of Hale White and Mrs. Gaskell it is mainly changes in society that challenge the intuitional morality, in George Eliot it is something different and something deeper. That her fundamental moral attitude is intuitional is shown by many recurring features in her novels: the constant appeal to sympathy and insight, the great importance given to the influence of a morally superior person in awakening the moral life of another, the stressing of motives and feelings rather than actions, the insistence on the distinction between a true conscience and a mere awareness of what others will think, are chief among them.[29] Nor does she construct a social world in which such a morality faces new sorts of problems. But throughout her

---

[27] *Catherine Furze*, ch. vi; and compare the comment in *The Revolution in Tanner's Lane* (1887), ch. ix, when Zachariah stifles a momentary doubt that arises from the callous treatment he gets when looking for a job. He is treated "as if he were not a person, an individual soul, but an atom of a mass to be swept out anywhere, into the gutter," and he wonders if God really looks after him. "But as yet his faith was unshaken and he repelled the doubt as a temptation of Satan. Blessed is the man who can assign promptly everything which is not in harmony with himself to a devil, and so get rid of it. The pitiful case is that of the distracted mortal who knows not what is the degree of authority which his thoughs and impulses possess; who is constantly bewildered by contrary messages, and has no evidence as to their authenticity."

[28] See the rejection of "philosophy" in *The Deliverance*, ch. vi. Rutherford insists on a deeper distinction between the higher and lower parts of our nature, and between right and wrong, than philosophy is capable of.

[29] "They would think her conduct shameful; and shame was torture. That was poor little Hetty's conscience" (*Adam Bede*, ch. xxxi). It is Arthur's also: we are constantly reminded of his dependence on the favorable opinion of others. It is significant that both Hetty and Arthur, who upset the moral balance of the community, are without strong family roots. It may be noted also that Arthur is rather utilitarian

work there is a strong sense of the influence of factors beyond the control of
the individual agent in determining his choices. Thus in one of the most
carefully analyzed decisions of the many George Eliot shows us, Gwendolen's decision to marry Grandcourt, we almost directly see the determining
forces at work; and they do not include some mysterious fiat of will working
in entire independence of Gwendolen's character and her past inclinations,
and able to check or change their tendencies. We do not need to rely on
George Eliot's letters and essays to attribute to her some kind of deterministic belief: it is a strong element in the sense of the world pervading her
novels.[30] I have pointed out that intuitionists strongly reject determinism on
the grounds that it makes truly moral distinctions impossible, while the
determinist replies that an interpretation of morality is quite possible on his
view, and that he at least is not burdened with the difficult concept of a
contra-causal freedom. The concept of freedom is of course quite crucial for
a moral view, even for a determinist one, and it is in her attempt to work out
a satisfactory portrayal of human freedom that George Eliot comes closest to
dealing in her novels with the conceptual tension between an intuitionist
attitude toward morality and a determinist attitude toward the universe
(unless it is a fatalistic view, alloting no place at all to human choice or
decision or effort; and this, it hardly needs saying, is not at all George Eliot's
version of determinism).

For the deterministic utilitarian, freedom exists when a man is not
prevented by anything outside his body or by any limits of bodily strength

---

in his outlook. He believes that an evil can be balanced by a greater good, so that one's transgressions can
all in principle be made up for (cf. ch. xxix). This is a view Adam explicitly disavows (ch. xviii); and at the
very end Arthur himself sees his mistake, and admits of Adam that "there is a sort of wrong that can never
be made up for." Like Adam he comes to disavow moral arithmetic and to realize that "feeling's a kind of
knowledge" (cf. ch. lii).

Felix Holt's reflection as the mob sweeps him into Treby Park is a miniature rejection of utilitarianism:
"As he was pressed along with the multitude into Treby Park, his very movement seemed to him only an
image of the day's fatalities, in which the multitudinous small wickednesses of small selfish ends, really
undirected towards any larger result, had issued in widely-shared mischief that might yet be hideous"
(ch. xxxiii). And as others have noted, if Holt is a radical, he is certainly not a Philosophic Radical.

[30] This is well brought out in the excellent discussion by George Levine, "Determinism and
Responsibility in the Works of George Eliot," *PMLA* 77 (1962), 268–79. The only difficulty with the
article is that it does not show any reason why we should take, as the philosopher who best articulates
George Eliot's position, J. S. Mill rather than someone like F. H. Bradley, who also includes the points of
her view that Levine brings out. Bradley, I think, is closer in general attitude to George Eliot than Mill is;
and there is consequently a closer correspondence in detail between his views and hers than between hers
and Mill's.

from doing what he wishes or would choose to do.[31] A man is free when he can do what he wants to do: is this George Eliot's view of freedom? If we are to judge by her characters who do as they please, the answer must be negative. *Daniel Deronda* (1876) is the novel in which freedom is closest to being George Eliot's theme; and in Gwendolen she gives us a brilliant portrayal of one whose whole aim in life is to do as she likes. Time after time George Eliot shows us that Gwendolen thinks she is free when she is living in this way. "My plan is to do what pleases me," she tells Rex, just after objecting to those who predict the actions of other people and saying boastfully, "I do what is unlikely" (ch. vii). She sees marriage with Grandcourt as "the gate into a larger freedom" (ch. xiv), because it will enable her to do more fully what she chooses. Just before accepting him she thinks that she can refuse him; and "Why was she to deny herself the freedom of doing this which she would like to do?" Then immediately after accepting him she "gains a sense of freedom" (ch. xxvi) as he tells her, and she believes, that "You shall have whatever you like" (ch. xxvii). After marriage, however, she rapidly finds out her mistake: "in seven short weeks her husband had gained a mastery" which she could not resist (ch. xxxv). Her submission to him is contrasted strongly with Mirah's very different kind of submission. Deronda says of Mirah that she is "capable of submitting to anything in the form of duty," and Gwendolen feels strongly the sense that "her own submission was something different...was submission to a yoke drawn on her by an action she was ashamed of" (ch. xlv).

The alternative to this dreary collapse of "doing as you like" into a slavery brought on oneself is presented through Deronda. To understand it we must understand his problem, which is precisely the problem one might expect to confront a sympathetic and imaginative determinist who is not prepared to be a utilitarian. "His early awakened sensibility and reflectiveness," George Eliot tells us, "had developed into a many-sided sympathy, which threatened to hinder any course of action" because he saw the human self in everyone and so could not really oppose anyone. Virtuous himself, yet "he hated vices mildly," being unable to separate them from

---

[31] Bain thinks the controversy between free-will and determinism is largely a verbal one, and recommends dropping both terms. "I am a moral agent," he says, "when I act at the instigation of my own feelings, pleasurable or painful, and the contrary when I am overpowered by force....We are not moral agents as regards the action of the heart, or the lungs, or the intestines. Every act that follows upon the prompting of a painful or pleasurable state, or the associations of one or other, is a voluntary act, and is all that is meant or can be meant by moral agency" (*The Emotions and the Will*, 564).

pitiful human lives. And, finally, "a too reflective and diffusive sympathy was in danger of paralyzing in him that indignation against wrong and that selectness of fellowship which are the conditions of moral force." It is this last point which is what the libertarian fears from the determinist. If Gwendolen shows us the purely selfish private will incapable of seeing any but its own ends, Daniel shows us a will so impartial and so impersonal that it is in danger of becoming, like the universe, incapable of seeking any ends or even of making any moral distinctions. What Deronda needed, we learn, was "an influence that would justify partiality, and make him what he longed to be, yet was unable to make himself—an organic part of social life" (ch. xxxii). Daniel's hope is that "the very best of human possibilities might befall him—the blending of a complete personal love in one current with a larger duty" (ch. 1). And what solves his problem is, of course, his discovery that he is a Jew. Here Sir Leslie Stephen dryly remarks, "Deronda's mode of solving his problem is not generally applicable," a complaint echoed by Dr. Leavis.[32] But this misses the point. What we are to see in Deronda, and in his mother as well, is that to be free is to bind oneself voluntarily to duty, to a task or calling. Daniel's mother, like Gwendolen, neglected family duties; but unlike Gwendolen she surrendered herself to the stern demands of art and so became the singer and actress she felt she was born to be. Daniel gives himself to duties he finds are hereditary because he can treat them as duties that he in particular was born to fulfill. The principle is the same in each case: one finds one's duty when one finds one's identity, whatever it may be; and one is free insofar as one is able to love one's duty and live for its sake. For one is then doing what one most desires to do, while at the same time, since this desire is the desire of the higher or better self, one is not a slave to one's passions.[33]

---

[32] Leslie Stephen, *George Eliot* (New York, 1902), 189. F. R. Leavis, *The Great Tradition* (New York, 1954), 107.

[33] One may think here of Spinoza's concept of the free man, and one does not entirely lose the connection with Spinoza when one thinks also of F. H. Bradley's Hegelian version of Freedom, tentatively suggested in *Ethical Studies*, ch. i. The whole essay is relevant; I quote a paragraph from the notes appended to it: "'*My* self,' we shall hear, 'is what is *mine*; and mine is what is *not* yours, or what does not belong to any one else. I am free when I assert my private will, the will peculiar to me.' Can this hold? Apart from any other objection, is it freedom? Suppose I am a glutton and a drunkard; in these vices I assert my private will; am I then free so far as a glutton and drunkard, or am I a slave—the slave of my appetites? The answer must be, 'The slave of his lusts is, *so* far, not a free man. The man is free who realizes his *true* self.' Then the whole question is, 'What is this true self, and can it be found apart from something like law?' Is there any 'perfect freedom' which does not mean 'service'?"

It is an interesting coincidence that George Eliot's most sustained attempt to bring together in one coherent vision both her intuitional morality and her determinist sense of the world should have appeared in the same year as Bradley's attempt to overcome the nineteenth-century English controversy between the two schools in a synthesis of a Hegelian variety, and only two years after Sidgwick's more painstaking attempt to reconcile the two schools. The concept of freedom which she tries to develop in the novel may in the end be as unsatisfactory philosophically as the hero is aesthetically. But the fact that she attempts to portray the sort of reality that would justify such a concept of freedom illustrates in a striking manner the way in which conceptual difficulties may operate in a literary medium, and gives us, as a result, an important example of one more way in which philosophical understanding may help in the understanding of a work of art.

.

PART III
On the Historiography of Moral Philosophy

4

Moral Crisis and the History of Ethics

The history of philosophy is not usually seen, in English-speaking circles, as a major tool for the resolution of philosophical problems. It is admitted to be useful for understanding classical authors. But it is not seen as offering direct aid in deciding whether their views are true or false. Still less is historical study taken to be a necessary step in analyzing current social and political problems. This commonplace stance is one of many challenged in Alasdair MacIntyre's original and wide-ranging book, *After Virtue*.[1] He believes that the history of moral philosophy is indispensable for understanding and criticizing any ethical theory, including those now current. He also holds that ethical theories mirror or articulate the actual moral structure of society and that problems in moral philosophy are inseparable from problems in moral life. Consequently, he thinks that the history of ethics must be understood if we are to improve the condition of society.

These are large claims. Their interest is increased by the extreme position MacIntyre takes about the theories and problems of our times. He sees current Anglophone ethics as obsessed with moralities of rule or principle and hopelessly mired in varieties of emotivism. These facts, he argues, reflect the extensive and deeply rooted moral malaise of our culture. Modern liberalism, and the individualism that infects both it and contemporary Marxism, are illnesses that have now become unendurable (AV viii). None of the current political approaches offers any hope. To find a cure for

Versions of this paper have been read at Harvard, the New York Philosophy Club, and the Washington Area Philosophy Club. I am grateful to members of those audiences, and to Prof. Richard Flathman of Johns Hopkins University, for helpful comments and criticism.

[1] *After Virtue* (Notre Dame, Ind.: University of Notre Dame Press, 1981). All page references to this book will be given in the text, indicated by the letters AV.

our ailment, we must first diagnose it properly. The diagnosis will show that we must abandon the views that dominate modern analytical ethics. We must return to a morality centered on the virtues and to the corresponding Aristotelian tradition of moral philosophy. At the end of his book, MacIntyre suggests, darkly, that our only hope is to work our way back to smaller, more unified kinds of community than we now have, in which lives structured by such a morality will be possible.

In backing these claims MacIntyre attributes a central role to historical argument. The main support for the virtue-centered theory elaborated in the latter half of the book is that it alone offers a proper way out of our present unhappy condition, and MacIntyre says that it is historical analysis that both reveals the nature of our present situation and shows us what the alternatives are. I do not believe that MacIntyre's positive theory can provide solutions to the problems he sees.[2] But in this paper I will examine only the line of reasoning through which he hopes to persuade us that we must accept that theory. I first examine it as a straightforward historical argument. I sketch a different way of looking at the history of modern ethics and indicate that it suggests a different analysis of our current moral situation than MacIntyre's. I then try to bring out some assumptions underlying MacIntyre's approach and to show that there is reason to doubt that his historical argument is what really carries the weight of his position.

I

MacIntyre tells us that both the language and the practice of morality in our times are in a state of "grave disorder" (AV 2) and that we cannot understand their condition unless we see the essential steps in the history that led to it. Two features distinctive of modern morality show that it is chaotic. One is the occurrence of numerous debates over important moral issues. The examples MacIntyre gives are controversies over what constitutes a just war, whether abortion is permissible, and the extent to which it is right to limit freedom to increase equality of opportunity. What is distinctive is not the extensiveness of the debate about these issues. It is that the arguments

---

[2] I argue this in "Virtue, Narrative, and Community: MacIntyre and Morality," *Journal of Philosophy*, vol. 79 (1982).

cannot be settled. A perfectly valid case can be made to support either side of any issue, but each case depends on premises the other side does not accept. And "the rival premises are such that we possess no rational way of weighing the claims of one as against the other." Hence, MacIntyre thinks, it is appropriate to say that the premises are "incommensurable." The second distinctive feature of our morality is that, while it is articulated in language that claims impersonal objectivity, its terms are, in fact, used manipulatively for private purposes. This reflects our inability to provide "unassailable criteria" for our selection of even our own moral premises (AV 8–9; cf. 38). And it leads MacIntyre to say that emotivism, although false as a theory of the meaning of moral language, is true of the way in which objective-sounding moral terms are actually used in our culture (AV 17). Thinkers of the emotivist persuasion—MacIntyre includes Hare, Sartre, and Nietzsche along with Stevenson—tell us that morality must always rest on arbitrarily chosen principles, and modern analytic philosophers have been quite unable to show that this is false. But both emotivists and their critics suffer from a crippling lack of historical perspective. This prevents them from seeing that, while emotivism is supported by our culture in a striking way, not every culture would have been accurately articulated by it. There was a time, MacIntyre holds, when authoritative rational justification for morality could be given and when its objective language provided genuine impersonal standpoints for judgment. Now, it seems, this is not so. History must tell us how we got from then to now.

The crucial events took place during a period that MacIntyre locates roughly between 1630 and 1850. It was then that "the project of an independent rational justification of morality" became and remained central not only to philosophy but "to Northern European culture" as well (AV 38). The end of the period is marked by Kierkegaard's decisive revelation that the project had failed. Kierkegaard shows us that no reason can be given for preferring the moral life to the aesthetic life: if one adopts either, one does so by making an arbitrary choice. But morality presents itself to us as that which claims our allegiance regardless of personal choice. So its authority cannot be explained by saying we just choose to be moral (AV 39–41). Kierkegaard was responding, MacIntyre says, to Kant, who was too sensitive to the distinctive claim of morality to try to found it on mere choice. Rejecting revealed religion and the pursuit of happiness as also unsuitable to ground morality, Kant tried to show that it springs from reason alone. It was the complete failure of his effort to show how the contents of morality can be derived from such a base that forced Kierkegaard into his position (AV 42–5). And Kant, in turn, was responding to the challenge posed by Hume and Diderot. They tried to "found morality on the passions" (AV 47) and failed, as Kant saw. All four of these thinkers held a common view of the substance of morality, which they shared with their culture. Hence, the collapse of their efforts shows that "the project of providing a rational vindication of morality had decisively failed; and from henceforward the morality of our predecessor culture—and subsequently of our own—lacked any public, shared rationale or justification" (AV 48).

We are not to suppose that this failure was a mere accident, that cleverer thinkers might have done a better job. The problem is intractable. It springs from the Enlightenment rejection of Aristotelianism in all its shapes. Briefly put, MacIntyre's analysis goes like this: On Aristotle's view, we humans have a *telos*, or goal, built into our nature. "Human" is therefore a function word, like "hammer." Function words pick out both physically identifiable characteristics of that to which they refer and criteria for the goodness of function of that sort of thing. Thus, the notion of "hammer" and that of "good hammer" are interdependent. And both the criteria identifying hammers physically and the criteria identifying their good functioning are, MacIntyre says, factual.

Hence any argument which moves from premises which assert that the appropriate criteria are satisfied to a conclusion which asserts that "this is a good such and such", where "such and such" picks out an item specified by a functional concept, will be a valid argument which moves from factual premises to an evaluative conclusion   (AV 55).

Thus, in a culture, such as the Christian culture of the West, which accepts a fundamentally Aristotelian framework of thought, rational vindications of morality are available. Morality is to be understood in terms of three notions: "untutored human nature, man-as-he-could-be-if-he-realised-his-telos, and the moral precepts which enabled him to pass from one state to the other." Moral injunctions in a Christian culture say both what God ordains and what will lead to realizing the individual end. Since "the whole point of ethics . . . is to enable man to pass from his present state to his true end," the function of moral judgments is simply "to correct, improve, and educate" human nature (AV 52). And they do this while stating what is factually the case.

Now, the project of giving a rational basis to morality, as the Enlightenment understood it, arose because the teleological concept of human nature was dropped, along with the rest of Aristotle. The problem then was to find a new way of connecting the moral rules with human nature. But for two reasons this had become impossible. First, the moral injunctions inherited from the past were meant to be *at odds* with human nature as it initially is, so dropping the notion that human nature is meant to be something else leaves a code of rules radically unsuited for a human nature understood in no such way. Second, these now "incoherent fragments" cannot be given the kind of grounding they once had. Abandon the idea of essential human functions, MacIntyre says, and "it begins to appear implausible to treat moral judgments as factual statements." And if, as Enlightenment thinkers did, one gives up the idea that morality is a matter of God's commands or laws, the problem is made much worse. Hume's famous discovery of the impossibility of drawing a legitimate inference from factual premises to a conclusion about what ought to be done is not, as it is commonly thought to be, the uncovering of a timeless law of logic. It merely reveals the problem that emerged for the Enlightenment due to the abandonment of teleological and religious beliefs and the "impoverished moral vocabulary" that was the upshot (AV 55–6).

This "transition into modernity," MacIntyre says, "was a transition both in theory and in practice, and a single transition at that" (AV 58). The breakdown of the Enlightenment project in philosophical ethics gives expression to the collapse of the moral framework and so begins to explain the condition of morality in our own culture. Our interminable disputes arise because we cannot make rational sense of the "series of fragmented survivals from an older past" that constitutes our morality. Where an Aristotelian theory could relate rules and ends perfectly well, we cannot. The deontological aspect of morality is for us merely "the ghost of conceptions of divine law which are quite alien to the metaphysics of modernity." The teleological aspect is no better than a remnant of the abandoned Aristotelian belief in a human nature with a given end. Bentham, who saw the need for a new account of the teleological side of morality, failed to help the situation, because the way he tried to solve the problem—by appeal to the greatest happiness—involved a "notion without any clear content at all" (AV 62). The intuitionism that arose in opposition to utilitarianism as an effort to explain the deontological side of morality was actually the move that led to emotivism. For intuitionism in its practice, as opposed to its rhetoric, is in fact emotivist (AV 14–17, 63). And recent neo-Kantian attempts to ground morality must also be accounted complete failures, as witness the hopelessness of Gewirth's central argument (AV 64–5). Once we realize, however, that modern morality is nothing but an "incoherent conceptual scheme which we have inherited" (AV 66) we will not be surprised that "the problems of understanding and assigning an intelligible status to moral judgments . . . prove inhospitable to philosophical solutions" (AV 104–5). An anthropologist, not a philosopher, is the sort of expert who might make the condition of morality in our culture comprehensible (AV 106).

MacIntyre concludes the first, diagnostic, part of his book with the claim that Nietzsche, more clearly and devastatingly than anyone else, revealed the incoherence of our morality. By showing that none of the accepted moral stances of Europe had any rational justification at all, he made it finally impossible to ignore the actual manipulative purposes served by high-sounding enunciations of principle. He went further: he claimed that no morality could have any justification. And here, MacIntyre believes, Nietzsche "illegitimately generalised from the condition of moral judgment in his own day to the nature of morality as such" (AV 107). He therefore posed the question that MacIntyre thinks we must now face. If Aristotelianism in ethics is rejected, as it was by the Enlightenment, then it seems as though we are compelled to accept Nietzsche's conclusion. So the "key question" is: "Can Aristotle's ethics, or something very like it, after all be vindicated?" (AV 111). Instead of following MacIntyre in his construction of an affirmative answer to this question, I turn to an assessment of the diagnosis that, as he thinks, makes it necessary.

II

MacIntyre's sketch—it is, of course, meant to be no more—of the history of the collapse of morality is brilliantly conceived. It succeeds in making us see how we could understand our own culture as the natural concomitant of the conceptual shift involved in the rejection of Aristotelianism. It thus reinforces the descriptive diagnosis of our current condition with which MacIntyre begins. And that description, in turn, provides a focal point for a narrative that leads us to see it as an almost unavoidable outcome. If we are to assess MacIntyre's argument, we must separate his narrative of the past from his description of the present and examine them separately. How convincing, then, is his diagnosis of our current condition? As far as I can see, there are two lines of thought supporting MacIntyre's view, and neither of them seems compelling.

The first seems to be implicit in his repeated charge that the presence of interminable debates over moral issues shows that our morality is in grave disorder.[3] I suppose the idea here is the familiar Wittgensteinian one, that, if a language-bound practice like morality is to be in order, there must be agreement not only in definitions but also in judgments. But MacIntyre does not tell us in detail about how much disagreement can exist within a practice that is in good working order, though he suggests that a great deal can (AV 242). He does not advert to the extensive areas of agreement evident within ordinary morality. And, perhaps most strikingly for one with so historical an orientation, he never tries to compare the amount of disagreement in our culture with amounts in earlier times. I should have supposed, for example, that sixteenth-century debates about religious toleration and those about the duty to obey magistrates who ordered citizens to act against their consciences must have been, in MacIntyre's sense, interminable. But the morality of the sixteenth century, on his time scheme, is still "in order." So this line of argument, if MacIntyre means to suggest it at all, does not go very far.

The same is true for the more purely sociological discussions. That MacIntyre gives us an insightful and chilling version of one aspect of contemporary life no one can deny. His portrayals of the therapist, the aesthete, and the manager and his attacks on pretensions to social expertise speak to much of what is most worrisome in our times. But this is not followed by sociological data purporting to reveal the extent of the rot. For all that MacIntyre says, there might still be extensive areas of our common life—not merely of the life of surviving "pre-modern" groups—in which the uses of moral language remain in accord with the impersonal and objective meanings that he allows moral terms to possess. Would we, in fact, still have a common life or a common culture at all if this were not so? But if society has not wholly

___

[3] "The most striking feature of contemporary moral utterance is that so much of it is used to express moral disagreements" (AV 6). Indeed; and the most striking fact about modern science is that so much of it is concerned with problems we have not solved. Science is there to solve problems; morality, to resolve disagreements. Outside the classroom, why should we expect to dwell on what is settled?

disintegrated, then the manipulative use of moral language can be explained as the natural and normal parasite on its non-manipulative use; and the core areas of agreement can provide a model for the kind of settlement we hope to achieve where we currently disagree. There have, after all, been theories of morality—perhaps interpretable, in MacIntyrean fashion, as sociologies— that incorporate the facts of controversy and unsettleable differences of deep commitment into a vision of an ongoing moral community. MacIntyre mentions Berlin's version of this position but does not take it seriously enough to criticize it. The argument from contemporary behavioral patterns, like the argument from interminable debates, is thus inconclusive. The burden must be carried by MacIntyre's history.

III

What MacIntyre presents in his history of ethics is a study of the internal logic of its development rather than a narrative of its events. I have no objection to this way of viewing the past of moral philosophy. But I think that a different inner logic was at work in it. To break the powerful hold of MacIntyre's outline, I will indicate, very briefly indeed, the story I think is preferable.

It is a commonplace of intellectual history that the thought of the seventeenth and eighteenth centuries must be understood against the background of a deep, but deeply challenged, belief in God. God is purposeful, just, and good as well as omnipotent. He made the universe for a purpose, and every part in it has a purpose as well—a special function or role, a special contribution toward achieving the purpose of the whole. The *telos* He built into human nature is simply an instance of a general fact about created beings. It points out the special role we are to play in the cosmos. Natural laws structure this role for all created beings: inanimate objects have their laws, the lower animate beings have theirs, and we have ours—in a special way, because we alone in the world we know are guided through *consciousness* of our laws. Since God is just, He does not require us to do what we cannot do. So we must be able to know what we are to do, and we must be able to do it. Hence, every human has adequate instruction about the role that, qua human, he or she is to play in the cosmos. The laws of nature are written in our hearts or in our consciences. We may need special help in seeing how to apply them in complicated circumstances, but they provide a framework for common human life because we know that other humans have the same laws written in their hearts.

Now, given this general background, it is clear that the task for the moral philosopher or the theologian will not be one of the justification or vindication of morality. It will rather be one of explanation. The moral philosopher, in this period, is not sharply distinguished from the natural philosopher. Both seek the laws God built into his universe, and both show them to us, thereby revealing the order behind the apparent disorder of the world as we first see it. The laws are there and are recognized by everyone or will be once they are clearly articulated. The question of vindicating or justifying them has not arisen. Such a question arises only when there is a challenge to one's claim or a sheer absence of any conviction one way or another about it. That simply was not the situation facing the moralists of the period that concerns us. There was—as MacIntyre himself points out several times—consensus on what morality required, a consensus including Hume and Diderot (and Hobbes can be listed here, too). So the moral philosopher could explain what the laws of morality are—could, for instance, argue about whether they all reduce to one or whether several basic laws must be assumed—and could explain how it is that all of us receive adequate guidance from them—perhaps by knowing them, perhaps through feeling—but all of this is in aid of helping us to understand a moral world about whose existence we have no doubts.

A second important point arises from the fact that for the culture of our period the world is supervised by the Christian God. The religious under-standing of morality leaves a place for the individual's search for earthly happiness and an even more central one for the personal quest for salvation, which is what the Aristotelian *telos* is transmuted into under Christianity. But it also requires that we see the individual as linked through divinely ordained laws to other individuals, and to other kinds of beings, in a vast collaborative venture. MacIntyre says that the Aristotelian scheme of morality—humans as they are, being guided by rules to what they are to be—is "complicated and added to but not essentially altered when it is placed within a framework of theistic beliefs" (AV 51). My own view is rather that the longstanding incorporation of the older teleological tradition into the Christian framework is a matter of central importance. For a grasp of the logic of the relations of rules and ends in the special kind of collaborative endeavor Christianity sees us engaged in is indispensible for an understanding of the development of the moral philosophy of the period. I will try to explain this briefly, using the notion of cooperation to bring out the essential points. This notion is not fully appropriate for every stage of the history that concerns us, but it will do here as a rough first approximation.

Cooperation involves the division of labor. To divide up work is to accept the idea that each agent in a common venture has a special job or station. Performing the duties of that station is the agent's primary responsibility. It is only the joint or appropriately successive performance by all the agents of their duties that will produce the good at which the cooperative endeavor aims. Thus, no agent has a task properly described as producing the good. Consequently, in a well-run venture, no one has any business going beyond the assigned duties of his or her station. Those duties have at least a prima facie absolute deontic status just because of their functioning within a complex teleological enterprise. In ordinary cooperative ventures it is, of course, easy to see reasons for overriding the *prima facie* absolute status of one's duties. I may doubt the wisdom of the assignment of duties; I may see that someone else is failing to do a job without which mine would be pointless or harmful; I may note an opportunity to save everyone a lot of trouble by taking advantage of an unpredictable lucky break. In all such cases, of course, I must fully understand the good we are all trying to bring about and know a fair amount about how everyone else's contribution fits in. Otherwise, I would not be in a position to reason directly from my understanding of the goal to a decision about the means.

Now, in the strongest form in which we understand God's governance of the world, individual humans are never in the position I have just described. We do not understand God's glory, the goal of cosmic cooperation; we cannot challenge the wisdom, or the fairness, of His assignment of duties; we know that His providence and His omnipotence will make up for any failings by any of the imperfect agents we see; and in any case we have no idea of what the other parts of the universe are really meant to be doing or of how they contribute to the goal. Hence, for us our duties must always have an absolute deontic status, although—as Butler points out—God may well be utilitarian and may understand the laws of morality in that sense. If we weaken some of these assumptions about God and His governance, we can see a tension develop between deontology and teleology. Suppose the aim of the enterprise is human happiness, rather than cosmic displays of God's glory: then we can begin to understand the goal. Suppose God no longer intervenes in particular cases in the world: then we cannot be sure He will make up for failures by our fellows; then each of us has some degree of responsibility to see to it that the end is indeed brought about by doing our duty. The absolute deontic status is gone; we are required, morally, to judge to some extent by results. Thus, the inner logic of a cooperative venture carries us toward utilitarianism as an explanation. But there is a counter-vailing pull toward "intuitionism," that is, toward reassertion of the absolute deontic status of moral demands, for it is essential in this special cooperative venture—since it is a just one, given its Creator—that everyone be equally able to be aware of what is demanded. If morality demands that each agent figure out what is for the best in each case, it is extremely difficult to see how this can be maintained. But on the assumption that intuitive truths are equally available to everyone, or that moral feelings are, we can maintain the justice of the cooperative venture by arguing that everyone is aware of dictates that are deontically absolute.

I think this dynamic helps us understand many of the actual positions of eighteenth-century moralists, and it carries us to further developments as well. God's role may be taken over by Nature (as MacIntyre notes, AV 217) if we think that Nature has so constructed us that our sentiments will coordinate our actions toward a common good and that our own happi-ness will be found in the course of so acting. But if Nature, too, becomes unavailable to play this role, the problems of morality begin to take on a new shape. For if we live in a neutral universe, not in a just world, we can have no rational assurance that our moral sentiments or our intuitive convictions will lead us to coordinate our actions with those of others to a common end: our duties, even if somehow separately possessing a cognitive warrant, may not have a rational point. And we cannot be sure, even if this problem is resolved, that acting on moral directives will also be for our own good, as in the just world we could be assured it had to be. It is at this point, with the emergence of the very different views of Kant and Bentham—and not, as MacIntyre seems to think, earlier—that the rational justification of morality becomes an important issue. With it there emerges also the problem posed by the rationality of concern for one's own good in its distinctively modern form. The reason is the same in both cases. At this point it becomes clear that the way things go in the moral world is up to us. It is all our responsibility, and we must be able to justify whatever we do.

IV

The aim of MacIntyre's narrative is to lend support to his diagnosis of our present moral condition as one of disorder and confusion. Today's chaos is yesterday's order, wrecked by the loss of its foundation, the fixed human *telos*. To make sense of moral life, history shows, we must find a way to restore that base. Otherwise, the rules of morality will continue to seem arbitrary, the debates go on forever, moral discourse merely mask personal aims in impersonal language. In opposition to this, I have suggested that we should not accept MacIntyre's portrayal of morality as being, prior to the collapse, centered solely on directing agents to their naturally determined individual good. Morality was seen to have another function as well, that of coordinating efforts toward a good that could only come about through cooperation. So, the disappearance of the fixed-*telos* view of human nature did not leave behind it a morality whose substance was totally at odds with the nature of the agents whose actions it was to guide. As Hobbes makes evident, cooperation is as much a necessity for persons viewed mechanistically as for persons viewed teleologically. The nature of the good they must cooperate to produce may differ, but in either case it is indispensable.[4] And the existing morality, since it had functioned to guide cooperation when framed in teleological terms, could continue to guide it even when framed quite differently.

Thus, the continuity, of which MacIntyre makes so much, between the content of the older, "Aristotelian," morality and its Enlightenment descendant is no surprise, still less evidence of radical incoherence. What the continuity shows is that the vitality of the morality itself is greater than that of what MacIntyre views as its foundations. People cannot avoid living together and therefore cannot avoid having a morality. When an old common understanding of it ceases to be viable and supportive, there is a need to replace it with a new one, which will do better at helping people continue the effort to sustain a just moral world. Changes in science and

---

[4] MacIntyre thinks that the "notion of the political community as a common project is alien to the modern liberal individualist world" (AV 146). This is a more complex issue than MacIntyre allows. The persistence in our schools of courses in civics and American history suggests that we still think it essential to educate our children to understand the special values of our form of democratic society, even if we think of the political community in a libertarian, minimalist way as being no more than the communally guaranteed safe arena for pursuit of private good. This does not make us into a Greek city-state. It does give us some shared values.

religious belief may have eroded the old understanding, and the new one may have to accommodate new criteria of what is generally acceptable to reasonable people, but morality itself sets some of the criteria. It does not merely respond to those established by scientific practice. To ignore this is to fall victim to one of the deeper prejudices of contemporary analytic philosophy, that of seeing morality as always the dependent variable in the history of thought. MacIntyre seems, surprisingly, to have constructed his history on this basis. But the facts to which he has drawn attention suggest that it is not obvious that moralities are abandoned because what we now locate as their foundations have been.

If we examine our present situation and its dynamics in this light, it will not look quite the way it does from MacIntyre's historical perspective. A number of issues might illustrate this. I will touch briefly on a few, beginning with a point about the language of morality.

If morality provides the framework for just cooperation, we need not see its language as being in the grave disorder that MacIntyre portrays. The distinction between impersonal and personal appeals to others and the idea that morality involves reasonable objective standards make sense in terms of the belief that those to whom we are speaking share with us the wish to sustain a moral community. Our very use of moral language is to be taken as an indication that we draw a distinction between aims, ideals, interests, and desires that can be publicly accommodated within such a community and those that cannot. We do not need to have a fixed human *telos* or an authoritative divinity to make sense of this distinction or to see that there continues to be a point in making it. Of course, some people will use the language of morality for private (or class-based) manipulative purposes. But history does not give us any reason to suppose that the language itself has lost its function and is therefore in disorder.

The "interminable" current debates about different views of justice, abortion, war, and so on, which MacIntyre takes as further evidence of moral disintegration, also look different in the perspective of a more adequate history than his. If deliberate cooperation is to be possible, the cooperating agents must be able to rely on one another. This requires, among other things, that each be able to be sure that others have both appropriate instructions about what to do and appropriate motivation to do it. In a neutral universe, there is only one way in which we can be sure that others have the appropriate moral instructions—which must be the same for everyone. That is by relying on received opinion, the positive morality of one's community. But to be sure that everyone has a stake in the cooperative venture, and so is motivated to try to continue it, that venture must represent everyone's concerns fairly. In a neutral universe, there is no *a priori* reason to suppose that common-sense morality does so. In fact, in particular areas we have good reason to suppose that it does not. The problem facing modern morality in this respect can, therefore, be described as that of sustaining a common core of received opinion while reforming it so as to make it responsive to the deepest concerns of all who are to live according to it. The moral community must respond to hitherto unrecognized interests of persons who are already members but some of whose aspirations have in the past been flouted, suppressed, or rejected as immoral. And it must look toward increased interaction with other moral communities with vastly different historical backgrounds, working out common moralities with them. It may be argued that both of these difficulties are greater now than they have been at any time in the past, though one should perhaps be suspicious of a claim of this kind, which seems to be made by every generation. But at any rate we need not look at these "interminable debates" as showing that the fabric of morality is in tatters. We can see them, rather, as testing the extent to which different concerns can be publicly accommodated within a single moral community.

As I indicated earlier, debates of this kind have been a recurrent feature of the history of morality. Their upshot is not to destroy it but to alter received opinion so as to include within it new sets of understandings concerning some vexed area of life, such as lending money at interest or divorce or voting. We cannot know *a priori* what interests or principled commitments or ideals people will try to incorporate publicly into our common life, and so we cannot know *a priori* what tests a sense of moral community will have to sustain. We can be sure that we will bring our existing understandings to current debates, and we will naturally try to make them explicit by stating them as rules or principles. Explicit articulations make sense where unspoken consensus seems to have reached its limits. An appeal to principle is a way of seeing whether that consensus can be projected into a novel area of controversy. Statements of rules and principles thus have a social function in this sort of context, one quite different from that often envisaged by moral philosophers but important nonetheless. If the deontic and teleological aspects of morality are not MacIntyrean fragments left alone of a temple once complete, neither are they simply contenders for the dignity of being the epistemological starting points of moral knowledge. They are, as we would expect from our historical perspective, inevitable functional elements in what we view as a complex cooperative enterprise. Debate about them is a way of discussing the stresses that arise when the justness of some feature of the enterprise is challenged or when it is questioned whether its point is adequate. It is not simply a futile endeavor by all the king's philosophers to put Humpty-Dumpty together again.

V

I have argued that MacIntyre does not present compelling reason based on current data to accept his portrayal of our culture as in a state of moral collapse, and that an historical narrative more adequate than his would not lead to that conclusion either. If this is correct, then we are not forced to choose between an unacceptable Nietzschean nihilism and MacIntyre's revised Aristotelianism. But MacIntyre holds that "arguments in philosophy rarely take the form of proof, and the most successful arguments on topics central to philosophy never do" (AV 241). He insists from the beginning that his view will necessarily seem implausible and that presently accepted philosophical stances will not enable us to find truly basic "disorders of moral thought and practice" (AV 2–5). My criticisms thus far may seem, therefore, to have failed to touch the nerve of his position. They look like just one more reassertion of precisely that modernist stance that MacIntyre is attempting not to refute but to undermine. To come to grips with this we must examine the nature of his own enterprise.

   The key is to be found in MacIntyre's notion of an epistemological crisis.[5] Such a crisis arises, he says, when a new discovery casts doubt not just on a particular belief or a set of beliefs but on a whole conceptual scheme, including "criteria of truth, intelligibility, and rationality" (EC 455). For example, one might face such a crisis on learning that one's spouse does not and never did love one. Then, one's whole past would have to be reinterpreted, because one would be faced with "alternative and rival

---

   [5] For this I draw on his "Epistemological Crises, Dramatic Narrative, and the Philosophy of Science," *The Monist*, vol. 60 (1977), 453–72. Page references are given in the text indicated by the letters EC.

schemata which yield mutually incompatible accounts" of what happened (EC 454). The crisis is resolved only when the agent can construct a new narrative of the past, one that "enables the agent to understand *both* how he or she could intelligibly have held his or her original beliefs *and* how he or she could have been so drastically misled by them" (EC 455). MacIntyre uses this idea to illuminate "epistemological progress" generally (EC 456) and in particular to cover scientific revolutions. Galileo's work, he says, shows how a new, more adequate theory enables us to understand older theories that we now see to be inadequate, for only after Galileo could we distinguish real counter-examples to medieval theories from mere anomalies justifiably handled by "ad hoc explanatory devices." Nor is it an accident that a successful theory enables us to do this. "The criterion of a successful theory," MacIntyre asserts, "is that it enables us to understand its predecessors in a newly intelligible way" (EC 460). MacIntyre's aim is to combine a modified Kuhnian view of scientific revolution with a narrativist perspective to show that scientific reason is "subordinate to, and intelligible only in terms of, historical reason. And," he adds, "if this is true of the natural sciences, *a fortiori* it will be true also of the social sciences" (EC 464; cf. 467). This general idea, I believe, guides MacIntyre's study of morality. Society is in a moral crisis—the practical equivalent of an epistemological crisis—and only historical understanding, arising ultimately from a new theory, will enable us to see where we are and where to go.

This brings together a number of features of MacIntyre's position. It gives a broader base to his insistence on the importance of narrative history for understanding moral problems.[6] It explains why he stresses understanding different societies through their stories (such as AV 201), for he also holds that what ends up as science begins in the "myths or fairy stories which are essential to a well-ordered childhood" (EC 456). It puts in its rightful central place MacIntyre's concern with deep shifts in the entire framework of morality, rather than disagreements within a shared scheme (such as AV 161–2). It helps us to understand his very strong view on the unity of theory and practice in morality. And it enables us to see why MacIntyre is so willing to say that his diagnosis of our times is one that is necessarily implausible, masked by the present structure of the academic disciplines

---

[6] It is worth noting that MacIntyre develops an additional theory of the role of narrative in knowledge and understanding in the latter part of his book. It is used to provide a foundation for part of his view of virtue. See especially ch. 15 of *After Virtue*.

(AV 4). For he says that the structure of an epistemological crisis and that of a paranoid frame of mind are not wholly dissimilar (EC 462–3).

There is some difficulty in mounting direct arguments against a critique of our culture and its philosophy that has this structure, and I do not propose to embark on criticism of MacIntyre's general theory of epistemological crisis. Still, there are two kinds of consideration that might tell against the paradigm change that MacIntyre is recommending. The first uses a test that MacIntyre himself proposes for the superiority of one theory or paradigm over another. We have, in fact, already traversed this ground, since the test he proposes is historical. It is, he says, rational to accept a later theory or paradigm and reject an earlier one if from the standpoint of the later, "the acceptance, the life-story, and the rejection of the previous theory or paradigm can be recounted in more intelligible historical narrative than previously" (EC 467). My historical sketch was meant to raise doubts that MacIntyre's history, inspired by a virtue-centered theory, is more intelligible, or better, than one not so inspired. The second kind of consideration has to do with the coherence of MacIntyre's execution of his project. The key question here is what it takes, on his view, for morality to be "in order." I am not at all sure that I have found the answer to this question. Several possibilities are suggested by the text.

Because of the stress on the significance of disagreement in showing that we are in a moral crisis, we naturally think first that MacIntyre would consider a morality "in order" only if it contained a method for obtaining rational agreement on any moral question that might arise. This would make him an ally of Kant and Bentham at their most extreme. But he criticizes Aristotle for not allowing for tragic conflict within morality and makes ample room for it in his own theory (AV 153, 183). Moreover, he insists that "there are bound to be occasions on which no formula is available in advance" to give clear guidance (AV 143). So, this cannot be what he requires for a morality to be "in order." The next plausible candidate for the criterion of order is the existence of a rational justification or vindication of the basic principles of morals. MacIntyre presents the failure of Enlightenment philosophers to come up with such a justification as the central episode in our culture's sorry descent into moral crisis, and he repeatedly tells us that it is the absence of such a justification that makes us all into emotivists in practice (AV 38, 111). But it would be puzzling if this were MacIntyre's criterion, for, in his own neo-Aristotelian theory, he does not offer anything readily recognizable as such a justification. He finds rock bottom in a functional vocabulary whose terms moral agents use to think of their own deepest personal identity. These terms, he says, are inherited from the community in which one is born and educated. As his own historical study of the virtues makes clear, such terms change through time and vary from community to community. It is, therefore, hard to see how they can have any purely rational justification or vindication.[7]

We may, nonetheless, have a clue here to MacIntyre's implicit criterion. He may think that morality is "in order" only if it somehow rests on a shared vocabulary that simply cannot be put in doubt. (He tells us that even Descartes was unable to doubt what he inherited in the languages he used [EC 458].) If we must use an inherited, shared vocabulary for self-description and if, as MacIntyre tries to make out, the terms of that vocabulary are functional, then we will have that shared, unquestioned framework for evaluations that is so sadly lacking from contemporary culture. This idea of what MacIntyre thinks it takes for morality to be "in order" fits in well with his denunciations of emotivist selves with "no necessary social content" or identity (AV 30). It also enables us to make sense of the otherwise baffling claim that Diderot, Hume, Kant, Kierkegaard, Bentham, and Gewirth all tried to work out some one thing called a foundation for morality, which MacIntyre himself has alone found. What, after all would come even close to describing all of the endeavors referred to in that assertion if not the statement that they are all quests for something indubitable?

If this, or anything like it, is MacIntyre's root thought about what it would take for morality to be "in order," then two observations are called for. First, there is a striking discrepancy between MacIntyre's treatment of morality and his treatment of science. He tells us that in science we must think that the theory we presently accept is a closer approximation to the truth than earlier views, but we need not think that we have now arrived at a final truth. Satisfactory and workable acceptance of a scientific theory is compatible with admitting both that we might be mistaken and that future radical changes might be necessary (EC 464–7). In short, no unquestionable vocabulary or principle is required for science to be "in order." Morality is

---

[7] MacIntyre promises us a new theory of practical rationality (AV 242). Perhaps when we have it, this difficulty will vanish.

required to meet a sterner test. It is because it currently fails to do so that MacIntyre tells us we have no rational vindication for it and are emotivist in practice. But, if we are to see science as having moved away from any need for unalterable foundations and unquestionable vocabularies, why should we not see morality as making a similar transition? If we did so, we could interpret meta-ethics generally as part of the experimentation involved in learning to live cooperatively in a world in which we cannot have certainties of the kind our predecessor culture had. Philosophical emotivism might be seen historically as having arisen from exaggeration of the contrast between morality and science, from noting an absence of unshakable foundations in morality while believing them to be present in science. MacIntyre's criterion would require us to exaggerate the difference in the other direction. But it is unclear why we should insist on this difference at all.

Second, MacIntyre does not put his criterion for morality's being "in order" in any historical perspective. He is prepared to be historicist to the extent of relativizing the truth of some basic ideas about the status of morality to the moralities embedded in different cultures. He has given us a historical account of the rise of the demand for a rational vindication of morality as it affected our predecessor culture and affects our own. But his account does not cover certain vital features of that demand: that it was from the start apparently a demand for an indubitably certain foundation and that it became a demand for a principle capable of supporting a comprehensive method for decision-making. He himself seems to have abandoned the latter of these demands while retaining the former. As I have frequently said, he uses this demand as the basis for his critical diagnosis of our culture. But he has given us no historical account that might justify the demand by showing that the conditions that once made it appropriate still obtain. And, if, as I have argued, a more comprehensive picture of the history of ethics than his does not lead to his diagnosis, then he must admit, I think, either that his diagnosis is badly off the mark or that history is quite irrelevant to it.

5

Modern Moral Philosophy: From Beginning to End?

Philosophers who ask, "Why should anyone be moral?" are often chided for supposing that being moral is simply a means to something else. Once it is admitted that being moral is valuable, perhaps supremely valuable, in itself, the question's crassness becomes evident, and we stop asking it. We might treat the question, "Why should anyone study the history of philosophy?" in the same dismissive way. Asking how it pays to study that history is like asking why one should read masterpieces. The question assumes that the activity must be good for something beyond itself. Surely, the assumption is philistine and should be dismissed.

There is something right about these responses, but since people keep asking both questions something else may be at issue. In the case of morals, the questioner may be asking about the place of morality within the whole economy of the active life, or what it is about morality that gives it unquestionable claim on our rational adherence. These questions deserve answers, not dismissals, and the answers help us understand our own involvement in morality. Similarly, good reasons may exist for asking why the history of philosophy is worth study, and the answers may help us understand what we are doing when we engage in philosophy. The desire to know how our forebears thought about these things needs no justification; but the work to which it leads may have philosophically important results that go beyond satisfying this deeply human desire to sustain the connection to our past.

I think this is indeed the case, but since I can find no single satisfactory account of what it is to do philosophy, I can give no single explanation of how historical study fits into that activity. Some who engage in historical inquiry claim they do so only because their predecessors often turn out to have had good ideas about solving perennial philosophical problems. For them, it is merely accidental that history is useful to philosophy as we do it today. Others see philosophical views as arising and developing within enduring separate traditions of inquiry, and they believe that it is only within such traditions that rational inquiry can be carried on. For them, since deeply rooted disagreements can only be understood as involving whole traditions, history is indispensable. I am inclined to think that those who rummage in the past merely to salvage usable bits and pieces from the junk heaps underestimate the degree to which the problems that engage them are historically conditioned, and that those who see all philosophical inquiry as enmeshed in traditions are trapped by a totalizing demand for comprehensive systems, which is itself philosophically questionable. But as an historian I have no desire to outlaw these approaches. Each of them has generated valuable investigations. Those of us whose primary interest is in finding out how people thought about these things in the past can take what they have to offer and see how helpful it is in our inquiries.

In studying the history of philosophy, I think it is more helpful to suppose that different aspects or areas of current work bear different relations to their pasts than it is to assume that there must be some single relation between past and present for any two values of those variables. The best way to learn about the instrumental value and the philosophical role of the history of philosophy is through case studies, and it is such a study that I shall present here. I shall discuss some aspects of the history of ethics; useful results of the kind that I think emerge from *this* piece of history may or may not be found to result from studying the history of other parts of philosophy.

The project from which this study emerged began as an effort to find out what questions about morality Kant himself thought his ethical theory answered. While working on the topic, I came to think that in uncovering this aspect of the development of Kant's ethics I was learning something about the origins of modern moral philosophy itself and of the morality implicated in it. I begin with a stripped-down account of why Kantianism is so central.[1]

---

[1] I offer a fuller account in "Autonomy, Obligation, and Virtue: An Overview of Kant's Moral Philosophy," in Chapter 14 of this volume.

I

At the heart of Kant's ethical theory is the proposition that normal adults are capable of being fully self-governing in moral matters, which are matters of supreme practical importance. Kant speaks of this capacity as displaying our "autonomy"; and autonomy, as he understands it, has two components. The first is that no authority external to ourselves is needed to constitute or inform us of the demands of morality. All of us are equally able to know without tutelage what we ought to do because moral requirements are those we impose on ourselves. The second component is that in moral matters we can effectively control ourselves, even though we do not always do so. The obligations we impose on ourselves override all other constraints or requirements on action and frequently run counter to our desires. We nonetheless find in our knowledge of what morality requires a sufficient reason to act as we ought. No external sources of motivation, no threats of punishment or promises of reward are needed for our self-legislation to have the potential for guiding our conduct.

Other eighteenth-century philosophers besides Kant argued for the equal ability of normal adults to be fully self-governing in moral matters, although none of them tried to explain it in terms of self-legislation. Richard Price and Thomas Reid would have agreed with Kant about the supremacy of morality and about our ability to know what morality calls for and to be moved by that knowledge. But they would have strongly rejected Kant's claim that we create moral requirements by imposing them on ourselves.

Kantianism and intuitionism were two of the main determinants of nineteenth-century debate in moral philosophy. The third was utilitarianism. It is not so clear that Bentham's version of that view allowed him to assert the full and equal moral competence of all normal adults. But the later Benthamites felt a need to work out a way in which allegiance to the utilitarian principle could be fitted together with the assertion of such competence. John Stuart Mill's theory that the rules of common-sense morality are really summaries of the experience of the human race about the typical beneficial and harmful consequences of action was an effort to show how ordinary people could know what it is right to do without having to carry out immense calculations prior to action. And his associationist explanation of how we build an immediate attachment to morality into our desires was meant to show why external rewards and punishments are not, as Bentham seemed to suggest, necessary for moral knowledge to be efficacious. The utilitarian acceptance, however difficult and perhaps tenu-ous,[2] of the belief in equal moral competence that Kant and Reid shared made it the general background assumption of the work we do and the courses we teach in what we call ethics or moral philosophy.

It is also central, I think, to modern morality itself. If we do not believe that everyone alike is "essentially" or by nature a fully competent moral agent, we believe that we ought to educate everyone to be so. We are uneasy about the idea of moral experts. We remain so despite the widespread desire for carefully focused moral advice reflected in the rapid growth of the studies known vaguely as "applied ethics." Much of what the "ethicist" does is to put specialized knowledge of some field of technical practice, such as medicine or engineering, at the service of specific moral inquiries. The *moral* competence of those involved in and affected by the moral decisions is presupposed, since a substantial amount of agreement from them is required for the alternatives or policies proposed by the ethicist to be acceptable. Ours is a society in which the idea of a moral authority is at best marginal.

It would be absurd to say that modern moral philosophy is the sole source or cause of our belief that in moral matters everyone's views have to be considered equally. But in the course of its development, modern moral philosophy produced the major ways in which this belief came to be articulated and defended. The study of its history is therefore the study of the emergence of one central aspect of our self-understanding.

II

Our belief in the full and equal moral competence of normal adults would have surprised a good many seventeenth-century philosophers. We do not usually appreciate the distance that separates all of us on this matter from what was widely believed during that period and well into the eighteenth century. It is worth being reminded. What I take to be the standard early

---

[2] Consider R. M. Hare's account in *Moral Thinking* (Oxford: Oxford University Press, 1981) of two levels of moral thinking, one for "proles" and one for "angels." The terminology as well as the doctrine betrays a certain unease about ordinary moral thinking.

view was expressed with unusual clarity by an important political theorist of
the early seventeenth century, Johannes Althusius. His major work, *Politica
methodice digesta atque exemplis sacris et profanis illustrata,* was first published in
1603. In the course of discussing "the knowledge imprinted within us by
God, which is called conscience," Althusius cites Saint Paul's central pro-
nouncement from Romans 2:14–15, asserting that the Gentiles, though
lacking the law, do by nature what the law requires because the law is
written in their hearts, and because their consciences disturb and accuse
them when they act wickedly. Commenting, Althusius says:

There are different degrees of this knowledge and inclination. For law is not
inscribed equally on the hearts of all. The knowledge of it is communicated
more abundantly to some and more sparingly to others, according to the will and
judgment of God. . . . Nor does God urge and excite all persons to obedience of this
law in the same manner and to an equal degree. Some men exert themselves more
strongly, others less so, in their desire for it.[3]

A more admiring view of ordinary people's ability to see for themselves how
to live was not to be found among the privileged few who professed to be
aiming at the life of a Stoic or Epicurean sage, or of an equable Skeptic.
"Good, in good truth," says the Stoic Du Vair, "is not so placed that all the
world may see and perceive it."[4] The knowledge required of the sage was
never thought to be something that everyone could acquire, nor was the
continuous dosage with antithetical arguments needed to preserve the
indifference of the accomplished Pyrrhonian Skeptic. Whatever the originators of these ancient sects thought, their Renaissance and early modern
inheritors did not think themselves to be delivering a path to the good that
was equally available to everyone. They were writing for an elite.

We would expect to find a more generous attitude within more orthodox Christianity. But the passage from Althusius shows it was possible to
admit that all men have consciences without admitting that all of them have
equally capable consciences; and the Roman Catholic practice of casuistry,

---

[3] *The Politics of Johannes Althusius*, trans. Frederick S. Carney (London: Eyre and Spottiswoode, 1964),
135–6.
[4] Guillaume Du Vair, *The Moral Philosophy of the Stoics,* trans. Thomas James, ed. R. Kirk (New
Brunswick, N.J.: Rutgers University Press, 1951) 54. Excerpts are to be found in J. B. Schneewind, ed.,
Moral Philosophy from Montaigne to Kant, 2 vols. (Cambridge: Cambridge University Press, 1990), 1: 202–14.
Page references to this book, indicated as *MPMK*, are given where relevant.

tied to confession[5] and continued by some Protestant groups well into the seventeenth century, presupposes that most consciences need to be directed.

In natural-law theories, the foundations for this belief are clear. We can see this view in the work of Francisco Suarez (1615), the greatest of the Spanish neo-Thomist system builders. To be properly binding, Suarez says, laws must be adequately promulgated; and those of God's laws that are binding on all people alike are promulgated through the natural light of reason,[6] which in this case exercises itself through conscience.[7] The light of reason shows us three classes of truths. There are "primary and general principles of morality, such principles as 'one must do good, and shun evil.' . . . " Other principles, which Suarez describes as "more definite and specific. . . . are also self-evident," such as that justice must be observed and that God must be worshiped. And the third class contains inferences from principles of the first two groups. Some of these conclusions are fairly easily grasped and so are available to many people, for example, that adultery and theft are wrong. But "other conclusions require more reflection, of a sort not easily within the capacity of all, as is the case with the inferences that fornication is intrinsically evil, that usury is unjust, that lying can never be justified, and the like."[8] The law works more frequently, Suarez adds, through these hard-to-infer proximate principles than it does through the obvious, very general ones.[9] And while ignorance of the latter is not possible, ignorance of the former is. Moreover, ignorance respecting the precepts that require greater reflection can be invincible, "especially," Suarez says, "on the part of the multitude."[10] The preface to his great treatise makes it clear that the theologian is the ultimate source of knowledge of law because he is the one concerned with everything to do with God, and the moral law is simply one manifestation of God in our lives. The need for an educated clergy instructing the consciences of "the multitude" is thus evident.

Low views of the multitude were not confined to Jesuits with an interest in defending casuistry; they also are prominent among natural-law theorists. Grotius does not say much about the matter, no doubt because it could be

---

[5] See John Mahoney, *The Making of Moral Theology* (New York: Oxford University Press, 1987).

[6] Francisco Suarez, *De Legibus ac Deo Legislatore* (*On Laws and God the Lawgiver*), trans. and ed. Gwladys Williams et al. (Oxford: Oxford University Press, 1944) II.vi.24; *MPMK*, 1:79.

[7] Suarez, II.v.10; *MPMK* 1:75.

[8] Suarez II.vii.5; *MPMK* 1:80; cf. II.viii. 3, *MPMK* 1:82–83.

[9] Suarez, II.vii.7; *MPMK* 1:81.   [10] Suarez, II.viii.7; *MPMK* 1:84.

taken for granted. "For alike children, women, and men of dull intellect and
bad education are not well able to appreciate the distinction between just
and unjust."[11] Hobbes thinks the masses must be reminded by constant
sermons of what they ought to do; he also thinks it seditious, within civil
society, to teach that every private person is judge of good and evil.[12]
Pufendorf leaves us in no doubt about the ordinary man's capacity for
moral knowledge. The first principles of natural law can be understood by
all, he says, at least after those principles have been properly explained. But
most men, not knowing how they are to be demonstrated, usually learn and
observe the law by imitation. Pufendorf finds no problem here: "As for the
common throng," he says, "the authority of their superiors . . . should be
enough to make them certain regarding [the law]."[13]

At times, Locke writes as if he agreed with his fellow theorists of natural
law. The basic precepts of morality, he says in a late work, could not have
been discovered by unaided human reason—witness the failure of the
ancient philosophers to find them—and had to be taught us by a divine
mediator. And even now that we know them, and think them perfectly
reasonable (as in his view they are), we cannot teach them as purely rational
precepts. Even if philosophy had "from undeniable principles given us
ethics in a science like mathematics, in every part demonstrable," it would
not avail.

The greater part of mankind want leisure or capacity for demonstration; nor can
carry a train of proofs, which in that way they must always depend upon for
conviction. . . . And you may as soon hope to have all the day-laborers and trades-
men, the spinsters and dairy maids perfect mathematicians, as to have them perfect
in ethics this way. Hearing plain commands is the sure and only course to bring
them to obedience and practice. The greatest part cannot know, and therefore they
must believe. . . . And were all the duties of human life clearly demonstrated, yet I
conclude, when well considered, that method of teaching men their duties would

---

[11] Hugo Grotius, *Law of War and Peace*, trans. Francis W. Kelsey (Oxford: The Clarendon Press, 1925)
II.II.xxxi.1, 497.

[12] Thomas Hobbes, *Leviathan*, ed. Richard Tuck (Cambridge: Cambridge University Press, 1991)
II.29.

[13] Samuel Pufendorf, *The Law of Nature and of Nations*, trans. C. H. Oldfather and W. A. Oldfather
(New York: Oceana, 1964) II.iii.13, 204. For an earlier statement, see Pufendorf's *Elements of Natural
Jurisprudence* (1660, 1672), trans. W. A. Oldfather (Oxford: The Clarendon Press, 1964) II.iv.1: "as
human society coalesces and is preserved by the law of nature, so this is by no means the least fruit of
societies already established, that, in them, through instruction from others and by its very exercise, even
the duller may learn the law of nature" (240).

be thought proper only for a few, who had much leisure, improved understandings, and were used to abstract reasonings. But the instruction of the people were best still to be left to the precepts and principles of the Gospel.[14]

Similar views are found in the rationalists—in Samuel Clarke and, earlier, in Malebranche and Spinoza, whose belief in "the stupidity of the masses, and their failure to think,"[15] underlies Spinoza's interpretation of our common moral vocabulary as showing only a deep confusion about necessity. And the widely influential predecessor of Kant, Christian Wolff, taught an ethic that made knowledge of the metaphysical constitution of the universe essential to right action. Admitting that most people could not acquire this knowledge "from their own reflections," he added that "it is not necessary that all men be discoverers." There are those among the learned, like himself, who will do the hard work, and then teach the others rules they can memorize and follow, and that will suffice.[16] In his view, it is obligatory for the more gifted to spread their learning; his own writing, he tells us, is intended to carry out this obligation.[17]

An episode from the life of Salomon Maimon will make clear one implication of this kind of view. The impoverished Maimon, invited as a needy scholar to the home of a wealthy merchant for dinner, was taken to the son's room after the meal. The son reports:

As he told me that the purpose of his trip to Berlin was only to pursue knowledge, I showed him some mathematical books, from which he begged me to read him aloud some sentences. I did so; but never was I so shaken as then, when I saw tears flowing from his eyes, and heard him weep aloud. O, my son, he said to me, weeping, how happy you are, to have and to be able to use, when you are so young, the tools for the perfection of your soul. Lord of all the world! If achievement of perfection is the vocation of man [as Wolff taught], pardon me the heavy sin if I ask, why until now the means for living true to my vocation were kept from poor me. . . .[18]

<hr>

[14] John Locke, *The Reasonableness of Christianity, Works* II.535; *MPMK* 1:194–6. There has been a good deal of controversy about Locke's position on this point; in other writings he expressed different views.

[15] B. de Spinoza, *A Treatise on Religion and Politics*, trans. A. G. Wernham (Oxford: Oxford University Press, 1958), 83; *MPMK* 1:243.

[16] Christian Wolff, *Vernünftige Dedancken von der Menschen Tun und Lassen (Reasonable Thoughts About the Actions of Men)* (1720) 1733, sect. 150; *MPMK* 1:341.

[17] Wolff, sec. 233; *MPMK* 1:343.

[18] *Salomon Maimons Lebensgeschichte*, ed. Zwi Batscha (Frankfurt: Insel, 1984), 344–5, quoted from a memoir about Maimon published in 1801.

Maimon did not know of the work of the British moralists, and he was unaware that Kant had already hit on a principle that he thought would enable anyone, even the simplest and least-educated, to know what morality requires.

III

The clearest view of seventeenth-century beliefs about normal moral motivation comes from a look at the prevailing understanding of the concept of obligation. It was generally agreed that somehow or other recognition that one has an obligation or feels obliged to do a certain act motivates one to do that act. It was also accepted that there must be a distinction between actions that we do at our own discretion, because we please, or because we want to, and actions we do whether we want to or not because we have to or because they are necessary. The latter constitute our obligations. A theory of obligation had to explain the motivational force of obligations and the kind of necessity involved in them.

Suarez offered one influential account. The necessity involved in obligation, he held, is the necessity of using the means needed to attain an end.[19] The laws of nature, in pointing out our obligations, show how we must all act in order to attain the good proper to humans generally, and the laws a sovereign lays down are aimed at securing the good proper to us as members of the commonwealth. But pointing out how a good may be attained is not the same as obligating someone to act. Giving someone such information is only advising or counseling him. A teacher or someone who is one's equal might give such instruction, but doing so does not obligate the hearer to act. Only a superior can obligate.[20] A superior obligates someone when the superior, possessing sufficient power to help or harm him, promulgates a rule pointing out acts that will achieve an appropriate good and demands compliance, under threat of penalties for disobedience.[21]

Suarez explains the motivational force of obligation in terms of the threat of penalties. I have already noted that he thinks many people are unable to understand the rationale for the laws that govern them. This means that they

---

[19] Suarez, I.iii–iv; in part in *MPMK* 1:70–3.   [20] Suarez, I.xii.4; *MPMK* 1:74.
[21] Suarez, II.vi.6; *MPMK* 1:76–7.

will not see the good that compliance brings about, and therefore that they cannot be moved by a desire to attain that good. In its place Suarez puts the motive of avoiding threatened punishment. We can know, he holds, that God will be displeased by disobedience, and so will punish it, even if we do not know anything in detail about the punishments.[22] Obligatory acts are necessary to attain the main end of our common life, but the compelling reason people have for carrying out their obligations is the necessity of avoiding a personal evil.

Suarez's analysis of obligation enables him to distinguish between advising someone and obligating someone, and to show how God's existence and concern for the world are indispensable to morality. It also enables him to avoid the charge that God's imposition of obligations on us is arbitrary. God commands only acts that in themselves are suitable for bringing about human felicity.[23] But acting from one's own recognition of that suitability itself is not acting as an obedient subject. And Suarez takes it as evident that intellectual creatures, in virtue of being created, have a superior whom they are to obey.[24] The concept of obligation as Suarez understands it thus carries the idea of our status as creatures who are meant to obey.

The elements of the Suarezian view are to be found in a wide range of seventeenth-century theories. Time does not permit me to trace the steps through which the picture altered, but I must mention the main development.[25]

Seventeenth-century philosophers accepted the view that what moves us to act when we are being reasonable is the belief that some good will be attained by our action.[26] The common theory of obligation results from the thought that the agent can see no good in obedience except the good of avoiding his own punishment. The natural-law thinkers agree that what we are obligated to do under the laws of nature is a means to a good, and that in most cases the agent cannot see this. But the laws of nature are supposed to be rational guides of conduct. The only reason the agent can have to obey, it seems, is the fear of punishment. Obedience not grounded on this

---

[22] Suarez, II.ix.3.   [23] Suarez, II.vii.7; *MPMK* 1:81.   [24] Suarez, I.iii.3; *MPMK* 1:71.

[25] For Pufendorf's views on obligation, see my "Pufendorf's Place in the History of Ethics," *Synthese* 72 (July 1987): esp. 143–8.

[26] Locke began to break with the common view when in the second edition of the *Essay*, II.xxi.31ff., he argued that it is a present uneasiness that moves us rather than a desire for a future good. *MPMK* 1:186–9.

consideration would be simply irrational. Spinoza—not himself a natural-law thinker—gives a very clear statement of a widely accepted view: "The real object of law," he says, "is seldom obvious to more than a few; most men are practically incapable of seeing it.... Thus in order to bind all men equally[,] legislators have wisely introduced another motive for obedience ... by holding out the sort of reward [and] penalty ... that appeals most strongly to the hopes and fears of the masses. . . ."[27] The common view of obligation carries a definite sense of the need in human life for a strong superior power to keep order, and this sense rests on a specific view of ordinary human moral capacities. Dissatisfaction with the common view expressed different political and moral estimates. There were religious thinkers, among them the Cambridge Platonists, who held that this theory of obligation accorded less dignity to human beings than God intended them to have, and that it left no proper room for action out of love, which was after all central to Christianity. Admitting, however, that many people usually did not act lovingly, they were unable to construct a theory of obligation that would show how all of us equally can have obligations even if some of us do not need to be made to comply by threats of punishment. The political implications of the Pufendorfian theory of obligation, which look uncomfortably similar to those of its predecessor, the Hobbesian view, motivated others to seek some alternative view. Their common move was to abandon the legislative model of law and to work with a different model. One way in which this thought was developed had crucial bearings on the psychology of obligation. Those who appealed to self-evident moral laws were ultimately forced to make a drastic revision of the common seventeenth-century moral psychology.

Although Samuel Clarke modeled moral law on the laws of mathematics, he was not as clear about the shift in psychological theory required by this move as was Richard Price. Price claimed that action can be rationally motivated in two ways, not just one. It is reasonable to act in pursuit of some good; it is equally rational to act at the behest of principles whose own rationality the agent perceives. Only by accepting this psychology, Price held, can we give an adequate account of the scope of the obligations we all acknowledge. In asserting that "the perception of right and wrong does

---

[27] Spinoza, *Treatise on Religion and Politics*, trans. A. G. Wernham (Oxford: Oxford University Press, 1958), 240; *MPMK* 1:240.

excite to action, and is alone a sufficient *principle* of action,"[28] he is claiming for us a sense of duty different in kind from any sense of what is good. There is no need for a lawgiver for this sort of law, and no need of a law enforcer to set up an effective reason for carrying out one's obligations.

In different ways, Reid and Kant developed views similar to Price's. Kant in particular worked out the thought that we can be motivated by our recognition of the constraints rationality imposes on action, without any thought of good or ill to be derived from the action. And he went beyond Price and Reid in the clarity of his recognition that this way of construing human motivational capacities has its justification in the requirements of morality itself. We all acknowledge that there are some categorical obligations arising from our own rational agency, and we can see that unless we were free to act as those obligations require us to, this would be impossible. We must therefore conclude that we are free—are able—to act as morality requires. The picture of the moral self that Kant draws is one whose main lines are determined by the needs of a morality that does not permit us to see ourselves as ruled by another.

IV

On the remaining point about morality as we think of it now, its supremacy, it is not easy to elicit a consensus from seventeenth-century thinkers. But here the difficulty is not that earlier thinkers would directly disagree with what I have supposed to be our present general understanding. Rather, insofar as the question of the supremacy of morality arises in the seventeenth century, it does not have its modern meaning.

The natural-law thinkers could indeed give the question a sense. "The laws of nature," one of them might say, "which constitute the moral laws as distinct from divine and human positive laws, are God's laws. Hence, they are supreme in the sense that they override any human laws. If your concern is with a conflict between morality and self-interest, since morality is the truest prudence, the only thing to say is that morality takes precedence over shortsighted self-interest. If you are asking whether there is some other sense

---

[28] Richard Price, *Review of the Principal Questions of Morals*, ed. D. D. Raphael 3d edn. (1787) (Oxford: Oxford University Press, 1948), chap. 8, 185; *MPMK* 2:600.

in which the natural laws are supreme, we can only suppose that you mean to ask whether God himself could make exceptions to, or abrogate, the laws of nature, or whether he can grant dispensations from them. Perhaps you have in mind God's dispensation to Abraham exempting him from the fifth commandment, or some of the other episodes in the Bible. We are divided on this issue. Some—the voluntarists—believe that God could do away with the whole force of the law. Others hold that this is impossible, but that at least some of the inferred precepts of the natural law could be abrogated, or that God could grant dispensations from them. And there are those who hold that even this latitude is not permitted. I suppose the strictest of these latter thinkers might be said to hold that the moral law is supreme in something like your modern sense."[29] Suarez himself took a strong line, denying that God could abrogate the laws of nature, and therefore held them to be always in force. Grotius follows him; but Pufendorf as late as 1672 is eager to defend a voluntarist position. He takes the view that God, in fact, never will abrogate the laws of nature—but not that he cannot.[30]

The issue is yet more complex. One thing Kant meant by saying that the moral law is supreme—perhaps it is something we do not now wish to mean ourselves—was that compliance from the right motive entitles one to happiness. And since the entitlement is plainly not honored in the present, Kant notoriously if quite unoriginally argued that it must be cashable in a life to come. Now if this is what is meant by the supremacy of morals, then it was certainly challenged by all of those who in the seventeenth century took to heart the denunciations of Pelagianism by Saint Augustine and many later religious thinkers. The whole question of salvation by faith or by works, and of the extent of the human need for grace, is involved here. And though the reformed confessions insisted more absolutely than the Roman on the absolute need for grace to be given to each individual as such before that person could do anything meritorious, the Catholic Church also held that without grace man can do nothing acceptable to God. Even if moral standards are the highest standards for our action, devoted obedience to them is either not possible without divine assistance or is not sufficient to entitle us to the highest kind of merit.

---

[29] On this issue, see the complicated discussion in Suarez, II.xv.

[30] On the tradition that lies behind Pufendorf's position, see Francis Oakley, *Omnipotence, Covenant, and Order* (Ithaca, N.Y.: Cornell University Press, 1984).

V

During the seventeenth century, then, and indeed for many thinkers of the eighteenth century, moral philosophy did not proceed on the assumptions about the capacities of moral agents that have dominated the subject since Kant, Reid, and the later utilitarians. What led to the changes was not—at least not in the earlier stages—a conscious aim of bringing them about. The changes began as a response to a specific view of the central problem for practical philosophy. This understanding of the problem, I suggest, was itself a major change from earlier views; and it has remained central to our own thinking about morality.

The accepted distinction between modern moral philosophy and its ancient predecessors is one given classical formulation by Henry Sidgwick more than a century ago. The ancients, he said, "argued, from first to last," about the good taken generically and about its relations to its different species, among which they counted the right. "Their speculations," he continued, "can scarcely be understood by us unless with a certain effort we throw the quasi-jural notions of modern ethics aside and ask (as they did) not 'What is Duty and what is its ground?' but 'Which of the objects that men think good is truly Good or the Highest Good?' "[31] Accepting this as far as it goes, I want to suggest that we need to deepen it. We need to try to see what is behind the shift from an inquiry about the highest good to an inquiry about duty, where the latter is conceived to take, as Sidgwick says, a "quasi-jural" from. And to do this, there is no better place to begin than the work of the founder of modern natural law, Hugo Grotius.[32]

Grotius's major work, *On the Law of War and Peace* (1625) is a treatise on international law, not on moral philosophy. His central subject is conflict. The very first paragraph of the treatise tells us that the topic is controversies, not only those that culminate in formal ways, but "such controversies, of any and every kind, as are likely to arise."[33] In that period of religious and

---

[31] Henry Sidgwick, *The Methods of Ethics*, 7th edn. (London, 1907), 106. The passage is in all editions, from the first (1874, p. 94) on. Sidgwick claims that there are two further differences between ancients and moderns. One is that the ancients assumed that rational individuals aim at their own good, while the moderns regard it as rational to have other aims (*Methods*, 91–2). The second is that the ancients thought there to be only one regulative faculty that is the faculty of Reason, and the moderns think there are two—"Universal Reason and Egoistic Reason, or Conscience and Self-love" (*Outlines of the History of Ethics* [London, 1896], 198).

[32] In what follows here and in the next section, I elaborate on points on which I have touched briefly in the introduction to *MPMK* and in "The Misfortunes of Virtue," Chapter 10 of this volume.

[33] Grotius, I.I.i.; *MPMK* 1:96.

commercial warfare, it is hardly surprising that Grotius built the problems of rivalry and strife into the heart of his theory. What is surprising is that Grotius did not try to show that warfare and its personal counterparts might be eliminated. Instead, he presented a view of the moral psychology of the individual according to which we should expect conflict to be ineradicable. His hope was that he also could show the psychological resources which would enable us to confine it within bearable limits. Grotius was not interested in the problems of individual decision-making or character-assessment as such. Moral philosophy entered his work as a continuation of politics by other means.

Grotius was educated as a humanist and knew the classical authors well. But in building a theory of how people are to live with one another, he simply ignored the way in which the ancients framed the questions of ethics. His dropping of the question of the highest good is memorable for its casual brevity. In the course of discussing the issue of the people's sovereignty, he remarked:

Just as, in fact, there are many ways of living, one being better than another, and out of so many ways of living each is free to select that which he prefers, so also a people can select the form of government which it wishes; and the extent of its legal right in the matter is not to be measured by the superior excellence of this or that form of government, in regard to which different men hold different views, but by its free choice.[34]

Grotius here takes it for granted that there will be disagreement about ways of living, and he has no intention of entering into a debate. Our controversies with one another and their possible resolution are what engage him, and he simply assumes that these cannot be solved by discussing the individual good.

That the control of strife is for Grotius the central issue becomes plain when we look at his discussions of various laws of nature. The very first law he derives says that war is not against the law of nature. It is not so because it is in accordance with the innate tendency of each animal to try to preserve itself and its body intact. Our rational nature requires us to add that war is only just if it does not infringe on society or try to take away someone's rights. Thus, the first law provides a basis for the many ways in which

---

[34] Grotius, I.III.viii.2; *MPMK* 1:102.

conventions about limiting war can be arranged, but Grotius makes no effort to ban war. He is saying: men will fight, but the fighting can be contained within certain limits, and the point of the law of nature is to set those limits.

It is worth noticing how very different Grotius's understanding of natural law is in this respect from that found in the Thomist tradition. For Saint Thomas, as later for Richard Hooker, the universe is taken to be governed by an all-powerful and all-knowing deity who intends that the good of the whole be brought about in ways that assure the good of its parts taken separately. God includes in his care the inanimate as well as animate creation, the lower animals as well as man and other higher created beings. Hooker compresses the point into a memorable sentence: "For we see the whole world and each part thereof so compacted, that as long as each thing performeth only that work which is natural unto it, it thereby preserveth both other things and also itself."[35] God governs not by giving individual and special direction to each particular thing, but through laws. To explain his governance, the term "law" must be taken in a very broad sense. Saint Thomas tells us that law is to be defined as "an ordinance of reason for the common good, promulgated by him who has the care of the commu- nity."[36] Hooker follows him, defining law as "a directive rule unto good- ness of operation"[37] and discussing without any sense of ambiguity laws that govern everything from stones to angels. The law, he says, directs things to their own perfection, but "another law there is, which toucheth them as they are sociable parts united into one body," bidding them serve the needs of other things, even at their own expense: "as we plainly see they do, when things natural in that regard forget their ordinary natural wont; that which is heavy mounting sometime upwards of its own accord . . . even as if it did hear itself commanded to let go the good it privately wisheth, and to relieve the present distress of nature in common."[38] Similarly, the angels care for both their own good and for what concerns them "as they are linked into a kind of corporation amongst themselves, and of society or fellowship with men."[39]

[35] Richard Hooker, *Of the Laws of an Ecclesiastical Polity* (1594) I.ix.1. I cite from the edition by John Keble (Oxford, 1845).

[36] Thomas Aquinas, *Summa Theologiae*, I.II.90.4a.   [37] Hooker, I.viii.4.

[38] Hooker, I.iii.5.   [39] Hooker, I.iv.2; cf. I.xvi.3–4.

Grotius, by contrast, does not consider natural law to be giving us rational guidance to the perfection of our nature, nor does he see each person as a member of an essentially harmonious community with a part to play in bringing about a common good. He does think, with his predecessors, that "if the authorities issue any order that is contrary to the law of nature or to the commandments of God, the order should not be carried out."[40] But, typically, this claim is made in the context of answering whether it is permissible for those subordinate to a sovereign to wage war against him. It is not a conclusion drawn from a view about the proper natural order in the universe and its inviolability.

When Hobbes made avoiding the war of all against all the central problem for his version of natural-law theory, he was showing his Grotian allegiance. The extreme to which he pushed the vision of individuals as inherently prone to conflict with one another, and the drastic remedy he proposed, made the subject inescapable for his successors. I do not mean to suggest that every modern moral philosopher saw social disharmony as the central question for his theory. Spinoza, for instance, clearly returned to the quest for the highest individual good, which Grotius and even more drastically Hobbes had rejected; and if Spinoza was largely ignored during the formative period of modern moral philosophy, there were other, more influential writers who approached morality through the problem of the highest good. Nor do I mean that everyone accepted the natural-law view that conflict is ineradicable. What is true, however, is that the impact of Hobbes and even more of Pufendorf gave preeminence to the natural-law understanding of morality as the solution to the question of how to sustain the sociability that we quarrelsome and unsociable creatures want and need. Even those who wished to deny that this was the central problem could not ignore it.

VI

The dominant practical problem for those who thought about politics and morality during the seventeenth century differed from the practical problems that occupied earlier theorists. The new problematic does not explain

___

[40] Grotius, I.IV.i.3; *MPMK* 1:102.

everything about the development of moral thought from that starting point to the assumptions that are common now, but it helps us understand a number of prominent features of that development's outcome—to see, that is, why modern moral philosophy came to be as it is. I will touch briefly on the points I have said are central to modern morality and its moral philosophy. I must, of course, take them separately, although they are actually intertwined.

Consider first the issue of the extent of the availability of awareness of what morality requires. Denial that such awareness is equally available to everyone is more likely to perpetuate than to confine conflict. If people are prone to controversy, then no matter what starts a quarrel—whether it concern who owns what or what religious beliefs or ceremonies are to be accepted[41]—appeal to moral norms will be useful for containing or settling it only if the norms are not seen as something that one party to the quarrel can use and the other cannot. In a society where people understand themselves as existing in potentially conflictual relations, the claim of a writer like Wolff to the authority to tell the masses how to behave must seem to be simply a covert rationale for domination. The belief that people are unalterably prone to conflict thus generates a pressure toward allowing that moral awareness must be open to everyone. And if it is to be so, the basic principle of morals must not only be simple enough for all to understand but easy enough for everyone to use. In showing how awareness of morality is generally available, Kantian and intuitional theories and the later forms of utilitarianism make sense as a response to the Grotian problematic.

The centrality of obligation, with its emphasis on what must be done regardless of its motivation, can be understood in a similar way. For the Grotian, the very existence of society will be threatened unless people respect certain minimal conditions in their interactions. A society organized around obligations and rights recognizes this truth. But a conception according to which obligations can exist only if there is some authority, human or otherwise, who can impose them is more likely to exacerbate than to settle conflict. Any understanding of God or of a secular authority may be open to challenge. And anyone may need to appeal to rights and duties to protect important interests. The obligations grounding such

---

[41] The existence of ineradicable disagreement about ecclesiological matters is as important to Locke's overall position as is the tendency for disputes about property to threaten the possibility of social life.

appeals cannot helpfully be derived from challengeable authorities perceived as partial to one party or another. In a Grotian society, obligation must be independent of sanction, as Grotius himself presciently held that it was.[42] The kind of reconstruction of the older, sanction-tied conception, which in fact occurred during the development of modern moral philosophy, represents an intelligible solution to one aspect of the problem that Grotius brought to the foreground.

Finally, the eventual acceptance of the supremacy of morality over other kinds of directive also fits into the pattern I have been sketching. This acceptance stands out most clearly, I think, if we contrast belief in the supremacy of moral norms with a very different view, articulated in radical form by Luther and Calvin but shared in essentials by Catholics. "God has ordained two governments," Luther says,

> the spiritual, which by the Holy Spirit under Christ makes Christians and pious people, and the secular, which restrains the unchristian and wicked so that they must needs keep the peace outwardly, even against their will. . . . these two kingdoms must be sharply distinguished, and both be permitted to remain; the one to produce piety, the other to bring about external peace and prevent evil deeds. . . . [43]

Modern moral philosophy eventually constructed a third realm, one where we are each governed by ourselves and where our conflicts can be adjudicated by something other than the magistrate's laws and God's commands. It is a social space that limits the authority of the magistrate as well as the demands of those who speak in the name of religion. It had to be the source of directives superior to those emanating from the other two kingdoms precisely because those directives were open to challenge in the Grotian world, and a conflict-settling body of norms had to be admitted somehow if society was to continue. What emerged as a solution to the problem was a domain of discourse in which the ruling vocabularies of justification and guidance are neither religious nor political nor prudential, but something else. They are what we now call moral.

---

[42] This is the point of Grotius's famous declaration that what he has been saying—that people have rights—would have a certain degree of validity even if (what is not possible to conceive) there were no God. Rights impose obligations on others, he is saying, regardless of the existence of sanctions, divine or otherwise. Grotius, *Prolegomena*, sec. 11; *MPMK* 1:92.

[43] Martin Luther, *Secular Authority: To What Extent It Should Be Obeyed*, vol. 4, *Martin Luther: Selections from His Writings*, ed. John Dillenberger (New York: Doubleday/Anchor, 1961), 370–1.

VII

Since the work of Kant, Reid, and the post-Bentham utilitarians, moral philosophy has been concerned with the self for whose construction they supplied alternative means. Of course, the idea that the bearers of morality are fully competent moral agents conflicting as well as cooperating with one another has been frequently attacked. But that has been the idea requiring consideration by moral and political theorists, whether favorably, as in the mainstream of British and American thought, or unfavorably. I do not believe that either ancient or medieval moral thought revolved around anything like the same complex idea. Consequently, I believe that it makes sense to consider the period of the emergence, defense, and critique of this idea as constituting a distinctive epoch in Western thought about ethics.

If a new problematic and a new range of solutions to it can emerge as the focal point of discussion, they also can drop out of sight. Modern moral philosophy is the target of widespread opposition at present. Is there reason to suppose that we are coming to the end of the period whose beginning I have tried to point out? And what help can a historical grasp of modern moral philosophy give us in answering this question?

I shall begin with the second question. Effective criticism of the program of modern moral philosophy must obviously be directed at what is central or essential to it. How, then, are we to distinguish the superficial from that which matters? It is not helpful to suppose that there is an "essence" of moral philosophy, some unchanging question such as "how should one live?"[44] around which moral philosophy has always turned. That assumption obscures the kinds of differences between periods of philosophy that I have been trying to highlight. We can only determine what is and is not central by looking at history. But, from my view, what are we to look at the history of? Of discussions, I reply, whose participants have seen themselves as linked in carrying on controversies or working out theoretical programs about issues on whose importance they agree. We see ourselves as carrying on a conversation in which Kant, Reid, and, say, Bentham were important participants, and they saw themselves as engaging the Grotians and their

---

[44] See Bernard Williams, *Ethics and the Limits of Philosophy* (Cambridge, Mass.: Harvard University Press, 1985), 1. This is an enduring question. But taking it as the question with which we are to be concerned blurs important distinctions.

critics. This discussion is what constitutes modern moral philosophy, and its history must serve to show us what is superficial and what is essential in it. Without a good grasp of the history, we cannot tell whether a criticism of the enterprise is important or not.

To illustrate this claim, I shall touch briefly on a few of the recent challenges to modern moral philosophy. I do not mean to mount a comprehensive defense, but I hope my comments will round out and suggest the usefulness of the portrait of the form of moral philosophy that still engages us.

1. *The antifoundationalist criticism.* The objection is that modern moral philosophy, like its counterpart in epistemology, has been caught up in the age-old effort to find unshakable cognitive justification for some morality, and since we now see this endeavor to be futile, we must shift to something new if we propose to continue doing ethics.

No reference has been made to the search for cognitive foundations in my account of the emergence of modern moral theory because that quest, insofar as it existed, seems to come second to the effort to find some set of principles that are adequate for settling or delimiting conflict which reasonable people would have to hold in common. The standard term for the faculty that yields results everyone must accept was and is "reason"; but the importance of Hutcheson and Hume in the development of Western ethical thought should remind us that reason and cognitive foundations are not the only conceivable sources of shared moral awareness.

2. *The neglect of virtue objection.* Numerous writers, beginning with Elizabeth Anscombe in 1958,[45] have objected that modern moral philosophy is fundamentally flawed because it omits consideration of virtue and the virtues. I have argued elsewhere against this allegation.[46] But it is surely true that virtue in the Aristotelian sense as requiring something like the educated insight of the virtuous agent, incapable of being captured in rules, was granted a relatively minor place in the moral thought of the period. It is not hard to see why. If conflict between individuals, groups, or countries is the chief issue, an appeal to the inarticulate insight of a virtuous man is not going to be of much help. There will be those on both sides who claim to be

---

[45] Elizabeth Anscombe, "Modern Moral Philosophy," *Philosophy* 33 (1958). In 1928 Max Scheler made similar complaints about modern moral philosophy, but I doubt that he helped to stimulate the contemporary English-language debates.

[46] "The Misfortunes of Virtue," Chapter 10 in this volume.

virtuous; and the classical virtue theories available to seventeenth- and eighteenth-century philosophers had little or nothing to say about the kind of rational discussion that could take place between them. So it is easy to see why theorists of the early modern period might think that if morality were wholly a matter of virtue, we would be constantly involved in shouting matches that would do nothing to settle the conflicts bound to arise.

3. *The communitarian or anti-individualist objection.* The objection is that modern moral philosophy assumes individuals who are prior to and not formed by the communities of which they are members, and that if this assumption were given up, the ties we have to one another would be seen to be more vital than the interests that separate us. The autonomous agent is only needed, so the objection goes, to counteract the falsifications of individualistic liberal psychology. In response, it must be agreed that much modern moral theory does suppose individuals who have a certain constitution regardless of their community. Like the social contract whose theory so often accompanies this kind of individualism, the abstract individual of moral philosophy is to be considered a theoretical device through which we may obtain some kind of understanding of the conflicts that in fact are so endemic to the societies in which we actually live. If the communitarian psychology or ontology of the individual is correct, it must be our communities that engender this conflict, and then either the problem remains to be solved, or the communitarian theory turns into a recommendation to change our societies so that they no longer create conflict-prone members. Aside from the feasibility of such a recommendation, there are grave questions about its desirability.

4. *Finally, the unified subject objection.* Modern moral philosophy and the liberalism with which it is often associated rest, it is said, on belief in the unified subject, a self that is separate from and able to control desires and actions. Once we show this belief to be the myth that it is, we eliminate the possibility of the kind of moral philosophy that has so far dominated modern thought.

It would take a lengthy discussion to deal adequately with this objection. Here, I can suggest only the rudiments of an answer.[47] In the case of Kant,

[47] In what follows, I find myself in agreement with Charles Taylor, *Sources of the Self* (Cambridge, Mass.: Harvard University Press, 1989), 514. See my "The Use of Autonomy in Ethical Theory," in Thomas C. Heller, Morton Sosna, and David E. Wellbery, eds., *Reconstructing Individualism*, Stanford, Calif.: Stanford University Press, 1986), 64–75. Christine M. Korsgaard has given a much fuller

the unified self is the free self and is indeed above and able to control desires and actions. Kant defended this view by claiming that it is the way in which we must conceive ourselves in order to understand our own moral commitments. The transcendental moral self is not a metaphysical given, prior to the moral order, but a necessary presupposition of that order. I have been suggesting throughout this essay, in fact, that the distinctive conflict-prone and morally competent individual of modern ethics was primarily constructed in response to social realities and to moral and political demands, not because of metaphysical or epistemological needs. Criticism of modern moral philosophy and the morality it has helped to create is superficial if it does not address, even if only to dismiss, the practical problems and normative pressures that led to the modern construal of the moral individual.

R. G. Collingwood long ago tried to teach us that we cannot understand past thinkers unless we know what questions they were trying to answer, and that we must not assume that their questions were the same as ours. He also held that we will not understand our own aims and achievements until we become aware of the historically specific presuppositions from which they arise. In the case of moral philosophy, it seems to me, Collingwood was right. But Collingwood offered philosophical reasons for holding that his view must be true for all philosophical issues.[48] I think we will be able to tell only by doing historical study of the issues one by one.[49]

---

interpretation of the Kantian position on this matter in "Morality as Freedom," in Y. Yovel, ed., *Kant's Practical Philosophy Reconsidered* (Kluwer: Dordrecht: Kluwer Academic Pubs., 1989), 23–48.

[48] For a brief account, see R. G. Collingwood, *An Autobiography* (New York: Oxford University Press, 1939), ch. 7.

[49] A somewhat different version of this essay was presented as a Gauss Seminar at Princeton University in February 1990. I have benefitted from the discussion there in preparing the present version.

6

No Discipline, No History:
The Case of Moral Philosophy

How are we to understand the history and the historiography of moral philosophy? As a number of recent works in ethics show, philosophers think that more than our knowledge of the past is at issue. In these works, interpretations of the history of ethics play an important part in the construction of an acceptable view about morality. MacIntyre, Williams, Donagan, Taylor, Irwin, and Annas offer various views about whether moral philosophy has made progress or not. They ask whether we are now doing better at the subject than our predecessors did, and they offer answers—quite different answers, to be sure, but that is no surprise in philosophy. Historians are apt to be uncomfortable with this question. To ask it is to suppose not only that there is some common enterprise engaging earlier and later moral philosophers, but also shared standards by which we may judge improvement or decline. Historians tend to think that such assumptions are not their business, and that in any case they make for "Whiggish" or "triumphalist" history. They are thus likely to be uncomfortable with histories of moral philosophy written with such philosophical assumptions; philosophers are likely to think histories written on any others are irrelevant.

In this paper I shall raise some questions about the supposition that there is enough significant continuity in the concerns of moral philosophers to warrant discussions of progress and regress in the discipline. I should like also to indicate why it is not possible to consider the history of moral philosophy seriously without some views that, properly speaking, can be adjudicated, if at all, only within the discipline itself. It seems obvious that if there is no single discipline of moral philosophy there cannot be a history of it; it may seem less obvious that unless you are pretty well versed in, and have views about, moral philosophy—unless you have acquired the discipline—you cannot properly study whatever history it may have. The history and the discipline, I shall argue, are inseparable.

I

The version of the history of moral philosophy that is most commonly accepted today goes back at least as far as Xenophon. He tells us that Socrates broke with his predecessors by attending to a new set of issues. He did not dispute, as they did, about the cosmos and the nature of things in general. He asked instead about human affairs.[1] Cicero elaborates on the point. Socrates, he says, "was the first to call philosophy down from the heavens and set her in the cities of men . . . and compel her to ask questions about life and morals and things good and evil."[2] In the eighteenth century Thomas Reid taught his pupils that Socrates "has always been reckoned the Father of Moral Philosophy."[3] In the opening paragraph of *Utilitarianism* (1861), John Stuart Mill calls upon this tradition. "From the dawn of philosophy," he says, "the question concerning the *summum bonum* or . . . the foundation of morality, has been accounted the main problem of speculative thought . . . And, after more than two thousand years, the same discussions continue, philosophers are still ranged under the same contending banners, and neither thinkers nor mankind at large seem nearer to being unanimous on the subject than when the youth Socrates listened to the old Protagoras, and asserted . . . the theory of utilitarianism against the popular morality of the so-called Sophist."

Mill offers a theory to account for the fact that the question of the first principle of morality remains open after so many centuries of inquiry. In all the sciences, he says, much information and many low-level theorems come to light long before the most basic principles are discovered. Mankind learns many more or less general truths from experience; only later does careful analysis enable us to extricate the fundamental concepts and principles of a science from the mass of details. Moral beliefs are like others. Hence it is not

---

[1] Xenophon, *Socratic Memorabilia*, I.11–12.   [2] Cicero, *Tusculan Disputations*, V.iv.10–11.
[3] Thomas Reid, *Practical Ethics*, ed. Knud Haakonssen (Princeton: Princeton University Press, 1990), 110.

surprising that common sense should possess some sound *beliefs* about moral rules even though we will not have secure *knowledge* about morality until we discover its true foundations.[4]

It is still standard to say that moral philosophy began with Socrates and has been carried on continuously ever since. Thus Bernard Williams begins his important study *Ethics and the Limits of Philosophy* (1985) as follows: "It is not a trivial question, Socrates said: what we are talking about is how one should live. Or so Plato reports him, in one of the first books written about this subject.... The aims of moral philosophy ... are bound up with the fate of Socrates's question ... " (1). Although we have not reached agreement about the basis of morality, the Socrates story draws on a clear picture of the tasks that moral philosophers should undertake. We are trying to answer the question Socrates raised: how to live. People have always had opinions on the matter, but it is very hard to get an indubitable answer based on an undeniable foundation. It is so hard that skeptics ask us to doubt that there is an answer, or even a real question. Perhaps, as Mill says, the difficulty exists in all disciplines. Or perhaps, as others think, there are special problems about morality that make the task of developing its theory harder than the tasks facing physics. These problems may account for the fact that we seem not even to have made any generally accepted progress toward the answer, much less found it. Still, the issues are there, and we should continue working on them. If we study earlier moral philosophy, it is because we may gain some insights from our predecessors, or learn at least to avoid their errors.

II

Because the Socrates story is simply taken for granted today it is important to be aware that it is not the only possible narrative of the history of the subject. For many centuries an alternative view of that history was widely held. Like the Socrates story, it carries with it a distinctive view of the tasks of the discipline. The underlying thesis of the alternate history is that the basic truths of morality are not the last to be discovered. They have been known as long as humans have been living with one another. Whatever moral

---

[4] John Stuart Mill, *Utilitarianism*, I. §§1–2.

philosophy is, therefore, it is not a search for hitherto unknown scientific knowledge.

The alternative narrative takes two forms, one religious and one secular. The religious version is the older. It gives importance to a question most of us would not naturally ask. We will be inside the story once we see why we might ask it. The question is: Was Pythagoras a Jew?

The question arises from two assumptions. One is that the biblical narrative provides the unquestionable framework within which all human history must be located. Bossuet's *Discourse on Universal History* (1681) is perhaps the greatest modern monument built on this assumption. As Santinello's study of Renaissance histories of philosophies shows, it was long common to assume that all wisdom comes from God. One major task for historians, therefore, was to explain its presence in cultures not directly descended from the Jews.[5] Those who undertook these enterprises believed that philosophy is an important human activity, which must have a providentially assigned role. They had a special problem about morality and its relation to moral philosophy. The truth about morality was revealed very early in human history, and it has not changed. William Law, arguing against Mandeville, gives us a clear eighteenth-century statement of this point:

When Noah's Family came out of the Ark, we presume, they were as well educated in the Principles of Virtue and moral Wisdom, as any People were ever since; . . .

There was therefore a Time, when all the People in the World were well versed in moral Virtue. . . .

He therefore that gives a *later* account of the Origin of moral Virtue, gives a *false* account of it.[6]

Belief that the Noachite revelation was the origin of moral knowledge itself would make it natural to ask why we have moral philosophy anyway. It would also lead us to wonder about how the Greeks could have been the ones to start it.

   [5] See *Models of the History of Philosophy*, ed. Giovanni Santinello, vol. 1: *From Its Origins in the Renaissance to the "Historia Philosphica"* by Francesco Botten et al., trans. C. W. T. Blackwell *et al.* (Dordrecht: Kluwer Academic Publishers, 1993), 21, 26, 28, and especially the discussion of Thomas Burnet, 330ff. See also Peter Harrison, *"Religion" and the Religions in the English Enlightenment* (Cambridge: Cambridge University Press, 1990), ch. 5, for discussion of the "single source" theory of religion. D. P. Walker, *The Ancient Theology* (Cornell, 1972), is another important study of this kind of view.
   [6] William Law, *Remarks upon . . . the Fable of the Bees*, in *Works* (London, 1762, 1892), 2:7.

The answer to the first question lies in human sinfulness. Our nature was damaged by the fall. It not only dimmed our faculties, lessening our ability to become aware of God's commands and understand them. It also unleashed the passions. Evildoers, driven by their lusts, seek to avoid the pangs of conscience, so they blind themselves to its clear dictates. They also strive to veil and confuse the moral thoughts of those whom they wish to entangle in their wicked schemes.[7] Bad reasoning is one of their basic tools. Now reason is one of God's gifts to humanity. Among other things it enables us to hold on to at least some of the moral knowledge we need, once revelation has ceased. If reason makes moral philosophy possible, pride leads men to try to outdo one another in inventing schemes and systems of morality, and morality itself gets lost in their struggles. Since the causes of the misuse of reason and of bad philosophy are now ingrained in our nature, there will be no final triumph of good philosophy until after the last judgment. But the battle must be kept up. Moral philosophy is to be understood as one more arena for the struggle between sin and virtue.

As to the Greeks, it may be mysterious *why* God chose them to be the first to philosophize. We can, however, find out *how*, lacking the Noachite and the Mosaic revelations and being as corrupt as the rest of mankind, they could have done as well as they did with morality (how well they did being, again, a subject of debate).

The first part of the answer is due to a frequently cited remark attributed to Aristotle. In *Magna Moralia* 1.1 he says that Pythagoras was the first who attempted to treat of virtue. Thomas Stanley, the first English historian of philosophy to write in the vernacular, repeats the claim, citing this source.[8] Given Aristotle's standing as the first historian of ancient thought, it seems that one could hardly ask for more impressive testimony. We can discover the importance of Pythagoras's priority from a parenthetical remark that Scipion Dupleix inserts in his assertion of it. In his *L'Ethique ou Philosophie Morale* of 1603 he says that although Socrates is praised for his discussion of

---

[7] "There has ever been an uninterrupted succession of men, who, seduc'd by a secret desire to shake off the troublesome yoke of duty; and to indulge themselves in the gratification, if not of their sensual and gross Desires, yet at least of their more delicate and refined Inclinations, have employed all the Faculties of their Souls, in extinguishing the Evidence of those Truths, which were most clear... in order to involve in their Ruin all certainty of the Rules of Virtue." From Jean Barbeyrac, *An Historical and Critical Account of the Science of Morality*, trans. Carew (London, 1729) §III, p. 5.

[8] Thomas Stanley, *The History of Philosophy*, (1655–62) (London, 1721), 395. The passage from *Magna Moralia*, 1182a12–14, is cited in full below at the opening of sect. 4.

the rules delivered by moral philosophy, he was not the first in the field: "it is certain that Pythagoras himself, whom the Greeks took for a philosopher of their nation (although St. Ireneus assures us that he was Hebrew and had read the books of Moses) had worthily treated of morality" before Socrates did.[9] Here as elsewhere Dupleix was unoriginal. Ficino, for example, thought he recalled that St. Ambrose "showed that Pythagoras was born of a Jewish father;" and there were others.[10] Thus the problem of transmission is solved. If Pythagoras was the one who initiated moral philosophy among the Greeks, and he was a Jew, it is clear how the Greeks managed to get the subject going.

Not everyone thought Pythagoras was actually Jewish; but there were second-best stories. It was a commonplace that the Greeks got much from the Jews.[11] John Selden, who traced our grasp of natural law back to the Noachite commandments, devoted long pages of his *De Jure Naturali et Gentium* of 1640 to analyzing the testimony of Jewish and Christian writers about the Jewish influence on Pythagoras. He preferred the Greek authorities to the Jewish, as having, he thought, less of a vested doctrinal interest in proving such a debt to the Jews. His conclusion is that the weight of the evidence makes it clear that Pythagoras,

the primary teacher of Greek theology and the first to be called a philosopher, to whom some also attribute the first doctrine in Greece concerning the immortality of the soul . . . and others wish to credit the first disputations about the virtues, that is, the principles of moral philosophy . . . consulted and heard the Hebrews.[12]

---

[9] Scipione Dupleix, *L'Ethique, ou Philosophie Morale* (Paris, 1603, 1632), 4. Dr. Sebastian Brock informs me that to the best of our knowledge St. Irenaeus said no such thing.

[10] I owe these last references to the excellent book by S. K. Heninger, *Touches of Sweet Harmony* (San Marino: The Huntington Library, 1974), 201–2. Heninger lists (229, n. 5) half a dozen studies from the seventeenth and eighteenth centuries that contain bibliographies on Pythagoras's debt to Moses.

[11] Herodotus and other ancients attested to Greek debts to Eastern thought generally, and Isocrates held that Pythagoras in particular had brought into Greek the philosophy he learned from the Egyptians. See W. K. C. Guthrie, *A History of Greek Philosophy*, vol. 1 (Cambridge: Cambridge University Press, 1962), 160, 163. Guthrie devotes nearly two hundred pages to reviewing the difficulties of studying Pythagoras and Pythagoreanism and summarizing the results of modern scholarship.

Heninger's fifth chapter, 256–84, gives a full and fascinating account of various views of what specifically the moral philosophy of Pythagoras, or of the Pythagoreans, was supposed to be, and the many ways in which Pythagorean views were given Christian legitimacy and propagated widely. But although he has earlier noted Pythagoras's alleged debts to the Jews for his moral thought, he does not explore the bearing of claims about the debts on the historiography of moral philosophy.

[12] John Selden, *De Jure Naturali et Gentium iuxta disciplinam Ebraeorum, Collected Works* vol. 1, col. 89. The examination of testimonies occurs in cols. 82–5 and elsewhere. I am deeply indebted to Michael Seidler for having put Selden's passages concerning Pythagoras into quotable English. Selden offers an

Selden thinks it quite possible that Pythagoras was taught by no less a figure than the prophet Ezekiel.

Henry More is also explicit about the importance of Greek philosophy's debt to the Jews:

Now that Pythagoras drew his knowledge from the Hebrew fountains, is what all writers, sacred and prophane, do testify and aver. That Plato took from him the principal part of that knowledge, touching God, the soul's immortality and the conduct of life and good manners, has been doubted by no man. And that it went from him, into the schools of Aristotle, and so derived and diffused almost into the whole world, is in like manner attested by all.[13]

We have here the germ of a history of moral philosophy. I do not know how old it is.[14] But I think that some version or other of the Pythagoras story, as I shall call it, must have been assumed, however indistinctly, by a great many philosophers. There is a large amount of room for maneuver within this kind of historical schema. Even the religious version leaves a role for reason while not making revelation superfluous.[15] Locke and Clarke in England, and Crusius in Germany, all concerned to defend the view that morality *at present* is not dependent on revelation, are still determined to keep revelation historically essential. They replace Pythagoras's Noachite revelation with Christ's, as that through which alone we became able to know the full truth about morality. It seems, Locke says, that

---

explanation of why "we do not find many vestiges of Hebrew doctrine in the writings of the Greek philosophers—indeed, that nothing at all occurs there which sufficiently retains the pure and unadulterated nature of its Hebrew origin." The various Greek sects themselves commingled so much, and splintered the old teachings so greatly, that the result is everywhere a hodge-podge. But, he adds, no one doubts that in Platonic as well as Pythagorean doctrine there are teachings derived from the Hebrews (col. 91).

[13] Henry More, *Enchiridion Ethicum*, English translation of 1690 (London), 267. For More and the "ancient theology" see Peter Harrison, cited in n. 5 above, 133–5. He does not discuss the Pythagoras story about moral philosophy; the ancient theology was concerned less with moral matters than with such doctrinal concerns as trinitarianism.

[14] Josephus, in *Against Apion*, trans. H. St. J. Thackeray, Loeb Classical Library, (Cambridge: Harvard Univ. Press, 1926, 1966), claims the Greeks learned much of their science and law from the East, and specifically from the Jews; he mentions Pythagoras in this connection but does not explicitly claim that he was the originator of moral philosophy. See I.13–14, I.165, II.168, where the translator suggests that the dependence of Greek on Jewish thought was first suggested by Aristobulus. Eusebius in the *Preparation for the Gospel* gives a famous description of Plato as Moses Atticizing; but he does not tie Pythagoras to the origins of moral philosophy.

[15] More himself says that the eternal son as the *Logos*, or human reason, as well as revelation, can enlighten us about morals.

'tis too hard a task for unassisted reason to establish morality in all its parts upon its true foundation . . . We see how unsuccessful in this the attempts of philosophers were before our Saviour's time . . . And if, since that, the Christian philosophers have much outdone them, yet we may observe that the first knowledge of the truths they have added [is] owing to revelation.[16]

Now that Christ has revealed the truth, we can see for ourselves the reasonableness of his teaching, and can even turn our knowledge into a demonstrative science. A truth is reasonable and philosophical, Crusius says in 1744, when it can be proven by valid arguments from rational starting points. It does not matter where we first learned it. "The duties that the Christian religion imposes on us are grounded in reason. Because our knowledge of them was dimmed by our corruption [*Verderben*] they had to be repeated. . . . we learn the extent of human corruption from the fact that without divine revelation we would not have grasped the most important and most fully-grounded rational truths."[17]

III

Neither Locke nor Clarke nor Crusius say anything at all about Noah or the idea that Pythagoras had a Jewish connection. Yet in holding that the Greek philosophers were never able to get very far in figuring out what morality requires, they share with the Pythagoras story the belief that reason without revelation could not discover morality. The Pythagoras story's explanation of the role of moral philosophy is implicit in their work as well. With it in mind, we can see, for instance, that Clarke's standard description of Hobbes as "the wicked Mr. Hobbes" is not just an incidental expression of personal revulsion. But none of them gives any account of the history that leads up to their own moral theories.[18]

---

[16] Locke, *Reasonableness*, *MPMK* I.194–5.

[17] C.A. Crusius, *Anweisung vernünftig zu Leben* (1744), reprint ed. G. Tonelli (Hildesheim: Olms, 1969), "Vorrede," fol. b4 and following.

[18] John Locke, *The Reasonableness of Christianity* (1695), ed. I. T. Ramsey (Stanford: Stanford University Press, 1958), β241, 60–1. Samuel Clarke, *The Unchangeable Obligations of Natural Religion* (London, 1705), VII.1. For Clarke it is the "wicked Mr. Hobbs" whose evil philosophy makes his own virtuous philosophical activity necessary. Reid does not say that the heathens could not have discovered the principles of morals; but he does say that revelation allowed Christians to surpass the heathen in matters of natural religion. Reid, *Practical Ethics*, 108–9.

Jean Barbeyrac is of great interest because he gives an only partly secularized version of the history embodying the basic philosophical assumption at work in the religious Pythagoras story.[19] Following Pufendorf, Barbeyrac assumes that the basic truths of morality are always readily accessible to human reason. They must therefore have been known in the earliest ages, so that no revelation of morality was necessary. But Barbeyrac also believes, with the religious Pythagoras story, that human sinfulness leads men to try to evade the demands of morality and to use reason in the effort. It is worth looking at some of the details as they are spelled out in his 1706 *Historical and Critical Account of the Science of Morality*.[20]

Since the first inhabitants of the world lived in the "Eastern Countries," he says, it must have been among them that there originated "the most general Notions of Morality, and the other Sciences... The Greeks," he adds, "for all their Vanity, were forc'd to own themselves Debtors for these notices, to those, they call'd Barbarians." As for Pythagoras, he travelled in the East, among the Egyptians, Persians, and Chaldeans, and brought back "many of his Notions" as well as his symbolic and enigmatic way of teaching (Barb., 37,45,47). Barbeyrac also cites the important sentence of Aristotle, on which the whole tradition hangs (Barb., 50). If he does not explicitly say that Pythagoras was a Jew or studied the books of Moses, he clearly has something like it in mind.

The problem that gives the structure to his *Account* shows his divergence from the purely revelational account of the origins of moral knowledge given in the older Pythagoras story.[21] In his first two chapters he tells us that the principles of morality are so simple that they are within the reach of everyone. His adherence to Pufendorf's natural-law view of morality requires him to add that in thinking of morality we must also be thinking of God, but he finds no problem with this because he thinks it easy to

[19] Richard Tuck rightly finds his history important for its part in the propagation of Grotian natural-law theory, but does not discuss the historiography as such. See Tuck, *Natural Rights Theories* (Cambridge: Cambridge University Press, 1970).

[20] The English translation of Barbeyrac's 1706 French work serves as a lengthy introduction to the fourth edition of Kennett's English translation of Barbeyrac's French translation of Samuel Pufendorf's *Of the Law of Nature and of Nations* (London, 1729). Barbeyrac's *Account* is hereafter cited in the text, with the abbreviation "Barb."

[21] I am greatly indebted to Dr. Jennifer Herdt for her comments on an earlier version of this paper, in which I failed, in the present section, to notice Barbeyrac's adherence to what I am calling the "secular" variant of the Pythagoras story. Her remarks led me not only to correct this error but to rethink the whole paper, which is, I hope, improved as a result.

acquire the natural knowledge that God exists and actively governs our lives (Barb., 1–2). Morality is not only plain and simple; it is also, as Locke showed, demonstrable (Barb., 4–5). Why, then, has the science of morality remained so backward? And what use are philosophers?

Here Barbeyrac falls back on the older history. Sin provides the answers. Barbeyrac cites Hierocles—significantly, he cites a comment on Pythagoras—to say that sinful people can have clear ideas about many things while still being blind to morals (Barb., 6). Not only self-interest, but long-standing custom or tradition can also conceal moral truth from us, as can prejudices acquired in early education. We might think that priests would at least teach morality properly, but it has not been so. Pagan priests had such misguided ideas of the divinity that they could not hope to get morality right. The Jewish priests were too busy with ceremonial and civil affairs to teach adequately "the revelation of which they were the depositaries." Their carnal prejudices, moreover, kept them tied to the letter of the law. Although Christ re-established morals in all their purity, there were false teachers even in the time of the Apostles who corrupted his doctrine. Barbeyrac goes on at great length about the decay that followed and about the awful morals of the Christian Fathers. He includes St. Augustine among those condemned: did not Augustine write in defense of persecution? Barbeyrac was a Huguenot, and he could hardly excuse Augustine for this failing (Barb., 24).

IV

Although Barbeyrac cites him as an authority for Pythagoras's priority as student of virtue, Aristotle—if indeed it was Aristotle who wrote the *Magna Moralia*—does not make a very strong claim about it.[22] The whole of what he says on the matter is this: "Pythagoras first attempted to speak about virtue, but not successfully; for by reducing the virtues to numbers he

[22] Guthrie presumably thinks that the *Magna Moralia* is spurious, since he does not list its remark about Pythagoras and the study of virtue in his review of sources concerning Pythagoras. Heninger also thinks that the *Magna Moralia* is spurious (277 n. 2)—a thesis John Cooper challenges in "The *Magna Moralia* and Aristotle's Moral Philosophy," *Amer. J. of Philology* 94.4 (Winter 1973), 327–49. For my purposes it does not, of course, matter whether the attribution to Aristotle is correct; it suffices that in the sixteenth and seventeenth centuries it was thought to be so.

submitted the virtues to a treatment which was not proper to them" (1182a12–14). Socrates and Plato are also mentioned as having attempted to understand virtue, but with similar lack of success; and we are left with the distinct impression that Aristotle sees himself as the first to succeed in moral philosophy. When Barbeyrac cites the passage in his text, he omits the words "but not successfully," although he plainly knew they were there. Pythagoras was in any case something of an embarrassment. Little of his writing survives, and that little obscure. He was the subject of fantastic stories. Stanley unquestioningly repeats some of the stories contained in Diogenes Laertius and in the (alleged) Aristotelian fragments—that he showed his golden thigh in public, was in Croton and Metapontum at the very same time, and convinced an ox to stop eating beans forever by whispering in its ear.[23] The lack of clarity in Pythagoras's writings and the other mists that shroud him may have made him ideally suited for construal as the link between God's revelation to the Jews and the ability of the Greeks to have and philosophize about a proper morality. But by the end of the seventeenth century he was evidently beginning to seem a broken reed.

The Pythagoras story, however, still kept its hold. Adam Glafey, a German historian of natural law writing some thirty years after Barbeyrac, refuses to report on the thought of the Eastern nations because they left no adequate written accounts. But he takes Pythagoras as the first of the Greek thinkers to give serious attention to morality, and after discussing his philosophy remarks that "we can see in general from this short summary of Pythagorean morality that, just as this man borrowed much from the Jews and the Egyptians, so also the succeeding Greek philosophers themselves made use of his doctrine."[24]

Vico found it necessary to challenge a number of stories about Pythagoras, among them the one about his having learned from the Jews. Quite aside from the difficulty of accepting the tales of Pythagoras's numerous travels, there is the strong probability that like priests everywhere, the

---

[23] Stanley, *The History of Philosophy*, 360–1. For Aristotle, see Fragments 190–1, in Barnes, ed., *Complete Works of Aristotle* (Princeton: Princeton University Press, 1984) vol. 2, 2441. Stanley partly follows Diogenes Laertius, *Lives*, VIII.11, who includes other wonders. The "Golden Verses" once taken as evidence about his moral doctrine is a much later composition wrongly attributed to him. See Heninger, who gives Stanley's translation of them (260–1) as well as a rich note on the controversies about them (278–9 n. 18).

[24] Adam Friedrich Glafey, *Vollständige Geschichte des Rechts der Vernunft* (Leipzig, 1739, reprint, Aalen: Scientia Verlag, 1965), 26–8; on Selden, 23–5.

Jewish priests kept their mysteries secret. Vico holds that it was "by grace of a most sublime human science" that Plato and Pythagoras "exalted themselves to some extent to the knowledge of the divine truths which the Hebrews had been taught by the true God."[25] He thus denies the essential presupposition of the Pythagoras story, that knowledge of morality could only have been acquired at first from a divine revelation.

Vico was not widely read; and it was not until the end of the eighteenth century that the Pythagoras story was critically examined and dismissed. In 1786 the German scholar Christoph Meiners published a history of the sciences in which he devoted much space to a critical examination of the alleged Pythagorean writings, dismissing almost all of them as unreliable.[26] An effective positive replacement for the Pythagoras story was not published until 1822, in what I think should be considered the first comprehensive *modern* history of moral philosophy, Carl Friedrich Stäudlin's *Geschichte der Moralphilosophie.*[27]

Stäudlin opens with a brief remark suggesting that morality arises from the interaction between the native powers and dispositions of the human mind and our situation in the world. Its origins lie so far back in antiquity that there is no use speculating about them. There was morality everywhere before there was philosophizing about it, and there were unsystematic and poetic articulations before anything rational appeared.[28] We are as naturally moved to reflect on our own powers as on the world in which we act, and that reflection, carried far enough, is philosophy. Moral philosophy begins with the Greeks: pre-eminently with Socrates.[29]

---

[25] Giamabattista Vico, *The New Science*, trans. Bergin and Fisch (Ithaca: Cornell University Press, 1948), 43. This is the 3rd edn. of 1744, §94–5. Leon Pompa, *Vico: Selected Writings* (Cambridge: Cambridge University Press, 1982), gives comparable passages from the 1st edn., 1725; see §§36, 39, 86.

[26] I have not been able to consult Meiners's work; I rely on Lucien Braun, *Histoire de l'Histoire de la Philosophie* (Paris: Editions Ophrys, 1973), 173–7. By the end of the eighteenth century another German scholar produced a brief history of ethics in which Pythagoras is mentioned along with Aristotle's claim about him, lacking, again, the phrase "but not successfully." But he says nothing about any link between a first revelation of moral truth to the Jews and its elaboration by the Greeks. See Johann Christoph Hoffbauer, *Anfangsgründe der Moralphilosophie und insbesondere der Sittenlehre, nebst einer allgemeinen Geschichte derselben* (Halle: Kümmel, 1798), 295–6.

[27] Adam Smith surveys part of the history of moral philosophy in Part VII of *The Theory of Moral Sentiments*. Although showing what I here describe as a modern attitude, it makes no effort to be comprehensive.

[28] Vico in *New Science*[3] says that human thought begins in particulars, not in theorizing, and that it was a mistake to think that universal laws were the most ancient form of the direction of action: 498–501.

[29] Carl Friedrich Stäudlin, *Geschichte der Moralphilosophie* (Hannover, 1822), 22. Referred to hereinafter as Stäudlin.

Stäudlin gives Pythagoras a chapter; but in it he expresses great admiration for the work done by Meiners (whom on other points he attacks) enabling us to dismiss all the old claims about his importance. Allowing that Pythagoras had some interesting thoughts about morals, he himself is not willing to concede that there is any live issue about a Jewish connection. Yet he notes several recent writers who do, and the amount of effort he devotes to getting rid of the Pythagoras story suggests that it is still a live option.[30]

What makes Stäudlin's work modern is not mainly its dismissal of the Pythagoras story and its kin. That, after all, is a scholarly position that might alter. Thus there is a more recent version of the Pythagoras story—surely not intended as such—according to which Zeno, the founder of Stoicism, was himself the son of a Jew. Giovanni Reale says that both Zeno and Chrysippus were Jewish and hypothesizes that the Stoic notion of *kathekonta* reflects Zeno's effort to bring Jewish moral categories into Greek philosophy.[31] What makes Stäudlin's work modern is essentially its attitude toward error. He treats error in moral philosophy as like error in any science, no more due to wicked desires or self-aggrandizing tendencies than blunders in mathematics. Error comes not from original sin, but from the great difficulty of the subject. The function of moral philosophy is not to defend God's revelation from sinful and perverse reasoners. Like Kant, Stäudlin holds that it expresses the human tendency to reflect on our own powers and dispositions. The Greeks, Stäudlin thinks, exhausted almost all the possibilities and explored almost all the blind allies. Only rarely does a new insight, such as Kant's, enable us to advance. With such insights moral philosophy may increase our grasp of moral principle from time to time, or correct honest mistakes made along the way, and so contribute to the progress of morality as well as of moral philosophy.

Stäudlin was a Kantian; and Kant would have agreed with much of his approach. But he would have added that reflection also has an important moral function. He thinks that we have all always known the basic principle

---

[30] Stäudlin, 1–3; on Pythagoras, 32–59.

[31] See Reale's *The Systems of the Hellenistic Age*, trans. John Catan (Albany: SUNY Press, 1985), 209, 216, 280–1. He refers to Max Pohlenz as his authority for Zeno's Jewishness. See Pohlenz, *Die Stoa* (Göttingen, 1948–49), 1.22, 24–5, 28, and the evidence, rather scant and with an anti-Semitic tone, 2.14n. For doubts about the thesis, see Brent Shaw, "The Divine Economy: Stoicism as Ideology," *Latomus* 44 (1985), 20 n. 8.

of morality. Because of our tendency to selfishness, however, a natural dialectic arises in which we try to convince ourselves that prudential reason is the only practical reason there is.[32] The philosophical reflection that shows the reality of pure practical reason therefore has its own practical importance. Kant has developed his own version of the secularized Pythagoras story.

V

Both the Socrates story and the Pythagoras story (in its secular as well as its religious versions) illustrate the interconnections among our conceptions of the aim or task of moral philosophy, the proper understanding of its history, and the nature of morality. The two grand narratives are similar in holding that moral philosophy has essentially a single task, though each assigns it a different one. But the assumption that there is one single aim that is essential to moral philosophy gives rise to difficulties for both views.

One difficulty lies in formulating the aim. Perhaps it is plausible to hold that we and Socrates are asking the same question if the central issue is described as Williams describes it. Yet we might wonder whether identifying the question of moral philosophy as "How should one live?" is useful for those interested in the history of the subject. The Socratic question, so stated, is extremely general. To take it as locating "the aims of moral philosophy" we must surround it with a number of unspoken assumptions. For instance, we must not take it to be a question about how one should live with respect to health, or income, or eternal well-being. Are we then to take it as a general question about how we should live in order to be happy? We have only to think of Kant's ethics to see that this will not identify an inquiry central to all moral philosophy.

The single-aim view seems to rest on a theory about the essences of philosophical disciplines which is itself contestable. If we look historically at what moral philosophers have said they were trying to do, we do not come up with a single aim uniting them all. Compare, for instance, Aristotle's claim that moral philosophy should improve the lives of those who study it

---

[32] *Grundlegung zur Metaphsik der Sitten*, Kant, *Gesammelte Schriften* (Berlin), 4:405.

with Sidgwick's belief that "a desire to edify has impeded the real progress of ethical science."[33] Recall the Stoic aim of finding the way to personal tranquillity; Hobbes's aim of stabilizing a society put in danger by religious fanaticism; Bentham's aim of locating a principle to show everyone the need for major political, social and moral reform; Parfit's aim of developing a new, wholly secular, science of morality.[34] Unless we leave the statement of the aim quite vague, it will be difficult to find one on which these thinkers agree. If we are more definite, then it seems that we will be required to say that anyone not sharing the favored aim is not really doing moral philosophy. Whatever the single aim assigned to the enterprise, we would be forced to deny the status of moral philosopher to many thinkers usually included in the category.

Those holding a Pythagoras story version of moral philosophy's single task face some additional difficulties. They must assume that the moral knowledge which is always to be defended can be identified in some way that does not presuppose the truth of any specific theory, and that it is always and everywhere essentially the same. Yet it is implausible to claim that Greek morality, the morality of the Decalog, and the liberal morality of modern Western democracies are in essence identical. The claim can be made out, if at all, only by proposing as "the essence" of these moralities some interpretation of them, probably in philosophical terms, which was not available to some or all of those whose moralities are at issue.

These objections to single-aim views about moral philosophy are themselves both historical. The historian will have a further problem with the outlook. It implies that since we and past moral philosophers share aims and goals, the best way to understand the work of our predecessors is to look at them in the light of our own view of the truth about morality. Even allowing, as some philosophers do, that our own views may not be the last word, it is still tempting, on a single-aim approach, to suppose that ours is the best word yet, and that therefore no other standpoint is needed for examining what has gone before.

The historian will complain that insistence on describing the views of past thinkers in our own terminology forces us into anachronism. If we are interested in what our predecessors were doing and thinking, we must try to

[33] Aristotle, *Nicomachean Ethics*, 1179a35–b4; Henry Sidgwick, *Methods of Ethics*, 7th edn. (1930), vi.
[34] *Reasons and Persons* (Oxford: Oxford University Press, 1984), 453.

understand them in terms they themselves had available. It is obvious that Hume could not even have conceived the aim of "anticipating Bentham." But it is just as misleading to describe him as "trying to develop a rule-utilitarian theory of justice." Although he discovered some of the important differences between the morality of actions within social practices and the morality of independent actions, the idea of utilitarianism as well as the distinction between "act" and "rule" versions of it are much later inventions. We may have good reason for thinking of his theory in terms like these, but we are not, in so doing, giving an historical account of it. Worse, we may be overlooking its historical distinctiveness by forcing it into our own molds.

VI

We cannot, it seems, write a history of moral philosophy without having some philosophical idea of the aims of the discipline; and we cannot have a well-grounded idea of its aims without having some awareness of its origins and history. The difficulties for the historian arising from this conclusion are not wholly avoidable. But they are less acute if we give up thinking of moral philosophy as having some single essential aim and suppose instead that philosophers at different times were trying to solve different problems.

As historians, we can work with a very general concept of morality, taking it vaguely and imprecisely as the norms or values or virtues or principles of behavior that seem to be present in every known society. We will study those who try to reflect philosophically on the matters thus described. No doubt our idea of what counts as "philosophical reflection" will be marked by our present conception. But we will not try to impose much more uniformity on past efforts than is carried by these two reference points. We will not need to decide whether common-sense morality, ancient or modern, is mere opinion or genuine knowledge. We will not, in particular, suppose that everyone who thought about morality in a way we consider philosophical was trying to solve the same problem or answer the same questions. We will think instead that the aims of moral philosophy—the problems that moral philosophers thought required reflection—are at least as likely to have changed as to have remained constant through history.

Why might there be such alterations in the questions or problems that set the differing aims of philosophical reflection about morality? One answer is that there have been times of upheaval when the norms involved in our common life have been called into question by social, religious, and political changes. The need to blend Christian belief with an inherited culture coming from Greece and Rome is one such case. The problems arising from the disintegration of even the appearance of a unified Christendom was another. Perhaps Parfit's concern to work out a wholly secular morality is another. Perhaps the apparent fact that there is no hope for agreement on conceptions of the good presents another such juncture. The history of moral philosophy, we may think, itself provides important clues to the eras at which the stresses on widely accepted norms and values became overwhelming and change was necessary. If philosophers do little to bring about the strains, they sometimes provide means to diagnose or even to cope with them.

If we take this approach we will be led naturally to ask some kinds of question about the history of moral philosophy that we may overlook if we think the discipline centers on only one question. On the single-aim assumption we will suppose we always know what moral philosophers were trying to do. They were trying to solve the essential problem. Without this assumption, we will need to ask what past philosophers were doing in putting forward the arguments and conclusions and conceptual schemes they favored. We will ask about the point or purpose of using these arguments. The answers will have to be historical. Holding that the answers to such questions may vary from time to time, we will ask just how the thinkers we study differ from earlier thinkers and from those of their contemporaries whose work they knew. What our subjects refused to ask or assert will matter as much to us as their positive claims. Knowing the former will enable us, as knowing the latter alone will not, to understand what their aims for moral philosophy were. To know what they refused to include we must know what they might have included, and did not. Here only historical information—not rational reconstruction of arguments in the best modern terms—will tell us what we need to know.

One benefit of this approach is that it gives us a way of checking on our interpretations or readings of past moral philosophy. There is historical evidence about the vocabularies available to our predecessors, and about the issues that mattered to them and to their publics. We may lack documentary evidence about a philosopher's own specific intentions in publishing a given book. But we can assume that he meant to be understood by a living audience, and not just by posterity; and what writers as well as readers could have understood is set to a large extent—not wholly—by the language they already possessed. Even innovative terms and concepts require some sort of introduction via existing notions. To learn what resources were available to a philosopher, we must look outside his writings, and outside of philosophy. If we do not check our accounts of a past philosopher in this manner, we are in serious danger of mistaking our own fantasies about what he "must have meant" for what he really did mean.

Single-aim theorists may reply that on this view there is no continuing subject of moral philosophy whose history we can try to write. But to say this is to oversimplify. Continuities are quite compatible with the discontinuities that arise from changing problems and aims. It seems highly probable that all societies complex enough to generate philosophical reflection must handle certain problems of social and personal relations. Views about the fair or proper distribution of the necessities of life, or about the relative praise- or blame-worthiness of individuals, seem always to arise in such societies. Study of different ways of structuring such views is a constant theme that gives moral philosophy some of its identity amidst its differences.

Some arguments and insights about what makes for coherent views of morality may carry over from one situation to another. They provide further elements of continuity in the work of moral philosophers. One illustration must suffice. When Cudworth said that "good" could not be defined as "whatever God wills," he turned against Descartes and Hobbes the same kind of argument that Plato's Socrates sketched against Euthyphro. G. E. Moore later presented other arguments against the definability of "good." Cudworth was trying to preserve the possibility of a loving relation between God and man that could not have concerned either Socrates or Plato. A century later Diderot appealed to the same argument precisely because it "detaches morality from religion."[35] Moore had still other aims in view. One could write a useful history concentrating simply on the

---

[35] Diderot makes this remark in one of his contributions to Raynal's *Histoire des Deux Indes* (1772 and later editions). I cite from Denis Diderot, *Political Writings*, ed. John Hope Mason and Robert Wokler (Cambridge: Cambridge University Press, 1992), 211.

question of definability.[36] But to do so would be to ignore historically crucial differences in the uses to which the point was put. I do not wish to minimize the importance of portable arguments. They do indeed provide a major set of linkages between past and present moral philosophies. But they do nothing to support the claims of the single-aim historian. Praxiteles and Brancusi both used chisels, no doubt, but we do not learn much about their art from noticing the fact.

Single-aim philosophers will undoubtedly feel that more significance must be assigned to these portable arguments. They will say that such arguments represent what moral philosophy is all about—the discovery of the truth about morality. Plato and Cudworth and Moore all saw the same thing, even if they described somewhat differently what they saw and put their discovery to different uses. They did not discover a mere tool for carrying out some external aim. They themselves say that they are in search of the truth about morality itself, and it is quite possible that they found an important part of it. Progress in moral philosophy, as in science, involves replacing false and one-sided theories with true and comprehensive ones about the designated subject matter of the discipline. History is useful only when philosophical assessment of the arguments of past philosophers helps us with our present projects.

Histories of moral philosophy can of course be written on such assumptions; and at the very least it is true that assessment of arguments given in the past is indispensable. The historian needs to know what led to the alteration or abandonment of various views. Since failure to achieve coherence or to produce valid supporting arguments may explain it in some cases, the historian who is not sensitive to such matters will write defective history. If the single-aim view is asserting only that knowledge of the discipline is prerequisite to writing its history, one cannot object to it. But the single-aim view leaves unexplained a great deal that the historian will naturally wish to consider. Why do some theories emerge and flourish and then disappear? Why do some recur? Why is there so little convergence, what does moral philosophy as a practice or discipline do in and for the societies in which it is supported? It is more useful for the historian to turn away from the single-aim view and adopt a variable-aim approach instead.

<hr/>

[36] See Arthur Prior, *Logic and the Basis of Ethics* (Oxford: Oxford University Press, 1949).

VII

If we take the variable-aim view of the subject, we will not be strongly inclined to make much of the question of progress or regress. We will look at the enterprise of rationally examining norms and virtues as one of the tools that various societies have used to cope with different problems they faced in shaping or preserving or extending a common understanding of the terms on which their members could live with one another. We will not think of moral philosophy as standing apart from and above the moral discourse of a society. We will take it as being simply one voice in the discussion of moral issues. In moral philosophy we will hear the voice that asks us to stand back from current issues and look at them in the most general terms we can call upon—or invent. Its hope is that by so doing we can reformulate the problems in more manageable ways. The very stance seems to make it natural to use an atemporal mode of discourse, but the rhetoric of moral philosophy need not conceal the fact that those who use it are located in their own times as well as in a timeless web of abstractions.

It is not hard to understand how questions that were of great importance at one time may lose their hold at another. The conditions giving the questions urgency may have altered. Or new and more pressing problems may have emerged. The abandonment of one question and the move to consider a new one may itself be a major kind of progress in moral philosophy. Perhaps only the assessment of questions can keep moral philosophy from the sterility and irrelevance that we sometimes call "scholasticism."

7

Teaching the History of Moral Philosophy

Undergraduate courses called History of Modern Philosophy in most American and British philosophy curricula are generally courses on the history of epistemology and metaphysics from Descartes through Kant. They rarely cover the ethical thought of the philosophers they study, and the curriculum almost never includes an introductory course on the history of ethics that parallels the course on the history of epistemology and metaphysics. There may be courses on the history of ethics at a more advanced level. But the Descartes-to-Kant course is usually required for majors, and comparable historical coverage of moral philosophy is not.[1] In this paper I first raise some questions about the rationale for giving such curricular priority to the history of epistemology and metaphysics. I go on to offer some suggestions for one-term undergraduate courses that might serve both as introductions to the history of ethics and to satisfy the history requirement in philosophy departments. The courses I outline sometimes involve texts not usually studied these days. And they all involve context-ualizing the philosophy by relating it to the social, religious, and political situations in which philosophers understood themselves to work. I discuss briefly some reasons for teaching the history in this fashion. And I end with some remarks on the significance of teaching moral philosophy and its history in the undergraduate curriculum as a whole.

---

[1] Mr. Todd Beattie of Princeton University examined 200 college catalogs and found that almost all philosophy departments require a course in the history of modern philosophy for the major. In most cases, this is a course on the history of epistemology and metaphysics. Only about eight schools allowed a course on the history of moral philosophy to count. I am grateful to Princeton High School for permission to use its collection of college catalogs and to Mr. Beattie for his assistance.

I

The standard Descartes-to-Kant course reflects the histories of their subject that philosophers have written. In these histories, the history of moral philosophy has typically received little if any coverage. Aristotle studied the metaphysics of his predecessors historically but not their ethics. Brucker wrote far less about the history of ethics than about the history of the religious, metaphysical, and epistemological aspects of philosophy.[2] Dugald Stewart's *Dissertation exhibiting the Progress of ... Philosophy* (1815) falls into the same pattern, as do more recent histories of philosophy. There are seventeenth-century histories of natural-law theories, of which Tim Hochstrasser has written an important study, but it was not until the nineteenth century that separate histories of moral philosophy began to appear.[3]

One possible rationale for this state of affairs lies in the religious heritage of the West. If morality contains God's instructions to us, then it might make sense to precede our study of it by asking what we know of God and how we know it.[4] If the questions here are not purely theological, they would fall to philosophical metaphysics and epistemology. More generally, if we supposed that morality must be rooted in metaphysical aspects of the universe, it would again seem to make sense to study these before moving to the ethics dependent on them.

This is the vision suggested by Descartes's famous tree of knowledge. "The roots [of knowledge] are metaphysics, the trunk is physics, and the branches emerging from the trunk are all the other sciences ... medicine, mechanics, and morals," he says.[5] If moral knowledge is dependent on knowledge about the metaphysical and physical nature of the world, including human nature, then morality and its philosophy will be comprehensible only once we understand their foundations and our ability to know them. On this view it may be reasonable to suppose that histories of philosophy should reflect the dependence of moral philosophy on what analytic philosophers view as the core disciplines: metaphysics and epistemology.

---

[2] See the explanation of this in T. J. Hochstrasser, *Natural Law Theories in the Early Enlightenment* (Cambridge: Cambridge University Press, 2000), 174.

[3] The first, to my knowledge, was C. F. Stäudlin's *Geschichte der Moralphilosophie* of 1822. The only nineteenth-century history still in use is Henry Sidgwick's *Short History of Ethics*, 1886.

[4] But well before Kant, both Lord Herbert of Cherbury and Pierre Bayle held that we must use moral knowledge to determine whether an alleged divine command really comes from God or not.

[5] Preface to *Principles of Philosophy*, in *Philosophical Writings* I, trans. Cottingham *et al.* (Cambridge: Cambridge University Press, 1985), 186.

It may be possible to revive the view that all sound thinking must begin by acknowledging God and the limits of human abilities to understand him.[6] But secular thinkers would hardly appeal to such claims to justify the subordination of ethics to epistemology and metaphysics. And general foundationalist views of a Cartesian kind have been widely criticized and rejected in recent years. If we abandon foundationalism, we also give up the assumption that there is a natural order of knowledge, in which some disciplines are essentially more basic than others. Then it is hard to see on what *a priori* grounds we could insist that the history of epistemology or metaphysics must be studied before getting on to the history of other parts of philosophy.

Whatever we think of foundationalism, when we are teaching history it is not very useful to presuppose that modern moral philosophy is best understood as an offshoot of views about more general or allegedly more fundamental theories in epistemology and metaphysics. Such foundationalist views may blind us to possibilities about the history that interests us. We need to be ready to examine the thought that just as changes in scientific belief may have stimulated new philosophizing about knowledge, so changes that upset accepted moral belief may have been the occasion for philosophical rethinking of morality. We will then want to explore the possibility that moral philosophy has a history of its own, which may have exerted its influence on other developments in philosophy and not merely been dependent on them.

Our thinking about the history of moral philosophy is constricted not just by religious or philosophical preconceptions of the proper order of knowledge but also by certain views about what moral philosophy is or does. Philosophers often write as if moral philosophy has always had a single aim or function, but for teaching the history of the subject, this is not a helpful assumption. Aristotle thought that "a knowledge of the Good is of great importance for the conduct of our lives," since we all aim at the good and are more likely to get it if we have the kind of clear knowledge of our target that philosophy can give.[7] Sidgwick urged us to reject Aristotle by making the improvement of knowledge, not of practice, our philosophical aim. In Sidgwick's opinion, "The predominance in the minds of moralists of a desire to edify has impeded the real progress of ethical science." We should

---

[6] See, for example, Nicholas P. Wolterstorff, "What New Haven and Grand Rapids Have to Say to Each Other." In *Seeking Understanding* (Grand Rapids, Mich.: William B. Eerdmans Publishing Co., 2001).

[7] Aristotle, *Nicomachean Ethics*, I.i.

instead approach the issues with "the same disinterested curiosity to which we chiefly owe the great discoveries of physics."[8] Sidgwick's view was reinforced by logical positivism. In 1930 Moritz Schlick said that moral philosophy "is a system of *knowledge* and nothing else . . . the questions of ethics . . . are purely theoretical problems." The philosopher, he urged, "must forget that he has a human interest as well as a cognitive interest" in morality. Moral philosophy is "in essence, theory or knowledge," and therefore "its task cannot be to produce morality, or to establish it, or to call it to life."[9] Schlick here assumes both that moral philosophy has only one aim or purpose and that the purpose is simply to obtain knowledge about morality. Twentieth-century meta-ethics even after positivism worked on the same assumption.

We need not accept Sidgwick's suggestion that the sole alternative to treating moral philosophy as a search for theoretical understanding is to treat it as an effort to edify. Pierre Hadot, Michel Foucault, and Alexander Nehamas have argued that in antiquity, moral philosophy was treated as the source of a "way of life."[10] More recently, Ian Hunter has argued that at least some of the major contributors to early modern moral philosophy also had highly practical aims in publishing their theories and that their aims were as diverse as their theories.[11] John Stuart Mill agreed with Auguste Comte that most people take their opinions from experts and that "the moral and intellectual ascendancy, once exercised by priests, must in time pass into the hands of philosophers and will naturally do so when they become sufficiently unanimous, and in other respects worthy to possess it."[12] American moral philosophy from the early decades of the nineteenth century until the end of the Civil War was supposed to provide a system of values and goals that all citizens ought to pursue.[13] All of this goes beyond an effort at edification, with its suggestion of individual religious uplift and encouragement.

[8] Henry Sidgwick, *The Methods of Ethics* (London, 1874), vi–vii. Hegel, in the Preface to the *Phenomenology of Mind*, trans. A. V. Miller, says, "Philosophy must beware of the wish to be edifying" (Oxford: Oxford University Press, 1977), 6.

[9] Moritz Schlick, *Problems of Ethics*, trans. David Rynin (New York: 1939) (original in German, 1930).

[10] Pierre Hadot, *Philosophy as a Way of Life*, ed. Davidson. (Oxford: Blackwell 1995); Michel Foucault, *The Care of the Self*, trans. Robert Hurley, (New York: 1986); Alexander Nehamas, *The Art of Living* (Berkeley, Calif.: 1998).

[11] Ian Hunter, *Rival Enlightenments* (Cambridge: Cambridge University Press, 2001).

[12] John Stuart Mill, *Autobiography*, ch.VI, ed. Stillinger, 126–7.

[13] See D. H. Meyer, *The Instructed Conscience* (Philadelphia: 1972).

An open mind about foundationalism and a natural hierarchy of knowledge suggests that philosophy departments have no compelling philosophical grounds for refusing to give the history of moral philosophy equal weight in the curriculum with the history of epistemology and metaphysics. Awareness that some of the moral philosophers took their task to be practical and not solely or even centrally theoretical leads to the thought that even an introductory survey of the history of modern moral philosophy should present the philosophical writings in relation to the varying practical problems about morality and social life that different philosophers may have aimed to address. I begin by sketching some of the ways one might structure a one-semester course on the history of seventeenth- and eighteenth-century moral philosophy, keeping these points in mind.

II

Any good undergraduate course in the history of philosophy needs a story line—a narrative with beginning and end. Both will be to some extent arbitrary, dictated by current interests as well as by our understanding of the sources. For an undergraduate offering that can serve as an alternative to the Descartes-to-Kant course, I suggest a history of moral philosophy from Montaigne to Kant.[14]

Montaigne makes a good beginning. It is not the least of his merits that students like to read him. To the instructor he gives an excellent reason to present a brief review of both ancient and Christian ethics before launching into early modern efforts to rethink the whole subject. Montaigne himself looks to classical moral philosophy to provide a way of life, but he gives up that effort. "Men are diverse in inclination and strength," he says. "They must be led to their own good according to their nature and by diverse ways."[15] He stresses the importance of the goods of this life, including the bodily pleasures. He expresses distaste for enthusiastic otherworldliness,

---

[14] My view of the history of moral philosophy is set out at length in *The Invention of Autonomy* (Cambridge University Press, 1998). My anthology, *Moral Philosophy from Montaigne to Kant* (Cambridge University Press, 1990), now reissued in a single volume, contains sufficient excerpts to keep students busy for more than a term, but the selections are not long enough to make possible the detailed study of any of the authors included.

[15] Montaigne, *Essays*, trans. Donald Frame. "Of Physiognomy" (Stanford, Calif.: Stanford University Press, 1958), 805.

whether it comes as Socrates' appeal to his daimon or as extreme religious devotion. He says that although many thinkers assert that there are universal moral laws of nature accepted everywhere, he has never been able to find one. And he claims that each of us can discover a ruling pattern within which suffices as a guide. Well before Descartes asked each of us to make a clean sweep of the clutter of our inherited beliefs about the world, Montaigne gave an example of someone doing just that with the main positions on morality that were then available. In doing so, he opened up *leitmotifs* that run through much of modern moral philosophy.

Why end with Kant? It is not necessary to do so. It would be more fun to end the course with the Marquis de Sade's critique of modern moral philosophy. But he was not influential in the respectable and increasingly academic circles that produced later moral philosophy.[16] Those who mattered were Reid, Bentham, and Kant. They superseded or overshadowed the work of their early modern predecessors. And it was their work that became the starting points of moral philosophy after the French Revolution. If departments sponsored a second course, covering the history of moral philosophy from Kant to Rawls, instructors could avoid the anguish of trying to cover Kant in a short time at the end of a term. (They would exchange it for the perhaps worse anguish of having to do so at the beginning of a term.) But Kant introduced some utterly new ideas into ethics, as neither Reid nor Bentham did. So it is worth trying to include him in the one-term survey, as we do in the counterpart history of epistemology and metaphysics, which could also end with Reid.

Even when we have decided on a beginning and an end, we can shape the narrative in different ways. We might treat it as a story of progressive enlightenment, showing morality's breaking free from subordination to religious belief and ending with three paths that independent ethics took in the nineteenth century. We could go further in this direction and allow our own preferences to let us endorse one of the three, declaring Benthamism, say, the triumphant outcome of our story. But we need not be progressivist. We could see the history of moral philosophy as a falling away from insights once possessed. MacIntyre, explaining how a Thomist might account for Nietzsche's genealogical attempts to unmask morality as a

---

[16] For de Sade as precursor of nihilism, see Winfried Schröder, *Moralischer Nihilismus* (Stuttgart-Bad Cannstatt: 2002), ch. V.

front for the will to power, suggests that the Thomist would begin with what Aquinas says about the roots of intellectual blindness in moral error, with the misdirection of the intellect by the will, and with the corruption of the will by the sin of pride—both that pride that is an inordinate desire to be superior and that pride that is an inclination to contempt for God. Where Nietzsche saw the individual will as a fiction that conceals from view the impersonal will to power, the Thomist can elaborate out of the materials provided in the *Summa* an account of the will to power as an intellectual fiction disguising the corruption of the will.[17]

If we choose to work out the history of moral philosophy in terms like these, we would be in line with a criticism of Locke published in 1697.

[God has] imprinted all natural truths in created beings ... from whence, by the vehicles of our senses, they are copy'd and transcribed into our minds ... Thus was mankind put into a plain roadway of gaining clear intellectual light [by developing logic] ... But ... the crooked bias of men's wills perverted their reason and made them disregard this well-grounded and regular method, given them by the Author of Nature.[18]

III

The way we teach the history of ethics is almost unavoidably affected by our assessments of modernity and the current state of morality. Those with strong convictions on the matter may well decide to make their views explicit and embed them in their historical narrative. But that is not inevitable. Narratives of progress or of decline in moral thought suppose that the narrator knows the truth. So too does a Weberian position that reserves for natural science the categories of progress and the obsolescence of old theories and that views philosophy as more like art. But the historian does not have to be sitting in some assured judgment seat. We can avoid this, I suggest, by treating past moral philosophers as responding to large-scale practical problems that were urgent in their time. We do not need to decide on the truth or falsity of the views we discuss. We can teach the critical skills the students need by showing them how to assess the

---

[17] Alasdair MacIntyre, *Three Rival Versions of Genealogy* (Notre Dame), 147.

[18] John Sargent, *Solid Philosophy Asserted against the Fancies of the Deists*, 1697, A2–A3.

philosophers' arguments and positions in the light of the questions that actually concerned them.[19] It takes historical work to unearth those questions and to avoid substituting for them the issues that we consider central now. But this can be done, and the students need to learn how to do it. We can also use the criticisms later philosophers made of their predecessors to get students to discuss the merits of positions. Butler's objections to egoism, Hume's to cognitivism, and Reid's to Hume's sentimentalism all provide important introductions to major disputes in ethics and are excellent exercises for students.

Setting moral philosophy in the context of the issues disturbing the philosopher's culture allows us to be on the watch for the kinds of discontinuity or rupture that Kuhn and Foucault stressed. Nearly a century ago, Dewey put a similar point quite forcibly.

Intellectual progress usually occurs through sheer abandonment of questions together with both of the alternatives they assume—an abandonment that results from their decreasing vitality and a change of urgent interest. We do not solve them: we get over them.[20]

The history of moral philosophy is a good place to go to observe philosophers abandoning old questions.

What then might a course on the history of moral philosophy from Montaigne to Kant look like? Here is a start, organized for three sessions per week in a 13-week semester.

History of Moral Philosophy: Montaigne to Kant

    I. 1. Introduction; 2. Montaigne; 3. Montaigne
   II. 1. Modern natural law: Grotius; 2. Hobbes; 3. Hobbes
  III. 1. Hobbes; 2. Hobbes; 3. Hobbes
  IV. 1. Pufendorf; 2. Pufendorf; 3. Pufendorf
   V. 1. Intellectualism: Leibniz; 2. Leibniz; 3. Leibniz [Wolff]
  VI. 1. Self-interest and morality: Nicole; 2. Mandeville; 3. Gay
 VII. 1. Moral sense: Hutcheson; 2. Hutcheson; 3. Butler

---

[19] We will show what we consider to be important or unimportant as much by the practical issues we choose to highlight as by the philosophers we read and those we skip.

[20] John Dewey, "The Influence of Darwinism on Philosophy," 1909, *Middle Works* vol. 4, (Carbondale, Ill.: 1977), 14.

VIII. 1. Butler; 2. Butler; 3. Hume
   IX. 1. Hume; 2. Hume; 3. Hume
    X. 1. Common-sense intuitionism: Reid; 2. Reid; 3. Reid
   XI. 1. Utilitarianism: Bentham; 2. Bentham; 3. Bentham
  XII. 1. Kantianism: [Crusius]; 2. Kant; 3. Kant
 XIII. 1. Kant; 2. Kant; 3. Kant

What carries the students through these authors is a narrative nicely opened by Montaigne's ambivalence about human beings. At the end of the essay on Sebond, Montaigne uses Seneca and Plutarch to say that man is a "vile and abject thing" if he does not "raise himself above humanity" and that he cannot do this unless he renounces his own means and relies on God to lend him a hand: only Christian faith can help. But in "On Repentance" he rejects the thought that he ought to regret being human. His conscience is "content with itself," he says, "not as the conscience of an angel or horse but as the conscience of a man." The judgment comes from his own "court and laws," and he does not look elsewhere. The *Essays* thus move from a view of man as lowly and needing external control to a much higher estimate of our capacities, particularly our ability to govern ourselves. I take this movement to be central to the development of modern moral philosophy. Not surprisingly, Kant provides a fitting end to the story.

To introduce the course, I discuss the Reformation and the religious wars tied to the ideological splits it introduced or exacerbated. Religious controversy is a *leitmotif* throughout. Even after the worst of the wars were over, confessional controversy remained. And with it there remained the need—desperate, for those who remembered the horrors of war—to find a morality that could be widely accepted despite confessional differences. Most people could not live a morality to which God was irrelevant, but at the risk of renewed bloodshed, God, whose will naturally had to be passed on by his official ministers, could not play an active role in it. This forms a large part of the context in which I try to explain the history of moral philosophy.

It is important not to overdo the amount of departure from religion that occurred in the seventeenth and eighteenth centuries. If Bentham gives us a wholly secular morality, neither Reid nor Kant do. One function of the course, therefore, is to correct misleading views of "the enlightenment and secularization" that are still current. Another is to explore the different ways in which religion has been taken to be of importance for morality and to raise questions about what morality might be without it. The rise of science was of course important, as was religion. I do not make much of it in this course, but the Newtonianism that gave Hume the model for his naturalism and the rhetoric in which he explained his philosophical ambitions deserves brief mention.

As general background, and to be helpful for understanding Montaigne, then, I say something about St. Thomas's views on natural law and about the strong positions of Luther and Calvin on our sinful condition. A lecture, with or without brief selections, suffices for Grotius, but it is important to bring in at the start his views on human sociability and the difficulties put in its way by our tendency to overreach ourselves. Hobbes goes further than Grotius in his estimate of the difficulty we have in living together. Comparing his view of the state of nature with St. Augustine's, visible in *The City of God*, highlights his Montaignian refusal to call us sinful. And his view of how we give effect to the dictates that become morality is a step on the path toward showing how we can construct our own governance. Pufendorf brings out the voluntarism that Hobbes himself espouses more overtly and fully than Hobbes does, and argues—against Montaignian skepticism—that international and not just national law is a possibility.

I choose Leibniz to speak for intellectualistic perfectionism partly because Spinoza is harder to understand and partly because Leibniz's criticisms of Pufendorfian voluntarism exemplify a major theme in the development of modern moral philosophy. (One could use Cudworth's critique of Cartesian voluntarism for this purpose as well, but his own positive views are hard to extract and present briefly.) The disagreements between Pufendorf and Leibniz raise serious questions about what sort of foundation, if any, a moral outlook should have. Pufendorf himself might have offered reasons for not being convinced by Leibniz's critique. Leibniz is useful also because his views, mediated and somewhat transformed by Wolff, were important in Kant's development. It is, however, quite possible to teach Spinoza instead, using material from the *Theological-Political Treatise* and the *Ethics*. When I do teach him, I confess that I do not expect the students to master the arguments for the propositions in the latter work. I aim at most to give them an overview of the position. Either Leibniz or Spinoza will introduce the students to the view that moral improvement comes only from clarified and increased knowledge.

I put three mischief makers next—Nicole, Mandeville, and Gay—partly because the students get a kick out of them. And of course most of those who wrote later tried to come to terms with them. Hutcheson is direct in doing so and is easier to read than Shaftesbury. Butler, though students find him difficult, is vital. More clearly than many other thinkers, he uses the major alternative to voluntarism or divine command theory for keeping God essential to morality. God, for Butler, is the supervisor of the universe who makes sure that if each of us does our duty, as it is made evident to us through conscience, all will be for the best. Thus God is a utilitarian though we cannot be. In addition, Butler's arguments against egoism, his claims about the superior authority of conscience as distinct from its strength, and his pluralistic critique of Hutcheson's view that benevolence is the whole of virtue raised issues that have not yet disappeared from moral philosophy.

Hume's distinction between natural and artificial virtues builds from Pufendorf's distinction between imperfect and perfect duties, and his conventionalist theory of justice is a response to Butler's objections to Hutcheson's quasi-utilitarianism. His insistence that approval is directed primarily at motives, not at acts, is a direct disavowal of the severe protestant position that in order to show us our need for grace, God could command us to act in ways that we are unable to act. Putting Hume in this context helps students see his originality. And it gives them a good sense of how his sentimentalism goes far beyond the thought of his predecessors in developing a way to understand ourselves as capable of self-governance. In connection with Hume's theory of justice, it is worth pointing out that Hume wrote on economics and was concerned about the severe underdevelopment of his native Scotland.

Reid presents a different picture of self-governance as well as a host of arguments against Hume. And Bentham fires a huge battery of objections at all of his natural-law, intuitionist, and sentimentalist predecessors. When he is done with them, utilitarianism seems to be the only show in town. But of course he did not know Kant. Like Bentham, Kant hoped to eliminate the views of all of his own predecessors, many of them the same as those of Bentham. I sometimes try to talk a little about Crusius to help the students see that Kant did not come just out of the blue and that he was using as well as criticizing earlier work. But time presses at the end of term, and there is enough to do in getting the students to have some understanding of morality as autonomy as it is spelled out in the first two sections of the

Groundwork. I do not try to get them through the third section, though I summarize it for them.

There are several themes that keep coming up in the authors I have proposed for study. Montaigne abandons the search for a highest good that will be the same for all human beings, and Grotius follows him. Hobbes vehemently denies that there is any such thing. Even Bentham does not claim that there is, as his "pleasure" is merely a placeholder for preferences, and his defense of homosexuality makes it clear that he knew how varied those could be. Kant insists that we each be allowed to pursue the good as we ourselves see it—within limits, of course. The problem of finding a common morality without relying on a highest good is thus one central issue.

Here is another: Montaigne does not deny the authority of the Catholic Church in moral matters but sets it aside; Hobbes subordinates religious teaching to the secular ruler. This provides a reason to bring in the emergence of moral philosophy as a discipline independent of moral theology.[21] It is worthwhile occasionally to point out that moral philosophy—as our curriculum conceives of it—is itself a discipline that emerged during the debates the course is covering. For the natural-law theorists, morality was just a part of law. It was separated out by thinkers I have usually not tried to include: Malebranche and Thomasius. But one cannot cover everything in one semester.

Is this a course on the rise of enlightenment moral philosophy? Yes, indeed, but it is an open question how useful it would be, while teaching it, to make enlightenment a major theme. To do so, one has to give an account of what enlightenment was. Using Kant's account in a semester ending with his ethics makes the voyage all too obviously destined for that goal from the start. If we take pure opposition to religion as the dominant focus of enlightenment, we will have a skewed approach to the moral philosophers who insisted on somehow keeping God involved in morality but who still must be considered enlightened. It is worth playing the enlightenment motif from time to time, but to do it full justice would pull the course away from its central subjects.

---

[21] On this, see Wilhelm Schmitt-Biggeman, "New Structures of Knowledge," in *A History of the University in Europe*, ed. Hilde de Ridder-Symoens (Cambridge: Cambridge University Press, 1996), 489–529. And note Ian Hunter's objections to his views, *Rival Enlightenments*, (Cambridge: Cambridge University Press, 2001), 20–1, 37–8.

Another way of presenting the history of moral philosophy would be to offer alternating courses: one on the seventeenth century (roughly) and one on the eighteenth. They could be taught in alternate years and allowed to satisfy the same requirements. A seventeenth-century semester, starting with the religious controversies and Montaigne, could give more time to the natural lawyers and to the rationalist theorists than the course already outlined. Stoicism could get a little time, with some Lipsius or DuVair as text, and Spinoza can be presented partly in this light. Students are quite intrigued by Malebranche, but one can avoid his metaphysical oddities and teach Clarke instead as a sort of finale. For the eighteenth century Shaftesbury, Mandeville, and Butler make a good beginning; Hume and Reid show the kinds of position against which Bentham specified his view; and Rousseau can be enjoyed for a week or two before landing at Kant's doorstep.

A rather different kind of course on the history of moral philosophy could begin with Machiavelli by using material on the classical republic from the *Discourses* as well as a little on unscrupulousness from *The Prince*. The absence of Christianity from his treatment of social life provides a view of human self-governance against which to teach some Aquinas, Luther, and Calvin. I would then move to Hobbes's rejection of republicanism together with his subordination of religion to the ruler. Pufendorf might come next, raising questions about the importance of religion in society, to be followed by Mandeville, whose cynical take on morality as political manipulation links him more to Machiavelli than to Hobbes. Shaftesbury asked questions about what sort of moral psychology is presupposed in the citizens of a modern classical republic. Butler can be fitted into this narrative, though not, I think, as interested in the political bearing of his moral psychology. Hume rejected republicanism; Rousseau revived it; and Kant gave it a new shape. Here the religious themes would be less prominent, and questions about politics, moral psychology and the relation of individual and community would be more prominent than they would be in the other courses I have suggested.

Another approach to the history of moral philosophy would be to concentrate on modern views about virtue.[22] Here Machiavelli might be a good starting point, since he uses a term translated as *virtue* but does not use it to mean quite what the ancients meant by it. The development in modern

---

[22] For an argument against those who claim that modern moral philosophy ignored virtue, see my "Misfortunes of Virtue," Chapter 10 of this volume.

times away from Machiavelli's understanding of *virtù* is a good story—one that can be set in the frame of the decline of admiration for the nobility and their warrior virtues, the rise of new views of courtesy independent of courts, and the admission of shopkeepers and other ordinary folk into the ranks of those who might possess all the important virtues. Montaigne is again important, since he comments on many ancient views of the virtues and is highly critical of the preeminence accorded to the character of the ruthless soldier or military leader.[23] Grotius's critique of Aristotle on virtue could be the focus for a brief discussion of his thought, followed by Hobbes's concerns about virtue in connection with republicanism and his attempt to create a law-centered alternative. Pufendorf's category of imperfect duties is best explained as his way of making room for something like the virtues of concern for others. In Shaftesbury, Hutcheson, Butler, and Hume, virtue takes center stage, and Rousseau deserves an important place in this narrative, bringing back Machiavelli's admiration for the classical republic but with a distinctly different twist. In ending with Kant, one would need to give the students some pages from his *Doctrine of Virtue* to supplement the usual reading in the *Groundwork*.

IV

Any of these courses would give students a good idea of the richness of the traditions of modern moral philosophy. My suggestions show that I am not favorably disposed to the sometimes popular course on "the British moralists" as a first survey of the history of modern ethics. That has long been a standard offering, partly because anthologies of seventeenth- and eighteenth-century English-language ethics have been available for over a century. Moreover, the British writings are accessible to beginners, and it is easy to link the main authors in a narrative going from Hobbes to Bentham and Reid. Nonetheless, to teach the history of modern moral philosophy in this way is to leave out as much of what shaped its course as we would omit if we tried to teach only British thinkers in the other introductory history class.

---

[23] See David Quint, *Montaigne and the Quality of Mercy* (Princeton, NJ.: Princeton University Press, 1998).

To put it another way, British moral philosophers were deeply involved with many Continental thinkers. Including them in the introductory history course is one way of broadening the context in which we locate the philosophers. I have suggested also some of the non-philosophical contexts in which I would try to situate the moral philosophy. A comment is now in order about why I propose to give so much emphasis to the broader cultural issues with which modern moral philosophy has been involved. Why, in a word, do we need the new histories of moral philosophy that I have been proposing?

Quentin Skinner and John Pocock have done more than anyone else during the past several decades to bring us to recognize the importance of situating philosophical thought in relation to historically local issues to which the philosophers were responding.[24] In working on the history of moral philosophy in the seventeenth and eighteenth centuries, I have been influenced by their writings. But I must make two comments about their views in connection with undergraduate teaching.

First, their complex rationales for contextualizing the works we study do not need to be explained in any detail in a beginning course on the history of moral philosophy. It suffices, I think, to make a comment now and again about the need a writer has to be understood by the people he wishes to affect and about the ways in which this need requires us to understand his language as he and his readers would have understood it.

Second, I have found that the history of moral philosophy requires a somewhat different approach to contexts than those that Skinner and Pocock take when they discuss the history of political thought. To put it briefly, I cannot always find specific cultural or political events to which philosophers were responding when they worked out what we now take to be their moral philosophy. And even when specific needs for rethinking ethics can be located, the philosophical inquiries go beyond what initially occasioned the work. Hobbes was indeed concerned about the English civil wars spurred by religious controversies, and Spinoza and Pufendorf were responding to different religious controversies in different social and political settings. But all of them were aware that the issues went beyond the local controversies that

---

[24] See Quentin Skinner, *Visions of Politics*, vol. I (Cambridge: Cambridge University Press, 2002), for Skinner's papers, and *Meaning and Context*, ed. James Tully (Princeton, N.J.: Princeton University Press, 1988), for discussion. See John Pocock, *Virtue, Commerce, and History* (Cambridge: Cambridge University Press, 1985), ch. 1, for one of Pocock's several accounts of his approach.

provoked their theories. Their concerns extended to the more general issues that were made specific in different ways in England or the Netherlands or Germany. Those issues, as well as the particular embodiments of them, changed over time. We can bring out the pastness of past moral philosophy by relating it to the large-scale issues prominent at the time. They will frequently not be the same as the questions that concern us now.

Context is indeed vital if we are to be historically careful about the meanings of the assertions of past philosophers. For undergraduates, context has an additional kind of importance. Explaining the different sorts of practical problems in which philosophers hoped to make a difference helps students see that what they are reading was not intended to be of merely academic interest. Philosophy nowadays does not have a large appeal to the public, not even to the undergraduate public. If we are to make the history of moral philosophy significant now for students, we need to show them that it mattered in its own time for reasons that went beyond the classroom. What that suggests is that moral philosophy might be as important now as it was then.

V

A basic one-semester course in history of moral philosophy could have a role in the curriculum like that of the course on the history of epistemology and metaphysics that has been standard for nearly a century. For many students the history course is an introduction to the problems of philosophy as well as to its history. Any of the history courses I have outlined introduces central problems of ethical theory and allows as much scope for their discussion as the Descartes-to-Kant course allows for its problems. At least as many students are interested in moral issues as are concerned about problems of knowledge. And the writers treated in the courses I have outlined are basic for the moral philosophy that follows. Aside from pre-conceptions about what is basic and what is derivative, a course on the history of moral philosophy seems as well suited as the traditional one to serve the purposes of a basic history course.

To allow such a course to satisfy the departmental history requirement would not, however, be a minor change. The standard history course serves, among other things, to prepare students for more advanced work in the subjects whose history it covers. There is more in the standard curriculum on epistemology and metaphysics than on ethics. Even advanced historical courses on rationalism or empiricism are not mainly, if at all, about the moral thought linked to these orientations. Giving history of moral philosophy a weight equal to the weight that has been given to epistemology and metaphysics might necessitate changes in the advanced offerings that have presupposed participation in the standard history course: less metaphysics, more ethics. Curricula are not easy to change in any case. And in this case, the curricular pattern displays some deep, or anyway old, currents in philosophy and in higher education that call for rethinking.

During much of the nineteenth century, American college education, like its British counterpart, was designed to prepare a leadership elite for positions of responsibility in the ministry, government, or business. In the United States, the capstone course during the senior year, often given by the college President, was a course on ethics. It provided an orientation to life in the form of a comprehensive overview of Christian morality. It criticized philosophical positions believed to be inimical to that morality and provided at least a rudimentary rationale for what the young men who took it were supposed to be assured of otherwise through revelation.[25] College presidents do not teach that course any more, and neither do philosophy departments. Colleges and universities on the whole no longer present themselves as preparing their students for leadership roles. Many students think that the idea that they might go into politics is bizarre or foolish. And the thought that philosophy courses might help prepare them for such a career would seem equally if not more bizarre.

Philosophy's own contribution to this situation is complex. In ancient times, as I suggested earlier, philosophers were looked on as sources of wisdom about the overall care of the self, about how to conduct oneself in matters familial and sexual, about how to use power and how to lose it, and about how to sustain either success or misery with dignity.[26] We do not now expect philosophers to be wiser about practical matters than other people are: indeed, probably the contrary. Christianity took over the guidance of life from pagan philosophy, and modern moral philosophy never took it back.

---

[25] See Meyer, referred to in n. 13.
[26] See the work of Hadot, Foucault, and Nehamas referred to in n. 10.

For this failure or refusal there were several reasons. One was that the Reformation ensured that it would be at least as hard for moderns to achieve agreement about the good life as it had been for the ancients. Moreover, there were urgent public problems about morality and politics, about which philosophers hoped to have more useful things to say than they could about the good life. Priests and ministers might continue to claim the authority to direct the private lives of individuals, but the universities in which philosophers came to be at home did not confer any such authority on them. And the academicization of philosophy also played a part in moving philosophers away from the kind of claim that John Stuart Mill made in the last third of his century: that philosophers should shape public morals. To sustain funding for the work of philosophy in twentieth-century universities dominated by science, it seemed necessary to make the subject look like the sciences. Analytic philosophy seemed just the right way to go for this purpose. It enabled Anglophone moral philosophy to present itself as a tough-minded discipline with an agenda of difficult and purely theoretical problems. But the civil rights movement, the Vietnam war protests, the women's movement, and developments in biology and medicine have moved different questions to the front. Rawls's moral and political thought and the rise of applied ethics have brought about remarkable changes in what can now count as serious work within the discipline.

What might justify allowing the history of moral philosophy to share the place traditionally accorded the history of epistemology and metaphysics? I have claimed that moral philosophy itself has had different aims and purposes over its long history. Study of the history of the subject has had a much shorter life span, and we have no good examination of it.[27] But insofar as the history has been taught, its teaching has also had varying aims. For Sidgwick, one point of the function of the historiography of ethics was to show that there really was—that there always had been—the discipline of moral philosophy; it therefore should have a secure place in the curriculum. Today, I think, we need a different service from study of the history of moral philosophy. We need it to show us how moral philosophy at different times has served different practical purposes. Historicizing the past of the discipline raises questions about what is being done now. Is the debate

---

[27] See Norman Fiering, *Moral Philosophy at Seventeenth Century Harvard* (Chapel Hill, N.C.: 1981), and *Jonathan Edwards's Moral Thought and Its British Context* (Chapel Hill, N.C.: 1981).

about deontology, consequentialism, and now virtue ethics still worth continuing? Or are there other issues that might well be addressed? Can moral philosophy address the larger issues of the time? Or is it at best part of the training for the new casuistry of applied ethics?

Moral philosophy no longer needs to present itself as the spectator sport it was in the heyday of analytic ethics. Philosophy departments have not completely caught up with this development. If our universities and colleges were more interested in preparing students for leadership positions than they now seem to be, they might ask more of ethics courses and of courses on the history of moral philosophy than they now do. Philosophy departments themselves might even take the lead in bringing back this ancient and honorable function of their institutions. If they do, they will find that courses on the history of moral philosophy will need to occupy a far more central place than they do now.

PART IV
Seventeenth- and Eighteenth-Century Moral Philosophy

8

The Divine Corporation and the History of Ethics

I

In studying the history of philosophy we are often tempted to project our current concerns with problems and methods backwards. One reason we may do this is that we cannot read any text intelligently without having some interpretative approach of our own, however inchoate it may be. In contemporary Anglo-American philosophy, both learning and teaching have been largely ahistorical. In looking at earlier texts, consequently, the framework we use to try to understand them naturally tends to be the one we use in our daily philosophical work. It is likely to seem obviously appropriate, and perhaps we do not have another one available.

There are particular drawbacks to this approach in studying the history of ethics. It is widely held that modern philosophy begins with Descartes and is essentially defined by its epistemological concerns. These in turn are seen as motivated by the new science and the cognitive challenge it contained for religious doctrine. Of course it is recognized that morality was involved in religion. But Bacon and Descartes and Locke did not make ethical issues central to their philosophy, and it seems to be Christianity as a theory of the world, rather than as a way of life, that is ultimately at issue in their writings. So when we teach a course called "the history of modern philosophy", we usually teach the history of epistemology and metaphysics, and we do not ordinarily offer a comparable course, held to be of equal importance, on the history of modern ethics. The history of ethics is seen, if it is seen at all, as a dependent variable. This accords well with that strain of contemporary ethics which sees moral philosophy as centering on those close relatives of

I am most grateful to J. J. Katz, Thomas Nagel, Quentin Skinner, David Sachs, Richard Rorty, and John Rawls for their comments on earlier versions of this paper.

epistemology, the topics of meta-ethics. In this connection it is interesting to note that there is a widely accepted pattern for teaching the history of modern epistemology and metaphysics from Descartes to Kant (one whose own history was explored by Professor Kuklick in the volume in which this essay first appeared[1]), but no similar widely accepted pattern for teaching the history of modern ethics. Of course it is possible that there is no really independent life to the history of thought about morality, that modern ethics simply arose out of changes in the best views available about knowledge and the ultimate constitution of the universe. I believe, however, that this is not so. And if it is not, then an interesting question arises as to why it has so long been assumed that it is. Rather than speculate on that issue here, I shall concentrate on sketching an alternative way of looking at the history of modern ethics.

The period with which we will be concerned begins at the end of the sixteenth century, with the work of Montaigne, who opens up the modern era in moral thought, and Hooker, who gave the older view its last great articulation in English. It extends through the time of Kant, Bentham, and Reid two centuries later. I will indicate how we can see the course of philosophical thought about morality during this period as centering on certain specifically ethical issues—issues of cooperation, justice, and responsibility. I do not want to deny that changes in metaphysics and epistemology, as well as in religious belief, were vitally important to thought about morality. But morality sets its own requirements for an adequate theory, and changes in those other areas of thought have their importance for morality through the medium of a dynamic arising out of those requirements. That dynamic is what gives the history of modern ethics its central problem and therewith its independence.

Before moving to my main theme, I want to make a remark about the kind of help I hope this paper can give. To use the terms now current, I seek predominantly an internal rather than an external explanation of the history of ethics between approximately the time of Montaigne and that of Kant. An internal explanation of a succession of philosophical positions sees the succession as developing from argumentative or rational considerations, using for the most part, common terms, and resting—consciously or not—on shared assumptions. An account which involves holding that

---

[1] "Seven thinkers and how they grew" in *Philosophy in History*.

some common assumption was dropped by a later thinker will still be largely an internal account if it stresses ways in which the later view is best understood as working out the consequences of dropping one, but not others, of the beliefs earlier thinkers held. In giving priority to a search for an internal explanation, I do not mean to suggest that external considerations are unimportant or unavailable—far from it. But I think we must have the best internal explanation we can get of an historical development in philosophy before we are in a good position to look for external explanations.

One reason for this is that we would like to understand the work of earlier thinkers as philosophers. On our own understanding of what philosophy is, it involves argument and the working out of the full logical implications of a principle or a position. So we want the historian of philosophy to explain earlier thinkers, and their conversations, in ways that bring out their philosophical aspects. We are not content if we are told simply that they came to hold certain views—never mind why—and that these views influenced later writers—never mind how. An important intellectual historian tells us, for example, that the Enlightenment was "always moving from a system of the universe in which all the important decisions were made outside of man to a system where it became the responsibility of man to care for them himself".[2] This may be true. Indeed I think it is. But I do not understand it philosophically until I can see what rational steps led various thinkers from the earlier "system" to the later one. And to see this is to have an internal explanation of the change.

More generally I think that the most satisfying account possible of why someone believes something is one which shows that what is believed either is true or is the proper outcome of a compelling argument from premises the person accepts, and that the person was in a good position to notice this. We may need to appeal to external factors to explain why the thinker was in a position to notice a truth or to see previously unnoticed implications of some of his beliefs. But we feel—surely correctly—that the fact that someone noticed the truth of some proposition or saw the soundness of an argument from his own beliefs to a new conclusion must be a strong explanation of why the person came to believe what he did. If such an explanation is available and correct, it seems to make unnecessary any search

[2] Venturi, Franco *Utopia and Reform in the Enlightenment* (Cambridge: Cambridge University Press, 1971), I; 2–3.

for further, non-rational, accounts of why the person held the belief. It seems then that it is only where internal explanations of the history of thought cannot be found that we must turn to external explanations; and if this is so, then it is evident why we should begin our work by seeking internal accounts.

Now this view leads, as one historian of political thought rightly complains, to "a kind of history which always tends essentially to trace things back to their origins, to the first beginnings of the ideas which it sees at work . . . Philosophers are tempted to push upstream until they arrive at the source. Historians must tell us how the river made its way, among what obstacles and difficulties."[3] The danger of supposing that philosophical views must be shown to be simply developments of one absolute originating point is real. So is the danger that the contexts in which philosophical positions develop will be ignored. If we really want to be historians, even when our subject is philosophy, we must be aware of these dangers. We must be ready to look for and acknowledge points at which there are radical discontinuities within the history of philosophy. But one way to locate such points is to push the search for internal explanations until we fail to find them. Then we will be in a situation where we must look for external explanations. Certainly many of the considerations which help us understand how a thinker came to be in a position to grasp a new truth or new argument are external. Questions about why certain issues become salient at a given time, about why some once common assumptions are generally abandoned but others are not, about why a line of thought took one turn but ignored another that was equally available, may often require externally based answers. But there is no *a priori* way to tell what sort of explanation will be available. Only detailed study of particular developments can tell.

II

It is uncontroversial that a long-standing Christian view of morality dominated thought at the beginning of the period I shall be considering. But an inadequate grasp of the logic of that position has hampered our ability to see

<hr>

[3] Wade, Ira O *The Intellectual Origins of the French Revolution.* (Princeton: Princeton University Press), 1971, 21; where the view is attributed to Cassirer.

its role in future developments. It is often supposed that the one essential issue about a religious morality is whether or not it is voluntarist or intellectualist: whether morally right acts are right simply because God commands us to do them, or whether, by contrast, God commands us to do them because they are, in themselves, right. This problem, of significant concern to theologians, is of considerably less moment to morality as such. Interest in it, sometimes rekindled by concern with the so-called naturalistic fallacy, simply serves to distract attention from what is a far more important aspect of morality when that is viewed as under the aegis of a Divinity of the sort Christianity teaches. My effort to present a heuristic for the history of ethics must begin, therefore, with a sketch of a model of the religious position which brings out the features I think more important. I say "model" because, while I think my outline captures the important features of a wide variety of actual positions, it deliberately leaves open a number of options about how the details are to be filled in. My sketch ends by portraying what I label "the Divine Corporation", but it begins simply with some remarks about the division of labor and about cooperation. What I say should be obvious—perhaps painfully so—but nonetheless true for all that.

Consider, then, the idea of a cooperative endeavor, in which agents join to produce a good that no one of them could produce alone. Each participant has a task or set of tasks. The tasks for each can be set out in rules laying down the duties of a station. It is the joint or successive performance by each of the duties of his or her station that brings about the good. There may or there may not be a separate, higher order, station, or set of stations, for the function of supervision or management. But neither a supervisor nor a first-order worker is personally responsible for the production of the good. Still, it would be unreasonable, in many instances, for participants to limit themselves strictly to their formally stated responsibilities and to refuse to go beyond them. We usually suppose that each agent has a general responsibility—over and above those listed as the duties of his or her station—to keep an eye on the way things are working out, and to step in to make up for the defective performance by others, or for unforeseen contingencies. So even though no single worker has an assigned responsibility described as "bringing about the good which the group aims at producing", each has some vague responsibility for keeping that good in view and adjusting his or her activities accordingly. And each participant would be liable to censure or perhaps penalty should this general responsibility be ignored.

That each agent should have this vague general responsibility for the outcome is not a necessary feature of cooperative ventures. On the contrary, it can only reasonably be attributed under certain conditions. These conditions may be present or absent in varying degrees. It seems plain, for instance, that as the participants understand less and less about the good to be produced, their liability to be criticized if they simply do their specific duties decreases. The less each understands about the contributions the others are to make, the less each is liable to criticism for minding his own business. To the extent that there is, and is known to be, a strong back-up system, so that misfortunes or failures by others will be remedied, one's vague general responsibility for adjusting one's actions by keeping an eye on the results will be decreased. If one's supervisor has made it very clear that one is paid for carrying out one's own duties strictly, looking neither to left nor to right, then, again, one's liability to criticism for doing this is minimized.

Imagine, then, that you have a job with clearly defined responsibilities within a huge cooperative venture. Your supervisor must coordinate the efforts of large numbers of other workers, who are unknown to you. The supervisor in turn reports to a still higher director, one of many, all ultimately controlled by a brilliant administrator, who is known to keep the vast international ramifications of the complex, multi-faceted, covert operation under review. You would, I think, be quite wrong in interfering with the tasks of others. It would be inexcusable for you to suppose that you could see well enough what was meant to result from another's work to intervene, to think that the chief administrator had failed to foresee all the contingencies, or to arrogate managerial responsibilities to yourself. In such a case one's responsibilities set strict limits to one's liability to criticism or penalty. Or at least this is true within the sphere of operation of the corporation. A sergeant who carries out direct orders from his company commander and assigns all-night garbage pail washing to a rambunctious platoon in sub-zero weather may not be liable to military criticism if two of the men catch pneumonia and die. But it is arguable that he has incurred other liabilities. A secret service agent may carry out his duties impeccably, winning nothing but praise from the Firm, and yet be open to serious reproach from other points of view. If we want an organization within which our responsibilities set a *complete* limit to our liabilities—where we should do our own duty, regardless of the consequences—we must take some further steps. The good we are helping to produce must be supremely important, yet far too complex for us to understand. The supervisor must be supremely efficient. He must never make mistakes about how to divide the labor. He must foresee every contingency and must be powerful enough to cope with any emergency. He must be so fair that there can be no doubts about his employment practices. Thus he must give all the agents adequate instructions about their tasks; he must assign them jobs within their powers; and he must reward them on the basis of their merits. Last, but not least, he must be too good ever to assign any duties that would be improper from any point of view. This just cooperative endeavor is the Divine Corporation, and its administrator is obviously unusual. In the Western world, indeed, he is generally thought to be unique.

III

The vision of the universe as a Divine Corporation carries with it a certain understanding of moral laws which in turn has important implications for the task of the moral philosopher.

The laws by which God structured the inanimate and subhuman parts of the cosmos and those through which the human and higher parts were ordered are not basically different in kind. They are God's bidding to his creatures, and all must obey. But there is a difference between the ways in which they do so. The inanimate and non-rational parts of the universe conform to their laws (to the extent they do: one cannot expect perfect conformity in less than perfect beings) automatically, without requiring any sort of conscious awareness of those laws. Rational creatures—humans, and presumably angels—conform through conscious choices, guided by some degree or kind of awareness of their laws. The difference in the role consciousness plays in keeping natural and moral agents acting in appropriate ways leads to one significant difference between the laws of the two realms. Both sorts of law must be universal. They must determine how every entity of the kind they govern is to behave. Thus laws governing humans, like those governing other natural kinds, must apply to all humans as humans, whatever special laws there may be for subgroups within the species. (The Divine Corporation does not as such require a hierarchical or class structure within human societies.) Moreover, both sorts of law must be the supreme determinants of behavior for the beings they govern. God's designs cannot, after all, be thwarted. But in addition to being universal and supreme, the laws governing humans must have a feature which laws for non-rational creatures need not. They must be such that humans can knowingly and deliberately do what the laws require. For if people could not act in accordance with moral laws, those laws could not structure the human contribution to the cosmic good at all; and if we could not act in full awareness that we are doing as they direct, the difference between rational and non-rational creatures would disappear. This third feature I shall label with the barbarous term "performability".

These three features of the laws of the moral world can also be seen as natural consequences of a Divine Corporation view of morality. It is a requirement of such a view, as I said, that the head of the firm be completely just. To guarantee our motivation, the tasks he sets for us are of supreme importance to each of us. It is therefore only just that we should be able to know what they are and be able to do them. If performance is the condition of our obtaining our wages, it would be unfair if some had harder and some easier tasks, or if some were better equipped to do their jobs and therefore found them less onerous. For the reward is essentially the same for each worker. So the work we must do to qualify for it must in some fundamental respect be the same for everyone, and everyone must be equally able to do it. On this view, therefore, the moral world is a just world, and as members of it we are involved in a just cooperative venture.

The natural philosopher then has the task of explaining the non-rational world. Perceptible disorder and irregularity exist in it, but they must be understandable somehow in the light of underlying order and purpose. Moral philosophy has an analogous task with respect to the moral world— the world of agents governed through their awareness of universal, supreme, and performable laws. There, too, apparent disorder and irregularity must be shown to be explicable in terms of order and of subservience to God's designs. There is no sharp discontinuity between natural and moral philosophy, but there are some differences. The moral philosopher tells us the substance of the laws of the moral world, as the natural philosopher does those of the natural world. In addition the moral philosopher must offer an account of the universality, supremacy, and performability of the moral laws—must, that is, explain how there can be a distinctive moral world. But in an important way moral philosophy, unlike natural, does not tell us anything new. The natural philosopher will discover hitherto unknown aspects of the workings of the natural world, and his instruction about them may teach us new ways of using the part of creation God made to serve us. Moral philosophy, by contrast, is corrective rather than instructive. Its usefulness lies not in discovering novelties but in removing the errors into which we are persistently tempted to fall. It thereby clears the way for us to live by the untheoretical guidance which must be available to all of us.

Not everyone, either before our period or during it, would have agreed that there is a moral world. But the Christian view of morality leads naturally, as I have indicated, to the conviction that there is, and offers a powerful account both of its inner structure and of its apparent disorder. As Christian beliefs came under attack and were weakened or wholly abandoned, the accounts that could be given of the structure and possibility of the moral world were forced to shift also. My main suggestion is that we will best explain the development of modern ethics by seeing it as resulting from attempts to defend belief in the reality of the moral world, viewed as a just cooperative venture, while accommodating changes in, or departures from, the religious underpinnings of that belief.

IV

I have tried to show that an important principle is involved in the dynamics of any venture in which people are at work to produce a good which no one of them alone could produce. The principle is that individual responsibility for the successful outcome of a joint endeavor varies inversely as the complexity of the enterprise and the perfection of the director. The Divine Corporation embodies this principle no less than other such ventures. But the idea of the Divine Corporation as I have so far sketched it is ambiguous or loose in a number of important ways. The Corporation requires a number of elements, each of which can be interpreted in various ways. Differing views about one element will require different ways of understanding other elements, or the relations among the elements, if the structure of the Corporation is to be preserved. This ambiguity or openness to multiple interpretations is what makes it possible to use the model in understanding a wide range of positions. I will give some examples.

Let me begin with the good to be produced by the agents working in the Corporation. So far I have talked as if their work must result in a product which is different from the work itself. This is the view of it held by the many Divine Corporation theorists who took the product to be the happiness of humanity. But other positions are possible. The Corporation might be considered on the analogy of a ballet company or an orchestra, where the product is not in the same way separable from the activities of the performers. It might then be held that our contribution to the cosmic order, or to displaying the full glory of God, is simply our behaving in the ways God has shown us to be fitting. This view of the purpose of the cooperative endeavor shades over into another one, which, like it, plays down the importance of consequences. God, it may be noted, can bring about any conceivable state of affairs, except one, regardless of our cooperation. The one thing he cannot produce by himself is our free decision to cooperate, our voluntary choice of doing as God directs. Perhaps the unique contribution humans make to the cosmic display of God's glory is the proper ordering of their own soul or wills.

Next there is, of course, the question of the nature and status of the laws governing the moral world—surely one, if not the sole, element of significance. It may be held, perhaps on theological grounds, that moral principles are laws made necessary by God's decree and transmitted to us as marking out our roles in declaring his glory. Then we would have neither a rational grasp of the laws themselves nor much understanding of how our assignment contributes to the cosmic good. Alternatively, it might be argued that each principle taken by itself must be inherently reasonable, and that God enforces the principles because they are so. Then their rationality might be self-evident to us, even though we still might not understand fully how the role they define for us makes its cosmic contribution. If on the other hand we suppose that the purpose of the cooperative venture is to make everyone happy, then it is natural to think that moral laws are, at least from God's point of view, general rules about utility. From the human perspective such rules always have exceptions. So to preserve universality we might argue that God always requires his creation to work by general laws. Or we could hold that the laws are absolute for us simply because of our subordinate position within the Corporation.

These options about the nature or status of the laws of the moral world are of course closely linked to the options about how agents can come to be aware of what they are to do. Here major constraints are imposed by the need to account for performability. If, for instance, moral laws are taken to be discoverable by reason, the philosopher must explain how it is that all people have essentially equal abilities to know moral truths. The cognitive theorist will probably move to an intuitionist position, at least as regards morality, since it seems plain that people do not have equal ability to reason about complex issues; and it was commonly held that people do have equal ability to grasp intuitive truths. To avoid intuitionism, with its connection to theories involving innate ideas, or else as one way of accommodating theological voluntarism, the theorist might offer a non-cognitivist account of moral awareness. This may give an easy account of performability, since it can help with the motivational issue as well as the availability of guidance. But then the requirement of universality demands an account of why moral emotions or the moral sense should be the same in everyone. In any case a Divine Corporation theorist will tend to hold that there is a *consensus gentium* about morals, and will need to explain any serious exceptions there seem to be to this.

Perhaps the most interesting feature of epistemology in Divine Corporation theories is that its main task is to help in explanation. Justification of moral principles as such is not the issue. The assumption is made that all or most of us are aware of what we ought to do, and are in agreement on the main points. Epistemology is called in to show why this is so. There is no call to generate, or to remove, deep skeptical doubts about morality as a whole. Arguments, epistemological and otherwise, are given about which specific principles best reveal the substance of the moral world. And a philosopher may well produce an argument to show that moral principles are rational or are purely emotional. But the point in either case is to support some particular explanatory account of the just cooperative venture of which we are all a part.

Finally there is the interpretation of the motives of the agents in carrying out their assignments—the old question of human nature. To indicate the full range of ambiguity involved here I must point out that the Corporation as so far sketched might involve only the *coordination* of the work of various agents, and need not involve their full cooperation. If someone were employing workers to produce a good which only joint effort could bring about, but the employees did not know that they were working with others on such a project, we could not say they were *cooperating* with one another.

Allowing the employees to know there are other agents beside themselves, even allowing them some knowledge of the aim or point of the joint enterprise, still would not entitle us to call their work cooperative. It is at best coordinated. The agents are cooperating only if in addition to the conditions so far given, it is also true that at least one of the reasons each agent has for doing his or her work is a desire to help bring about the good which the venture is meant to produce.

Consider first workers in a merely coordinated venture. They are presumably working solely for their own ends: each has taken the job for its wages, and so far none has a basis for questioning his or her assignment. If each knows there are other employees and knows something of the point of the joint venture, but is still working solely for the wages, it turns out that there is an analog of the principle I have said is at work within a truly cooperative venture. We can see this by imagining a worker in a coordinated venture who wants to increase his wages. He knows there are others involved and knows the point of the venture. If the employer is fair, he can reasonably suppose that he will be rewarded in proportion to his contribution to the good which, for whatever reasons, the director wants brought about. The worker might then reasonably think he could increase his contribution by making up for slackness in the performance of others, or by doing things that are important but are being left undone. But the more complex the venture is and the more perfect the director, the less reasonable it is for the employee to think that he can really increase his contribution to the good and thus come to merit higher wages by going beyond his responsibilities. In the limiting case of the Divine Corporation he would have no reason to think he could increase his wages in this way. The employee's duties would be absolute for him, despite the fact that God sees his work as being for a purpose. The Divine Corporation can thus model some features of morality whether we take the corporation to involve coordination or full cooperation.

Consider, then, the questions that arise if cooperation is involved. Here at least part of the motivation for participating is a desire to help bring about the good. This need not be the same as a desire for that good itself, though it may be. If the good to be jointly produced is truly a common good—one which is a good for each and all of the agents, in addition to being the good for which God created the whole enterprise—then any of several accounts may be offered of how we each find our own happiness in that good. If it is not a common good in this way, then a different account will have to be offered of why we participate. We may also see this as the question of whether the persons who are the agents in the Divine Corporation have within them a source of order, essential to their nature, which leads them to act as members of a just cooperative venture, or whether, as in a coordinated enterprise, they must be induced or compelled to act appropriately by external sanctions and rewards. On any account of motivation, the need to explain the supremacy of moral laws is as important as the need to account for their performability; and the philosopher must also leave room for an account of why we do not always act in accordance with the laws of the moral world.

V

So far I have kept my discussion of the Divine Corporation away from historical realities. I have only tried to show how the idea might be embodied in a wide variety of positions having the common essential feature of relying on the logic of coordination or cooperation under a perfect supervisor. I do not mean to suggest that every possible variant was actually exemplified. Nor do I want to say that Divine Corporation ethics was dominant at the beginning of our period in the unqualified and bare form I have given it. On the contrary, religious doctrines about the necessity of Divine grace, in stronger, anti-Pelagian, or in weaker, semi-Pelagian, forms always raised difficulties about performability, while skepticisms of various kinds led to doubts about universality, and Stoicism and Machiavellianism raised questions about supremacy. But I do want to claim that the Divine Corporation represents what became increasingly central to the moral teaching of Christianity. As a result, the model can serve some useful purpose for the historian.

First, it helps us understand the structural and dynamic features of an important succession of actual, influential positions. St. Thomas Aquinas and his numerous followers in the natural-law tradition, both on the Catholic and on the Protestant sides, through Suarez and Hooker, hold views which are modelled by the Divine Corporation. So too do the "modern" natural-law thinkers descending from Grotius. We do not find thinkers like Pufendorf, Burlamaqui, and Vattel of great philosophical interest today, because the philosophical part of their work, as distinct from their concerns with politics and international law, so often merely repeats what had been worked out earlier. But they represent what I believe to have been the common framework of thought of the educated part of the world during the seventeenth and eighteenth centuries. The philosophers we study from that period draw our attention in part because they modify, depart from and eventually abandon that framework. It is crucial to our understanding of them to know what they were departing from, to see why they departed, and to note how far they went. Thus the Divine Corporation is useful not only as a starting point but also as a benchmark. To the extent a philosopher stays close to it we may view him as conservative; to the extent he breaks away, as innovative. This gives us some rough measure of change in moral philosophy in terms that could have been used by the thinkers of the period we are trying to understand, and not just in our own terms.

Second, the idea of the Divine Corporation helps us to see the history of ethics as controlled by a concern for the moral world as a just cooperative enterprise. By bringing before us the complex whole into which the elements of the moral life must fit, whatever philosophical interpretation of them is given, it reminds us not to attach undue explanatory importance to philosophical debates about any one of the elements alone. A change in interpretation of one element will require other changes in a philosophical explanation of the moral world. A grasp of the dynamic that links these changes is perhaps the most important tool that the idea of the Divine Corporation gives us for understanding the history of ethics during our period.

In what follows I shall try to illustrate this by tracing very hastily the changes that led to the positions of Reid, Bentham, and Kant. With their work we come, I believe, to the culmination of the classical period of modern ethics and to the transition to a new period. If the idea of the Divine Corporation can help to explain how their positions emerge reasonably from earlier views, it has served its purpose.

VI

The basic change in religious thought during the period that concerns us was the rejection, to as great an extent as possible, of appeals to mystery and incomprehensibility as central to adequate accounts of the Christian faith.

This change leads to dramatic results for the explanation of morality within the Divine Corporation. When we can understand neither the corporate good to which we are contributing nor our own role in producing it, and when we believe in constant providential supervision of life, it is only rational—so I have argued—to treat our duties as absolute. This holds whether we are each motivated solely by self-interest or not. Consequently the philosopher explaining the moral world needs an account of those duties which yields such a view of them. As God's purpose comes to be thought more comprehensible, and as our part in helping it becomes plainer, there is less and less reason to treat duties in this way. This is particularly true as one moves away from seeing God primarily as a just judge, and toward thinking of him rather as the Benevolent Author of Nature. Then his end will be our happiness, not an incomprehensible display of infinite glory; and if happiness is the goal, our part in bringing it about is more easily grasped. This tendency is reinforced when, like the theists and deists, one insists that after the Creation God intended the world to operate without unpredictable special providences—that he set the world-machine going, and then let it alone. For then we must cease to think that an intelligent power rectifies our errors and omissions and makes up for accidents. More of the responsibility for doing so must rationally be thought to be our own. There is thus more and more good reason to understand morality in terms of our responsibility for looking to the *point* of our duties—to the good our cooperative efforts are to produce—for direct guidance in action.

At the same time there are good reasons to resist this utilitarian tendency. As we would expect, it can be challenged on the ground that utilitarianism finds it hard to explain how each of us can know what to do. We also find another kind of reasoning. Our moral experience, and not appeal to religious doctrine, is used as a source of argument against utilitarian views. Our moral experience carries rational weight because, in a Divine Corporation theory, God must have given us ways of being aware of what is required of us. Hence the experience through which each of us learns how to act must reflect the realities of the moral world. And as that experience is equally available to all of us, it gives us common data from which to argue reasonably. Butler is the *locus classicus*. Admitting that the only positive moral character we can attribute to God is goodness, he agrees that God looks at the world as a utilitarian. But we are not in God's position. We do not know enough to be utilitarians, and our moral experience shows us that we have particular duties of other kinds:

> As we are not competent judges, what is upon the whole for the good of the world, there may be other immediate ends appointed us to pursue, besides that one of doing good, or producing happiness. Though the good of the creation be the only end of the Author of it, yet He may have laid us under particular obligations, which we may discern and feel ourselves under, quite distinct from a perception that the observance or violation of them is for the happiness or misery of our fellow-creatures. And this is in fact the case.[4]

Butler elsewhere gives ample detail in support of this last contention. His target is in part Hutcheson, who argues that while we have a moral sense to guide us—thus avoiding worries about performability—its dictates are best mapped by a utilitarian law. If Butler makes the latter conclusion implausible, others criticize the non-cognitivism as unable to account for universality. The predictable result of these moves is a reassertion of intuitional views in Price and ultimately in Reid.

Reid gives us the last and most minimal of Divine Corporation theories in the eighteenth century. Indeed it is doubtful whether he should be thought of as a Divine Corporation theorist at all. He holds that moral principles are self-evident, and that everyone has sufficient intuitive grasp of them to guide action by them. Intuition is construed in a way that gives it the same role in explaining our knowledge of nature as it has in explaining our knowledge of morality. Since Reid thus has quite general grounds for allowing that ordinary moral beliefs carry rational weight, it looks as if he need not rely on the Butlerian belief that our moral faculty is God-given. And it also looks as if Reid does not think that action in accordance with the self-evident principles of morality is meant to serve any end whatsoever beyond conformity itself. He thus seems to advocate the kind of deontological view later made familiar by Prichard and Ross. But if in this respect he is out of the realm of Divine Corporation theory, there is another side to his position that is not. He holds that our ordinary moral beliefs are the test we are to use when we try to construct theories about the general laws of morality. And with this test in mind he concludes, against Hume, that no simple basic law is adequate. There are some seventeen intuitively evident axioms of morality. No reduction of them to any one principle is possible.

---

[4] *The Works of Bishop Butler*, vol. I, ed. J. H. Bernard (London: Macmillan, 1900), 166n.

At this point Reid's independence of reliance on the deity ends. Reid must have God available to guarantee that our intuitions reveal a moral world, not a chaos. God is needed to assure us that the apparently arbitrary list of moral axioms is complete and that the axioms do not conflict. In particular, Reid appeals to God to show that prudence, which is self-evidently required, does not conflict with the demands of benevolence, justice, and the other equally self-evident principles of morality. Against the monistic utilitarianism of someone like Bentham, who will not allow of any appeal to God as an explanatory entity, Reid could have only two lines of argument. One is to claim that the best explanation of the fact that we all share the same moral beliefs is that they result from accurate perception of underlying moral reality. The other is the appeal to self-evidence. But Bentham claims that the best explanation of such common moral beliefs is that they arise simply from social and psychological conditioning. Reid is thus left with only the epistemology of general intuitionism as the basic line of defense of a pluralism of moral principles against utilitarian monism. At this point we begin to face the issues that became central in the next phase of the history of ethics.

VII

The task for secular moral theories during the period from Montaigne to Kant is set by the ability of Divine Corporation theories to account for morality as it is present in the society of the times; and that morality had largely been shaped by teachings which were informed by the presuppositions of the Divine Corporation. Thus secular moralists were forced to duplicate in their theories many of the features of Divine Corporation views. This is strikingly evident in the work of Hobbes, and is a feature of Hume's view as well. A brief comment about them will help to bring out the originality of Bentham and Kant, and show why I take these later thinkers to mark the end of one understanding of the problems of moral philosophy and the beginning of another. I think it obvious that both Hobbes and Hume find ways to replicate that relation between absolute moral laws and a good which is produced by coordination or cooperation, which is essential to Divine Corporation views. It is also clear that each finds a surrogate to take on at least some of the functions of God in such views.

The point I want to stress here has rather to do with their view of the task of moral philosophy. Amid many differences between them, this is a point of agreement.

Their agreement is that the moral world does not hold together only because each individual within it understands the whole explanation of morality, far less because each deliberately uses the philosophical account of morality in making moral decisions. Indeed, Hobbes and Hume would agree that there would be considerable danger to the moral world if such a thing should occur. The citizens, for Hobbes, are to understand morality as a matter of the Golden Rule, supplemented by carefully regulated preaching of the laws from the pulpit. His own books are addressed to the ruler—not to the masses for further debate. Hume, without thinking so much central control is needed, sees the moral world as held together by our sentiments. He explains how they are naturally coordinated to do the job, but he does not suggest that each of us should transform his explanation into a principle which we would then use in making our decisions. There may possibly be some room for "correcting our sentiments" at the margins of the moral world, but deliberate use of theory is not what gives the moral world its basic order.

The rejection of this view of the limits of moral philosophy, and its replacement by the belief that each agent can deliberately contribute to a proper moral order by consciously using a principle of action discovered by a philosopher, is the work of Bentham and Kant.

With Bentham the change does not result so much from internal philosophical motivation as from a deep conviction that the social world needs to be reformed. Accepting no cosmic principle of order, Bentham abandons the Divine Corporation stance entirely, since he sees no reason to suppose that our moral beliefs up to this time have any value as guides in this endeavor. Before we can know their value, we must have a rational criterion which we can deliberately use to assess them. He thinks, of course, that he has such a criterion. Not only can it be used by rulers to lead the reshaping of their societies, it can be used by individuals making their own decisions. Bentham thus does not offer the utilitarian principle as the explanation of a moral world which we can be confident we already, somehow, inhabit. It is rather to guide us in making by ourselves and for ourselves a community which will be moral. There is no one else who can take the responsibility for doing so.

Bentham shows us how radically the task of the moral philosopher changes if we do not suppose that there is anything like the supervisor for a Divine Corporation, not even Nature. The philosopher must now also give rational grounds for this principle, strong enough to convince people who may very well hold convictions opposed to it. Questions of how each agent can figure out or come to know what to do in particular cases acquire an importance they did not have in Divine Corporation theory and its secular analogs. And questions about how, and whether, a moral first principle of this description can be proven come to have a new and far greater significance. Once again we are at the beginning of a new period of moral philosophy.

VIII

My story must end with Kant; and in the light of that story, his position is extraordinarily complex and, I believe, profoundly ambivalent. Only necessity drives me into the folly of trying to present an analysis of his place in the history of ethics at the end of a paper.

If Kant were the deontologist pure and simple that he has often been taken to be, he would have gone even further than Reid in abandoning Divine Corporation views of morality. He would have extracted the element within such views that stresses the absoluteness of one's duties and made it into the whole of what is distinctively moral. He would thus have denied the teleological significance of absolute duties which is central to Divine Corporation views. He would have shown that one can account for the universality of moral demands by noting their transparent rationality. He would have avoided Reid's need to use God to guarantee the coherence of morality by showing that there is only one moral principle. He would have shown that performability can be assured because it is easy to apply the one principle, and because we are free always to do as morality demands. And he would have guaranteed the supremacy of morality by his insistence on its uniquely categorical character. It is of course this last claim that leads readers to think Kant sees morality as entirely cut off from any concern with the teleological point of performance of duty. But this reading of Kant is not adequate. Numerous commentators have shown why, and the matter is perhaps no longer in doubt. I want here only to note a way of bringing it out that shows simultaneously an important respect in which Kant is still deeply inside the Divine Corporation tradition.

We can see this by noting Kant's frequently repeated view that virtue or moral goodness is to be understood as worthiness to be happy. It is important to see that this is a seriously question-begging account for Kant to use. One of his avowed aims is to show that morality is binding on us regardless of whether (we believe that) God exists and rewards and punishes us. But the notion of deserving something—good or bad, reward or punishment— only makes sense in a context in which some system of distributing goods and evils according to pre-established rules or criteria is in force. Given such a practice, then it is indeed obvious that those who abide by the rules or meet the criteria (or do so "best", if that is pertinent) deserve the established rewards, and that those who break the rules deserve the punishments. Lacking such a context, no sense can be given to the notion of desert. The assertion that someone deserves a better break than life has given him really comes to no more than the use of a metaphor to express the feeling that it would be nice if the person had had a better life. Thus in simply taking it for granted that virtue can be defined in terms of deserving happiness, Kant reveals how thoroughly he assumes a point of view which makes perfect sense in a just world of which a Divine Corporation view is true, but makes none if we live in a neutral universe.

Of course there is an important way in which Kant does not simply take it for granted that we live in a just world. Rather, he argues that morality requires us to believe that we do. Our moral actions, he holds, are not to be done for the sake of their consequences. They are to be done simply because they are required by the moral law. Nonetheless, all rational acts have purposes, and so must the acts required by morality. Kant thinks he can show that the world required by morality as its outcome is one in which happiness is distributed according to merit. Now if it is not reasonable to act purposelessly, and if we cannot take as our purpose something we know or believe to be impossible, then we must believe that such a world is possible. And to believe that a just world is possible, we must—so Kant notoriously concludes—also believe that there is a God who can make it so, for humans alone cannot control those aspects of Nature which must fall into line if a just moral world is to be brought about. In short Kant cannot conceive of morality except in a world structured as the Divine Corporation structures it. Instead of seeing the absolute character of the demands of duty as resulting from prior knowledge that we live in such a world, he sees those demands as giving us our sole justification for believing that we do.

It is well known that this part of Kant's general position created enormous difficulties for him. I do not refer to his moral arguments for the existence of God and the immortality of the soul, which bother us more than they worried him. I refer rather to his difficulty in explaining convincingly how morality can be perfectly independent of religious belief and its assurances of rewards for virtue, while at the same time holding that morality requires us to project a religious view of the world in which we act. If Kant's refusal to give up the latter part of this complex belief testifies to the tenacity of his commitment to a Divine Corporation view of morality, there is another side of his thinking that shows plainly his reluctance to remain within those confines. Kant always believed that the ability of the parts of God's world to direct themselves as parts of an ordered whole gave more sublime proof of God's glory than would a need for his constant intervention and direction. The upshot of this in Kant's mature thought is not only the Rousseauvian conviction that moral insight is equally available to every normal human. It is the belief that conscious use of articulated knowledge of the moral law would not disrupt, would instead strengthen, moral order. He sees his principle, therefore, both as explanatory of our deepest moral convictions—as in Divine Corporation theory—and as directive of our choices—as in Bentham's view. But in his historical and political writings, the directive function comes to have more and more of a role. We are to think of ourselves as being like God in one respect. We are required to make the world into a just moral community. The moral law shows us the conditions to which it must comply if it is to be one in which we as rational agents can willingly participate. Kant thus seems increasingly to treat the moral world as an historical task rather than as a metaphysical or religious assurance. That his view is indeed a descendant of the Divine Corporation is borne out by this turn in his thought. As I have pointed out, it is a result of the dynamic of the Divine Corporation that as God's supervision and activity lessen, man's responsibility increases. Like Bentham, though in a much more complex fashion, Kant did not really think we could leave it up to God.

9

Natural Law

In Heinrich von Kleist's play *The Broken Pitcher* (1808), an elderly character remarks offhand, "The world, our proverb says, gets ever wiser; and everyone, of course, reads Pufendorf." Pufendorf's most important work, a massive Latin treatise, *De jure naturae et gentium (On the Law of Nature and of Nations)*, appeared in 1672. Most audiences today, even in Germany, would probably not catch the reference, but Kleist may well have thought that his contemporaries would. For well over a century, Pufendorf was the most widely studied writer in Europe on natural law, morality, political theory, legal philosophy, and international law. Current German law still embodies some of his recommendations concerning the structure of a legal system. But aside from scholars, who study his impact on the history of modern thought about his subjects, not many people remember him today.

Samuel Pufendorf, born in 1632 in Saxony, was the son of a poor Lutheran pastor. While studying at Leipzig and Jena, he decided not to enter into his father's profession. In 1658 he assumed the position of tutor to the children of Sweden's minister to Denmark, and when war broke out between those two countries, he was imprisoned. There he wrote his first book, an attempt to demonstrate the principles of politics in geometrical fashion. The *Elementa jurisprudentiae universalis (Elements of Universal Jurisprudence)* was published in 1660. In the following year, Pufendorf began teaching international law at the University of Heidelberg. His most important publication during the Heidelberg years was a historical analysis of the states within the decaying Holy Roman Empire. Published in 1667 under a pseudonym, the book was so critical of the German political structure that it was banned from German universities. In 1670 he moved to the University of Lund, in Sweden. There he completed *On the Law of Nature and of Nations* as well as a short summary of it for students, *De officio hominis et gentium* (1673; *On the Duty of Man and Citizen*). This brilliant textbook went through more than one hundred editions in Latin and was translated into every European language.

In 1677 the king of Sweden appointed Pufendorf his official historian. During his time in Sweden, he published several historical works and a treatise on religious toleration and the relations between church and state. He dedicated the latter to Frederick William I, the ruler of Prussia, who in 1688 summoned him to Berlin to serve as his historian. Angered, the Swedish king held on to one of Pufendorf's manuscripts. Pufendorf's trip to Sweden to retrieve it, in 1694, ended in disaster. Scandinavian weather was too much for him, as it had been for Descartes and for Grotius. He died of illness contracted on the return journey, leaving a widow with very little money.

In 1648, when Pufendorf was sixteen, the Peace of Westphalia ended a thirty-year period of devastating warfare. The religiously motivated strife had destroyed innumerable villages, ruined agriculture, and depopulated large parts of the German-speaking lands. In England, civil war, centered on religious differences, continued for another dozen years. Rulers throughout Europe had to cope with fierce sectarian struggles as they tried to consolidate their power. The emergence of the modern nation-states and a growing intolerance for sectarian differences increased the need for rethinking the principles that had traditionally shaped individual conduct and public law.

Pufendorf's *Law of Nature and of Nations* was by far the most detailed and comprehensive of numerous seventeenth-century attempts to address the problem. In it, he offers a way of justifying morality he thought would be acceptable to every religious confession. A theory that puts morality on a sound footing, he argues, also provides the best view of political authority. He further claimed that his principles could be extended to develop the basic elements of international law, particularly the laws of war and peace. His system was structured to meet the specific problems of his era.

Despite the damage done by religious hatred, atheism was not openly acceptable in the seventeenth century. Hence one crucial problem social theorists of the time faced was how to show that God's existence was essential to human life while, at the same time, minimizing the danger that sectarian differences would carry over into disagreements about morality and politics. Pufendorf tried to solve the problem with two basic claims.

First, he holds that we must analyze moral obligation in terms of divine commands. Aristotle was wrong to think that nature gives ends to all things, and that these suffice to guide human action. Physical events can help us or harm us; they can be naturally good or bad. But recognition of good and evil alone does not tell us what we ought to do. God has given us commands to govern our action, and these are the original source of morality. Having created a physical universe, Pufendorf says, God *imposed* moral properties on it. Morality is not a matter of advising people to do what is for their own good. It involves obligating someone to do something, like it or not. To obligate someone is to issue a justifiable command backed by the threat of punishment for disobedience. Only God is in a position to issue commands that are binding on all humankind. And morality is constituted by precisely such norms. God is central to our lives because in acting as we morally should, we are obeying him.

Second, Pufendorf points out that since no one can command God, there can be no moral obligations binding on him. He is essentially unrestricted in his laying down laws for us. We therefore cannot understand his reasons for imposing on us the morality we have. The Christian revelation has not been given to all humans, so we cannot base morality on it. The only way we can hope to learn God's will is by looking at the evidence he has given us. We must consider our nature as showing how he meant us to live. To discover natural law, we must study human nature.

The knowledge we need is ordinary, empirical knowledge. It is not affected by our religious beliefs. It consists of facts that, Pufendorf thinks, no one can deny. We are weak beings with many needs. The world can supply the things we need, but we must cooperate in order to get them. We tend to be quarrelsome and selfish, but we also need one another's help and enjoy one another's company. From this we can infer that God wills us to live sociable lives. Because he gave us reason, we are unlike other animals in two crucial respects. We have language, and we are able to understand and share rules and laws. We must conclude, then, that God wills us to live together under laws that govern all reasonable beings.

The chief obstacle is our insufficient sociability. So the first divine command that reason discovers is that we must increase our sociability. We are enjoined to do whatever makes us better able to live together peacefully under the laws. This is the first law of nature, and all others are derived from determining what we need to do in order to carry out this law.

Pufendorf begins by considering the simplest sort of social life, a condition without conventions or laws, with no one in authority over anyone. Following a long tradition, he calls this "the state of nature." All humans in this state face the same task of increasing their sociability. Once we discover how these common problems can be solved, we recognize the laws God wills for everyone. Pufendorf thinks, moreover, that once he sees why people want to leave the state of nature for a society under government, he can also determine what kind of political regimes are justifiable.

Even the first people were under obligation to obey God. Solitary or not, they had to have control over material objects in order to survive. God, of course, owns the entire creation; but he gave everything in the world to humans. He did not assign shares. That was up to human decision. We come to realize that physical possession does not suffice for a secure social life. We need a way of being sure that no one will take anything from us when we are not guarding our possessions. So we invent a variety of ways of assigning things to particular people—of giving them property rights. God dictates only that such parceling out should take place. He leaves it to us to decide whether property rights should be held by individuals or groups.

However the first humans came into existence, it is plain that the sexual impulse is one of our strongest drives. God thus meant us to live in families. The law of nature does not require monogamy, but it plainly requires one person to be in charge in each family. To Pufendorf it was obvious that the male, being stronger and wiser than the female, should rule. Children, slaves, and servants as well as wives must obey him, and the husband must take good care of them all.

God's laws assign rights even under conditions where a central authority to enforce them is lacking. Pufendorf thinks of humans in the state of nature as slowly developing tools and skills to serve their needs, as becoming increasingly agricultural and then starting to trade surplus crops for things they need or want but do not grow or make themselves. Commerce develops from these simple beginnings into complex forms of interaction. The pleasure we take from the company of others also leads to the development of different forms of society, and eventually to the arts and to luxury. All this begins and grows without governments; but it cannot endure.

In contrast to Aristotle, Pufendorf holds that humans are not naturally sociable. We are not law-abiding by nature. Some people develop sociability but many never do. As property rights become more important, people come to realize that something needs to be done to protect those rights against those who disregard them. Man is the greatest help to man, Pufendorf says, but also the greatest threat. Governments are human devices constructed to cope with the dangers of violation of rights, first from those within a society and eventually from other societies.

Governments possess authority, not mere strength. To create authority, the will of many must concur in assigning power to a person or group. Governments, therefore, must arise from consent or contract. One of several pacts needed to constitute a state specifies the kind of government to which consent is given. The law of nature imposes no limits on what might be a legitimate form of government. Those who live under a regime thereby signify their implicit consent to it. If rulers propose bad laws or become corrupt, the citizens cannot appeal to the contract in order to oust them. Bad government is like bad weather; it just has to be endured.

Rights for one person are meaningless, Pufendorf holds, unless they impose duties on others. And rights as well as duties arise from laws: first God's laws, then those imposed by the magistrate. Pufendorf spells out in great detail the many forms the command to increase sociability takes under different conditions of social life. He works out natural-law principles for positive laws concerning marriage, children, inheritance, contract, punishment, the distribution of honors and offices, international treaties, the exchange of ambassadors, the treatment of prisoners, and the conduct of war. The particulars of human legislation will vary from time to time and from society to society. Since God commands that we have rulers, all positive laws reflect God's will to some extent. But the magistrate never needs to appeal to God or revelation to find out what laws should be enacted.

At first sight it seems that protection of individual rights is all that matters to Pufendorf. But this is too simple. Sociability is a character trait. It is for Pufendorf the basic virtue, and its increase is the first order of law. Moreover the rights and duties the laws impose on individuals are meant to improve all of society. Pufendorf is no utilitarian. He never speaks about the greatest possible happiness. But rulers should strive to enact laws that will benefit the whole. We must obey their laws as well as God's out of respect for authority, not out of fear of sanctions. Although Pufendorf believes that our free will enables us to do so, he also thinks that people are selfish and that few will act out of respect for the law. Harnessing their energies to a system of individual rights designed for the good of all, therefore, is the best we can do.

Although Pufendorf centers his system on law, he also assigns an important role to love. He takes sociability itself as a form of love. And within his system of law, he distinguishes two kinds of rights and duties, the perfect and the imperfect. Perfect rights are entitlements that can be stated with considerable precision, and performance of the duties related to them can be exacted by force. Imperfect rights cannot be precisely specified, and performance of the duties tied to them must spring from love and so cannot be compelled. Perfect duties are duties of justice. Typical are those which arise from a contract. Imperfect duties are duties of love, exemplified in obligations to charity and gratitude. Society cannot exist unless most people carry out their perfect duties, but their performance entails no special merit. Duties of love, by contrast, make society pleasanter. The more we do of imperfect duty, the more merit we acquire—merit that Pufendorf thinks might even carry weight with God.

Pufendorf's theory of morality as arising from divine command was the first extended attempt to see how the worldview of the new physics would allow for the existence of norms that are central to a distinctively human life. His elaboration of the contrast between perfect and imperfect duties was drawn on by most major moral philosophers up to and beyond the time of John Stuart Mill. His learned and meticulous consideration of positive law gave his *Law of Nature and of Nations* unrivaled authority as a work of jurisprudence. His hypothetical history was used by many later writers. Its influence is evident, for example, in the thought of Jean-Jacques Rousseau and Adam Smith. His insistence that morality requires obedience to universal law for its own sake, and that free will enables us to act from that motive, raised questions that Kant eventually thought he had to answer. It is unlikely, of course, that there will again be a time when we all read Pufendorf. But he deserves to be a little less forgotten.

10

The Misfortunes of Virtue

In recent years a number of moral philosophers have been critical of what they take to be the striking neglect by their predecessors of the topic of virtue and the virtues. It is not always clear exactly what period is meant to be covered in this indictment, but a statement by Philippa Foot gives us a clue: "For many years the subject of the virtues and vices was strangely neglected by moralists within the school of analytic philosophy. The tacitly accepted opinion was that a study of the topic would form no part of the fundamental work of ethics; and since this opinion was apparently shared by philosophers such as Hume, Kant, Mill, G. E. Moore, W. D. Ross, and H. A. Prichard, from whom contemporary moral philosophy has mostly been derived, perhaps the neglect was not so surprising after all."[1] Another of the friends of virtue, G. H. von Wright, shares Foot's view. "Virtue is a neglected topic in modern ethics," he says, and implies that Kant is one of the culprits.[2] The suggestion is that virtue has been neglected ever since the period of moral philosophy that culminated in the theories of Hume and Kant. Such widespread and protracted indifference would indeed have to count as a misfortune for virtue; if it actually occurred an historian of ethics

A very early version of this paper benefited from the careful scrutiny of William Frankena and from discussion at the University of Michigan. Various revisions were presented at Princeton University, Virginia Commonwealth University, Notre Dame University, Johns Hopkins University (where Michael Slote commented on it), the University of Virginia, the University of Pittsburgh, and the University of California, Berkeley. I am grateful for the many criticisms and suggestions I received at these institutions. I have also received valuable assistance from Richard Rorty, Rüdiger Bittner, and Stephen Hudson, who discussed various versions with me; and I am especially grateful to David Sachs, for insightful suggestions and protracted discussions.

[1] Philippa Foot, "Virtues and Vices", in her *Virtues and Vices* (Oxford: Basil Blackwell, 1978), 1.

[2] G. H. von Wright, *The Varieties of Goodness* (London, 1963), 136. Von Wright continues: "Kant's famous *dictum* that formal logic had made no appreciable progress since Aristotle, could be paraphrased and applied—with at least equally good justification—to the ethics of virtue."

might well be expected to try to explain why. But I doubt very much that it did occur. In this article I shall argue that at least during the seventeenth and eighteenth centuries, the formative period for modern moral philosophy, virtue did not suffer from neglect. Its misfortune was something rather different.

I

It is not easy to collect from present exponents of virtue-centered views of morality an agreement about what distinguishes their position from others. Some idea of the difference is, however, necessary if we are to discuss virtue's misfortunes. At the risk of oversimplification, I will lay out a set of differences between virtue-centered views, on the one hand, and what I shall call "act-centered" or "rule-centered" views on the other.[3]

It seems to be commonly agreed that a virtue-centerd view sees character at the core of morality and supposes that the central moral question is not "What ought I to do?" but "What sort of person am I to be?" The first point about a virtue-centered view is that the primary or central moral judgments are judgments about the character of agents. The virtuous person, as one commentator put it, is someone "for whom proper conduct emanates characteristically from a fixed disposition".[4] There is not much agreement on exactly what sort of disposition a virtue is, but this much at least we might take as common ground: that virtuous dispositions lead virtuous agents to be sensitive to the goods and ills to which people are exposed in particular situations and to respond by bringing about good and preventing harm.

Second, on the epistemological side, the virtue theorist holds that the perceptions of the virtuous person are the original and central source of knowledge of how much good to pursue, for whom, in what circumstances, and how vigorously. We may be able to formulate rules which crudely map the decisions of the virtuous person, but no set of rules will exactly capture them or anticipate every decision in a new situation. Nor does the virtuous

---

[3] I take rules (and laws) to require acts, and therefore, for the purposes of this article, do not consider the differences between the names I assign to be significant.

[4] L. A. Kosman, "Being Properly Affected: Virtues and Feelings in Aristotle's Ethics", in Amélie O. Rorty (ed.), *Essays on Aristotle's Ethics* (Berkeley and Los Angeles, 1980), 103.

person have any algorithm.[5] We may educate children into virtue by teaching them some simple rules, but mature moral agents do not need them.

Third, virtue is natural to humans, not in the sense that it need not be learned or that it is easy to acquire, but in the sense that virtuous agents individually, as well as the community they compose, benefit from virtue. This fact indicates our social nature. Living alone, and living without virtue, are both harmful to us.

By contrast to virtue-centered views of morality, act-centered views see the point of morality as directing what we do. We may acquire habits of acting in the right ways, and these habits may be called virtues. But their value lies in their ensuring correct action, and if we are praised as virtuous, the praise derives from the value placed on what we do.[6]

The act-centered theorist then explains how we can know what to do by appealing to rules, laws, or principles which spell out or give us a method for finding out what is right, or permitted, or obligatory. The rules or principles can be known and applied by someone who has no desire or concern for acting on them. Such a person could mimic the actions of someone who had, behaving correctly without valuing such behavior for itself. There is thus no counterpart in an act-centered theory for the epistemological privilege of the virtuous agent in a virtue-centered view.

Finally, since the principles of morality provide the structure of morally decent common life, virtuous people will tend to contribute to the common good. How well each individual will fare in so doing is to some extent an open question, though it seems obvious that everyone has a better chance of living a good life in a society dominated by virtuous people than in one where there are few.

An act-centered morality will naturally welcome the virtues, construed in its own way, as subordinate to the explicit rules or laws that require specific actions. So if a virtue-centered ethic is to be significantly different from an act-centered ethic, it needs to show that the virtues which are most important to morality have a life of their own, which is independent of rules or laws.

---

[5] "If one were to ask Aristotle how to decide how to act on particular occasions, his initial answer would be that one must do so by bringing to bear the intellectual excellence of (practical) wisdom. If we then ask in what wisdom consists, we shall get a long answer. . . . There is no simple decision procedure for the wise man to use" (J. O. Urmson, "Aristotle's Doctrine of the Mean", in Rorty (ed.), *Essays*, 162).

[6] Or on the results of what we do.

II

It is sometimes suggested that the first misfortune of virtue was the collapse of Aristotelian teleological thinking as a result of the rise of the new science in the sixteenth and seventeenth centuries. But Christian teleology was available to replace Aristotle's, and in any case this diagnosis overlooks a much earlier misfortune: Christianity itself. Thomas Reid reminds us of the opposition between virtue ethics and Christian ethics. "Morals have been methodized in different ways," he remarks. "The Ancients commonly arranged them under the four cardinal virtues of prudence, temperance, fortitude, and justice. Christian writers, I think more properly, under the three heads of the duty we owe to God, to ourselves, and to our neighbor."[7] Christianity, as Reid indicates, teaches a morality of duty, not of virtue, and it understands duty in terms of acts complying with law. A contemporary authority agrees with this point. "Any consideration of Christian morality", he remarks, "must acknowledge that the idea and the connotations of law are all-pervading and appear all but indispensable to the subject."[8] From the earliest days of the practice of confession in the sixth century through the great flowering of casuistry in the sixteenth and seventeenth centuries, Catholic moralists were preoccupied with specific acts which might or might not be sins, and with the appropriate penalties for them if they were.[9] If ever there was an ethics of acts and quandaries,[10] it was here.

It is no surprise to find, therefore, that there is a commonly accepted understanding of virtue and the virtues in the seventeenth century which makes them secondary to laws or rules. Though many sources might be cited, I will let John Locke articulate what had long been a commonplace: "By

---

[7] Thomas Reid, *Essays on the Active Powers of Man* (Edinburgh: University of Edinburgh Press, 1788), Bk. 5, ch. 2. The contrast between Christian and heathen did not end with Reid. "Many have heard so much of the *danger* of trusting to good works . . . that they . . . consider that the less they think about them the better. The word virtue sounds to them heathenish" (*Miscellaneous Remains from the Commonplace Book of Richard Whately, D.D.*, ed. E. J. Whately (London, 1865), 239). "It is true that the classic origins of the doctrine of virtue later made Christian critics suspicious of it. They warily regarded it as too philosophical and not Scriptural enough. Thus, they preferred to talk about commandments and duties rather than about virtues" (Josef Pieper, *The Four Cardinal Virtues* (Notre Dame, Ind., 1966), p. x, referring to what he evidently regards as a still-living attitude).

[8] John Mahoney, *The Making of Moral Theology: A Study of the Roman Catholic Tradition* (Oxford, 1987), 224.

[9] See ibid. 30–1 and ch. 1 generally.

[10] See Edmund L. Pincoffs, *Quandaries and Virtues* (Lawrence, Kan., 1986), esp. ch. 2.

whatever standard soever we frame in our minds the ideas of virtues or vices . . . their rectitude, or obliquity, consists in the agreement with those patterns prescribed by some law."[11] In the previous century the Puritan divine William Perkins had the same thing to say: "Universall justice, is the practise of all vertue: of that, whereby a man observes all the commandements of the Law."[12] It is arguable that the idea goes back as far as Saint Thomas's attempt to bring classical natural-law doctrine and Aristotelian virtue theory into some kind of union. However that may be, the dominance of an act-centered or legalistic account of morality is to be found in numerous Protestant writings, clerical as well as lay, throughout the period that concerns us.[13] It even affected the way Aristotle was understood, as we can see from a comment in the notes of an early seventeenth–century Cambridge tutor taking his students through the *Nicomachean Ethics*. "The other day we proposed a definition of virtue," he says. "It is a constant disposition of the soul to live according to law."[14] The assumption almost universally made is that if the virtues are important it is precisely because they are the habits, however formed, of obeying the moral laws—or the moral law, if, as with Cumberland and Samuel Johnson, the writer reduces them all to one.[15] A virtuous person is one whose standing dispositions lead her to do the acts required by the laws of morality.

The natural-law thinkers whose work dominated seventeenth-century moral thinking and exercised a powerful influence well into the eighteenth

---

[11] John Locke, *Essay concerning Human Understanding*, ed. Peter H. Nidditch (Oxford: Oxford University Press 1979), 358, 2.28.14.

[12] William Perkins, *The Whole Treatise of Cases of Conscience*, in *William Perkins*, ed. Thomas F. Merrill (Nieuwkoop, 1966), ch. 6, 231. Merrill does not give the date of this treatise; Perkins died in 1602.

[13] Alasdair MacIntyre tells us that Hume's "treatment of the virtues" contains "a quite new conception of the relationship of virtues to rules. . . . Virtues are indeed now conceived of . . . as being just those dispositions necessary to produce obedience to the rules of morality" (*After Virtue* (London, 1985), 216). If that were Hume's view—and I argue below that it is not—it would hardly be new.

[14] William S. Costello, SJ, *The Scholastic Curriculum at Early Seventeenth-Century Cambridge* (Cambridge, 1958), 65–6.

[15] Samuel Johnson is a telling case of the general point I wish to make. Although in numerous essays he speaks of the virtues as means between extremes, he has no clear view about them. In the review of Soame Jenyns, *A Free Inquiry into the Nature and Origin of Evil* (1757), he espouses a version of what we call "rule utilitarianism", and he seems to think of its rules as the laws of nature laid down by God and revealed through conscience. These are at the core of morality for him. He does not mention virtue or the virtues in the 1748 allegory "The Vision of Theodore, the Hermit of Teneriffe", which he once said he thought was his finest work. That tale shows Reason guiding us with the aid of Conscience, which is the emissary of religion; habits are almost always bad; and it is clear that man's natural dispositions, uncorrected, would do no one any good.

were not, therefore, introducing a new emphasis into the subject by seeing law as the focal point of the moral life. But their apparent neglect of the topic of virtue makes them look like paradigm cases of act-centered or law-centered theories in which character is assigned no importance. This impression is strengthened when we examine the criticisms of Aristotle on virtue offered by the founder of so-called modern natural law, Hugo Grotius.

In the Prolegomena to his *Law of War and Peace* of 1625, Grotius devotes three paragraphs to a criticism of Aristotle's doctrine that virtue consists in a mean in passion and action. The theory of the mean is a crucial point of difference between virtue-centered and act-centered views of morality, because it is one way of articulating the virtue theorist's belief that no antecedently stable set of rules or laws can substitute for virtuous character in leading people to act properly. Grotius plainly wants nothing to do with it.

His criticisms are brief. He points out the implausibility of the doctrine of the mean with respect to virtues such as truthfulness (said to be a mean between boastfulness and dissimulation), but his main fire is reserved for justice.[16] Aristotle himself, says Grotius, could not make the doctrine work when it came to this virtue. For he could not point to a mean in any appropriate passion, or any action coming from the passions, which could plausibly be said to constitute justice. So he resorted to making claims about the things justice is concerned with—possessions, honors, security—because only about these would it be reasonable to say that there could be a too much or a too little. And even here, Grotius continues, the doctrine of the mean fails. A single example shows this. It may be a fault not to take what is my own property—for example, if I need it in order to support my child—but it is surely not doing an injustice to another to claim less than is mine. Justice consists wholly in "abstaining from that which is another's". And Grotius adds that "it does not matter whether injustice arises from avarice, from lust, from anger, or from ill-advised compassion". What matters is only whether one is taking what another has a right to.[17] Grotius concedes that some virtues do keep passions under control, but this is not due to the nature of virtue. It is due, rather, to the fact that "right reason, which virtue everywhere

---

[16] Hugo Grotius, *On the Law of War and Peace*, trans. Francis W. Kelsey (Oxford, 1925), Prolegomena, sect. 43.

[17] Ibid., sect. 44.

follows" sometimes prescribes moderation. At other times, as in worshipping God, or in hoping for eternal bliss, it does not. These cannot be excessive, any more than hatred of sin can be too great.[18]

The immediate target of the attack, the doctrine of the mean, need be no part of a virtue-centered theory, but Grotius is rejecting more than that doctrine. He is saying that a central feature of such theories is wrong. The motive of the just agent does not matter. To be just is simply to have the habit of following right reason with respect to the rights of others. It does not matter why the agent has and sustains the habit. And rights are not, for Grotius, the kind of good which virtuous dispositions regard. Rights are or spring from—Grotius is not entirely clear—a special moral attribute attaching to human nature, which even God must respect.[19] They make acts required or forbidden regardless of the natural good brought about by respecting them.

Grotius rejects yet another important aspect of an ethics of virtue, its attribution of a privileged status to the insight of the virtuous agent. He does not think the laws of nature determine what we are to do down to the last detail. Where the law is indeterminate, however, what operates is not insight but discretion. In such cases we choose freely among permissible acts. Grotius brings this out in direct confrontation with Aristotelianism. Because so many complexities enter into morals, he says, and circumstances always alter cases, it comes about "that between what should be done and what it is wrong to do there is a mean, that which is permissible; and this is now closer to the former, now to the latter.... This is what Aristotle means when he says: 'Oftentimes it is hard to decide what choice one should make.' "[20] The virtuous are simply those who obey the law where it is specific, and stay within the bounds of the permissible where it leaves room for choice. In the Grotian morality of rule and act there is no room for any special cognitive ability arising from virtue.

Grotius was accepted as a major authority on morality and law. His followers saw him as the founder of a new school of thought, and even

---

[18] Ibid., sect. 45. Saint Thomas Aquinas, *Summa theologiae* 2a–2ae.27.6, makes the point that the theological virtues faith, hope, and charity cannot be excessive. In *On Charity*, trans. Lottie H. Kendzierski (Milwaukee, 1984), Aquinas says that the theological virtues are not means between extremes and that only the moral virtues are (art. 2, reply to objections 10 and 13, p. 31).

[19] Grotius is here opposing the voluntarist view of the laws of nature. On Grotius on rights, see Richard Tuck, *Natural Rights Theories* (Cambridge, 1979).

[20] Grotius, 2.23.1.

Dugald Stewart, who did not admire natural-law theory, allowed that Grotius "gave a new direction to the studies of the learned".[21] His most important successor was Samuel Pufendorf, by far the most widely disseminated of the natural-law writers of the seventeenth century, and the most widely and persistently taught.[22] Like Grotius he claimed that there is a methodical, non-intuitive, way of deriving knowledge of the rules of morality.[23] He went even further than his master in actually spelling out these rules in considerable detail. To read his treatise, or the treatises of his imitators and commentators, is to see how the moral life looks as if it is viewed as overwhelmingly a matter of learning the rules and acting as they direct.

There were of course critics, among them those who defended Aristotle and his theory of virtue against the Grotian attacks.[24] But the defenses, however justified, seemed to have had little effect. We need not think that Grotius and Pufendorf had refuted Aristotle; we must allow that for the cultivated Europe of their age and much of the eighteenth century they displaced his understanding of morality with another one. The culture seems to have been hungry for a morality giving the kind of explicit guidance that rules and laws provide. The triumph of the Grotian version of natural-law theory thus seems to constitute exactly the kind of misfortune that the friends of virtue suppose must have happened at some point during this period.

III

The triumph of natural law was not, however, an unmitigated misfortune for virtue. The natural lawyers provided in their own way for an aspect of

---

[21] Dugald Stewart, *Dissertation Exhibiting the Progress of Metaphysical, Ethical and Political Philosophy* (1815), in *Works*, ed. Sir William Hamilton (Edinburgh, 1854), i. 170.

[22] Horst Denzer, *Moralphilosophie und Naturrecht bei Samuel Pufendorf* (Munich, 1972), lists nearly forty editions of Pufendorf's major work, the *de Jure Naturae et Gentium* (1672), in Latin, French, English, and German, and nearly a hundred of the shorter work, *de Officio Hominis et Civis* (1673), in every major European language. His figures are probably quite low. See also Sieglinde C. Othmer, *Berlin und die Verbreitung des Naturrechts in Europa* (Berlin, 1970), 136–42, for tabular information about translations and editions.

[23] See J. B. Schneewind, "Pufendorf's Place in the History of Ethics", *Synthèse*, 73 (1987), 122–55, for fuller discussion.

[24] For example, Samuel Rachel, *Dissertations on the Law of Nature and of Nations* (1676), trans. John Pawley Bate (Oxford, 1916), devotes some seventeen pages in "Of Moral Virtue" (sects. 17–44) to defending Aristotle and showing that Grotius's criticisms can all be answered.

the moral life where action is not governed by rules and where the agent's character and motives are central. Nor was this an unimportant aspect of morality. On the contrary, it was here that the lawyers, who with the exception of Hobbes were serious Christians, made room for the operations of that love which their religion made so important to them. Constructing natural-law theory, they could not appeal to revelation: all the more significant, then, their insistence that there is a requirement of love which cannot be understood in the ways in which other kinds of requirement are. It was by means of their distinction between perfect and imperfect rights and duties that they made room for love in their general theory. And because they understood imperfect duties as they did, the discussions of them covered much of the ground which in the vocabulary they rejected was discussed in terms of virtue.

This now familiar distinction was first made by Grotius, in terms of rights. Some rights, such as those involved in property ownership or conferred by contract, entitle their possessors to use force to obtain that to which they have the right if it is not otherwise forthcoming. Other rights, such as the right of a beggar to your alms, do not carry this entitlement: they are thus "imperfect", that is, not full and complete.[25] Pufendorf develops the distinction in terms of duties. He sees perfect duties as those whose performance could be compelled, either by force (prior to the existence of political society) or through court action. He adds that what is owed under a perfect duty is always quite specific: precisely so much money or such and such services. Imperfect duties, for both Grotius and Pufendorf, are not precisely specifiable. They fall under what Grotius calls the law of love, which tells us to benefit others but does not specify how much, or to whom, one ought to give.[26] Giving must be the expression of one's direct concern for the good of another. To give in order to be rewarded for so doing is to take away an essential element of imperfect duties.

Pufendorf adds an important point to Grotius's sketch. Perfect duties are those which must be carried out if society is to exist at all. Imperfect duties serve to improve the quality of life, but society could continue to exist even if they were ignored. But if performance of the former is more

---

[25]   Grotius, 1.1.4–8, 35–7.
[26]   Grotius, 3.13.4, p. 759; 2.25.3, sects. 2–3, pp. 579–80; 1.2.8, sect. 10, p. 75; 2.12.9, sect. 2, p. 347.

urgent, it does not entitle the agent to merit, whereas genuine execution of imperfect duty is meritorious.[27] Functionally speaking, perfect and imperfect duties thus have complementary roles in facilitating social life. As Pufendorf puts it: "The law of humanity or charity, and the agreements of men, mutually supplement each other by way of their duties and guarantees, in that what is not or cannot be secured by charity is secured by agreements, while in cases where agreements are not possible, charity offers its services."[28]

It is significant that Pufendorf uses the term "charity" here. He is following Grotius in transforming the theological virtue of charity into a secular virtue, detaching it from its Thomistic sense of friendship with God, and seeing its importance not in its role in personal salvation,[29] but in its ability to improve social life. It is equally important that he does not say that love should infuse the other areas of the moral life. Perfect duties, or duties of justice, need not be carried out in a loving spirit. They are fully executed when a perfect right is respected, and the man who regularly carries out all his perfect duties is a just man even if he dislikes acting justly. What matters is the performance, not the spirit behind it.[30]

IV

The idea of imperfect duties allowed for the accommodation within natural-law theory of many of the features of the moral life stressed by virtue-centered outlooks. So although the friends of virtue will of course protest that much is altered or omitted, I think that they cannot fairly say that natural-law theory involved the complete neglect of virtue. The distinction between perfect and imperfect duty has another importance for virtue as well. It provides the context for understanding the two

[27] Samuel Pufendorf, *The Law of Nature and of Nations*, trans. C. H. Oldfather and W. A. Oldfather (Oxford, 1934), 1.1.19–20, pp. 18–20; 1.7.7–9, pp. 118–21.

[28] Ibid. 3.4.1, 380.

[29] Or not only so: he thinks the merit one acquires from performing imperfect duties will count with God.

[30] Moreover it is not the case, as it is in Luther, that only those given divine grace are expected to act from love, while the rest are subjected to compulsion. In the state of nature as well as in political society everyone is expected to perform some imperfect duties, and everyone is under laws which threaten the use of force to exact compliance.

most original and profound of the modern discussions of the subject—the theories of Hume and of Kant.

Hume acknowledges a debt to Grotius in his second *Enquiry*, and there is no doubt that he was familiar with Pufendorf and other natural-law writers as well.[31] A full analysis of his debt to them remains to be made. Here I will suggest only that his distinction between the artificial and the natural virtues is clarified by seeing it in connection with the distinction between perfect and imperfect duties. We should see Hume as trying to show that a theory making virtue rather than law the central concept of ethics can give a better account of the distinction than that given by the natural lawyers who invented it.

Hume tells us that in explaining morality, as in explaining anything else, one must account for the data by the smallest number of laws possible.[32] He seems to have been convinced that the Grotian tradition, in distinguishing between perfect and imperfect duties, had correctly located a definite pattern in the moral approvals and disapprovals constituting his data and that the pattern had to be explained. This becomes clear when we note which approvals Hume links to the different types of virtue. The coincidence between his two patterns and the Grotian dichotomy is striking.

The artificial virtues, for Hume, include justice, fidelity to promises, and allegiance to government. Of the natural virtues Hume gives several lists: in one place he includes "generosity, humanity, compassion, gratitude, friendship, fidelity, zeal, disinterestedness, liberality", which he sums up as beneficence (T 603). Elsewhere he lists meekness, charity, clemency, moderation, and equity as natural virtues (T 578). These lists make it evident that Hume's artificial virtues, like perfect duties, cover the domain of clear and definite claims which may be enforced by law. This is obvious in the case of justice and of duties owed to government in Hume's view of them, and becomes so with regard to promising when we note that Hume views it chiefly as concerned with "the interested commerce of mankind" (T 522), that is, with contracts.

---

[31] See the discussion in Duncan Forbes, *Hume's Philosophical Politics* (Cambridge, 1975), esp. ch. 1.

[32] David Hume, *Treatise of Human Nature*, ed. L. A. Selby-Bigge and Peter H. Nidditch (Oxford: Oxford University Press, 1978), 473, 578. References will hereafter be given in the text, identified as T.

One of the arguments Hume uses to show that justice must be "artificial" appeals explicitly to the fact that in its domain clear and sharp distinctions are required: "All natural qualities", Hume says, "run insensibly into each other, and are, on many occasions, indistinguishable" (T 530). This is true of "all kinds of vice and virtue" as well—or almost all kinds: "Whatever may be the case, with regard to all kinds of vice and virtue, 'tis certain, that rights, and obligations, and property, admit of no such insensible gradation, but that a man either has a full and perfect property, or none at all, and is either entirely obliged to perform any action, or lies under no manner of obligation" (T 529). So if you admit that justice has this preciseness, Hume holds, you must agree that it is artificial, not natural.

Finally, Hume takes over yet a further aspect of the Grotian tradition. As for Pufendorf the perfect duties are those which are indispensable for the existence of society, so for Hume the artificial virtues are the ones required if society is to exist, that of justice, concerning itself with property, being the most important of all (T 491). Hume's natural virtues plainly map the imperfect duties, which serve rather to ameliorate or embellish social life. Both sorts of virtue, like both sorts of duty, produce good results. But instead of taking the distinction between the precise and the imprecise, or that between the enforceable and the unenforceable, to be the core of the difference between the artificial and the natural virtues, Hume takes the distinction to be that the good arising from the natural virtues is normally brought about in every case of their exercise, while the good arising from the artificial virtues comes about only as a result of the existence of a general practice of exercising them, and so may not come about in each particular case.[33]

Hume's distinction of kinds of virtue has often been taken as showing that he anticipated the distinction between act and rule utilitarianism, and opted for the latter. From a historical perspective it is more accurate to describe it as Hume's attempt to show how perfect as well as imperfect rights and duties can be explained by a non-teleological virtue-centered theory. His larger aim in doing this is to free our understanding of morality throughout from

---

[33] This is one important reason for calling them "artificial". Their exercise involves in each case the thought that others will similarly exercise them and that these others will have the thought that I and others will exercise them, and so on. This is not true of the natural virtues, which need not involve the virtuous person's awareness of participating in a social practice.

any need of appeal to supernatural origins or maintenance. Natural-law theory, even when it was not voluntaristic as Pufendorf's was, tended to invoke divine wisdom to explain the fit between moral laws and human good, and divine sanctions to explain the nature of obligation. Hume argues that a narrative of natural development will explain both of these features. And the key to his narrative is the adequacy of human nature to evolve its own directives and controls. Hume's point is that morality need not be imposed upon us from without. It is our own creation, though not, to be sure, our *conscious* doing until fairly late in the game.

In his effort to show how much human nature "can do by itself",[34] Hume, looking back to classical antiquity for an alternative to natural-law theory, portrays morality as emerging from character unaided by supernatural forces. This is the point of his insistence that the motive determines the moral character of action. "No action can be virtuous, or morally good," he famously says, "unless there be in human nature some motive to produce it, distinct from the sense of its morality" (*T.* 479; cf. p. 518). This principle serves to undermine the natural-law position of Grotius and Pufendorf because it requires a connection between motive and obligatory action which they did not clearly supply for the cases they take as central, perfect duties. Grotius explains the duties in terms of respecting rights but says nothing of the motive that moves us to respond to rights as such. Pufendorf speaks in terms of obligations and is at best unclear about what motive we all always have for carrying them out—other than divine sanctions, which are not only an embarrassment for a natural-law theorist but which, to be justifiable, must also presuppose the obligatoriness of the acts to which they move us. That presupposition is what Hume challenges. Acts, for him, can only be obligatory if there are prior praiseworthy standing motives whose natural expression is doing them, and those motives will be virtues. Only the egoist would see any problem in saying that our natural affections for others are the motives that correspond to imperfect duties. Are there comparable motives which will allow Hume to explain that the perfect

---

[34] Montaigne, *Essays*, trans. D. Frame (1957; repr. Stanford, Calif., 1976), 3.12, "Of Physiognomy", pp. 793–4: "It was he [Socrates] who brought human wisdom back down from the heavens, where she was wasting her time... even the simplest can recognize in him their means and their strength; it is impossible to go back further and lower. He did a great favor to human nature by showing how much it can do for itself."

duties are morally significant because of the admirable natural dispositions they express?

Hume argues that there are at least no natural motives that will do the trick. There is no natural tendency to respect property, to obey the laws, and to abide by our promises and contracts, as there is a natural tendency to be (say) nice to our children or generous to those in need. Given the principle of the priority of virtue in motive to virtue in actions, Hume's problem is to explain why we feel moral approval of acts which display respect for property, obedience to law, and fidelity to contract. His explanation has been discussed many times. I will therefore recall only the nub of it, concentrating on justice, which Hume himself takes as the paradigm.

Justice originates when individuals become aware that stability of possession would be beneficial to each of them individually but is only possible if all and each steadfastly refrain from disturbing one another's transferable goods. As this awareness spreads and becomes more reliably effective in the behavior of one's fellows, there comes to be what is in effect a convention by which each respects the possessions of others. Only then can the ideas of justice and injustice arise and, with them, the ideas of property, rights, and obligations (T 489–91, 497–8). Self-interest, redirected by the realization that one's own interest cannot be forwarded unless one controls one's avidity for possession when others do so as well, becomes the motive out of which we initially act when we act justly.[35]

The practice called "justice" arises without any activity of the moral sentiment. Its name acquires positive moral connotations only when agents reflect on their common behavior and through sympathy with the benefits others enjoy are moved to approve of the disposition in each agent from which such good consequences flow (T 498–500). The man who lacks this socialized sense of his own interests may notice the lack, and hate himself for lacking it. When he does so, he will be able to show respect for the possessions of others out of a hatred for himself for lacking the normal motive, and in that case he will be acting from a sense of duty. This cannot be the standing motive in the case of just actions, any more than it can for other virtuous acts: it is only "on some occasions" that "a person will

---

[35] Knud Haakonssen has provocatively disputed this view and offered an alternative interpretation— admittedly hypothetical—of what Hume has in mind (see his *The Science of a Legislator* (Cambridge, 1981), ch. 2, esp. 33–5).

perform an action merely out of regard to its moral obligation". The standard case is that where there is some definite principle "capable of producing the action and whose moral beauty renders the action meritorious" (T 479)—and in this case it is the socialized self-interest on which we eventually bestow moral approval.[36]

Hume certainly sees justice as requiring us to obey the laws or customs concerning property which are current in our society, and one might think this a lapse on his part to a natural-law view. But if individuals may actually possess goods before there are customs or laws, we can see that the latter come to be invented to codify and clarify the convention of respecting possession and to make it more easily transmissible to the young. So what underlies justice is not our ability to form habits of compliance with rules but our ability to extend our sense of self so that self-interest comes to include the interests of others with whom we form a cooperating society. We come, that is, to have an interest in the good of others, which, though mediated and indirect, is akin to the interest the natural virtues lead us to show in their good. When that interest is gratified, not only are our private ends forwarded, but we also receive gratification from the very existence of the institution of justice. Justice by its very nature thus benefits its possessors as well as their society. And if Hume cannot attribute any special cognitive status to the virtuous agent, as Aristotle does, the friends of virtue might think this a small price to pay for a rehabilitation of virtue that does not rely on Aristotelian assumptions we can no longer accept.

Despite its brilliance, however, I think that Hume's view must be considered one of the misfortunes of virtue. It failed to convince those who accepted Grotius's assumptions that it was an adequate alternative to an act-centered or juridical approach to morality. Its weakness becomes apparent if we follow its fortunes in the work of the one major thinker who might be taken as something of a follower of Hume's in ethics: Adam Smith.

---

[36] At one point, Hume expresses indifference about whether we consider the motive to justice a vice or a virtue (T. 492). He says this only in order to dismiss the whole question of whether man is innately good or evil: since self-interest controls itself, if self-interest be vicious, then vice controls itself in our nature and makes us social, and if it be good, then a good motive has that effect. In all other contexts Hume makes plain his belief that the settled disposition to respect the possessions of others out of socialized self-interest is a virtue.

V

The eulogy of Grotius as the founder of international law with which Smith concludes *The Theory of the Moral Sentiments* is by no means the only indication of his indebtedness to natural-law thinking.[37] He had a different view of the nature of moral laws or rules and of how they are to be derived, but he shared the Grotian belief that society could not function properly without clear and precise rules for the guidance of action. In working out the implications of this belief he relied extensively on the natural-law distinction between perfect and imperfect duties.

These points stand out sharply in Smith's criticism of the views of virtue he attributes to Plato, Aristotle, the Stoics, Clarke, Wollaston, and Shaftesbury. All of them, he says, place virtue in the propriety of the affections, but "none of these systems either give, or pretend to give, any precise or distinct measure by which this fitness or propriety can be ascertained or judged of". Yet to direct such judgments is "the great purpose of all systems of morality" (*TMS* 7.2.1.1, p. 267; 7.2.1.47–8, p. 293). A natural-law outlook is also plain in his account of the importance of moral rules. These rules are no more than summaries of the judgments which morally sensitive people make of individual cases. They matter because although most people are not able to make delicate moral discriminations they are usually able to "behave very decently" by acting "merely from a regard to what they saw were the established rules of behavior". Even if one's own sentiments do not make one aware of the proper gratitude to show a patron, one can do everything appropriate simply from the motive of "reverence for the established rules of duty, a serious and earnest desire of acting, in every respect, according to the law of gratitude". Even good manners would be rare without explicit guidance; and in a strongly Pufendorfian passage Smith remarks:

But if without regard to these general rules, even the duties of politeness, which are so easily observed . . . would yet be so frequently violated, what would become of the duties of justice, of truth, of chastity, of fidelity . . . ? But upon the tolerable observance of these duties, depends the very existence of human society, which would crumble into nothing if mankind were not generally impressed with a reverence for those important rules of conduct   (*TMS* 3.5.2, p. 163).

[37] Adam Smith, *The Theory of Moral Sentiments*, ed. D. D. Raphael and A. L. Macfie (Oxford, 1976), 7.4.37, pp. 341–2. Citations hereafter in text as *TMS*. The work appeared first in 1759; the edition I cite, the last edition (1790), was much altered.

If the natural lawyers' stress on actions and on perfect duties is thus apparent in Smith, so too is their preference for the clear and definite over against that which must be left to the discretion of the agent. "The general rules of almost all the virtues," he says, "The general rules which determine what are the offices of prudence, of charity, of generosity, of gratitude, of friendship, are in many respects loose and inaccurate . . . it is scarce possible to regulate our conduct entirely by a regard to them." Smith here of course refers to Humean natural virtues; and he promptly points out that there is at least one virtue which is not like them: justice.[38] Its rules "are accurate in the highest degree, and admit of no exceptions or modifications, but such as may be ascertained as accurately as the rules themselves". The duties of justice must be regarded as sacred, and are best performed when done from "a reverential and religious regard to those general rules which require them". The other virtues require us to "consider the end and foundation of the rule rather than the rule itself", and to use our judgment accordingly. But in matters of justice, "the man who refines the least and adheres with the most obstinate steadfastness to the general rules themselves, is the most commendable and the most to be depended upon" (*TMS* 3.6.9–10, pp. 174–5).

Virtue is thus once again discussed in terms of perfect and imperfect duties. The significance of this for Smith shows in two further views of his, one about the importance of examination and discussion of the virtues, the other about the importance of the virtues in society.

Moral philosophy, Smith says, has three parts. One is ethics, whose task is to describe the virtues and vices, pointing out the "propriety and happiness of the one" and the "deformity and misery of the other", exhorting us to love the former and refrain from the latter. Ethics can be eloquent but not accurate; it is useful mainly in educating the young (*TMS* 7.4.3–6, pp. 328–9). Next comes jurisprudence, which is "the endeavor to lay down exact and precise rules for the direction of every circumstance of our behavior". It has two branches. Jurisprudence proper considers the person to whom an obligation is owed and asks what he may exact by force. Casuistry considers the person obligated and asks what he ought to think himself bound to do so as neither to wrong his neighbor nor to violate "the integrity of his own character" (*TMS* 7.4.7–8, pp. 329–30). Now casuistry,

---

[38] He thinks that of all the imperfect duties, that of gratitude has the most precise rules with the fewest exceptions.

says Smith, "ought to be rejected altogether" (*TMS* 7.4.34, p. 340). In other words, discussions of virtue and character, ethics and casuistry, are either eloquence useful for children or totally useless; and only examination of the rules whose observance is necessary for society is worth one's time. At the very end of *The Theory of the Moral Sentiments* Smith proposes to move on to jurisprudence.

Pufendorf held that imperfect duties did much to ameliorate the life we are enabled to live together when we carry out our perfect duties. In *The Wealth of Nations* Smith did not deny this, but he offered a quite different view of how social existence is enhanced. In a much-quoted passage he remarked:

It is not from the benevolence of the butcher, the brewer, or the baker, that we expect our dinner, but from their regard to their own interest. We address ourselves, not to their humanity but to their self-love, and never talk to them of our own necessities but of their advantages.... It is by treaty, by barter, and by purchase, that we obtain from one another the greater part of those mutual good offices we stand in need of.[39]

If justice establishes the framework for the moral world and self-interest makes life better, the role for the imperfect duties—for what is left of virtue—is small indeed.

VI

Adam Smith shows in a particularly clear way the vulnerability of Hume's virtue-centered ethic when it is faced with a demand for clear and definite moral guidance. I think an awareness of its inability to sustain itself in the face of such a demand enables us to see why Hume's moral philosophy, for all its brilliance, was one of virtue's misfortunes.

Hume presents himself as flouting the natural-law tradition. If we are virtuous, we will not need any moral rules to guide our action (though of course the law of the land is another matter). Hume therefore writes as a theorist bent only on explaining the moral life, not as offering direction nor

---

[39] Adam Smith, *An Inquiry into the Nature and Causes of the Wealth of Nations*, ed. R. H. Campbell and A. S. Skinner (1976; repr. Oxford, 1979), 1.2.2, pp. 26–7.

even as showing us where to get it. He does not claim that his theory gives guidance, still less that it contains a rule book or a single principle which each person could use for decision-making. Nonetheless he has practical purposes in mind, as his denunciation of the "monkish virtues" makes clear. The theory is not really neutral with respect to all the data about what people approve.

A Humean moral outlook therefore presents us with a dilemma. If we insist that moral philosophy cannot and should not offer direction, we condemn it to irrelevance in the eyes of those who share Smith's Grotian sense that there is a need for the kind of directive that only laws or rules can give—and the popularity of Pufendorf suggests that there were many who felt this need. But if we allow that moral theory is to provide us with such guides, a still worse problem arises. Hume's drive for Newtonian economy of explanation led him to conclude that natural goods and evils are the ultimate determinant of the content of morality. The core of the virtues, artificial as well as natural, is concern (however mediated) for the good of others or of oneself. What makes something into a good for someone is that person's desire for it or enjoyment of it. And desires and enjoyments are what they are regardless of morality.[40] Since Hume refuses to believe in the sinfulness of our passions he holds that the content of morality must in the end be determined by facts about what is desired and enjoyed. They automatically carry moral weight because, for Hume, there is no principle in us wholly independent of those facts which might point us in other directions. Take a Grotian approach to Hume's explanatory principle, and what emerges is Benthamism. And Benthamite utilitarianism has, of course, no room for virtues in the traditional sense. It provides a rational decision procedure for every case, so that there is no room for the imprecisions of the imperfect duties, still less for the insight of the virtuous agent, or for any attribution of value to certain kinds of character other than an instrumental value in reliably producing good results. There may or may not be room for moral laws; but the virtues on such a view are at best derivative.

---

[40] I think Hume holds that we have a second-order desire that our own character should be such that others and we ourselves can approve of it. But this is only a minor emendation to the statement in the text.

VII

Like Hume, Kant worked in a philosophical culture in which the distinction between perfect and imperfect duties was a commonplace.[41] He himself recurs to it throughout his life. He discusses it as an illustration of his views on negative quantities in an essay of 1763.[42] He reflects on it in marginalia both early and late.[43] In 1766 in *The Dreams of a Spirit Seer* he refers to the distinction as that between the strong law of duty and the weaker law of love (A ii. 335). He brings the problem up in the ethics lectures he gave from 1764 on (A xxvii *passim*). He discusses the matter in the *Groundwork of the Metaphysics of Morals*, and touches on it briefly in the second *Critique*. But until the late *Metaphysics of Morals*, where it is given a major treatment, it played much less of a role in his thinking than I have argued that it did for Hume.

In the *Groundwork* Kant discusses the distinction between perfect and imperfect duties only briefly. In a footnote he remarks that a perfect duty is "one which allows no exception in the interest of inclination" (A iv. 421 n.), thus suggesting that the sole special feature of imperfect duties is that we may carry them out or not, as we prefer. The other way in which the distinction is drawn is more adequate. Kant distinguishes between maxims which cannot be coherently thought as universal laws, and maxims which can be thought but not willed as laws. Maxims of the first kind are in conflict with strict or narrow or irremissible duty, maxims of the second with broader or meritorious duty. A maxim of not repaying a deliberately contracted debt illustrates the former, a maxim of never helping those in need the latter (A iv. 424). Kant is here clearly restating the traditional perfect/imperfect distinction in his own terms.[44]

At this point in his thinking, however, Kant can make no room for love. Love as inclination or feeling or tender sympathy is dismissed in one

---

[41] In what follows I am much indebted to Wolfgang Kersting, "Das starke Gesetz der Schuldigkeit und das schwächere der Gütigkeit", *Studia Leibnitiana*, 14 (1982), 184–220.

[42] *Kant's Gesammelte Schriften* (30 vols.; Berlin, 1902), ii. 172, 174. Subsequent references to this *Akademie* edition are in parentheses in the text and are referred to as A.

[43] For example, ibid. xix. 10 (#6457), 17 (#6469), 30 (#6498), and 51 (#6517–19), which are all quite early; pp. 94 (#6582), 102 (#6597), 105 (#6603), 125 (#6653), 138 (#6709), and 152 (#6760), probably from the late 1760s and early 1770s, pp. 261 (#7165) and 308 (#7309), late notes.

[44] In discussing the duty to help others, Kant contrasts duties necessary for the continuation of "mankind" and duties going beyond that to helpfulness—a version of the Pufendorfian explanation of the distinction (ibid. iv. 430).

sentence. It cannot be commanded. It must be replaced by "beneficence from duty", which is practical love (A iv. 399). The love commandment of the New Testament is conceptually incoherent if it is understood as requiring a feeling.

I have pointed out that, as traditionally understood, doing one's imperfect duties would earn merit because they go beyond strict obligation and are done from love. In the *Groundwork* Kant calls imperfect duties meritorious but does not explain how they guide us or what motivates us to do them. That we are not to act on a maxim which cannot be willed as a universal law does not tell us what we are to do. I cannot rationally will never to help others, Kant thinks, but this alone will not lead me to think that a given particular act of helping someone is required by the moral law, so that I could then do it solely for that reason. Kant needs to say more about the imperfect duties if he is to retain anything like the traditional distinction.

The additions are made in the *Metaphysics of Morals*. We now have two principles, one governing duties of law or justice (*Rechtspflichten*), the other, duties of virtue or morality (*Tugendpflichten*). Legal duties require us to perform external actions, moral duties to have certain maxims. The principle of legal duties is that we are to act externally only in ways that allow "the freedom of the will of each to coexist together with the freedom of everyone in accordance with a universal law" (A vi. 230). The principle of virtue is that we are to "act according to a maxim of *ends* which it can be a universal law for everyone to have" (A vi. 395).[45] These ends, Kant says, are our own perfection and the happiness of others. The idea of compellability, strikingly absent from the *Groundwork*, is tied to the principle of legal duties. We can be compelled to perform external actions, but not to adopt ends; and Kant thinks he is asserting an analytic proposition when he says that acts to which someone has a right may properly be obtained by compulsion. He thus rejects the Pufendorfian way of drawing the distinction between perfect and imperfect duties altogether. It is legality and morality which are distinguished by the propriety or impropriety of using compulsion, not these kinds of duty.

A distinction between the two kinds of duty is however assigned a significant place in morality. The principle of perfect duties enables us to

---

[45] Translations of citations from pt. 2 of the *Metaphysics of Morals* are from Mary Gregor, *The Doctrine of Virtue* (New York, 1964).

determine *a priori* with fair precision what action is required, but that of duties of virtue does not. As Kant puts it, when juridical duty is in question, "then the Mine and the Thine must be determined on the scales of justice with quasi-mathematical precision . . . but so long as this knowledge concerns a mere duty of virtue, this is not necessary" (A vi. 375n.).[46] We can therefore have perfect duties to ourselves as well as to others, though we can only be compelled to carry out those to others. Imperfect duties to ourselves, like those to others, require us to have certain ends, but we cannot determine on *a priori* grounds alone what to do in order to achieve them or what acts would best express our attachment to these ends. Consequently, in these cases, "what is to be done cannot be determined according to rules of morality . . . only judgment can decide this according to rules of prudence (pragmatic rules)" (A vi. 433n.).[47]

In the *Metaphysics of Morals*, then, an ethic of rule and an ethic of admirable disposition or virtue are presented as dividing the moral life between them, as in the natural-law tradition. Since the ends involved in virtue are generated by obedience to the moral law, they will presumably never lead us to plan acts that would transgress the limits of legality; and legality always leaves open more ways than one for us to try to achieve our moral ends. It is worth noting that Kant does not rely on Pufendorf's thesis, which is also Hume's, that the perfect duties are more important for the existence of society than the imperfect. The perfect duties are prior to the imperfect in that they spell out the conditions under which we may act to carry out our imperfect duties. But the imperfect duties are the ones we must carry out to acquire merit, and with it a title to happiness.

The crucial point to be noticed about the new position is that a direct concern for the good of others may now play an immediate motivational role in morality. We do not act with the thought that we are doing our duty when we act to carry out the duties of virtue. If we have performed a duty of virtue, we have made (say) the well-being of a friend our own end. In acting to bring it about, therefore, our purpose is not "to do our duty", but "to bring about the well-being of our friend". If this is not quite acting from love, it can come to be so: "Helping others to achieve their ends is a duty. If a man practices it often and succeeds in realizing his purpose, he eventually comes to feel love for those he has helped. Hence the saying: you *ought* to

---

[46] Ibid. 31.   [47] Ibid. 97–8 n.

love your neighbor . . . means . . . *do good* to your fellow-man, and this will give rise to love of man in you" (*A*. vi. 402).[48]

Kant's reconstruction of virtue seems to be an even more brilliant achievement than Hume's. It does not face the problem which threatened Hume's view of being irrelevant to those who accept the Grotian view of the importance of moral laws because it does contain a directive law, and it argues that there are necessary limits to the range within which such a law can guide our action. It does not have the practical instability of Hume's view because it does not rest morality on some non-moral good to the realization of which character might be merely instrumental. It makes inner motivation to morality central and allows for different kinds of motivation. How then does Kant's late view fit into the story of the misfortunes of virtue?

VIII

If the misfortune is that virtue was neglected by moral philosophers, then part of the answer to this question is that it was the *Groundwork*, not the *Metaphysics of Morals*, that until recently got most of the attention. Perhaps this is because the latter book is so badly written and so hard to understand. Whatever the reason, Kant was almost always seen as arguing that all morality falls under a single principle which is capable of giving guidance over the whole range of the decisions we have to make as moral agents. So discussion of his ethics came to center on the now familiar questions: can we really get definite results from the categorical imperative, and if so do we get all and only those we want? If not, will some other principle do the same thing, or are we forced to rely on a plurality of ultimate principles? But in that case, are we not liable to allow convention and prejudice to pass as morality? There was post-Kantian discussion of these issues in Germany, which was much like the controversy in Britain over the Benthamite assertion of the principle of utility as the sole principle of morals; and in similar fashion the terms of the question made the topic of virtue and the

---

[48] Translations of citations from Pt. 2, 62–3. Kant was saying similar things in his ethics lectures at a much earlier stage (see, e.g., xxvii, 417 II: 10–9; 419 II: 5–7.)

virtues unimportant. From this point of view, Kant was one of virtue's misfortunes because he perhaps unintentionally made it uninteresting.

The friends of virtue think that Kant was much more of a misfortune. The virtuous agent, for Kant, has no epistemological privilege: when she exercises her virtue she is simply choosing at her discretion among alternative ways of helping others or improving herself; she is not displaying insight as to the morally best thing to do. Moreover, Kant sees virtue in a most un-Aristotelian way, as always a struggle, never a settled principle. Kant's vision of the divided self is the villain here, with morality springing from an impossibly pure reason in conflict with reprobate passions forever calling for discipline. Virtue is not so much the expression of our nature at its most developed as it is the triumph of one part of it over another. The connection between virtue and the agent's own flourishing therefore cannot be made out on Kantian terms except by means of some notoriously questionable postulates. And perhaps worst of all, virtue has at best a partial role to play in morality, dividing the realm with perfect duties which are the archetype of everything the virtue theorist rejects. Kant's theory is a misfortune for virtue, on this view, not because his theory of virtue was ignored but precisely because of what that theory was.

If we take this view—and obviously I cannot assess it here—we must ask just one more question. To what extent is virtue itself involved in creating this misfortune? Here, I think, the history I have been tracing offers us a clue.

If we ask why the project of the Grotians was to establish a law-like code of morals, the answer must be that they took the central difficulties of life to be those arising from disagreement—disagreement involving nations, religious sects, parties to legal disputes, and ordinary people trying to make a living in busy commercial societies. It is not an accident that the very first word in the body of Grotius's text is "controversiae".[49] I have tried to show that the natural lawyers did not think this the only morally pertinent problem area. They saw that there is an important part of our lives in which the problem arises not from disagreement but from the scarcity of resources for helping others. No single person, perhaps not even any society, can help everyone who is suffering or in need. But some can be helped even if not all can. The theory of imperfect duties provides one way

---

[49] Grotius. I.I.I.

of thinking about how we are to distribute resources in situations where only some can be helped. The serious issues involved here seemed less urgent to the natural lawyers than the problems arising from disagreement about strict justice, which they took to pose threats to the very existence of society. They therefore gave first priority to what they thought might assist with those controversies.

In tackling these problems, classical virtue theory is of little or no use. Aristotle does not tell us what a virtuous agent (*phronimos*) is to do to convince someone who is not virtuous to agree with him, other than to educate him all over again. He does not suggest criteria which anyone and everyone can use to determine who is a virtuous agent and who is not. He does not discuss the situation in which two virtuous agents disagree seriously with one another. And consequently he does not notice what seems to be an implication of his view: that if two allegedly virtuous agents strongly disagree, one of them (at least) must be morally defective.

The Aristotelian theory may have been suited to a society in which there was a recognized class of superior citizens, whose judgment on moral issues would be accepted without question. But the Grotians did not believe they lived in such a world. Moreover, since virtue theory must treat disagreement with the virtuous agent as showing a flaw of character, it discourages parties to a moral dispute from according even *prima facie* respect to differing points of view. It encourages each, rather, to impugn the character of the other rather than listen to the other's case. And it gives no distinctive guidance about how to analyse a dispute so as to find the common ground from which agreement can be peacefully reached. Natural-law theory tries to do precisely that. It reminds us of the basic needs we share, and the difficulties, inherent in our nature, to overcoming them. It gives us laws showing us what we have to do to solve the problems. And it instructs us to apply those laws either to resolve our disputes in their terms (in a state of nature) or to construct civil laws which will give us more specific instruments for reaching agreements.

The Grotian approach, in short, leads us to ask how we are to handle serious disagreements among equals. If it is addressing the right problematic, then Kant's moral theory is not one of virtue's misfortunes. He did as well for virtue as could be done, given the deficiencies of classical virtue-centered views. It may well be that the friends of virtue think some other problematic is more relevant to our current situation than the Grotian, or that they see more resources in the classical tradition of virtue-centered ethics than I have noticed. I hope that they will at any rate realize that virtue was not neglected during the seventeenth and eighteenth centuries. It is up to them to show that it was not virtue's own weakness that brought its misfortunes down upon its own head.

11

Voluntarism and the Foundations of Ethics

Philosophical theories respond to specific problems about their subject. The problems determine in large part what can count as an adequate theory. If the problems change, so do the requirements that an acceptable philosophical view must meet. In the seventeenth century a new problem about morality came to seem inescapable to many philosophers. It arose from the voluntarist account of God's relations to morality. The issue was not about revelation and reason. Voluntarists as well as their critics agreed that we are to be guided by principles discoverable by reason. The critics, however, saw grave moral and political deficiencies in voluntarism. It was apt to corrupt character, and it had dangerous political implications. Theologians were not its only exponents. There were philosophers who made it their business to defend it; others, of course, tried to defeat it.

   The critics had a twofold task. They plainly had to replace the morality of voluntarism with a substantive morality that did not suffer from its alleged defects. Not surprisingly, different philosophers proposed different basic moral principles. But they agreed that voluntarism made it imperative to show that morality could be given a justifying foundation of a kind not previously claimed for it; and each tried to explain how his own substantive ethical theory could be given that sort of justification. The ethical theories most distinctive of modernity—utilitarianism, intuitionism, and Kantianism—were all initially proposed as ways of understanding morality that would defeat voluntarism. In ancient moral philosophy there are no counterparts to these

Presidential Address delivered before the Ninety-Second Annual Eastern Division Meeting of The American Philosophical Association in New York City, New York, December 29, 1995.

   I am grateful to Richard Rorty, John Cooper, Ian Hunter, Susan Wolf, and Richard Flathman, who commented helpfully on early versions of this paper. I have also benefitted from discussion of the paper at departmental colloquia at McGill and at Johns Hopkins Universities.

theories because the normative issues that generated the modern concerns about principles and foundations had not been raised.

The attacks on voluntarism thus illustrate an important point about the history of ethics. Modern thought about our moral convictions and about the psychology and metaphysics presupposed by them was profoundly shaped by moral and political concerns. Philosophers did not simply apply to morality the theoretical views they developed in response to problems posed by skepticism and the new science. Rather, substantive moral beliefs imposed conditions on theories of knowledge. The priority of morality to epistemology is central to much of the history of modern ethics. Nowhere is it more striking than in the development of theories concerning the epistemological foundations of morals.

1. Voluntarism and Its Failings

For an account of voluntarism we need look no further back than Luther.[1] "God is he," says Luther, "for whose will no cause or ground may be laid down as its rule and standard . . . What God wills is not right because he ought or was bound so to will; on the contrary, what takes place must be right, because he so wills."[2] Luther's view is part of his characteristically voluntarist belief that God is beyond human comprehension. We are here to obey his commands, not to understand his ways. Voluntarism also underlies Calvin's predestinarian view of God's incomprehensible distribution of grace.[3] During the seventeenth century several voluntarist theories about morality were put forward. The Catholic Suarez incorporated a significant element of voluntarism in his presentation of natural law. Descartes made much stronger voluntarist claims, asserting God's absolute power over the laws of morality as well as those of thought. Puritan theologians, Hobbes, Pufendorf, and Locke all proposed different kinds of voluntarist moral theory. King's popular *de Origine Mali* (1702), and, ironically, Leibniz's

---

[1] A fuller account would take us back to Duns Scotus and William of Ockham, and lead through the many scholastic writers who influenced Calvin as well as Luther.

[2] Luther, *Bondage of the Will*, in *Martin Luther: Selections from his Writings*, ed. John Dillenberger, (Garden City, 1961), 195–6.

[3] See Calvin's *Institutes of the Christian Religion*, ed. John T. McNeill, trans. Ford Lewis Battles, (London, 1961), vol. II.23, 2–7.

attack on it, kept awareness of voluntarism alive in the early decades of the eighteenth century; and in the 1740s it was powerfully restated by Crusius, whose work Kant knew.

Voluntarists claimed that their view is the only one compatible with God's omnipotence, because it alone leaves God absolutely untrammelled in creating the world. The way this interpretation of omnipotence affected seventeenth-century moral philosophy stands out very clearly in Pufendorf's version of natural-law doctrine, published in 1672, and for over a century more widely studied throughout Europe than any other systematic account of morals and politics.

On Pufendorf's view God created all physical beings by an absolutely arbitrary fiat. These objects and their movements, including the movements that make up human actions, have no inherent moral attributes. It is only because God imposes what Pufendorf calls "moral entities" on us that there are attributes such as right and wrong, and normative positions such as ruler and subject. God is the supreme authority, and therefore his laws create moral attributes and positions binding all people alike. But we ourselves can create additional moral entities of more limited scope. We do so whenever we set up rule-governed practices.

Since God is not subordinate to any superior, he is under no law and therefore has no obligations. He keeps his promises because it pleases him, and not, as we do, because there is a law requiring it. More generally Pufendorf insists that there can be no morality common to God and us. He illustrates the point forcefully. "For who," he asks, "dare reason thus? Pay your debts, because God pays his. Be grateful, because God is kind to them that serve him. Obey your Governors, because God is subject to his superiors. Honor your parents, because God honors his. Are not these reasonings manifestly absurd?"[4]

Pufendorf was not the only target of Leibniz's criticism of voluntarism. In the *Theodicy* he attacked Hobbes and King, hoping "to banish from men the false ideas that represent God to them as an absolute prince employing a despotic power, unfitted to be loved and unworthy of being loved."[5] That view "despoils God of all goodness and all true justice," he declared, and

---

[4] Samuel Pufendorf, *On the Law of Nature and of Nations.* trans. B. Kennett, (London, 1729), II.iii.v, p. 123 and n. 5. The illustrations, given in the note, are taken from one of Pufendorf's controversial writings and added by Barbeyrac, the translator.

[5] G. W. Leibniz, *Theodicy*, trans. Huggard, (LaSalle, 1985), sect. 6, 127.

"represents him as a tyrant, wielding an absolute power, independent of all right and of all equity."[6] These statements make clear the central aspects of the moral objection to the voluntarist view of God. A despotic ruler causes servility in his subjects, not love. But God must be loveable if the basic Christian moral commandment is to be one we can obey. Since mutual love between God and human beings is the source of love among humans, the voluntarist view would make a proper moral community impossible. God must be included in that community, because, as Leibniz put it, "God is not a kind of imaginary metaphysical being... God is a definite substance, a person, a mind."[7] We can avoid a loveless morality of despotism and servility only if God and we form a community whose members know that they all accept the same morality.

The Cambridge Platonists were the earliest moderns to raise objections of this kind against the voluntarists.[8] Before 1652 John Smith introduced a complaint that was frequently repeated when he contrasted the "servility" required by voluntarism with the "freedom and liberty of soul within us" that comes from a "right knowledge of God."[9] In 1678 Cudworth charged that voluntarists "slander human nature and make a villain of it" in order the better to excuse political despotism.[10] All anti-voluntarists strongly rejected what they took to be the voluntaristic moral denigration of human nature; and the fear that voluntarism had unacceptable political implications was never out of sight. The implications were plain in Hobbes. His mortal deity, the Leviathan, would be as untrammelled as the immortal one in legislating for selfish human beings. As late as 1765 Diderot underlined the link between Hobbes's political claims and his voluntarism. "All these ideas on the sovereignty and justice of God," Diderot says, "are the same as those he established about the sovereignty and justice of kings."[11] Voluntarism seemed to pose a problem for anyone who shared these moral and political concerns.

---

[6] *Theodicy*, 402; cf. 237–8.

[7] Leibniz, *Philosophical Papers and Letters*, ed. Leroy E. Loemker, (Dordrecht, 1969), 158.

[8] Luther and Calvin were aware of such objections. See e.g. Calvin, Inst. III.xxiii.2.

[9] John Smith, *Select Discourses*, (1660), 28; see also 362, 364, 424. Smith died in 1652.

[10] Ralph Cudworth, *True Intellectual System*, (London, 1845), vol. III, 497.

[11] For Cudworth's charge see the last chapter of *True Intellectual System*, (London, 1845), vol. III, 497. Diderot's article *Hobbisme* is reprinted in his *Oeuvres*, ed. Laurent Versini, vol. I, (Paris, 1994); I translate from p. 445. 1765 is the date of publication of the volume in which the article appeared; it seems to have been drafted as early as 1753.

II. The Need for New Foundations

In Adam Smith's history of systems of morality in the last part of *The Theory of Moral Sentiments*, Cudworth is identified as the originator of modern ethical rationalism. Cudworth attributed the origins of morality to reason, Smith says, in order to refute Hobbes; and it then became "the popular doctrine" that morality consists in conformity with reason.[12] Popular or not, it is true that rationalist moral theorists from Cudworth on were typically opposed to voluntarism. It is also true that opponents of voluntarism all adopted central elements of rationalism in constructing their theories. William Law puts concisely the point they all want to make: "It is this rationality of our Nature that makes us . . . obliged to practice moral Virtue, and brings us into a kind of Society with God and all other intelligent beings."[13] The nature of the problem the anti-voluntarists faced made their appeal to rationalism inevitable.

The voluntarists and their opponents agreed on two points. The first is that any satisfactory theory must explain how God is essential to morality. Denial of this would be tantamout to atheism. The second is that God expects us to use reason to discover the moral principles by which he intends us to live. But the antivoluntarists converge on three claims that their opponents reject.

First, they agree that the basic moral principle or principles must assign a definite moral status to every action. If morality fails to cover every possible action, then God has scope for arbitrary choice; and it is against precisely this possibility that the anti-voluntarists wanted to guard. This is a new demand on a basic principle of ethics. Neither the classical theorists nor the mediaeval natural-law writers thought of morality as centering on principles of such power.

Second, the critics all assert that the basic moral principle or principles must be necessarily true, and applicable to all moral agents. Contingent principles might hold only for us. But to assure moral community with God, in the next life as well as in this, we must know that he reasons from the same principles we do. Pufendorf's illustrations of his claim that God

---

[12] Adam Smith, *The Theory of Moral Sentiments*, ed. Raphael and McKie, (Oxford, 1976), 319 (VII.iii. ii.4–5).

[13] William Law, *Remarks upon the Fable of the Bees*, (1723), in Law's *Works*, Privately Reprinted for G. Moreton, (New Forest, Hampshire, 1892), vol. II, 16.

and we stand under no common law make the difficulty here quite plain. No principle tied to contingent features of our lives would serve the critics' purpose. They were forced to appeal to the most general conceivable principles of morals. But the necessary and most general principles of a science must be self-evident. There is nothing from which they can be inferred. The anti-voluntarists consequently held that morality must rest on necessary and universal self-evident truths.

Third, the opponents of voluntarism take an *a priori* position about moral motivation. God has none of our finite needs or desires. Hence he must be moved simply by his awareness of moral principle. Unless this is true, we cannot be sure that God will not arbitrarily disregard morality. And as God's actions cannot be compelled, this motivational force of moral knowledge must be compatible with freedom. Only a priori knowledge about God's perfection can give us this assurance. And if rational knowledge can move God to free moral compliance, it must be able to do the same with us. We can act for the same kind of reasons that move God.

For the anti-voluntarists, it is through reason that we resemble God. Moral principles bind God and humans alike just because they embody the universal features of practical reason as such. Their justification is their rationality. The Stoics had a similar view. But the rationalists gave it a dramatically new turn to accommodate their belief, not shared by the Stoics, in a deity who is an agent like human agents in that he must make specific decisions. In what follows, I discuss some of the ways in which rationalist moralists tried to spell out ethical principles that would both rule out moral arbitrariness and be justified as demands of practical reason.

III. Rationalist Theories of Morals

Leibniz gives the simplest theory that meets the new requirements. God, he says, necessarily takes increase of perfection as his reason for acting. Since perfections are commensurable, the more perfection an act can realize, the stronger the reason for doing it. Because no two states of affairs can be identical, no two can contain equal amounts of perfection. God's omniscience, therefore, enables him to single out the best possible world and his goodness makes it necessary for him to make that world real. No other view is acceptable. "If the will of God had not as its rule the principle of the best, it would tend towards evil . . . or else it would be indifferent somehow to good and to evil, and guided by chance."[14]

Both of the latter alternatives deny God's own perfection. Thus the principle of practical reason that governs God's will can have no gaps: it directs every conceivable choice.

Since we think like God, the same principle holds for us. Like God we necessarily aim at increasing perfection as much as we can. Hence the only conceivable moral directive for us is to increase perfection as much as possible; and justice and the other parts of morality are nothing but specifications of this requirement. We cannot suppose that God might pursue only some perfections and not others. That would involve the irrational policy of pursuing less rather than more perfection in some cases. But to hold that God's willing need not be guided by the best reasons opens the way to voluntarism.

Leibniz is a perfectionist who requires us to bring about the best possible consequences, but he is not yet a utilitarian. Cumberland is traditionally, and I think correctly, seen as taking the first steps toward a principle that requires bringing about the greatest possible amount of pleasure. The voluntarism he opposes is that of Hobbes. Hobbes's view that God's authority comes from his power "evidently leads men to seek dominion over others by Force, or Fraud" and must be rejected.[15] Cumberland sees God as a loving being who wants us to love one another. To love others is to desire to do them good, and more good is always better than less. Hence God wants us to have the heartfelt aim of "promoting the common good of the whole system of rational agents."[16] We are able do so because Hobbesian psychology is mistaken. Like God, we have desires for the good of others. We can act from the same kind of love that God has; and we should increase that love as much as we can. We can include God among those whose good we are to maximize, because although he has no needs he derives "joy or complacency" from seeing his creatures obey his laws. Cumberland's morality tells us to maximize such feelings in order to ensure that God and we are embarked on a common enterprise that we both understand.

---

[14] *Theodicy*, 387.
[15] Richard Cumberland, *A Treatise of the Laws of Nature*, (1672). trans. John Maxwell, (London, 1727), 319.
[16] Cumberland, Introd. ix. 16.

Cumberland is a distinctive case, because he explicitly refuses to argue along the then available rationalist lines. He does not disavow the Platonism developed in Cambridge, but he thinks that since Hobbesians would reject its assumptions he will do better to talk in their empirical terms. Much of his *de Legibus Naturae* of 1672 is devoted to arguing not only that empirical evidence disproves Hobbes's psychological egoism, but also, and far less plausibly, that it shows that God aims at the greatest happiness of all rational beings. Hence it shows us God's law for us. But quite surprisingly, given his aim of meeting Hobbes on his own terms, he thinks that we learn an eternal and necessary moral law from this evidence. And he argues that even though God has no superior, he is not above the law, as the voluntarists claimed. There is, Cumberland says, an "intrinsic propension of the divine will" making it impossible for God not to pursue what he perceives as the greatest available good. Since God cannot fail to know an eternal and necessary truth, his infallible knowledge of the good is "analogous to a natural law." It imposes a necessity upon him, and obligation just is moral necessity. God is thus bound by "the immutability of his own perfections." Cumberland here joins his thesis that empirical evidence shows us necessary moral truth to an *a priori* claim about God's will to justify his anti-voluntarism. Empirical evidence alone would not justify it.[17]

How can necessity of this kind be compatible with divine freedom? Cumberland replies that God's freedom, which is what the voluntarists wish to defend, consists in his ability to choose to create one world out of a group of equally good possible worlds, all of which would be better than any world not in the group.[18] Leibniz would rule out this way of explaining God's freedom as leaving room for arbitrary divine choice. But Leibniz failed to convince his critics that he had an adequate account of moral freedom. His view that God and we necessarily pursue what we think the greatest perfection was widely held to exclude it. Those who wanted to defend a richer conception of freedom thought that they had to explain practical rationality as involving more than finding means to an end given us by theoretical reason. Samuel Clarke tried one way of making explicit what more is involved.

Clarke is quite explicit about his opposition to voluntarism. The Calvinist preachers of "absolute Predestination and unconditionate Decrees," are as

---

[17] Cumberland, ch. 7.vi, 317–19.   [18] Cumberland, ch. 7.vii, 320.

much his enemy as Hobbes. In making God's goodness and justice different from ours, Calvinism makes him incomprehensible.[19] Voluntarists, moreover, place too much stress on the purely positive duties of ritual, forgetting that "the end and design of all Religion...is the practice of virtue." Doctrine for Clarke is to be judged by a moral test, and voluntarism fails.[20] But how are we to understand the morality common to God and us?

We are to understand it, first of all, in terms of eternal fitnesses of things, unalterable relations of appropriateness between agents and actions. They are the ultimate basis of reasons for action. God sees them in the same way we do and is necessarily governed by them. Human obligation is our form of this necessity: we ought to act as God necessarily does act. Moreover, awareness of the fitnesses generates in us, as in him, a motive to act as they require.[21] And as intelligent beings we have a free will that enables us to choose whether to act from promptings of desire or from the moral motive. God, as intelligent, is also free. Although he is never faced with our kind of choice, he has room for free decision of another kind.

In his correspondence with Leibniz, Clarke argues that God can freely choose among alternatives that do not differ in degree of goodness. For instance, he can decide how to arrange three "equal particles."[22] Are there then absolutely no rational or moral constraints on this divine power? Clarke replies that while one of the eternal fitnesses is the maximizing principle that "every rational creature ought...to do all the good it can to its fellow-creatures,"[23] there is another, equally compelling principle. We are to treat like cases alike. This is the principle forbidding inequity, which, Clarke says, "is the very same in action as falsity or contradiction in theory; and the same cause which makes the one absurd makes the other unreasonable."[24]

Clarke thus finds two kinds of rational constraint on choice.[25] God can choose freely only where the options are equally good; and he cannot choose

---

[19] Sermons X, XIV, XVI (*Works*, (London, 1738), vol. I) contain these points as do many others.

[20] Sermon XL, 250 ff.; CX, 703.

[21] Clarke does not explain how this happens.

[22] *The Leibniz-Clarke Correspondence*, ed. H. G. Alexander, (Manchester, 1984), 30.

[23] Clarke, *Works*, (London, 1738), vol. II, 621.

[24] Clarke, *Works*, vol. II, 619–20. Cumberland had earlier made the same point.

[25] In the first edition of *The Methods of Ethics*, Henry Sidgwick used Clarke's language in presenting the axioms of ethics he thought self-evident. Sidgwick is another of those who adopted a rationalistic stance in morality because of a concern with religion. He embarked on moral philosophy in an effort to resolve his well-known doubts abut the existence of God. He thought that if common-sense morality

capriciously. The principle of equity requires, for instance, that if God chooses to save one undeserving soul, he cannot damn another who is no more undeserving. Leibniz suggested that the eternal damnation of some may be justified because their sufferings are outweighed by the enjoyments of those who are saved.[26] For Clarke this was unacceptable. Practical reasoning by its nature requires equity and so rules out Calvinist predestination as unjust.

Richard Price took Clarke's line of thought a step further. The theological voluntarism he opposed wore a new garb. He thought that voluntarism was implied by Hutcheson's sentimentalist view of morals. A well-known passage in a letter from Hume to Hutcheson shows exactly what Price feared. "[Since] Morality, according to your Opinion as well as mine, is determin'd merely by Sentiment," Hume wrote, "it regards only human Nature and human Life . . . . What Experience have we with regard to superior Beings? How can we ascribe to them any Sentiments at all? They have implanted those sentiments in us for the Conduct of Life like our bodily Sensations, which they possess not themselves."[27] It is to ward off this limitation on morality that Price insists that it must rest on necessary truths. They alone can assure us that we and God share a common set of principles; and without that, Price thinks, we cannot love God and try to live in friendship with him.[28]

For Hutcheson, as Price reads him, our moral faculty is a mere instinct contingently planted in us. On that view we could have no reason to suppose that God has a moral sense like ours. Indeed we could not conclude that God has "any moral character at all." Price stresses the point that moral truths are necessary truths. He thinks that only their necessity enables us to have knowledge of God's principles. Empirical evidence will not suffice. Even a wicked or characterless deity might just happen to produce the amount of good we observe in the world. Moreover we must know "what prevails universally and eternally." A merely empirical inference would not

---

showed increasing development toward Christian teaching, this would be evidence of the truth of that religion. He thought common sense could be made coherent as implicitly utilitarian, and that utilitarianism follows from some necessary self-evident axioms. He thus rejected the contingent empiricist basis that Bentham and Mill had given to utilitarianism, in favor of an *a priori* foundation that would enable him to reach into the heavens—if only it had not been so seriously at odds with itself.

[26] *Theodicy*, pp. 134–5. Leibniz takes the issue up again at pp. 385–6, but does not address Clarke's concern for equity.

[27] Hume, *Letters*, ed. J.Y. T. Greig, (Oxford, 1932), vol. I, 40.

[28] Richard Price, *Review of the Principal Questions in Morals*, ed. D. D. Raphael, (Oxford, 1948), 266.

tell us about the after-life. Only rational necessary truths about God's nature will.[29] Sentimentalism about morals would bar us from such knowledge.

Price follows Clarke in holding that several basic moral truths are self-evident, that awareness of them provides us with motivating reasons for action, and that our free will enables us to control desire and to act as we ought.[30] Unlike Clarke, however, he denies that morality directs us to bring about the greatest amount of good we can. "Happiness is the *end*, and the only end conceivable by us, of God's providence and government," Price insists, "but he pursues this end in subordination to rectitude. . . . *Justice* and *Veracity* are right as well as *goodness*, and must also be ascribed to the Deity . . . *justice* is not merely a mode of goodness, or an instance of [benevolence's] taking the most effectual method to accomplish its end."[31]

With Clarke, Price claims that the right and the good offer different kinds of reasons for God's actions and ours. What he adds is that the right takes precedence and that it can limit the amount of good that may permissibly be produced. He defends this analysis of practical reason because he thinks no other will show that God's morality can be fully intelligible to us. What leads Price to this new claim about morality is his concern with the problem of evil.[32]

On this issue, Price thinks, Leibniz must have been right. Only a voluntarist or an atheist can hold that this is not a perfect world. Admittedly there is much suffering and evil-doing in the world. But God's moral principles are ours, and he is all-perfect. Unless we can explain how such a deity could refuse to prevent some evil, or to cause some good, when he might, we leave matters in voluntaristic mystery. The explanation requires a more complex view of the perfection of the universe than Leibniz's. We cannot deny God's providence, and if God cares for any one event in nature, then he takes all the care that it is possible to take for all events.[33] But once we see that morality requires God to be just before he is benevolent, we can also see

---

[29] Price, *Review*, pp. 236–43.   [30] Price, *Review*, pp. 185–7, 207–10.

[31] Price, *Review*, pp. 250–1; cf. 252.

[32] Malebranche is the first philosopher who tried to work out this line of thought; Price's views are strikingly similar to his, and Price in all probability knew his work. For Malebranche, God is not moved solely by concern for the good. In acting, as he does, to bring about good for us, Malebranche's God respects the 'order' determined by the relative worth of the eternal ideas in his mind, which we also perceive in moral insight. Malebranche introduces this claim because it, along with the claim that God acts always by "general wills," enables him to solve the problem of evil.

[33] Richard Price, *Four Dissertations*, (London 1768), rep. (Bristol, 1990), 17–18. Hereafter referred to as Diss.

that his care of the world is governed by moral principle. "Rectitude, under the government of a being of perfect rectitude," Price declares, "I may be sure, shall take place invariably, universally and for ever; and this is all I ought to wish for."[34] If unmerited suffering occurs in this life, we may be sure it will be recompensed in another, just as the apparently successful scoundrel will get his due there. The voluntarist thinks punishments and rewards are essential to the very constitution of moral obligation. For the anti-voluntarist they are not. Rational necessity suffices to obligate, all by itself. But sanctions are essential to show that God ensures the fairness of his world by making up for the individual costs of acting justly.[35] The priority of the right to the good was first propounded in purely rational terms in order to make God's providential care morally intelligible.

IV. Keeping God in Morality

I have tried to show how several of the major modern theories of morality originated in the moral struggle against voluntarism. I have not, however, shown that this was the main motivation for them. Rationalist theories might have been proposed simply as the best explanation of common-sense morality. I should like to give one reason for thinking that this would not adequately account for them.

In doing so I can also indicate how the anti-voluntarists satisfied the need to show God to be essential to morality. As they well knew, voluntarism, holding that God's free choice creates morality, can easily seem to be the only view that does so. If morality rests on necessary truths which are eternally valid, then it would exist without God's creative fiat. And if our moral knowledge can move us to freely chosen compliance, divine sanctions seem unnecessary.

To show that, despite all this, God is essential to morality, anti-voluntarists all appealed to the same point. Moral principles by themselves do not guarantee that things will turn out as they should when we apply them. But rational practical principles cannot require pointless or self-defeating action. Divine providence is needed to make the world hospitable to action from rational principle. God sees to it that all will be for the best even if

---

[34] Diss. 96.   [35] Diss. 132–3.

wicked people are successful, or good people are weak-willed or morally obtuse, or natural events wreck all plans.

This way of keeping God essential to morality was not the exclusive property of rationalists.[36] Price and the sentimentalist Adam Smith hold essentially identical views on the matter. For Price, we must follow conscience, or our best insight into what the eternal truths of morality require; we often do not know the consequences of our doing so; but we may be sure that all will work out as it ought because God is there to supervise everything.[37] Adam Smith holds that we distinguish right from wrong by our sympathetic feelings. Reason, however, enables us to form summaries of the feelings sensitive moral agents have, and then, when we ourselves have no such feelings—and Smith thinks this is very often the case—we can simply act on the rules. We do not deliberately aim at human happiness when we act from sympathetic approval or from respect for the rules. But we are always under the aegis of the God to whom Smith refers as "the great Superintendent of the universe." He guarantees that our rule-following actions work out for "the happiness of mankind" and other rational creatures.[38]

Price and Smith thus agree that common-sense morality tells us to follow rules discovered by reason even when we do not know all the consequences. They both assign to providence the job of seeing to it that such rule-following, with all its short-comings, will still bring about the best results. Their disagreement about rationalism and sentimentalism thus does not arise from disagreement about the way common-sense morality works in daily life. It arises because Price is deeply concerned about the voluntarist view of God, and Smith is not. Smith is content with empirical indications of God's purposes for us and is not worried about defending the possibility of community with him. The point is general. Sentimentalist thinkers are not concerned about voluntarism, and those who oppose sentimentalism are.[39]

---

[36] It could also be invoked by voluntarists.   [37] Price, *Review*, 244.

[38] Smith, *Theory of Moral Sentiments*, 161–8; 236, 277, 290.

[39] Was not Shaftesbury, however, a sentimentalist who opposed voluntarism? In fact he helps my case. He is indeed out to supplant voluntarism. He thinks it abases and degrades both God and us to think of God in voluntarist terms. But his sentimentalism is not pure. Through moral feeling Shaftesbury thinks we discern eternal harmonies which are independent of the feelings and of anyone's will. It is these harmonies that provide the test of the morality of any allegedly divine command. Only a command that matches the harmonies can come from God. Shaftesbury again illustrates the point that moral concerns motivate moral epistemologies.

V. Kant

Kant was on the side of the rationalists. He knew of voluntarism through Crusius's defense of it as well as through Leibniz's reports and criticisms of it. His early marginalia display his detestation of servility, and in the *Metaphysics of Morals* he tried, as other anti-voluntarists did not, to show what is not merely distasteful but morally wrong about it. Some of the "pre-critical" writings make it evident that he gave serious consideration to treatments of morality within the terms of empiricism. His a priori ethic fits the pattern I have pointed out in the anti-voluntarists who preceded him. Like them he defends a moral law drawn from the very nature of practical reasoning. "We must be able to know," he says, "in every possible case, in accordance with a rule, what is *right* and what is *wrong*."[40] Since the rule is a pure necessary moral law, a rational deity is governed by the same morality that binds us. Kant moves beyond Clarke and Price by deriving the requirements of benevolence as well as justice from a single law. To ensure that the law can motivate us as well as God, he claims that the one truly moral motive arises directly from awareness of the law and does not depend on the accidents of our empirically given nature. To keep God essential to morality, he argues that the moral agent must believe "in the cooperation or management [*Veranstaltung*] of a moral world-governor" who guarantees that action from the moral law, no matter how frustrated in politics or how costly in personal terms, will not be futile.[41] And he defends the thesis that this is the best possible world while insisting, with Price, that God is just before he is benevolent.[42]

If we see Kant as standing with the anti-voluntarists in the controversy over voluntarism, we can understand an otherwise quite puzzling comment he makes in the Preface to the *Groundwork of the Metaphysics of Morals*. He claims that it is "self-evident" (*leuchtet von selbst . . . ein*) from the common ideas of duty and of the moral law that there must be a pure moral

---

[40] Kant, *Critique of Pure Reason*, trans. N. Kemp Smith, at A477=B505.

[41] Kant, *Religion within the Limits of Reason Alone*, trans. Greene and Hudson, (New York, 1960), 130 (VI. 139).

[42] In the essay "On the failure of all possible theodicies" Kant argues that there can be no proof that this is the best possible world; but in the *Lectures on Philosophical Theology*, trans. Wood and Clarke, 1978, pp. 137–9 he suggests that there are general rational considerations about purposiveness that entitle us to see the world as being organized in the best possible way, and he also suggests a moral argument for the conclusion. At pp. 112–13 he asserts that God is a judge, and hence is just, not merely benevolent.

philosophy, independent of anything empirical. Everyone will admit, he says, that if there is a genuine moral law, then it "does not apply to men only, as if other rational beings had no need to observe it."[43] Since Kant knew that many theorists would have denied these claims, how could he have thought them obvious? The commentators, to the best of my knowledge, have not tried to explain.[44] But if Kant assumed without question that the moral community must include God, then it would naturally have seemed "self-evident" to him that there must be a moral law that applies to all rational beings, not to humans only, and a pure *a priori* moral philosophy to explain it.[45]

VI. Voluntarism and Anti-Foundationalism

So far I have considered only how *opposition* to voluntarism gave rise to a distinctively modern debate about the foundations of morality. I want now to suggest that at least some voluntarist views had a positive impact on the subject. The voluntarists differed from the rationalists, not by trying to do the same thing in a different way but by refusing to seek the kind of foundation that the rationalists thought was needed. They first proposed what we would now call anti-foundationalism.

On the voluntarist view, we must treat God's decision to create this world as ungrounded. He could as justifiably have created a world whose parts had other natures; and because he does not act in vain, he would then have ordained other laws suited to those natures. Since God's commands are tailored to our contingent nature, the moral laws they impose are themselves also ultimately contingent.[46] The voluntarists thus think that it is a

---

[43] *Grundlegung zur Metaphysik der Sitten*, AA 4.389.9–11, 12–16.

[44] Most commentators do not discuss the Preface in detail. Rüdiger Bittner gives it a careful examination, in "Das Unternehmung einer Grundlegung zur Metaphysik der Sitten," in Ottfried Höffe, ed., *Grundlegung zur Metaphysik der Sitten: Ein kooperativer Commentar*, Frankfurt am Main, 1989, pp. 13–30. He argues that neither Kant's exclusion of all empirical grounds for the moral law, nor his extension of its validity to all rational beings follows from the necessity he attributes to it; but he does not take up the claim that it is self-evident that there must be a pure moral philosophy and a pure morality binding all rational beings (See p. 25). Ludwig Siep, in "Wozu Metaphysik der Sitten?" in the same volume, pp. 31–44, also discusses the Preface but, again, without considering the relevant lines.

[45] Despite his opposition to voluntarism on these points, Kant is in many ways a voluntarist himself.

[46] Scholars of the subject stress the importance for voluntarists of the contingency of nature, and tie this to the origins of empiricism generally.

mistake to look for the sort of necessary and universal principles for morality that their critics insist on. They do not think that morality arises solely from the requirements of practical reason. It is intended to guide beings with our empirical nature, physical and emotional as well as rational. Morality for them can have neither the sort of foundation nor the universal and necessary scope that the rationalists require.

The rejection of rationalist foundations does not imply, for these voluntarists, that reason has no role in our morality. On the contrary: one of their chief aims was to show that moral controversies can be settled rationally. But they held that empirical observation, rather than rational intuition, is at the heart of moral reasoning. What experience shows us entitles us to believe that God created us and meant us to enjoy life on earth. Our nature must point to God's purposes for us and is therefore an indicator of his laws. We can discover what the laws are by determining our special needs and abilities and considering how we can respond to them in ways that preserve us in our actual surroundings.

Price thought that unless we could be sure that we share a common morality with God we would feel abandoned in a "forlorn and fatherless" universe.[47] Voltaire gave a quite different, and more positive, construal, to God's leaving us alone. Like his hero Locke he was a voluntarist insofar as he had a coherent moral view, and *Candide* was among other things a voluntarist tract. His *Philosophical Dictionary* contains a classic summary of the moral point of the doctrine: "When Nature created our species," he says, "and gave us instincts—self-regard for our own preservation, benevolence for the preservation of others, love which is common to all species, and the inexplicable gift of being able to combine more ideas than all the other animals put together—after giving us our portion, she said to us: 'Now do the best you can.' "[48] God created nature, and nature created us with the ability to guide our own affairs.

The pre-Kantian rationalists were not willing to confine us to nature in this way. The arguments they used to support their moral objections to voluntarism make this clear. They argued that even our moral concepts require us to reject voluntarism. We understand the distinction between authority and mere power; and ever since Plato's *Euthyphro* we have been

---

[47] Diss. 97–8; so also Smith, *Theory of Moral Sentiments*, 235.
[48] Voltaire, *Philosophical Dictionary*, trans. Gay, (New York, 1962), 364.

able to see that when we say that God's will is just, we are not saying that God wills what he wills. Plainly, then, will cannot be the source of morality. And our ability to see this shows that we have the power of grasping simple moral concepts. However we explain this intuitive power, our possession of moral concepts shows its existence; and once we admit that much, we must also admit that we can see the truth of the necessary universal principles they carry with them.

Neither Hobbes nor Pufendorf nor Locke confronted criticisms of this kind head on. But they did object to the kind of view about language and concepts presupposed by them. They thought that God left us to create our own language, and they rejected innate ideas. Hobbes says that we make up our words and then make our theories from them. A good moral theory will draw strict deductive consequences from the words, but its ultimate test will be whether or not it serves our purposes, keeping us alive and preserving peace.[49] Similarly, Pufendorf holds that we make up moral terms to stand for the moral entities that we create, and Locke thinks that moral words name mixed mode ideas that we ourselves assemble from experientially given simples.

On grounds like these the voluntarists consciously rejected all platonizing theories of meaning. They tried to treat meaning as one natural phenom-enon among others. They might agree with their critics that words like "ought" and "right" pose a special problem. But they would not concede that to solve it we must appeal to an ability to share in God's mind or to grasp eternal mind-independent verities. If they did not solve the problems involved in giving a naturalistic account of the concept of "ought" or of the distinction between power and authority, they at least began to see the issues. Whatever Mandeville's other affinities may have been to voluntaristic natural-law thought, he is fully in line with it in telling his story about how a group of schemers invented the language of morals in order to gain lasting, non-coercive power over others, and in arguing that everyone benefitted from the invention.[50]

---

[49] See, for example, Hobbes, *De Cive* XVIII.4; *Leviathan* IV and V; and *Leviathan* XLVI, explaining philosophy as knowledge about causes "to the end ... to be able to produce ... such Effects, as humane life requireth."

[50] Like Pufendorf, Mandeville holds that we cannot attribute any of the human virtues to God. William Law's comment, quoted above, is in his reply to Mandeville and is directed at his naturalism, of which his anti-rationalism is a part.

The rationalists gave voluntarism a great deal of bad press. They accused it of denigrating human nature, turning God into a tyrant, and making morality impossible. They failed to see, or deliberately overlooked, important aspects of the constructive side of voluntarist moral theory. Here we must distinguish varieties of voluntarist. The purely theological voluntarists and their closest philosophical ally, Crusius, agreed with the rationalists in trying to defend a rather severe and demanding Christian morality. Other voluntarists had rather different moral and political motivations. Hobbes and Locke and Voltaire were far more humanistic. They thought the point of morality lay in the satisfaction of our natural desires. They did not require us to strive for God-like perfection. They hoped that religion would cease to cause turmoil in human life and saw their voluntarism as a tool to achieve that result. Our ignorance of almost everything about God is vital for Hobbes's minimalist view of what we must believe to be saved and for Locke's and Voltaire's defenses of toleration.[51]

In denying rational foundations to morality these voluntarists, if not the others, aimed to show that morality does not bring eternal truths or patterns into our lives. They considered it as offering the best solution to a set of practical problems arising from contingent facts about us. It does not have to supply principles that resolve every problem. We need only enough to enable us to get along peacefully with one another and to make social life more than minimally bearable. They think that if moral philosophers can invent a language that enables us to articulate general principles that we are all willing to use in solving our common problems, they will have provided the only foundations morality needs or can have.

VII. Conclusion

I have tried to show how some major epistemological claims involved in modern moral philosophy arose out of moral and political convictions. During this period at least, epistemology and metaphysics were not core disciplines that set the agenda for the rest of philosophy. Skepticism, both

---

[51] Richard Flathman has argued convincingly that theological voluntarism is both an important forerunner of political liberalism and a repository of useful ways of developing modern liberal theory. He discusses, as I do not, the importance of will in the psychologies that stem from theological voluntarism. See *Willful Liberalism*, (Ithaca: Cornell University Press, 1992), P. 2, chs. I and II.

ancient and Cartesian, did indeed raise problems to which some moral philosophers thought they had to reply.[52] But the distinctive engagements of modern moral philosophy with foundations of morality were more than a response to skepticism, and more than the application of epistemology or metaphysics or philosophy of language to moral issues. On the matter of foundations modern moral philosophy began with specific normative beliefs that in turn set their own constraints on the epistemological and other theoretical views that would be acceptable.

The problem that gave rise to the innovations I have been tracing was itself a new one. Voluntarism, originally a response to St. Thomas's way of systematizing Catholic theology, was given new social and political significance by the Reformation and by Catholic replies to Luther and Calvin. The enormous power that organized religion had over the lives of everyone in seventeenth- and eighteenth-century Europe made it a matter of the deepest and most urgent importance to settle how much influence Christian morality was to have, and how its content was to be determined. Whether one defended or objected to the weight of religious authority in everybody's life, its social reality meant that it had to be addressed by moral philosophy.

Institutionalized religions and personal religious beliefs are now more varied and have a much more differentiated hold on practice in the world we inhabit. Moral philosophers today do not need to keep an eye on the theological implications of our debates about morality, as our predecessors had to. Partly because we live amidst so much variation in religious belief, we must explore the different issues involved in the question of how we are to understand a fully secular and naturalized morality. Even those who share this concern might, no doubt, continue to search for universal and rationally self-evident principles to serve as the basis of morality, but they would have to give a new account of why such principles are needed. Sidgwick provides a brilliant example of how this might be done. Others might follow the natural lawyers in seeking to ground principles for all human beings on general features of human life. Still others might think it sufficient to explore ways in which the practices and virtues of groups less extensive than all of

---

[52] Richard Tuck, in *Philosophy and Government*, (Cambridge, 1993), ch. 7, and elsewhere, stresses the role of skepticism in the work of Grotius and Hobbes. James Tully pointed out to me that the minimalism of the morality put forward by the natural lawyers may be due in part to their effort to defeat skepticism. I think this is correct, but the claim in the next sentence in the text still stands.

humanity can be exemplary for a pluralistic morality and sufficient for human needs. All of these become live options when we shift from a morality that must relate God and the human community to one that can be confined to human needs.

Philosophical explorations of a purely secular morality could barely get a hearing during the formative period of modern ethics. Today the legitimacy and importance of the question is acknowledged, however contested a secular morality itself may be. The kind of major social change that made this shift of philosophical interest possible seems to me to be far from uncommon. In our lives, at least, such changes are occurring at an ever greater rate. When major alterations of the social world occur, serious strains on the accepted morality of the society are likely to come as well. If they provoke moral philosophers to ask new questions, the strains may lead to helpful rethinking of the situations and issues that trouble the society. Some day we will have better scientific accounts of how we know, feel, and decide; and then theoretical philosophical efforts to understand these aspects of human existence may simply fade away. But no amount of advance in the empirically based disciplines will show us how to organize the social world. That world is to a large extent a result of our own work. In the past, moral philosophy helped to create and reshape it. It did not try to leave everything as it was. If we can combine conceptual imagination and rigorous thinking with sensitivity to changing human issues, moral philosophy can continue to have a creative role as long as social crises occur.

12

Hume and the Religious Significance of Moral Rationalism

Hume notoriously criticized religion and its defenses, and in particular Christianity. The *Dialogues*, the *Natural History*, the chapters on miracles and on providence in the first *Enquiry*, some of the essays, and many passages in the *History* are usually taken to be the main presentations of his objections. As Edward Craig points out, it adds up to a great deal—to more than Hume wrote on any other single philosophical subject.[1] There are in addition several obvious attacks on religious beliefs in the *Treatise*. But it is not noticed in the literature that a number of Hume's arguments in the *Treatise* tell against propositions that are important for religion even when they are not labelled as being so. I give only one example. In the course of arguing that causes must precede their effects, Hume remarks that everyone accepts the principle "that an object, which exists for any time in its full perfection without producing another, is not its sole cause." The point reappears later as one of the rules for judging cause and effect.[2] At neither place does Hume make explicit one of the implications: that either God is not the sole cause of his creation, or else the creation is co-eternal with God. Both of these alternatives would of course be unacceptable to Christians.

In this paper I argue that Hume's critique of moral rationalism is yet another unlabelled attack on religion. I do not propose to add to the literature assessing the arguments against rationalism. I raise instead a question about their point in Hume's campaign against religion. John Balguy

---

The first draft of this paper was written for the 24th Hume Conference, July 29-August 2, 1997. I am grateful to the audience who responded to the paper and to others who have heard it since for questions and comments that have, I hope, led to some improvements.

[1] Edward Craig, *Hume on Religion* (Shimla: Indian Institute of Advanced Study, 1997), 9.

[2] *A Treatise of Human Nature*, ed. L. A. Selby-Bigge, 2nd ed., rev. by P. H. Nidditch (Oxford: Clarendon Press, 1978), 76, 174. References hereafter in the text, indicated as T.

voiced a commonplace eighteenth-century view of the relations between religion and morality when he remarked that "whatever promotes the cause of revealed religion befriends morality, and whatever strengthens morality adds force to religion."[3] Hume, everyone agrees, was trying strenuously to separate the two; and he knew he was bound to be understood as threatening both in so doing. A look at the religious signficance of rationalist moral thought should bring out some of the philosophically pertinent motivations he had for attempting to destroy this view of morality.

It may also add some clarity to the vexed issue of what Hume himself "really" thought about God. On this matter, as we all know, the variety of opinion is considerable. Was he, as his early critics charged, an atheist? Was he a concealed believer—a theist perhaps? Did he hold some version of deism? For present purposes the question of the relation between Hume and deism is central. It is not unusual to identify Hume as an adherent of this movement. Thus Gawlick cites an extensive German literature from the eighteenth century onward which treats Hume, more or less hesitantly, as a deist. Gawlick himself thinks the matter is debatable. What chiefly separated Hume from deism, Gawlick thinks, "was not his rejection of rationalism" but his own "final despair" about attaining the defining goal of the deists, which he takes to have been ridding the world of superstition, intolerance, and clerical authority.[4] Agreeing about Hume's pessimism on the practical matter, Gaskin argues nonetheless that Hume is an "attenuated deist," and that what separates him from the deists is his "attack on two arguments: that from design and that from first cause."[5] Foster agrees with Gaskin.[6]

I think that both of these views about Hume's relation to deism are mistaken. Of course no one thinks it matters much exactly what label we attach to Hume's religious position. He is not apt to fit into a pre-existing category so in any case we will have to explain what our label means. But in order to understand Hume's standpoint we must be able, like the sympathetic moral spectator, to put ourselves imaginatively into the position of those most affected by the debates that he was entering. We need to

---

[3] John Balguy, *A Collection of Tracts* (London, 1734), 371. This is from *The Law of Truth*. Cited in the text hereafter as Balguy.

[4] Guenter Gawlick, "Hume and the Deists: a Reconsideration," in G. P. Morice, ed., *David Hume* (Austin: University of Texas Press, 1977), 128–38. See n. 10 and p. 133.

[5] J. C. A. Gaskin, *Hume's Philosophy of Religion*, 2nd edn. (Atlantic Highlands N.J.: Humanities Press International, 1988), 223.

[6] Stephen Paul Foster, *Melancholy Duty* (Dordrecht: Kluwer, 1997), 23–4.

understand the map of religious options on which Hume's readers would have located him. Whether he accepted the common options or not, he would have known them and taken them into account in his presentation of his views—and in his understanding of what their shock value would be. I think that previous discussions of his ethics have not given enough weight in this connection to the religious signficance of moral rationalism.

Commentators from Sir Leslie Stephen on have located many of the points that need to be considered here. But there is one element of Hume's thought whose significance for his contemporaries has, to the best of my scanty knowledge, been universally neglected, although the feature of Hume's thought that makes it pertinent has been widely noticed. It is frequently noted in commentary on Hume's views of God that while Hume seems grudgingly to allow some causal power to whatever deity reason leads us to accept, he uniformly denies any moral attributes to that deity. I shall suggest that when we put this Humean negation in the context of the alternative views of religion available at the time, we will have a better understanding of Hume's rejection of Balguy's commonplace claim about the inseparability of morality and religion. We will also see why moral rationalism was so important to its religious adherents.

The religious view that I think the commentators have neglected is sometimes called "voluntarism" and more frequently "divine command ethics". In *The Invention of Autonomy* I argue that this position was centrally important in the development of modern moral philosophy.[7] In what follows I try to supplement the argument in the book by showing that fear of voluntarism kept the problem it posed a live issue in Britain as late as the 1730s, when Hume was working on the *Treatise*. We will not find the fears and worries about voluntarism stated with great precision, nor do later articulations of them seem to differ much from earlier ones. Like the dread of "communism" in the United States during the 1950s, the early eighteenth-century rejection of the voluntarist position needed less to know its enemy in detail than to display its own propriety by the firmness with which that enemy was cast out.

The labels I have given to the position that caused the concern are not nearly as old as the doctrine itself, which originates in the work of Scotus and Occam and was revitalized by Luther and Calvin. Both of the great

---

[7] (Cambridge: Cambridge University Press, 1998).

"reformers" hold that God's untrammeled will is the source of the principles of morals. I give one illustrative passage from Calvin. God's ways, he holds, are far beyond human understanding. That it was predestined from eternity that Adam would sin, that in his sin all mankind would be ruined, that out of the mass of totally undeserving beings some would mercifully be chosen for salvation, that those not chosen would be left to suffer the anguish of permanent separation from God—all this is God's justice and is incomprehensible to us. How, then, can we be sure that it is just?

God's will is so much the highest rule of righteousness that whatever he wills, by the very fact that he wills it, must be considered righteous. When, therefore, one asks why God has so done, we must reply: because he has willed it. But if you proceed further to ask why he has so willed, you are seeking something greater and higher than God's will, which cannot be found.[8]

In the seventeenth century the most widely influential philosophical exposition of moral voluntarism was Pufendorf's.[9] He holds that God imposed "moral entities" after creating the natural world and that his purpose in imposing them was to give human beings guidance about how we are to live. He explicitly rejects Cartesian rationalism and allies himself with empiricism. Empirical evidence allows us to infer that God exists and gives us commands. God could have made an entirely different kind of world and imposed different moral directives upon those who lived in it. Empirical evidence allows us to infer what he actually commands in this world, and therefore how we ought to live. But since moral entities were imposed for the sole purpose of guiding human action, they do not allow us to infer anything about God's moral attributes.

Theories of this kind seemed to many Christians to have two major defects. First, they turned God into a tyrant and a despot, and thus made him a dangerous political model for earthly sovereigns, who are all too likely to want to satisfy Hobbes's description of the ruler as a mortal deity. Second, by making God tyrannical they made him unloveable. But since Christ commands us to love God above all else, a theory making such love impossible must be mistaken. To show that it is mistaken, the rationalists

---

[8] I cite from John Calvin, *Institutes of the Christian Religion*, ed. John T. McNeill, trans. Ford Lewis Battles (London: S. C. M. Press, Ltd., 1961); see II v 12, III xi 7, III xxiii 2.

[9] For the discussion that follows, see *The Invention of Autonomy*, ch. 7 i, 7 vi, on Pufendorf, and ch. 12, iv–v for objections to his views.

tried, in various ways, to explain the principles of morality as not only truths that reason could discover—Pufendorf agreed with that claim—but as *a priori* necessary truths, truths that would have to be recognized by any rational agent, no matter how situated, and so by God as well. Leibniz, for example, in both his *Theodicy*, which Hume plainly knew, and his attack on Pufendorf, tries to confute voluntarist views; and Malebranche, whose work was important in Hume's development, was also opposed to such theories.

Theological as well as philosophical use of voluntarism became rare by the end of the seventeenth century, but the feeling of the threat did not go away. We can see its persistence by noting the efforts to show that God's will is not arbitrary or tyrannical but is governed by eternal measures of justice and goodness.

Philosophers were not the only ones with this concern. Here, for instance, is William Sherlock, Dean of St. Paul's, a prolific seventeenth-century controversialist, considering God's power in his *Discourse concerning the Divine Providence* of 1694. He characterizes it as "absolute power," the technical phrase used by voluntarist thinkers to refer to the total absence of limits on what God might originally ordain. Sherlock then notes the fears that go with the claim that God's power has no bounds: "mankind...judge of God's absolute power by the arbitrary and tyrannical government of some absolute monarch. But," he hastens to add, "true absolute power can do no wrong."[10] The unity of God, he says, shows that his goodness and his will are the same thing; but it makes things clearer for us to reject the thought that God's will makes things just and good and to "make good and evil antecedent to the will of God and the rule of his will and choice." Otherwise we imply that "justice and goodness has no stable nature of its own."[11]

The Cambridge philosopher Cudworth was one of the major seventeenth-century opponents of voluntarism. His *Treatise concerning Eternal and Immutable Morality* is devoted wholly to attacking it.[12] The fact that it was first published in 1731, over four decades after his death, suggests that voluntarism was still a live issue. Clarke's sermons attacking Calvinist predestinarianism make his anti-voluntarism plain, as do his frequently reprinted 1705 Boyle Lectures demonstrating what their title calls "the

---

[10] William Sherlock, *A Discourse concerning the Divine Providence*, 5th edn. (London, 1715), 86–7. Cited hereafter as Sherlock.
[11] Sherlock 95–6.   [12] (London, 1731).

unchangeable obligations of natural religion."[13] And Clarke's follower and defender John Balguy makes his opposition to voluntarism equally plain in a series of tracts gathered into a single volume in 1734. He challenges one central voluntarist claim, that because God can have no superior no law can bind him, in terms reminiscent of both Cumberland and Clarke: "God has no superior to prescribe laws to him, and yet is eternally bound by the rectitude of his own nature; that is, the rules of right reason. These are so many laws to him . . . they strictly and formally oblige him" (Balguy 5). And he attacks Locke by name for holding views that would make God "arbitrary in all his procedings" (Balguy 145).

Clarke and Balguy were serious Christians, not simply deists. Many deists shared their moral rationalism. But some eighteenth-century British deists were empiricists. Toland and Collins proclaim themselves Lockeans. Was Hume perhaps within their camp? Bolingbroke, attacked at length for his deism in Leland's *View of the Principal Deistical Writers*, sounds as if he holds a Lockean view. Leland reports that he describes as absurd enthusiasts those who hold that there is "a moral sense or instinct by which men distinguish what is morally good from what is morally evil. . . . This may be acquired in some sort by long habit . . . but it is whimsical to assume it to be natural."[14] Bolingbroke is thus plainly separating himself from Hume. It seems evident that Hume's readers could not easily have taken him to be a deist of the empiricist sort.

There are, however, enough important deists who do hold to a full-blown moral rationalism to allow us to treat such adherence as a major deistic strategy. They owned it, after all, by inheritance. Hume claimed, in an often-cited footnote, that Malebranche was the originator of the "abstract" or rationalist theory of morals afterwards followed by Cudworth and Clarke.[15] But that honor should in fact go to Lord Herbert of Cherbury. And Leland takes him to be, if not the originator of deism, "the most eminent of the deistical writers, and in several respects superior to those that succeed him" (Leland 1: 3).

---

[13] See n. 26 for citations.

[14] John Leland, *A View of the Principal Deistical Writers*, 5th edn., 2 vols. (London, 1766), 2: 29. Hereafter cited as Leland. The first edition was published in 1754.

[15] David Hume, *Enquiry concerning the Principles of Morals*, ed. L. A. Selby-Bigge, 3rd edn., revised by P. H. Nidditch (Oxford: Clarendon Press, 1975), 197n. Hereafter cited as EPM.

Herbert holds that we are all equally equipped with a basic, unique moral concept, and that we can all equally know intuitively what the fundamental principles of morality are.[16] We can moreover use this knowledge to test any alleged revelation. God cannot have a morality other than ours, he thinks, and so any putative divine directive that contravenes our moral insights must be spurious. Herbert is aware of the implications of his view for the authority of the clergy, which he aims to subvert. He thus has the reformist political concerns that Gawlick places at the center of deism; and his view of the need for a moral test of revelation is one that later deists made central. He also shows himself deeply opposed to voluntarist predestinarian doctrines. Herbert's arguments can work only if justice is the same in God and in humans; and a rationalism that places *a priori* necessary truths at the foundation of morality, as Herbert did, supports that claim. After Pufendorf and Locke it became clear to opponents of Calvinism that empiricism was, to put it mildly, not a reliable ally.

The deists were as troubled by enthusiasm, or Protestant sectarianism, as Locke was, and as opposed to superstition, their term for Roman Catholic belief; and they found Herbert's views useful for fighting both these opponents. They acknowledged the existence of God and agreed that he ought to be worshipped, but they held, as one of them put it in *The Oracles of Reason* (1693), "that our obedience consists in the rules of right reason, the practice whereof is moral virtue."[17] Right reason shows all humans the same thing, the writer continues. Our eternal happiness depends on our living as it requires, and on nothing further. Since no revelation less universal than that of reason can be admitted, the Bible can have no special standing; nor can the special claims of any confession.

Matthew Tindal's *Christianity as Old as the Creation* (1730) is probably the major exposition of eighteenth-century British deism. His opposition to voluntarism is plain. It disrupts the moral relation between God and us. "[I]f the relations between Things, and the Fitnesses resulting from thence, be not the sole Rule of God's actions, must not God be an arbitrary being? and then what a miserable condition will Mankind be in! . . . tis not in our Power, tho' ever so often commanded, to love the Deity, while we

[16] For what I say about Herbert I draw on *The Invention of Autonomy*, ch. 9 ii–iii, where I give references for my account of his views.

[17] [Charles Blount and others], *The Oracles of Reason* (London, 1695), 195; this piece is not by Blount.

conceive him an arbitrary being acting out of humor and caprice."[18] His commitment to a rationalist account of morality is equally plain. We discover God's will, he says, by discovering the "law of nature or reason" which is "perfect, eternal, and unchangeable." And his final chapter is a lengthy discussion of Clarke, whose moral philosophy he finds acceptable although he does not want to draw from it some of the conclusions Clarke draws, and to which I shall return.

Less sophisticated than Tindal, Thomas Chubb, writing in 1730, is no less Clarkean in his deistic defense of the precedence of the moral obligations of religion over its positive obligations concerning the proprieties of worship. He expressly appeals to Samuel Clarke on his opening page, and argues that even the positive obligations stemming from "the will and pleasure of God" must be founded on reasons, or else they would be "tyrannical impositions, unworthy of God."[19] John Clarke of Hull holds that God's will is the sole source of the *obligation* of the moral law, though he allows that its *content* is not due purely to will. Chubb will have none of this, insisting, with Samuel Clarke, that "the obligation of the moral law does not arise from the positive will of God, but from the reasons and fitnesses of things."[20] Like Tindal and Chubb, the deist Thomas Morgan appeals again and again in *The Moral Philosopher* (1737) to "the moral, eternal reason and fitness of the things themselves" as central to arguments in support of religion.[21]

Moral rationalism is thus central to the thought of some of the major representatives of deism. It is so precisely because it provides grounds for rejecting the voluntarist view of God. This rejection was recognized as one of their central aims by no less a figure than William Law, who in 1731 published a long pamphlet attacking Tindal.[22] In it he goes beyond criticism

---

[18] Matthew Tindal, *Christianty as Old as the Creation* (London, 1731; reprinted New York: Garland, 1978), 30–1.

[19] Thomas Chubb, *The Comparative Excellence and Obligation of Moral and Positive Duties* (London, 1730), 1, 24.

[20] John Clarke, *The Foundation of Morality in Theory and Practice Considered* (York, 1726), 10, 20; Chubb, 17–18.

[21] Thomas Morgan, *The Moral Philosopher* (London, 1737), 86.

[22] William Law (1686–1761) is best known as the author of *A Serious Call to a Devout and Holy Life* (London, 1729), a classic of English devotional literature. A mystic and later a follower of Jacob Boehme, he wrote numerous polemical as well as religious works and had a wide readership. See E. Gordon Rupp, *Religion in England 1688–1791* (Oxford: Clarendon Press, 1986), ch. 15, which however does not discuss Law's philosophical views. In "William Law and the Christian Economy of Salvation," *English Historical Review* 111 (1994): 308–22, B. W. Young touches on Law's attack on Mandeville's ethics but does not discuss his voluntarism.

to provide a positive sketch of voluntarism as providing the key to the proper understanding of morality. His critical point can be put briefly. Suppose, as Tindal and Clarke do, "that there is a fitness and unfitness of actions founded in the nature of things and resulting from the relations that persons and things bear to one another", and also, as Tindal says, that these fitnesses are "the sole rule of God's action." It still does not follow that the relevant fitnesses will be comprehensible to us, because one of the terms of the fitness relation must be God's nature, which is infinite and incomprehensible. So some acts could be fitting for such a being without our being able to have a rational grasp of their fitness. In fact, Law says, if God is to act on what is fit for a being with his "divinely perfect and incomprehensible nature" then he must necessarily act by a rule above all human comprehension. He must do so precisely because he is not arbitrary but acts according to what fits the particular case of his own actions. "We have from this argument," Law concludes, "the utmost certainty that the rule or reasons of God's actions must in many cases be entirely inconceivable by us, and in no cases perfectly and fully apprehended."[23]

Law has so far drawn a voluntarist conclusion from the fitness theory itself on the assumption that its proponents think that God's own nature must be the rule of his action. But, he goes on, these theorists in fact appeal instead to "I know not what eternal, immutable reasons and relations of things ... which are a common rule and law of God and man." In opposition to them he argues that the nature and the relations of things are created by God, so that his willing cannot be based on them (Law 82–3). God's omnipotent action certainly suits the causes and effects he has created, but it cannot be "founded upon" their nature "because neither causes nor effects have any nature but what they owe to omnipotence." And the same is true of moral relations between rational beings (Law 84).

To Tindal's assertion that we could not love God were we to think him an arbitrary being acting out of caprice, Law replies: God's will is as opposed to caprice as his omnipotence is to weakness. It is the highest perfection, and therefore "we have the highest reason to love and adore God, because he is arbitrary, and acts according to his own all-perfect will." Because his will is as all-perfect as God himself is, it needs nothing outside itself for guidance,

---

[23] William Law, *The Case of Reason, or Natural Religion* (London, 1731), as it appears in *The Works of the Reverend William Law*, 9 vols. (Brockenhurst, Hampshire: G. Moreton, 1892), 2: 63–3. Cited in the text hereafter as Law.

and particularly nothing moral. Law emphatically declares that "Nothing has a sufficient moral reason or fitness to be done, but because it is the will of God that it should be done." Even when God wills that certain acts are fit to be done, this does not make them fit in themselves: their continuing fitness depends as thoroughly on God's continual willing of it as the existence of things depends on God's sustaining them (Law 86–7; cf. 68).

Law suggests that reliance on our own reason rather than on God for our guidance is the worst sort of pride (Law 59). The deists, he points out, claim that our own reason shows each of us all we need to know about how to live and what salvation requires. But this is as absurd as if we claimed that our own reason teaches us our language. We learn to speak from others, acquiring in the process whatever knowledge or insight past experience has given our culture. The same is true of morality. The powers of reason in people generally can be learned only by experience, and that shows them to be generally weak. There is no evidence of an inner light that guides us all, as the deists claim. And if we need the help of other humans in order to know anything at all, why might we not need the help of God if we are to know the most important things of all (Law 115–21)?

Here Law comes to the central point of his polemic against Tindal. It was a point that united all Christian opponents of deism: the need for revelation. Tindal is very clear that reason shows us morality and that morality suffices for salvation. Deists from Lord Herbert on argued that to think otherwise is to think God could be unjust, since revelation has not been given equally to all people. It was, however, generally agreed that the Christian doctrines of the fall and inherited sin, the incarnation, and salvation through Christ, were available to us only through revelation, not through natural religion. It is no surprise, therefore, that the devout Leland says that Herbert's central failing is to make no room for revelation (Leland 1: 6ff). But the need for revelation to support the special teachings of Christianity gives rise to a problem.

Moral rationalism seems to rule out revelation. But if morality is not centered on *a priori* necessary truths, or if performance of positive duties beyond those of morality is required for salvation, the door is open to the voluntarist version of Christianity and to the fear that God is after all only an arbitrary tyrant. The problem for Christian apologists was how to use moral rationalism to ward off voluntarism without falling into the deism that threatens Christian revelation—and with it Christian institutions and ministers.

The difficulty confronted Catholics as well as Protestants, and the first effort I know of to get around it comes from Malebranche. I shall not discuss here his effort to defend the need for divine revelation and for a unique church to bring that revelation to all mankind. I turn instead to Samuel Clarke, who hardly wished to defend the Roman church but who shows in clear form the source of the general line of thought that the moral rationalists used to defend revelation—and some priesthood or other.

The reasonableness of Christianity concerns Clarke at least as much as it did Locke. "Christianity," he says, "presupposes the truth of natural religion,"[24] and he holds that even the efficacy of divine grace is to be understood as the gift of the ability to understand the arguments that should move one to belief.[25] With a rational morality at the core of religion, what room is left for anything more than the deists would have admitted? Clarke devotes far more of his second set of Boyle lectures to arguing for the truth and necessity of the Christian revelation than he gives to demonstrating the existence of unchangeable moral obligations.[26] Having proved to his own satisfaction that the morality of Christianity is embodied in eternal moral truths, he then goes on to argue that most people cannot understand and appreciate these gifts of reason. The widespread weakness of reason, a sure sign of human corruption, is clear evidence that there was need for a revelation;[27] the Christian revelation best fills that need; and if this does not convince the reader of the truth and certainty of its message, nothing will.

Clarke offers arguments to support the belief that there must be a future life in which the virtuous will be rewarded and sinners punished.[28] Without that hope virtue could not be widely practiced. Yet most people are so enslaved by lusts and desires, so swayed by prejudice, so governed by superstition, that they cannot follow arguments like these. So although "the great obligations and the principal motives of morality are indeed certainly discoverable and demonstrable by right reason," most people

---

[24] *The Leibniz-Clarke Correspondence*, ed. H. G. Alexander (Manchester: Manchester University Press, 1956), 6.

[25] Sermon XXX, in Samuel Clarke, *The Works of Samuel Clarke, D.D.*, 4 vols. (London, 1738; reprinted New York: Garland, 1978), 1: 187.

[26] See the summary of the argument in *A Discourse concerning the Unchangeable Obligations of Natural Religion* (cited hereafter as *Obligations*), in *Works* 2: 596–600. In these lectures issues of moral philosophy as such are discussed only under the first proposition; under the remaining fourteen Clarke argues for the truth of specifically Christian doctrines and the need for a revelation.

[27] *Obligations*, lecture 15, *Works* 2: 730–1.   [28] *Obligations*, lecture 3–5, *Works* 2: 642–52.

must be instructed about them and about the future rewards and punishments they lead us to expect.[29] Moreover, such instruction must come from someone who can speak with *authority*. Reason alone and the philosophers have never been able to do so.[30]

Neither the knowledge of the morality of natural reason nor its motivating power, then, can reach the world it should govern, and "[f]or these reasons there was plainly wanting a divine revelation."[31] It is often thought that miracles must provide the main support for claims that the religion to whose revelation they attest is to be accepted.[32] What Clarke gives instead is an argument in support of revelation from the moral need for one. Moreover, he goes to great lengths to demonstrate that the Christian revelation supplies, more perfectly than any other, exactly what is needed. Not the least of the reasons for accepting it is that it centers on an authoritative teacher on whose word even the simplest will accept the truths that enable them to act morally. Happily that authority has been passed on to others, who have carried it down the ages. So long as reason remains weak in the many, the clergy will be there to see to it that virtue has its champions.[33]

Thomas Morgan tells us that the religion of nature consists only of "the eternal, immutable Rules and principles of moral Truth, Righteousness, and Reason." He rejects the other kind of religion, the revealed kind (Morgan 94). John Balguy thinks the deists wrong on exactly this point. He supports his opposition to voluntarism in part by showing some of its unpalatable implications. The voluntarist must think that we could learn about morality only through revelation. This would subvert natural religion as well as morality; and since it opens the possibility that God's will changes, it would require a new revelation every instant. We could not predict future duty from present (Balguy 365–6). But since morality does not depend on God's will, we can see that "the obligations of religion depend, and are entirely founded on the obligations of reason." Religion is simply obedience to God's commands; and obedience is owed, out of gratitude, only to justified commands (Balguy 383–4). But though eternal moral truth grounds revealed religion as well as natural, there are two problems about the purely

[29] *Obligations*, lecture 5, *Works* 2: 652–6.   [30] *Obligations*, lecture 6, *Works* 2: 656–7.
[31] *Obligations*, lecture 7, *Works* 2: 666ff.
[32] See, for example, Gaskin's Introduction to his edition of Hume's *Dialogues* in David Hume, *Principal Writings on Religion* (New York: Oxford University Press, 1993), xii.
[33] *Obligations*, lecture 5, *Works* 2: 655–6.

natural kind. First, "the fierceness and headiness of mankind will not ordinarily be restrained by the mild laws and pure dictates of reason" (Balguy 393). Revealed religion teaches us means of bringing "distempered minds" to act not only for reward but from an internal concern for rightness and truth. Reason could not have discovered these means; revelation is needed to show us how to perfect ourselves in complying with the rational dictates of natural religion (Balguy 403–4). Second, revelation is needed because most people are unable to see for themselves the rational truths at the core of both morality and natural religion. If moral obligation is a kind of force, "it is not, like corporeal attraction, effected at a distance." Moral reasons cannot operate where they are not known; revelation brings them to everyone, as reason cannot.

Moral rationalism extends moral community to God, and voluntarism confines it to humans. The Christian moral rationalists get God in but are forced to restrict the number of people who are equal members of the moral community. Sin or stupidity forces most people to take their morality at second hand, even though it is in principle available to reason. If reason were less feeble in the masses, the special gifts of Christianity would seem unnecessary.

I need not spend much time in pointing out the implication that religious readers would have drawn from Hume's sentimentalist view of morality. Hume goes out of his way to show that he leaves them with only a voluntarist understanding of God. The very way in which he poses the issue between sentimentalism and rationalism in the third paragraph of the second *Enquiry* suggests this. The question, he says, is whether "morals" have foundations that "should be the same to every rational intelligent being; or whether . . . they be founded entirely on the particular fabric . . . of the human species." The pertinent other rational intelligent being is of course God. To hold that morality rests on "eternal fitnesses" is to imply, as Hume points out, that immutable moral standards "impose an obligation . . . on the Deity himself," but of course he rejects such theories (T 456). God, moreover, is not our equal and does not share with us in the circumstances of justice. In relation to him we are like those rational but feeble creatures whom Hume imagines, who are too weak to make resentment of us effective. We might be gentle to such beings, but we could not enter into relations of justice with them (EPM 190). Pufendorf had made exactly this point. "A right," he says, "which is to have power among persons equal in nature" cannot be patterned after the relations between persons as drastically unequal as humans and God.[34] In a footnote to one of his additions to the *Treatise* Hume says the kind of thing that infuriated religious readers of Locke: "The order of the universe," he there says, "proves an omnipotent mind; that is, a mind whose will is constantly attended with the obedience of every creature.... Nothing more is requisite to give a foundation to all the articles of religion"—so that, notably, moral attributes are not requisite (T 633n.).

Hume's treatment of the problem of evil, in the *Dialogues concerning Natural Religion*, also belongs in the voluntarist camp.[35] Leibniz and Malebranche try to show that evil poses no moral difficulties for God's character. The voluntarists have no need to try. They simply do not think that God has to be morally intelligible. Hume's speakers argue that we cannot admit that evil exists and also have any justifiable views about God's moral attributes. Rather than proposing a solution to this problem Hume's discussion exacerbates it. If in the end he allows us any rationally grounded religious belief, it is belief in a deity so attenuated and so incomprehensible as to have no resemblance to the God of either Leibniz or Clarke.[36] We can hardly speak about Hume's deity in literally meaningful terms, and we certainly cannot be assured that we live in a moral community with him. And to make matters still worse, Hume's sentimentalism undercuts the intellectualist defense of revelation that the Christian moral rationalists invoke.

Hume is plainly aware of the voluntarist implications his view would have for believers. He is in effect telling his readers that, if there is to be any religion, it must be of a kind most of them would reject. His anti-religious aims were not hard to see. I have argued that he could not have been mistaken for an empiricist deist, and I hope it is now evident that he was not

---

[34] Samuel Pufendorf, *On the Law of Nature and of Nations*, trans. C. H. Oldfather and W. A. Oldfather (Oxford: Clarendon Press, 1934), II iii 5, p. 186.

[35] See M. A. Stewart, "An Early Fragment on Evil," in M. A. Stewart and John P. Wright, eds., *Hume and Hume's Connexions* (University Park: Pennsylvania State University Press, 1994), 160–70, for evidence that Hume was concerned with the problem of evil from the early stages of his philosophical work, not only after the *Treatise*.

[36] *Dialogues* 10 and 11 contain the discussion of the problem of evil; in 12 Hume suggests that the cause or causes of the world probably have some remote analogy to human intelligence. Whichever speaker represents Hume's own position, if any one of them does, the voluntarist religious implications of empiricism are made plain. See also EPM 294, where Hume says that the standard of rational truth is unalterable "even by the will of the Supreme Being," while the moral standard, arising from an animal constitution, "is ultimately derived from that Supreme Will," which made each kind of being have the nature it has.

a rationalist deist either. He did not need to be taken for an atheist to be read as posing a devastating problem for Christian believers. In the eighteenth century it would suffice for him to be a voluntarist. I do not know whether or not he was one, since I do not know how seriously to take his various assertions about belief in the existence of God. But if he meant to be taken as a believer, it is clear how his readers would understand the God he accepted. And I am confident that his devastating attack on moral rationalism was intended as a major part of his campaign to destroy all the foundations of religion, revealed as well as natural.

PART V
On Kant

13

Why Study Kant's *Groundwork*?

Kant's *Groundwork for the Metaphysics of Morals* is a very hard book to understand. But everyone who teaches moral philosophy believe that it's worth trying to do so. Why? There are three reasons.

First, Kant created a dramatically new way of thinking about morality and about ourselves as moral beings. He held that all previous attempts to spell out the principles of ethics had been mistaken. In the *Groundwork* he presented the fundamentals of a different vision of morality. And in later writings he showed how to work out the details of morality using his new formulation of its basis. To understand Kant's ethics historically is to come to see the emergence of a major new option in Western thought.

Second, Kant's ethical thought has been profoundly influential. It is one of the two or three most important contributions that modern moral philosophers have made to our culture. The *Groundwork* has always been the main text used to learn about Kant's ethics. Anyone who wants to understand the history of nineteenth- and twentieth-century moral philosophy and its importance for society has to understand this book.

Third, the positions Kant took in the *Groundwork* are very much alive in moral philosophy today. A renewal of scholarship, commentary, and philosophical discussion concerning the book began around the middle of the last century.[1] Many misunderstandings have been cleared away, and Kant's other writings on ethics have been brought in to illuminate this one. New philosophical insights from recent work are being used to show the depth and importance of what Kant said. Kantian views of morality are a

---

[1] H. J. Paton's *The Categorical Imperative* (London: Hutchinson, 1947) is a landmark in the modern revitalization of Kant scholarship. It was preceded by a few German contributions. John Rawls's *A Theory of Justice* (Cambridge, Mass.: Harvard University Press, 1971) showed how much some Kantian ideas could be used to help with current issues. Much of the current discussion of Kantian ethics reflects developments of Rawls's ideas.

central topic of contemporary moral philosophy. In developing Kant's positions to bring out their pertinence today, advocates of Kantian views depart more or less from what he himself actually said. But an understanding of the *Groundwork* is indispensable for anyone who wants to take part in current discussions of ethics.

These are strong claims about the importance of a short book. It would take another book, and a longer one, to support them all. Here I will try first to sketch Kant's epoch-making break with the past and then to indicate some of the developments underlying his importance for contemporary moral philosophy.

I. Kant's Historical Revolution

Two quotations will get us going. The first comes from St. Thomas Aquinas, the great thirteenth-century synthesizer of Roman Catholic doctrine. The second is from Kant.

Law directs the actions of those that are subject to the government of someone. Hence, properly speaking, none imposes a law on his own actions.

(Summa Theologiae IaIIae 93.5)

The rational being must always consider itself as giving law in a realm of ends ... Morality thus consists in the reference of all action to that legislation through which alone a realm of ends is possible. But the legislation must be encountered in every rational being itself, and be able to arise from its will.   (G 4:434)

Aquinas and Kant agree that morality centrally involves law and obedience to law. Both could agree with an important passage in St. Paul's Epistle to the Romans (2:14–15): "when the Gentiles, which have not the law, do by nature the things contained in the law, these, which have not the law, are a law unto themselves: Which shew the works of the law written in their hearts, their conscience also bearing witness." The gentiles do not have the written Jewish law, but they find an unwritten law in their hearts or consciences. For Aquinas, the law is put there by God. He finds it unthinkable that human beings might legislate the moral law that we are all to obey. Kant thinks that our own reason gives us the law. Morality can be understood only if we see that each of us is equally a law-giving member of the group of those who must also obey the moral law. He holds that each of us is both to legislate the law and to obey it.

Kant's remark comes from a part of the *Groundwork* in which he introduces the term "autonomy" to indicate what is distinctive about his own
view. The word had long been current in political discussions. An autonomous state was one that ruled itself. It could make its own laws without
asking permission from rulers of other states. Kant took the term from
political discourse and changed its meaning. He applied it to individuals
and to the morality that ought to govern the relations of persons to
themselves and to one another, regardless of the political laws under
which they lived. He said that morality is a human creation. It is the
legislation that comes from our own rational will.

We can see what a radical innovation this was by looking briefly at the
history of moral philosophy. Ancient thought about ethics from Socrates to
the time of St. Augustine centered on the question of human flourishing
(a translation of the Greek *eudaimonia*). What is the best life for a human?
Classical philosophers all thought that having good relations with others
constituted a major part of the kind of life anyone would want to live.
Consequently they held that in pursuing a good life for ourselves we would
not only have to control our own passions and desires; we would also have
to act thoughtfully and justly toward others. On this view virtue and
happiness are inseparable.

Christianity gave a new twist to the search for a good life. Our ultimate
good, theologians held, is to be found in a loving union with God. God
made us so that we all seek such a union. We may not realize that that is
what we want. But we are always dissatisfied with earthly goods. And this
dissatisfaction shows that the pagans were wrong to think that we might find
happiness in the present life. Moreover we are deeply flawed and sinful
beings. We ought to live in loving friendship with other people. But we are
dominated by selfish desires. Morality teaches us what we ought to do, but
we find in ourselves a stubborn resistance to doing it. Instead we seek what
we misguidedly think is our own individual good. We must be made to
obey God's laws by threats of punishment. Morality thus becomes something external to our own nature—at least to our fallen nature. It does not
come from within us, emerging as our own concern in the course of our
natural development. It has to be imposed on us.

What is God's relation to the laws he imposes on all human beings—the
laws of nature, as they came to be called? Aquinas held that God's intellect is
the source of these laws. God commands us to obey them because he knows

that they contain the core of justice and virtue. Two other medieval thinkers, Duns Scotus and William of Ockham, proposed an alternative. God is inscrutable and beyond human understanding, and he imposes on us whatever laws he chooses. The laws of nature contain the core of justice and virtue simply because God wills that we obey them. Later historians labeled these positions "intellectualism" and "voluntarism." Both positions were very much a part of arguments about morality with which Kant was familiar. Martin Luther's teaching derived from the thought of the medieval voluntarists, and Kant was raised a Lutheran. The German philosopher Leibniz and his follower Christian Wolff were strongly opposed to volun-tarism, and Kant learned Wolff's views from his first philosophy teachers.

Luther puts his view bluntly and forcefully: "God is he for whose will no cause or ground may be laid down as its rule and standard; for nothing is on a level with it or above it . . . What God wills is not right because he ought or was bound so to will; on the contrary, what takes place must be right, because he so wills."[2] This side of Lutheran teaching has a prominent place in the thought of Samuel Pufendorf, whose work on natural law was studied throughout Europe for over a century after its publication in 1672. His central point is simple. Christianity, as St. Paul shows, teaches that morality is obedience to law. Law is the command of a superior, and only God's commands can establish a morality for all humans. But then there cannot be moral requirements binding God, because—obviously—God can have no superior. It follows that there can be no morality common to God and humans. Pufendorf ridicules the very idea. "For who," he asks, "dare reason thus? Pay your debts, because God pays his. Be grateful, because God is kind to them that serve him . . . Honor your parents, because God honors his. Are not these reasonings manifestly absurd?"[3]

Pufendorf expresses what was then a widespread Christian feeling: we should humbly adore and obey God even if we do not understand him. Morality is simply obedience. There were many other Christians who found this position deeply disturbing. It puts God in the position of a tyrant and makes us into servile subjects. But Christ taught that the essence of the law is love: we are to love God above all and our neighbor as ourselves.

---

[2] *Martin Luther: Selections from His Writings*, ed. John Dillenberger (Garden City, N.Y.: Doubleday, 1962), 195–6.

[3] Quoted in J. B. Schneewind, *The Invention of Autonomy* (New York: Cambridge University Press, 1998), 140.

And a Pufendorfian God, who lays down arbitrary laws and gives no rationale for them, is not, the critics said, a God who can be loved. If we are to love God we must understand his moral commands as expressions of his love for us. It must be possible for us to understand morality as common to God and ourselves, however mysterious other aspects of God's activity may be. If we govern ourselves by following laws that we see are just and right, we will be acting as nearly in God's way as we can. This is what it means to say that we are made in God's image. It seemed impossible for the voluntarists to explain how this could be so.

In Kant's time there were very few atheists. Most people not only believed in God but also agreed that he was somehow indispensable for morality. The Scots philosopher David Hume was an exception. He developed a view of morality in which God played no role. He saw human feelings as the source of morality. Purely natural explanations could be given of those feelings. And there is nothing about us that takes us out of the realm of nature. We must see ourselves and our morality as causally determined parts of a causally determined nature.

Hume's view avoided the problems of the relation of God to morality, but it seemed to many people to deprive humans of any special dignity or worth. For Hume, we are only a kind of animal—cleverer than the rest, but otherwise not very different from them. Religious believers could not see morality in this way. They could not accept the idea that the natural world is the only world there is. We must belong to a supernatural spiritual world, they held, in which God is supreme. They therefore had to face the problem of how to preserve human dignity in a universe governed by the kind of God they could not give up.

The intellectualists thought that the voluntarists could not solve the problem but that they themselves could. If we can know the eternal truth about morality and are able to bring ourselves to follow its directives just from concern for righteousness, then we are self-governed. We have a special relation to God. We are the only part of his creation that can obey his laws just because we know what they are. It is because of our knowledge—especially our moral knowledge—that we are entitled to think that we are made in God's image.

Some intellectualists held that there are eternal self-evident principles governing morality. They compared such principles to the axioms of geometry. God knows the moral axioms and so do we. God necessarily governs himself by them. When we have an intuitive grasp of the moral axioms and work out how they apply to the case at hand, we are self-governed when we act as they direct. Other intellectualists made no appeal to such intuitively evident axioms. They held that God always acts for the best. He created the most perfect possible universe, and we are to be like him. We are to bring about the most perfect results we can. To do so we need to know which of the options before us will bring about the greatest increase in perfection. We are self-governed when we know what is best and decide to bring it into existence. Both sorts of intellectualists rejected purely naturalistic theories of the world and used their moral philosophies as part of their defense of a religious outlook.

Kant rejected Hume's naturalism and insisted that we are not merely natural beings, like the animals. Morality itself shows us that we have free will. Kant shared the intellectualists' aim of defending human dignity and argued that free will gives it to us. But he feared that the intellectualists were all too likely to think that only people with superior minds could be morally good. The moral feelings that Hume saw as central could be shared equally by everyone, but plainly some people are much smarter than others. Does it follow that moral knowledge is not equally available to everyone alike? It is hard to understand geometry; it may be equally hard for many to understand morality. It would also be difficult for most people to calculate which among the choices before them will bring about the greatest increase in perfection. In either case not everyone can be self-governed. Most people will have to obey the few who knew the truth about morality. This was a view that Christian Wolff held. Kant found it abhorrent. Hume's reliance on sentiment was part of a naturalistic view that Kant rejected. A purely intellectualist morality apparently led to an elitism that he also found unacceptable. He thus seemed to be forced into a voluntarist view. But Kant rejected the servile attitude that seemed to go with that theory. His new idea of the autonomy of the will gave him a way to resolve this complex problem. He accepted the voluntarist claim that morality stems from will, but he transformed the conception of will by making it into a special form of rationality—practical rationality. He could then say that because the will is itself rational it contains a law within it, governing all its activities. We do not need to grasp eternal truths or to calculate complex consequences. A simple formula governs our legislative activity. It enables us to test our plans for action and to reject some and accept others. And just as we can think out for ourselves what we ought to do, so we can motivate ourselves to do it. We do not need rewards or threats from others to make us act morally. God's will and ours are alike in these respects. What God necessarily wills is what we ought to will. We and God are fellow legislators of a single moral community. We are equal to God, not merely his servile subjects, because of our moral autonomy.

II. Kant's Current Importance

The conception of morality as autonomy was Kant's fundamental innovation in moral philosophy. In working out his vision of humans as autonomous agents Kant developed new ideas about freedom and the nature of action that are still being discussed. His view also had important implications for longstanding positions about the structure and content of morality. One of these implications accounts for much of the significance of Kantianism in current discussions. It is that no principle of human happiness can be the foundation of morality or show its point. Utilitarianism is the label most commonly applied to views that make happiness central to morality. Kantianism is opposed to all such views.

Kant never denied the importance of happiness. He criticized the Stoics for thinking that the pleasure of self-approval arising from awareness of living a virtuous life was happiness enough for human beings. Happiness is the satisfaction of desire, he held, and he insisted that finite beings such as we are need to have our desires satisfied. He held it to be an important duty for each of us to help others achieve happiness as they understood it. But he denied that morality is simply the set of virtues or directives that lead to happiness, either our own or that of everyone affected. He held that morality has a different role in our lives. Morality's function is to set the limits within which it is permissible for us to seek our own happiness and to help others pursue theirs.

Kant had several reasons for rejecting a morality of happiness. One of them is this. We have little if any control over what desires we have. To say that what we ought to do is determined by what people want is to subordinate ourselves to our causally determined nature. It is, in other words, to abandon our autonomy. But the moral law forbids us to do so. More generally, Kant thinks that we cannot accept any morality holding that the goods relevant to deciding what to do are made good, and can be known to be good, without any appeal to what is morally right or obligatory. Kant holds, against this, that only pleasures and pains that are allowed by the moral law are morally relevant. In order for a pleasure to count as relevant in deciding what to do, it must be one that can be obtained by a morally permissible act. So there must be a way of determining what acts are permissible or impermissible prior to knowing what goods in the situation are morally relevant. And Kant thought, of course, that there is such a way. The categorical imperative tells us whether or not we may act on any plan of action, and from this we can learn what acts we may or may not do.

Kantianism is thus an alternative to utilitarianism. It is not the only one. Various forms of intuitionism hold that we can grasp a number of self-evident moral truths by which to guide our actions. One of these truths tells us to be benevolent, or to help others attain happiness, but that is not the only principle. We are also to tell the truth, keep promises, and be just. Principles like these may come into conflict with the principle that tells us to increase the happiness of others. And it is far from self-evident that in cases of such conflict benevolence ought always to win out.

Intuitionism often seems to be the best account available of the common-sense morality that most of us share. We do not come to philosophy with some single universal principle that we use to get answers to all our moral questions. And we do seem to think that it is just obvious that we should keep promises, tell the truth, help others in need, be just, and so on. Yet intuitionism has defects. It does not suggest any mode of reasoning for settling controversies with other people about what to do. And it does not give us any way of critizing our pretheoretical moral convictions. Yet we know that people in the past have thought it "just obvious" that women should obey men, that people of color were inferior to white people, and that gay and lesbian practices were abhorrent and unnatural. It is hard to escape the thought that some of our "obvious" beliefs might be as benighted as these. But how can we tell?

One appeal of utilitarianism and of Kantianism is that each promises a way of arguing about moral disagreements and of criticizing socially accepted moral beliefs. During much of the nineteenth century British and American philosophers took utilitarianism and intuitionism to be the major alternatives in moral theory. Kant played little if any role in English-language ethics. And during much of the twentieth century,

English-language moral philosophers did not discuss the substantive issues of morality. They were concerned rather with whether moral beliefs were susceptible of rational proof. Was morality, as Hume held, simply a matter of sentiment? If it was rational, in what way? Was moral language used to express thought that could be true or false, or was it, rather, used just to express emotions?

These debates took place against the background of a widely shared assumption that utilitarianism captured the content or substance of morality, whether morality rested on reason or on feeling. Many philosophers were convinced, however, that utilitarianism led to morally unacceptable conclusions. But to oppose it they had little but intuitions or strong convictions. The first major effort to go beyond intuitionism and provide a systematic alternative to utilitarianism was John Rawls's *A Theory of Justice* (1971). Rawls presented a way of arguing in support of principles of justice that did not derive them from the good consequences that would follow from obeying them. Instead his principles could be used to determine the relevance of alleged goods and harms to moral decisions. He asserted what is now called "the priority of the right to the good," and he linked this strongly with Kant's moral views.

Rawls's work led to a great deal of constructive philosophical interest in Kant's ethics. Building on the scholarly work that had been published since the 1940s, American and British philosophers produced a substantial body of work influenced strongly by Kant's moral thought. New interpretations of almost every aspect of Kant's ethics were soon followed by important works applying Kant's insights to contemporary problems, such as world hunger. The English-language moral philosophy of the past decades has revolted to a large extent around controversies concerning Kantian moral philosophy, and Kant's views continue to vitalize discussions.

14

Autonomy, Obligation, and Virtue: An Overview of Kant's Moral Philosophy

Kant invented a new way of understanding morality and ourselves as moral agents. The originality and profundity of his moral philosophy have long been recognized. It was widely discussed during his own lifetime, and there has been an almost continuous stream of explanation and criticism of it ever since. Its importance has not diminished with time. The quality and variety of current defenses and developments of his basic outlook and the sophistication and range of criticism of it give it a central place in contemporary ethics.[1] In the present essay I offer a general survey of the main features of Kant's moral philosophy. Many different interpretations of it have been given, and his published works show that his views changed in important ways. Nonetheless there is a distinctive Kantian position about morality, and most commentators are agreed on its main outlines.[2]

   I should like to thank Richard Rorty, David Sachs, Larry Krasnoff, Paul Guyer, Fred Beiser, and Richard Flathman, who read this essay at various stages of its development and made helpful suggestions.

[1] Contemporary English-language study of Kant's ethics owes a great deal to the important commentaries of H. J. Paton, *The Categorical Imperative* (London: Hutchinson, 1946), and Lewis White Beck, *A Commentary to Kant's Critique of Practical Reason* (Chicago: University of Chicago Press, 1960), both of which helped stimulate German scholarship as well. John Rawls's widely read *A Theory of Justice* (Cambridge, Mass.: Harvard University Press, 1971) showed one direction in which Kantianism could be revised, and was a major impetus to the use of Kantian insights in developing general ethical theory and in handling concrete current issues.

[2] Although Kant did a great deal of thinking about ethics during his early years, he wrote little about it before the publication of the first *Critique*. That *Critique* contains some discussion of moral philosophy, but the major works are the following:

Groundwork of the Metaphysics of Morals (1785), reference to *Akademie* edition volume and page followed by the page number of the translation by H. J. Paton, *The Moral Law* (London: Hutchinson, 1948).

I

At the center of Kant's ethical theory is the claim that normal adults are capable of being fully self-governing in moral matters. In Kant's terminology, we are "autonomous." Autonomy involves two components. The first is that no authority external to ourselves is needed to constitute or inform us of the demands of morality. We can each know without being told what we ought to do because moral requirements are requirements we impose on ourselves. The second is that in self-government we can effectively control ourselves. The obligations we impose upon ourselves override all other calls for action, and frequently run counter to our desires. We nonetheless always have a sufficient motive to act as we ought. Hence no external source of motivation is needed for our self-legislation to be effective in controlling our behavior.

Kant thinks that autonomy has basic social and political implications. Although no one can lose the autonomy that is a part of the nature of rational agents,[3] social arrangements and the actions of others can encourage lapses into governance by our desires, or heteronomy. Kant, as we shall see, found it difficult to explain just how this could happen; but he always held that the moral need for our autonomy to express itself was incompatible with certain kinds of social regulation. There is no place for others to tell us what morality requires, nor has anyone the authority to do so—not our neighbors, not the

---

Critique of Practical Reason (1788), references followed by page numbers of the translation by Lewis White Beck (Indianapolis: Bobbs-Merrill, 1956).

Metaphysics of Morals, in two parts, known as the *Doctrine of Right* and the *Doctrine of Virtue*, which were published separately in 1797; references when quotations are from the *Doctrine of Virtue* followed by the page number of the translation by Mary Gregor (Philadelphia: University of Pennsylvania Press, 1964).

Religion within the Limits of Reason Alone (1793), references followed by the page number of the translation by Theodore M. Greene and Hoyt H. Hudson (1934; 2d edn., New York: Harper & Row, 1960).

Kant's essays on history and politics are important sources as well. There are two useful collections: Lewis White Beck *et al.*, *Kant on History* (Indianapolis: Bobbs-Merrill, 1963), and Ted Humphrey, *Perpetual Peace and Other Essays* (Indianapolis: Hackett, 1983). References are followed by H and page number from the Beck translation.

Volumes 27 and 29 of the *Akademie* edition of *Kants gesammelte Schriften* contain over a thousand pages of student notes on Kant's classes on ethics, which he taught between twenty and thirty times from 1756–7 to 1793–4 (see Emil Arnoldt, *Gesammelte Schriften* [Berlin: 1909], vol. V, 335). The earliest notes come from 1763–4, the latest from 1793–4. Notes taken in 1780–1 are available in English: *Lectures on Ethics*, trans. Louis Infield (originally 1930) (New York: Harper & Row, 1963).

The student notes offer many insights into Kant's ethical thought, but they also pose several new interpretative problems. In this essay I concentrate on the published works.

[3] Not only humans: Kant thinks any rational agents would be autonomous.

magistrates and their laws, not even those who speak in the name of God. Because we are autonomous, each of us must be allowed a social space within which we may freely determine our own action. This freedom cannot be limited to members of some privileged class. The structure of society must reflect and express the common and equal moral capacity of its members.

Kant's interest in the social and political implications of autonomy is shown in many places. In the short essay "What is enlightenment?" Kant urges each of us to refuse to remain under the tutelage of others. I do not need to rely on "a book which understands for me, a pastor who has a conscience for me." We must think and decide for ourselves. To foster this, public freedom of discussion is necessary, particularly in connection with religion. An enlightened ruler will allow such discussion to flourish, knowing he has nothing to fear from it (7:35, 40ff / H 3–4, 8ff). Later in "Perpetual Peace" Kant expressed the hope that eventually all states will be organized as republics, in which every citizen can express his moral freedom[4] publicly in political action (7:349ff / H 93ff).

What stands out in Kant's vision of the morality through which we govern ourselves is that there are some actions we simply have to do. We impose a moral law on ourselves, and the law gives rise to obligation, to a necessity to act in certain ways. Kant does not see morality as springing from virtuous dispositions that make us want to help others. He sees it as always a struggle. Virtue itself is defined in terms of struggle: It is "moral strength of will" in overcoming temptations to transgress the law (*Morals*, 7:405 / 66–7). Law is prior to virtue, and must control desires to help others as well as desires to harm.

It has sometimes been thought that the salience of law and obedience in Kant's view shows that he had an authoritarian cast of mind. Some unpublished early notes show quite clearly that the moral stance behind his emphasis on obligation was very different. "In our condition," he wrote around 1764,

when universal injustice stands firm, the natural rights of the lowly cease. They are therefore only debtors; the superiors owe them nothing. Therefore these superiors are called gracious lords. He who needs nothing from them but justice and can hold them to their debts does not need this submissiveness.[5]

---

[4] The term "his" is used advisedly here: Kant had unfortunate views about women. He also thought servants were not sufficiently independent to be entitled to full political status.

[5] This is from marginal notes Kant jotted down as he was reading Rousseau's *Social Contract* and *Emile* during 1763–4 (20:140–1; I have added some punctuation). It is largely from these notes that we know of the considerable impact that Rousseau had on Kant.

A society built around the virtues of benevolence and kindness is for Kant a society requiring not only inequality[6] but servility as well. If nothing is properly mine except what someone graciously gives me, I am forever dependent on how the donor feels toward me. My independence as an autonomous being is threatened. Only if I can claim that the others *have to* give me what is mine by right can this be avoided. Kant makes the point even more plainly in a comment written a few years later:

Many people may take pleasure in doing good actions but consequently do not want to stand under obligations toward others. If one only comes to them submissively they will do everything; they do not want to subject themselves to the rights of people, but to view them simply as objects of their magnanimity. It is not all one under what title I get something. What properly belongs to me must not be accorded to me merely as something I ask for.[7]

Kant did not deny the moral importance of beneficent action, but his theoretical emphasis on the importance of obligation or moral necessity reflects his rejection of benevolent paternalism and the servility that goes with it,[8] just as the centrality of autonomy in his theory shows his aim of limiting religious and political control of our lives.

II

Kant's attribution of autonomy to every normal adult was a radical break with prevailing views of the moral capacity of ordinary people. The natural-law theorists whose work was influential through the seventeenth and much of the eighteenth centuries did not on the whole think that most people could know, without being told, everything that morality requires of them. The lawyers were willing to admit that God had given everyone the ability to know the most basic principles of morality. But they held that the many are unable to see all the moral requirements implicit in the principles and often cannot grasp by themselves what is required in particular cases. Like Kant later, the natural lawyers thought of morality as centering on obligations imposed by law. For them, however, God is the legislator of moral

---

[6] 20:36, "kindnesses occur only through inequality."   [7] R 6736, 19:145.
[8] See Kant's late remarks on servility in *Morals*, 6:434–6; 99–101; see also Thomas E. Hill, Jr., "Servility and Self-Respect," *Monist* 57 (1973), 87–104.

law, and humans his unruly subjects. Most people are unwilling to obey the laws of nature, and must be made to do so through the threat of punishment for non-compliance. This view was built into the concept of obligation as the natural lawyers understood it. They held that obligation could only be explained as necessity imposed by a law backed by threats of punishment for disobedience. They would accordingly have thought Kant's view that we can make and motivate ourselves to obey the moral law not only blasphemous but foolish.[9] They would also have wondered what kind of account of moral necessity Kant could give, once he refused to appeal to an external lawgiver or to sanctions.

A number of philosophers before Kant had begun to reject the natural lawyers' low estimate of human moral capacity, and to present theories in which a greater ability for self-governance is attributed to people. A brief look at the philosophers whom Kant himself has told us were important in his development will help us see how far beyond them he went.[10]

In deliberate opposition to natural-law views, the British philosophers Shaftesbury and Hutcheson portrayed virtue rather than law and obligation as central to morality.[11] They argued that to be virtuous we have only to act regularly and deliberately from benevolent motives that we naturally approve. Because approval is naturally felt by everyone, and because we all have benevolent motives, we can all equally see and do what morality calls for, without need of external guidance or of sanctions. Christian Wolff, whose philosophy dominated German universities when Kant was a student, tried to reach a similar conclusion by a different route.[12] He argued that we can be self-governed because we can see for ourselves what the

---

[9] In the essay "On the Common Saying: 'That may be true in theory but it does not work in practice'," Kant says that in connection with our moral self-legislation "man thinks of himself according to an analogy with the divinity" (8:280 n.). The essay is translated in Hans Reiss, ed., *Kant's Political Writings* (Cambridge: Cambridge University Press, 1970).

[10] The standard work on the development of Kant's ethics is Josef Schmucker, *Die Ursprünge der Ethik Kants* (Meisenheim am Glan: Anton Hain, 1961). There is no reliable study of the subject in English.

[11] For selections from Shaftesbury and Hutcheson, see. D. D. Raphael, *The British Moralists*, 2 vols. (Oxford: Oxford University Press, 1969), and J. B. Schneewind, *Moral Philosophy from Montaigne to Kant*, 2 vols. (Cambridge: Cambridge University Press, 1990). Their works were available in German, and Kant owned the translations of Hutcheson's most important writings.

[12] There are no studies of Wolff in English, and little of his work has been translated. Lewis White Beck, *Early German Philosophy* (Cambridge, Mass.: Harvard University Press, 1969) discusses his general philosophy but says little about his ethics. For an excellent study of the early German enlightenment and Wolff's place in it, see Hans M. Wolff, *Die Weltanschauung der deutschen Aufklärung* (Bern, 1949). For selections in English of his ethics, see Schneewind, *Moral Philosophy from Montaigne to Kant*, vol. I.

consequences of our actions will be, and can tell which action will bring about the greatest amount of perfection. Since we are always drawn to act so as to bring about what we believe is the greatest amount of perfection, Wolff says we are bound or necessitated to do what we think will be for the best. And this seems to him to explain the necessity we call "moral," or our moral obligation. In political matters we are obligated or obliged to act by sanctions imposed by a political ruler; but in morality we oblige ourselves to act through our perception of perfection. Hence in morality we are self-governed. We need no sanctions to move us to act for the best.[13]

Kant came to hold that neither of these kinds of moral theory was acceptable. They imply that the only necessity involved in morality is the necessity of using a means to an end you desire. If you do not want the end, there is no need for you to do the act that leads to it. But Kant thinks it is just a contingent empirical fact that you have the desires you have.[14] If so, then on these views it is a matter of happenstance whether or not someone is bound by any moral necessity. Obligation becomes a matter of what one wants to do. But true moral necessity, Kant held, would make an act necessary regardless of what the agent wants.

One philosopher prior to Kant, the Lutheran pastor C. A. Crusius,[15] had taken moral necessity to be independent of our contingent ends. There are, Crusius said, obligations of prudence, which arise from the need to act in a certain way to attain one's end. But there are also obligations of virtue, or moral obligations, and these make it necessary to act in certain ways regardless of any of one's own ends. Both the knowledge of these require-ments and the motive to comply with them are available to everyone alike

---

[13] These views are compendiously presented in Christian Wolff, *Vernünftige Gedancken von der Menschen Thun und Lassen* (1720).

[14] Kant holds that it is necessarily true that each of us desires his or her own happiness, and he sometimes equates happiness with the satisfaction of the totality of our desires. But no single desire is a necessary feature of any particular individual. This is a point on which many of Kant's recent critics, particularly those sympathetic to Aristotle, disagree with him. They would argue that some desires or motives or active dispositions are essential to the individual identity of the person. See, for example, Jonathan Lear, *Aristotle: The Desire to Understand* (Cambridge: Cambridge University Press, 1988), p. 189. Kant would think that if you must have some specific effective desire then you are not free with respect to it. Kant does not think, as some of his critics believe, that the free will constitutes the whole identity of each individual. But he does think that whatever constitutes individual identity does so only contingently.

[15] Crusius was a leader of the anti-Wolffian movement. His moral philosophy is contained in his *Anweisung, vernünftig zu leben* (1744). There is good discussion of his general position in Beck, *Early German Philosophy*. For translated selections, see Schneewind, *Moral Philosophy from Montaigne to Kant*, vol. II.

because certain laws are incorporated in the structure of our will, and carry their own impetus to action. Because everyone has a will, everyone can always know what morality requires; and when we act accordingly we are determining ourselves to action. Crusius thus explains the idea of moral obligation in terms of an unconditional necessity, and claims that because this necessity binds our will by its own nature we need no external guidance or stimulus to be moral. Crusius's aim in asserting our high moral capacity was in fact to show that we are fully responsible for our actions before God. He took the laws structuring our will to obligate us because they are God's commands; and he believed that obedience is our highest virtue. If Crusius provided Kant with some of the tools he used to work out his idea of autonomy, he was not the inspiration for that idea.

It took a radical critic of society, Jean-Jacques Rousseau, to suggest the idea. Rousseau convinced Kant that everyone must have the capacity to be a self-governing moral agent, and that it is this characteristic that gives each person a special kind of value or dignity.[16] Culture in its present corrupt state conceals this capacity of ours, Rousseau thought, and society must be changed to let it show and be effective. In the *Social Contract* he called for the construction of a community in which everyone agrees to be governed by the dictates of the "general will," a will representing each individual's truest and deepest aims and directed always at the good of the whole. The general will would have to be able to override the passing desires each of us feels for private goods. But, Rousseau said, "the impulse of appetite alone is slavery, and obedience to the law one has prescribed for oneself is freedom."[17] Previous thinkers had frequently used the metaphor of slavery to describe the condition in which we are controlled by our passions, but for them the alternative was to follow laws that God or nature prescribe. Rousseau held

---

[16] There is considerable difficulty in interpreting Rousseau's influence on Kant. As indicated above, the most important evidence comes from the notes Kant made when he first read *Emile* and the *Social Contract* during 1763–4 (20:1–192). One of the most frequently quoted notes compares Rousseau's clarification of the hidden aspects of human nature to Newton's uncovering of the hidden aspects of physical nature (20:58–9). Another is more personal: "I am myself a researcher by inclination. I feel the whole thirst for knowledge and the eager unrest to move further on into it, also satisfaction with each acquisition. There was a time when I thought this alone could constitute the honor of humanity and I despised the know-nothing rabble. Rousseau set me straight. This delusory superiority vanishes, I learn to honor men, and I would find myself more useless than a common laborer if I did not believe this observation could give everyone a value which restores the rights of humanity" (20:44).

[17] *Social Contract*, I. viii.§4, in *On the Social Contract*, ed. Roger D. Masters, trans. Judith R. Masters (New York: St. Martin's Press, 1978), 56.

that we make our own law and in doing so create the foundation for a free and just social order. This thought became central to Kant's understanding of morality.

III

The problem Kant faced was to show how such law-making is possible. In particular he had to explain how we can impose a necessity upon ourselves. If my obligations arise simply through my own will, how can there be any real constraints on my action? Cannot I excuse myself from any obligations I alone impose? Rousseau had nothing to suggest beyond the thought that conscience is a sentiment that moves us without regard for our own interest; and we have already seen why Kant could not accept that suggestion. Someone might not have conscientious sentiments, or might get rid of them. Then on such a view no obligations bind her. Moral necessity could not be explained on that basis. Kant eventually found an explanation by comparing moral necessity to the necessity involved in the laws governing the physical universe. Kant was a Newtonian. He held that the sequence of events in the world is necessary. But its laws involve no commands and no sanctions. Morality, however, is not science. Science shows us how the world has to be. Morality tells us how it ought to be. How can the model of scientific laws help us understand morality?

Kant had read Rousseau and rethought morality before he came to the breakthrough that led to the critical philosophy.[18] In developing his new view of morality he used the tools the critical standpoint gave him. In the *Critique of Pure Reason* he argued that perceptual experience of the world shows only what *does* happen. Since laws say what *has to* happen they must involve a non-experiential, or *a priori*, aspect, and it must be this that explains the necessity they impart. How is this non-experiential aspect of lawfulness to be explained? The mind, Kant answered, involves the activity of imposing different forms of order on the perceptual material that its passive receptivity gives it. The forms of order are not externally imposed

---

[18] In the 1763–4 notes (see n. 5 in this chapter) there are several attempts to formulate the principle behind what Kant later called the categorical imperative. There are also clear indications both of the distinction between it and the hypothetical imperative and of the idea that the former is central to morality.

on the mind. They are an aspect of itself, the aspect through which it makes experience lawful. And they are "pure" or devoid of any empirical content in themselves. Their constitution is independent of their actual forming of perceptions into lawfully ordered sequences.

The question then is whether there is an aspect of the mind that does for action what the mental activities revealed in the first *Critique* do for experience. Thinking in terms of separate faculties of the mind, Kant attributes the initiation of action to the will, responding to desires. Desires, he assumes, are not rational as such. They arise in us because we are finite beings, with bodily and other needs. If there is to be rationality in action, the will must be its source. Kant therefore equates the will with practical reason. Does the faculty of practical reason have an inherent structure in the way that the faculty of pure reason does? If it does, and if it imposes form on the givens we feel as desires, then we have a clue to an explanation of exactly how and why we are autonomous. Taking the activity of practical reason as the source of the necessities that we impose on our willed behavior would show that these necessities are no more escapable than those that give structure to the physical world. They could therefore constitute our morality.

IV

To translate this idea into a moral theory, Kant had to show that the main concepts of morality can be explained in terms of a self-imposed necessity. We can begin to see how he does this by examining the way he relates three ideas central to morality: the ideas of the moral worth of an agent, of the rightness of an action, and of the goodness of the states of affairs that are the goals or outcomes of action.

One way of relating these ideas is to take as basic the goodness of states of affairs that can be brought about by human action. We consider, say, that being happy, or having fully developed talents, is intrinsically good. Then a right act can be defined as one that brings about good states of affairs, or brings them about to the greatest extent possible; and a good agent is one who habitually and deliberately does right acts. In such a scheme, right acts will have only an instrumental value, and we can and indeed must know what is good before we can make justifiable claims about what acts are right. Such a scheme is a common feature of the work of Kant's predecessors. Kant rejected it.

He rejected it because it makes autonomy in his sense impossible. Suppose that a kind of state of affairs is intrinsically good because of the very nature of that kind of state of affairs. Then the goodness occurs independently of the will of any finite moral agent, and if she must will to pursue it, she is not self-legislating. Suppose the goodness of states of affairs comes from their conformity to some standard. Then the standard itself is either the outcome of someone's will—say, God's—or it is self-subsistent and eternal. In either case, conformity to it is not autonomy.[19] Conformity would be what Kant calls heteronomy.

An alternative way of relating the three moral concepts became available to Kant through the idea that moral necessity, as embedded in the laws of morality, might have a pure *a priori* status akin to that of the necessity characterizing Newton's gravitational laws. While the mind imposes necessity in both cases, in morality the relevant aspect of mind is the rational will. This leads Kant to take the concept of the good agent as basic. Think of the good agent as one whose will is wholly determined *a priori*, and think of the pattern of that determination as the moral law.[20] Then we can say that it is necessarily true that whatever acts such an agent does are right acts; and whatever states of affairs such an agent deliberately brings about through those acts are good states of affairs. Kant makes it clear in the second *Critique* that this is his position:

the concept of good and evil is not defined prior to the moral law, to which, it would seem, the former would have to serve as foundation; rather the concept of good and evil must be defined after and by means of the law.

(*Practical Reason* 5:62–3 / 65)

For Kant, then, the rightness of acts is prior to the goodness of states of affairs, because only outcomes of right acts can count as good states of affairs. We do not discover what is right by first finding out what is good. Indeed we cannot determine what states of affairs are good without first knowing what is right.

---

[19] Those who insisted that God laid down the laws of morality by absolute fiat argued that unless that were true, God would be limited by something external to himself. They thought that even eternal moral standards would be an intolerable constraint on God's absolute freedom.

[20] Pure theoretical reason is an activity determined *a priori*, and one might think of one of its patterns of activity as embodying the "causal law." The causal law, in this sense, explains why every event must have a cause, but does not alone tell us what event causes what other event; to obtain this knowledge we need data of experience in addition. Similarly, as I explain later, the moral law does not by itself tell us which specific acts are obligatory; we must use it to test maxims in order to learn what we ought to do.

In order to know what is right all we need to know is what the perfectly good agent would do. Then whenever there is an act that a perfectly good agent could not omit, it is an act anyone in those circumstances has to do.[21]

Kant thinks one more step must be taken before we can obtain a full account of the moral concepts. So far we have considered a will completely determined by its own inner lawfulness. Because this law is a law constituting practical reason, such a will—unlike ours—would be perfectly rational. We finite beings do not have what Kant calls a "holy will," a will so fully determined by its inner lawful constitution that it acts spontaneously and without struggle. Our desires clamor for satisfaction whether they are rational or not. Hence for us the operation of the law in our rational will is not automatic. We feel its operation within us as a constraint, because it must act against the pull of desire. In finite beings, Kant says, the moral law "necessitates," rather than acting necessarily (*Groundwork*, 4:413–14 / 81). The terminology is not helpful, but Kant's thought here is familiar. If you were perfectly reasonable, you would go to the dentist to have that aching tooth looked at; and if you do not go because you fear dentists, you will find yourself thinking that you really ought to go. This is a prudential illustration of something that holds in the purely moral realm as well. When we see a compelling reason to do an act we are reluctant to do, we may not do it; but we admit we ought to.

The term "ought" is central to our moral vocabulary because the tension between reason and desire is central to our moral experience. "Ought" can be defined, on Kant's view, by saying that whatever a holy will, or perfectly rational will, necessarily *would* do is what we imperfectly rational agents *ought* to do (*Groundwork*, 4:413–14 / 81; *Practical Reason*, 325: / 32–3; *Morals*, 6:394–5 / 54–5). When we speak of our obligation to do something, we are referring to the necessity of a given act, without specifying which act is necessary; and to call an act a duty is to say that it is an action that is obligatory. It is Kant's belief in the importance of struggle in the moral life that leads him to his view that virtue cannot be defined as a settled habit or disposition. God, Kant thinks, necessarily acts morally and for that reason cannot have virtue. Only beings who find morality difficult and who develop persistence in struggling against the temptations can be virtuous.

---

[21] Some theorists have taken the rightness of acts as basic, defining a good agent as one who has a conscious habit of doing such acts, and good states of affairs as those intended to be the outcome of right acts. This view tends to go along with intuitionist explanations of how we know what is right. Thomas Reid's *Essays on the Active Powers of Man* (1788) offers one theory of this kind.

We finite beings will never get to the point at which we do not need the strength to resist desire. We are neither angels nor animals. Virtue is our proper station in the universe (*Morals*, 6:405–9 / 66–71).

V

If we grant Kant his account of the central moral concepts, we want next to know what the moral law is, and how and to what extent it can serve as a principle for showing us what we ought to do. Many critics, from Hegel to the present, have argued that Kant's principle cannot yield any results at all, because it is a formal principle.[22] Are they right?

I have tried to explain why, in order to assure the autonomy of the moral agent, the moral law must be pure and *a priori*. This means, Kant insists, that the law must be *formal*. Like the logical law of contradiction, which rules out any proposition of the form "P and not-P", the moral law must not itself contain any "matter" or content. Nonetheless, Kant thinks form without content in morality is as empty as he thinks it would be in our experience of nature. There must be content, Kant holds, but it can only come from outside the will—from desires and needs, shaped by our awareness of the world in which we live into specific urges to act or plan for action. Our finitude makes the needy aspect of the self as essential to our particular mode of being as is the free will. It takes the two working together to produce morality. But all that the moral law can do is to provide the form for matter that comes from our desires.

---

[22] A brilliant account of Hegelian objections of this kind, as well as other criticisms, is given in F. H. Bradley, *Ethical Studies* (1876; 2d edn., Oxford: Clarendon Press, 1927) ch. 2. The literature on the subject is extensive. The best book in English is Onora (O'Neill) Nell, *Acting on Principle: An Essay on Kantian Ethics* (New York: Columbia University Press, 1975), to which I am much indebted. For a sample of other criticisms of Kant see C. D. Broad, *Five Types of Ethical Theory* (London, 1930), ch. 5. See also the articles by Jonathan Harrison, "Kant's Examples of the First Formulation of the Categorical Imperative," *Philosophical Quarterly* 7 (1957); Julius Ebbinghaus, "Interpretation and Misinterpretation of the Categorical Imperative" (1959), repri. Robert Paul Wolff, ed., *Kant: A Collection of Critical Essays* (Garden City, N.Y.: Anchor/Doubleday, 1967), 211–27; Jonathan Kemp, "Kant's Examples of the Categorical Imperative," *Philosophical Quarterly* 8: 63–71 (1958); Nelson Potter, "Paton on the Application of the Categorical Imperative," *Kant-Studien* 64 (1973): 411–22; Ottfried Höffe, "Kants kategorischer Imperativ als Kriterium des Sittlichen," *Zeitschrift für philosophische Forschung* 31 (1977): 354–84; and the following books: Paton, *The Categorical Imperative*; Marcus G. Singer, *Generalization in Ethics* (New York: Alfred A. Knopf, 1961); Bruce Aune, *Kant's Theory of Morals* (Princeton, N.J.: Princeton University Press, 1979); and John Atwell, *Ends and Principles in Kant's Moral Thought* (Dordrecht: D. Reidel, 1986).

Our urges to act come to the will through what Kant calls "maxims." A maxim is a personal or subjective plan of action, incorporating the agent's reasons for acting as well as a sufficient indication of what act the reasons call for. When we are fully rational, we act, knowing our circumstances, in order to obtain a definite end, and aware that under some conditions we are prepared to alter our plans. Because circumstances and desires recur, a maxim is general. It is like a private rule. A maxim might look like this: If it is raining, take an umbrella in order to stay dry, unless I can get a ride. We often do not think explicitly about the circumstances or the contingencies when we are acting, and Kant does not always include them in his examples of maxims. Sometimes we do not even think of the purpose or goal of an action, only of what we are intent on doing. But if we are rational our action always has a purpose, and we are responsive to the surroundings in which we act. A full maxim simply makes all this explicit. A rational agent tests her maxims before acting on them. To do so she uses the laws of rational willing.

Kant thinks there are two basic laws of rational willing. One governs goal-oriented action generally, and is easily stated:

Who wills the end, wills (so far as reason has decisive influence on his actions) also the means which are indispensably necessary and in his power.

(*Groundwork*, 4:417 / 84–5)

This simply says that when a rational agent is genuinely in pursuit of a goal, she must and will do whatever is needed to get it. Otherwise she is not really pursuing the goal. Now whenever there is a law determining a perfectly rational being to action, there is a counterpart, couched in terms of "ought," governing the actions of imperfectly rational beings such as ourselves. Kant calls such "ought" counterparts of the laws of rational willing "imperatives." He uses this term because the laws of rational willing appear as constraining us in the way that commands do. The "ought" counterpart of the law of goal-oriented willing is easily stated:

Whoever wills an end ought to will the means.

Kant calls it the "hypothetical" imperative. It is hypothetical because the necessity of action that it imposes is conditional. You ought to do a certain act *if* you will a certain end.[23]

---

[23] The formula given indicates the essential form underlying all particular hypothetical imperatives ("If you want to preserve your health, you ought to go to the dentist"). What makes an imperative

Given Kant's claim that means–ends necessity is inadequate for morality, it is plain that he must think there is another law of rational willing, and so another kind of "ought" or imperative. The kind of "ought" that does not depend on the agent's ends arises from the moral law; and Kant calls the imperative version of that law "the categorical imperative." The moral law itself, Kant holds, can only be the form of lawfulness itself, because nothing else is left once all content has been rejected. The moral law can therefore be stated as follows:

A perfectly rational will acts only through maxims which it could also will to be universal law.

When this appears to us in the form of the categorical imperative, it says:

Act only according to that maxim through which you can at the same time will that it should become a universal law.   (*Groundwork*, 4:421 / 88)

We might think of Kant as recommending a two-stage testing of maxims. First test a maxim by the hypothetical imperative. Does the proposed act effectively bring about a desired end? If not, reject it; and if it does, test it by the categorical imperative. If it passes this test, you may act on it, but if it does not, you must reject it. It is not hard to see how to apply the test of prudential rationality. The question is whether the test of morality, the categorical imperative, actually enables us to decide whether or not we may act on a maxim.

Kant gives us a formulation of the categorical imperative that he thinks is easier to use than the one I have already cited:

Act as if the maxim of your action were to become through your will a universal law of nature.   (*Groundwork*, 4:421 / 89)

Now suppose you need money. You think of getting some by asking a friend to lend it to you, but you have no intention of ever repaying him.

---

hypothetical is not the appearance of an "if" clause in its formulation. Such clauses might appear in categorical imperatives: "If you are asked a question, you ought to answer truthfully." And they need not appear in hypothetical imperatives: "Eat whenever you are hungry." The sole defining feature of a hypothetical imperative is that it obligates the agent to an action only on condition that the agent has desire for something that the action would bring about. For an excellent discussion, see Thomas E. Hill, Jr., "The Hypothetical Imperative," *Philosophical Review* 82 (1973), 429–50.

You plan to make a false promise to repay. Your maxim (omitting circum-stances and conditions) is something like this: Use a lying promise to get money I want. Suppose this passes the prudential test. You then consider whether your maxim could be a universal law of nature, whether there could be a world in which everyone was moved, as by a law of nature, to make lying promises to get what they want. It would have to be a world in which it is prudentially rational to make a lying promise to get money. Well, if everyone made lying promises it would be pretty obvious, and people would stop believing promises. But in a world where no promises are trusted, it cannot be rational to try to use a promise in this way. Thus you cannot coherently think a world for which your maxim is a law of nature. You are therefore not permitted to act on it (*Groundwork*, 4:422 / 89–90).

Another example shows a different way in which the categorical impera-tive works. I pass someone collapsed on the street, and decide not to help him. My maxim is something like this: Ignore people in need of help, in order not to interfere with my plans. Kant says that I can coherently *conceive* of a world of people indifferent to one another's distress. But he believes that I cannot *will* the existence of such a world. Look at it this way. As a rational agent I necessarily will the means to any of my ends. The help of others is often a means I need for my own ends. So it would be irrational to will to exclude the help of others as a possible means when I need it. But if I universalize my maxim, I will to make it a law of nature that no one helps others in need. I would therefore be willing both that others help me when I need it and that no one help others when they need it. This is incoherent willing. Hence I may not act on my maxim (*Groundwork*, 4:423 / 90–1).[24]

When we use the categorical imperative in these cases we suppose that we are examining a maxim embodying the agent's genuine reasons for propos-ing the action, rather than irrelevancies (such as that the act will be done by a gray-bearded man) that might let it get by the categorical imperative. A vocabulary for formulating our plans is also presupposed (though that vocabulary itself might be called into question, as when we reject racist language).[25] Given these assumptions, the examples show that if maxims of the kind they involve are what the categorical imperative is to

[24] There are many other views about how universalizability or the application of the formula of universal law should be understood. For an excellent discussion, see Christine Korsgaard, "Kant's Formula of Universal Law," *Pacific Philosophical Quarterly* 66 (1985), 24–47.

[25] See Barbara Herman, "The Practice of Moral Judgment," *Journal of Philosophy* 82 (1985), 414–35.

test, then the moral law is not empty. There are at least some cases in which we can assess the moral permissibility of a plan simply by considering its rationality, without basing our conclusion on the goodness or badness of its consequences. The Kantian position is a real option for understanding morality.

VI

The categorical imperative can be formulated in several ways. Kant thinks they are all equivalent, and insists that the first formulation, the one we have been considering, is basic. Though the others bring out various aspects of the moral law, they cannot tell us more than the first formula does. It concentrates on the agent's point of view. The second formulation draws our attention to those affected by our action:

Act in such a way that you always treat humanity, whether in your own person or in the person of another, never simply as a means, but always at the same time as an end.   (*Groundwork*, 4:429 / 96)

Kant is saying that the ends of others—if morally permissible—set limits to the ends we ourselves may pursue. We must respect the permissible ends of others, and we may make others serve our own purposes only when they as moral agents assent to such use, as when someone willingly takes a job working for another. Thus we may not pursue our own ends if they impermissibly conflict with the ends of others.[26] We are also to forward the ends of others, a point to which I will shortly return.

The third formulation instructs us to look at agent and recipient of action together in a community as we legislate through our maxims:

All maxims as proceeding from our own law-making ought to harmonize with a possible kingdom of ends as a kingdom of nature.   (*Groundwork*, 4:436 / 104)

Here we are told always to think of ourselves as members of a society of beings whose permissible ends are to be respected, and to test our maxims

---

[26] See Christine Korsgaard, "Kant's Formula of Humanity," *Kant-Studien* 77 (1986), 183–202.

by asking whether, supposing the maxims were natural laws, there would be a society of that kind.[27]

Because the richer formulations of the categorical imperative can take us no further than the formula requiring us to test our maxims by asking if they could be universal laws, we must ask how well that principle can serve to show us the way through all of our relations with one another.

The categorical imperative clearly requires a kind of impartiality in our behavior. We are not permitted to make exceptions for ourselves, or to do what we would not rationally permit others to do. But it would be a mistake to suppose that Kantian morality allows for nothing but impartiality in personal relations. The maxim "If it is my child's birthday, give her a party, to show I love her" is thinkable and willable as a law of nature, as are some maxims of helping family members and friends rather than helping others. Of course our actions for those we prefer must be within rationally allowable limits, but within those limits Kantian ethics has nothing to say against the working of human affection.

A broader point is involved here. Although the categorical imperative operates most directly by vetoing proposed maxims of action, it is a mistake to suppose that it does nothing more. It is usually true that from its prohibitions alone no positive directives follow. Whatever is not forbidden is simply permitted. Sometimes, however, a veto forces a requirement on us. Where what is forbidden is *not* doing something—for instance, not paying my taxes—the veto requires me to do something, to pay my taxes, because it is not permitted not to do so. Beyond this, the categorical imperative can set requirements that are not so specifically tied to prohibitions. Kant gives us more detail on this in the *Metaphysics of Morals*.

He there divides morality into two domains, one of law or right (*Recht*), and one of virtue (*Morals*, 6:218–21 / 16–19). The domain of law, which extends to civil law, arises from maxims that are vetoed because they cannot even be thought coherently when universalized. The rejection of such maxims turns out to provide a counterpart to the recognition of the strict rights of others. We may not interfere with their legitimate projects, may not take their property, and so on. The domain of virtue involves maxims that can be thought but not willed as universal laws. Most of what morality requires as action rather than abstention is a requirement of virtue.

---

[27] Kant seems to assume that those who apply the categorical imperative to their maxims will come out with answers that agree when the maxims tested are alike.

We have already seen why Kant thinks we cannot will a maxim of universal neglect of the needs of others, even though such a maxim is thinkable as a law of nature. Now the denial of this vetoed maxim is not the maxim "Always help everyone." It is rather the maxim "Help some others at some times." Kant thinks that further argument from this point will show that it is morally required that one of our own ends be to forward the ends of others. He thinks it can be shown in similar fashion that we must make the perfection of our moral character and of our abilities one of our ends (*Morals*, 6:384–8 / 43–7).

The differences between the domain of law and that of virtue are significant. To be virtuous, I must be acting for the sake of the good of another, or for my own perfection, and viewing these ends as morally required. In the domain of law it does not matter why I do what I do, so long as I abstain from violating the rights of others. Because the motive does not matter in legal affairs, if I do not perform as I ought, I can rightly be compelled to do so. I obtain no moral merit for carrying out legal duties. I simply keep my slate clean. In the domain of virtue, by contrast, there is nothing to which I can be compelled, because what is required is that I have certain ends, and ends must be freely adopted (*Morals*, 6:381 / 39). Moreover, in the realm of virtue there are no requirements about specific actions. It is up to me to decide which of my talents to improve, where my worst moral failings are, and how, when, and how much to help others. Of course I may only do what is permissible within the limits of my legal duties. But the more I make the required ends mine, the more I will do. In the realm of virtue, moreover, I can become entitled to moral praise through my efforts for others. My merit increases as I make their goals my own.

Kant thus makes a place for a concern for human well-being as well as for negative respect for rights.[28] What is to be noted is that he does not base the requirement of concern for others on the goodness of the results virtue brings about. And he does not require us to bring about as much happiness (or as much of our own perfection) as we possibly can. He allows that we will have permissible ends that will compete for time and resources with the morally required ends. Morality does not tell us how to decide between them. It only tells us that we must pursue the required as well as the personal ends, staying always within the limits of justice.

---

[28] He also shows how the basic principles of morality can be extended to handle cases where agents do not comply with the moral requirement of acting from respect for the law. The treatment even of those who are indifferent to morality falls under an extension of the moral law.

How adequate, then, is the categorical imperative as a moral guide? One might wish to reject the whole vocabulary of law and obligation, and with it Kant's principle, on the grounds that it gives a skewed and harmful portrayal of human relations.[29] But even if one does not wish thus to set aside or subordinate the moral concerns that led Kant to make that vocabulary central, one must allow that there are problems with Kant's claims for the categorical imperative. I note only two.

First, Kant held that his principle leads to certain conclusions that many sensible people do not accept, such as that lying, suicide, and political revolution are always prohibited. If his inferences to these moral conclusions are valid, then his principle is questionable. If he is not right, then a question must be raised about his claim that his principle is so easy to apply that an ordinary person, "with this compass in hand, is well able to distinguish, in all cases that present themselves, what is good or evil, right or wrong. . . ." (*Groundwork*, 4:404 / 71–2). It is not clear that any single principle can do all that Kant claims for the categorical imperative.

Second, if the adequacy of the categorical imperative for cases involving only relations between two people is hard to determine, its adequacy for helping settle large-scale social issues is even more so. Kant thought that individual decision-making would be able to guide people to coordinated action on matters of general concern. This seems extremely doubtful. It does not follow, however, that there is no way of revising the Kantian principle so that it might handle such issues in a way that preserves the intent of Kant's own formulation.[30]

VII

Kant held that the proper way to proceed in moral philosophy is to start with what we all know about morality and see what principle underlies it. The *Groundwork* accordingly begins with an examination of common-sense

---

[29] For strong representations of this point of view, see Alasdair MacIntyre, *After Virtue* (Notre Dame, Ind.: Notre Dame University Press, 1981), and Bernard Williams, *Ethics and the Limits of Philosophy* (Cambridge, Mass.: Harvard University Press, 1985).

[30] For an excellent example of an attempt to use the Kantian thinking to deal with a major social issue, see Onora O'Neill, *Faces of Hunger* (Oxford: Basil Blackwell, 1986).

opinion. From it Kant extracts the motive that is central to morality as well as the basic principle of decision-making.

He begins with the claim that we all recognize a kind of goodness different from the goodness of wealth, power, talent, and intellect, and even different from the goodness of kindly or generous dispositions. Under certain conditions any of these might turn out not to be good. But there is another kind of goodness that stays good under any conditions. This is the special kind of goodness a person can have. It is shown most clearly, Kant thinks, when someone does what she believes right or obligatory, and does it just because she thinks it so. Someone lacking kindly feelings, pity, or generosity, and not even caring about her own interest any more, may nonetheless do what she thinks right. The special sort of merit we attribute to this person is the goodness central to morality. It is best thought of as the goodness of a good will (*Groundwork*, 4:393–4 / 61–2).

Reflection on the agent of good will brings out an important point. Her value does not depend on her actual accomplishments. And because she is moved by a desire to do the act or to bring about its results, her value cannot depend on the results she intended either. Her value must depend, Kant says, "solely on the *principle of volition*" from which she acted. And the only principle available, because she is not moved by the content of her action, must be formal. The agent of good will must therefore be moved by the bare lawfulness of the act. Kant puts it by saying that she is moved by respect or reverence (*Achtung*) for the moral law (*Groundwork*, 4:400 / 68).

Common-sense beliefs about the moral goodness of the good agent show us, Kant thinks, that the categorical imperative is the principle behind sound moral judgment. Kant also thinks he obtains from beliefs about the good agent his view about the motivation proper to morality. Historically the latter was as revolutionary as the former, and systematically the two aspects of the theory are inseparably linked. But the motivational view leads to some new problems for Kant.

The psychological doctrine prevalent in Kant's time held that what motivates us in voluntary rational action is desire for good and aversion to evil. Granting that people often fail to pursue the good either through mistake or through perversity, the view implies that if we do not act from a desire for some perceived good, we are acting wrongly or at least irrationally. Of course it was allowed that people sometimes do their duty just because they ought to. But since doing one's duty was understood to be productive of good—the good of the community—even conscientious action was seen as motivated by desire for the good.[31]

Crusius broke with this tradition when he said that we could obey God's laws simply because they are ordained by him.[32] Kant's assertion that in obeying the dictates of the categorical imperative we could be motivated by what he called respect for the law accepts this decisive break with the older view. Respect, as we have seen, is a concern not for the ends or goods of action, but for the form. So when we are moved by it, we are not pursuing good. But neither are we acting wrongly or irrationally. The central moral motive therefore does not fit the standard pattern.

Respect is unlike other motives in two further ways. First, it is a feeling that arises solely from our awareness of the moral law as the categorical imperative. And it always arises from such awareness. While other motives may or may not be present in everyone at all times, every rational agent always has available this motive, which is sufficient to move her to do what the categorical imperative bids. Second, other motives, such as fear of punishment, greed, love, or pity, can lead us to act rightly. But it is merely contingent if they do. Love, like greed or hatred, can lead one to act immorally. The sole motive that necessarily moves us to act rightly is respect, because it alone is only activated by the dictates of the categorical imperative.

It is easy to see the place of respect in Kant's portrayal of autonomy. Respect provides an answer to the claim, made famous by Hume but probably known to Kant through work by Hume's influential predecessor Francis Hutcheson,[33] that reason cannot motivate us. On the contrary, Kant replies: practical reason generates its own unique motive. External sanctions, of the sort the natural-law theorists thought indispensable to give obligation its motivating power, are unnecessary, at least in principle, because we all have within ourselves an adequate motive for compliance. Respect also makes up for the inequities of nature. Some people are naturally loving, friendly, and thoughtful. Nature has not been so generous to others. If only natural motives were available to move us to do what

---

[31] If you obey the natural law only because of fear of God's sanctions, you are still motivated by desire for good—the good of avoiding punishment.

[32] There are unclear and wavering anticipations of the Kantian move in Pufendorf and Samuel Clarke, but Crusius was the first to make the point central to his moral psychology.

[33] See Dieter Henrich, "Hutchenson und Kant," *Kant-Studien* 49 (1957–8): 49–69, and "Über Kants früheste Ethik," *Kant-Studien* 54 (1963), 404–31.

morality requires, then some, through no fault of their own, would be unable to comply with it. Kant's doctrine implies that no one need be prevented by the niggardliness of nature from attaining moral worth.

If the attractions of the doctrine of respect are plain, it nonetheless gets Kant into difficulties. It leads him to think along the following lines. If I act from any motive other than respect, I am simply doing something I find myself wanting to do. My action may be right, but if so that is merely contingent. Even if it is, I show no special concern for morality when I am moved by my desire. All that is shown by a right act done from a non-moral motive is that morality and my interest here coincide. Consequently I deserve no praise unless I act from respect. Action from respect is the only kind of action that shows true concern for morality. No other motivation entitles me to count as a virtuous agent.

As critics have frequently pointed out, this seems a paradoxical position.[34] It seems to make almost every aspect of character unimportant to morality, because it denies any moral worth to actions springing entirely from feelings of love, loyalty, friendship, pity, or generosity, and seems to rule out mixed motives as sources of moral worth.[35] Worse, it suggests that kind or loving feelings can get in the way of our achieving moral merit. If merit accrues only when we act from a sense of duty, it seems that human relations must be either unduly chilly or else without moral worth. Did Kant really hold this view? There are passages that suggest he did,[36] and others where he

[34] The poet Schiller first made this kind of criticism. Schiller's and related objections are discussed at length in Hans Reiner, *Duty and Inclination* (The Hague: Martinus Nijhoff, 1983). A considerable literature has grown up on the subject. For recent discussion of it, see Michael Stocker, "The Schizophrenia of Modern Ethical Theories," *Journal of Philosophy* 73 (1976), 453–66; Richard Henson, "What Kant Might Have Said: Moral Worth and the Overdetermination of Dutiful Action," *Philosophical Review* 88 (1979), 39–54; Barbara Herman, "On the Value of Acting from the Motive of Duty," *Philosophical Review* 90 (1981), 359–82; Marcia Baron, "The Alleged Moral Repugnance of Acting from Duty," *Journal of Philosophy* 81 (1984), 197–220; Judith Baker, "Do One's Motives Have to be Pure?" in Richard Grandy and Richard Warner, eds., *Philosophical Grounds of Rationality* (Oxford: Oxford University Press, 1986), 457–74; and Tom Sorrell, "Kant's Good Will," *Kant-Studien* 78 (1987), 87–101.

[35] Kant says that action from any of these desires is heteronomous. This is not because he thinks the desires are not part of the self. It is because through these desires action is governed by something other than the self. In these desires the self pursues good and avoids ill. It is therefore governed by the features of things that make them objects of desire or aversion, and these features are, of course, independent of our wills. Thus in describing heteronomy Kant speaks of the object determining the will "by means of" inclination (*vermittelst der Neigung*) (*Groundwork*, 4:444 / 111).

[36] He rejects the feeling of love as a proper moral motive (*Groundwork*, 4:399 / 67); he usually treats the passions and desires as if their aim is always the agent's own pleasure or good (for example, *Groundwork*, 4:407 / 75); and at one point he says it must be the wish of every rational person to be free of desire (*Groundwork*, 4:428 / 955–6).

asserts a much more humane view.[37] The most plausible alternative to the extreme position is one that allows conditional mixed motives: I may have merit when moved by the motive of pity, say, if I allow pity to operate only on condition that in moving me it leads me to nothing the categorical imperative forbids, and if respect is strong enough in me to move me were pity to fail. Because the texts show a change of mind, the best interpretation depends on systematic considerations, of which not the least is whether one accepts Kant's belief that there is a unique and supremely important kind of merit or worthiness, the moral kind.

VIII

So far I have tried to explain the principle Kant takes to be central to morality and the motivation he thinks is unique to it. I have said nothing about the justification he thinks he can give for claiming that the principle really holds. We are thus at the point Kant reaches toward the end of the second part of the *Groundwork*. He there says that so far all he has done is to show what ordinary moral consciousness takes morality to involve if there is such a thing. But is there? A parallel question about prudential rationality would be easy to answer. The law of prudence is true by definition, or analytic. To say someone is a "perfectly rational agent" simply means (in part) that she "uses the means needed to attain her goals." But the moral law is not analytic. The concepts "completely good will" or "perfectly rational agent" do not include "acts only through universalizable maxims." And we cannot base the moral law on experience. It is a necessary proposition, and experience alone never grounds such propositions. What basis then is there for the moral law?[38]

---

[37] This is particularly evident in the *Religion*. See 6:28 / 23, where the natural dispositions in human nature leading us to sexual activity and to strive for social superiority are said to be dispositions for good, though they can be misused; and 6:58 / 51: "Natural inclinations, *considered in themselves*, are *good*, that is not a matter of reproach, and it is not only futile to want to extirpate them but to do so would also be harmful and blameworthy."

[38] Kant here raises the questions of whether a transcendental deduction of the moral law is possible. The problem differs from that involved in constructing a transcendental argument for, say, the principle that every event must have a cause. We experience a spatiotemporal world of stable and interacting objects, and can therefore ask under what conditions such experience is possible. But we are so far from experiencing a stable moral world that we cannot point with certainty, Kant thinks, to even one case where someone was motivated by respect alone.

The problem as Kant sees it is to discover something through which we can join the subject of the moral law—"perfectly rational agent"—and its predicate—"acts only through universalizable maxims." He sees a possible solution in the idea of freedom of the will. Freedom has a negative aspect: If we are free, we are not determined solely by our desires and needs. But freedom is more than the absence of determination. A will wholly undetermined would be random and chaotic. It would not allow for responsibility, nor consequently for praise and blame.[39] The only viable way to think of a free will, Kant holds, is to think of it as a will whose choices are determined by a law that is internal to its nature. Such a will is determined only by itself, and is therefore free. But we have already seen that the only self-determined actions are actions done because of the universalizability of the agent's maxim. So if we could show that a rational will must be free, we would have shown that a rational will acts only on universalizable maxims.[40] We would have proven the first principle of morality.

Given Kant's Newtonian model of the physical world, a strong claim about freedom of the will raises problems. Our bodies as physical objects are subject to Newton's laws of motion. If they are moved by our natural desires, this is unproblematic, because desires themselves arise in accordance with deterministic laws (as yet undiscovered). Morality, however, requires the possibility of action from a wholly non-empirical motive. We never know whether real moral merit is attained, but if it is, the motive of respect must move us to bodily action, regardless of the strength of our desires. Is this possible?

In the first *Critique* Kant argued that no theoretical proof (or disproof) of free will can be given. In the *Groundwork* Kant thinks he can give at least indirect support to the claim that we are free. When we as rational beings act, he says, we must take ourselves to be free. He means that whenever we deliberate or choose we are presupposing freedom, even if we are unaware of the presupposition or consciously doubtful of it. More broadly, whenever we take ourselves to be thinking rationally (even about purely theoretical matters) we must take ourselves to be free, because we cannot knowingly

---

[39] Freedom of that kind, Kant thinks, would be terrifying, not something to cherish. See 20:91 ff., 27:258, 1320, and 1482.

[40] On the thesis that a free will and a will governed by the moral law are one and the same, see Henry E. Allison, "Morality and Freedom: Kant's Reciprocity Thesis," *Philosophical Review* 95 (1986), 393–425, and, more fully, the same author's *Kant's Theory of Freedom* (Cambridge: Cambridge University Press, 1990).

accept judgments determined by external sources as judgments we ourselves have made. Now anything that would follow about us if we were really free still follows for practical purposes if we have to think of ourselves as free. Because freedom entails the moral law, we must think of ourselves as bound by it (*Groundwork*, 4:447–8 / 115–16).[41]

Can we both take ourselves to be free and believe theoretically in a deterministic universe? Kant's answer appeals to his first *Critique*. Theoretical knowledge has limits. It applies only to the world as we experience it; the phenomenal world. We cannot say that the determinism holding in the realm of phenomena holds beyond it as well, in the noumenal world. If we think of ourselves as belonging to the noumenal as well as the phenomenal world, then we can see how in one respect we may be beings bound in a web of mechanistic determination, while in another respect we are the free rational agents morality supposes us to be. Our theoretical beliefs and our practical presupposition of freedom do not come into any conflict.

There are many difficulties with this argument. One of them is this. The argument seems to suppose that we are free just when we are acting rationally. But then if we act irrationally, we are not free. Immoral action is, however, irrational. So it seems to follow that we are responsible only when acting as the moral law requires, and not responsible when we do something wicked. Kant might have had a reply to this objection, but if so he did not give it. In his later writings, he introduced a distinction between the will and the power of choice (*Wille* and *Willkür*), which was meant to remove the problem.[42] He held that the will is simply identical with practical rationality and is therefore the home of the moral law, but that we have in addition a power of choice, whose task is to choose between the promptings of desire and the imperatives stemming from the will. It is in the power of choice that our freedom, properly speaking, resides. The will itself is neither free nor unfree.

Kant not only developed his view of free will considerably; he changed his mind about how to argue in support of it.[43] In the *Critique of Practical Reason* Kant continued to hold his earlier view that if we are free we are under the moral law, and if we are under the moral law we are free.

---

[41] For an attempt to unpack this difficult argument, see Thomas E. Hill, Jr., "Kant's Argument for the Rationality of Moral Conduct," *Pacific Philosophical Quarterly* 66 (1985), 3–23; and Allison, *Kant's Theory of Freedom*, ch. 12.

[42] See *Religion*, 6:21–6 / 16–21; *Morals*, 6:213–14 / 10–11; 6:225 / 25.

[43] For discussion, see Karl Ameriks, *Kant's Theory of Mind* (Oxford: Oxford University Press, 1982), ch. 6.

But he now argues that what he calls "the fact (*Faktum*) of reason" is what shows us that we are free. There is considerable difficulty in clarifying just what Kant supposes the fact of reason to be.[44] One possible interpretation starts with Kant's claim that the fact of reason is revealed to us through our moral awareness that we are bound by unconditional obligations. Because we know we are bound by such obligations, we know also that we can do what we are obligated to do. This means that we can do it, no matter what the circumstances and no matter what has gone on before. In other words awareness of categorical obligation contains awareness of freedom. But it is awareness of freedom as it expresses itself in imperfectly rational beings. The fact of reason, we might take it, is pure rationality displaying itself as immediately as it can in imperfectly rational beings.[45]

In the *Critique*, therefore, Kant treats freedom as the ground of our *having* moral obligations, and our awareness of categorical imperatives as the ground of our *knowledge* that we are free. He thus gives up the one attempt he made to support the principle of morals by appeal to something other than itself—rationality in general—and he uses our awareness of morality as a foundation from which we can extend our understanding of ourselves and our place in the universe.[46]

Kant is not here retracting the claims he made in the first *Critique* about the limits of knowledge. Our justified assurance that we are free is not theoretical knowledge. While we are entitled to that assurance for practical purposes, we cannot infer from it anything of pertinence to our theoretical understanding of the world. Indeed Kant thinks that without the positions established in the theoretical *Critique* the moral outlook he aims to defend would be impossible. Unless we see that knowledge is limited, we will think that the kind of theoretical knowledge science gives us is all the knowledge

---

[44] For valuable assistance, see John Rawls, "Themes in Kant's Moral Philosophy," in Eckart Förster, ed., *Kant's Transcendental Deductions: The Three "Critiques" and the "Opus postumum"* (Stanford, Calif.: Stanford University Press, 1989), 81–113; Henry E. Allison, "Justification and Freedom in the *Critique of Practical Reason*," ibid., 114–30; and the discussion of both papers by Barbara Herman, ibid., 131–41.

[45] See Dieter Henrich, "Der Begriff der sittlichen Einsicht und Kants Lehre vom Faktum der Vernunft," in *Die Gegenwart der Griechen im neueren Denken*, ed. Dieter Henrich et al. (Tübingen: J. C. B. Mohr Paul Siebeck, 1960), 77–115; and "Die Deduktion des Sittengesetzes," in *Denken im Schatten des Nihilismus*, ed. Alexander Schwann (Darmstadt: Wissenschaftliche Buchgesellschaft, 1975), 55–112.

[46] Whether this marks the failure of an attempt to ground morality or a wise realization that morality needs no grounds beyond itself is of course a matter of considerable philosophical disagreement. For extended discussion, see Gerold Prauss, *Kant über Freiheit als Autonomie* (Frankfurt am Main: Vittorio Klostermann, 1983).

there can be. Then a theoretical understanding of our own behavior will become inevitable. Kant held that if we think of ourselves solely in empirical and deterministic terms we will necessarily think of ourselves as heteronomous, as moved by our desires for this or that, and never solely by respect for law. This thought would be debilitating to our effort to be moral.[47] But the first *Critique* showed that the deterministic stance of theoretical reason is valid only within the bounds of experience. Theoretical reason has no jurisdiction over the beliefs morality requires us to hold.

IX

Kant calls this the primacy of practical reason (*Practical Reason*, 5:119–21 / 124–6). If the categorical imperative requires us to think of ourselves and the world in certain ways, then the limitations on speculative reason cannot be used to deny that we have any warrant for those beliefs. Our nature as rational agents thus dominates our nature as rational knowers. There are two matters, other than freedom, on which practical reason requires us to accept beliefs that can be neither proven nor disproven theoretically. One concerns our hopes for our own private futures, the other concerns our hopes for the future of humanity. In one case we are led by morality to have certain religious beliefs; in the other, to have certain views about history and progress.

In the second *Critique* Kant argues not only that we must think of ourselves as free moral agents but also that we must see ourselves as immortal, and as living in a universe governed by a providential intelligence through whose intervention in the course of nature the virtuous are rewarded and the vicious punished. We must have these beliefs, Kant holds, because morality requires each of us to make ourselves perfectly virtuous—to give ourselves a character in which the dictates of the categorical imperative are never thwarted by the passions and desires. And it also requires that happiness be distributed in accordance with virtue.[48] The former cannot be done in a

---

[47] The second *Critique* is a critique of practical reason generally, and not only of *pure* practical reason, because it examines, among other things, the claim of empirical practical reason—means/end reasoning—to be the only practical reason there is. The establishment through the fact of reason of pure practical reason disproves this claim.

[48] "The proposition: Make the highest good possible in the world your own final end! is a synthetical proposition *a priori*, which is introduced by the moral law itself" (*Religion*, 6:7 n. / 7 n.). Kant's argument for this is to say the least unclear.

finite amount of time, so we must believe that we each have something like an infinite amount of time available for carrying out the task, or at least for approaching closer and closer to completion. The latter is not possible if the mechanisms of nature are the sole ordering force in the universe, nature being indifferent to virtue and vice. Hence we must believe that there is some non-natural ordering force that will intervene to bring about what morality requires (*Practical Reason*, 5:122–32 / 126–36).

In his essays on history[49] Kant argues that theoretical reason can never determine whether mankind is progressing or not. War and the innumerable ghastly ways in which people mistreat one another seem sometimes to be waning, sometimes to be increasing, sometimes simply to go through an endless see-saw of more and less. But morality requires us to try to bring it about that there is peace in the world, and that the standing form of government is everywhere one in which individual autonomy is publicly acknowledged and respected. We must therefore believe that it is possible to bring this about, and we must see history as moving, however slowly, and at whatever cost to innumerable individuals throughout countless generations, in this direction. Thus within the world constituted by theoretical reason, practical reason directs us to form a moral world by imposing moral order on the whole of human society as well as on our individual desires.

Kant is not saying that moral agents come to believe these propositions about religion and history through arguments. He is saying rather that each moral agent will find herself acting as if she saw the world as Kant's propositions portray it. Morality, as Kant understands it, makes sense only if certain background conditions are met. Unless these conditions hold, a form of *pointlessness* threatens action dictated by the categorical imperative; and the rational agent cannot act while thinking her action pointless. The belief in freedom is needed first of all, because otherwise we would lack the assurance that we can do what the categorical imperative requires. The other morally required beliefs ward off a different kind of pointlessness.

What is evident in all of these other beliefs to which we are led on practical grounds alone is a concern for human happiness. Kant is often

---

[49] In addition to the collections cited in n. 2, see the important essay "An Old Question Raised Again: Is the Human Race Constantly Progressing?" in the *Streit der Fakultäten* (7:77–94); a translation is included in the Beck collection and in *The Conflict of the Faculties*, trans. Mary Gregor (New York: Abaris Books, 1979).

thought to hold that happiness is not valuable, and even to have ignored it wholly in his ethics. This is a serious mistake. It is true that for Kant moral worth is the supreme good, but by itself it is not the perfect or complete good.[50] To be virtuous, for Kant, is to be worthy of happiness: and the perfect good requires that happiness be distributed in accordance with virtue (*Practical Reason*, 5:110–11 / 114–15). Happiness, or the sum of satisfaction of desires, is a conditional good. It is good only if it results from the satisfaction of morally permissible desires. But it is intrinsically valuable nonetheless. It is valued by a rational agent for itself, and not instrumentally.[51]

Atheism and meaninglessness in history threaten to make morality pointless. A holy will necessarily aims at the perfect good, and we imperfect beings therefore ought to do what we can to bring it about. But it seems simply irrational to devote serious effort to bringing about a goal that one believes cannot be brought about. If reason showed the perfect good to be a required but unattainable goal, reason would be at odds with itself. The moral agent, knowing herself required to act in ways that make sense only if certain ends can be achieved, finds herself simply taking it that the world must allow the possibility of success. Since this attitude is not translatable into theoretical knowledge, the agent cannot have any details about *how* her effort will help bring about the ends. All that is needed is the confidence that it will. Philosophy helps, Kant thinks, by showing that nothing can prove the attitude unwarranted.

---

[50] Kant repeatedly criticizes the Stoics for making the mistake of thinking virtue the perfect good. The Epicureans, he held, made just the opposite mistake, taking happiness to be the complete good. His view synthesizes the two in the proper way (*Practical Reason*, 5:111–13 / 115–17).

[51] A basically virtuous person takes as her fundamental maxim to pursue her own good only on condition that doing so meets the requirements of morality. A basically vicious person reverses the order, and takes as fundamental the maxim of doing what morality requires only if it is not in conflict with the pursuit of her own good. See the discussion in *Religion*, 6:36–7 / 31–2 and 6:42–4 / 37–9.

15

Kant and Stoic Ethics

Having agreed to explore teleology and deontology in Stoic and Kantian ethics, I find I am forced at the very outset to voyage between the Symplegades, the clashing rocks. On the one side there are Kantians who tell us to stop thinking of Kant as a deontologist.[1] On the other side loom the students of ancient ethics who tell us that it is a mistake to think that Stoic thought was teleological in any way that contrasts meaningfully with deontology. If we accept both these views, we should conclude that the route for my expedition is impassable. Can it be opened by fending off the rocks? Displaying a no doubt deplorable exegetical conservatism, I shall try. I begin by rejecting the position of the Kantian revisionists. I then go on to argue that ancient ethical theories are indeed teleological in contrast to something that is not so in Kant. If we can get past the clashing rocks into calmer waters, we may find ourselves rewarded with views of the significance of some of the differences between the Stoic theory of morality and Kant's.[2]

I am much indebted to John Cooper for lengthy discussions of Stoicism, as well as for comments on a draft of this essay. Needless to say I have probably failed to learn much of what he tried to tell me. I owe thanks to Gisela Striker, whose essays on Stoicism I have found particularly helpful and who kept me from making a serious mistake about the doctrine. My thanks go also to the Hopkins graduate students who took my seminar on Stoic and Kantian ethics in the fall of 1993 and whose comments on an early version of this essay were acute and instructive. I benefited from the discussion in Pittsburgh throughout the symposium for which this essay was written, and from questions raised by John Simmons and Richard Rorty at the University of Virginia.

[1] Just when we began doing so is unclear. As Robert Louden points out in a forthcoming paper, Bentham used the term "deontology" but not in the way now common. The current use seems to have been started by C. D. Broad in his 1930 commentary on Sidgwick in *Five Types of Ethical Theory*.

[2] I bear in mind Brad Inwood's warning concerning overconfidence in constructing out of our multiple, often fragmentary, sources a picture of "an orthodox Stoicism teaching internally consistent doctrine, grounded on clear general principles." See his "Seneca and Psychological Dualism," in J. Brunschwig and M. Nussbaum, eds., *Passions and Perceptions* (Cambridge: Cambridge University Press, 1993), 152. A similar caution is needed about treating Kant as if he never changed his mind.

I

Teleological views are supposed to put value at the center, or the base, of morality, while deontological views put duty there. Hence, neither label captures Kant's view. Duty for him is of course a derivative notion; but so is value. Kant explicitly allows for two kinds of goodness, or value, and gives an admirably clear account of them in the second *Critique*. Both kinds of "good" and "bad" on Kant's view are *relational* predicates. To be good is to be the necessary object of a will according to a rational principle. If the necessity of willing an object is conditional on a prior desire, then the object's goodness falls into the category of *das Wohl* (well-being or natural good). If an object is necessarily willed in complete independence of any desire, then its goodness falls into the category of *das Gute* (moral goodness). Necessary rational objects of aversion fall into two similar classes (V 58–60).[3]

Goodness and value, on this reading of Kant, are always explained in terms of rational willing. They cannot themselves be used as final explanations of what it is rational to will. To say this is to say that for Kant nothing possesses the kind of intrinsic value that G. E. Moore thought would belong to a beautiful world even were there no observers of it.[4] The only sort of thing that can be, as Kant says, "simply good...in all respects and without qualification" is the manner of acting—the maxims—of someone who acts from respect for the law (V 60).[5] This manner of acting is "simply good" because under any and all circumstances it is what is necessarily willed by anyone willing in accordance with the moral law. It is thus unconditionally good, and in that sense absolutely good, but it is not intrinsically good. When at the beginning of the *Groundwork* Kant says that the good will is unconditionally good, he is not implying that it possesses a value that is independent of the moral law. We recognize its value because, as we ultimately learn, we recognize that the law unconditionally requires maxims that make the will good. Good will does not have some other value that might provide a moral motivation different from the respect to which Kant standardly appeals.

---

[3] Otherwise undesignated note and parenthetical text references are to Kant's works using the volume and page numbers of the *Gesammelte Schriften*.

[4] G. E. Moore, *Principia Ethica* (Cambridge: Cambridge University Press, 1903), 83–4. My thanks to T. E. Hill Jr. for suggesting the use of this comparison.

[5] The phrase "simply good" translates Kant's *schlechthin gut*, which Beck misleadingly translates as "absolutely good."

In an important paper entitled "Kant's Morality of Law and Morality of Freedom," Paul Guyer challenges this conventional interpretation. He argues that "the fundamental but indemonstrable value of freedom itself is the heart of Kant's moral theory."[6] The categorical imperative obligates us because "it is the principle which we must follow in order to give full expression to our unique freedom in the phenomenal sphere" (G 45). Guyer does not think that we bring about our freedom as an effect of obligatory action: "Our duty is not to create freedom but to enhance the circumstances for its exercise" (G 64). In elaborating his conviction that "the foundation of Kant's entire moral philosophy is his belief in the absolute value of the freedom of rational beings," he speaks of conformity to the categorical imperative as that through which "this intrinsically valuable freedom can be preserved and enhanced" (G 70). And he thinks that Kant at times considers seriously the idea that the requirement of universalizability is "necessary in order to maximize the exercise of this freedom and thus maximally realize its potential intrinsic value" (G 71–2). These passages suggest that Guyer sees Kant as treating an increase in the display of freedom as the outcome of action that justifies requiring the actions that produce it.

Guyer does not directly challenge the kind of reading I have just sketched, nor does he try to explain how his own fits in with the passages on which that reading relies. He comes to his interpretation because he believes that Kant has not explained what motive we have for compliance with the categorical imperative. He thinks the second *Critique* "profoundly unsatisfying" because after laying down a necessary and universal law that must be formal, it says that we can comply with it "without explaining in what sense we have any *reason* to do such a thing" (G 53). It does not explain how the moral law can motivate us by giving us a reason. The *Groundwork* likewise leaves "the underlying motivation for adhering to the moral law a mystery" (G 57). If freedom is an absolute and intrinsic value, however, then those who possess it "provide an end ... for the sake of which any rational being would see fit to adopt the moral law" (G 61). The formula of the end in itself, therefore, gives Kant what he needs: not "an end which the antecedent adoption of the principle of morality could

---

[6] Guyer's essay is in R. M. Dancy, ed., *Kant and Critique* (Dordrecht: Kluwer Academic, 1993), 43–89. Page references will be given in the text, indicated by G.

force a rational being to adopt," but "an end the intrinsic and absolute value of which would compel any rational being to adopt the principle of morality" (G 60). Even if we can only take the absolute value of freedom as a regulative principle, it can "serve to motivate our practical behavior and to guide it towards rational coherence" (G 85–6).

Commentators frequently find Kant's respect unsatisfactory. Perhaps this is because they assume that all action must be explained in terms solely of desire and belief. But Kant does not accept that psychological model; and it seems to me that his view of the role of respect in our motivational economy is at least not mysterious. Respect is meant to explain how we humans can respond to the constraints that we ourselves in our rational aspect impose on the goal-oriented projects proposed by ourselves as dependent sentient beings. The constraints are not themselves goal-derived, but they *have a point*. The point is to create conditions for action that we can approve of unconditionally. Our own appreciation of this point is shown in the "special joys" (*besondere Freuden*) that the moral agent feels from the effort to act as morality requires (V 117–18).

None of this, of course, shows the adequacy of Kant's account of the motive for complying with the categorical imperative. But it indicates that Kant himself did not think that some additional intrinsic kind of value was required to explain it, and that we need not, therefore, insist that he thinks that there is some intrinsic value that compels rational agents to adopt the moral law. It is worth noting that others beside Kant made the same kind of claim. Clarke, Crusius, Price, and Reid were among those attempting to develop a moral psychology allowing that we can be moved by the claims of practical rationality not only in using means to ends, but in restricting and setting ends. Kant's way of going about it is certainly unique, but the concerns to which he is responding are common to an important group of eighteenth-century philosophers.

II

Barbara Herman urges us to leave deontology behind as we read Kant.[7] Her interpretation seems intended mainly as a way of moving toward a more

---

[7] References to Herman are to her "Leaving Deontology Behind" in *The Practice of Moral Judgment* (Cambridge, Mass.: Harvard University Press, 1993), indicated by PMJ.

fully defensible Kantian ethic than we get from attributing to Kant the principle of the priority of law to good. So I read her claim that "[w]hatever it is that makes Kantian ethics distinctive, it is *not* to be found in the subordination of all considerations of value to principles of right or duty. In this sense, Kantian ethics is not a deontology" (PMJ 210).[8] Like Guyer, she thinks that "[w]ithout a theory of value the rationale for moral constraint is a mystery." If we do not answer the question "why?" about such constraint, we invite mere skepticism. Herman also holds that a theory of value is needed if a Kantian ethic is to enable us to deliberate successfully "in circumstances containing competing moral considerations" (PMJ 210–11). She fills in her second rationale in illuminating detail.[9] But she insists, rightly, that "negotiating the casuistry is not enough." The kind of defense that she thinks is needed by deontological constraints must involve us in consideration of "the place of morality in our self-conception as rational agents" (PMJ 212). I discuss only this part of her essay.

The value that Herman thinks Kant needs as a rationale for observing deontological constraints on action is not "some other good that this way of acting promotes or brings about." The Kantian must hold that appropriately lawful action itself has value. So we need to know "how or in what sense refraining from acting in a way that rational beings could not accept is in any way *good*" (PMJ 215). Herman is not asking merely about the relation of such action to the moral law. She is pushing for a deeper account of why formal lawful willing should be held to be something we can think of as basic and central to our lives as moral agents (PMJ 215). Unless we can see that, she thinks, we will be left wondering about the rationale for morality.

Her response is that Kant's principles of rational action themselves perform "the role a conception of value is to play in action and judgment." How can the principles of rational willing be a final end? Herman answers that "if we accept that the defining feature of ends is that they are sources of reasons that shape action, then principles can be ends" (PMJ 216).

Her main point, if I understand her, is that acting from reasons is itself a value whose realization in our lives is vulnerable to certain kinds of dangers, among them assault from other agents. Rational agents, Herman says, are

---

[8] Taken literally Herman's claim is correct. Considerations of right and duty are themselves subordinate to the moral law, as are considerations of value. But I take it that Herman aims to displace the principle of the priority of law to good.

[9] Guyer has a different and equally interesting program for using his theory of the value of freedom in developing a Kantian casuistry, including a politics.

agents who must take themselves to be, as she puts it, "acting for reasons 'all the way down.'" This is what shows that rational agents "can fully determine their actions according to reasons." They are not simply *caused* to act by their desires; desires must be adopted by the will before they become ends. And "the adoption of an end is an activity of will undertaken for a reason." Herman thinks the reason for adopting an end is always a principle. "We act," she says, "on such principles as desire satisfaction, or even this-desire satisfaction, is good. Our adoption of ends always has a principled basis" (PMJ 228–9). Anything that prevents our acting from reasons will violate the very possibility of our being agents of the distinctive kind that Kant thinks we are. There is thus a value inherent in compliance with the categorical imperative—the value of protecting our sense of ourselves as agents. Deontology is left behind.

Herman shows admirably how to use this reading of Kant in making the application of the categorical imperative more perspicuous. I think, however, that we cannot accept the move as Kant's own. Kant does not think that freedom is a vulnerable possession. Thorny issues are raised if it is taken to be so.[10] If our very capacity to act for reasons can be threatened, is our status as end-in-itself equally vulnerable? If there are degrees of agency, are there also degrees of being an end in itself? If I am deprived of agency can I then rightly be treated as means only? Herman does not consider these issues. Her interest lies in the extent of our ability to act for reasons.

There is a sense in which Herman is right in saying that for Kant we act for reasons all the way down. On his view what is not done from reasons is simply not a human action. Desires suggest maxims but maxims must be freely adopted if behavior ensuing from them is to count as action. But although we act for reasons, the sources of our reasons are not usually themselves reasons, or even rational. They are desires; and we do not choose our basic desires.

Here again Kant is involved with a problem that concerned many other philosophers of his time. For Kant, as for Locke and his followers, desires are non-rational causal forces varying idiosyncratically from person to person, and in any one person from time to time. Since happiness for Kant comes from satisfaction of desires, the range of components out of which we can choose to flesh out our conception of happiness is not up to us. But for

---

[10] Among them is the relation of the noumenal to the phenomenal will, since plainly—as Herman says in a footnote—we cannot interfere with noumenal freedom (PMJ 229 n. 36).

Kant, as for Locke and Price and Reid, there is a difficulty concerning the choice of desires to include in the conception of happiness I decide to pursue.

Without desires I would not have my non-moral reasons for acting. I would lack most of the reasons I have. Reason directs me to satisfy as many desires as I can without infringing on the moral law. But it cannot tell me which ones to reject from my conception of happiness unless it first privileges some whose satisfaction would be excluded by adding new ones; and it cannot tell me which desires should have this status. I can indeed refuse to act to gratify any desire I have. If the rejected desires are strong and persistent enough, that will simply leave me unhappy. I can decide to remain so, but I cannot decide desires into or out of existence, even if sometimes I can get myself to have new ones.[11]

For Kant, then, it seems, I can give reasons down to my desires but not any further. My desires are as much a part of me as my rationality, and are as essential to my being a distinctively *human* agent. They are not by themselves reasons for action, but without them my rational will could not move me in any specific direction. The self as knower requires percepts as much as concepts; and however it may be with a holy will, the human self as agent requires desires as well as the rational will. What makes human agency unique, for Kant, is not simply that it is the eruption of pure rationality into the causal order. It is rather that it is the sole point at which pure rationality can direct the part of the causal order most intimately tied to our identity. A morality that required reasons "all the way down" could not be a morality for human beings. Since the categorical imperative always requires the contribution of the desires in order to yield specific directives, it is not by itself a complete source of reasons. Hence, it does not, by Herman's own account, play the role that a conception of value plays in human agency.

The natural disarray of the passions and desires is a given in Kant's ethics, as the content of sensation is in the theoretical philosophy. The material of our lives, the substantive happiness we pursue, comes from forces we can neither create nor (as Kant eventually came to admit) eradicate.[12] Moral agency brings a kind of unity to our lives that prudential agency alone could never bring. Thus, there is a role for pure practical reason, although having

---

[11] For instance, if out of duty I make the well-being of others my end, I may come in time to feel genuine affection or love for those I decide to help.

[12] Contrast *Groundwork* IV.428 with *Religion* VI.58, 28, and 36.

and exercising it is not the whole point of our lives. If the principle of the priority of law to good encapsulates this position, then we can see why Kant need not have thought the law's claim on us mysterious. Perhaps we may call this aspect of Kant's position deontological.

III

The rocks on the other side now call for attention. Here I have in mind Julia Annas's powerfully argued views about Stoic and Kantian ethics in *The Morality of Happiness*.[13] She allows that there are important differences between the two, but the similarities as she portrays them are quite striking. Stoicism presents itself, as does all of ancient ethics, as an answer to a question any reflective person asks: "What should my life be like?...am I satisfied with my life as a whole, with the way it has developed and promises to continue?" (MH 27, 28–9). It offers a way to happiness. But despite being cast as a morality of happiness, the Stoic theory is neither hedonistic nor egoistic nor teleological. It assigns virtue a value of a unique kind, incommensurable with any other sort of value, and it takes this value to override other kinds of value (MH 122–3, 171, 185). Thus, it holds that desires are to be satisfied only if virtue permits. It requires the virtuous agent to be impartial in her concern for everyone (MH 128, 174, 265). And it claims that virtue is constitutive of the end, not merely instrumental in achieving it (MH 37).

If this is not quite Kantianism, it is certainly not the kind of morality of happiness the textbooks usually find in ancient ethics. And Annas finds further similarities between Stoic and Kantian views. The Stoics make the "very Kantian" claim that whoever understands the kind of value involved in virtue also realizes that this gives "a reason to act which is different in kind from a reason that merely promotes one's own desires and projects" (MH 263; see also 398, 432).[14] The brave person does the brave act "just because it is brave, and not for any ulterior reason." This is the counterpart to the

---

[13] New York, Oxford University Press, 1993; references given in the text are indicated by MH.

[14] Earlier Annas suggests that the values involved in virtue are in fact commensurable with non-virtue values, only they are so very much greater that it would be the height of folly to compare them (MH 122). However, she more frequently asserts that the kinds of value involved are incommensurable.

modern demand that the moral agent act for the moral reason, not for any ulterior reason. In each case the reason is to motivate by itself, not owing its force to "any more basic reasons." Annas adds that "in a way reminiscent of Kant, the Stoics represent the recognition of the force of a moral reason as a kind of respect for law" (MH 175).[15]

A further point of similarity, Annas claims, emerges more clearly in earlier than in later Stoicism: the secondary role of metaphysics. We are not required just to take our principles from nature. Nature may suggest a principle, but we must work it into a theory before we accept it. "There is an analog here to Kant's insistence" on avoiding heteronomy (MH 162). Cosmic nature is not a principle within ethics for the Stoic. The content of ethics is "already established" before we get to appeal to nature (MH 165). Even if Stoic theology might help "the advanced student" to understand the moral point of view, "what matters for morality is already obvious before we do any metaphysics, as indeed it is for Kant" (MH 169 n. 37).

Annas thus rejects the kind of contrast between ancient ethics and distinctively modern "morality" that Bernard Williams draws. She argues at length that "ancient [ethical] theories are theories of what modern moral theories are theories of" (MH 14; cf. 12, 47, 120ff.). Ancient thought about virtue plays the role in reflection on life that modern thought about morality plays. We can therefore usefully set one against the other. Annas seems to think that, when we do, the moderns come out looking rather badly. Leaving that issue to one side, I want to raise some questions about the commonalities that Annas sees in Stoic and Kantian thought. To do so I shall follow the Great Boyg's advice to Peer Gynt, and go round about.

IV

There is no doubt about Kant's admiration for the Stoics. Indications of agreements with them are scattered in many of his writings. They saw that

---

[15] Like Guyer and Herman, Annas finds an obscurity in the modern version of this view. Ancient ethics, unlike modern, she says, "does not give up at this point" by failing to explain the source of these reasons. For ancient ethics the brave person sees that acting bravely is part of the good of her life—or, as Herman and Guyer might put it, sees a value in acting bravely (MH 75). There is enough similarity between ancient and modern views for Kant to lose by the comparison.

the principle of morality must come from reason, and that happiness ought to be the result of virtue.[16] Their terms give the appropriate characterization of the outcome of moral strength. Virtue requires courage, to fight the monsters opposing it; moral courage constitutes honor and wisdom. "Only in its possession is a man "free", "healthy", "rich", "a king", and so forth, and can suffer no loss by chance or fate" (VI.405). Their doctrine of apathy is sound. One should never be in a state of emotional agitation, not even over one's best friend's misfortunes (VII.253; cf. VI.408–9). The Stoics point the way not only to the moral life but to the healthy one as well (VII.180). They were the best of the ancient philosophers, and "[i]n moral philosophy, we have not come any further than the ancients" (IX.32; cf. XXVII.484).

Kant's reservations about Stoicism were as pervasive as his appreciation of it. "Man fancifully exaggerates his moral capacity," Herder reports Kant as telling his class in the early 1760s,

and sets before himself the most perfect goodness; the outcome is nonsense; but what is required of us? The Stoic's answer: I shall raise myself *above myself*, . . . rise superior to my own afflictions and needs, and with all my might be *good*, be the *image of godhood*. But how so, for godhood has no obligations, yet you certainly do. . . . Now the god departs and we are left with *man*, a poor creature, loaded with obligations. *Seneca* was an impostor, *Epictetus* strange and fanciful.[17]

Human beings can hope at most to increase in virtue, not to attain it fully, Kant thinks, but he refuses to say, with the Stoics, that without perfect virtue one is not virtuous at all. The Stoics neglect our needs, the Epicureans do not. If a Stoic moral regimen is a useful tool, it is not sufficient. In being virtuous we should have the kind of cheerful heart that Epicurus recommended. Kant rejects "monkish ascetics," as Hume did (VII.484–5). Like Descartes, Kant claims that he can reconcile the two great schools of antiquity.[18] Happiness, the satisfaction of desires, is indeed second in rank to worthiness to be happy, assured only by virtue; but it is nonetheless indispensable for needy dependent beings such as we are.

---

[16] V.41, XVII.1402.29–31; see also V.60, and cf. *Refl.* 6630, XIX.118.
[17] XXVII.67, Immanuel Kant, Lectures on Ethics., ed. Peter Heath and J. B. Schneewind, trans. Peter Heath (Cambridge: Cambridge University Press, 1997), 32.
[18] For Descartes, see the letters to Queen Christina, November 20, 1647, in Cottingham *et al.*, *Philosophical Writings of Descartes* (Cambridge: Cambridge University Press, 1991), vol. III, 325, and to Princess Elizabeth, August 18, 1645, vol. III, 261.

The Stoics did, of course, allow for the satisfaction of needs, allowing them to count as a secondary kind of good.[19] But Kant gives no discussion of the Stoic view of these goods. He does not try, for instance, to relate them to the goods to which we are directed by hypothetical imperatives. He is simply not interested in giving a full assessment of Stoic theory.[20] For him Stoic views are useful primarily as ways of describing his attitudes and locating his own position. Consequently his explicit comments about Stoicism do not teach us much about its relations to his philosophical ethics. We can get further by seeing what Kant thought of Leibnizian moral philosophy.

If Leibniz was not a Stoic, there are nonetheless a number of striking resemblances, some closer and some more distant, between his position and Stoicism. Like the Stoics, Leibniz is a determinist who rejects fatalism. His doctrine that all things represent all other things, however indistinctly, is a counterpart to the Stoic doctrine of the infusion of divinity in everything. He thinks our reason and God's are the same in kind. Like the Stoics he holds that the mind is all of a piece. It is its representations; the clearer and more distinct they are, the more perfect we are and the more virtuously we act. Leibniz does not accept the Stoic doctrine that virtue is an all-or-nothing affair, but he agrees in holding that virtue is a function of knowledge about the constitution of the universe. These Leibnizian views were available to Kant in the *Theodicy* and other writings.[21]

Clearly Kant disagrees with many of the points on which Leibniz and the Stoics seem to agree. Kant accepts determinism only for the phenomenal world, leaving room for freedom as noumenal, and offers a moral argument for belief in the latter. He intends the kind of freedom he defends to differ from the kind Leibniz himself thought he could defend. He denies that theoretical claims about God can be warranted, and places such rational

---

[19] See A. A. Long and D. N. Sedley, eds., *The Hellenistic Philosophers* (Cambridge: Cambridge University Press, 1987), §58, 354–7.

[20] Kant developed his own basic ideas about morality before reading Adam Smith's *Theory of the Moral Sentiments*, but he seems to have read it in the German translation of 1770, and he evidently admired it. Smith gives a detailed account of Stoicism in his historical account of systems of moral philosophy. His discussion, in Bk. VII, ii.1, §§15–47 of the *Theory*, which is much fuller than that of any other theory he considers, is a judicious and, on the whole, favorable estimate. Kant gives no such overview of Stoicism—or of any other moral philosophy.

[21] References to the *Theodicy*, given in the text by T and section number (§), are to the translation by E. M. Huggard, ed. Austin Farrer (LaSalle, Ill.: Open Court, 1985).

investigation of divinity as we can carry out within morality, rather than within physics. Insofar as we are entitled to believe that we live in a rationally ordered universe, our grounds are moral. The nature of the divine order that Kant thinks us morally required to believe in is also not the same as that thought warranted either by the Stoics or by Leibniz. Here we come to a point of some importance.

Leibniz and Kant share a concern about a problem that could not have had the same meaning for the Stoics, the problem of the relation of morality to the divine will. The Stoics were no doubt aware of the dilemma put by Plato in the *Euthyphro*. But for them the issue did not carry the baggage it carries for moralists in Christian times. Voluntarism, asserted in modern times by Descartes, Hobbes, Pufendorf, King, and less overtly, by Locke, seemed to many thinkers then to be a major danger. It threatened to undermine relations between humans and God, turning him into a tyrant whom one could obey only blindly and out of fear, and toward whom one could not feel the appropriate kind of love. Since God's relations to his creation could serve as a model for the sovereign's relations to his subjects, voluntarism seemed to offer support to despotism and tyranny in earthly politics. Cumberland and Leibniz both oppose voluntarism by arguing that God is moved by his awareness of the goodness of options before him, choosing always the best. Since what we are required to do echoes what God necessarily does, both of them propound strongly consequentialist theories of morality. Like the Stoics, they think that some states of affairs are good regardless of whether they are desired or willed; and they hold that God acts to bring these about and wills that we should do so as well.

Kant, like Pufendorf, rejects the equation of Being with Goodness that Leibniz defends and comes down on the side of the voluntarist. He holds, as I have noted, that to be good is to be the object of a will. By taking the divine will to be governed by the moral law, he guards himself against the standard objections to the voluntarist thesis. Kant's God is not arbitrary, although we cannot come to any conclusion about whether he does or does not create the best of all possible worlds. We have no moral need for a decision on that point. We need think only that the divinity is just and sees to it that the increasingly virtuous become ever happier. An important part of what makes it morally necessary to conceive of God in this way is the belief that nature has no necessary connection to moral worth. And for

Kant, as I have said, happiness comes only from the satisfaction of natural desire, to which the Stoics give a more limited role.

Through this deliberate rejection of Leibniz, Kant in effect rejects a major aspect of Stoicism as well. The metaphysics of Stoicism is profoundly important for its ethics. Regardless of the extent to which any particular moral principle is derived from the metaphysics, Stoic metaphysics grounds at least the *a priori* assurance that when we act from reason as far as we can, everything of concern to us will be well.[22] Kant simply takes for granted an anti-Leibnizian, anti-Stoic acceptance of the indifference of the natural world to rational human concerns.

The indifference of the natural world to human meaning is also involved in a major disagreement between Kant and both Leibniz and the Stoics concerning the passions.[23] Plutarch tells us that the Stoics "suppose that the passionate and irrational part [of the soul] is not distinguished from the rational by any distinction within the soul's nature, but the same part of the soul (which they call thought and commanding-faculty) becomes virtue and vice as it turns around and changes in passions ... and contains nothing irrational within itself."[24] Leibniz would not have found this objectionable. Kant would have preferred Plutarch's own view: "In us the faculty of judging and the faculty of feeling emotion are different ... that within us which follows is different from that which it follows when persuaded, or ... fights against when it is not persuaded."[25]

On the Stoic theory of *oikeiōsis* our natural development points us toward a harmonious set of desires within ourselves, leading eventually to the dominance of reason and, ideally, to full virtue.[26] We are part of the universe and can in principle become as harmonious as it is. For Leibniz, as we increase our knowledge of the divinely ordered world we cannot fail to become more harmonious ourselves, because our minds, including our pleasures and our desires, are nothing but representations of that world. The

---

[22] On these points, see John Cooper, "Eudaimonism, the Appeal to Nature, and 'Moral Duty' in Stoicism", in Stephen Engstrom and Jennifer Whiting, eds., *Aristotle, Kant, and the Stoics* (Cambridge: Cambridge University Press, 1996), 261–84.

[23] Guyer, pp. 84–73, has an excellent discussion of Kant's efforts in the *Critique of Judgment* to see how far we can think away the indifference of nature.

[24] See Long and Sedley, *The Hellenistic Philosophers*, vol. I, 61B.9, p. 378.

[25] Plutarch, *On Moral Virtue* 449 C–D, trans. W. C. Helmbold (Loeb Classical Library, Cambridge, Mass.: Harvard University Press, 1929).

[26] See Long and Sedley, *The Hellenistic Philosophers*, §57, 346–50.

Stoics and Leibniz thus think that there is an order of goods or perfections that we have but to track to find peace and harmony. Ignorance of this real existing order is the cause of our unhappiness and disorder. If we enlighten our passions they will misrepresent good and ill less; and to the extent that they represent the values of things accurately, they will bring the order of the universe into our lives, both personal and social.

This picture of motivation gives us reason to doubt Annas's suggestion that something like respect for moral law is a central moral motive for the Stoics. For them reasons for action are all perceptions, more or less clear, of various goods or ills. They are thus commensurable. What the brave person sees when she is brave for the sake of bravery and for no ulterior reason is the goodness of being brave in that way. Even when the virtuous person is moved by the thought that Zeus directs her to act bravely, she is thinking of Zeus's directions as something it is good for her to follow. But for Kant respect is not the perception of some good. It is a unique feeling caused by being humbled by a law that we know we must follow and whose directives are incommensurable with those arising from our desires. Respect, Kant says, is that law itself "regarded subjectively as an incentive" (V.72–6). If an incentive of this kind is an essential part of Kant's deontology, then we may take a theory that lacks it or would deny it as teleological.

For Kant there is no natural harmonious order to be carried into our lives. Even if there were, the passions and desires would not carry it by representing it. On his view, the passions are not confused or indistinct representations of good or ill; they are not representations at all. They are, as in Locke and Hume, urges toward or away from various objects or states of affairs represented by the understanding. In themselves they can be neither rational nor irrational.[27] For the Stoics the thoughts embedded in desires are open to assent or dissent in virtue of their implicitly propositional nature. Leibniz's view does not differ in essentials. But for Kant, desires must generate maxims if reason is to enter as that which, in Plutarch's phrase, they are to follow. Kant says that we do not need to explain how desires and inclinations arise from pleasure, and how maxims arise from these through the cooperation of reason (IV.427). But we can see how his naturalistic theory of the passions leads him to another step away from Leibniz.

---

[27] Hume gives a well-known account of what we can mean when we call a desire irrational. Kant also has an account of this (see VII.254, 265, VI.408).

Leibniz has no need for a faculty of will that is different in kind from desire, because for him all desires are desires for more or less of the same thing, perfection or good. "The will is never prompted to action," he says, "save by the representation of the good, which prevails over the opposite representations" (T §45). When and if we reflect, whichever desire emerges as offering us the most good becomes our strongest desire, and hence our will. For Kant our desires do not all aim at objects under a common description, seeking more rather than less of the same thing. What we desire we call good, and we expect pleasure from it; but the object of our desires is not some prior goodness or abstract pleasant sensation. It is, for example, flute playing, or glory, or benefit to others. If we do not accept the view that we are moved by the strongest desire, we need to allow the existence of a different power—a will—enabling us to decide which desire to act on and which to rule out.

To explain how we can possess a will able not only to explain observable choices, but to account for the possibility of morality, Kant thinks he must invoke the whole noumenal apparatus. Morality, he thinks, requires that the self must be a free agent, not tied to the universe like a dog to a cart. We can see why he turns to the transcendental for a solution, however little it may seem to us to offer one.

V

Kant is not trying to answer questions about how one's life is going. Still less is he setting up to know better than ordinary folk where they should place their happiness. He does indeed hold that as we improve morally we can come to take satisfaction in our behavior, deriving tranquillity and even a kind of contentment from it. But such self-satisfaction is not positive enough to be more than an analog of happiness. Arising from our exercise of free will, it is something like "the self-sufficiency which can be ascribed only to the Supreme Being" (V. 117–18). But Stoic though this sounds, it is still unlike Stoic *eudaimonia*: it leaves us with much to desire. And Kant, unlike the Stoics, thinks that when we try to help others attain happiness, we should accept their own conception of happiness, not impose ours on them.

Given Kant's view of happiness, with its deep roots in his understanding of nature, the venture that Annas says is central to ancient ethical theory does not make much sense. Kant sees regularity in the physical world, and in the operations of the mind considered as part of that world.[28] But the regularity does not include any humanly meaningful order among the impulses that are the desires and passions, even though they are part of the natural order. In the third *Critique* Kant draws a strong implication from this view. We cannot, he says, form any realizable idea of happiness, or of the complete gratification of our desires. Even if nature obeyed our every wish and our powers were unlimited, our idea of happiness is too wavering and fluctuating to allow us to attain what we think we seek. And even if we aimed at no more than satisfying "the true wants of nature in which our species is in complete and fundamental accord," what we mean by happiness would remain unattainable. "For [man's] own nature is not so constituted as to rest or be satisfied in any possession or enjoyment whatever" (VI.430). It is not an accident that Kant never offers us a rational principle for constructing a substantive conception of happiness.

Kant allows that one might discover simple rules that add to happiness for certain kinds of people—rules about how to stage a dinner party for maximal enjoyment, for instance. But he did not propose anything like a philosophical theory that does better in guiding everyone to happiness than common-sense notions do. Kant himself remarks that among the moderns "the concept of the highest good has fallen into disuse or at least seems to have become something secondary" (V.64). Though he offered a view of the structure of the complete good, he did not intend to give a detailed answer to questions about how one's life might go well as a whole.

In assigning a different task to moral philosophy, Kant is not even claiming to know something important about morality that ordinary people do not know. As he says, "Neither science nor philosophy is needed in order to know what one has to do in order to be honest and good...the philosopher...has no principle which the common understanding lacks" (IV.404; cf. V. 8n). This most un-Stoic position reflects Kant's view of the enterprise of moral philosophy.

Kant thinks it has two functions. One is simply to sort out the place of morality in the universe, and to understand what it shows us about the human mind. The theoretical task gets some urgency from a practical need.

---

[28] The impossibility, as Kant saw it, of a science of psychology is not due to any lack of determinism in the temporal flow of mental happenings.

Human corruption induces us to use, among other things, bad philosophy to undermine the demands of morality. Kant explains this not by an appeal to original sin, but by the dual nature of the human constitution. Unavoidably concerned for our happiness, equally responsive to the inescapable voice of our own pure practical reason, we find in ourselves a natural dialectic that leads us to try to obfuscate the call of the latter so that we may pursue the former without limits. The problem of explaining the relations of the two voices must have been the same for Socrates as it is for us. Kant thinks that there is still work left for us to do even if the Stoics did better at dealing with that issue than any of the other ancients. Of course, he—like many another philosopher—thought that he himself had pretty much wrapped it up.

VI

If I have fended off the clashing rocks, then we can see one reason why the contrast between Kantian deontology and ancient teleology is significant. Even the Stoics are teleologists in a way that Kant is not. Kant's deontology reflects his quite modern lack of confidence in the natural world. Nothing but our powers of reason can regulate our natural inclinations and wishes so that we can act as we must if we are to live in a society of free and equal agents. Kant's theory of freedom as rooted in our transcendental nature may not seem acceptable. We may wish to replace it with a fully naturalized account of moral motivation. But he at least opened the way to a question of great importance to us. It is the question of how we are to shape our lives and our societies once we see that their structure is not imposed on us by any natural constraints. Metaphysical confidence in the rational order of nature made this a question that the Stoics could not have raised.

From here we can also see one aspect of the philosophical importance of debates about assimilating Kant to Stoicism, or to any other ancient philosophy. It concerns our approach to the history of moral philosophy. Like Annas and many others, we can approach that history with the assumption that throughout its course philosophers have all been attempting to answer the same basic question, or solve the same set of problems. We might say that just as the interaction of mind and body, or our perception of color, has always needed an explanation, so morality has always called for one.

We might then think of the historian of moral philosophy as tracing different theoretical efforts to understand the domain of the moral. This might lead us to try to minimize differences between ancient and modern ethics.

I find it more useful to take another approach. We can ask whether at different times the salient questions differed. Perhaps the Stoics saw different issues facing individuals than Plato or Aristotle saw. Perhaps the problems that Grotius and Hobbes made central were problems that could not have arisen for Epictetus or Seneca. Even if we grant that there are facts about the human situation that call for some sort of norms in any society, the construal of these facts may alter drastically. It is after all our *socially meaningful* life whose facts are the concern of morality and moral philosophy. These facts are thoroughly and richly conceptualized before they come to the philosopher's attention, and the conceptualizations may be different at different times. Old ways of talking about how to live together and how to settle differences without fighting may cease to be useful under drastically altered circumstances, such as the introduction of a new religious vocabulary for discussing such matters. Moral philosophies can be viewed as sets of tools some cultures develop for coping with various deep problems in the ways we talk about or understand our common life. On that view the changes will be as important as the continuities.

Some of the essays in Engstrom and Whiting (cited in n. 22) seek commonalities between Kant and Aristotle, even when they allow for some differences. In claiming that the differences may be more revealing than the similarities, I do not mean to be implying anything about the superiority of Kant over the Stoics, still less of Aristotle. I do want to suggest that to assess the significance of what we find in the texts and arguments we need to ask what the philosophers at different times thought they were doing. If we simply assume that what they were doing was trying to solve the same "philosophical problem," we have a ready answer. But that answer does not get us down to the level of detail where we can see real history happening.

We can take the blurry notions of deontology and teleology to point, however inadequately, to profoundly different conceptions of the tasks of moral philosophers. Kant saw a world in which divisions within Christendom made an ethic centering on the highest good highly problematic. He saw a world of contestation around rights. He saw a crumbling of the authority of old social elites, including those claiming to be the sole source of proper moral guidance for the ill-educated and poor. When he took ideas from his predecessors, he reworked them to handle issues that Aristotle and Chrysippus and Cicero could not even have formulated. By pointing out that Kant was not alone in his times in trying out a deontological view, I mean to suggest that where so many seek a radically new approach, it is worth looking for a new issue.

One might lack interest in the history of moral philosophy construed in this way. One might be interested in philosophers of the past only to the extent that their work helps us now with ours. Even so it may be important to look beyond what the old philosophers said to the situation in which they said it. We need to ask what issues they saw in their society's ways of handling private lives and personal relations. And we need to relate their philosophy to these issues. To take just one example, *eudaimonia* in ancient theory is not the same as Kantian *Glückseligkeit*. Why did Kant find it necessary to use a conception of what makes life worthwhile that differs so significantly from the conception the Greek philosophers used? Why did he think it necessary to construct a realm of the moral radically distinct from that of prudence and happiness? Answers to these questions may lead us to consider problems—such as that of rebuilding a distinctive eudaimonistic theory—that we might not otherwise have taken up. It may also lead us to question our assumptions about the problems we put at the center of our own work.

16

Toward Enlightenment: Kant and the Sources of Darkness

The title page of Christian Wolff's *Vernünftige Gedancken von Gott, der Welt und der Seele des Menschen* of 1720, the so-called "German Metaphysics," shows a brilliant sun beaming through dark clouds above a peaceful rural landscape. A Latin phrase over the sun explains the picture: "light restored after clouds." Many other philosophy books published in Germany during the first part of the eighteenth century carried similar pictures. In at least two the word *Dispellam* is shown at the top.[1] Enlightenment or *Aufklärung* was the sun dispelling the clouds. The sun was reason; the clouds were ignorance and false belief. The darkness they caused was favorable to despotic government, overbearing priests, misguided religiosity, abusive nobility, repressive laws backed by ferocious punishments, unjust taxation, and stultifying economic practices. Enlighteners opposed these by trying to reform legislation, government, and penal systems, to increase religious toleration and the freedom to think and publish, to spread scientific knowledge, to improve education, and to rationalize economic policies. Success, they thought, depended on removing the dark clouds inherited from the past. Reason was the tool for the job. And philosophers were taken to be among those best equipped to show what reason could do and how it could help.

Kant's essay "An Answer to the Question: What Is Enlightenment?" is widely taken to be a classic statement of enlightened thinking, and he himself to be one of its great advocates.[2] While this is broadly speaking

My thanks to Eckart Förster, Sean Greenberg, Don Rutherford and Rüdiger Bittner for helpful suggestions and comments.

[1] Werner Schneiders, *Hoffnung auf Vernunft*, (Hamburg: Felix Meiner Verlag, 1990), Wolff on p.87, the others on Schneiders pp. 84,85, from books by Gundling, 1715, and Thomasius, 1726.

[2] The "Enlightenment" essay is in *Gesammelte Schriften*, 8, pp. 33–42, trans. in Immanuel Kant, *Practical Philosophy*, trans. Mary Gregor (Cambridge: Cambridge University Press, 1996), 17–22, cited

correct, Kant's stance toward *Aufklärung*, as toward almost everything else, is very much his own. One way of seeing how he differs from his enlightening predecessors is to compare his view of the sources of darkness with theirs. I begin with a few general comments about Enlightenment. In the second section, I review briefly some of the thinkers who express views on the sources of darkness—not all of them do. In the last part, I look at Kant's complex position.

I. Enlightenments

The reforming outlook toward which I gestured above was consciously shared by many thinkers and activists whom we classify as enlightened. It is, however, a matter of scholarly debate whether they should all be thought of as participating in a single movement of Enlightenment.[3] Expressing a now common view, one scholar argues that if enlighteners were reformers, the national differences in the institutions to be reformed must have made a significant difference to the ideas they used to question established beliefs. He is defending the claim that there was a uniquely Scottish Enlightenment: "Since there is demonstrably something distinctively Scottish about the large institutions...which informs the experience that supports and motivates the thinkers' reflections, there will also be something distinctively Scottish about those reflections about the concepts...and values" involved in the institutions.[4]

---

hereafter as PracP. With one exception references to Kant are to volume and page numbers of the Akademy edition of the *Gesammelte Schriften*; the one reference to the *Critique of Pure Reason* follows the standard practice of using A and B page numbers for 1st and 2nd edn. references.

Allen Wood says that Kant was "perhaps the greatest philosophical proponent" of the Enlightenment. (*PracP*, p. xxiii)

[3] For a most illuminating look at the whole category, see James Schmidt, "Inventing the Enlightenment: Anti-Jacobins, British Hegelians, and the *Oxford English Dictionary*", in *Journal of the History of Ideas*, 64.3, July 2003, pp. 421–45. Schmidt shows that the Germans had in *Aufklärung* a word that long preceded the English *Enlightenment* as the name of a historical period. Schmidt's anthology, *What is Enlightenment?* (Berkeley: Univ. of California Press, 1996), is a useful collection to which I am indebted.

[4] Alexander Brodie (ed.), "Introduction" to *The Cambridge Companion to the Scottish Enlightenment* (Cambridge: Cambridge University Press, 2003), 2–3. For a more specific contrast between Enlightenments in Scotland and Germany see Fania Oz-Sulzberger, "Scots, Germans, Republic and Commerce" in *Republicanism*, ed. Martin van Gelderen and Quentin Skinner, vol. II (Cambridge: Cambridge University Press, 2002), 107–226.

There is much to be said for this view. German philosophers, for instance, lived under a wide variety of political regimes, with several religions permitted and sometimes backed by the different governments.[5] In France, by contrast, a central government imposed one religion, while in England a central government more or less tolerated a number of them. Nonetheless, there were commonalities that crossed political boundaries. Jonathan Israel has argued powerfully that we should take Enlightenment to be "a single highly integrated intellectual and cultural movement" occurring all over Europe, coming at various times but centered on the same problems and often stimulated by the same books.[6]

Israel also argues that what he calls the early radical Enlightenment, which developed in the latter part of the seventeenth century, was decisive in shaping European and eventually world thought thereafter. Nationality, for him, is not deeply significant. What does matter is that some groups of thinkers advocated far more sweeping changes in thought and action than others. The radical enlighteners were atheistic, materialistic, and naturalistic. They advocated governments that would be much more liberal and democratic than any under which they lived. For Israel, their most influential philosopher was Spinoza. Because he rejected all the main points of Jewish and Christian conceptions of God, he was seen as an atheist, even though he called the basic substance of the universe "God or Nature." His views were spread by innumerable pamphlets, books, letters, discussion circles, and clandestine manuscripts.

More moderate enlighteners were appalled by the radical Spinozistic program, seeing it as a threat to the religion many of them still accepted as well as to morality and public order. But even moderates found much

---

[5] For an older but still useful view of the peculiarities of *Aufklärung* in Germany, see Lewis White Beck, *Early German Philosophy*, (Harvard, Mass.: Harvard University Press, 1969), 244–7. Schneiders, cited in n. 1 above, pp.45–8, distinguishes four stages in the Aufklärung: an early stage from 1690 to 1720, stimulated largely by Thomasius; high Aufklärung, centered on Wolff, from 1720 to 1750; a popularizing Aufklärung, from 1750 to 1780, in which ideas were spread by less rigorous thinkers; and late Aufklärung from 1780 to 1800.

Ian Hunter argues for differentiation of Enlightenments *within* Germany, distinguishing between a movement aiming at making government wholly non-religious and indifferent to the private beliefs of its citizens and another trying to preserve an older view in which the state must protect religion and concern itself with the spiritual welfare of its citizens. He sees Pufendorf and Thomasius as the main thinkers favoring the civil enlightenment, Leibniz and Kant as theorists of the metaphysical Enlightenment. See *Rival Enlightenments* (Cambridge: Cambridge University Press, 2001).

[6] Jonathan I. Israel, *Radical Enlightenment* (Oxford: Oxford University Press, 2000), v.

darkness in the practices of religion. Their aim was to bring light to drive away what they saw as harmful excrescences on much-needed belief rather than to eliminate it altogether. Kant himself was neither atheistic nor materialistic nor naturalistic. He devoted much of his work to arguing that these views were not supportable. He has consequently been thought by some scholars not to belong to the *Aufklärung* at all.[7] But metaphysically based antireligious claims are not the only markers of Enlightenment.

Whether radical or moderate, enlighteners used a common vocabulary to identify what they rejected. Ignorance was not the only enemy. It simply opened the way for mistaken beliefs that were more directly the causes of the practices the enlighteners opposed. In religious matters, they tended to think of these beliefs as falling into two main categories: superstition and enthusiasm. By "superstition," the enlighteners sometimes meant any religious belief, but often they meant belief in the value of the worship of saints, the use of relics and images, and the necessity of priestly intercession to obtain salvation—all of which they took to be distinctively Roman Catholic. By "enthusiasm," they might mean any sort of religious fanaticism, but often they meant the largely Protestant belief that individuals could receive inspiration—and political instruction—directly from God.[8]

Superstition and enthusiasm were tied to what the enlighteners called "prejudice." By this they meant, not negative and hostile attitudes toward "other" people, but inherited beliefs and practices with the authority of long acceptance behind them. The term had a wide application. In the *Ethics*, published in 1677, Spinoza said that the belief that everything in nature acts for an end, as humans do, is foremost among the prejudices he wishes to remove.[9] D'Alembert spoke of prejudices in favor of Aristotle opening the

[7] See Panajotis Kondylis, *Die Aufklärung im Rahmen des neuzeitlichen Rationalismus*, (1981) (Hamburg: Meiner Verlag, 2002), 639–42.

[8] In an early work Kant distinguishes fanaticism from enthusiasm, reserving the first term for the feeling of immediate contact with a higher being and the second for an abnormally high degree of attachment to any principle whatsoever. He ties superstition especially to Spain and thinks it more pernicious than fanaticism. *Observations on the Feeling of the Beautiful and Sublime*, 2. 250–1 and n. In *Religion within the Boundaries of mere Reason*, Kant ties enthusiasm to "supposed inner experience (effects of grace)." 6.53; cf. 6.174. I use the translations of Kant's writings on religion by Allen W. Wood and George di Giovanni in Immanuel Kant, *Religion and Rational Theology* (Cambridge: Cambridge University Press, 1996). Future references to *Religion within the Boundaries* will be given in the text, indicated as RR.

[9] The remark about prejudice occurs at the beginning of the Appendix to Part I of the *Ethics*, in *The Collected Works of Spinoza*, ed. and trans. Edwin Curley (Princeton: Princeton University Press, 1985), 439. Cited hereafter as Curley.

way to benighted scholasticism.[10] Some students at Jena, inspired by the French Revolution, formed a group "to set Reason on the legislative throne that she deserves." They proclaimed that "Reason tolerates no prejudices, which mock her. Dueling is such a prejudice."[11] In the *Critique of the Power of Judgment*, Kant identified prejudice with the passivity and hence the heteronomy of reason. He added that "the greatest prejudice of all is . . . **superstition**."[12] Later I present more evidence of the importance of these Enlightenment concepts in Kant's thinking.

II. The Sources of Darkness

Why do the religious prejudices that form the dark clouds have such a strong hold? After all, most of these beliefs impose severe regimens, call for sacrifice, interfere with one's life. Why do people hold to them with such tenacity? Why is the struggle for Enlightenment so difficult? Does the answer lie in our psychology? Kant says that while it is permissible to represent the corrupter of mankind as external to us, that is, as a devil, the ultimate source of corruption is within: after all, "we would not be tempted by [the devil] were we not in secret agreement with him" (RR 6.60). What attracts us to superstition and enthusiasm, and makes us cling to our prejudices? What are the sources of darkness?

Spinoza opens the preface to his *Theological-Political Treatise* (1670) with some suggestions of an answer. Men would not be held by superstition (*superstitione*), he says, if they could control their own lives and had rules by which to govern their actions. But they often have no idea about how to cope with the difficulties fortune puts in their way. They fluctuate between hope and fear, and grasp at any belief that offers help. They wonder at anything unexpected, and take it as a sign or a portent of the will of the gods requiring sacrifice. But if greed and fear are the main source and sustainer of superstition, they are aided by statecraft. It profits despotic rulers to keep

---

[10] Jean le Rond D'Alambert, Preliminary Discourse to the Encyclopedia of Diderot, trans. Schwab and Rex, 1963, 71.

[11] Quoted in Nicholas Boyle, *Goethe. The Poet and the Age*, vol. II (Oxford: Oxford University Press, 2000), 112.

[12] *Critique of the Power of Judgment*, trans. Paul Guyer (Cambridge: Cambridge University Press, 2000), 5. 294. Cited hereafter as CJ.

their subjects in thrall by religion. Spinoza's aim in the book is to show that only freedom of thought, fostered by freedom in society, can lead to true piety and to civil peace and order. To do so he must convince the masses of the truth of these views.[13]

Later, he explains why the task is so difficult. The best way to convince people of the truth of anything is to prove it, deducing it rigorously from self-evident principles. But most people find arguments of this kind too hard to follow. They prefer to take their beliefs from experience. The main points of true religion can be brought to the masses, whose minds cannot perceive ideas clearly and distinctly, only by embodying the ideas in stories. And while the masses need stories that move them to obedience, they cannot themselves judge which are best for this purpose. Hence they always need "pastors or ministers of the church" as their guides. Otherwise they attend to trivial narrative details and not to the lessons to be learned.[14]

Even with such guides, men's minds are easily led astray. In the *Treatise on the Emendation of the Intellect* and the *Ethics*, Spinoza says the masses have at best perceptions of kinds that allow for error.[15] In the *Ethics*, he adds that falsity "consists in the privation of knowledge which inadequate, or mutilated and confused, ideas involve."[16] Confused ideas constitute the passions and desires that drive most people. The masses think God made everything for their benefit. They develop their own ways of trying to influence God to direct all of nature to satisfy their own "insatiable greed." Thus the prejudice that everything in nature works for an end "was changed into superstition" and lodged firmly in men's minds. We would all have remained in this sorry state had not mathematics, which is not concerned with ends, "shown men another standard of truth."[17] It will take a clear deductive demonstration of the truth, such as his own *Ethics*, to free men from their superstitions; but this is exactly the kind of thinking most people cannot follow.

---

[13] *Tractatus Theologico-Politicus*, ed. and trans. Günter Gawlick and Friedrich Niewöhner (Darmstadt: 1989), with facing Latin text, 5–11.

[14] *Tractatus*, Ch. V, pp. 179–85; also in Benedict de Spinoza, *The Political Works* ed. and trans. A. G. Wernham (Oxford: Oxford University Press, 1958), 99–105.

[15] Curley, *Treatise*, pp. 12–16; *Ethics* II.40 Schol.2, 477f.   [16] Curley, *Ethics* II.35, 470.

[17] Curley, *Ethics*, I, Appendix, pp. 440–1, and Book III generally.

Locke discusses the sources of darkness in religious matters in many places.[18] Here I can consider only a little of what he says. Unlike Spinoza, he believes that we have been given a genuine divine revelation and he defends a version of Christianity. The domain of faith begins where reason cannot deliver knowledge, but faith cannot require us to believe anything that goes against clear reason. Moreover, our acceptance of claims as divinely revealed must rest on our having reasons for believing that the revelation does indeed come from God. A proper understanding of the relations between reason and faith, and due reliance on reason, is essential if we are to avoid superstition.[19] But few men care to reason or to seek truth for its own sake. Their passions and interests all too often dictate their beliefs; and in religious matters, this leads to enthusiasm. Having disregarded both reason and Christian revelation in imposing beliefs on themselves, they proceed to impose them on others. They set up the "ungrounded fancies" of their own brains as "a Foundation both of opinion and Conduct." Becoming an authority for others without going to any trouble "flatters many Men's Laziness, Ignorance, and Vanity": hence the great appeal of being an enthusiast and claiming immediate divine inspiration.[20]

Locke thinks that failure to reason is in general a major source of error. Men hold many beliefs without grounds, even when grounds are available. Many people are unable to think well enough to assess evidence and follow arguments. There is "a difference of degrees in Men's Understandings . . . to so great a latitude . . . that there is a greater distance between some Men, and others . . . than between some Men and some Beasts." Some just refuse to consider reasons for and against various claims. And many are content to give up their own ability to reason. They simply accept the "current Opinions, and licensed Guides" of their country.[21] Many do not have time and energy to think after their exhausting work. But the truths about God and morality needed for right living are so easily accessible that most people could think their way to them. And those who cannot—farm hands and dairy maids—can learn them from the preacher.[22]

---

[18] He discusses these matters in his *Conduct of the Understanding*, in *Thoughts concerning Education*, and in *The Reasonableness of Christianity*, as well as in the *Essay concerning Human Understanding*, which I cite in the edition of Peter Nidditch, (Oxford: Oxford University Press, 1975), cited as Locke.

[19] Locke, IV.xviii, 696.   [20] Ibid. xix.3, 698.   [21] Ibid. xx.3–5, 707–9.

[22] Locke, *The Reasonableness of Christianity*, (1695) ed. I. T. Ramsey (Stanford: Stanford University Press, 1958), 66.

It is not just ignorance or confusion that is the source of darkness for Locke. It is mainly the inability or unwillingness to think clearly. In his writings on education and the conduct of the understanding, he repeatedly says that most people can reason, that it is lack of desire or practice that leads them to fail to seek grounds for their beliefs, and that sound education can do much to remedy the defect. Spinoza does not seem to share his optimism on this point. Nonetheless, both he and Locke are rejecting strong Calvinist views about the inability of sinful humans to reason clearly or to improve their faculties.[23] Neither attributes the darkness to the depravity that Calvinists thought we inherited from Adam. They are offering not a supernatural view of the tendency to accept corrupt forms of religion, but naturalistic accounts. Contingent facts about human energy and ability, not divinely imposed punishment, explain the darkness. Something can be done about it.

Whether Hume himself was or was not wholly without religious belief—a much-discussed question—he seems to have allowed that there is some reason to accept a minimal single deity, the first cause of the universe, but otherwise barely describable. The rich variety of religious belief beyond this is caused by ignorance, hope, and fear. With almost no knowledge of a causal order in nature, surrounded on all sides by threats to life and happiness, and with "a universal tendency...to conceive all things like themselves,"[24] humans first invented a variety of deities whom they could blame for misfortune and supplicate for aid. Monotheism emerged only slowly. And "whoever thinks it has owed its success to the...reasons, on which it is undoubtedly founded, would show himself little acquainted with the ignorance and stupidity of the people, and their incurable prejudice in favor of their particular superstitions."[25] Nor do irrational forces cease to work once monotheism is reached. Religious belief is unstable: it tends "to rise from idolatry to theism, and to sink again from theism into idolatry."[26]

The consequences are not trivial. On the whole, polytheists are tolerant of other religions, and monotheists are not. Human sacrifice was practiced

[23] See W.M. Spellman, *Locke and the Problem of Depravity* (Oxford: Oxford University Press 1988), and John Marshall, *John Locke: Resistance, Religion, and Responsibility*, (Cambridge: Cambridge University Press, 1994), whose criticisms of Spellman I follow.
[24] David Hume, *The Natural History of Religion*, ed. J. C. A. Gaskin, (Oxford: Oxford University Press, 1993), III, 140. Referred to hereafter as Hume.
[25] Ibid. 153.   [26] Ibid. 159–60.

in "barbarous nations" but it nowhere equaled the horrors of the Inquisition. And the proclivity of monotheists to attribute infinite superiority of every kind to their deity leads them into a submissiveness and passivity that takes them far from the virtues displayed by the heroes of antiquity. Moreover, as theism is more in accordance with sound reason than polytheism is, it more easily coopts philosophy. But theology insists on limiting the scope of reason. Religion—or the clergy—must have "Amazement...Mystery...Darkness" in order to keep the masses in awe.[27] Hume delights in pointing out absurdities in the beliefs and practices of monotheistic religions, especially Roman Catholicism. He also argues that every religion tends to corrupt its adherents. Votaries, he says, "will still seek the divine favor, not by virtue and good morals, which alone can be acceptable to a perfect being, but either by frivolous observances,...by rapturous extasies, or by the belief of mysterious and absurd opinions."[28] Were there to be so unlikely a thing as a religion insisting that only pure morals can be pleasing to God, "the people's prejudices" are so strong that they would find ways to make even attendance at moral instruction into a superstitious means of ingratiating themselves with their deity.[29]

There is no way we can escape religious controversies except to leave the different superstitions to quarrel among themselves, while we turn to "the calm, though obscure, regions of philosophy."[30] But in fact on Hume's view there is more room for hope than this remark suggests. Ignorance, combined with fear and desire, creates religion. If Newtonian accounts of natural events become widely known, they will dry up the sources of superstition. Whatever his skeptical doubts in the obscure regions of philosophy, Hume holds to the Enlightenment belief that scientific knowledge will dispel the darkness.[31]

"Man is unhappy only because he mistrusts Nature," declaims Baron d'Holbach at the opening of his *System of Nature* (1770). "His mind is so pervaded with prejudices that one might believe him forever condemned to error...It is time to seek in Nature the remedy for the ills that enthusiasm

---

[27] Hume, 166.   [28] Ibid. 179.   [29] Ibid. 180.   [30] Ibid. 185.
[31] See Stephen Buckle, *Hume's Enlightenment Tract*, (Oxford: Clarendon Press 2001), for strong development of this point.

has made for us."[32] The *System* is perhaps the fullest Enlightenment account of the sources of darkness. In it Holbach makes a comprehensive effort "to scatter the clouds that prevent man from walking with a sure foot on the path of life."

His undefended starting point is empiricism. All knowledge comes from sensory experience, Holbach holds, and so do all ideas. We should strip the language of words with no determinate ideas attached to them. If we do, we will get rid of beliefs in a mind distinct from the body, free will, and purely spiritual beings—all of them props for religion. Holbach has no interest in tracing the experiential pedigrees of ideas he takes to be sound. His main effort is to show how we came to have the harmful ideas and beliefs that enable princes and priests to tyrannize over us. And he has no doubt about where the trouble lies: "It cannot be too often repeated, it is in error that we find the true source of the ills by which the human race is afflicted...not Nature; not an irritable God; not hereditary depravity; it is only error."[33]

Holbach vehemently denies that religion does any good. Religion and theology, "far from being useful to mankind, are the true sources of the ills that afflict the earth, of the errors that blind it, the prejudices that benumb it."[34] There is no rationale for religious belief: Holbach examines the arguments of Clarke, Descartes, Newton, and Malebranche and proclaims them worthless. Hence a causal, naturalistic account of religious belief is needed.

The account Holbach gives is close to Hume's. Mankind begins with almost total ignorance of nature's ways. And "it is solely ignorance of natural causes and the forces of nature that gives birth to the gods."[35] Our sufferings, our fears and needs, and our tendency to model everything on our own feelings lead us to attribute extraordinary powers to natural objects and events that we do not understand. Religion is "always a system of conduct invented by imagination and ignorance to win favor from the unknown powers to which Nature is supposed to be submitted...[T]hese crude foundations support all religious systems."[36] Priesthood originated when

<hr>

[32] Paul Henri Thiery Baron d'Holbach, *Système de la Nature*, 2 vols., 1770, I. 11–12; references to the edition published by Fayard, Paris, 1990, referred to hereafter as Holbach. The English transl. by Samuel Wilkerson, 1820, repr. Garland, 1984, is not fully reliable.

[33] Holbach, I. 360; cf. I.12.   [34] Holbach, II. 280.   [35] Ibid. 24.   [36] Ibid. 21.

old men started supervising offerings to the deities. Eventually they told stories about the gods, and then developed elaborate theories to explain their contradictory ways. They "enveloped [the gods] in clouds...and became the masters of explaining as they pleased the enigmatic being they made to adore."[37] In all this they were aided by the regrettable fact that men love mysteries and marvels, and so are complicit in spreading the system that oppresses them. Men "need mystery to move their imaginations," Holbach says, and once they have the mysteries they spend their time praying, rather than investigating nature.[38]

To improve matters, education is clearly needed. But we cannot easily get rid of the error and ignorance that are the sources of the harmful beliefs. The abstract arguments that would clarify our thinking cannot be understood by the masses. "It is not...for the multitude that a philosopher should propose to himself either to write or to meditate; the principles of atheism or the system of Nature are not made...for a large number of people." Still, the advance of science, exemplified especially by Newton's work, can give us hope. For science always drives out superstition: thus astronomy has put the alchemists out of business and science more generally has destroyed the credibility of magicians. A wise sovereign will be needed as well, to spread the light and drive away the clouds. But advanced ideas come to be accepted only slowly. The most we can hope for now is that people will lose interest in religious and theological controversies. "It is this indifference, so just, so reasonable, so advantageous to states, that healthy philosophy can propose to introduce little by little on earth."[39]

Nearly a quarter of a century after Holbach's *System* appeared, the Marquis de Condorcet wrote a classic Enlightenment account of the progress of knowledge and its effects in dispelling the clouds of prejudice and superstition. He holds that the history of error is an important part of the history of the progress of knowledge. And much more than his predecessors, he attributes both progress and opposition to it to structural features of social life, particularly to struggles for power. Individual psychology plays only a small part in the formation of the clouds that knowledge will eventually drive away.

---

[37] Holbach, II. 61.   [38] Ibid. 178–82.   [39] Ibid. 372–5.

There are two points on which individual psychology matters. Our faculties develop only slowly, and some prejudices served a useful purpose in their time. But "they have extended their seductions . . . beyond their season because men retain the prejudices of their childhood, their country and their age" even when enough is known to reject them.[40] To mental inertia Condorcet adds a feature of early thought that he does not explain. When some men came to know enough to be the leaders and teachers of others, two classes were formed, one trying to place itself above reason, "the other humbly renouncing its own reason and abasing itself to less than human stature."[41] This self-abasement helped in the rise of the priesthood. Since then that class has clung to power, terrifying the masses with super-stitious fears of penalties in an afterlife for disobedience and fiercely oppos-ing the progress of knowledge that would disabuse subjects of their belief in clerical superiority.

The priestly class sometimes sought to increase knowledge, but its aim was "not to dispel ignorance but to dominate men."[42] The death of Socrates, Condorcet says, "was the first crime that marked the beginning of the war between philosophy and superstition," a war still continuing.[43] Aristotle discovered the principle of empiricism, but did not take it very far. Under the Roman Empire, the claims of reason were swamped by the triumph of Christianity, "to which the great mass of enthusiasts gradually attached themselves." Condorcet says the converts were the slaves and the poor, but offers no further account of why they adhered to the new faith.[44]

To sustain their power, the medieval priests exalted religious virtues above natural ones and kept the populace in ignorance. Their only achieve-ment was "theological daydreaming and superstitious imposture." The Arab revival of science offered some hope, but was defeated by "tyranny and superstition": there was no way to defend it from "the prejudices of men who had already been degraded by slavery."[45] It was only with the inven-tion of printing and the consequent wide dissemination of the advances of the new science that knowledge began what Condorcet considers a now irreversible advance. "There is not a religious system nor a supernatural

---

[40] Antoine Nicholas de Condorcet, *Sketch for a historical Picture of the Progress of the Human Mind*, trans. Barraclough (London, 1955), 11. Hereafter referred to as Condorcet.
[41] Ibid. 17–18.   [42] Ibid. 36.   [43] Ibid. 45.   [44] Ibid. 71.   [45] Ibid. 77–87.

extravagance," he says, "that is not founded on ignorance of the laws of nature." Science will end the reign of darkness.[46]

III. Kant

Kant begins to offer a view about the sources of darkness in the opening paragraph of his "Enlightenment" essay. To be enlightened is to have left the condition he calls self-incurred minority or tutelage (*selbst verschuldete Unmündigkeit*). "This minority is *self-incurred*," he continues, "when its cause is not in lack of understanding but in lack of resolution and courage to use it without direction from another" (*PracP*, 8.35). The imperative, "Have the courage to use your own reason!" is the motto of *Aufklärung*. If Enlightenment is thinking for oneself, the source of darkness would be the "laziness and cowardice" which hinder us from doing so. At least, that would be the source within individuals. Freedom to make public use of reason seems to be what it takes for a whole society to be enlightened. Here the sources of darkness would be efforts of rulers and clergy to prevent open critical discussion of their policies and decisions.

Kant devotes much of the essay to distinguishing between public and private uses of reason, and the critical literature has accordingly examined the distinction in detail. But the opening paragraphs raise questions about the inner source of darkness that Kant does not answer in the essay, and it is these that I shall explore.

When we think for ourselves, what are we to think *about*?[47] Religious beliefs are Kant's main concern in the essay. But he does not explain why it takes courage to think about them for oneself. It is also unclear what Kant means by saying that our being in a condition of minority or tutelage is self-incurred. Shortly after the "Enlightenment" essay was published, J. G. Hamann wrote a letter criticizing it and especially "that accursed adjective *self-incurred*."[48] Though Kant uses the adjective two more times

[46] Condorcet, 163.

[47] Rüdiger Bittner raises important questions on this point in "What is Enlightenment?", reprinted in James Schmidt, ed., *What is Enlightenment?*, Berkeley, Ca.: University of California Press, 1996, 345–58. Bittner's criticisms of Kant helped me to reach the interpretation offered here.

[48] The letter, dated Dec. 18, 1784, is translated with annotations by Garrett Green in Schmidt's anthology (n. 3), 145–53. The German text is reprinted and given detailed commentary in Oswald

in the essay (at *PracP*, 8.40 and 8.41) and plainly thinks it important, the essay itself does not offer much help in understanding it. Irresolution and cowardice may keep most people under tutelage, but are they also self-incurred?

The imperative of Enlightenment seems to be addressed to individuals.[49] Yet Kant also says that "it is hard for any single individual to work himself out of the life under tutelage." What is needed is a society in which citizens have the freedom to make public use of their reason (*PracP*, 8.36). If I do not live in such a society, is my tutelage still self-incurred? Do I personally bear the responsibility for it? We do not yet live in an enlightened age, Kant allows, but only in one going through the process of *Aufklärung*.[50] We still lack much that would be required for men to use their own reason in religious matters. The obstacles to escape from self-incurred minority are being removed, but not all at once. In what way then is our remaining in the condition of tutelage self-incurred? Kant does not here say.

A similar juxtaposition of individual and community responsibility occurs in Kant's "Conjectural Beginning of Human History." He there sketches a history of the awakening and gradual development of moral reasoning. In the course of this development, "man . . . has cause to ascribe to himself the guilt (*Schuld*) for all the evil that he suffers and for the bad that he perpetrates." Yet the suffering is unavoidable. It is part of nature's way of teaching the human race the moral lessons it needs to learn. Kant thinks we must "admire and praise" it.[51] Perhaps; but it is still hard to see how the individual can be responsible for all these evils.

An endnote to the final page of the "Orientation in Thinking" essay gives us vital help with Kant's view in "Enlightenment." I quote it in full here:

Thinking for oneself means seeking the supreme touchstone of truth in oneself (i.e. in one's own reason); and the maxim of always thinking for oneself is **enlightenment**.

Bayer, "Selbstverschuldete Vormundschaft" in Dieter Henke, Günther Kehrer, and Gunda Schneider-Flume, eds., *Der Wirklichkeitsanspruch von Theologie und Religion*, (Tübingen: J. C. B Mohr, 1976), 3–34. I am grateful to James Schmidt for pointing out the significance of Hamann's letter and for other advice. Bittner has a sharp paragraph criticizing Kant on this point, p. 346.

[49] And is so taken by e.g. Gordon Michalson in his valuable study *Fallen Freedom* (Cambridge: Cambridge University Press, 1990), 15.

[50] On *Aufkärung* as process rather than as historical period see the essay by Schmidt referred to in n. 3 above.

[51] 8.116, trans. Ted Humphrey, *Perpetual Peace and other Essays*, (Indianapolis: Hackett Publishing Co., 1983), 54.

Now there is less to this than people imagine when they place enlightenment in the acquisition of *information*; for it is rather a negative principle for the use of one's faculty of cognition, and often he who is richest in information is the least enlightened in the use he makes of it. To make use of one's own reason means no more than to ask oneself, for everything that one should assume, whether one could find it feasible [*wohl thunlich finde* = find it doable] to make the reason why one assumes something, or the rule from which there follows what one assumes, into a universal principle for the use of one's reason. This test is one that everyone can apply to himself; and with this examination he will see superstition and enthusiasm disappear, even if he falls far short of having information to refute them on objective grounds. For he is using merely the maxim of reason's *self-preservation*. Thus it is quite easy to ground enlightenment in *individual subjects* through their education; one must only begin early to accustom young minds to this reflection; for there are external obstacles which in part forbid this manner of education and in part make it more difficult.   (RR 8.146n.)[52]

Kant is here saying that Enlightenment consists in or requires the adoption of a maxim. Maxims, for Kant, are our most general practical principles. Enlightenment thus belongs within the domain of practical rather than theoretical reason. More specifically, Enlightenment is not a matter of getting more information. We do not need detailed information to accept or reject a proposed maxim. As Kant's whole ethical theory shows, there is an *a priori* test for such maxims. By identifying *Aufklärung* with adopting a maxim, Kant rejects all views holding that the clouds are dispelled simply by the removal of factual or scientific ignorance.

The Enlightenment maxim is "a negative principle in the use of one's faculty of cognition." By this Kant means that the Enlightenment maxim will lead us to reject certain cognitive claims—those made by the advocate of superstition or enthusiasm. The maxim directs one to use a test for whatever one is asked to assume (*was man annehmen soll*), and Kant says that everyone can use this test. Kant's phrasing suggests a possible procedure for applying the Enlightenment maxim: formulate a principle that would lead one to assume whatever it is that the advocate of superstition or enthusiasm says one should assume. Then ask if one could will that the principle be a universal principle of one's reason. Could the principle guide

---

[52] I have slightly modified Allen Wood's translation, in Immanuel Kant, *Religion and Rational Theology*, trans. Wood and diGiovanni (Cambridge: Cambridge University Press, 1996), to make it conform more literally to the text.

all of one's thinking? If not, reject it; and since it is this principle that would lead to acceptance of the advocate's claim, reject his claim as well.

By way of example, Kant says only that if one uses the test, superstition and enthusiasm will disappear. He does not tell us what reasons or rules would ground one's acceptance of the advice their advocates give us. He does however say that we do not need to bring "information" (*die Kennt-nisse* = pieces of knowledge) to bear in order to reject the claims of the advocate of superstition or enthusiasm. We reject these claims not because we can prove them false on empirical grounds, but because the self-preservation of reason requires their rejection. Reason would contradict itself in some way were we to accept the principle that would lead us to accept what the advocate urges upon us. What exactly this means will become clear later, when I identify the sort of principle that the Enlightenment maxim tells us to reject.

Kant ends the note with a distinction between individual enlightenment and the enlightenment of an age, indicating the possibility of one and the difficulty of the other—but not in quite the same way he does in the "Enlightenment" essay itself.

An equally packed passage in the third *Critique* reinforces these points. Enlightenment, Kant there says, is thinking for oneself, which is "the maxim of a reason that is never passive." Superstition demands passivity of mind as an obligation. Hence it is the preeminent case of prejudice, and liberation from it is at the core of Enlightenment. In the note to this passage, Kant says that Enlightenment is in one way easy, in another way hard. "Always being legislative,"—active—is easy for someone who does not want to go beyond his essential end and seeks no knowledge which is beyond understanding. For Kant, our essential end is a moral end: that happiness should be distributed in accordance with virtue. Belief in God and immortality have no theoretical basis, but we can accept the beliefs on practical grounds. If we ask for knowledge beyond that, there are many who will promise it. Kant says that we will find their promises tempting. Hence we find it hard to stay enlightened; that is, to maintain the critical stance, toward what they offer us for belief. And this will be especially difficult for a whole public (CJ 5.294–5).

In both passages Kant treats being enlightened as having adopted a maxim, or as a matter of practical reason. In both he distinguishes between achieving enlightenment as an individual and achieving it as or for a whole public. In neither does he help us to understand just how our persistent condition of minority or tutelage can be self-incurred. But now that we know that we are considering matters within the domain of practical reason, we can see a parallel between the struggle for Enlightenment and the struggle for virtue. Virtue is strength of maxims in doing our duty. The opposition to doing so comes from within us, from our inclinations; and, Kant adds, "it is the human being *himself* who puts these obstacles in the way of his maxims" (*PracP*, 6.394). Moral difficulties, like the condition of tutelage, are self-incurred. But so far we do not see Kant explaining why we put these inclinations in the way of virtue, or why we are tempted by the thought of extra-moral knowledge of God, or why it is so hard to adopt the Enlightenment maxim. Thus in these passages he does not fully explain the source of darkness.

To find Kant's account of it we must look at his *Religion within the Boundaries of Mere Reason*. In part one, Kant presents his view of the radical evil that dwells in each of us. This resuscitation of what looks like the doctrine of original sin shocked many contemporaries. Kant, wrote Goethe in a frequently quoted passage, "after spending a long life cleansing his philosophical mantle of various grubby prejudices, has wantonly besmirched it with the infamous stain of Radical Evil so that Christians too can after all be lured up to kiss its hem."[53] Even his critics should admit, however, that Kant's radical evil is not St. Augustine's original sin. Kantian evil leaves us with our ability to see our duty and choose it, which strong views of Christian depravity did not. Kant says nothing of predestination, and he rejects prevenient grace. Even so, it is a surprising view for a philosopher of *Aufklärung* to hold.

That Kant is nonetheless a philosopher of *Aufklärung* is, however, nowhere clearer than in part four of the *Religion*. He there gives his fullest account of why we should reject the aspects of religion that enlighteners attacked. In doing so he puts the doctrine of radical evil to a surprising use. My suggestion is that radical evil is for Kant the ultimate source of the superstition, enthusiasm, and priestcraft which constitute so large a part of the darkness to be dispelled by *Aufklärung*. In what follows I try to support this suggestion.

---

[53] Quoted in Boyle, vol. II, 162; also in Michalson, 17.

I give only a brief reminder of Kant's view of radical evil. That we are evil is not a strict necessity of our nature, but a contingent fact, although it holds of all of us (RR 6.32). Our being evil is not a matter of our having impulses to preserve and benefit ourselves which are often stronger than the impulse derived from our awareness of the moral law. This is simply human frailty. The inclinations themselves are not evil, but good (RR 6.58). Nor is our being evil constituted by our complying with the requirements of the moral law out of incentives other than the law itself. This is merely impurity. Our depravity or corruption is rather "the propensity of the power of choice to maxims that subordinate the incentives of the moral law to others...it reverses the ethical order as regards the incentives of a *free* power of choice" (*RR*, 6.29–30). The good agent makes compliance with morality the *condition* for action from a non-moral incentive. The evil agent makes compliance with a non-moral incentive the condition for doing what morality requires (RR 6.36).[54]

We need not retrace the qualifications and explanations with which Kant surrounds the claim that we are all inherently evil. It is important, however, to note that he is not talking of specific individuals when he makes this claim. He rules out the thought that some people might be inherently good, and only some evil. He is speaking of "the whole species" (RR 6.25). And although he holds that we all start in corruption, he also insists that "[t]he human being (even the worst) does not repudiate the moral law ... The law rather imposes itself on him irresistibly" (RR 6.36). Awareness of the moral law is bound up with our freedom and "through no cause in the world" can anyone lose that freedom. Kant puts the point quite strongly:

> However evil a human being has been right up to the moment of an impending free action (evil even habitually, as a second nature), his duty to better himself was not just in the past: it still is his duty *now*; he must therefore be capable of it.
>
> (RR 6.41; cf. 6.45)

The question of the proper order of moral and other maxims as related to faith recurs frequently in the rest of *Religion*.[55] Kant repeatedly contrasts rational religion as a pure moral position with statutory faiths which try to

---

[54] In the first *Critique* Kant says that "the moral disposition, as a condition, first makes partaking in happiness possible, rather than the prospect of happiness first making possible the moral disposition." (A813–14/B841–2, trans. Guyer-Wood).

[55] See, for example, RR 6.118–19; 6.174–5; 6.185 and n.

ignore or bypass or downgrade morality in favor of other means of appealing for the favor of the deity. He distinguishes "*religion of rogation* (of mere cult)" from "*moral religion*, i.e. the religion of *good life-conduct*" (RR 6.51); ecclesiastical faith from the pure faith of religion (RR 6.109); and faith as commanded from religion as compliance with morality understood as God's commands (RR 6.163–4). Kant is eager to show that historical faith, transmitted by learned scholars, can be of assistance to moral religion. He accepts the claim that rituals and prayers in a limited community may help realize the moral religion that must ultimately be common to all. But whenever we think we can become well pleasing to God by something other than pure morality—when we think that living according to ancient prescriptions transmitted in a book, or carrying out rituals demanded by an ecclesiastical authority, will replace morality as a means to divine favor—we are getting things in the wrong order. The language is revealing: "to deem this statutory faith . . . essential to the service of God in general, and to make it the *supreme condition* of divine good pleasure toward humans" is itself what Kant calls "a delusion of religion" (RR 6.168, my emphasis; cf. 6.170–1). It is the root error that leads to the darknesses of superstition and enthusiasm, and opens the way to priestly tyranny.

A noted authority on Kant's religious thought says that "The general subjective ground of religious delusion lies in the human tendency to anthropomorphism."[56] Kant does indeed say that we tend to think that God can be swayed as we can by entreaties and gifts. And his explanation of the strength of this tendency is tied to his accounts of superstition, enthusiasm, and priestcraft. All of them display the pattern characteristic of radical evil. Good life-conduct, Kant reminds us, is the only thing well pleasing to God. We know that in this life we cannot bring ourselves into complete compliance with the demands of morality. Hence we hope for some sort of aid beyond ourselves that will enable us to make progress in a task we cannot morally escape. Reason shows us, Kant says, that God will count sincere effort as sufficient to entitle us to divine grace. But because morality requires hard work and we are greedy for assurance of salvation, we look for other ways of obtaining it. We know that people can be bought off. So we think that we might obtain grace by some less arduous service to the divinity, and

---

[56] Josef Bohatec, *Die Religionsphilosphie Kants in der "Religion innerhalb der Grenzen der reinen Vernunft"*, (1938) (Hildesheim: Georg Olms, 1966), 507.

that then moral virtue will be added to it. We grant that grace might come in a mysterious way. We offer sacrifices which, however costly, are less demanding than morality. And we persuade ourselves that we can tell that we are feeling the effects of the grace our sacrifices and prayers have won us.

"The delusion that through acts of cult we can achieve anything in the way of justification before God is religious *superstition*," Kant says, "just as the delusion of wanting to bring this about by striving for a supposed contact with God is religious *enthusiasm*" (RR 6.174). Superstition is using natural means, themselves not tied to morality, to bring about nonnatural, moral, effects. Enthusiasm calls on something not within human powers—immediate contact with the divinity—to effect nonnatural goals (RR 6.174–5). Superstition at least offers many people the ability to try for grace, since it uses natural means. Enthusiasm, by contrast, is more irrational: because it ends as an appeal to inner feeling (RR 6.114), it is "the moral death of reason without which there can be no religion" (RR 6.175).

Priests simply formalize and reinforce the delusions at work in superstition and enthusiasm. There is no difference in principle between the refined priest of Europe and the primitive shaman of Asia. What they both want is "to steer to their advantage the invisible power which presides over human destiny" (RR 6.176). As I noted, Kant thinks that morality can benefit from churches, rituals, and prayers. But when they, and the revelation that prescribes them, are made necessary to the inner life and not treated as mere means to enhance morality, the result is what Kant calls fetishism. The priest takes just this step. He turns what should be merely means into an end, and thus tells us to join means and true end in the wrong order.

Priestcraft is the constitution of a church devoted to fetishism. In such organizations the clergy rules, dispensing with reason and claiming authority over all the laity, including the secular ruler. Everyone must pretend to receive benefits from clerical rule, so unconditional obedience to priests undermines "the very *thinking* of the people." The hypocrisy necessary under such a regime even undermines the loyalty of subjects. Instead of bringing peace and order, it brings about their opposite (RR 6.179–80). Ritualized service and moral effort may indeed be joined. They are both good things, but, Kant warns, "[s]o much depends, when we wish to join two good things, on the order in which we combine them!" "It is in this distinction," Kant significantly adds, "that true *Aufklärung* consists" (RR 6.179).

Wherever Kant notes the temptation to treat aspects of religion which are at best means to morality as more important than morality, in the hope of currying divine favor, he indicates that this is the wrong ordering: it subordinates morality to desire for one's own happiness. Everywhere the pattern is that of radical evil. Then, at the end of the book, Kant characterizes the delusions of religion as "self-deceptions" (RR 6.200). The self-incurred tutelage of the essay on Enlightenment may, I suggest, be understood in the same way. The failure of courage to use our own reason is a moral failure. Radical evil is the ultimate source of the darkness resulting from the failure so far of all our efforts at *Aufklärung*.

What will the enlightened agent think when confronted by a superstitious or enthusiastic person? The enthusiast claims to have direct divine inspiration about a non-moral way to become well pleasing to God. The superstitious person claims to know that attention to certain rituals or relics or saints will enable one to become well pleasing to God. To accept what they urge upon us, we must accept the principle that there is some non-moral way of pleasing God. This is what enlightened agents reject. When thinking for themselves, they will always reject any claim grounded on the belief that there are non-moral means to God's approval. In this application, the Enlightenment maxim has a negative outcome for the use of our faculty of cognition, as Kant says it has: we conclude that we do not know what the religious advocates claim to know. In this way the maxim leads, as Kant also says, to the death of both aberrant forms of divine service.

Can this point be broadened to take in other aspects of *Aufklärung*, as Kant suggests in the "Enlightenment" essay? To make this out, we have to think that the book or spiritual adviser that does our thinking for us, or the ruler, or the physician (*PracP*, 8.35), all urge us to courses of action that require placing our own interest ahead of morality. Perhaps our pastor directs us to persecute members of a group he thinks ungodly and despicable; perhaps our commanding officer tells us to kill the wives and daughters of the enemy as well as their soldiers; perhaps our physician urges us to bribe the pharmacist to give us priority for some important medicine in very short supply. To see that they should reject such directives, enlightened agents need not question any factual or quasi-factual claims that the priest or ruler or physician may make. They can see that the reasons underlying advice of the kinds I have imagined always involve placing self-interest, or special group interest, above moral principle. Mature agents cannot accept the basic reasons given for this sort of advice as rules for their own practical reasoning. Since practical reason gives morality precedence over other kinds of direct- ive, to do so would be to use practical reason to destroy itself. Enlighten- ment thus ensures the self-preservation of reason. Enlightened agents can, however, accept church ceremonies or political directives or medical advice as long as these do not require overruling morality. The agent is free to decide by using prudential reason whether to accept or reject directions from any authority, insofar as their directives concern the use of means that lie within the bounds of morality. And he can decide simply to take the authority's advice without trying to think for himself about it any further than to see that it is morally permissible.

For Kant, the ultimate source of darkness—of our persistence in the unenlightened condition of tutelage—is, I have argued, the radical evil that besets all human beings. Emergence from radical evil is up to us. If we decide to reject it, we do so in a realm beyond experience. Nothing can be known of how the choice is made. The same is true if we decide not to emerge from radical evil. Our ignorance here spreads to other aspects of Kant's philosophy. Moral improvement requires steady refusal to place self- interest ahead of morality. *Aufklärung* requires steady adherence to the maxim of thinking for oneself, refusing to obey any authority that directs us to place morality in second place. Both moral improvement and Enlight- enment must essentially be freely chosen. But if the choice of the right course is free, so is the choice of the wrong. And in that case, are we not always in the condition of thinking in practical terms for ourselves—of being not under tutelage but enlightened?[57] No theoretical answer to these difficulties is possible, on Kant's view. We cannot have a theoretical under- standing of why the condition of tutelage is self-imposed. Kant can only say that we are morally required to think it is, because we are morally required to think that improvement is always possible.

The contrast between Kant's account of the source of darkness and the accounts of the other enlighteners whom I have discussed is striking. For them, darkness comes from cognitive failure of one sort or another. Enlightenment requires improvement in our theoretical grasp of the world. They therefore offer clarification of ideas, or improvement of reasoning, or

---

[57] Rüdiger Bittner raised this question in correspondence.

increase of scientific knowledge as ways to dispel the darkness. And even those who, like Holbach, ardently defend the rights of man, preserve the idea that an intellectual elite of some sort must lead the rest of us toward the light. For Kant, the source of darkness is a moral failure of will. In moral matters we are all equally failures; but we all have essentially the same ability to get things right.

Kant advocates a republican form of government as best suited to express our essential moral freedom. He thinks we all have a duty to work toward a world federation of republics as most likely to preserve peace. But however enlightened Kant's goals may sound, he nowhere suggests practical steps anyone might take toward reaching them, except for improvement of moral education. He thinks that political revolution is never morally permissible. He praises Frederick the Great in the "Enlightenment" essay, but says nothing to challenge the ruler's authoritarian regime. It is his view of the source of darkness that provides the rationale for this quite minimal program of *Aufklärung*. What is essential is individual moral improvement. Political action cannot improve matters. Kant can offer only the morally necessary hope that we are moving ourselves through history toward Enlightenment.

17

Kantian Unsocial Sociability: Good Out of Evil

> There is nothing so unsociable and so sociable as man: the one by his vice, the other by his nature.
>
> Montaigne[1]

Schopenhauer tells us of a group of porcupines who huddled together for warmth on a cold winter day, only to be driven apart by each other's quills. Separated, the need for warmth forced them together again—and so on repeatedly, huddling and withdrawing. "Thus", he comments, "the need for society which springs from the emptiness and monotony of men's lives drives them together; but their many unpleasant and repulsive qualities . . . once more drive them apart." Politeness is what enables us to put up with one another. Those who have sufficient internal warmth will "prefer to keep away from society."[2]

This nineteenth-century parable sums up nearly two centuries of debate about sociability. It is easy to suppose that living sociably with other people is the natural and normal condition for human beings. But Kant, along with many of his predecessors, sees it as problematic. Kant baptized the problem with the memorable phrase "unsocial sociability".

In the first three Propositions of his "Idea for a Universal History with a Cosmopolitan Purpose," (*Idea*) Kant tells us that nature intends all natural human capacities to be developed to their fullest in the species, though not in the individual. Moreover, humans are meant to provide by their own

---

[1] Michel de Montaigne, I.39, Of Solitude, in *Complete Essays of Montaigne*, trans. Donald M. Frame (Stanford: Stanford University Press, 1965).

[2] Arthur Schopenhauer, *Parerga and Paralipomena*, trans E. F. J. Payne (Oxford: Oxford University Press, 1974), vol. II, 651–2.

efforts whatever they enjoy of happiness and perfection (8.18–20).[3] In the Fourth Proposition Kant lays out the means nature employs to bring about this result: the "unsocial sociability" [*ungesellige Geselligkeit*] of men.[4] We have, he says, a "propensity to enter into society". But we also have a "thoroughgoing resistance" to this tendency so that we are always liable to isolate ourselves and tear society apart (8.20).

This seems a regrettably porcupine-like combination of basic character traits. But Kant sees in it the goad needed to make us overcome our natural laziness. We do not want to live solitary lives. But we find in ourselves a strong desire to have everything go as we want it to. We know we would resist this desire coming from others, so we expect the others with whom we want to live to resist our desire. The resistance stirs us to try to overcome it. To get our way, we strive for superiority in possessions or honor over those others who are our antagonists but whom we cannot do without. The energies we devote to showing others how much stronger and smarter we are lead us to create ingenious inventions and brilliant new ideas that gradually enrich and enlighten our strife-ridden common lives.

Without all this competition we would enjoy an idyllic pastoral existence of ease and idleness. But envy and our insatiable desires for property, honor and power force us to develop our natural abilities, which would otherwise remain hidden and useless. Nor is that the end of it. If at first only threats of punishment prevent us from destroying one another, we eventually develop our inherent ability to think in moral terms. And then we replace a social union kept in order by fear with a union which is freely willed and thus moral. All this, Kant says, points to a divine purpose in our being so unsociably sociable (8.21–2).

I

Sociability was a recurrent topic in early modern moral philosophy, and Kant joined the discussion after much had been said about it. We need to know something of how the conversation went before he entered it.

---

[3] All references to Kant are identified by giving the volume and page number of the Academy Edition of Kant. For *Idea* I use the translation by Allen W. Wood.

[4] We may suppose that by "men" Kant intended to refer to all human beings, but he rarely takes notice of women, and then not very favorably.

Theories of sociability and our unsociable resistance to it arose as attempts to account for the historical development of society. Ancient philosophers had some views on the growth of society. But they did not explain it in terms of tension between sociable and unsociable character traits. The Epicureans held that the primary human motivation is the desire for our own pleasure. Interest in procuring it drives us to cooperate with others. In *De Rerum Natura* Lucretius presents a full and vivid picture of human development from an animal level of existence into our present sophisticated societies. We started, he says, with the simplest needs, for food, sex, shelter. We learned slowly how to make tools, use animal skins, cultivate vegetables, build shelters, and make boats. At first we did not "look to the common good . . . did not know now to govern . . . intercourse by custom and law." (5.958ff). Eventually we learned these things too, each being driven always by desire for a more enjoyable life. As we formed larger groups, we began to seek the pleasures of eminence and honor, we engaged in political struggles, and at some point law and punishment were invented and a more orderly and peaceful society established (5.1105–60). In this story we learn to cooperate with one another for the satisfaction of our personal desires. Lucretius allows that we come to love our spouses and children, but he does not speak of a wider sociability.

The Stoics tell a different story. They deny that we always seek our own pleasure. All living beings strive to preserve themselves, and we as young animals do so as well. Pleasure is just a by-product of success in this endeavor. It is proper to begin with simple self-concern.[5] But "it is wrong for man to begin and end where the non-rational animals do." As we mature, reason and the ability to use language lead us to concerns for others and not just for ourselves. We come to understand ourselves as part of the divinely ordered cosmos and this alters our initial motivations. When mature, we desire to live in accordance with nature, and by nature we are "an animal which is rational, sociable and gregarious".[6] We are suited to form unions with other people who are at ever-increasing distance from ourselves. As we come to have more insight into our own nature, we understand that living in accordance with our nature requires living as part of a society which includes all other humans as fellow members.[7]

---

[5] Epictetus, in A. A. Long, and D. N. Sedley, *The Hellenistic Philosophers* (Cambridge: Cambridge University Press, 1987), vol. I, 63E, 396.

[6] Stobaeus, Long and Sedley, 67W, 433.   [7] Cicero, Long and Sedley, 57F, 348.

We will marry and take part in civic affairs of our own society because it is right and proper, and not, as the Epicureans think, for our own pleasure.[8]

Epicureanism and Stoicism were important influences on early modern moral philosophy. What gave the contrast between the sociable and the unsociable aspects of our nature its modern importance was not, however, the thought of the ancients. It was the work of Hugo Grotius. (1583–1645).[9] He was a Dutch lawyer who developed a new kind of theory of natural law and who is regarded as the founder of current understandings of international law. The "Preliminary Discourse" to his *The Rights of War and Peace* (1625, 2nd edn., 1631) contains his central assertions on the topic.

Grotius says he must begin a treatise on the law of nature by refuting those who deny that there is any such thing. Allowing that man is an animal, and so a part of nature, he adds that man is an animal of a higher order. "Now amongst the Things peculiar to Man," he continues, "is his Desire of Society, that is, a certain Inclination to live with those of his own kind . . . peaceably, and in a Community regulated according to the best of his Understanding." (Prelim. § VI, 79–81) In the first edition, Grotius says that nature leads each animal "to seek its own interests" and that this is true of man also "before he came to the use of that which is special to man". Grotius is not making the Epicurean claim that each of us is always essentially self-interested. He is rather reworking the Stoic view, that as animals we begin with a drive to sustain our own existence and then as human beings we naturally develop a broader concern, which shows what is "special to man." We come to have a "care for society in accordance with the human intellect." This care, he stresses, is not due only to the needs we have for help from one another. It expresses the special nature of man. And it is the source of law or right, properly so called.[10] Sociability, he says in the second edition, is "this care of maintaining Society in a Manner conformable to the Light of human Understanding." (Prelim. § VIII, 85–6).

Grotius never loses sight of our concern for our own interests, however. It is not surprising that in a treatise focused on rights of war and peace our

---

[8] For useful surveys of Epicurean and Stoic ethics and social thought, see Keimpe Algra *et al.*, Jonathan Barnes, Jaap Mansfield, and Malcolm Schofield, eds., *The Cambridge History of Hellenistic Philosophy* (Cambridge: Cambridge University Press, 1999), chs. 20–22.

[9] In what follows in this section I draw on my *The Invention of Autonomy*, chs. 4–7, 14–16.

[10] Hugo Grotius, *The Rights of War and Peace*, Richard Tuck, ed., (Indianapolis: Liberty Fund, 2005), *Prolegomena* to 1st edn., vol. III, 1747 (there were no paragraph numbers in this edition). The term *jus* can be translated as "law" or as "right" and so poses difficulties for all English versions of Latin texts on the subject.

"differences" (*controversiae*) are a principal topic (I.I.1, 133). One of the major sources of these differences during Grotius's lifetime was religion. Europe in 1625 was in the midst of wide-spread, vicious, decades-long war over sectarian disagreements. Politics was inextricably combined with confessional disputes.[11] If there was to be agreement on international law, there had to be an understanding of it that did not rely on contested religious claims. Scriptural interpetations would not do, nor would arguments ending with claims about God's will in particular matters. Grotius simplified the issues with a brilliant stroke. We are sociable creatures and want to live together, he said, but we have endless differences over property and power, both personal and national. Let us take natural law to be a set of empirically discoverable ways in which sociable but quarrelsome beings such as we are can get along together. These laws will not rule out warfare—far from it. But they will regulate its conduct and the conduct of every other area of life in which strife threatens the peace of society, either international or at home.

From this understanding of natural right Grotius worked out an entire system of rights—not just political rights but also those we would think of as moral. A few decades later Thomas Hobbes (1588–1679) used a similar approach to warrant a rather different set of rights. In doing so Hobbes made no appeal to any natural sociability. Indeed in a famous comment he rejects the long-held Aristotelian view that we are by nature "born fit for society".[12] Our most basic drive, he held, is our fear of death. Anybody, however weak, can kill anybody else, however strong (since everyone has to sleep at some point). Thus we all have reason to fear one another. So we seek power to secure our own safety; and no amount of power is enough. Hence without a strong ruler we would have to be forever prepared to fight one another—a condition of war. A life of permanent war would be a life without cooperation. It would be completely horrid. But fear would make cooperation impossible. We would never trust anyone to stick to a bargain after we had kept our part of it first. We have enough wit, however, to see that a strong ruler can make people carry out their side of a bargain. That would alleviate our fears enough to make social life and collaboration possible. We have no desire of society for its own sake. We are simply driven into it by our desperate need for peace. The first law of nature,

---

[11] For an illuminating history of Reformation thought and politics, see Diarmaid MacCulloch, *The Reformation* (London: Penguin Books, 2003).

[12] Thomas Hobbes, *De Cive*, edited by Bernard Gert (Indianapolis: Hackett Publishing, 1991), I.2.

Hobbes says, is simple: to seek peace. The other laws of nature—there are many—are all derivable as means to obtaining and preserving peace.[13]

For Hobbes, then, sociability is an imperative, not a basic desire. It is even more explicitly an imperative in the theory propounded by Samuel Pufendorf (1632–94). His *De Jure Naturae et Gentium* (1672) (*Of the Law of Nature and of Nations*)[14] was one of the most widely read of the works of modern natural-law theorists. In it Pufendorf presents a whole system of law for both domestic and international affairs; and like Grotius and Hobbes, he bases it on facts about human nature. For him the first central fact about man is that "he is an Animal extremely desirous of his own Preservation . . . unable to secure his own Safety and Maintenance without the Assistance of his Fellows, and capable of returning the Kindness by the furtherance of mutual Good." The second fact is that man is "often malicious, insolent, and easily provoked, and as powerful in effecting Mischief, as he is ready in delighting in it." Because we are weak we need the help of others; because man is "an animal seething with evil desires . . . unruly and deviant passions",[15] we put difficulties in the way of obtaining it. Pufendorf takes these empirically discovered facts to be the rationale for the first law of nature: "Every man ought . . . to promote and preserve a peaceful Sociableness with others." By "sociableness", Pufendorf explains, he does not mean a mere willingness to join with others. He means a more active disposition that supposes each united to others "by Benevolence, by Peace, by Charity, and so, as it were, by a silent and a secret Obligation" (LNN II.III. xv, 136–7).[16]

Why does the combination of our weakness and our unsociable character traits warrant us in affirming the requirement of sociability as the first law of nature? Like Grotius and Hobbes, Pufendorf believes that religious disagreement must not be allowed to hamper our agreement on laws of nature. Still, he takes it for granted that everyone will agree that God exists and has laid down laws for us. God has also enabled us to come to know them. We learn them by treating the salient facts about ourselves as pointers to God's

---

[13] Thomas Hobbes, *Leviathan*, Richard Tuck, ed., (Cambridge: Cambridge University Press, 1991), I. 13–14.

[14] Samuel Pufendorf, *Of the Law of Nature and of Nations*, trans. Basil Kennett (London, 1729). Hereafter LNN; I will cite this work by book, chapter, and section number as well as by page.

[15] Samuel Pufendorf, *The Whole Duty of Man, According to the Law of Nature*, Ian Hunter and David Saunders, eds., (Indianapolis: Liberty Fund, 2003), Preface, 10.

[16] For a useful discussion of Pufendorf on sociability and the development of society, see Istvan Hont, "The Language of Sociability and Commerce: Samuel Pufendorf and the Theoretical Foundations of the 'Four-Stages Theory,'" in Anthony Pagden, ed., *The Languages of Political Theory in Early-Modern Europe* (Cambridge: Cambridge University Press, 1987), 253–76.

will. And it is from ordinary experience, available to everyone, that we learn what these salient features are. We need neither theology nor biblical exegesis to see that man is quarrelsome and self-interested but weak and in desperate need of help from others. If these—in addition to our ability to think and use language—are our distinctive features, then an inference to the first law of nature, Pufendorf thinks, is quite obvious.

Pufendorf's ideas were spread by translations into all the modern European languages and by innumerable editions of his works. They were also spread by less original thinkers who made briefer and simpler versions of them available. One widely read disseminator of Pufendorfian thought was the Swiss professor of natural law, Jean-Jacques Burlamaqui (1694–1748). His French treatise on *droit naturel* (1747) was combined after his death with his work on *droit politique* (1752). Translated as *Principles of Natural and Politic Law* the two-volume work was popular in the British North American colonies. Burlamaqui added elements from many other views[17] but his basic idea about the foundation of natural law was Pufendorfian, though given a heavier dose of sentimentality than its source.

He notes the weakness of man as infant, his "rudeness, ignorance and confused ideas" when grown up, his liability to "spleen and melancholy" when without company. Following Pufendorf he suggests a somewhat Hobbesian condition of pre-civil society. But he notes ignorance and lack of education as the sources of its misery, mentioning "savagery" but without elaborating on it (I.4.4, 59). Thus we need society; and God has given us many talents that make us all useful to others. Moreover "our hearts are naturally bent to wish for the company of our equals." And it is only in society that man can feel the social affections—"benevolence, friendship, compassion, and generosity"—from which "our purest enjoyments arise." Society would not exist or be happy unless we had the sentiments of "affection and benevolence for one another". Plainly it is God's will that we should have these feelings. They are what is commonly referred to as our sociability. And because God wills that we should have them, sociability is "the true principle of the duties which the law of nature prescribes to us in respect to other men" (II. 4. XII–XV, 152–5). All our other duties to others

---

[17] See Patrick Riley's brief sketch of Burlamaqui as offering a "kind of compendium of Enlightenment thought", in Mark Goldie and Robert Wokler, eds., *The Cambridge History of Eighteenth-Century Political Thought* (Cambridge: Cambridge University Press, 2006), 60–1.

flow from the principle of sociability (II.4.XVI). So too do the principles of international law (II.6.VII, 175).[18]

II

Outside the natural-law tradition many philosophers engaged with the concept of sociability. Among reinterpretations the most significant are those that take sociability to be essentially a matter of sentiment or feeling. The third Earl of Shaftesbury (1671–1713) leads the way to this revision. He thinks sentiment important in our moral responses to one another, and he rejects the Hobbesian vision of the state of nature. Isolation is not possible for humans, he holds, since we are born weak and dependent and remain so for years. More significantly we are born with natural affections drawing us to others, and parents are naturally kind and loving to their children.[19] We can find our own good only in virtue, in forwarding the good of others. Man, indeed, is "not only by nature sociable within the limits of his own species or kind". He extends his love to the universe, which he perceives as divinely ordered, and he accepts whatever it may bring him.[20]

The sentimentalist version of sociability developed further partly because it was so severely challenged by Bernard de Mandeville (1670–1733).[21] He scorns it, no matter how it is understood. What makes man a sociable animal, he says, in his *Fable of the Bees*, "is not his desire of Company, Good Nature . . . and other Graces of a fair Outside". What is needed to fit man for society is rather his "vilest and most hateful Qualities" (I.4). Sociability is just a taste for human company. It is found most often in people with weak and uninventive minds, or bad consciences, who cannot stand to be alone. Sensible people would rather be solitary than put up with the noise and rudeness of gatherings and crowds. And even if everyone had a taste for company, it would not prove "some Intrinsic Worth in Man not to be found in other animals" (I, 340–41). Elsewhere Mandeville says that such sociability

---

[18] Lynn Hunt sees Burlamaqui as having wide influence in the American colonies and in Europe: *Inventing Human Rights*, 118, 120–1.

[19] Anthony Ashley Cooper, third Earl of Shaftesbury, *Characteristics of Men, Manners, Opinions, Times*, Lawrence E. Klein, ed., (Cambridge: Cambridge University Press, 1999), 285–8.

[20] Shaftesbury, 433.

[21] Bernard Mandeville, *The Fable of the Bees*, F. B. Kaye, ed., 2 vols. (1924) (Indianapolis: Liberty Classics, 1988).

as we have simply springs from "self-liking", a passion which may seem utterly "destructive to Sociableness and Society" (II. 175) but is not so. Our concern for our own "Ease and Security" and our desire to improve our own condition are enough to explain our fondness for society.

Mandeville grants that man naturally has a "desire . . . after Company". But he has it, Mandeville adds, "for his own sake", hoping to improve his condition by it (II, 180,183). Such a desire, moreover, explains nothing important about our lives together. Only governance—the use of power to keep us in order—explains social life. Once that comes into being, children are raised to be pliable by being taught that it is to their own advantage to obey. Of course we may say that God made us for society. We may also say he made grapes for wine, but that does not prove that there is wine in each grape. It takes human invention to make wine out of grapes and society out of individuals. The fermentation that makes wine has its social counterpart in our commerce with one another. "Men become sociable," Mandeville says, "by living together" (II, 185–9). There is no need to suppose that natural sociability plays an important role in our lives together.

Replying to Mandeville and thus indirectly to Hobbes is a major enterprise for Francis Hutcheson (1694–1746). He criticizes psychological egoism and argues for the existence of disinterested and other-regarding desires. But in his widely read works on morality and on the passions, he uses the term "sociability" little if at all. His inaugural address at the University of Glasgow, however, was entitled "On the Natural Sociability of Mankind". His aim is to show that society is natural to us because its suits our nature as individuals. He notes that many writers have seen that we are naturally sociable and have taken sociability to be the source of natural law. But they have not given an adequate account of what is meant by sociability. It does not mean, he says, with a slap at Mandeville, simply that men like to pass their time in crowds (201). Nor does it mean simply that we have many abilities that contribute to sociable living. He rejects what he calls Pufendorf's epicurean view, that social life is natural because it is advantageous to each of us. This ignores the fact that men have many desires which directly "depend on the company of others" (203). And our sociability is not exhausted by these. What shows most strongly that we were meant for society is that our nature is "in itself immediately and primarily kind, unselfish, and sociable without regard to its advantage or pleasure." We have many passions that "look directly to the felicity of others" (205). And, not least, what is honest and decent is natural to us: the virtues that help others are gratifying to us just as such (205–7).

Jean-Jacques Rousseau (1712–94), like Mandeville, gives a genealogy of sociability—and a subtler and more destructive one at that.[22] Rousseau is deeply opposed to the natural-law theories of Grotius and Hobbes, and attacks Pufendorf as well. They are wrong about the state of nature. If there ever were such a condition, Rousseau says, humans living in it would just be animals. They would try to keep themselves alive, they would show some rudimentary pity or concern for other animals, especially humans, who were sick or wounded, and they would mate and help with newborns. Aside from that they would ignore one another. But it is from the combination of these two principles—self-preservation and pity—"without it being necessary to introduce into it that of sociability"—that the rules of natural right arise (*Second Discourse*, Pref, 127).

There is society before there are laws, on Rousseau's view. Desire for the company of others, beyond the most minimal, is non-existent in the state of nature. It develops only slowly, and then for the most part unfortunately. Arising from sexual desire, it turns into striving to show oneself superior to rivals for love, by being a better dancer or singer or hunter. When society gets more complex, humans invent the idea of private property. Then the striving for superiority turns into the kind of obsessive greed for power and possessions that Hobbes mistakenly thought existed in the state of nature. Sociability develops with a vengeance: the struggle for social distinction makes us slaves to our need to impress others in whatever ways we can.

The only way out, Rousseau holds, is by a total transformation of society. Politics must enter. A will for the general good must supplant the will for one's own good in each of us. We can then come to live as equals under law, secure in our possessions and free because we are obeying only laws that we ourselves enact. Only then can we come to be sociable without endless competition and an oppressive class system.

III

Plainly, then, there were many conceptions of sociability and of unsociability circulating in early modern Europe. For Grotius, sociability is a desire or

---

[22] The chief source here is the *Discourse on the Origin and Foundations of Inequality*, in Jean-Jacques Rousseau, *The Discourses and Other Political Writings*, Victor Gourevitch, ed. and trans. (Cambridge: Cambridge University Press, 1997).

inclination to live in a reasonable way with other reasonable people. It is opposed by our self-interest and our tendency toward controversy with one another. Hobbes sees no sociable inclination in our make-up. Our desperate need to keep alive fosters our distrust of one another and hence leads us toward a condition of unrelenting hostility. Only fear of death drives us into society.

Like Hobbes, Pufendorf finds no original sociability in us. He finds us, in fact, inclined to be overly concerned with our own good and quarrelsome toward others. Hence the natural-law requirement that we increase sociability prescribes that we correct our first impulses and cultivate a disposition we do not naturally have, a disposition to "accept social life with ease" and to develop our sense of duty to others.[23] Burlamaqui speaks of our many social affections, particularly benevolence; somehow these are also the principle from which natural laws are derived. Shaftesbury also stresses our social sentiments, as does Hutcheson, who focuses on benevolence. Mandeville denies that any such feelings are part of our original nature. Some people take pleasure in crude or boisterous crowds as an escape from their own emptiness; otherwise, he seems to think we may be brought up to pay at least lip service to generous affections, if not really to feel them. For Rousseau the closest feature of our constitution to sociability is a notion of our uncultivated tendency to pity unfortunate living beings if we come across them. But it is not involved in generating sociality. In the corrupt society in which we now find ourselves, it is hard to find any genuine feelings for the good of others. And when we reform ourselves under the general will, what holds us together is not a sentiment of any sort, nor a principle of sociability urging us to cultivate benevolence. It is a rational principle requiring us to treat ourselves and others as all free and equal citizens capable of governing ourselves.

Where, if anywhere, amidst these differing views of sociability, can we locate Kant? Here there are three main questions. First, what is the role of unsocial sociability in Kant's thinking, and how does it compare with its role in the views of those of his predecessors who used it? Second, what more can be said about the psychology of unsocial sociability? And third, what place, if any, does unsocial sociability have in the Kantian philosophical system?

1. Kant's natural-law predecessors use conceptions of unsocial sociability to pose and resolve what they see as the central problem of social cohesion.

---

[23] Pufendorf, *The Whole Duty of Man*, 1.5.1–2.

We want or need to live together but we are all hard to get along with. Natural laws show us how to cope with this problem so that despite the unsociable aspects of our make-up we can nonetheless be sociable. The framework they provide is based in human nature. It is therefore the same for everyone. Its most basic directives are what we would think of now as constituting morality. The laws of morality allow room for differences among societies in the positive laws they enact. But because the laws of nature are the same for all humans, they are the grounding for universal laws governing all countries—the law of nations or, as we would now call it, international law.

Kant sees the central function of unsocial sociability quite differently. He allows that it points toward a problem that morality and law must be used to solve. But he does not try to derive moral laws or laws of nations from sociability, as Pufendorf and Burlamaqui do. For Kant, of course, moral imperatives are binding on us independently of any ends or purposes we may have. But the natural-law theorists treat the laws of nature as justified because they help bring about the good of society. Even God, on Pufendorf's view, must see his commands as meant to guide men to a good beyond their obedience. The natural-law view, in treating morality as a matter of hypothetical imperatives, misses the whole point.

The main role of unsocial sociability, for Kant, is as a permanent spur to personal and social improvement. He frequently makes this claim about unsocial sociability. Thus he tells his students that "[t]he purpose of nature would appear to be promoted by this, that providence has implanted in mankind an impulse to mutual emulation among themselves in order to compel them to be active in enlarging and cultivating their powers." And emulation has both pro-social and anti-social aspects. Kant puts the double-edged point strongly: emulation brings out "a side of human nature that has become malignant, notwithstanding that the purpose of emulation really lay in inciting men to constant cultivation of greater perfection in themselves, by comparison with others" (LecEth 27.678–9).

Our unsocial drives never disappear, even when society improves.[24] Kant correspondingly holds that progress toward the perfection of the species is nowhere near being accomplished. At times it even seems to recede after we think we are approaching it. Hence we may be tempted to think that history is

---

[24] This point is also made by Howard Williams, *Kant's Critique of Hobbes* (Cardiff: University of Wales Press, 2003), 121.

just a to-and-fro of progress and regress. Kant thinks this a foolish view.[25] We cannot, however, hope to refute it by appeal to experience.[26] Kant claims that it is nonetheless a moral duty to hold on to the belief in progress. It is a duty to do what we can to move mankind forward, and we cannot be expected to do our duty here unless we have a reasonable hope that progress can be made.[27] We must look at unsocial sociability and the "conflict of individual inclinations, which is the source of all evil," in this light. (T&P, VIII.312)

2. Kant thinks that our desires and motivations are largely opaque, to ourselves as well as to others.[28] Moreover he sees no possibility of applying mathematics to the inner appearances in the soul. And since he holds that scientific knowledge can be obtained only of phenomena susceptible of mathematical treatment, he concludes that there can be no science of the soul—no scientific psychology.[29] Perhaps because of this, his accounts of the psychological states that display our unsociable and our sociable impulses are scattered. His most thorough discussion of human psychology is given in his lectures on anthropology, but even there he provides no such thorough and complex theory of the passions as Hume gives.[30]

We can put flesh on the bones of unsocial sociability by looking at Kant's views of some of the virtues and vices. What in our make-up favors sociability? We have, for one thing, a tendency to seek friends. "*It already lies in human nature,*" Kant says in a lecture, "to love something *outside oneself,* and especially another human being." (LecEth 27.682) Thus we are psychologically disposed to carry out some semblance of the duty to love other humans. That duty does not require feeling. It requires a firm will to act for the good of others, or beneficence. We are also required to show gratitude toward those who help us—but we seem to have less of an emotional tendency to be grateful than we have to be benevolent. He also finds in us a disposition to sympathize with others, to have "sensible feelings of pleasure or displeasure" due to the joys or sufferings of others. He does not wish to rest much on these feelings alone, however. As with love of others, he moves promptly to

---

[25] He calls it "the abderitic hypothesis" because the Abderites pf ancient Greece were supposed to be a group of fools. Kant's younger contemporary Christoff Martin Wieland (1733–1813) wrote an engaging novel called *The History of the Abderites* (1774), thus bringing the name back into circulation.
[26] See "An Old Question Raised Again", VII, 83.   [27] See *Perpetual Peace*, VIII, 386.
[28] See e.g. MS 6.441, 447; *Anthropology* VII, 121, 143.   [29] G, IV.471.
[30] For an excellent account of Hume's psychology bearing on unsocial sociability see Gerald J. Postema, " 'Cemented with Diseased Qualities': Sympathy and Comparison in Hume's Moral Psychology," *Hume Studies* 31.2 (November 2005), 249–98.

consider what the moral law can require of us in these matters. Action from duty to help those in need is the chief thing. If someone acts beneficently often enough, Kant thinks, "he eventually comes actually to love the person he has helped." Love follows from acting sociably (MS 6.402). But we are also to take steps to cultivate our compassionate feelings, fostering them as means to active helpfulness (MS 6.456–7).[31]

These virtues attract us to one another, Kant holds, and they require to be balanced by virtues that keep us at a proper distance from one another—virtues in which we show our respect for one another. Mutual love urges us to "*come closer* to one another," while respect leads us to keep ourselves "*at a distance* from one another*". Respect requires that we not make excessive demands on others—that we show modesty toward them. We must not injure the just self-esteem of others. And we must maintain our honor as law-abiding citizens (MS 6.462–5). Guided by these two principles we can construct a moral world, just as physical principles of attraction and repulsion make the natural world (MS 6.449).

All these virtues plainly belong among our tendencies to sociability. Our unsociable vices also fall into groups. One arises from hatred of others. We are prone to envy—"a propensity to view the well-being of others with distress, even though it does not detract from one's own." We fall into jealousy, and as I have just noted we tend also toward ingratitude. Worse is to come. Malice, "the direct opposite of sympathy", lurks in the soul. It is brought out by haughtiness and self-conceit in others but it can also take the form of desire for revenge (MS 6.458–61). Another group of unsociable vices are those coming from refusal of the duty to respect others. The main ones that Kant considers are arrogance and its associate, contempt; the tendency to defame others, which is an effort to lower the respect they deserve; and the related urge to ridicule others (MS 6.465–8).[32]

In *Idea* Kant does not elaborate on how we know about unsocial sociability. He says simply that we learn about it from experience. The facts we learn from even the small portion of endless history with which we are acquainted point toward a pattern, which emerges in classical Greece and appears in later eras as well. It shows how our unsociability drives us into what we can now see is progress (8.27;50; 8.29; 52). The other works in

---

[31]   And see also "The End of All Things", VIII, 337–8.
[32]   See also the quite full discussion of vices in LecEth 27.686–698.

which Kant discusses unsocial sociability also treat our knowledge of it as empirical. There is however one passage in which Kant offers what sounds like a different account of our knowledge of at least one aspect of unsocial sociability. In the *Doctrine of Right*, Kant says:

It is not from experience that we learn of the maxim of violence in human beings and of their malevolent tendency to attack one another before external legislation endowed with power appears, thus it is not some deed that makes coercion through public law necessary. On the contrary, however well disposed and law-abiding human beings might be, it still lies *a priori* in the rational idea of such a condition (one that is not rightful) that before a public lawful condition is established individual human beings, peoples and states can never be secure against volence from one another, since each has its own right to *what seems right and good to it* and not to be dependent upon another's opinion about this.

(MS 6.312)

Prior to establishment of a public lawful condition humans are in a state of nature (MS 6.312–13). In it there might be familial societies but there is no public authority to safeguard possession (MS 6.242). Hence there is mutual fear and suspicion, and there cannot be true property. At this point the postulate of public right holds for everyone: "when you cannot avoid living side by side with all the others, you ought to leave the state of nature and proceed with them into a rightful condition, that is, a condition of distributive justice" (MS 6.307; cf.6.237).

In general Kant holds that awareness of the moral law and of specific instances of the categorical imperative provides agents with a sufficient motive to do what is required: in this case, to begin to live sociably. Taken together, then, the two passages I have just quoted suggest that however it may be with the sorts of unsocial sociability that arise from our passions and desires and about which we learn from experience, there is another kind. This kind arises from the right to act on one's own judgment of what is "right and good". In a state of nature we cannot expect convergence in different agents' judgments. But we can each understand that we are morally required to enter into a condition that will remove the potential for conflict due to our conflicting judgments of what is right and good. Kant does not explicitly mention unsocial sociability in either of the discussions from which I have given the key passages. But I think we may take them to imply that one of its forms is *a priori* necessary.

3. The fullest account Kant gives of unsocial sociability in its relation to the rest of his views occurs in *Religion within the Boundaries of Mere Reason*. There are, Kant says, three original predispositions toward the good in our nature: toward animality, humanity, and personality. Our predisposition to animality explains "merely *mechanical* self-love", our automatic tendencies toward self-preservation, sex and procreation, and sociability. Reason is not required for any of these drives. (Thus this is like the Stoic view of our initial tendency toward self-preservation.) By contrast, our predisposition to humanity depends on our possession of reason. It expresses itself in a self-love in which we compare our condition with that of others. This first gives rise to our inclination to "gain worth in the opinion of others". We begin by thinking of all people as equal, but our anxiety about others lording it over us leads us to seek superiority over them. And then jealousy and rivalry arise. Nature intended these to generate a competitiveness that would have the effect of increasing our degree of culture. But because we are always spurred on by our fear that others will gain ascendency over us, we move toward vices like envy and ingratitude. We have no original inclination to these. It is our fears for our own security that give rise to them (R 6.27).

Reason is also central to the third predisposition, that to personality. It is shown in our openness to being moved by awareness of the moral law, which, of course, for Kant is the core of practical reason. While the second predisposition uses reason to serve our non-moral desires, the third expresses the sufficiency of practical reason to move us regardless of these desires (R 6.27–8). This leads to another point about the way Kant must see our unsocial sociability. When fully developed it is a result of what Kant calls our inborn "radical evil".

Kant explains his view of evil in Part One of *Religion*. We are not evil just because we sometimes need non-moral motives to cooperate with the moral motive if we are to act morally. In cases like this we show what Kant calls the "impurity" of our hearts. We are fully evil, however, only when we adopt maxims that "subordinate the incentives of the moral law to others (not moral ones)." In doing this we show a propensity to act as morality requires only if it suits our non-moral desires. The tendency to this improper ordering of motives must be considered, Kant says, to be a result of a free choice made by each and every person. Kant thinks we learn from experience that everyone makes this choce. The whole history of humankind shows us that everyone tends to subordinate morality to non-moral desires. Experience thus shows us that evil in this sense is "radical", "woven into human nature" and inseparable from us (6.30). Because it is due to a free choice, morever, the propensity cannot be explained.

By the time the desires and passions that make us unsociable are fully developed, we have also experienced the awakening of our moral sensibilities.[33] Mature humans, Kant holds, cannot avoid being aware of the moral law. At some level we are always aware of its bearing on our maxims. Consequently we cannot help noticing that the moral law prohibits acting from our harmful, unsociable desires. Throughout *Idea* Kant makes it clear that he considers the acts that display our unsocial sociability to be free. In such behavior we are freely choosing to act on a maxim or plan that we know is prohibited by the moral law. This is precisely what constitutes being morally evil.

What makes us unsocial in our sociability is thus not mere animal instincts for which we are not responsible. It is rational choices, for which we are. Our difficult personality is therefore not only a natural ill of the human condition; it is a moral evil as well. Yet this very evil, Kant thinks, gives us reason to hope for the moral good of a morally well-ordered society and ultimately for a politically well-ordered world.[34] At the end of the essay Kant suggests that his *Idea* enables us to see the wisdom of God in the human world as well as in the natural world. *Idea* is thus intended as a theodicy, an account of how God has arranged things so that what strikes us as only an evil is nonetheless a major source of good. Kant is unique in seeing unsocial sociability in this light.

IV

The problems left behind by the concept of unsocial sociability continued to be discussed after Kant. But the terms changed. A history of the descendants of unsocial sociability would occupy a large volume. I point to only three of the topics that would need to be considered.

1. In Kant's *Idea*, the progress which he sees as resulting from unsocial sociability is not the intention of any of the agents whose often wicked actions contribute to bringing it about. He is thus working with a conception

---

[33] For the awakening of sophisticated desires and sensibilities, see Kant's "Conjectures on the Beginning of Human History" (MA 8:109–23), translation in Hans Reiss, *Kant: Political Writings*, trans. H. B. Nisbet, 2nd edn. (Cambridge: Cambridge University Press, [1970] 1991.)

[34] Kant says that the history of nature begins with good, as the work of God, but "the history of *freedom* begins with evil, for it is *the work of man*." "Conjectures" in Reiss, 227, MA 8. 115.

of what later came to be called "the unintended consequences of intentional action". It would take a history of the social sciences and of the philosophy of history to follow the uses of this fruitful notion. Adam Smith sees improvement in society's material well-being as coming from private and purely personal endeavors to make a living. In Hegel's philosophy of history, progress toward freedom for all is the unintended outcome of innumerable struggles, most of them with far more limited goals. For Smith a "hidden hand" brings about the fortunate result; for Hegel it is the dialectical self-development of *Geist* or Spirit. Hegel sees the course of history as a kind of vindication of God. Karl Marx leaves God out of the story. He takes over Hegelian dialectic but transforms it into the work of economic forces, not spiritual ones. Darwin eventually led most thinkers to drop the idea that history has a point or a goal. For him evolution has no purpose. It is driven by chance and its ever-changing outcomes have no necessary relation to human purposes or values. Many sociologists have tried to explain the mechanisms bringing about social conditions which look as if they were the outcome of human planning, but which, they think, cannot be explained solely in terms of individual psychology.[35]

2. For Kant, unsocial sociability serves first and foremost to explain human inventiveness and industry. By doing so it gives him grounds for celebration of divine providence. Aside from Hegel, post-Kantian thinkers who reconstruct versions of unsocial sociability leave out the theodicy. Certainly neither Nietzsche nor Freud bring it in. But both of them invoke different versions of unsocial sociability in explaining some of the major features of society.

"Every animal," Nietzsche says, "instinctively strives for an optimum of favorable conditions in which fully to release his power and achieve his maximum of power sensation."[36] Unlike Hobbes, Nietzsche thinks that some human animals are naturally more powerful than others. The strong enslave the weak and construct a society to their own liking. As true nobles, they value spontaneous outpourings of energy in hunting, in warfare, and in tormenting others. But the weak learn how to strike back. Their values come from a deep resentment[37] of the strong. (OGM 91) Out of this

---

[35] A classic modern study of historicism and the various uses of the idea of the unintended consequences of intentional action is Karl R. Popper, *The Poverty of Historicism*, (London, 1957).

[36] *On the Genealogy of Morals*, 3.7, ed. Keith Anselm-Pearson, trans. Carol Diethel (Cambridge University Press, 1994), p. 81. Further references are given in the text, indicated as OGM.

[37] Nietzsche uses the French term *ressentiment* but "resentment" is a close enough translation for present purposes.

resentment they invent life-denying values like "poverty, humility, chastity" (OGM 82). They form an ascetic ideal in opposition to the ideal of unselfconscious enjoyment of life expressed by the strong. And the weak use their ideal to triumph over the strong, convincing "the happy, the successful, those powerful in body and soul to begin to doubt their *right to happiness*" (OGM 97). The fullest expression of the resentful attitude to life is Christianity, which has imposed its slave morality on all of Europe.

For Nietzsche, the strong use the weak as material for expressing their power. The weak must then struggle to control the strong in order to have a society they can bear. The conflict in this version of unsocial sociability never ends. Kant, as I have said, does not use unsocial sociability as a basic explanation of morality. Nietzsche, by contrast, uses the struggle between weak and strong to show us how the dominant slave morality of western Europe came into being. He thinks his narrative presents a new standpoint from which we can assess that morality. If we ourselves are strong we will come to despise it as he does.

Among the values trumpeted by the slaves is the value of impersonal truth, valid for everyone. Nietzsche holds that this value is illusory. Every version of how the world is comes from some standpoint and expresses the perspective of those who accept it. The slave mentality in pursuing impersonal truth has created modern science, which becomes yet another instrumentality for keeping the strong subordinate to the weak. What Kant sees as one of the great positive outcomes of unsocial sociability is for Nietzsche another episode in the struggle between slave and noble mentality.

In *Civilization and its Discontents* Freud claims that the benefits of civilization come at great cost to individuals. We all need protection against nature and we all desire loving community with other people. Civilization provides these, but to get them we must suppress some of our deepest and most insistent urges. Sex is one: from birth on we are forced to give up intense pleasures and repress desires that society finds unacceptable. Aggression is another. It is not merely a response to the frustration that comes from repression of desire. It is, Freud says, "an original, self-subsisting instinctual disposition in man and . . . it constitutes the greatest impediment to civilization."[38]

---

[38] Sigmund Freud, *Civilization and its Discontents*, (1930) transl. James Strachey, W. (New York: W. Norton & Co., 1961), 81. Further references in text marked as CD.

Kant holds that the categorical imperative requires us to work for a world federation of republics. Because duty calls us to forward this end, we must think it can be achieved—and this despite the unsociable aspect of our sociability. Freud says that "civilization is a process in the service of Eros, whose purpose is to combine single human individuals, and after that families...into one great unity, the unity of mankind." The aggressive instinct, "the hostility of each against all", opposes love's program. History is essentially the struggle of these two forces, welling up from within individuals and shaping society (CD 81–2). Freud is not at all sure of what the outcome will be (CD 112). He calls on no providence, not even one assured only by moral requirements, for consolation. Unlike Kant he aims at no theodicy.

Freud's individuals are internally riven by the conflicts between the search for pleasure and the instinct of aggression, whose destructiveness leads him to identify it with a deep wish for death. The energy from the suppression of egoistic desires is transferred to an increasingly tyrannical conscience, which creates feelings of guilt and anxiety even in the absence of actual deeds for which remorse might be appropriate. Freud sees Christian morality, with its insistence on love of neighbor, as voicing the impulses of one part of our nature. But unlike Kant he does not call love good and aggressiveness evil. And unlike Nietzsche he does not locate the impulse in one kind of human, the slave kind, and the opposition to it in another kind. With Kant he sees each of us as torn by the conflict between sociable and unsociable drives. Kant does not comment on the results of the conflict for personal happiness. Freud sees it as making guilt-free enjoyment of life just about impossible.

3. Recent theorists are engaged with a problem that may be a descendant of the problem raised by unsocial sociability but that has no ties to religion or history. The question as they see it is that there are two aspects of practical rationality. It is wholly rational, on this kind of view, to try to increase one's own good as much as possible. It is also rational to to hold that other agents have as much right to consideration as one has oneself. Or, put another way, it is rational to be equally concerned for the good of all. The problem is that these two rationalities can and do yield conflicting answers to questions about what one ought to do. And this seems to show that practical reason is deeply at odds with itself.[39]

---

[39] For the classic statement of this view, see Henry Sidgwick, *The Methods of Ethics*, London (1874) 7th edn., 1907, Bk. IV, Concluding ch.

Kant avoids this incoherence because he holds that moral im_
rationally override self-interested imperatives, but he fails to convince
everyone. Egoists equally fail to convince everyone that self-interest is
always rationally entitled to defeat moral requirements. Other philosophers
think that while morality may rightly override personal projects in some
cases, there are also cases where it does not. None of these thinkers consider
that concern for one's own good or one's own projects is vicious or wicked.
It is tempting to say that the problem of unsocial sociability continues to be a
presence in recent moral philosophy because of the lively discussion of the
relations between these two aspects or kinds of rationality. But in reading
past authors who discuss unsocial sociability we should not impute to all of
them the specific form of the problem occupying attention now. We should
not ignore the strand of past thought in which the conflict was not just
between two forms of rationality, but between good and evil.

PART VI
Moral Psychology

18

The Active Powers

In 1751, in the *Discours préliminaire* for the great encyclopedia he and Denis Diderot were editing, Jean d'Alembert proclaimed a simple scheme for organising "the sciences of man". The divisions of this science, he said,

are derived from the divisions of his faculties. The principal faculties of man are the *understanding* and the *will*; the *understanding*, which it is necessary to direct toward *truth*; the *will*, which must be made to conform to *virtue*. The one is the object of *logic*, the other is that of *ethics*.[1]

D'Alembert's dichotomy was not one of the novel ideas put forward in the *Encyclopédie*. It had forerunners in antiquity, and Descartes used a revised form of it. Locke seemed to use a similar classification, but he stated it in different terms, and for good reason. If we speak of understanding and will as faculties of mind, he said, we may be tempted to suppose that the words "stand for some real Beings in the Soul, that performed those Actions of Understanding and Volition". But the idea that there are "distinct Agents" in us breeds nothing but confusion.[2] Locke chose to talk of the powers of the mind and, without making a fuss about it, sometimes classified them as active and passive (see, for instance, *Essay concerning Human Understanding*, II.xxi.72).

Leibniz also objected to the "personification or mythology" in which the will is imagined as "alone active and supreme . . . like a queen . . . whose

For comments on drafts of this essay, I would like to thank Knud Haakonssen, Elijah Millgram, Susan James, and Charles Larmore. I am particularly grateful to Natalie Brender for her comments and for her expert assistance on numerous matters of detail.

[1] Jean le Rond d'Alembert, *Discours préliminaire de l'Encyclopédie* (Paris, 1894), translated as *Preliminary Discourse to the Encyclopedia of Diderot*, trans. R. N. Schwab and W. E. Rex (Indianapolis, IN, 1963), 149. D'Alembert did not use the label "psychology" for the systematic study of the understanding and will. In 1732, Christian Wolff published his *Psychologia empirica*, and in 1734 his *Psychologia rationalis*. The books initiated the use of the term as the name for a distinct discipline, but it was slow to catch on.

[2] John Locke, *An Essay concerning Human Understanding*, ed. P. H. Nidditch, (Oxford: Clarendon Press, 1975), II.xxi.6, 20.

minister of state is the understanding, while the passions are her courtiers". Taken literally, the view would be incoherent, leading to an endless multiplication of faculties to explain how the will can take account of reasons produced by the understanding. The truth is that it is "the soul, or the thinking substance" that understands, feels, and decides to modify its active force (*sa force active*) in producing our actions.[3]

Later writers tended to follow Locke and Leibniz in explaining mental life in terms of varied powers of a single mind. They thereby avoided the difficulty of explaining the unity of mind posed by explanations in terms of different parts or faculties.[4] In what follows, I outline the various ways in which philosophers from Locke and Leibniz through Kant understood the mental powers associated with "the will" or connected with action. I suggest that the opposition between Leibniz and Locke set the terms for eighteenth-century discussion of these issues. Hence, after noting briefly, in Section I, the changing metaphysical background to discussions of human activity, I present (Section II) the view sketched by Leibniz and worked out by Wolff and then (Section III) that given by Locke. The Leibnizians held the basically Stoic view that the activities of the mind, including its desires and decisions, naturally tend toward order because all of them represent some aspect of an objectively good and orderly universe. Locke found no such natural, inherent tendency toward order in our decisions. They can be controlled, he held, only by deliberately imposed sanctions. Most of those who accepted Locke's denial that the desires and the will are naturally ordered were repelled by his thesis that external intervention is essential to bring order into human action. Morality, they held, can come from within. Their efforts to show how this is possible fall roughly into three groups.

Some asserted that natural self-interest is so strong that it enables us to govern the passions. Knowledge of where our true private interest lies is thus what gives us control of ourselves.

---

[3] Gottfried Wilhelm Leibniz, "Remarques sur le Livre de l'origine du mal, publié depuis peu en Angleterre", in *Philosophischen Schriften*, 6: 400–36 at 416, translated as "Observations on the Book concerning 'The Origin of Evil' ", in *Theodicy: Essays on the Goodness of God, the Freedom of Man and the Origin of Evil*, trans. E. M. Huggard, ed. A. Farrer (London, 1951), 405–32 at 421.

[4] See, for example, Law's note in William King, *An Essay on the Origin of Evil* (*De origine mali*, 1702), trans. E. Law (London, 1731), 153n.; Abraham Tucker, *The Light of Nature Pursued* (1768), 4 vols. (Cambridge, MA, 1831), 1: ch. 1, §17, p. 46; Johann Nicolas Tetens, *Philosophische Versuche über die menschliche Natur und ihre Entwicklung* (1777), in *Die philosophischen Werke*, 2 vols. (Leipzig, 1777).

Those who rejected egoism held that we possess unselfish as well as selfish desires. We also have a moral faculty or sense capable both of showing us the proper ordering of our desires and of helping us to achieve it.

Proponents of both these lines of thought, such as the Wolffians, accepted determinism. Against them, a third school asserted that we possess a unique kind of agency because we have a free will. We are able to order our decisions in accordance with the eternal moral truths discerned by our intellect, regardless of the strength of our desires.

The actual history was, of course, not as simple as the categories suggest. In Sections IV through VII, I discuss the complex British debates on the issues. German philosophers who opposed Wolffianism took the third line. In Section VIII, I discuss the first major German philosopher to oppose the Wolffians with a strong doctrine of free will: Christian August Crusius. In Section IX, I turn to the views of J. N. Tetens, who used both Lockean and Leibnizian ideas in constructing an empirically based libertarian view. Then, in Section X, I describe Kant's views about freedom and desire, which responded to all these discussions among his predecessors. In Section XI, I conclude with a brief look back and then comment on the turn the post-Kantians gave to Kant's view of the will.

I. Activity and Passivity

The concepts of activity and passivity as they were used in classifying human powers during the eighteenth century were themselves the outcome of complex and protracted arguments about science, religion, and metaphysics. Aristotle held that active powers enable whatever has them to transmit new forms to substances possessing the passive power to receive those forms. In *Les passions de l'âme* (*The Passions of the Soul*), Descartes rejected this way of understanding action and passion. Whatever happens or is done, he said, "is generally called by philosophers a "passion" with regard to the subject to which it happens and an "action" with regard to that which makes it happen".[5] For instance, matter, on Descartes' view, is caused to move at first by God; thereafter, physical change is no more than the transmission of

---

[5] René Descartes, *Les passions de l'âme*, in *Oeuvres*, 11: Pt. I, §1, translated as *The Passions of the Soul*, in *The Philosophical Writings of Descartes*, trans. J. Cottingham *et al.*, 3 vols. (Cambridge, 1984–91), 1: 328.

motion to new configurations of corpuscles, each of which is passive when receiving motion and active when passing it on. In this sense, an active body does not differ in any essential way from a passive body. Another Cartesian distinction between action and passion does involve essentials. God's will is wholly active; so too is the human will, the feature of our constitution making us resemble God. In some circumstances, such wills can determine themselves to act in entire independence of anything external to them. This spontaneous exercise of active power differs in kind from the activity displayed by things without wills, which is simply the passing along of motion originating elsewhere.

Descartes' theory of the will helped provoke a sharp reaction. Nicolas Malebranche, the foremost opponent of the belief that anything in the created world could possess genuinely active power, argued that it would be impious and dangerous to locate real power anywhere except in God. If we believe that created beings—particularly human beings—can cause happiness, we might begin to worship them instead of God. Moreover, only God has such power that what he wills *necessarily* occurs. Any other alleged cause serves only as the occasion on which God exerts his power to bring about what we call the effect. We can see this because we can understand what it would be like for the cause to occur without the effect occurring. If a genuine cause makes its effect come about necessarily, then only God is such a cause. Piety as well as logic thus requires the admission that only God possesses truly active power.[6]

Leibniz argued strongly against Malebranche's occasionalism. Locke simply ignored it. He unhesitatingly ascribed active power to created beings and proceeded without apology to track down the source of our idea of it.[7] Newton likewise attributed active powers to natural objects without any fear of irreverence. Thus the greatest scientist of the period as well as its two most influential philosophers validated the thought that humans may—among other things—be truly active.

[6] For Malebranche's views, see *The Search after Truth* (*De la recherche de la vérité*, 1674–5), trans. T. M. Lennon and P.J. Olscamp (Columbus, OH, 1980), VI.ii.3, 446–52; *Discourse on Metaphysics* (*Entretiens sur la métaphysique et sur la religion*, 1688), trans. W. Doney (New York, NY, 1980), Seventh Dialogue, 145 ff.

[7] For Leibniz, see *On Nature Itself* (1698), in Gottfried Wilhelm Leibniz, *Philosophical Papers and Letters*, trans. and ed. L. E. Loemker (Dordrecht, 1969), 498 ff. Locke did not discuss the occasionalism when he criticized Malebranche in his posthumous *Examination of P. Malebranche's Opinion of Seeing All Things in God*, in *Posthumous Works of Mr. John Locke* (London, 1706), 141–213.

In doing so, however, they opened the way to a further problem. Leibniz held that all events in the world are determined by some antecedent cause. Newton's theory was widely taken to give determinism and even mechanism the support of the most successful science ever seen, and Locke avowed himself a supporter of Newton. The question then was whether human beings exert their powers only in accordance with deterministic laws such as Newton's laws of motion. If active powers are always caused to act by something outside themselves, then their possessors are not truly originators of their actions.[8] How then can they be capable of moral responsibility or possess any more dignity than stones or trees or horses? Newtonian science seemed to make a Cartesian will just as unthinkable as Malebranchean metaphysics did. Eighteenth-century inquiry about the domain of the will was framed by the question of whether between God and nature there is any conceptual room for powers in the human mind that make our agency different in kind from that of natural objects.

II. The Leibniz-Wolff Theory

Leibniz was deeply critical of Newton's physics and Locke's philosophy. For our purposes, the disagreements between Leibniz and Locke on action, will, and passion are of central importance. They determined the basic outlines of eighteenth-century thought on these topics. Leibniz's position, expounded unsystematically in scattered writings, was drawn together into a massive system of unsurpassed thoroughness and scope by Christian Wolff. Accepting the main Leibnizian views—about monads, the principle of sufficient reason, and the pre-established harmony—he elaborates their consequences far more fully than Leibniz himself ever did. He analyses the passions, he gives an account of will and its place in action, and he argues for a specific way of understanding the difference between being active and being passive. In doing so, he explains freedom, showing how there can be

---

[8] For a clear statement, see Clarke's Fifth Reply in his correspondence with Leibniz: the question of liberty, he says, is "whether the *immediate physical Cause* or *Principle of Action* be indeed *in* him whom we call the *Agent*; or whether it be some *other Reason sufficient*, which is the *real Cause* of the Action, by operating upon the Agent, and making him to be, not indeed an *Agent*, but a mere *Patient*". Samuel Clarke, *Works*, ed. B. Hoadly, 4 vols. London, 1738), 4: 674.

alternatives for the will to choose between and how the will can be the source of its choice.

In Germany, the Leibniz-Wolff philosophy remained the dominant academic orthodoxy until the middle of the eighteenth century. Locke produced no similar orthodoxy, but his admirers all rejected the major points contained in the Leibniz–Wolff understanding of the metaphysics and psychology of action. If we understand the kind of view they rejected, we shall have a better grasp of the positive points they were making. Wolff's exposition of the Leibnizian theory in his *Vernünfftige Gedancken von Gott, der Welt und der Seele des Menschen* (Reasonable Thoughts on God, the World, and the Soul of Man) is a serviceable guide.[9]

The soul, on this view, is a simple, non-corporeal substance. Like any existing thing, its essence is constituted by its power, and because it is simple, it can have only one power (*Gedancken*, §§742–5). Basically this is the power of representing the world as the world impinges on the soul via the body associated with it. Representations (*Vorstellungen*) can have different degrees of clarity and distinctness, but whether clear or dark, explicit or obscure, they all essentially carry propositions about the world (§§198–9, 206, 209). The senses, imagination, memory, reflection, understanding, desire, and will are all to be understood as different ways in which the soul represents the world (§747).

Wolff's position thus entails that each specific instance of each kind of mental activity, from sensation to conceptual reasoning, from desiring to willing, is constituted by two factors: its definite propositional content and the degree of its clarity and distinctness. Since there is only one power in the soul, and content and degree of clarity and distinctness are the only dimensions of manifestations of that power, there is nothing else from which mental states can get their identity. Sensations, for instance, may be clear representations—I see clearly that green is not red—but they are indistinct

---

[9] Christian Wolff, *Vernünfftige Gedancken von Gott, der Welt und der Seele des Menschen, auch allen Dingen überhaupt* (1719–20), ed. C. A. Corr, in *Werke*, I.2 (1983). Hereafter cited as *Gedancken*, followed by the section number. Wolff had a European audience through his own lengthy Latin versions of his works and also through French versions. Jean Deschamps published French summaries of the foundations of the system in 1741 and 1743 and abridgements of the two Latin psychology volumes in 1747. Jean Henri Samuel Formey's six-volume *La belle Wolfienne*, which appeared between 1741 and 1753, covered most of Wolff's teaching. Alexander Gottlieb Baumgarten's *Metaphysica* (1739 and many later editions), a textbook from which Kant regularly taught, contains a comprehensive outline of the Leibniz–Wolff philosophy. It was translated into German by G. F. Meier in 1766 for use in his own classes.

(*undeutlich*) since I cannot say exactly what constitutes the difference between red and green (§214). Yet there is some set of truths about that difference, and if I perceived colors distinctly I would know it. Memory and reflection, involving reiterated operations on representations, enable us to have clearer and more distinct concepts, to form judgments, and to make inferences. To see how passions and will arise from representations, we must bring in a new consideration.

Like Leibniz, Wolff sees the world and everything within it in terms of perfection and imperfection. "The harmony of the manifold" is Wolff's definition of the perfection of things (§152). Complex entities contain a number of parts working harmoniously together to attain an end. The more parts they contain and the simpler the principles of their organisation toward that end, the more perfect they are. This world, Wolff argues, is the most perfect of all possible worlds since all its parts work together as fully and as simply as possible to express God's glory (that is, his infinite perfection) (§§982, 1045, 1049–51). If Voltaire's *Candide* made a laughing stock of Leibniz's view that this is the "best of all possible worlds", it was for him, as for Wolff, a direct *a priori* inference from the proposition that God, being infinitely wise, powerful, and good, could not act without a reason and so could not choose to create any world other than the best possible one. I discuss later the problems this thesis raises for freedom of the will. Here we must note the way in which degrees of perfection are involved in the passions.

The tie is quite direct. When we recognise, or think we recognise, perfection, we feel pleasure. Indeed, to feel pleasure is just to have an intuition of perfection (*ein Anschauen der Vollkommenheit*) (*Gedancken*, §404).[10] In speaking of intuition, Wolff refers to an uninferred representation without intending to imply that no error is possible. We can get pleasure from mistaken representations of perfection as well as from accurate ones (§405), and the amount of pleasure we feel must be absolutely proportional to the amount of perfection we intuit.[11] Pleasure and displeasure or pain (compare §§417–18, 421) are tied to good and ill through the central

[10] "*Voluptas* est intuitus, seu cognitio intuitiva perfectionis cujuscunque, sive verae, sive apparentis", in Christian Wolff, *Psychologia empirica* (Frankfurt, 1738), §511. In *Werke*, II.5, Wolff says we owe the idea to Descartes.
[11] As Jean École notes (*La métaphysique de Christian Wolff*, 2 vols., in *Werke*, III.12.1–2: 269), Wolff sometimes speaks of pleasure and pain as consequences of intuitions. If he means to treat pleasure and pain as non-representative states of mind, he is departing from his basic theory rather seriously. In either case, the feeling will be proportional to the perfection perceived.

definitional claim that "what makes us and our condition more perfect is good" (§422). Thus the intuitive awareness of good is what brings, or more accurately constitutes, pleasure. And pleasure and pain, so understood, are the building blocks out of which the passions are constituted.

We can clearly tell pleasure from pain, but both of them remain indistinct representations of perfection, or good and ill (§§432–3). Insofar as they are indistinct, they give rise to sensuous desire. Such desire is "an inclination of the soul toward something of whose goodness we have an indistinct conception" (§434). Just as we can tell green from red without being able to say what makes each the color it is, so can we tell that we like the taste of a specific wine without being able to say what it is in the wine that makes it more perfect than a wine we dislike. Our pleasure represents the good confusedly and indistinctly, and the inclination to drink, Wolff says, is thereupon necessary since the soul is necessarily inclined toward whatever pleasure represents to it as good (§878).

The specific passions are essentially characterised by the kind of good or pleasure that constitutes them, taking into account also the relations in which we stand to that good. Desire and aversion arise directly, Wolff maintains, from pleasure and pain (§§434, 436). When we are disposed to take pleasure in the happiness of another person, we are said to love that person, and such love in turn can give rise to notable happiness or unhappiness on our part, according to whether the other fares well or ill (§§449–53). Wolff is careful not to suggest that in loving another we are seeking only our own enjoyment or benefit. (Leibniz thinks that the pleasure we get from acts of love is essential to our being moved to perform them, thus allowing a strain of egoistic thinking to enter his psychology.)

Wolff gives brief and conventional accounts of the other passions. Envy, for instance, is the disposition to see another's misfortune as good—that is, to take pleasure in it. Sympathy, by contrast, is the disposition to be pained by the misfortune of another (§§460–1). Remorse is displeasure at something we have done, shame a displeasure at the thought of the bad opinion others will have of us due to some imperfection of ours (§§464–5). These definitions of desires and feelings, very much in the vein of those offered by Descartes and Spinoza, lay the groundwork for the Leibniz–Wolff theory of the will.

When passions rise to a noticeable degree of strength, Wolff says, they are called affects (§441). Affects pull us this way and that, and we remain their slaves as long as they stay indistinct (§491). But there is a way out of such slavery. We can think something good through clear and distinct representations as well as through obscure and indistinct ones. The effort to attain more perfection is essential to our being. Hence, insofar as we are moved by indistinct representations, we are doing less of what we essentially will and are therefore passive. As our ideas become more distinct, we are acting more as we essentially will to act. Since distinct ideas give us more power than indistinct ones, they make us more active (§§115, 744, 748, 755–6).

Our essential striving toward perfection or good in general constitutes our will (§492). Will and desire are not different in kind from "the representative power of the soul" (§879). A representation of something as perfect is simply a representation that inclines us toward it. Will differs from desire only because in willing we compare amounts of perfection presented by different ideas and move toward the greatest. What finally moves our will is our reason for acting, and Wolff follows Leibniz in stressing that the will has no power of choice in the absence of a reason or motive (*Bewegungsgrund*).[12] It may seem that we can make choices where we are wholly indifferent, but this is never the case, although often the cognitions of perfection that move us are below the level of consciousness (§§496–8, 508–9). Moreover, we never choose what seems to us the worse in preference to what seems the better, though again we may not be aware of the sensuous desires influencing us (§§503–7).

The mind has no dispositions to act other than its motives. Hence we always necessarily act for what we represent as the greatest good or perfection available to us. Both Leibniz and Wolff, moreover, think that God has created the best possible world. Thus it seems that not only do our representations of good and ill determine our actions but that these representations could not have been other than they are and therefore that we could in no sense act in any way other than we do. How, within this framework, can we be free?

Leibniz's *Theodicy* is an extended answer to this question, and Wolff's views are very similar. Both theorists are concerned with making two points. One is that despite the determinism implicit in the "best of all possible worlds" thesis, we have alternatives from which to choose and we must make choices. The other point is that the determination of the will

---

[12] Wolff gives *motiva* as the Latin equivalent for *Bewegungsgrund*.

by representations of perfection allows conceptual room for action to be fully voluntary. These two points seem to Leibniz and Wolff to add up to a defense of human freedom sufficient to underpin morality, and Wolff adds that any less deterministic conception of freedom would in fact undercut morality.

Admitting that we necessarily choose what seems to us the best alternative, Leibniz says that the necessity involved is not absolute or metaphysical but hypothetical. Absolute necessity is the kind involved in mathematics, where the opposite of what is necessarily true is not even conceivable. Hypothetical necessity does not involve the inconceivability of the opposite. What is chosen is necessary as means to an end. Hence we know what it would be like not to do what we do even if, given our end, we necessarily do it. Even God has this choice when he makes the best possible world real: he must create that world, but not because no other choice is conceivable (*Theodicy*, 61, 334, 387). This world is necessarily chosen only on condition that God wills the best.

How, then, can we be free? Are we free to have or not have the ends we have? Could God have a different end? All one can mean in asking this, Leibniz thinks, is whether we are spontaneous when we act, or "have within us the source of our actions" (*Theodicy*, 303). We cannot be asking whether we choose to have the will we have. The will is a settled disposition to obtain the greatest good, and we cannot without absurdity ask whether we will to have that will, "else we could still say that we will to have the will to will, and that would go on to infinity" (151). Insofar as what we pursue is something that we distinctly perceive to be good, we are acting as we most want to act. No more than that could meaningfully be required in order for us to be acting from our own will, or voluntarily.

The will, Wolff says, is like a pair of scales, immovable if both sides are equal and moving only through greater weight on one side. Does this rule out freedom? Only, he replies, on a false conception of freedom as the ability to choose either of two alternatives without any reason for a preference (*Gedancken*, §§510–11). On that view, he asserts, all moral truth is destroyed. Morality requires that representations of good and bad have a reliable effect on human action:

If you throw that out of the window, then all certainty in morality collapses, since one cannot influence the human soul except through representations of the good and the bad. Even in the commonwealth, obligation as based on punishment rests on the fact that man does not want ill and does want good, and avoids what he thinks good in order to escape a greater ill.   (*Gedancken*, §512)

What we need for morality is freedom defined as "the ability of the soul through its own power of choice [*Willkühr*] to choose, between two equally possible things, that which pleases it most". (§§514–19)

III. Locke

Locke's theory of the passions and the will offered an empiricist alternative to the Leibniz–Wolff position. It also posed a problem which concerned philosophers throughout the century following its publication. Locke's account comes mainly from two chapters of *An Essay concerning Human Understanding*, in which he uncovers the origins of our ideas of the desires and the will and discusses the will's freedom.

The passions take their rise, he says, from pleasure and pain. Since these are simple, we can obtain ideas of them only from our own experience of them. We call "good" whatever is "apt to cause or increase Pleasure . . . in us", Locke says, but he does not say that the feeling represents its cause (*Essay*, II.xx. 1–2). Leibniz says he agrees with Locke's view that the good is "that which is apt to cause or increase pleasure", but the agreement is less than Leibniz makes it seem. In a later section, Leibniz speaks of "our inevitably confused ideas of pleasure and pain", discussing the advantage we get from their being confused and indistinct. But Locke does not speak of pleasure and pain as involving confusion and indistinctness. Indeed, because they are simple they cannot do so.[13]

When the thought of something produces pleasure, we feel the passion called love for that thing. Love, however, is not desire. Desire occurs only if we find ourselves uneasy in the absence of things we think of as pleasing. The uneasiness felt is what we call desire, and the strength of the desire is the strength of the uneasiness. We do not desire things in proportion to the

[13] Leibniz, *Nouveaux essais sur l'entendement humain*, eds. A. Robinet and H. Schepers, in *Sämtliche Schriften*, VI.6 (1962). Page citations refer to the translation, *New Essays on Human Understanding*, trans. and ed. P. Remnant and J. Bennett (Cambridge, 1981), II.xx.2, §6.

amount of good we think them to have. We can even know that something would please us without feeling any uneasiness at our lack of it. In a crucial passage, Locke remarks that "whatever good is propos'd, if its absence carries no displeasure nor pain with it; if a Man be easie and content without it, there is no desire of it, nor endeavor after it" (*Essay*, II.xx.6).

Locke uses his new account of desire to construct some quite standard illustrative accounts of particular desires and passions. Fear is uneasiness at the thought of a likely evil, anger is uneasiness "upon the receit of any Injury, with a present purpose of Revenge", envy is uneasiness caused by the thought of someone's having a good we want and think he should not have (II.xx. 10–13). Locke notes that passions have variable effects on the body—some people blush from shame and some do not—but excuses himself from giving a full treatment of the passions, thinking that these examples show how we get the ideas of the remainder.

The discussion of power, by contrast, occupies the longest chapter in the book. As Locke himself emphasises, he drastically revised his views after the publication of the first edition. Much of the revision is due to the thesis that we do not necessarily pursue what we think would be our greatest good (II.xxi.35, 71–2). Locke begins with the idea of power. We note changes in things affected by other things and note changes in our ideas when we choose to alter them. From these observations, we come to the idea of a power to make change and a power to receive it—active and passive powers. It is quite possible that matter has only passive power. In any case, the clearest source of the idea of active power is "reflection on the Operations of our Minds". We can alter our thoughts and also "barely by a thought of the Mind" we can make our bodies move. Noticing this experience gives us the simple idea of active power, and with it we can define the idea of will. It is the idea of our power to call up ideas for consideration and to prefer moving, or not moving, parts of our bodies. Voluntary acts thus are those "consequent to such order or command of the mind" (II.xxi. 1–5).

What then is liberty? Locke first gives a quite Hobbesian account. I am free if nothing outside me prevents me from doing what I will or makes me perform that action should I will to refrain. A free act is not the same as a voluntary act. If I prefer to stay in a room with someone whose company I like, I stay voluntarily even if the doors are locked. But I am not freely there because, should I will to leave, I could not (II.xxi.8–11). Leibniz objected that there is a sense of "freedom to will" that Locke here ignores. It stands for a condition opposed to that of "imposition or constraint, though an inner one like that which the passions impose.... [O]ne's mind is indeed not free when it is possessed by a great passion, for then one cannot will as one should, i.e. with proper deliberation" (*Nouveaux essais*, II.xxi.8). Locke does in fact take up the issue.

The will is a power of the mind, he reminds us, and since freedom is also a power, it makes no sense to ask whether the will is free. A power cannot have a power. The power of choosing or preferring is no more either free or unfree than the power of speaking or dancing (*Essay*, II.xxi. 14–19). But, because men wish to avoid all thoughts of guilt, they ask whether we are free to will. This question, arising from fear of damnation, entangles us in endless perplexities (II.xxi.22).

The answer is brisk. Where we are faced with a choice, we are not free not to will. We must choose one way or another. That would end the matter were it not that men persist: are we at liberty to will whichever alternative we please? Here Locke loses patience. The question is absurd; anyone who answers it must fall into an infinite regress since a will to will would itself need to be explained by yet a further willing, and so on (*Essay*, II.xxi.24–5).[14]

There is a further question about willing that Locke thinks is not absurd and which he answers. What determines the will to "this or that particular Motion or Rest?" What determines us to do this or that specific action? Locke's answer is that it is the strongest uneasiness presently felt. To elaborate on this, he returns to the view of desire outlined in the previous chapter of the *Essay*, chapter 20 (II.xxi.29).

Desire is felt uneasiness. Will is different from desire. Introspection shows it to be a different simple, and we can decide or will to do something we do not want to do. The will is determined by uneasiness at the thought of some absent good, but the uneasiness may not be aroused by "the greater good in view" (II.xxi.30–1). The drunkard knows sobriety would be better for him, yet he decides to drink; the sinner continues to sin although he knows that God rewards with infinite eternal joys those who reform. If the will were

---

[14] In *The Concept of Mind* (London, 1949), ch. 3, 62–82, Gilbert Ryle criticized the concept of volition or willing by arguing that it generates an infinite regress and is therefore useless in explaining action. Both Leibniz and Locke refuse to take willing as itself an action of the kind that requires a willing in order to be done. See Leibniz, *Nouveaux essais*, II.xxi.23.

determined by the prospect of the greatest good, behavior of this kind would be inexplicable (II.xxi.32–8). But if the greatest present uneasiness moves the will independently of the amount of good in view, it is no mystery.

Happiness is always what we desire, and happiness consists of "the utmost Pleasure we are capable of, and *Misery* the utmost Pain". But not all people are affected in the same way by the absence of various goods. One person may be indifferent to what another desires. Desire is only contingently aroused by various thoughts of goods, and "all good, even seen, and confessed to be so, does not necessarily move every particular Man's *desire*; but only that part . . . as is consider'd, and taken to make a necessary part of his happiness". There is no question of confusion and indistinctness here: "Men . . . may have a clear view of good, great and confessed good, without being concern'd for it, or moved by it" if they take their happiness to be complete without it (*Essay*, II.xxi.38–43). True enough, we all unfailingly seek to avoid severe bodily pain, and we avoid what other evils we can. But in desire and pursuit, there is no uniformity from person to person. Since "the same thing is not good to every Man alike", philosophers have wasted their time in debating about the highest good (II.xxi.54–5). In heaven, God will accommodate differences of taste in providing for our happiness. "For that being intended for a State of Happiness, it must certainly be agreeable to every one's wish and desire: Could we suppose their relishes as different there as they are here, yet the Manna in Heaven will suit every one's Palate" (II.xxi.65).

How does this bear on the issue of liberty? The most pressing removable uneasiness determines the will. But usually many uneasinesses are felt together. We find by experience that we are able to suspend action, and refrain from trying to remove our present uneasinesses, at least while we reflect on what makes us uneasy and consider which of the objects of desire will truly be best for us. This suspension of action, Locke says, is "the source of all liberty; in this seems to consist that, which is (as I think improperly) call'd *Free will*" (*Essay*, II.xxi.47). When we keep our uneasinesses from moving our will, we are not showing our indifference to good and ill.[15] Far

---

[15] Locke has some harsh words concerning those who claim that liberty of will essentially involves its "Indifferency" to good and ill; See *Essay*, II.xxi.48 and especially 71. But he thinks we can be indifferent in matters of no importance; see II.xxi.44.

from it: we are trying to assure that our will comes to be moved by the greatest good available to us. The power of suspending action, by increasing our ability to cause our will to be moved by the most durable uneasinesses, increases our freedom by leading us to do what we most want to do, which is to increase our happiness. Locke knew and was quite possibly influenced by Malebranche's view that the only action one can perform is to suspend action and do nothing while the amounts of good available to one pass before the mind and determine one to act.[16]

For both the Leibniz–Wolff view and Locke, then, will is to be explained in terms of reflection about our desires for specific goods. But there is a critical difference, shown in Locke's insistence that will is not itself a desire. On the Leibniz–Wolff view, will itself determines choices between desires because it is itself the standing desire for the greatest good, and all desires are commensurable in terms of the amounts of good they promise. To will is simply to go for the most good, or most perfection. For Locke, the matter is much more problematic. The greatest perceived good does not necessarily determine the will; the strongest removable uneasiness does. Suspension of action enables the uneasinesses to pull and tug until one wins. But beyond saying that some thought of good must be involved, Locke tells us nothing about what determines the strengths of present uneasinesses. Nor indeed could he. There is too much variability among people for any general truths about sources of desire to hold. We necessarily seek our own happiness, and it seems to be up to us to decide what goods to make part of our happiness; but once again Locke has no way of saying how we are to decide or what determines our decision.

The fact that we pursue our happiness does not settle the matter because until we make some pleasure part of our specific happiness its absence will not arouse uneasiness and hence not motivate us. Locke holds, moreover, that we can change our tastes. People can "correct their palates" or learn to like substances, such as tobacco, which are healthful even if at first distasteful (*Essay*, II.xxi.69). But of course we must first will to do so, and Locke says nothing about how we are to develop enough uneasiness at the absence of improved tastes to determine our will.

---

[16] See Jean Michel Vienne, "Malebranche and Locke: The Theory of Moral Choice, a Neglected Theme", in *Nicolas Malebranche: His Philosophical Critics and Successors*, ed. S. Brown (Assen and Maastricht, 1991), 94–108.

Hobbes took our overriding fear of death to impose some order on our passions. In the Leibniz–Wolff view, the objective amounts of perfection provide for inner order. But no positive ordering principle seems available for the Lockean inner world. The Lockean will, although an active power different from motives, has no inner rational ordering principle. The strengths of uneasinesses or desires are not necessarily proportional to the amounts of good in the ideas that cause them; and all the will does is to give the uneasinesses time to fight it out.

In his ethics, Locke invokes God's laws backed by threats of punishment and reward to produce more order in human affairs than civil laws and a concern for public opinion can create. Aside from its unpalatable implications for religion and human relations, it is not clear that this can work for Locke. Distance in time weakens the present uneasiness caused by threats (*Essay*, II.xxi.63); people are not, as we have seen, moved by the promise of heavenly rewards. Locke devotes much space to warning us about the dangers of miscalculation in deliberating about what to do. But he never explains what moves us to suspend action and deliberate, a point criticised by Leibniz and Collins.[17] Nor does he tell us how we can bring ourselves to feel a dominant uneasiness in the absence of our greatest good once we see where that is.

Locke's claim that the will is not determined by beliefs about the good amounts to saying that the springs of action are fundamentally irrational. If he is right, personal order as well as social stability seem to be attainable only through some sort of external pressure—either God's punishments or social sanctions. It is understandable that later thinkers, even while accepting much of Lockeanism, should have sought to explain human action in ways that show how we can control what we do.

At the end of Section I, I outlined the three main ways in which later thinkers who accepted Locke's view of the passions tried to respond to what they took to be his unacceptable theory of the will. In what follows, I discuss first, in Sections IV and V, the determinist alternatives and then the various versions of the third line of response.

---

[17] Leibniz, *Nouveaux essais*, II.xxi.47; Anthony Collins, in *A Philosophical Inquiry concerning Human Liberty* (London, 1717), 39. The objection still seemed worth making to Priestley in 1777: "a determination to suspend a volition is, in fact, *another volition*, and therefore, according to Mr. Locke's own rule, must be determined by the most pressing uneasiness" (Joseph Priestley, *The Doctrine of Philosophical Necessity Illustrated* (1777), §I, in *The Theological and Miscellaneous Works*, ed. J. T. Rutt, 25 vols. in 26 (London, 1817–32), 3: 447–540 at 461).

IV. Moral Sense and Egoism

The debates on these issues of passions, will, and self in morality were
touched off by the striking work of Anthony Ashley Cooper, third Earl of
Shaftesbury, who had been tutored by Locke. Shaftesbury reacted strongly
against Locke's motivational theory, which he thought no less egoistic than
Hobbes's, and against the Lockean belief that morality must invoke divine
sanctions. Locke portrays agents with no way of determining what goods to
make part of their own happiness and without any internal source of moral
self-control. Shaftesbury ties these issues together.[18] If I have no way of
telling which goods are to be included in my happiness, or which desires are
to constitute my self, Shaftesbury fears I will be left to the whims of passion
and have no stable self. "The man in anger has a different happiness from the
man in love."[19] If my passions are governed only by fancy, I am no better
than a madman. "If I vote with Fancy, resign my opinion to her command,
and judge of happiness and misery as she judges, how am I myself?"
(*Characteristicks*, III.ii, 209).

What, then, enables the self to distance itself from its fancies and impose
its own idea of happiness? Shaftesbury does not propose reason for the job.
"'Tis a due sentiment of morals which alone can make us knowing in order
and proportion, and give us a just tone and measure of human passion" (II.
iii, 181). Though he sometimes speaks of a moral sense, he gives no
elaborate theory about its nature, but its function is clear. It is to tell us
when our passions and desires form a harmonious whole. A harmonious self
elicits approval, and whatever is approved is virtuous. Inner harmony makes
the agent happy as well as virtuous. We understand what goods to make part
of our happiness when our moral sentiment tells us the virtuous relations
our desires should have to one another.[20]

Self-control for Shaftesbury is therefore not dependent on will, of which
indeed he has a low opinion. Even if there is a free will (he does not say
there is), "Humor and Fancy...govern it.... [I]f there be no certain
inspector or auditor established within us to take account of these opinions

---

[18] References to Shaftesbury are to page numbers in Anthony Ashley Cooper, 3rd Earl of Shaftesbury, *Characteristicks of Men, Manners, Opinions, Times*, ed. J. M. Robertson, 2 vols. (London, 1900).

[19] Treatise III, "Advice to an Author", in *Characteristicks*, vol. I, Pt. 3, §i, 192.

[20] Shaftesbury's main account is given in Treatise IV, "An Inquiry concerning Virtue or Merit", in
Characteristicks, vol. 1, especially Bk. I, Pt. 2, §iii and Bk. II, Pt. 1, §ii, 251–5 and 282–5.

and fancies...we are...little like to continue a day in the same will" (*Soliloquy: Or, Advice to an Author*, I.ii, 122). The internal auditor cannot be merely a calculative power or a Leibnizian will as a desire for the greatest good because, for Shaftesbury as for Locke, it is not the amount of good involved that influences action but the particular directions in which one seeks one's happiness. The moral sentiment alone, Shaftesbury thinks, can show us which way to go. But although the moral sentiment alone can give one enough unity so that one can be a single agent, Shaftesbury's psychology seems to be rather simply deterministic: the strength of our feelings is what explains which of them we act upon. What ultimately differentiates this view from Hobbes's is that for Shaftesbury we have genuinely altruistic impulses and an independent moral sentiment which can throw its weight into the balance as well. He does not use the vocabulary of active and passive power, nor does he so much as mention suspension of action by means of will and the inner liberty Locke thinks it gives us.

Numerous critics responded to Shaftesbury's rejection of the selfish theory of motivation. Probably the most famous, and certainly the liveliest, is Bernard Mandeville. In *The Fable of the Bees* (1714), he offered a witty and plausible alternative to Shaftesbury's portrayal of the generous other-directed sentiments.[21] Although he gives no systematic analysis of the passions, Mandeville sees both the principle and the particulars of our behaviour through the eyes of an egoist. "[I]t is impossible", he says, "that Man, mere fallen Man, should act with any other View but to please himself" (*Fable*, 1: 348). If we rescue a baby about to fall into a fire, "the Action is neither good nor bad, and what Benefit soever the Infant received, we only obliged our selves; for to have seen it fall, and not strove to hinder it, would have caused a Pain, which Self-preservation compell'd us to prevent" (1: 56). Man loves company, no doubt, but he loves it "as he does every thing else, for his own sake" (1: 341).

These comments suggest that Mandeville has a theory compelling him to find a way to analyse every action as being done at the agent's own pleasure and consequently directed toward the agent's own good. Yet at the same time he sets as a standard for judgment an austere morality demanding that we be completely self-sacrificing. If we are truly charitable, for instance, we

---

[21] References are to Bernard Mandeville, *The Fable of the Bees: or, Private Vices, Publick Benefits*, ed. F. B. Kaye, 2 vols. (Oxford, 1924).

transfer "part of that sincere Love we have for our selves" to others, with no expectation of benefit, not even gratitude or public recognition (*Fable*, 1: 253 ff.). Such virtue may be rare, but Mandeville seems to think it possible. If he really does, then his egoism is less an attempt at a pure theory than a device allowing him to mock pretensions to virtue while showing—in a fashion everyone took to be Hobbesian—that society could operate quite well if no one were ever benevolent or disinterested.

Although Shaftesbury tended to rely not so much on explicit argument as on the immediate appeal of his portrait of human nature, his position seemed convincing to innumerable readers, including the many who, like Kant, read him in French or German translation. In hard-line egoists such as Mandeville, and later Helvétius, Shaftesbury aroused only scorn. One of his admirers, Francis Hutcheson, set out to provide some argumentative back-ing for Shaftesburyan views in his *An Inquiry into the Original of Our Ideas of Beauty and Virtue* (1725) and other early works. Taking Mandeville as his open target, and assuming that even he would allow that we at least *seem* to have benevolent and disinterested affections, Hutcheson argues that appear-ances are not misleading. We respond so differently to benevolence and to pure self-interest—approving the former but not the latter and feeling affection for those who are kind but not for those who are purely selfish—that the unselfish affections must be allowed to have a real part in our lives. We cannot get ourselves to have such affections either by simply deciding to have them or by seeing that it pays to have them. Moreover, we do not appreciate the benevolence of others only for the benefits it brings us. We do not cease to love a generous friend the instant she loses all her wealth. We do not love indiscriminately anyone who could give us equiva-lent assistance. And it is plainly ludicrous to try to explain parental affection, ties to our neighbors, and love of our country by saying that we all think it benefits us to have them.[22]

A year after Hutcheson confronted psychological egoism with these inconvenient facts, Joseph Butler published some further objections to it. Perhaps the most significant are those that involve his distinction between self-interest and what he calls the particular passions. The former is our

---

[22] Francis Hutcheson, *An Inquiry into the Original of Our Ideas of Beauty and Virtue; in Two Treatises* (London, 1725). For these arguments, see Treatise II, "An Inquiry concerning Moral Good and Evil", §2, 125–49.

long-term concern for the attainment of our own happiness. By itself, it does not determine what will make us happy. It is our specific desires—our wants for some things and not others—that determine what will please or displease us. The particular passion of hunger has food as its object; other passions lead us to desire money or fame or the success of our children or the relief of suffering among the ill. Self-interest would have nothing to do were it not that the passions put us upon a variety of projects, but the passions are not themselves self-interested, nor do they aim always at the agent's own good or benefit. Once we understand the nature of particular passions, we have no difficulty admitting that while some of them may indeed move us to benefit ourselves, some move us directly to help others, and some, such as an obsession with gambling, motivate actions that can harm the agent.[23]

If self-interest is the desire for one's own happiness or one's own pleasure, we must admit that it is the particular passions that allow us to take pleasure in things or be made happy by having them. If I did not desire food, Butler says, I would not enjoy eating; if my only desire were the desire for happiness, nothing would make me happy since nothing could give me pleasure. Butler points out that any particular passion is obviously the agent's own passion. One might be tempted to slide from noticing this to thinking that when one acts from a passion, one is acting to gratify one's own desire, or to do exactly what one wants, from which one might conclude that whenever we act from a particular passion we are acting for our own interest or selfishly. This, however, is a mere verbal confusion: that I act from my own desire is a trivial truth, implying nothing about the object of my desire. But it is the object of desire that determines whether or not someone is acting for his or her own interest, and the facts make it plain that we often act for the good of others.[24] Butler here reveals the confusion that caused many writers—Leibniz included—to suppose that any desire that moves me must be a desire for my own pleasure, and so for my interest, simply because in acting from it I act as I please.

The critics of psychological egoism faced a problem the egoists did not. Among the many available springs of action, which should be followed? Butler claimed that conscience would tell us. He abstained, however, from

---

[23] Joseph Butler, *Fifteen Sermons Preached at the Rolls Chapel*, I, §§6, 7, in *Works*, ed. J. H. Bernard, 2 vols. (London, 1900), vol. 1: 27–31.

[24] Butler, *Sermons*, XI, §§5–9, vol. 1: 138–42.

giving any account of how exactly the directions of conscience might become efficacious. Although he believed in free will, he felt no need to develop a theory of how it is possible or how it works.[25] He thus left a problem for his libertarian followers Price and Reid, whose views I discuss later.

Hutcheson was not quite so reticent about the workings of the moral sense. For present purposes, it must suffice to say that he offers a deterministic account of its force. Whatever else it may be, distinctively moral approval is an enjoyable feeling. We want both the approval of others and our own approval. Since approval is caused only by benevolent desires, our own desire for approval is not selfish. It is rather a mark of our being made for society. Approval and disapproval are thus socially efficacious forces; and as the desire to be approved can motivate us to develop our own benevolence, the moral sense can shape our own character as well as guide us in action.[26]

Neither Hutcheson nor Butler forced the partisans of self-interest, even in Britain, to admit defeat, and one of them, John Gay, in 1731 offered an ingenious theory to show how one could concede Hutcheson's factual claims (he does not notice Butler) while still insisting that there is no need to admit original and irreducible benevolent desires in the human constitution. His theory rests on an appeal to the association of ideas, our tendency, noticed in antiquity and referred to by Descartes and Locke, to think of one thing upon seeing or thinking of something else with which the first has frequently been associated. Gay thinks we all pursue only our own happiness in all our voluntary actions. We take pleasure in the thought of what brings us happiness, and we learn that helping others pays off because those we help give help to us in turn. Hence we come to think with pleasure or approval of those who help us. Eventually we associate our own pleasure so strongly with the thought of benevolent action, both in ourselves and in others, that conscious awareness of our original selfish end is not necessary to awaken it. We are, Gay says, like a miser who initially

---

[25] On conscience, see *Sermons*, Preface, §§25–9, vol. 1: 11–13; also Sermon I, §8, vol. 1: 31–3; Sermon II, §§8–11, vol. 1: 44–7; Sermon III, §4, vol. 1: 63–4. On free will, see Butler, *The Analogy of Religion, Natural and Revealed, to the Constitution and Course of Nature,*, Pt. I, ch. 6, in *Works*, 2: 102–18.

[26] Hutcheson's first account of the moral sense is in the first part of *An Inquiry*, the "Inquiry Concerning Moral Good and Evil", §I, Pts. 1, 2, 4, 5; §II, Pt. 3; §V, Pts. 1, 3, and 7.

wants money for its purchasing power and comes to want it for itself. We retain out of habit principles of action and feeling originally acquired for reasons of private interest. Hutcheson's data thus do not force us to postulate original benevolent impulses: association provides a simpler and therefore more satisfactory explanation of the undoubted fact that we act and approve without conscious thought of our own benefit.[27]

Egoism, sometimes bolstered by associationism, became a major eighteenth-century articulation of the Lockean alternative to the Leibniz–Wolff theory of the passions. Gay's kind of associationist theory of the passions was elaborated at length by David Hartley, whose treatise, published in 1749, bears a title—*Observations on Man, his Frame, his Duty and his Expectations*—suggesting his plan to link psychology, morality, and religion. Hartley argued that through association we can move from crass selfishness to unselfish devotion to God and our neighbor.[28] In France, egoistic views were used not to defend religion but to attack it. Helvétius, for instance, acknowledging Hobbes as one of his sources, simply spells out the basic points of an egoistic theory with no sense that it had been criticised. Like Hartley, he thinks that our desires are educable and can be shaped in ways that lead us to help others. True virtue is nothing but a desire for the general happiness; men can be so trained or so situated that they find pleasure in bringing it about. We must not expect to make men virtuous by asking them to sacrifice their pleasure for the public good; one can make them so "only by uniting personal interest to the general interest".[29] In present society—and this is Helvétius's real point—almost everyone is corrupt, taking pleasure in purely private goods or in goods limited to some small group, such as the Jesuit order. His egoistic theory turns into a tool for unmasking hypocrisy. Allowing the possibility of genuine virtue—"probity", as he calls it—he hopefully finds room for the

---

[27] John Gay, *Preliminary Dissertation concerning the Fundamental Principle of Virtue or Morality*, in King, *Essay on the Origin of Evil*, xi–xxxiii.

[28] See also *An Enquiry into the Origin of the Human Appetites and Affections* (1747), in *Four Early Works on Motivation*, ed. P. McReynolds (Gainesville, FL, 1969), published anonymously and attributed to one James Long about whom nothing else is known. McReynolds publishes another development of Gay's kind of associationism which has also been attributed to Long; see McReynolds's introduction, xxvi–xxix.

[29] Claude-Adrien Helvétius, *De l'esprit*, (1758), Discours II, ch. 15, 119. See also the anonymous English translation, published in London the following year, 81.

existence of people who might desire to reform the corrupt system in which all now live.[30]

V. Hume: Order Through Nature

The most sophisticated and thoroughgoing of the empiricist replies to Locke's denial of any sufficient inner principle of order came from David Hume. He also gave the fullest determinist account of active powers or human agency. Claiming to apply Newtonian methods to the human realm, he portrays us as being fully part of nature, with all our behavior just as much caused by antecedent events as the behavior of stones. Nature, he finds, happens to be orderly without being purposive. We are made with a sympathetic ability to feel as others feel, numerous passions leading us to aid one another, and moral feelings reinforcing these passions. No threats from external powers are needed to make us virtuous. Were it not for misguided opinions, mostly about supernatural matters, our inner constitution would enable us to live happily together.

Hume uses "laws of association" to give reductionist analyses of central concepts such as cause, continuity of objects over time, and personal identity.[31] But, unlike Gay, he does not give reductionist analyses of the concepts involved in explaining feeling and action. For Hume, the desires and passions are not representational: they are essentially simple. Pride and humility, love and hatred, will, and the moral feeling are all indefinable impressions (*Treatise of Human Nature*, 2.1.2.1, 2.2.1.1, 2.2.12.1, 3.1.2.1–4, SBN 277, 329, 397, 470–2). Moreover, self-love does not serve for Hume, as it does for Gay, as a central explanatory principle. Hume disparages the very concept. The feeling of love, he says, is always directed toward some sensible being external to us; and when we talk of *self-love*, " 'tis not in a proper sense" (2.2.1.2, SBN 329). He accepts the existence of a Butlerian concern for our own good on the whole and even allows himself to call it

[30] On probity, see Helvétius, *De l'esprit*, Discours II, chs. 5 and 11. A similar use of psychological egoism is to be found in the work of d'Holbach. See Paul-Henri Thiry d'Holbach *Système de la nature ou Des loix du monde physique et du monde moral*, 2 vols. (London, 1770, but probably printed in the Netherlands).

[31] References to Hume are to *A Treatise of Human Nature*, ed. L. A. Selby-Bigge, 2nd edn., revised by P. H. Nielditch (Oxford: Clarendon Press, 1978).

self-love (3.2.1.10, SBN 480). For Hume, the desire of our own good is neither our sole nor our most important motivation, nor the basic explanation of the passions (3.2.2.5, SBN 487). In these ways, he is not an associationist about the passions.

Hume offers a psychology as complex as Butler's. Some of our central passions have ideas of good and ill among their causes, but others do not. There are desires that "arise from a natural impulse or instinct, which is perfectly unaccountable". Desires for revenge or for the happiness of friends, as well as hunger and lust, "produce good and evil, and proceed not from them" (*Treatise*, 2.3.9.8, SBN 439). Of desires that are directly caused by thoughts of good and ill Hume has little to say, and that little is conventional. The mind instinctively tends to "unite itself with the good". Desire of this type arises from thoughts of good considered alone. When we believe the good is certain or probable, we feel joy; the thought of certain or probable evil causes sorrow. Hume gives only hope and fear more than perfunctory attention (2.3.9, SBN 438 ff.). These passions themselves are not complicated by concepts other than those of good and ill, certainty and uncertainty. Hume is more interested in the feelings of pride and love, and their opposites, whose explanation involves many more ideas.

For Hume, pride is an "agreeable" simple impression that can arise not only from the thought of our own beauty, wealth, or power but also from the thought of our own virtue. It is a special feeling of being pleased with oneself caused by the thought of something especially valuable or admirable as having an especially close connection to oneself; and it causes no specific desire (*Treatise*, 2.1.7.7–8, SBN 297). Love is another agreeable simple impression, a feeling of pleasure in the thought of another person caused by the lover's thought of something especially good possessed by the one loved. Love is in itself not a motive at all. True, Hume thinks it is "always follow'd by a desire of the happiness of the person belov'd", but this separate benevolent desire requires that we think of the happiness of the object of love, which we do not always do. Love might have been conjoined with malevolence. Its connection with benevolence, Hume says, is just "an arbitrary and original instinct implanted in our nature" (2.2.6.3–2.2.7.1, SBN 367–8).

Pride as well as love helps to bind people to one another. To feel pride is, roughly, to take pleasure in other people's esteem, and esteem is a form of love (2.2.5.1 and 3.3.4.2n., SBN 357 and 608n.). Moral approval is also a form of love—of purely human love (see, for example, 3.3.1.19, 26, 30–1, SBN 584, 589, 591). We are approved, or loved with the distinctive feeling we call moral approval, on account of the aspects of our character that make us agreeable or useful to ourselves or others, not because we comply with divine commands or absolute laws. Our enjoyment of this love and our pride in our virtue as well as in our wealth, status, and outstanding abilities indicate our sociable nature. Morality and the economy of the passions thus function to benefit everyone in this life. The passions are naturally conducive to order.

Hume does not say that the impressions and ideas involved in the passions are indistinct or confused. Passions themselves may mingle, and one passion may be "mixt and confounded with" another (*Treatise*, 2.3.9.12, SBN 441).[32] But the causes or objects of the passions are not presented through confused ideas in such cases. Hume goes out of his way to explain the agitation involved in some feelings without any appeal to indistinctness of idea. Sometimes the passions are violent, producing great agitation and making us disregard long-term consequences. This is because similar passions when produced by related causes may reinforce one another. Uncertainty about the outcome of action may also produce agitation. But indistinctness in the ideas causing the passions does not figure among the causes of violent feeling (2.3.4.3–10, SBN 420–2).

Thus quite generally for Hume there are only contingent connections between beliefs (lively ideas) and feelings such as pride, or desires for specific objects. Because each passion is "an original existence . . . and contains not any representative quality" reason has only an indirect role to play in our active life. Reason, Hume is notorious for saying, is the slave of the passions (*Treatise*, 2.3.3.4–5, SBN 415). All it can do is present them with a set of beliefs that will trigger the force that constitutes desire. Reason does not determine the amount of force—the strength of the desire—its representations may cause. If it presents two alternatives, I may happen to prefer a greater to a lesser evil—destroying the world rather than getting my finger

---

[32] It is interesting that the few cases where Hume says that important ideas are confused concern theoretical issues, such as the relation of the taste of a fig to the physical fig (*Treatise*, 1.4.5.13, SBN 238) or aspects of our idea of liberty (2.3.1.13, SBN 404). In discussing curiosity, Hume likens the association of two ideas to a chemical mixture which produces a compound perceptibly unlike either of its elements (2.3.10.9, SBN 452). The chemical analogy became important to nineteenth-century associationists, but Hume does not use it elsewhere.

scratched, for instance—or I may not. Reason cannot decide me (2.3.3.6, SBN 416). To control a passion, we must bring some other passion to bear on it.

Our sympathetic responses to other people's feelings have just that function. To understand others is not merely to represent a counterpart of what they feel. It is to feel it; and the counterpart feelings affect our behavior. For instance, we feel with all those who benefit from stable property laws, and these feelings are stronger than those we get from feeling with those who benefit from breaking the laws. Hence we feel disposed to obey the laws, and our moral sentiments reinforce that disposition. Sanctions may be needed, but only at the margin. Sympathy and our own desire to have the approval of others and ourselves make us basically sociable. Order arises from the natural interaction of the feelings.[33]

We mistakenly think that the regularity in our lives is the work of reason, Hume suggests, because some passions are "calm" and only some are violent. A calm desire for, say, a career that demands long training may be strong enough to motivate someone for years, yet it may not erupt in conscious perturbations; a highly disturbing outburst of desire may not be sufficient to move us to act. It is easy to think of durable calm passions as "determinations of reason" because they feel more or less the same. No matter how they feel, what moves us is wholly different from the faculty that "judges of truth and falsehood" (*Treatise*, 2.3.3.8, SBN 417; see also 2.3.8.13, SBN 437–8).

As I have indicated, anti-egoists could be as determinist as associationist egoists or they could believe in free will. Hume, anti-egoist and admirer of Butler though he was, continues the determinist line of thought with no reticence. His treatment of the issue is the classical exposition of the claim that determinism is compatible with the only sort of liberty needed to sustain morality.

Hume agrees with Locke in considering will to be different in kind from desire. Will is a simple impression, Hume says, which "*we feel and are conscious of, when we knowingly give rise to any new motion of our body, or new perception of our mind*" (*Treatise*, 2.3.1.2, SBN 399). Unlike Locke, however, he gives the will no clear role to play, even though he treats it as the immediate cause of action. Hume never mentions suspension of action as something we can do because we have a will. He is interested in whether the will is causally

---

[33] For Hume's views on justice, see *Treatise*, 3.2.1–2; on sympathy, see 2.1.11 and 2.2.5.

determined, and if so by what; and his theory would proceed in the same way if he dropped the term "will" and asked only whether we are causally determined to act as we do and, if so, how.

Having argued in the first book of the *Treatise* that causation essentially involves no more than constant conjunction of the objects that are causes and effects and the habit in the observer of inferring from the idea of the cause to the idea of the effect, Hume uses this analysis to answer his question about the will or action. The point he makes seems simple. We find ourselves with desires for various ends and beliefs about how to attain them. When we act, desires, aroused by beliefs, serve as motives. Our actions follow our motives as regularly and predictably as stones fall when dropped. If the latter exemplify causation and necessity, so do the former. Nowhere is there less regularity in the human world than in the natural one. The confidence we all have that other people, and we ourselves, will act in predictable ways is evidence that we form habits of expectation about people no less than about things. If causal necessity governs what happens in the physical world, it therefore also governs what happens in the human world; if freedom is incompatible with necessity, then to assert human freedom requires a belief that a billiard ball freely chooses to move when hit (2.3.1.14, SBN 404).

For Hume, the only important kind of freedom is compatible with the only comprehensible kind of necessity. He has no desire to defend the liberty of indifference, the ability to choose without a reason. He is only concerned with "the liberty of *spontaneity*", or the liberty that comes from the absence of coercion (*Treatise*, 2.3.2.1, SBN 407–8). When we can do what we desire to do, we are as free as we can be or need to be. To insist on more, Hume says, would be to threaten morality and religion. His argument here is the same as Wolff's: laws, whether human or divine, are usually supposed to be "founded on rewards and punishments". If these had no necessary influence on our behavior, laws would be pointless. Moreover, if we possessed liberty of indifference, there would be only random ties between our character and our behavior. We could then hardly think of holding one another accountable for what would be chance actions. Determinism is not incompatible with morality; it is presupposed by it (2.3.2.5–7, SBN 410–12).

What, then, are "the influencing motives of the will" (2.3.3 title, SBN 413)? We have already seen that deliverances of reason are not among them.

The "actions of the will" (2.3.2.8, SBN 412) are caused by particular desires of whatever variety. The love of moral approval plays a role, as does self-interest. Custom, imagination, and distance in time and space from desired ends also affect what we do. Taking all these considerations together, Hume concludes that no specific laws of motivation can be stated. There are too many forces interacting within us, and the play of forces is diversified by too many factors, to be formulated. Philosophy must confess that the principles determining action are for the most part "too fine and minute for her comprehension" (2.3.8.13, SBN 438). The science of man demonstrates the certainty of determinism without giving us a single determinist law.

VI. Agency Revitalised

In France as in Britain, there were many other writers who worked out determinist views of action and passion along Lockean lines. Adam Smith's views are perhaps the most interesting. His analyses of the passions in *The Theory of Moral Sentiments* (1759) rest on a completely non-representational understanding of their nature. This comes out with great clarity in his account of the way we estimate the appropriateness or inappropriateness of feelings. We do so, Smith says, through our ability to feel sympathetically what another feels and to compare it with what we ourselves would feel in like circumstances. If our feelings would be as strong as the other person's, we approve; if we would feel less strongly, we say her feeling is excessive or exaggerated. There is no suggestion that we estimate the amount of good or evil to which the other is responding and approve or condemn her feelings or desires as they are or are not commensurate with that amount.[34] Subtle as his account of assessment is, Smith, like the far less imaginative French materialists and egoists, makes no effort to move the study of active powers beyond a determinist framework.[35] That effort was made by British and

---

[34]   Adam Smith, *The Theory of Moral Sentiments*, eds. D. D. Raphael and A. L. Macfie, in *Works* (1976), I.i.3–4.

[35]   See Long, *An Enquiry* (see note 31); Abraham Tucker (pseudonym Edward Search), *The Light of Nature Pursued* (1768), 4 vols. Cambridge, MA, (1831); Joseph Priestley, *Writings on Philosophy, Science and Politics*, ed. J. A. Passmore (New York, NY, 1965); Jean Offray de La Mettrie, *L'homme machine*, in *Oeuvres philosophiques*, 2 vols. (Berlin, 1774), vol. 1; and d'Holbach, *Système de la nature*.

German thinkers motivated by concerns about both religion and morality that they thought their determinist opponents could not accommodate.

Many Christian thinkers held that Locke's system, later aided by associationism, opened the door not only to determinism but to materialist exclusion of all spiritual reality, God's included. Neither Leibnizian nor Lockean accounts of will seemed to them able to explain how we could have the psychological resources to act independently of our desires. But this, they held, is what morality requires. They found it necessary to rethink action and to take Newton into account in doing so.

Hume was aware of the religious opposition to determinism. In presenting his theory, he was trying in part to undermine the views of two of its critics, Samuel Clarke and George Berkeley. These two disagreed deeply about morality, but they were at one concerning active power.

Clarke, a highly placed if unorthodox Christian minister, was also a successful expositor and defender of Newton's physics. His Boyle Lectures of 1704 and 1705 aim at refuting Hobbes and Spinoza, whose materialism and necessitarianism amount, he insists, to atheism. In attacking them, he is also seeking to go beyond Locke and Leibniz.[36]

Clarke begins by arguing that there must of necessity be one eternal, non-material, unchanging, infinite being who is the cause of all other things and who himself is a self-activating agent. This being must be free because "*Intelligence* without *Liberty*...is really...*no Intelligence* at all. It is indeed a *Consciousness*, but it is merely *a Passive One*; a Consciousness, not of Acting, but purely of being Acted upon". (Boyle Lectures, I.ix, 548). God's freedom enables him, as Clarke makes clear in his correspondence with Leibniz, to choose between alternatives even when it does not matter which alternative he chooses.[37] Newton had indeed thought that God intervenes in the world, restoring it to order. Hence for him the universe is not a closed clockwork mechanism. It is open to spontaneous action from the deity. And if from the deity, then why not from us? Clarke is drawing on such views in

---

[36] The first set of Clarke's lectures is titled *A Demonstration of the Being and Attributes of God: More Particularly in Answer to Mr. Hobbs, Spinoza, and their Followers*, the second *A Discourse Concerning the Unchangeable Obligations of Natural Religion, and the Truth and Certainty of the Christian Revelation*. I give references to the two sets as Boyle Lectures I and Boyle Lectures II, with proposition number and the page number in his *Works*, 2: 513–77 and 579–733. Other references to Clarke are to other volumes in the *Works*.

[37] See the Leibniz-Clarke correspondence in Clarke's *Works*, vol. 4.

his Boyle Lectures as well as in his later controversy with Leibniz. In general, however, there is a special kind of necessity underlying God's choices. It is a necessity of *fitness*, requiring that things be as they are in order not to diminish "the Beauty, Order, and Well-being of the Whole" (ix, 550). This is not an "absolute necessity", entailing that there is a contradiction in supposing the contrary (iii, 528). Alternatives are conceivable even if unfit. To act as one does because the fitness of things makes such action necessary is "consistent with the greatest Freedom and most perfect Choice. For", Clarke continues, "the only Foundation of this Necessity, is such an unalterable Rectitude of Will, and Perfection of Wisdom, as makes it impossible for a Wise Being to resolve to Act foolishly; or for a Nature infinitely Good, to choose to do that which is Evil" (ix, 551).

It is thus a mistake to argue that liberty is a conceptual impossibility because every event, including volitions, must have a cause. Those who say this "ignorantly confound *Moral Motives* with *Physical Efficients*, between which Two things there is no manner of relation". Avoid this confusion, Clarke is saying, and you can see that choices made from motives are free, while being morally necessary (ix, 553).

So much for God's freedom: now for human freedom. God is proven to be omnipotent, and from this it follows that he can give creatures the power of beginning movement (Boyle Lectures, x, 557). When we act, we experience ourselves as we would if we possessed the power of self-motion (x, 557–8). This no more demonstrates that we have the power than sensory experience proves the existence of an external world. But the bare possibility that we might be without such power, like the bare possibility that the material world does not exist, should worry no one. Against Malebranche, Clarke simply points out—as Reid was to do later—that our possession of self-moving power does not make us independent of God. He freely gives us the power, and he can take it away.[38] Since the power of self-motion coupled with intelligence is liberty, Clarke thinks he has done enough to show that our wills are free. What remains is to dismiss all arguments against it as being due to the "Fundamental Errour" of failing to distinguish clearly between "*moral Motives, and Causes Physically Efficient*" (I.x, 565 ff.).

[38] Clarke, *Remarks upon a Book, entitled, A Philosophical Enquiry concerning Human Liberty* (1717), in *Works*, 4: 734; Thomas Reid, *Essays on the Active Powers of Man*, in *Philosophical Works*, ed. W. Hamilton, 8th edn., 2 vols. in 1 (Edinburgh, 1895), 2: I.ii, 517b: "All our power is, without doubt, derived from the Author of our being; and as he gave it freely, he may take it away when he will".

Clarke's treatment of morality shows that he considers motives to be reasons, different in kind from felt desires and not dependent on them. God is guided by reasons given by his knowledge of certain self-evident axioms about the eternal fitnesses of things; we can and ought to be guided by them as well. Knowledge of the axioms, as such, serves as our motive. We do not need additional considerations of punishment and reward to be moved to do what "right Reason" moves us to do (II.i.7, 628). Thus the earlier argument to show that intelligence entails agency is transposed to human beings to support the claim that we can act from reasons arising not from desires but solely from knowledge of moral truths.

Clarke's liberty is not a Hobbesian absence of external impediments. It is a liberty we have even in prison (I.x, 566). It is an inner power different in kind from desire. It is not the Cartesian will, which necessarily assents to clear and distinct representations and can choose only where there is confusion and indistinctness.[39] It is neither the Leibnizian tendency to seek the greatest perfection nor the Lockean ability to suspend action. What is liberty, then? Clarke regrettably devotes more effort to refuting his opponents than to developing his own position. He is content to say that liberty consists in a person's "having a continual Power of choosing, whether he shall Act, or whether he shall forbear Acting". He does not tell us anything about how we choose whether to act or forbear. Nor does he tell us how the motives constituted by our knowledge of eternal fitnesses relate to the urges and impulses due to our needs and desires. What he does make clear is that morality depends on our ability to be moved by our knowledge of eternal truths. That ability is at the core of what he calls the "Power of Agency or Free Choice (for these are precisely Identical terms)" (I.x, 566).

In the phrase just quoted, Clarke makes what I believe is the first use of the term agency in its modern philosophical context. The *Oxford English Dictionary* shows only one earlier use, in 1658, which is not clearly a philosophical one. It then gives a citation from Jonathan Edwards dated 1762. As we shall see, Berkeley, Hume, and Price used the term before then, and in 1731 Edmund Law, referring to Clarke, described the word as "generally including the power of beginning *Thought* as well as *Motion*".[40]

---

[39] Assent to truth is a passive operation of the understanding, Clarke says, and it does not "determine" the active power. See *Works*, 4: 716–18 and *Remarks Upon a Book*, 722–3.

[40] King, *Essay*, 156n.

The view that humans are agents is of course not new, and Bishop Bramhall, controverting Hobbes a half century before Clarke, had supported views like his.[41] But Clarke brings a new consideration into his defense of liberty. For Leibniz, desires can be controlled directly by reason because they are themselves implicitly rational. Lockean desires are not, and they cannot be so controlled. Clarke agrees with Locke on this point. Leibniz and Locke think of the will as being determined by the strength of various desires. Clarke does not mention strength when he speaks of moral motives and the kind of necessity they involve. He thinks they are the wrong kind of thing to have that sort of property.[42] Knowledge of moral axioms and the desire for happiness are incommensurable, yet both enter into explanations of our action. Strength of desire is one kind of determinant of action. Knowledge of normative truth must be a different kind, playing a unique role in our decisions because it possesses what Butler later called authority. We experience ourselves as deciding which of these incommensurable kinds of consideration to follow. Clarke's innovation here is to see free agency as providing the only possible explanation of how we can do so.

Berkeley takes up Clarke's new term to raise an important problem. He is notorious for his thesis that the physical world is reducible without remainder to ideas, which exist only in the mind. Ideas are necessarily and by their nature, he thinks, wholly and utterly inactive: "there is nothing of power or agency included in them".[43] They cannot even *represent* action. Hence all change in the so-called physical world is due to God's action on ideas. Spirit alone, which is simple and substantial, is active. Only spirits understand and, more importantly, exercise will. We experience this because we know we can call up ideas at our pleasure. "This making and unmaking of ideas doth very properly denominate the mind active".[44]

The concept of will or agency poses a problem for Berkeley of which he is well aware. Ideas are passive and can only represent what is passive. If

---

[41] See John Bramhall, *A Defence of True Liberty from Ante-cedent and Extrinsecall Necessity* (London, 1655).

[42] See, for example, Clarke, *Works*, 4: 723, 734.

[43] George Berkeley, *A Treatise concerning the Principles of Human Knowledge* (1710), Pt. I [no more publ.], §25, in *Works*, 2: 51; see §32; *Three Dialogues between Hylas and Philonous* (1713), Dialogue III, in *Works*, 2: 231.

[44] *Principles*, §§25, 28.

spirit is active, we can therefore have no idea of it or of its components, understanding and will. We have instead what Berkeley calls notions, which, unlike ideas, cannot be perceived.[45] He does not make it clear just how notions are known and what relation the existence of imperceptible understanding and will have to the things whose existence is constituted by their being perceived.

Berkeley's difficulties on these matters point to an apparent problem for philosophers who tried to follow Locke in allowing legitimacy only to ideas that can be derived from sensory and introspective experience of ideas and reflection on it. If Berkeley is right, agency of the kind he and Clarke think necessary for morality is a notion that cannot be explained in those terms.

Hutcheson and Hume, of course, did not wish to make room for any such concept. Hume sees no need for the kind of agency Clarke invokes. He takes note of appeal to *"a false sensation or experience"* of liberty only to dismiss it (*Treatise*, 2.3.2.2, SBN 408). Moreover, in reinforcing his conclusion that reason is only the slave of the passions, he argues explicitly against Clarke's claim that knowledge of truth alone can motivate (3.1.1.18–26, SBN 463–8). Hume's theory of causation is itself directed in part against Clarke. Agency is just another synonym for cause, Hume says (1.3.14.4, SBN 157), and his analysis of causal necessity tells us all there is to know about it. There is, he insists, "but one kind of *necessity*, as there is but one kind of cause . . . the common distinction betwixt *moral* and *physical* necessity is without any foundation in nature" (1.3.14.33, SBN 171). Henry Home, Lord Kames, attacking Clarke explicitly, relies on Hume's denial that there can be different kinds of necessity, asserts that action is necessarily determined by the strongest desire or aversion, and assumes what Clarke is trying to combat, that "[a]ll our principles of action resolve into *desires* and *aversions*".[46]

Faced with Hume's systematic determinist account of action and morality, those who wished to defend the Clarke-Berkeley view of agency were forced into major attacks on the empiricist position.

[45] On notions, see, for example, *Principles*, §142.
[46] Henry Home, Lord Kames, *Essays on the Principles of Morality and Natural Religion* (Edinburgh, 1751), Pt. I, Essay III, 172–3, 174; see also 167, 193.

VII. Agency Defended

I shall consider here only two of the British philosophers who attempted to
defend a Clarkean view of agency and morality: Richard Price and Thomas
Reid. Both acknowledge a debt to Bishop Butler. They follow him in
distinguishing particular desires, whose objects are specific objects or states
of affairs, from more general principles such as self-love and benevolence, in
rejecting the thesis that all voluntary action is self-interested, and in refusing
to see all of morality as stemming from a single principle, such as that of
benevolence. They also accept another of Butler's central claims: that there
is a difference between the strength of a desire or principle of action and
what he calls its authority. We can see that the two are distinct, Butler says,
by considering that even when we do not have any desire to do something
for our own long-term good—for instance, visit the dentist—we recognise
that we ought to, and that recognition is our awareness of the authority of a
principle of prudence. Authority of a higher kind belongs to the dictates of
conscience, or our general awareness of moral directives. We can be guided,
Butler believes, by the authority of prudence or conscience even when their
strength is less than that of the desires they require us to control. He
thus claims, with Clarke, that the different kinds of considerations involved
in action are incommensurable, but he does not say how "authority" can
move us.[47]

Price and Reid go beyond Butler in elaborating the psychology of moral
action. "The human mind", says Price in his one philosophical work, the
exceptionally acute *Review of the Principal Questions in Morals* (1758),

> would appear to have little order or consistency in it, were we to consider it as only
> a system of passions and affections, which are continually drawing us different ways,
> without any thing at the head of them to govern them, and the strongest of which
> for the time necessarily determines the conduct. But this is far from being its real
> state.[48]

The Lockean vision Price calls up of the mind's lack of any internal principle
of order is falsified by the "moral faculty" which appropriately governs "all

---

[47] Butler, *Sermons*, II and III, in *Works*, 1: 40–60.
[48] Richard Price, *A Review of the Principal Questions in Morals*, ed. D. D. Raphael (Oxford, 1974),
215n.

our other powers" (215n.). To explain the operations of the moral faculty, Price finds that he must reject the Lockean epistemology and assert, with Cudworth, that reason is not, as in the works of Locke and Descartes, a purely passive power; it is an active power and is the source of our agency.

For our purposes, the key part of Price's rejection of Locke's epistemology lies in his claim that reason is itself a source of simple ideas. He is driven to this by what he takes to be the inadequacies of Hutcheson's account of moral approval. If Hutcheson were right, approval would simply be a sensation derived from the way our mind operates, telling us nothing about "the real characters of *actions*" (15).[49] We need not agree. Reason does what sense cannot. It generalises and compares where sense is confined to particulars. Reason discerns, sense merely suffers (21). Many of our ideas—of solidity, substance, duration, space, infinity, contingency, necessity, causation, or power—cannot be explained as originating from purely sensory information. Hume sees this but draws the wrong conclusion. The correct response is not to deny or redefine the ideas as he does but to admit the creative power of reason and the narrow bounds of sense (22–35). Reason, Price holds, gives us simple ideas by giving us intuitive truths of which the simple ideas are constituents. Thus actions, like other things, have a nature, and being right or being wrong is a necessary part of it. Reason, discerning this, gives us these moral ideas. We cannot coherently imagine a rational being unable to distinguish right from wrong and, if actions had no moral nature, God could have no grounds for performing one act rather than another or preferring one end to another (48–9). He could act only arbitrarily.[50]

Awareness of moral truth, Price allows, is always emotionally colored. But feelings are not all there is to moral ideas. Feelings are aroused by knowledge of moral truth, not constitutive of it. No new sense is needed to account for feelings of approval and the pleasure we take in contemplating virtue. Our cognitions cause them. These feelings also have a definite moral

---

[49] For Hutcheson, to feel approval is one way of taking pleasure in someone's action. He says it resembles liking a piece of music rather than contemplating a truth. See his *Illustrations of the Moral Sense*, ed. B. Peach (Cambridge, MA, 1971), §1, 136. The *Illustrations* was originally published as a supplement to *An Essay on the Nature and Conduct of the Passions and Affections* (1728).

[50] Price (*Review*, 20n.) refers for support to Ralph Cudworth's *A Treatise concerning Immutable and Eternal Morality* (London, 1731), published posthumously in aid of the Clarkeans. Cudworth died in 1688.

function. It is not that our moral ideas are confused and indistinct, but reason's deliverances would be too slow and weak in many cases to move us to act properly were they not seconded by feelings or what Price calls instinctive determinations. We need both "a *perception of the understanding*, and a *feeling of the heart*" to prompt us effectively (61–2).[51]

Moral sentiments are not the only feelings aroused by knowledge. Our passions and desires generally have conceptual origins. We cannot understand the idea of happiness without coming to desire it, regardless of who has it. Similarly, we must admire and desire truth, knowledge, and honor, once we understand what they are (70–3). Price's thought seems to be that when objects are conceived in certain ways, they awaken the appropriate feelings or desires. If such "affections" are strengthened by instinctive determinations, they are "passions", but in all cases grasp of a concept is the crucial source (74). Although brief on these matters, Price clearly disagrees not only with the Leibniz–Wolff approach, since he does not construe the passions as involving indistinct ideas, but with the Humean approach as well. The instinctive determinations do no more than add strength to affections which get their energy as well as their direction from rational concepts. Price goes so far as to claim that were we sufficiently rational, we would have no need of the instinctive appetites to move us to action (76–7).

Price brings this apparatus to bear on his central concern when he discusses the virtuous agent's motives. The virtuous agent must first possess liberty, "the power of *acting* and *determining*". By this Price means not that an agent's actions must have no cause but that the agent must be the cause of them. There cannot be a "*foreign* cause" for what I think of as my own volition. It is absurd to suppose that "I determine *voluntarily* and yet *necessarily*". Price thus thinks the Hobbesian view is obviously false. If we do not allow "*agency*, free choice, and an absolute dominion over our resolutions", there is no room for morality (181–2).

The second requisite for morality is intelligence. Self-motion or activity can exist without intelligence, but intelligence cannot exist without liberty. Since we are plainly intelligent, we must have liberty, or so Price suggests without spelling out his argument at any length (183–4). Liberty and reason

---

[51] Price here tries to correct Butler, who says that moral awareness may be considered as "a sentiment of the understanding, or as a perception of the heart; or, which seems the truth, as including both" ("Dissertation II: Of the Nature of Virtue", §1, in Butler, *Works*, 2: 287).

together make an agent capable of virtue, and Price argues that only the motivation arising from the belief that a given act is morally right or morally good—only the intention to do the act as one that is called for by morality—constitutes the agent's virtue. He has no doubt that we all "continually feel, that the perception of right and wrong excites to action". Excitement to action "belongs to the very ideas of moral right and wrong", and morally appropriate action will ensue from seeing that the ideas apply to a case "whenever there is nothing to oppose it". Price thinks that there is no sensible question to be asked about "why a *reasonable* being acts *reasonably*" (185–7).

Hume had argued that because moral awareness moves us to action, and reason alone never moves us, it follows that moral awareness does not come from reason. Price, agreeing that moral awareness moves us to action, insists that moral awareness comes from reason and so concludes that reason is an active power. Like Clarke, he distinguishes the motive or reason for action from "*physical efficients*" or causes. The former is the "*occasion*" upon which the agent determines to act, but not an external force moving her (183n., 211). Voluntary action always requires "the *physical possibility* of forbearing it", but this, he adds, is entirely compatible with its being quite certain that the act will be done (244–5).

Liberty, for Price as for Clarke, is an all-or-nothing attribute, not something we can have in varying degrees (209–10). When Price takes up the relations of moral and non-moral motives (which Clarke does not discuss), he creates a difficulty for himself. The two kinds of motive can cooperate in leading to an action, and they can conflict. The strength of our non-moral motives always threatens to overwhelm or outweigh the moral motive, but we can strengthen the latter indefinitely. Thus Price seems to allow, as Clarke does not, that reasons and desires operate in the same field of force. The "spring of virtue", he says, which should repel the forces of temptation, may be "relaxed or broken" (207). He seems to be defending agency in a Newtonian world by adding to physical forces those derived from concepts.

Price agrees with Butler in criticising Shaftesbury for treating motives only in terms of commensurable strengths. The latter failed to see that moral motives claim an *authority* over the others (190n.). Yet Price does not show how authority can be factored into the field of forces in which moral motives may lose. He recognises an incommensurability in considerations prompting us to action, but does not treat the will as that which explains how we can decide among incommensurable potential motivations. He treats it instead as that through which we are able to respond to reasons of a kind that override considerations coming from desires. Hence he does not explain how we can be acting freely when our moral reasons are not strong enough to win the day against non-moral or immoral reasons.

Thomas Reid published his *Essays on the Active Powers of Man* (1788) toward the end of a long academic career.[52] They were preceded by *An Inquiry into the Human mind on the Principles of Common Sense* (1764) and by the *Essays on the Intellectual Powers of Man* (1785). In all these works, Reid opposes Hume's reductionist version of empiricism and defends what he took to be "common-sense" beliefs, themselves rooted deeply in experience. Common–sense about action and morality turns out to be quite definitely Christian. In this respect as in many others, Reid's views are closely allied with those of Clarke and Price. Like them, he aims to defend moral accountability in a divinely ordered universe by showing that we can freely determine ourselves to live by the precepts of a code that requires more than the pursuit of happiness. In *Active Powers*, he fights not only Hume, whose necessitarianism he takes to entail atheism, but also Leibniz, who was not an atheist but as strongly necessitarian as Hume, and to be rejected just as emphatically (I.6, 624–5).

For our purposes, Reid's views center on two points: one concerns active power and causation generally and our status as agents, the other our ability to determine our will freely and the way in which this ability enables us to guide ourselves by considering reasons for action. Before turning to these points, we must note Reid's views on desires and other motivations.

Reid's position is as pluralistic as that of Butler and Price. Desires take all sorts of objects and are not reducible to any single principle. They are impulses toward objects as represented in thought. When they cause agitation and cloud thinking, they are passions, but Reid does not say that the thoughts eliciting them must be indistinct. All of them, even anger and resentment, serve good purposes when not excessive, and they do not exhaust our motivational repertoire. Reid follows Price in arguing that some rational ideas themselves motivate. It takes reason to construct the

---

[52] Citations of Reid are to page and column of these essays, indicated as *Active Powers*, in his *Philosophical Works*, ed. W. Hamilton, Edinburgh, 1895.

idea of our own good on the whole and to recognise the basic axioms of morality. These thoughts give us reasons to act which, as we shall see, can be effective in determining what we do. Hume is quite wrong in thinking reason is only the slave of the passions. Without reason we would lack some of our most important motivations.

The belief that some things act and others are acted on is one of the fixed points of common-sense belief that Reid refuses to doubt. The distinction is made in all languages. Everyone understands it, and so has the idea of power. It is absurd to speak of passive power: "passive power is no power at all" (Active Powers, I.3, 519a). The proper contrast with "active power" is "speculative power", the general ability displayed in seeing, hearing, recalling, judging, reasoning, and so forth (I.1, 515a). The idea of power is simple. It is not acquired through sense or reflection but is known only indirectly, through that which we observe it to bring about (I.1, 514a–b). If Locke was mistaken in many ways about power, he was correct in holding that "the only clear notion or idea we have of active power, is taken from the power which we find in ourselves to give certain motions to our bodies, or a certain direction to our thoughts" (I.5, 523a). Our power is what accounts for this ability, and when we attribute power to God, we think of him as being like us (IV.2, 604a).

Given that we have wills, how do we fit in with the causally ordered world in which we live? Reid never challenges the common-sense belief that every event or change must have a cause (IV.2, 603a). But he does raise questions about the common-sense way of speaking of one natural event as causing another. We must not take such language literally any more than we now take it literally when we say that the sun is rising. Because we cannot obtain knowledge of causation or power through our senses (here Reid accepts Hume's view), all that we really know about nature is law-like sequences of events. That is enough to gratify our curiosity, teach us what to expect, and show us how to make things happen (I.6, 526b; IV.3, 606b–7a). Regularities do not constitute causes, whatever Hume may think, but they give us all we need where nature is concerned. God may move natural things directly, or through intermediaries, or by means of an initial command; it is unimportant as well as impossible to decide. "It is only in human actions, that may be imputed for praise or blame," Reid says, "that it is necessary for us to know who is the agent", and here we can often enough tell (I.6, 527b).

What matters is the act of will, or volition. Desire and appetite can take almost anything imaginable as their objects, but will can take as its object only "some action of our own", either thinking or bodily movement, which we have a thought of and believe to be in our power (I.7, 531a–3a). To will it is to determine ourselves to do such an act. Only actions coming from the will are voluntary (I.7, 531a; IV.2, 601b). Reid freely allows that neither he nor anyone else knows how determinations of the will control thoughts or make the body move (I.7, 528a). The central question, for him as for Locke, is, what determines the will?

There are two alternatives. Any specific volition is determined either by the person whose will it is or by some other being. Reid thinks that in cases of free volition the person whose will is involved is the cause of the volition. Here he comes to his central claim about human active power. We simply possess the power to determine our wills to do this or that, to act or to refrain. Because causation is the exertion of a basic active power, and not constant conjunction, Reid offers no account of what this kind of determination is and sees no need for further inquiry about causes. To deny that persons can determine their own wills is to deny that persons are efficient causes, and so that they are free and accountable. To admit that they are agents is to admit that agents can cause their wills to opt one way or another. We may ask why they made the choice they made, but that, as we shall see, is not necessarily to ask what caused the agent to determine her will as she did. It may be a question of reasons (IV.1, 601a–4a).

A conception of agent causation is thus central to Reid's account of liberty and morality. Agency is not always involved in explaining our actions. Reflex acts, or what very young children do or what we do when seriously ill or corrupted by vicious habits, may not be explicable in terms of agency. But when our agency explains why we determined our will as we did, then, Reid says, we are free, and for the actions that ensue we are fully accountable.

It is no surprise that Reid does not accept the Humean position that motives necessarily determine the will. Like Clarke, he argues that motives are not efficient causes at all. A motive "is not a thing that exists, but a thing that is conceived", and so it is not the right kind of entity to enter into causal relations (*Active Powers*, IV.4, 608b). The necessitarians suppose the world to be composed of inert matter, never acting and always acted upon. Since they think the behavior of intelligent beings is part of such a world, they think motives work on will in proportion to their strength and direction. But if we consider rational beings as genuine agents, then we must say that motives *influence* action in the way that advice does, not that they cause it. Some of Reid's most effective arguments are directed against the necessitarian view that motives determine the will in accordance with their strength.

Reid raises, for the first time, the question of how we know the strength of a motive. If we know it only because of its outcome, then the claim that motives are effective in proportion to their strength is empty. If the contrary motives are of the same kind, we can compare strengths: a bigger bribe provides a stronger motive than a smaller bribe. But, Reid asks, "[W]hen the motives are of different kinds, as money and fame, duty and worldly interest, ... by what rule shall we judge which is the strongest motive?" (IV.4, 608b).

Reid offers two rules. Suppose I am hungry but afraid to eat. These feelings act directly on the will, bypassing my reason. That one is strongest which I find most difficult to resist. It wins the "animal test" of strength (IV.4, 611b). Now consider rational motives, which spring from our awareness of moral principles, or our thought of our own greatest good. The beliefs involved may not cause feelings in us, but they are motives nonetheless. Should these motives conflict, then that one is strongest which represents what is most our duty, or most for our interest. It passes the "rational test" of strength (IV.4, 612a).

Does the strongest motive always determine the will? Leaving aside cases where we determine our will with no motive—as when we pick one coin rather than another to pay a debt—the answer is negative. Sometimes the strongest animal motive prevails, sometimes the strongest rational motive (IV.4, 612a). Since we have the power of acting without a motive at all, "that power, joined to a weaker motive, may counterbalance a stronger" (IV.4, 610a). It is thus within our power to act as the *rationally* strongest motives advise. Good agents are those who habitually do so. Reid does not ask what brings it about that some agents are habitually good and others not.

Having explained the conceptual framework needed to make sense of free agency, Reid goes on to consider whether in fact we are free. Of the three arguments he gives to show that we are, two are familiar. Everyone, he says first, is conscious of deliberation and voluntary exertion, and our moral lives are structured around our experience of ourselves as free agents.

Reid here backs the Clarkean argument with his own general epistemological principle that fixed points of common sense must be true (IV.6, 616b ff.).[53]

The second argument rests on the thesis, for which Reid argues in earlier sections of the *Active Powers*, that morality imposes a unique kind of requirement upon us. Its demands are thus incommensurable with those involved in satisfying our desires. This brings out the significance of the fact that we accept accountability for our actions. On the common-sense view, accountability requires that we must be able to do what we see we ought to do (IV.7, 621a). Since frequently we ought to act in opposition to the motive that according to the animal strength rule is strongest, we can do so, although not so necessitated. Thus we can determine our own will either way, which means, of course, that we are free. Given accountability in this sense, moral praise and blame mean what common sense has always taken them to mean. In the necessitarian system, they must be given a new and quite unacceptable meaning (622b).

Finally, Reid points to prudence in support of his thesis. He accepts the Lockean assumption that there is among our desires no natural ordering toward the good, not even toward the agent's own greatest good. The fact that we can make and carry out long-range plans is therefore evidence that we are not mere mechanisms moved by the varying strengths of our desires, but agents able to determine our own wills (*Active Powers*, IV.8, 623b).

Reid's theory of the active powers provided the version of strong libertarianism most influential in British, French, and American thought in the early decades of the nineteenth century. The other eighteenth-century libertarian view that came to be widely influential developed in Germany, among thinkers aware of Locke, Clarke, Shaftesbury, Hutcheson, and Hume, but ignorant of Butler, Price, and Reid's work on active powers.[54] Its central opponent was the Leibniz–Wolff theory.

[53] Kames argued in 1751 that the feeling of having the ability to make a free choice is "delusive", and attempted to explain why we have been given such a misleading feeling; see Kames, *Essays*, 183–5. Jonathan Edwards replied, forcing Kames to modify his position. See Edwards, "Remarks on the Essays on the Principles of Morality and Natural Religion, in a letter to a minister of the Church of Scotland". In *The Works of Jonathan Edwards* (New Haven, CT, 1957–), 1: *Freedom of the Will*, ed. P. Ramsey, 443–65, especially Ramsey's introduction. Reid continues the attack.

[54] Only Tetens knew Reid's work, and he knew only the *Inquiry*. His own major work was published prior to Reid's late lectures on theoretical and practical philosophy. See Manfred Kuehn, *Scottish Common Sense in Germany, 1768–1800: A Contribution to the History of Critical Philosophy*, (Kingston and Montreal, 1987), ch. 7.

VIII. The Will and God's Laws

Aside from Wolff, the most interesting eighteenth-century German philosopher before Kant was Christian August Crusius (1715–75). A Lutheran pastor and the leading critic of Wolffianism, Crusius put his considerable philosophical ingenuity at the service of essentially reactionary Christian apologetics. Although his great treatise on ethics, the *Anweisung vernünftig zu leben* (*Guide to Rational Living*) was published in 1744, a year prior to his metaphysical treatise, *Entwurf der nothwendigen Vernunft-Wahrheiten* (*Sketch of the Necessary Truths of Reason*), the positions defended in the later work are obviously drawn on in the earlier one.[55] The philosophy of Crusius is highly systematic, deliberately opposing Leibniz and Wolff on almost every major issue.

Crusius is concerned above all with showing that human beings are accountable for their own acts and that their primary responsibility is to acknowledge their total dependence on God by freely obeying his commands. God created, sustains, and oversees the world, but it is a world containing various kinds of agents with their own powers. Something has a power when it contains the possibility or necessity of another thing. Only substances have powers. One substance has a power when there is something within it on account of which another substance can come or continue to be, or alter its condition (*Entwurf*, 112–13). There are passive as well as active powers, and, more importantly, basic as well as derived powers. Derived powers may be explained in terms of basic powers; basic powers belong to the essence of what has them and cannot be explained further (121–3). Some attributes are powers simply by existing. Thus the sides of a triangle make its angles what they are. In contrast with these existential powers, other powers change what exists, and these are active powers (*thätige Kräfte*).

Among active powers, some are self-activated, not set in action by anything external to their substance (*Entwurf*, 135–7). Crusius argues that

---

[55] References are to Christian August Crusius, *Die philosophischen Hauptwerke*, eds. G. Tonelli, S. Carboncini, and R. Finster, facsimile of Leipzig, 1744–7 edn. (Hildesheim, 1964–). vol. 1 contains *Anweisung, vernünftig zu leben*, in four parts, and vol. 2 contains *Entwurf der nothwendigen Vernunft-Wahrheiten*, in three parts. The main treatment of will is in *Anweisung*, Pt. I, "Thelamatologie", a term Crusius seems to have invented. Some of the material is reiterated in the *Entwurf*. Numbers refer to pages in the two respective volumes.

there must be such powers because otherwise there would have to be an infinite series of activators before anything could change. The acts originating in self-activation are called basic actions (139). God must, of course, have this kind of power, but we have it as well: it is the basis of our freedom and our accountability (140–3).

Crusius offers three arguments to show that we are free. First, we experience ourselves as originators, capable of acting or changing course or not acting at all, and we can choose between indifferents—equally good means to our ends, for instance (*Anweisung*, 51–2). Next, we know that there are divine moral laws and that we are obligated to obey them, but we could not be so obligated were we not free (53–4). Crusius's central argument is much more unusual. It is that unless the world contains agents with free will there would be no reason for God to create it. Without free agents in a world, everything in that world would really be done by God himself. Hence "created beings would obtain through their reality no other relation to God than what they already had in the mere state of possibility, namely, that their being and essence depended on him". This would mean that God could have no formal purpose in making a possible world real. But God does nothing in vain, and hence any real world must contain free agents (53). Because of free will, created beings can come into kinds of relations with God—moral relations—that would otherwise be impossible. Free will is the power making these relations possible, and they justify God in making a possible world real. Morality is the point of existence (*Entwurf*, 504–8, 638, 669–70).

What, then, is will? Crusius gives an original answer: will is "the power of a mind to act according to its representations". It is the effort to make real something represented (*Anweisung*, 4; *Entwurf*, 866). Will as active power contains various strivings, some constant and some intermittent. These are our desires, which are thus aspects of the will. Desire is not essentially due to need or lack. It is one form of the will's exercise of its activity. The representation that stimulates a desire serves as a potential end for us. To adopt a possible end is to decide to realise what is represented, to make it exist, or come to possess it. Thus, where the understanding moves from one idea to another, the will takes us beyond the realm of thinking and so is neither a part of the understanding nor simply derivable from it (*Anweisung*, 9–11; *Entwurf*, 867–9). The Leibniz–Wolff school is thus mistaken in holding that since all we can do is represent, every mental occurrence must amount to moving from one representation to another. For them, desire is the desire for new representations and will is the movement to new representations. But this change in what we think, as Crusius sees it, is not genuine action at all.

Acts of will, or volitions, for Crusius always bring to the representations that elicit them an otherwise absent thrust toward realisation. Beings who can think must have wills because otherwise their representations of the world would be pointless. "The understanding", Crusius says, in the first modern proclamation of the primacy of the practical, "exists for the sake of the will" (*Anweisung*, 4; *Entwurf*, 886).

Pleasure and good as well as desire are explained in terms of will. Pleasure is what we feel when we are in a condition we have willed (*Anweisung*, 24). The good itself is simply what is in conformity with a will or with desire (*Anweisung*, 29; *Entwurf*, 326–7). Good is thus a relative concept, unlike the concept of perfection. Things are more or less perfect as they are more or less able to be causes of other things or as they have more or less power (*Entwurf*, 296–300). Crusius thinks that we, like God, always desire perfection, and hence that the perfect is in fact the good, although the concepts are different. But the desire for perfection explains little because there are many kinds and degrees of perfection, and—contrary to Leibniz—no single "most perfect" or "best" state toward which we might aim. For Crusius it is, of course, pointless to say, as Leibniz and Wolff do, that we always will the good. Goodness presupposes but does not explain the activity of will. It is thus no surprise to find Crusius insisting that there are innumerable kinds of objects of desire and refusing to try to explain them in terms of self-interest or any other single factor.

Many of our desires originate from other desires, as the desire for a means does from the desire for an end. Since this cannot go on forever, there must be basic desires, and at least some of these must be essential to the mind. Basic desires, given to us by God, cannot be wicked and must be shared by all. As forms of will, desires require representations. Innate desires must therefore carry innate ideas with them (*Anweisung*, 109–15). But it is important to distinguish derivative desires from basic ones. The desire for happiness, for instance, is not basic. It is only the desire to enjoy the gratification of our specific desires and therefore presupposes their existence (119–28). Crusius holds that no general explanation of particular desires can be given (128–9).

Although the desire for happiness is derivative, there are basic human desires or drives. Crusius identifies three. The first is the desire to increase our own appropriate perfection (*Anweisung*, 133–4). Against the Leibniz–Wolff school's use of this desire, Crusius argues that it is the origin not of all striving but of the desires for truth, clarity, good reasoning, the arts, bodily improvement, freedom, friendship, and honor (135–44). The second basic desire is for community with those in whom we find perfection (145). This leads us, among other things, to feel a general moral love or a desire to help others (148–50). The third desire is "the natural drive to recognise a divine moral law" (157). This is evident in our drive of conscience (*Gewissenstrieb*), a sense of indebtedness which moves us to do our duty and carry out our obligations.

To act from our awareness of God's laws, Crusius thinks, we must be free, and he makes several points about the freedom that enables us to obey those laws. Freedom is not just the absence of external hindrances to doing as we please. Nor is it acting for what we perceive as the greatest available amount of good or perfection. If there were only Leibnizian freedom, he argues, "all our virtue would be turned into mere good luck" since it would depend on our having a constitution enabling us to acquire knowledge and on our being so situated as to get it (*Anweisung*, 46). Crusius thinks Leibniz does not avoid fatalism. If his "hypothetical necessity" is to offer real alternatives of action, then the ends involved must be chosen by genuinely self-determining agents of a kind for which Leibniz leaves no room (*Entwurf*, 203–10).[56] If we are truly free, then, even given constant antecedents and circumstances, we can determine ourselves to act in several ways (*Anweisung*, 44–5; see *Entwurf*, 140–5). "Whenever we freely will something", Crusius says,

we are deciding to do something for which one or several desires already exist in us. . . . Freedom consists in an inner perfect activity of will, which is capable of connecting its efficacy with one of the currently active drives of the will, or of omitting this connection and remaining inactive, or of connecting it with another drive instead of with the first. (*Anweisung*, 54–5)

In one way, the Crusian will is more like the Leibnizian than the Lockean one. It contains within itself its own rules for making choices among the

---

[56] He also accuses Leibniz of altering the meaning of "free" to suit his philosophy (*Entwurf*, Pt. III, ch. 1, §388, vol. 2: 752).

alternatives presented to it by desires and drives. These are all forms of will, but they are not commensurable. The drive of conscience, for instance, is different in kind from desire. Hence the Crusian will is much more complex than the Leibnizian. It does not direct us to maximise perfection. It tells us to follow a moral code as well as rules of prudence, both inherent in the will. When these rules seem to conflict, we are to follow God's laws above all else. What enables us to do so is, first, the fact that conscience provides a permanent basic drive and, second, the fact that our will is free. We feel the charm of the various representations to which the will's strivings respond, but we are not determined by them. We can turn the will away from them and "connect its efficacy" with our conscientious feeling of obligation.

What allows Crusius to make this claim is his distinction between physical causes and motives or exemplary causes, which are reasons justifying proposed actions. He argues that the Leibnizian principle of sufficient reason systematically and inexcusably overlooks this distinction, collapsing radically different kinds of reason (*Grund*), the physical and the moral, into one (*Anweisung*, 204–6; *Entwurf*, 112–55; see also 865–6). Crusius feels no hesitation in allowing cognitive reasons causal efficacy in moving bodies in a material world. Granting physical determinism a large part in explaining the behavior of inanimate objects, he thinks that total determinism is unacceptable. It allows neither for morality nor for miracles (*Entwurf*, 723–5). Mind, however, is spiritual substance, and both God and humankind must be able to alter the course of events. Indeed, in the end, only God and ourselves possess truly active powers (776–7). If determinism cannot account for these things, so much the worse for it.

IX. Empirical Evidence for Free Will

Crusius's incorporation of moral knowledge into the will implied a rejection of the classical distinction between understanding and will. In 1777, J. N. Tetens rejected it more elaborately in his *Philosophische Versuche über die menschliche Natur und ihre Entwicklung* (*Philosophical Essays on Human Nature and its Development*).[57] He replaced the classical dichotomy with

---

[57] Tetens, *Versuche* (see n. 4).

a threefold division not of faculties but of powers, making sensibility a separate power of receiving sensations from the external world or one's own body and giving it the function of supplying data to the other two powers, the understanding and the will (*Versuche*, 1: 618–26). Tetens also reassigned the attributes of passivity and activity, leaving sensibility alone purely passive and finding as much activity in the understanding as in the will (see 2: 20–1). Since Kant reportedly kept Tetens's work on his desk as he wrote the *Kritik der reinen Vernunft*, historians have understandably investigated this aspect of Tetens's thought, expounded in his first volume.[58] They have generally overlooked his reflections on free will and human perfectibility, the topics of the second volume and, for Tetens, the point and justification of the whole (*Versuche*, Vorrede, 1: xxxv–xxxvi).

Tetens, sometimes described as "the German Locke", knew the work of the British philosophers thoroughly, as well as the work of French theorists such as Condillac and Bonnet, who were influenced by them. He had, however, no single allegiance. Tetens admires Leibniz and Wolff and remarks at one point that the "foreigners" have left much obscure (*Versuche*, 1: 427). But he rejects the central Leibniz–Wolff thesis that all mental functioning including pleasure and desire can be explained in terms of representation. He is equally doubtful whether association can explain everything. He allows that knowledge must come from experience but takes experience to teach us far more than Hume admits. It teaches us, for instance, that causation is more than paired events always occurring in the same sequence. Real power is involved. We get the idea of power from our own feelings, but it is justifiable (Tetens never succeeds in explaining exactly how) to take our inner experience of necessary connection as showing that objective powers exist in external objects as well as in ourselves (1: 312–16, 322–7; 2: 564–8).[59]

The concept of the mind's self-activating power is central to all of Tetens's accounts of mental functioning. Self-activity is involved, for example, in transforming sensations into thoughts. Possession of it is also

---

[58] Ernst Cassirer, *Kant's Life and Thought*, trans. J. Haden (New Haven, CT, 1981), 194. For discussion of Tetens, see Lewis White Beck, *Early German Philosophy: Kant and His Predecessors* (Cambridge, MA, 1969); Kuehn, *Scottish Common Sense*; and Günter Gawlick and Lothar Kreimendahl, *Hume in der deutschen Aufklärung: Umrisse einer Rezeptionsgeschichte* (Stuttgart-Bad Cannstadt, 1987).

[59] The way Reid parallels these views is remarkable, but there is no reason to suppose that he had even heard of Tetens.

presupposed by the ability to act freely. Water flowing out of a hole in a jug displays a self-activating power, as does a tensed spring when it is released, but neither is free. Freedom is a power over oneself, going beyond the ability of the soul to have effects upon itself (as the Leibnizians think). "The *positive power* through which we have ourselves in our own control when we are active requires a *simultaneous inner capacity* or readiness to do, under unaltered circumstances, the opposite of what we do. This capacity to be otherwise active . . . persists during the whole action if this is a free action in its entirety to its end" (*Versuche*, 2: 6–7). Free agents thus possess more powers than merely self-activated agents. They possess the ability to initiate action, the ability to apply this ability, and the ability not to act, or to do something else entirely. Because they possess this third power, free beings are more fully the originators of their actions than merely spontaneous agents (2: 125).

Tetens rests all his basic claims on experience. The threefold division of mental powers is intended as an explanation of observable phenomena (*Versuche*, 2: 625). So also is the claim that some self-activating agents are free agents. This raises a difficult question. Since the power to do otherwise is never used, how do we know that anything has it? Tetens adduces several kinds of data, which serve as his arguments to show that we are free.

Most importantly, self-awareness gives us a sensation of being able to do otherwise. That sensation may be erroneous, as are some sensory data about the external world, but occasional error does not—despite Berkeley—show that the sensation is always wrong (*Versuche*, 2: 9–19, 131). Moreover, we experience the power to do otherwise as a series of impulses, interrupting the action, to do otherwise. Consequently, freely chosen actions do not proceed in the uninterrupted and unvarying way that unfree actions do (2: 16). Compare human action with the behavior of the famous automata that Vaucanson made: there are many more forces at work in the former and many more irregularities in their observable performances. When people are swayed by a single passion, and so not free, they act more nearly like machines (2: 126–7).

Observations such as these, made by the "experimental physics of the soul", require freedom for their explanation (*Versuche*, 2: 43). We should also like to know how it works. Tetens perhaps goes to unnecessary lengths to differentiate a stimulus that merely sets off an inherent self-activating power from an external power working through the capacities of the soul (2: 50–8). He has more difficulty in accommodating freedom to the fact that the power to act and the power to act otherwise are determined by reasons or motives.

Tetens does not deny that there are sufficient reasons leading these powers to act. The principle of sufficient reason is solidly based on experience, which shows that there is "a fully determining cause, a sufficient...reason" for whatever occurs (*Versuche*, 2: 131–2, 137). Motives provide such reasons for action. The sensation of freedom presents itself to us as the power to resist the temptation offered by motives (2: 32). In having motives, we of course have ideas of the acts they give us reason to perform. To act freely, we need not have distinct ideas. We can freely control ourselves even if we feel strong passions aroused by swarms of confused ideas (2: 37). In being motivated, we are presented with an idea of an act as pleasing or unpleasing to us, and our active power is generally stimulated to efficacy (*Wirksamkeit*) by what seems most pleasing to us. Even in cases where the alternatives are indifferent, something occurs to us as a reason to choose, perhaps only that first is best. Given the reason, we act, and the reason fully explains why we act. Sometimes we are overpowered by desire, but where we are free, this is because we could choose not to do what we do. How can this freedom-giving ability be efficacious while there exists a necessary connection between the reason for acting and the act?

Tetens's answer is not wholly clear. He explains that causal laws hold only if there is no hindrance to their operation. A falling cannonball will break a china jug, but not if someone removes the jug from its path. Similarly, it seems, the most pleasing thought of an action will invariably stimulate the agent's self-activating power to efficacy unless the equally present self-activating power to do otherwise intervenes. Hence even when the agent did the act, he had the full power not to do it and could have used his ability to apply that power—his *Willkühr*, or ability to choose—to activate it. But this is all that is required for the agent to be free. To deny that this is possible is to commit oneself to what Tetens takes to be the absurd view that no one could ever do what he did not do. Experience shows that agents could have done what they did not do.

Morality, like freedom, has its source in the self-activating power of the agent, and morality is not thinkable without freedom (*Versuche*, 2: 124).

A being that does *good* out of inner natural necessity—does it not possess a *splendid* nature? But yet this natural goodness is not *free* goodness, and a *free* being, with an *equal* power for good, will have *more inner goodness* and be a *greater* being, because it works with a greater inner power which also has the power to do evil. (2: 27)

Morality and freedom are also tied to reason, without which no ideas of alternative actions are possible. Virtue requires us to control our passions in the name of ideas of right and duty. "This inner self-power [*Selbstmacht*] of the soul over its sensations and drives, this ability to rule them according to distinct ideas, is the essence and true spirit of virtue" (2: 656). Goodheartedness without self-activation through these ideas can be wicked. Only insofar as goodness springs from reasoned self-control is it meritorious. A self-controlling fully active being is "the most sublime and most fully worthy of respect of God's creations" (2: 657–8). Tetens seems, in these remarks, to be preparing for an argument, like Clarke's or Price's, from the fact that we can decide between incommensurable reasons to the need for a special power. But he does not argue this way. His defense of free will rests on the empirical, not the moral, evidence for it.

X. Kant: Desire and Transcendental Freedom

Kant held that a truly scientific psychology is impossible, and he wrote no treatise on the passions.[60] Nonetheless, from his early cosmological treatise to his final "posthumous work", he showed a deep interest in the will and its relation to feeling and desire. In the *Kritik der Urtheilskraft* (1790), he

[60] *Metaphysische Anfangsgründe der Naturwissenschaft*/*Metaphysical Foundations of Natural Science* (1786), Vorrede, in Ak 4: 467–79 at 471. See also Kant's *Vorlesungen über Metaphysik*, Ak 28: 2.i, 679, translated as *Lectures on Metaphysics*, trans. and eds. K. Ameriks and S. Naragon, in *Works* (1997). Also cited are *Anthropologie in pragmatischer Hinsicht* (1798), Ak 6: 117–333, translated as *Anthropology from a Pragmatic Point of View*, trans. and ed. M. J. Gregor (The Hague, 1974); *Grundlegung zur Metaphysik der Sitten* (1785), Ak 4: 385–463, translated as *Groundwork of The Metaphysics of Morals*, trans. and ed. M. J. Gregor, in *Works*/*Practical Philosophy* (1996); *Kritik der praktischen Vernunft* (1788), Ak 5: 1–163, translated as *Critique of Practical Reason*, trans. and ed. M. J. Gregor, in *Works*/*Practical Philosophy*; *Kritik der reinen Vernunft* (1781), Ak 4; 2. Aufl. (1787), Ak 3, translated as *Critique of Pure Reason*, trans. and eds. P. Guyer and A. W. Wood, in *Works* (1998); *Kritik der Urtheilskraft* (1790), Ak 5: 165–547, translated as *Critique of the Power of Judgement*, trans. P. Guyer and E. Matthews, ed. P. Guyer, in *Works* (2000); *Metaphysik der Sitten* (1797–8), Ak 6: 203–493, translated as *The Metaphysics of Morals*, trans. and ed. M. J. Gregor, in *Works*/*Practical Philosophy*; *Die Religion innerhalb der Grenzen der bloen Vernunft* (1793), Ak 6: 1–202, translated as *Religion within the Boundaries of mere Reason*, trans. and eds. A. Wood and G. di Giovanni, in *Works*/*Religion and Rational Theology* (1996).

presented a theory about the kind of disinterested pleasure that we take in beautiful and sublime works of art and nature. His other discussions of these subjects show his concern with the practical bearing of affects and passions and with our need to control and guide them. He had definite views on health and the prudent conduct of life, but his overriding practical concern was morality.[61]

Kant arrived at the original central idea of his moral theory by about 1765, well before he had come to the main points of his critical views on knowledge.[62] Morality, as he came to think of it, requires us to act independently of our desires. It may dictate that we do what we have the strongest aversion to doing and what in no way serves even our long-term self-interest. Although we often fail to act as we ought, we must be able to do so. Hence we must have a power to do what we do not do. What is it, and how can we know about it?

We know that Kant found Tetens's views on freedom unhelpful, but he could hardly have been indifferent to the questions asked.[63] Moreover, Tetens's extended contrasts of the Leibniz–Wolff theory of the passions and the will with the more empirical British theories would have kept these positions fresh in Kant's mind while he was working on the *Kritik der reinen Vernunft*. He had defended an essentially Wolffian view of freedom in an important early essay[64] but also admired Crusius, so whether he knew Clarke's work or not, he was familiar with a non-Wolffian view of free will supported by moral and *a priori* arguments. His own views thus respond to all the kinds of theories we have been considering.

---

[61] For Kant's views on health, see "Versuch über die Krankheiten des Kopfes"/"Essay on Illnesses of the Head" (1764), Ak 2: 257–72. His manuscript notes, "De Medicina corporis, quae philosophorum est"/"On Philosophers' Medicine of the Body" (1786 or 1788), Ak 15: 939–53, are translated in *Kant's Latin Writings: Translations, Commentaries and Notes*, trans. L. Beck et al. (New York, NY, 1986), 217–43. See also *Der Streit der Fakultäten* (1798), §3, Ak 7: 97–116, translated as *The Conflict of the Faculties*, trans. M. J. Gregor and R. Anchor, in *Works/Religion and Rational Theology*. Kant's views on the conduct of life are scattered through his lectures on ethics; some are presented more compactly in the *Anthropologie*, for example, Pt. I, Bk. 2, §§60–6, and Bk. 3, §§75–6 and 82–8, in Ak 7.

[62] See Josef Schmucker, *Die Ursprünge der Ethik Kants in seinen vorkritischen Schriften und Reflektionen* (Meisenheim am Glan, 1961); Dieter Henrich, "Hutcheson und Kant", *Kant-Studien*, 49 (1957–8): 49–69, and "Über Kant's früheste Ethik", *Kant-Studien*, 54 (1963): 404–31.

[63] See the letter of Marcus Herz, April 1778, Ak 10: 125.

[64] *Principiorum primorum cognitionis metaphysical nova dilucidatio*/*A New Elucidation of the First Principles of Metaphysical Cognition* (1755), §11, Ak 1: 391–410, translated in Kant, *Works/Theoretical Philosophy 1755–1770*, trans. and eds. D. Walford and R. Meerbote (1992).

However Wolffian Kant was when young, he began to leave Wolff's views behind him under the influence of Shaftesbury, Hutcheson, and Hume. By 1764, he was using a Lockean view of the passions in analysing mental disturbances.[65] In later writings, he abandoned Wolff's view of the passions no less completely than he rejected his theory of knowledge and his theory of freedom. As opposed to the Leibniz–Wolff thesis that the mind has only one power, Kant holds that there are three quite separate aspects of its functioning: knowing, feeling, and desiring. I begin with a brief look at Kant's mature understanding of the last two.

There are three kinds of feeling that we call pleasure. The kind of pleasure connected with desire, Kant insists, is purely subjective. It carries no information about its causes outside us nor even any about us. We think otherwise only if we overlook the ambiguity of the word "sensation" (*Empfindung*), which may refer to the cognitive representations we obtain through our various senses or to the feeling (*Gefühl*) with which we respond to them (*Kritik der Urtheilskraft*, 5: 206). No logical inference from a representation or concept to a feeling of pleasure of this kind is possible (5: 170). What one person finds pleasant another may not. There can be no question of error here; tastes simply differ (5: 212). This kind of pleasure differs from both aesthetic pleasure and the pleasure that arises from morally motivated choice.

Because pleasure and pain show only the relation of a representation to the subject with the feelings, they "cannot be explained more clearly in themselves". We can make them "recognizable in practice", however, by specifying their results (*Metaphysik der Sitten*, 6: 212). To do so, we must look at a different aspect of the way the mind works, the *Begehrungsvermögen*, or capacity for desire (*Kritik der Urtheilskraft*, 5: 177–8).[66]

We must begin with Kant's explanation of a goal or end. He distinguishes two kinds of event. Some come about through natural causality. Others come about only because a conscious being first represents them and is then moved to bring them about by this representation of them. If we think that some state of affairs can exist "only through a concept of [it]", we are

---

[65] "Essay on Illnesses of the Head", Ak 2: 261.
[66] The German is often translated as "faculty of desire", but *Vermögen* means "ability", "power", or "capacity" as well as "faculty". The latter term should be avoided in view of its misleading connection with a faculty psychology which Kant did not accept.

thinking of it as an end. The thought of the effect here precedes the cause—someone's action—and determines the agent to cause the state of affairs to exist (5: 219–20). The faculty of desire is defined as "the faculty to be, by means of one's representations, the cause of the objects of these representations" (*Sitten*, 6: 211). When a representation of something causes in me an incipient effort to make it exist, I think of it as my end; I desire it. Since this is different both from having a non-moving thought of something and from taking pleasure in the thought or reality of something, Kant postulates a separate power in the mind to account for it.

How then is pleasure related to desire? There are various ways. Sometimes a pleasure precedes and causes a desire. Alternatively, I may have a propensity for the object of the desire, even before experiencing it and the pleasure it gives me. If I do, then after experiencing the object I will have a habitual desire for such things or an inclination toward them. I can also have desires for objects I have never experienced or thought of. These urges are instincts; pleasure does not cause them but may come from their gratification (*Sitten*, 6: 212; *Religion innerhalb der Grenzen der bloβen Vernunft*, 6: 28n.). In addition to these differing connections, one general link between feeling and desire is observable. When I feel prompted to leave the condition I am in, the state is painful; when I feel prompted to stay in it, it is pleasant. Kant thinks, in an almost Lockean way, that pain must precede enjoyment. I must be prompted to leave one state before I enjoy being in another one (*Anthropologie in pragmatischer Hinsicht*, 7: 230–1; see also 7: 235).

Since the capacity of desire is a capacity for a certain kind of causality, it is not passive receptivity as the capacity for feelings of pleasure and pain is. Even the excessive desires we call passions are not, for Kant, passive. Settled desires or inclinations are passions when they are so deeply rooted that they make it difficult for us to use reason to compare them with one another and with our other desires (*Anthropologie*, 7: 265; *Sitten*, 6: 408). Similarly, we are sometimes agitated by a feeling (*Affekt*) not because of its intensity but because it tends to make us fail to compare it with the rest of our pleasures and pains (*Anthropologie*, 7: 254). When we are unreasonable in having passions and emotions, for Kant it is not because they misrepresent the world, as the Leibnizians think, or are caused by false beliefs, as Hume holds. It is because they cause us to fail to use reason to put them in perspective.

If we were being reasonable, we would consider each of our feelings, desires, inclinations, and passions in the light of the totality of what we want. Since we possess reason as a part of our cognitive capacity, we tend to form idealised notions of totalities in practical as well as in theoretical matters. The idea of the satisfaction of all our desires is the idea of happiness. Kant would thus have agreed with Reid in thinking that the desire for happiness is a rational one. But whereas Butler thought that we all too often fail to desire it, Kant thinks it is naturally an inevitable object of desire.

The desire for happiness does not, however, provide an inner source of order. More strongly than Locke, Kant thinks our desires unstable. Each person's conception of happiness fluctuates so greatly that even if nature were at our command, no natural law could guarantee us satisfaction. Contentment is not possible. Human nature "is not of the sort to call a halt anywhere in possession and enjoyment and to be satisfied" (*Kritik der Urtheilskraft*, 5: 430; see *Anthropologie*, 7: 234–5). The problem is made worse, in Kant's eyes, because he thinks—here following Jean-Jacques Rousseau—that many of our desires and passions are social. They do not arise simply from bodily or other needs taken by themselves, as do our desires for sex, the well-being of our offspring, and human company. They arise when we begin to compare ourselves with other people. Envy, ingratitude, and spite are social in this way (*Religion*, 6: 27), as are our desires or manias for honor, power, and wealth (*Anthropologie*, 7: 268).

Although in the *Grundlegung zur Metaphysik der Zitten* Kant claims that a reasonable person would wish to be free of all inclinations, in the *Religion* he rejects this view. We cannot get rid of our desires, and they are not to be condemned. Morality requires us only to control them, and insofar as we get better at doing so, they may become more nearly capable of being satisfied. But there is no natural harmony among them, nor would theoretical knowledge of the world introduce it. If anything enables us to harmonise them, it is our rational capacity for prudence (*Religion*, 6: 58).

Moral as well as prudential self-control is possible because reason is as much a part of our nature as are the passions and desires. In its theoretical activity, reason enables us to know the world, while practically it enables us to direct our actions freely in a way that other living things in the world cannot. Kant's views on the nature of practical freedom and how we know of it changed significantly from book to book. They are among the most difficult of his theories, and commentators tend to disagree about them. Some points, however, are reasonably clear.

First, the freedom that Kant defends is not merely the ability to act as we choose but an inner ability to control our choices. Freedom does not require the absence of determining grounds for our choice. An indeterministic, lawless freedom—a power to act randomly—is thinkable, but Kant has no desire to defend it. He rather defends, like Leibniz and Wolff, freedom in the sense of spontaneity. A free act is one whose determining ground lies wholly within the agent. But, along with Crusius, Kant rejects the Leibnizian account of spontaneity. When Leibnizian agents act freely, they act on reasons, which they have because of a long chain of antecedent events, springing ultimately from God's decision to make the best world. Their choices, Kant thinks, are *pre*-determined, not merely determined. The determining grounds of their acts were in earlier times and are no longer in their power. Spontaneity requires that my grounds originate in me now.

Second, our knowledge that we are free cannot rest on any empirical grounds. The weakness of Tetens's empirical arguments may have helped to convince Kant of this. In any case, the systematic results of the *Kritik der reinen Vernunft* make it absolutely impossible to ground belief in freedom on experiences such as our feeling of freedom when we decide or on theoretical arguments concerning the need for an uncaused first cause. We must take our experienced world to be fully determined. Psychological events, like spatial events, necessarily follow from prior causes (*Grundlegung*, 4: 427). But the first *Kritik* argues that it is equally impossible for either experiential or *a priori* arguments to prove that we cannot have free will.

Third, since theoretical reasoning leaves open the question of freedom, only practical considerations can settle it. Here Kant agrees with the Clarkeans. Moral considerations are different in kind from grounds for action drawn from desires, yet we do make choices between them. We have empirical awareness of desires. Our awareness of moral considerations comes to us in what Kant calls "a fact of reason" (*ein Factum der Vernunft*) (*Kritik der praktischen Vernunft*, 5: 42). We are each unavoidably aware, he believes, of particular obligations to specific acts, regardless of what we feel or desire. Such obligations are unavoidable or, as Kant says, "categorical". They entitle us to complete practical assurance that we *can* do as we ought, and so warrant our belief that we are free in the requisite way. No

THE ACTIVE POWERS   399

antecedently determined grounds cause us to act. We can ignore our desires and act as we know we ought.

Fourth, in his *Die Religion innerhalb der Grenzen der bloen Vernunft* and the *Metaphysik der Sitten*, Kant speaks of two separate powers as being involved in the explanation of freedom. There is first the will (*Wille*), which is our own reason in its practical capacity. It functions to place permanent rational requirements on action, both prudential and moral. With Leibniz, and unlike Locke and Clarke, Kant sees the will as containing its own principles for decision-making. But with Crusius, and against the Leibnizians, he does not think the principles direct us to consider only the goods and ills that will result from the alternatives before us. Practical reason essentially requires formal consistency in our choices. We in our rational aspect demand this of ourselves as we consider the projects for action proposed by the desires that arise from ourselves in our empirical aspect.

It follows that whenever a desire prompts us to act for an end, the rational demand for consistency is also evident to us. The power of choice (*Willkür*) is what enables us to decide between them. We might have the power of choice even if we did not have the kind of practical reason we have. It would act where the alternatives are indifferent; otherwise, its choices would be determined by the relative strengths of desires and passions. As morality shows us, however, *Willkür* can be determined by purely rational requirements imposed by the self as rational. The will itself is neither free nor unfree. As pure practical reason, it always gives us the option of acting solely on internal spontaneous grounds. The power of choice, which can opt for morality or against it, is a free power. Because we can choose, we never have to accede to desires that, although certainly part of ourselves, are determined by what is not part of ourselves.

Of the many questions raised by Kant's view, I can consider only three. First, how can desires be tested for consistency? Since Kant thinks, with Hume, that desires are blind causal forces, which in themselves are neither rational nor irrational, he holds that they are not tested directly. Collaborating with reason, desires somehow present us with proposals for action. Kant explicitly declines to give any empirical psychological explanation of how this happens (*Grundlegung*, 4: 427). What results is a rationally testable "maxim", a proposal to act in a definite way in given circumstances to attain a specific end. Reason can test the maxim for consistency in ways that Kant explains in detail in his ethics. We use our power of choice either to adopt or reject the proposal, and we then act accordingly.

Second, what leads us to make the choices we do? We can choose to ignore the requirements of reason or to comply with them, in prudential or in moral matters. Is the free power of choice undetermined? Kant wrestles with this problem in the *Religion*. He gets as far as saying that we must suppose, given the empirical evidence about human behavior, that each of us makes a fundamental free choice whether to prefer actions in our own interest or those required by morality when the two conflict. Once this choice is made, the rest are explicable; why it is made as it is—for the worse—is inexplicable (*Religion*, 6: 32–9).

Finally, how is it possible that a demand for rational consistency, even elaborated as Kant thinks it can be into a full system of ethics, can have an empirically observable effect on our behavior? How can action determined by such a non-temporal reason be fitted into the determinist psychology Kant accepts? He tells us that no answer is possible. The *Kritik der reinen Vernunft* has set strict limits on what we can know. The aspect of the self that produces desires is phenomenal. The aspect that is the rational will is noumenal. Only transcendental argument can warrant it. Morality shows us that we possess the ability to act for reasons independent of desire. But nothing noumenal can enter into causal explanations of anything in the phenomenal realm. We here reach the limits of our ability to understand our active powers.

XI. Conclusion

Two issues dominate eighteenth-century debates about the active powers. One is whether our desires are themselves implicitly rational, as representations of good or perfection, or whether they are non-rational forces within the psyche. The other is whether all kinds of considerations that we take into account in making decisions are commensurable or whether morality gives us grounds for action that are incommensurable with grounds arising from desire.

If desires are inherently rational, then knowledge alone can produce moral order in them and in our actions. If, as the Lockeans held, they are not rational, then some other source of order must be found. Those who believed that all reasons for action are commensurable had no need to appeal to a strong separate power of willing to explain the decisions we make. They could argue that choice is determined by the strength of our desires, whether or not it is complicated by a moral sense that reinforces some desires and not others. Those who saw morality as requiring us to act regardless of desire had to postulate a will in order to explain the fact that we sometimes decide to act morally. They also felt forced to claim that such a will, or power of agency, must be independent of the causal laws that Newton had shown to determine the physical world.

Libertarians before Kant argued for an empirically discoverable freedom operating, in ways they never managed to explain, within the physical world. Kant thought their efforts failed. He shared with them, however, the belief in the incommensurability of moral and desire-based reasons and in our ability to act against our desires. To save agency in a determinist world, he exiled the source of our freedom to a realm beyond experience.

Kant's way of preserving agency had fateful consequences in German thought. Kant himself took the idea of a source of agency beyond all merely empirical appearances to be available only for practical purposes—only in connection with morality and never with speculative knowledge. Later thinkers dropped the restriction. In the works of Fichte and even more in those of Schopenhauer, the hidden source of freedom became a metaphysical principle explaining appearances. Active power, which the late seventeenth-century occasionalists chased out of the world, returned at the beginning of the nineteenth century as its inner essence.

PART VII
Afterword

19

Sixty Years of Philosophy in a Life

I dedicate this lecture to the memory of Richard Rorty. "There is no action or thought in which I do not miss him, as indeed he would have missed me. For just as he surpassed me infinitely in every other ability and virtue, so he did in the duty of friendship."[1]

Hume opened his autobiographical essay with a comment and a resolution: "It is difficult for a man to speak long of himself without vanity," he said, "therefore I shall be short."[2] He did indeed make his review of his own life "short". But he did not have to fill up the fifty minutes expected of a talk to a session of the APA. So I, with no boasting rights at all compared to Hume, shall not be as brief as he was. Still worse, if Galen Strawson is on target, I shall be inaccurate. In a recent article Strawson claims that "the more you recall, retell, narrate yourself, the further you risk moving away from accurate self-understanding, the truth of your being. Some are constantly telling their daily experiences to others in a storying way . . . They are drifting ever further off the truth."[3] Well, on this occasion it is a risk I must take. And Montaigne offers permission to try. "I speak the truth," he remarks, "not my fill of it, but as much as I dare speak; and I dare to do so a little more as I grow old, for it seems that custom allows old age more freedom to prate and more indiscretion in talking about oneself."[4]

   I am honored by the Eastern Division's invitation to give this year's Dewey lecture. Having accepted it, I shall prate away, perhaps indiscreetly. The Dewey

   I am grateful to Sharon Cameron, Mary Rorty, Sarah Schneewind, Victor Gourevitch, George Kateb, John Cooper, William Mann, Larry Seagull and David Brewer for their helpful comments and suggestions.

   [1] Montaigne, *Essays*, trans. Donald Frame, Stanford University Press, 1958, "Of Friendship", p. 143.
   [2] David Hume, *Essays*, ed. Eugene F. Miller (Indianapolis, 1985.), xxxi.
   [3] "Against narrative", *Ratio* XVII.4 (Dec. 2004), 447.   [4] *Essays*, "Of Repentance", 611.

lecturer is asked to "give a talk of an autobiographical sort . . . with perhaps some account of the way in which she or he was shaped by or shaped the profession".[5] So I shall say something about what led me to work on the history of moral philosophy, some ways in which my life and changes in the profession have been intertwined, and some friends who helped me along.

I

I must begin with something about my childhood, because I think it affected the ways in which philosophy functioned as part of my life. I was born in 1930 in a large town in Westchester. My parents were secularized American Jews from families long settled in the States. They were solid Roosevelt Democrats, but not active politically. My father worked for a large corporation in Manhattan, my mother raised my sister and me, and then, during the Second World War, took up substitute teaching. Shortly after my birth we moved to Pelham Manor. It was a pleasant little suburb of tree-lined streets and separate houses surrounded by well-kept lawns and filled with white Christians. They were mostly Protestant and mostly anti-Semitic. My parents learned that they could not join the country club. I learned that I could not play with all the other kids. From time to time I was chased home from school by boys throwing stones and shouting "Dirty Jew". Boys I thought were friends had birthday parties to which I was not invited. There was a dancing class to which I could not go. Compared to what was being done to Jews in Europe, this was completely trivial. But it made me aware that I was an outsider, excluded from whatever it was that the Christian kids shared.

One thing they shared was something called Sunday School. They were not available on Sunday mornings. I would see them going into their churches, the boys in jackets and neckties, but I did not know what they did there. I belonged to no formal religious group. There were one or two other Jewish families in Pelham Manor but there was no synagogue, and my parents would not have sent me had there been one. I had no formal religious education until I was a teenager, when I was sent, along with a few other Jewish religious illiterates, to a Bible reading group run by a believing Jew.

---

[5] From Richard Bett's invitation to give the lecture.

But early on I learned from miscellaneous reading that one thing Christians were taught in Sunday school was that they were to love one another.

I could not put this teaching together with what I knew of how my schoolmates acted, and of what Germans—presumably Christians—were doing to Jews in Europe. During the war my mother's father had helped get some of our European relatives to the States, and we had them to dinner from time to time. Their presence made the persecution of the Jews more vivid than the newspapers did. But they did not talk about their plight, still less how Christianity was involved in it. Even after Laura Hobson's 1947 novel, *Gentleman's Agreement*, made American anti-Semitism discussable, I heard no one try to explain how a religion of love could cause such hatred.

I was not raised in any religion and I have never had any religious beliefs. Am I an atheist or an agnostic? It would be more accurate to say that I am just not interested in assessing religious claims to truth. I have read many Victorian sermons and a fair amount of Christian theology. But I have not been looking for a faith I could accept. My aim has been only to understand how religion and morality have affected each other. My early experiences of exclusion in Pelham Manor led me to stay away from religion of any variety. It has always been morality that interested me first.

My interest in philosophical ethics and in the relations between religion and morality is largely due, I think, to my experiences of being an outsider because of a religious moral teaching whose workings I could not understand. I cannot be sure that this was what made me a philosopher. But it certainly left me with questions. Religious believers sometimes ask whether anyone can be moral without religion. If in my childhood I could have thought in such abstract terms, I would have asked instead: how can anyone be moral *with* religion? Either question can seem outrageous to partisans of one side or the other. Between them they point to issues that have concerned me all my life.

Eventually I came to feel strongly about other issues as well. I did not experience economic hardship or notice racial prejudice during my childhood. It was only later that I became aware of the injustices to which poverty and race give rise. If I have come to be moved by these issues it has been because anti-Semitism first taught me that however smooth the social surface may seem, there are terrible things going on beneath it. Being Jewish makes me feel that I share to some extent in the vulnerabilities of the oppressed.

In the early 1930s, Robert Hutchins, the new President of the University of Chicago, paid a visit to John Grier Hibben, a philosopher who was then President of Princeton. Hutchins asked how many Jewish students Princeton had; Hibben told him there were about two hundred. Hutchins writes that he then

asked about the number the year before. Hibben responded: "About two hundred." I said that was very odd and asked how it happened. He said he didn't know; it just happened. Mrs. Hibben was outraged and said, "Jack Hibben, I don't see how you can sit there and lie to this young man. You know very well that you and Dean Eisenhart get together every year and fix the quota."[6]

—the quota that kept the number of Jews so steady.

Jewish quotas were introduced in the 1920s by the President of Harvard, A. Lawrence Lowell. One of the main changes in academia since I entered it has been their disappearance and the coming of large numbers of Jews, as students, teachers and administrators. I wish that academe had done as well with racial minority members and with women. There are many more of both now than there were in 1947, but philosophy as a field has lagged behind other disciplines. Despite this, women and African-Americans have become noticeable and notable contributors to philosophy. That is a second major and happy change I have lived through.

In 1947, however, when I applied for admission, Harvard still had a Jewish quota. There is some evidence that the quota kept me out. I went instead to Cornell. And that is where philosophy entered my life.

I had never given the subject any thought. In high school I read Thoreau's *Walden* and was cheered by its encouragement of individuality, but I read nothing else even remotely philosophical. During my Freshman year I took no philosophy courses. I went to Cornell intending to be a chemist. In my first chemistry course, however, the woman who was my lab partner lost patience with me. My clumsiness, she said—quite rightly—was wrecking our lab work; I should go away and just use her results. While I was realizing my scientific ineptitude I was reading the *Book of Job* for a literature

---

[6] Jerome Karabel, *The Chosen* (New York: Houghton Mifflin Co., 2005), 128. This important book is full of information on the history and practice of Jewish quotas. For a study of Yale and selective admission, particularly in the latter half of the twentieth century, see Joseph A. Soares, *The Power of Privilege*, Stanford University Press, 2007. Soares argues that although Yale's President Kingman Brewster dropped the Jewish quota, he continued longstanding practices favoring a socio-economic elite, disguised as meritocracy.

course. That led me to write a term paper on the problem of evil. I was fascinated by the conceptual issues (as I later learned to call them). Next term I applied for an experimental tutorial program started by, among others, Max Black. The applicants were told that it did not matter what they majored in, as everyone would take the same courses. Many applicants wanted to major in literature, only a handful in philosophy. So I said, opportunistically, that I would be a philosophy major. I was accepted as such, and in the Fall of 1948 I took my first philosophy course. It was on moral philosophy, it was taught by Stuart Brown, and in it I read Kant's *Groundwork* for the first time. I did not understand it, and I have been struggling with it ever since. But I could see even then that it was addressing my concerns about the relations between morality and religion. I began to think that my decision to major in philosophy was luckier than I could have hoped.

I explored the subject with growing ardor. A third or more of my work was in philosophy courses. In my senior year I had a graduate seminar with Brown on the British moralists, another with Arthur Murphy on recent ethics, and a reading course, again with Murphy, on Kant. I studied history of philosophy and history of political thought with Gregory Vlastos. And I did logic and philosophy of language with Max Black. He was my advisor. I lived in dread of him. He was often cruel and cutting in his remarks to students. Nonetheless he was a most effective teacher. I learned far more about writing from him than from the required writing course. I was not good at logic—not at all—but out of pure terror I did well even in Black's advanced logic class. I had occasional nightmares about him for the next twenty years.

The few philosophy majors were a congenial group. I got to know some of the graduate students as well, in particular Bill Gass, who had not yet begun writing fiction. And I started going to the departmental colloquium. One day, during my junior year, it was attended by an elderly man in a plaid shirt. I thought perhaps he was the father of a faculty member. After a paper, there was silence. Finally the elderly man started to talk. He went on for about half an hour. I could not really follow his remarks, but I noticed that Black had not lit his usual cigar and that everyone was listening attentively. After the stranger stopped, Black said: "Professor Wittgenstein just suggested that . . . ". I had heard that name, though I knew nothing about him. (This was before the publication of *Philosophical Investigations*.) As we left after the discussion Black turned to me and said, ponderously, "Remember this meeting, my boy."

Aside from the philosophers, the student with whom I spent most time was one I had met early in 1948, Harold Bloom. We became close friends. I'd made the mistake of joining a fraternity, and I lived in the fraternity house during my sophomore year. Despite that I spent most of my time with Bloom. He was in the tutorial program and we had many classes together. During our junior and senior years we roomed together. He made me glad I was not studying literature. Bloom could read at an astonishing pace, with total recall; he remembered fully every poem he liked, including *Paradise Lost*; he scribbled off his term papers non-stop in long-hand and sent them to his sister to be typed without revising; and the papers kept winning prizes. At one point I was reading Popper and he was reading St. John of the Cross. One Friday evening we started arguing about rationalism and mysticism. By Sunday afternoon we decided to go a movie to take a break. Then we got thrown out of the theater because we could not stop arguing. I learned an enormous amount from Harold. After we graduated we kept on seeing one another for years, still arguing. But he went on to Yale, and I to Princeton.

II

Before getting to Princeton I had to explain to my parents that I was intending to become a philosophy professor. My father had not gone to college, and my mother went only long enough to get a teacher's licence. They had no idea of what philosophy was; and I could explain neither it nor my fascination with it to them—nor, indeed, to myself. My father asked if I could earn a living at it. I could only reply that Max Black earned enough to support a family so I supposed I might do so too. With some bemusement but no hesitation my parents backed my decision, and supplied enough money to supplement the meager fellowship I had been offered.

Princeton was still a men's school when I arrived in 1951; chapel was still required of undergraduates; the Graduate College, known as Goon Castle, was a long walk from the meagre opportunities for relaxation that the village offered; and New York City was too distant and too expensive to be any help. The Philosophy Department was at a low point in its history. I did not find there teachers as good as those I had at Cornell. But Princeton was not all a disappointment. It was there that I first saw wisteria in full bloom; and there that I met Rogers Albritton.

The wisteria grew on the walls of the Graduate College; its fragrance attracted bees in the daytime, and lonely graduate students in the evening. A love of wisteria has stayed with me ever since. And so has the effect of knowing Rogers Albritton. He was still a graduate student, but even then the magical philosophical interlocutor that I—and everyone else—found him to be in later years. He seemed able to divine my philosophical perplexities before I knew what they were, and to go a long way toward untangling or just getting rid of them. He attended all the sessions of a seminar on sense data that Norman Malcolm gave, as a visiting professor. Rogers and Norman debated intensively and unforgettably. Each week Rogers challenged some point Norman wanted to insist on. When Norman could not reply, he would say: "I'll have to think about that." Then the next week he would give an answer. He plainly had thought about the challenge. The two of them provided a model of protracted, acute philosophical debate. I got, for the first time, some real understanding of how attention to language could have important philosophical payoffs. Between them they demolished sense-datum theory.

When I started at Princeton there were only three other entering doctoral students in philosophy, and not a large number ahead of us. John Rawls had finished his dissertation just before I arrived, but was still there as an instructor for undergraduates. Despite his great personal modesty he already had an awe-inspiring reputation. He urged me one day to read Sidgwick, and I took his advice the next semester, with long-term consequences.

Most of my time was spent talking with Albritton, and with Jerry Schaffer. They and a few other students had taken a seminar with J. O. Urmson, who had been visiting the previous year. In it they had been introduced to the latest Oxford style of analysis of ordinary language. Then James Ward Smith, an assistant professor, returned from a stay in England with typescripts of Wittgenstein's still-unpublished Blue and Brown Books. The department had copies made; we got them and did our best to absorb them. The senior faculty did not join in this endeavor. Their indifference added to our sense that we were engaged in a new and exciting venture, one that could change our whole discipline.

I could not, however, understand Sidgwick's *Methods of Ethics*. Albritton was not interested in him. And the faculty were no help. Sidgwick said he was trying to reconcile the utilitarians and the intuitionists. When I asked who the intuitionists were, Walter Stace replied: "Oh, you know, Moore and Prichard." Well, Sidgwick had taught Moore but was dead before Prichard published. There was very little secondary literature on Sidgwick, so I decided that I would make him my dissertation topic. One trouble was that there was no one to direct it. In my third year C. I. Lewis came as a visitor, and I was assigned to him. He, however, perhaps in Harvard style, never said anything about the quality of what I submitted to him. After I gave him a long chapter outlining and criticizing what I took to be Sidgwick's main argument, he said only: "Mr. Schneewind, don't you believe anything?" He left me with no idea of whether or not my work was acceptable. I learned only some years later that Lewis himself was then working out a view in ethics very much like the Sidgwickian line I had criticized.

In Murphy's graduate seminar on recent ethics, which I had taken as a senior, we read Toulmin's book on the place of reason in ethics. R.M. Hare's *The Language of Morals* was published the next year, in 1952. I found "analytic ethics" less interesting than I thought moral philosophy should be; and I was repelled by Hare's claim that ethics "is the logical study of the language of morals."[7] Surely there was more to it than that? Analytic ethics was not addressing the questions about morality and religion that I thought I would find help with. I turned back to John Stuart Mill to see if he agreed with Hare on what ethics was about. It seemed to me that Mill had far more substantial moral and political aims in mind. But I did not have time to follow up on this thought. My generous third-year fellowship was running out and I had to find a job. Morris Lazerowitz and Alice Ambrose invited me to come up to Smith College for an interview. A couple of weeks later I got two job offers in the mail: one from Smith and one from the United States Army.

III

My two years in the army were spent mostly in Germany. I did clerical and administrative work, improved my German, evaded physical training and traveled whenever I could. There was almost no philosophy in my life. Sidgwick was completely set aside. But I was bothered by Morris Lazerowitz's

---

[7] R. M. Hare, *The Language of Morals* (Oxford: Oxford University Press 1952), v.

psychoanalytic interpretation of metaphysics, which he had explained to me at length during my visit to Smith. I kept thinking about the matter, so I covertly took time from my Army clerical job to read McTaggart's *The Nature of Existence*, that most metaphysical of treatises. By the end of my military service I was more or less ready to write a dissertation rebutting Lazerowitz and offering a new defense of metaphysics. Back at Princeton, John Yolton kindly agreed to read McTaggart and supervise my work. With his help and that of Gregory Vlastos, who had moved to Princeton, I was able to get a PhD by the end of my first year out of the army. In April of 1957 Warner Wick, who was visiting Princeton and along with me had been auditing Vlastos's seminar, offered me a job at the University of Chicago. In the Fall I embarked on the grown-up part of a life full of philosophy.

At Chicago, the Chairman allowed me to give a graduate seminar on Victorian moral philosophy. I began working seriously on Mill. Reading his early essays on "The Spirit of the Age" I saw that his moral thought was meant to respond to what he took as a need to rethink public morality in an age when religious certainties were fading. If he was interested in the logic of moral discourse, it was to aid his much larger project.[8] I wrote about this in introductions to two volumes reprinting Mill's shorter writings. Then Paul Edwards asked me to write several articles on Victorians for his *Encyclopedia of Philosophy*, including a long one on Mill. I was also asked to write a book on the cultural and religious backgrounds of Victorian literature.

When I tried to understand Sidgwick the next time around it was by taking a detour: finding out who those intuitionists were and what they were getting at. Chief among them was William Whewell. I had found his major work in ethics by sheer chance, in a used book store in New York, before I had ever heard of him. Whewell was not an easy read, but his opposition to utilitarianism was evident. Sidgwick was widely supposed to be giving the finest account of classical utilitarianism. It baffled me to find that he himself insisted that he was not defending utilitarianism. He was just examining common-sense morality. Why was he doing that? Why did utilitarianism nonetheless matter so much to him?

What I discovered from my round-about reading was that there were a number of Cambridge Anglicans—Whewell among them—who believed that evidence for God's existence could be found in the historical development

---

[8] See my "Introduction" to *Mill's Ethical Writings* (New York: Collier Books 1965), 13–17.

of ordinary moral consciousness. That development, so they claimed, was a progressive revelation of God to mankind. Sidgwick had suffered a classic Victorian loss of his childhood religious faith. His examination of common-sense morality—so I thought—made sense as an effort to test this Anglican claim. Was the conventional morality of plain unphilosophical people a site of progressive revelation? Was it coming ever closer to the ethics of Christianity?

The Cambridge Anglican claims about morality and revelation turned out to be the clue to Sidgwick's thought that I needed to get started on a book. Sidgwick's work, like Mill's, made much better sense to me when I could see how his arguments and positions were responding beyond philosophy to problems he saw in the culture of his own society. This insight, as I took it to be, shaped all the rest of my work. Like everyone else with an analytic background, I had had no training at all about how to work on the history of philosophy. Now I was learning that doing the history of moral philosophy required knowing a great deal about the philosophical, religious, and cultural contexts in which major works were written. Only so, I thought, could I grasp fully what the philosopher was doing, what were the problems he or she thought had to be addressed, and what lines of thought were or—more importantly—were not to be taken up and carried further. When I first met Quentin Skinner, many years later, I was already trying to understand the history of moral philosophy in ways similar to those he has so brilliantly defended for the history of political thought.

Mill's early work was not in print, so I was lucky that the libraries I could use enabled me to find it in the publications in which it first appeared. If I had not stumbled on to the Whewell book I would have lacked an absolutely necessary resource for my Sidgwick work. It is a book that many libraries, even at good universities, do not have. Those were primitive days. There were no skateboards, no cell phones, and no internet. There were also no modern editions of Hobbes or Locke or Hume. There were almost no reprints of minor writers, who were to be found only by hunting in used book stores (I enjoyed that hunting to excess). The *Wellesley Index to Victorian Periodicals* had just come out. John Robson's great edition of John Stuart Mill had just been started. Machine-searchable and web-based texts were not even dreamt of. One of the most significant changes in philosophical research in my life-time has been the increase in the accessibility and accuracy of historical texts and commentaries on them. It has totally transformed historical research. The problem now is not mainly to get the material. It is what to do with so much of it.[9]

At Chicago I had my first experience of job placement from the faculty side. In 1958 I was sent to the Western Division meetings (as they were then called) carrying an armload of student folders and trailed by a flock of hopefuls. More often than not they had just finished their Master's degrees; only a few had begun doctoral dissertations. Those were the glory days when undergraduate enrolments were expanding rapidly and demand for teachers—any plausible teaching bodies—was high. The reception on the first evening was called "the smoker", and almost everyone smoked. Placement officers roamed the floor, buttonholing colleagues who were seeking new employees. Personal acquaintance was very important. Interviews were conducted on the spot, or a day later. A good placement officer would be able to get a student five or six such contacts during the evening. That was the old-boy network.

It was fun working it all. But it seemed unfair to me. Those without well-connected protectors did not have much of a chance. Albritton, Rawls, Malcolm, and some six or eight more of the well-connected at big universities began worrying about the unfairness of the procedure. Open advertisement of vacancies was the obvious solution; and some major departments agreed to advertise if the others would. Where could ads be published? I was deputed to check out costs at the *New York Times*. I quickly learned that the price per vacancy notice was prohibitively high. Moreover, most of the senior well-connected professors liked the existing system and objected to changing it. What? Actually publish salaries? Give up our power over the young? Shocking! It was only some years after our feeble first effort that the

---

[9] The increased ease of access to historical sources has been only a part of the massive growth in philosophical publication. It is hard to get accurate figures but one well-informed estimate is that more than 5,000 philosophy titles are published yearly. There are now over 150,000 philosophy books. Some 500 journals are indexed annually in *Philosopher's Index*, which does not claim to cover everything. There are over 170 active philosophical societies in the United States alone. (I am indebted to George Leaman, Director of the Philosophy Documentation Center, for these figures.)

All this is part of an overwhelming flood of new publications in general: Robert Darnton tells us that in 2006, 291,920 new titles were published in the USA alone. (*New York Review of Books*, June 12, 2008, p.78) Internet publishing and reviewing are expanding so rapidly that any numbers I might report would be out of date. Myles Burnyeat writes of the 1960s as a time before philosophy "fell apart into specialisms". (See his introduction to Bernard Williams, *The Sense of the Past* (Princeton, NJ: Princeton University Press, 2006), xiii) Now we mostly ignore each others' areas: hard enough to keep up with one's own.

APA took on the task. The first issue of *Jobs in Philosophy* (as it was first called) came out in 1971.[10] It signaled a major change in the profession.[11]

IV

In 1960, for family reasons, I needed to be on the East Coast. Princeton kindly gave me a one-year position. Then, thanks to a paper on McTaggart, I was given a junior appointment at Yale, which later awarded me a third-year paid leave. One February morning in 1963 I asked John Smith, the department Chair, if I would be reappointed afterwards. "No", he replied, "but you must remember that Yale is a good place to leave from." He was quite right. At noon the same day I had lunch with Wilfrid Sellars, who offered me a tenured associate professorship at the University of Pittsburgh. I got married the next day, and in the Fall of 1964, after a leave, I began a happy decade in the growing Pitt department. Under the genial leadership of Kurt Baier, the department developed a stronger sense of common

---

[10] I am indebted to Janet Sample of the APA National Office for this and other information presented here.

[11] I do not think the change was motivated solely, or even mainly, by mounting awareness of the unfairness of the old-boy system. The number of academics was growing rapidly all over the country, as was the number of colleges and universities. The old-boy system could not handle so many places and people. Consider only the numbers of registered philosophers: in 1948 the APA had just over 1000 members. Divisional meetings could be held on college campuses: I remember going to one at Yale in 1960. But that turned out to be the last Eastern Division meeting held at a university. The next year we met in Atlantic City, and since then it has been hotels in big cities every year. (The *Journal of Philosophy* used to print the programs and papers for the Eastern Division meetings. It records the location of our meetings each year.)

By 1978 there were over 5000 APA members; now we have about 13,000. Regular session programs have gotten ever longer; and in 2007 more than eighty satellite organizations held their meetings when this Division met. Little wonder that arranging meetings has become a major chore. (Thanks again to Janet Sample, and to Linda Smallbrook, for help here.)

In 1949 there were about 1850 institutions of higher education in the United States. Fifty years later there were over 4000. Community colleges and more recently for-profit institutions multiplied, and with them the numbers of faculty who had neither tenure nor prospects of getting it. In 1975 over 55 percent of faculty were either tenured or on tenure track. In 2005 only some 30 percent were in that happy position. (For data, see Jack H. Schuster and Martin J. Finkelstein, *The American Faculty* (Baltimore, MD: Johns Hopkins University Press, 2006).) Professors at the elite universities mostly did not know those at less prestigious schools. As jobs became scarcer, however, it became increasingly important for even the top universities to be able to place their students outside the old charmed circles. Advertising became standard, as did arranging interviews through official placement services. Smoking ceased at the smokers—sorry, "receptions". If personal contacts did not vanish so completely, they mattered much less. The numbers to be served, and an increasing concern about sexual harassment and gender and racial prejudice, forced everyone into the much more impersonal system we now have.

involvement in philosophy and in teaching than I have ever found anywhere else. Baier asked me to propose a program for majors. With much
trepidation—recalling the rancor I had seen at Yale—I presented a detailed
plan. To my astonishment everyone just agreed that we should adopt it. Of
course we had philosophical disagreements. But they never carried over
into policy matters affecting everyone. Moreover, the department encour-
aged my research and waited patiently for a book on Sidgwick.

Meanwhile, civil rights movements and the Vietnam War were changing
the atmosphere for moral and political philosophy. Analytic ethics was
failing to interest undergraduates. Rawls' *A Theory of Justice* showed that
philosophers could leave moral language aside and work again on more
substantive issues. The development of what is called applied ethics began in
the 1970s. Philosophical discussions of the Vietnam War, and then of the
oppression of black people and of women, further enriched the field. A J.
Ayer's *Language, Truth, and Logic* was one distinctive mark of a definite era in
modern moral philosophy. John Rawls' *A Theory of Justice* initiated and
deeply influenced another.[12] That shift was the most significant change in
philosophical ethics that has occurred during my career.

I was already too deep into historical work for the new developments to
redirect my research. But something altogether outside academe altered my
life. In 1967–68 my family and I were in London where I was writing about
Victorian thought. On April 4, 1968, Martin Luther King was assassinated.
His death was the most important single event in shaping the place philosophy had in my life thereafter.

King's assassination made me ask myself if writing philosophy and its
history was doing enough—was doing anything—to help with the social
and political problems that were emerging in the turmoil at home. It seemed
clear to me that it was not. I knew I had no gift for real-world politics. No
matter what I might try, I would look and sound like a professor—not great
for getting votes. I had no idea what I might do. But I felt ever more
strongly that I ought not to remain just a passive observer.

Events provided me with what looked like an opportunity. Student protest
movements continued in 1969. During the spring, Pitt undergraduates

---

[12] See my "Ethics: Hooker to Ayer" in *Continuum Encyclopedia of British Philosophy*, Thoemmes
Continuum 2006, vol. 2, 1014–22. I have discussed the impact on philosophical ethics of Rawls, the
Vietnam War, and the civil rights movements of the 1970s in "La philosophie morale au xxme siecle", in
Un siècle de pilosophie 1900–2000, (Paris: Gallimard, 2000), esp. 150–9.

took over a new lecture hall built on a main street. I had been departmental major advisor, and some of the student leaders were my advisees. The Chancellor's deputy asked me to negotiate with them. After some difficulty, I got the administration to offer them the use of an older, less noticeable building for their headquarters and teach-ins. With more difficulty I got the student leaders to accept the offer. Three days later the Chancellor asked me to become Dean of the undergraduate college at Pitt. I had never considered administration and I had no experience of it. Still, Pitt educated poor kids. Helping them get a good education would not alone solve America's major problems. But I thought it might be doing something for social justice; and in that naive belief I accepted the position.

Much of my four and a half years as Dean was spent on efforts to change the curriculum and improve teaching. Cheered on by students, I led my faculty allies in battle against other faculty who I thought were impossibly conservative. We dropped the foreign language requirement, opened the way to new multi-disciplinary and "self-designed" majors, introduced new grading options, allowed students to vote on college policy matters, started having student evaluations of teaching . . . in short, carried out what was in fact the commonplace radical revisionism of the period. My partisans and I were sure our struggles were improving undergraduate education by giving the students far more freedom than they had ever had. A Hispanist political radical—Roberta Salper—whom I had appointed assistant Dean, asked me to help her start a Women's Studies program. Shaped as I was by John Stuart Mill's views on women, I agreed. We aroused much opposition, but we won. We created the first such program at a large public university, and it is still functioning. The nascent program in Black Studies similarly aroused much opposition, and I did what I could to help it survive. That program also lasted. Most of the other changes I convinced the College to adopt, however, disappeared to no one's regret, under my successor. I consoled myself with the thought that at least I had made the faculty think anew about their teaching.

My own interest in teaching had begun in graduate school. Although I had a third-year fellowship, I wanted to teach, and I convinced the Princeton department to allow me to take a section in Walter Stace's big introductory course. When I asked to teach again in the spring, the Chair decided that I ought to be paid. I think I was the first TA, at least the first paid TA, the Princeton department had ever had.

The job of undergraduate Dean made me realize that my own teaching, though well enough received, was quite conventional; and I tried to change it. More importantly, it made me aware that the APA itself had voiced no concern about teaching at all. In the early 1970s Maurice Mandelbaum, whom I had met while I was at Yale, was Chair of the APA Board of Officers. Despite his doubts about whether there was any need or any future for a committee on teaching, he gave me permission to form one on a temporary basis. Its innovative divisional programs were exceptionally well attended. After a year the Board conceded that the committee had some use, made it permanent, and appointed me its Chair.

At the end of my term as Dean my family and I returned to England, where I finally started writing that book on Sidgwick. By the time we came back home, I had nearly finished it. I let it be known that I was interested in administrative work at a school that aimed to educate poor city students. After some months, Jacqueline Wexler offered me the job of Provost at Hunter College CUNY. We moved to New York just as the city headed into a fiscal crisis. My first job as Provost was to cut the faculty by 10 percent. Then finances got much worse. I set up a committee to steer us through the mess. We decided that we would have to cut whole departments, and not rely on piecemeal attrition. It was impossibly difficult to decide which departments to close. At a climactic meeting the committee told me that they had voted to have me alone make the final decisions. On the day I was to tell the President what I had decided, she informed me that the state was going to take over the whole of CUNY. We would not have to make the cuts. "So don't tell me what you decided," she said, "I never want to know." I never told her.

I lasted six years in the Provost's job. During the first year I finished the Sidgwick book. As I had done when I was a Dean, I continued teaching. While giving a graduate seminar in 1977 I came across Josef Schmucker's study of the development of Kant's ethics. It had not been reviewed in English. I thought perhaps I'd write a critical essay about it. What I wrote, instead, after many years, was *The Invention of Autonomy*.

As Provost, I found what I had already experienced as a Dean: that many faculty members are not only distrustful but disdainful of administrators. I recall visiting a Pitt historian and his wife one afternoon right after becoming Dean, and being dismayed when she asked whether we could still be friends. Most faculty members are quite incompetent about the practical affairs of a university, and most have absolutely no idea of the budgetary and political problems from which the administration shields them. Their uninformed contempt for administration unfortunately tends to steer away from it the few faculty members who might do it well.

Besides teaching and mulling over a Kant project, there were additional ways in which philosophy occupied much of my life while I was Provost. I began to do a substantial amount of reviewing of grant and fellowship applications in philosophy. In 1977 I served for the first time on an external review committee for a philosophy department. In the next dozen or more years I chaired or worked on over twenty such reviews. One of the visiting committees I chaired examined the Johns Hopkins department. Eventually it accepted the committee's recommendation that it hire an outside person as Chair. In 1980 I was offered the job. Jacqueline Wexler had left Hunter. Donna Shalala, the new President, was not comfortable with me, nor I with her. In over ten years of administration I had accomplished little more than helping to keep two worthy colleges going through difficult times; but I felt I could return to the professoriate without the uneasy conscience that had led me to move out of it. In 1981 I joined the Hopkins faculty.

V

We spent some twenty-three years in Baltimore. Managing the department was not onerous. The university was generous with time and money for research; and I obtained fellowship support as well. I wrote most of *The Invention of Autonomy* at the Center for Advanced Study in Stanford, a marvelous haven of assistance and intellectual camaraderie. I finished it with further assistance from Hopkins in 1996. But my administrative travails were not over.

In 1994 I was elected Vice-President of our Division, and that, of course, led to the presidency for 1995–96. A few years later I was astonished to be asked if I would stand for election to the Chair of the National Board of the APA. I wanted to decline. I did not think I was of the philosophical eminence of those who had held the position previously. But knowledge-able friends, while not denying my point, said that the Board at this juncture urgently needed someone with administrative experience. And the Board Chair had to be a past divisional President. I felt indebted to the APA, and I agreed to stand. I was elected to what turned out to be the most nerve-wracking position I have ever had.

In 1998 the most pressing problem for the national office was one of personnel. Philip Quinn, the then Chair, told me that the members of the office staff were having trouble working together. The animosities were so great that it looked as if the collapse of the whole APA national operation was a real possibility. In cutting the budget at Hunter, I always worked as part of a large organization with many others sharing the burdens. I had no such support at the APA. A few of the divisional officers—particularly Bill Mann and Robin Smith—were helpful, and the staff who stayed after I made some personnel decisions were admirably loyal. But I felt that the burden of keeping the organization going was basically mine. I usually sleep soundly. I had one or two bad nights during the financial crises at Hunter College; but I lost much more sleep over the APA.

During the early stages of this tumultuous period, I frequently drove up to the national office at the University of Delaware in Newark to cope with the most urgent issues. Then I was lucky enough to get Richard Bett, a colleague of mine at Hopkins, to take over some of the responsibilities. His splendid performance relieved me of much work. Richard, however, did not want to continue on a regular basis. It was difficult to recruit someone for so unsettled an organization, but eventually we found an excellent person to take the job: Elizabeth Radcliffe.[13] She ran the office very effectively for a year and a half, so I thought the worst of our problems were over. But then she decided to return to teaching. It was even harder this time around to find candidates for the position. Somehow we managed, and when Judith Thompson took office as my successor I thought I was handing her an organization that was at least in running order. I learned later

---

[13] Until we appointed Radcliffe, the chief administrative officer of the APA had received only a half-time salary from us. We depended on our host university to hire this officer for enough part-time teaching to make up a decent income. We learned that we could not attract anyone with that kind of arrangement. Consequently we had to raise individual member dues and renegotiate the division of income received from book exhibits. It was not exactly easy to get the Board and the Divisions to go along with all this.

Other changes needed to be made as well—part of the growing pains due to the massive increase in the number of our members. We created the offices of Vice-Chair and of Treasurer, and started the committee on diversity to represent all the increasingly numerous groups of philosophers who felt themselves to be outside the main stream of the profession. A fine report from a committee chaired by Karen Hansen helped us to make other significant changes in the way the Board worked.

that this had been a serious delusion on my part. By the time I found out, the APA was no longer my responsibility.

VI

Over the course of sixty years in philosophy I have received much help from friends and colleagues. Richard Rorty was not only my closest friend; he was—after Kant—the most important influence on my thinking. We met in 1957. It was some years before we began discussing philosophy seriously; and when we did I was already largely on his side. At Chicago and Yale I had taught Peirce and been convinced by his early anti-foundationalist arguments; and I had published a paper arguing against foundationalism in ethics.[14] Rorty admired Dewey much more than I did, and Peirce much less. We argued for more than forty years about what philosophy—particularly moral philosophy—might do, and about the value of Kantianism. He frequently convinced me; I rarely managed to change his mind.[15] I think we both found our endless conversations edifying, as he would have said.

Mary Mothersill joined the Chicago Philosophy Department while I was there. In her uniquely droll and astringent way she provided me with much-needed guidance as well as encouragement. It was from her that I first learned of the very hard time women encountered when trying to pursue a philosophical career. We kept in touch over the years, and she never stopped advising and encouraging me.

John Rawls introduced me to Derek Parfit at an APA meeting in the early 1970s. When I was working on Sidgwick, Parfit's guidance was invaluable. He had already begun the thinking that led to his powerful *Reasons and Persons*, for which he had found Sidgwick very stimulating. He opened my eyes to much about Sidgwick's arguments that would otherwise have escaped me altogether. Rawls himself was also a constant source of support in my historical endeavors. He was always my ideal reader. His approval of my two books was the best reward I could have gotten.

---

[14] "Moral Knowledge and Moral Principles," delivered at the Royal Institute of Philosophy, London, Nov. 1968; published in *Knowledge and Necessity*, ed. G. N. A. Vesey (London: MacMillan, 1970).

[15] For a snapshot of our last conversations, see my essay on Rorty's ethics, and his reply, in the forthcoming Library of Living Philosophers volume on him.

I have already mentioned the support and encouragement I received from the Pitt department. Once John Cooper joined it, he and I became close friends. For years now I have relied on him for instruction and correction when I have rashly tried to write about ancient moral philosophy. Moreover, he took on the thankless task of being Vice-Chair of the National Board of the APA. His shrewd and level-headed advice on APA matters was of inestimable value.

For about ten years at Johns Hopkins I had the great benefit of the company of David Sachs. Upon learning that I had read all of Pufendorf's massive treatise on the law of nature and of nations he told me that I had a greater capacity for enduring boredom than anyone else he had ever met. Nonetheless, he patiently read my drafts, always seeing what I was trying to do and unerringly pointing out where I was failing to do it. I have always regretted that he did not live to shred more of my early efforts to get straight about Kant and his predecessors.

Along with all this help there were occasional personal discouragements. Warner Wick at Chicago said emphatically, in my hearing, that no one not raised as a Christian could really understand Christian thought. Derek Parfit relayed a remark by John Plamenatz, the Oxford historian of political philosophy, to whom he described my Sidgwick project. "No one can write such a book," Plamenatz said. Many years later I was introduced to the distinguished German Kant scholar Konrad Cramer. On hearing my plans for a book on Kant and earlier moral philosophy, he replied instantly: "Aber Herr Schneewind, so einen Buch können *Sie* bestimmt nicht schreiben".[16]

Remarks like these helped teach me a lesson everyone should learn: that one often has to ignore advice from one's elders and betters. What mattered more to me than such personal road-bumps was the general low esteem in which history of philosophy was held by philosophers. Quine thought historical work a waste of time for anyone seriously interested in philosophical problems. There were often-told tales of anti-history slogans on some office doors in major departments. The attitude was made vivid to me quite early in my career in a casual remark by William Frankena when I was talking with him at an APA meeting. I told him how much I admired his essays on the British moralists, and reported that Dick Brandt thought he

---

[16] "But Mr. Schneewind, *you* certainly can't write a book like that."

was going to expand them into a book. "Just like Brandt," Frankena snapped, "suggesting that I'm giving up philosophy and turning to history."

I was already sure that Frankena's disparaging contrast between doing philosophy and studying its history was misguided. I had no doubt that doing history of philosophy properly requires a philosophical understanding and assessment of what past thinkers have said. My own work on Mill and Sidgwick had convinced me that historical understanding was equally indispensable for any accurate reading of past philosophy. How could it be less so for our own? For a long time I felt that my historical concerns alienated me from the main stream of English-language philosophy. But in recent years anti-historical bias has noticeably decreased. A great deal of significant historical work has been published, including studies of neglected and "minor" past philosophers. More and more philosophers are realizing that their own work is as historically situated as that of the past major figures on whom we continue to comment. I take this to be at least the start of one more significant shift in professional philosophy, and I am happy to have made a small contribution to it.

J. B. Schneewind
Johns Hopkins University

J. B. Schneewind: Bibliography

Books

Backgrounds of English Victorian Literature. (New York: Random House, Inc., 1970).

Sidgwick's Ethics and Victorian Moral Philosophy (Oxford: Clarendon Press, 1977); repr., 1986.

The Invention of Autonomy: A History of Modern Moral Philosophy. (Cambridge: Cambridge University Press, 1998). Transl. into French (2001), Portugese (2001), Romanian (2002); Japanese (forthcoming), Spanish (forthcoming), Chinese (forthcoming), Korean (forthcoming).

Essays on the History of Moral Philosophy. (Oxford: Oxford University Press, 2009).

Anthologies and Editions

Mill's Essays on Literature and Society, ed. and introd. J. B. Schneewind (New York: Collier Books, 1965).

Mill's Ethical Writings, ed. and introd. J. B. Schneewind (New York: Collier Books, 1965).

Philosophic Problems: An Introductory Book of Readings, Edited by M. Mandelbaum, F. W. Gramlich, A. R. Anderson, and J. B. Schneewind, 2nd edn. (New York: Macmillan Co., 1967).

John Stuart Mill: An Anthology of Contemporary Opinion, ed. and introd. J. B. Schneewind (New York: Doubleday and Co., 1968).

David Hume, *Enquiry Concerning the Principles of Morals*. Edited and with an introduction by J. B. Schneewind. (Indianapolis: Hackett Publishing Co.), 1983.

Philosophy in History, Essays on the Historiography of Philosophy, eds., Richard Rorty, J. B. Schneewind, and Quentin Skinner. (Cambridge: Cambridge University Press, 1984).

Moral Philosophy from Montaigne to Kant, ed. J. B. Schneewind. 2 vols. (Cambridge: Cambridge University Press, 1990). Reprinted in one volume, 2002.

John Stuart Mill, *Basic Writings: On Liberty, Subjection of Women, Utilitarianism.* Introduction by J. B. Schneewind. (New York: The Modern Library, 2002).

Edited

Victor Lowe, *Alfred North Whitehead: The Man and His Work*, vol. II. ed. J. B. Schneewind (Baltimore: The Johns Hopkins University Press, 1990).

Reason, Ethics, and Society: Themes from Kurt Baier, with his Responses. ed. J. B. Schneewind (Peru, IL: The Open Court, 1996).

Giving. Western Ideas of Philanthropy, ed. and introd. J. B. Schneewind (Bloomington: Indiana University Press, 1996).

Immanuel Kant: Lectures on Ethics, eds. Peter Heath and J. B. Schneewind. Introd. J. B. Schneewind, trans. Peter Heath (Cambridge: Cambridge University Press, 1997).

Teaching New Histories of Philosophy. Proceedings of Princeton Conference 2003, ed. J. B. Schneewind (Princeton University Center for Human Values, 2005).

Articles

Review of Donald MacKinnon, "A Study in Ethical Theory", *Philosophical Review*, 69/2 (1960), 259–62.

Review of Dorothea Krook, "Three Traditions of Moral Thought", *Ethics*, 71/2 (1961), 136–9.

"Knowledge and Choice," *Review of Metaphysics* 14 (Mar. 1961), 520–42.

"Comment on Prior's 'Limited Indeterminism'", *Review of Metaphysics*, 16/2 (1962) 374–9.

"First Principles and Common Sense Morality in Sidgwick's Ethics," 45 *Archiv für Geschichte der Philosophie* (1963), 137–156.

"Moral Problems and Moral Philosophy in the Victorian Period," in *Victorian Studies*, Suppl. (Sept. 1965), 29–46.

"Responsibilities and Liability", *Journal of Philosophy* 62.No.21 (Nov. 4, 1965), 649–50.

"A Note on Promising," *Philosophical Studies*, 17/3 (Apr. 1966), 33–5.

Articles for *The Encyclopedia of Philosophy*, ed. Paul Edwards, (New York: Collier-Macmillan, 1967):

George Eliot, vol. 2, pp. 471–2.

John Grote, vol. 3, pp. 392–3.

James Martineau, vol. 5, pp. 169–7.

J. M. E. McTaggart, vol. 5, pp. 229–31.

John Stuart Mill, vol. 5, pp. 314–23.

F. W. H. Myers, vol. 5, p. 419.

Henry Sidgwick, vol. 7, pp. 434–6.

Leslie Stephen, vol. 8, pp. 14–15.

Review of Brian Barry's *Political Argument*. *Philosophical Review*, 76/4 (Oct. 1967), 508–11.

"Whewell's Ethics," *Studies in Moral Philosophy, American Philosophical Quarterly Monograph No. 1*, (Oxford: Basil Blackwell, 1968). 108–41.

Review of Alasdair MacIntyre, *A Short History of Ethics. Philosophical Review*, (Apr. 1969), 78/2, 261–5.

"Technology, Ways of Living and Values in Victorian England," *Values and the Future*, eds. K. Baier and N. Rescher (New York: Free Press, 1969), 110–32.

"Moral Knowledge and Moral Principles," in G. N. A. Vesey ed., *Knowledge and Necessity* (London: MacMillan, 1970), 249–62.

"Moral Progress," Tenth Oberlin Conference, April 1969; published in *Society and Reform*, eds. Robert E. Grimm and Alfred F. MacKay (Cleveland and London: Case-Western Reserve Press, 1971), 3–18.

Review of Edmund L. Pincoffs, ed., *The Concept of Academic Freedom. Southwestern Journal of Philosophy* 8/2 (Summer 1977), 167–170.

Review of Maurice H. Mandelbaum, *History, Man, and Reason: A Study in Nineteenth Century Thought*, in *Philosophical Review*, 83/4 (Oct. 1974), 528–33.

"Sidgwick and the Cambridge Moralists," *The Monist*, vol. 58, No. 3 (1974), 371–404.

"Two Unpublished Letters from J. S. Mill to Henry Sidgwick," *Mill Newsletter*, vol. 9, No. 2 (Summer 1974), 9–11.

"Concerning Some Criticisms of Mill's *Utilitarianism* 1861–1876," *James and John Stuart Mill: Papers of the Centenary Conference*, eds. John M. Robson and Michael Laine (Toronto and Buffalo: University of Toronto Press, 1976), 35–54.

"Philosophy Teaching: More Questions than Answers," Report on Teaching #3, *Change Magazine*, vol. 9, No. 1 (Jan. 1977), 48–9.

"Sociobiology: The Long View," *Sociobiology and Human Nature*, eds. Michael S. Gregory, Anita Silvers, and Diane Sutch (San Fransisco, 1978), 225–39.

"On 'On Tenure'," *Philosophical Forum*, vol. 10, (1978–79), 353–9.

"What Can We Make of Sociobiology?", *Dissent*, 26/2 (Spring 1979), 240–4.

Review of William C. Spengemann's *The Forms of Autobiography, MLN* 95/5 (Dec. 1980), 1392–5.

Review of John Stuart Mill's *Autobiography and Literary Essays*, ed. John M. Robson and Jack Stillinger. *MLN* 96/5 (Dec. 1981), 1231–5

"Virtue, Narrative, and Community," *The Journal of Philosophy*, vol. 79, No. 11 (Nov. 1982), 653–63.

Review of W. D. Hudson's *A Century of Moral Philosophy, Teaching Philosophy* 5/2 (Apr. 1982), 149–51.

Review of Anthony Ashley Cooper, 3rd Earl of Shaftesbury's *Complete Works, Selected Letters and Posthumous Writings in English with Parallel German Translation. Dialogue* 22(2) (Jun. 1983), 366–8.

"Moral Crisis and the History of Ethics," *Midwest Studies in Philosophy*, vol. 8, (1983), 525–39

"The Divine Corporation and the History of Ethics," in *Philosophy and History*, eds. Richard Rorty, J. B. Schneewind, and Quentin Skinner (Cambridge: Cambridge University Press, 1984), 175–91. Translated into Spanish in *La Filosofia en la Historia*, ediciones Paidos, Barcelona, 1990.

"Applied Ethics and the Sociology of the Humanities," *Applying the Humanities*, eds. Daniel Callahan, Arthur L. Caplan, and Bruce Jennings New York: Plenum Press, 1985, pp. 71–87.

"The Use of Autonomy in Ethical Theory," in *Reconstructing Individualism*, ed. Thomas C. Heller, Morton Sosna and David E. Wellbery, (Stanford: Stanford University Press, 1986), 64–75.

"Pufendorf's Place in the History of Ethics," *Synthese*, vol. 72 No.1 (1987), 123–55.

Review of Jeffrey Stout's *Ethics After Babel: The Languages of Morals and their Discontents. Canadian Philosophical Reviews* 8/12 (Dec. 1988), 498–500.

Review of Terence Penelhum's *Butler. Philosophical Review*, 97/3 (Jul. 1988), 425–7.

"The Misfortunes of Virtue," *Ethics*, vol. 101/1 (Oct. 1990), 42–63.

"MacIntyre and the Indispensability of Tradition," *Philosophy and Phenomenological Research*, vol. 51/1 (Mar. 1991), 165–8.

"Natural Law, Skepticism, and Methods of Ethics," *Journal of the History of Ideas*, vol. 52/2 (Apr.–Jun. 1991), 289–308; vol. 88 (Aug., 1991), 422–6.

Review of Charles Taylor, *Sources of the Self, Journal of Philosophy*, vol. 88/8, (Aug. 1991), 422–6.

"Modern Moral Philosophy," in Peter Singer, ed., *A Companion to Ethics*, (Oxford: Blackwell, 1991), 147–57

Articles for *Encyclopedia of Ethics*, eds. Lawrence Becker and Charlotte Becker, 2 vols., 2nd edn 2001 (New York: Garland Publishing Co., 1991).

Common Sense Moralists, 266–9

Crusius, 362–3

History of Western Ethics: seventeenth and eighteenth centuries, 730–9

Montaigne, 1106–8

Thomasius, Christian, 1711–12

"Autonomy, Obligation and Virtue: An Overview of Kant's Ethics," *Cambridge Companion to Kant*, ed. Paul Guyer (Cambridge: Cambridge University Press, 1992), 309–41.

"Seventeenth and Eighteenth Century Ethics," in Lawrence C. Becker and Charlotte Becker, eds., *A History of Western Ethics* (New York: Garland Publishing Co., 1992), reprint of article from *Encyclopedia of Ethics* 1991.

Review of John Skorupski's *John Stuart Mill. Philosophical Review* 101/4 (October 1992), 873–5.

"Modern Moral Philosophy: From Beginning to End?," in *Philosophical Imagination and Cultural Memory*, ed. Patricia Cook, (Durham, NC: Duke University Press, 1993), 83–103.

"Kant and Natural Law Ethics," *Ethics* 104 (Oct. 1993), 53–74.

"Henry Sidgwick," in *The 1890's: An Encyclopedia of British Literature, Art and Culture*, ed. G. A. Cevasco, (New York: Garland Publishing Co., 1993), 556–7.

"Classical Republicanism and the History of Ethics," *Utilitas*, vol. 5 No. 2 (Nov. 1993), 185–207.

"Locke's Moral Philosophy," in *Cambridge Companion to Locke*, ed. V. C. Chappell (Cambridge: Cambridge University Press, 1994), 199–225.

"Voluntarism and the Origins of Utilitarianism," ISUS conference, Tokyo, August 1994; in *Utilitas*, vol. 7 No. 1 (1995), 87–96.

Cambridge Dictionary of Philosophy, ed. Robert Audi, Cambridge (Cambridge: Cambridge University Press, 1995). Articles on
Classical republicanism
Crusius
Cumberland
du Vair
Filmer
Godwin
Grotius
Human Nature
Natural Law
Prichard
Pufendorf
Scottish common sense philosophy
Sidgwick
Stephen.

"Baier's Ethics: An Historical Introduction," in J. B. Schneewind, ed., *Reason, Ethics, and Society* (Peru, IL: The Open Court, 1996), 1–19.

"Barbeyrac and Leibniz on Pufendorf," in Fiametta Palladini and Gerald Hartung, eds., *Samuel Pufendorf und die europäische Frühaufklärung* (Berlin: Akademie Verlag, 1996), 181–9.

"Philosophical Ideas of Charity: An Historical Sketch," in *Giving*, ed. and introd. J. B. Schneewind (Bloomington: Indiana University Press, 1996), 54–75.

"Kant and Stoic Ethics," in *Aristotle, Kant, and the Stoics*, eds. Stephen Engstrom and Jennifer Whiting (Cambridge: Cambridge University Press, 1996), 285–301.

"Voluntarism and the Foundations of Ethics," *Proceedings of the Ameican. Philosophical Association*, vol. 70/2 (Nov. 1996), 25–42.

"Histoire de la philosophie morale," in *Dictionaire d'ethique et de la philosophie morale*, ed. Monique Canto-Sperber. (Paris: Presses Universitaire de Paris, 1996). 651–7.

"No Discipline, No History: the Case of Moral Philosophy," in *History and the Disciplines*, ed. D.Kelley, (Rochester, NY: University of Rochester Press, 1997), 127–42.

"Bayle, Locke, and the Concept of Toleration," in Mehdi Amin Razavi and David Ambuel, eds., *Philosophy, Religion, and the Question of Intolerance*, (Albany, NY: Suny Press, 1997), 3–15.

"Korsgaard and the Unconditional in Morality," *Ethics* 109 (Oct. 1998), 36–48.

"Henry Sidgwick: Bibliography", with Bart Schultz, in Joanne Shattuck, ed., *New Cambridge Bibliography of English Literature*, vol. 4 (Cambridge: Cambridge University Press, 1999), 1580–1.

"La philosophie morale au xxe siecle: quelques contributions de langue anglais," in *Un Siecle de Philosophie* (Paris: Gallimard edns, 2000), 121–74.

"Vom Nutzen der Moralphilosophie—Rorty zum Trotz," *Deutsche Zeitschrift für Philosophie*, 48. Heft 6 (2000), 855–66

Review of Peter Singer, *Writings on an Ethical Life*, in *NY Times Book Review*, (Dec. 17, 2000), 24.

"Hume and the Religious Significance of Moral Rationalism," *Hume Studies*, 26/, No. 2 (Nov. 2000), 211–23.

Comments on J. J. Thomson, in Amy Gutmann, ed., *Goodness and Advice* by Judith Jarvis Thomson (Princeton, NJ: Princeton University Press, 2001), 126–31.

"De l'historiographie de la philosophie morale," in Yves-Charles Zarka, *Comment écrire l'historie de la philosophie?* (Paris: 2001), 171–84.

Review of John Rawls, *Justice as Fairness. A Restatement*, in *New York Times Book Review* (Jan. 24, 2001), 21.

"Why Study Kant's *Groundwork*?," in Allen Wood, ed. and trans., *Kant's Groundwork of the Metaphysics of Morals*, (New Haven, CT: Yale University Press, 2002), 83–91.

"On the Historiography of Moral Philosophy," *Rivista di storia della Filosofia*, vol. 45/2 (2003), 323–34.

Review of W. J. Mander and Alan P. F. Sell, *Dictionary of Nineteenth-Century British Philosophers*, in *Victorian Studies* vol.45, No.3 (Spring 2003), 563–6.

"Kant on the Will," in *The Will and Human Action*, ed. Thomas Pink and M.W.F. Stone (London: Routledge, 2004), 154–72.

Critical Notice of Alexander Broadie, ed. *The Cambridge Companion to the Scottish Enlightenment* (Cambridge: Cambridge University Press, 2003), *The Journal of Scottish Philosophy*, 2/1 (2004), 78–83.

"Comments on the Commentaries," reply to discussants, *Utilitas*, 16/2 (Jul. 2004), 184–92.

"Natural Law," in David E. Wellbery, ed., *A New History of German Literature*, (Cambridge, MA: Harvard University Press, 2004), 325–32

"Teaching the History of Moral Philosophy," in J. B. Schneewind, ed., *Teaching New Histories of Philosophy*, University Center for Human Values (Princeton University, 2004), 177–97

"Montaigne and Moral Philosophy," in *Cambridge Companion to Montaigne*, ed. Ullrich Langer, (Cambridge: Cambridge University Press, 2005), 207–28.

"Globalization and the History of Philosophy," *Journal of the History of Ideas*, 66/2 (Apr. 2005), 179–88.

"The Active Powers," *Cambridge History of Eighteenth Century Philosophy*, ed. K. Haakonssen 2 vols. (Cambridge: Cambridge University Press, 2006), 557–607.

Review of *Analytic Philosophy and History of Philosophy*, ed. Tom Sorrell and G. A. J. Rogers, *Notre Dame Philosophical Reviews* (Mar. 15, 2006).

"Toward Enlightenment: Kant and the Sources of Darkness," in *Cambridge Companion to Early Modern Philosophy*, ed. Donald Rutherford (Cambridge: Cambridge University Press, 2006), 328–52.

"Ethics: Hooker to Ayer," in *Continuum Encyclopedia of British Philosophy*, Thoemmes Continuum vol. 2 (2006), 1014–22.

Review of John Rawls, *Lectures on the History of Political Philosophy*, Cambridge: Harvard University Press, 2006, in *Notre Dame Philosophical Reviews* (web) (Oct. 18, 2007).

Critical Notice of Michael Gill, *The British Moralists on Human Nature and the Birth of Secular Ethics*, (Cambridge: Cambridge University Press, 2006), in *The Journal of Scottish Philosophy*, 6/2 (2008), 209–17.

"Kant on Unsocial Sociability," in Amélie Rorty and James Schmidt, eds., *Essays on Kant's 'Idea for a Universal History'*, (Cambridge: Cambridge University Press, 2009), 94–111.

Forthcoming

"19th Century Moral Epistemology," with Allen Wood, for Allen Wood, ed., *Cambridge History of Nineteenth Century Philosophy*.

"Rorty on Moral Philosophy," in Randall E. Auxier, ed., *Richard M. Rorty*, Library of Living Philosophers, Chicago: Open Court Publishing Co.

"The Classical Heritage: Ethics," in Anthony Grafton, Glenn W. Most, and Salvatore Settis, eds, *The Classical Tradition: a Guide* (Cambridge, MA: Harvard University Press).

"Kant's Criticisms of Heteronomy," in Jens Timmerman, ed., *Kant's Groundwork: a Critical Guide*, (Cambridge: Cambridge University Press 2009).

"Sixty Years of Philosophy in a Life," Dewey Lecture, Dec. 29, 2008, *Proceedings of the American Philosophical Association*, 2009.

"What has Moral Philosophy done for us . . . lately?" in James Tartaglia, ed., *Richard Rorty: Critical Assessments of Leading Philosophers*, vol. 4 (London: Routledge).

Name Index

Abraham 96

Albritton, Rogers 411, 415

Althusius, Johannes, and unequal moral ability 88

Annas, Julia 107; her reading of Kant 284–5, 290, 291

Anscombe, G. E. M xii, xiv; and neglect of virtue 104

Aquinas, St. Thomas xiii; on divine governance 99, 133, 136, 161; on virtue and law 180, 220; on not making own law 240–1

Aristotle xiv; his virtue theory 68–9, 70, 81, 129, 180; on Pythagoras 111, 115–16, 120, 173; does not deal with disagreement 200, 295, 299; on active power 345

Austin, J. L. x, 8, 46n

Bacon, Sir Francis 149

Baier, Kurt 416

Bain, Alexander 51n, 59n

Balguy, John, religion tied to morals 223, 224; anti-voluntarism 226–7; against moral need for revelation 233–4

Barbeyrac, Jean, and the Pythagoras story 115–16

Beattie, Todd 127n

Bentham, Jerem xi, 6, 22, 34, 36n, 42, 43n, 44n, 49n; emptiness of his idea of good 69, 75, 81; and equal moral ability 86, 103, 121, 122; and teaching 132, 135–8, 150, 162; as turning point 165–7, 169

Berkeley 373–5

Berlin, Isaiah 72

Bett, Richard 421

Black, Max 409–10

Bloom, Harold 410

Bossuet, Jacques-Benign 110

Bradley, F. H. 42n, 44n, 50n, 52, 58n, 60n

Brandt, R. 423f

Broad, C. D. 39

Brodie, Alexander, on enlightenment 297n

Bunyan, John 51

Burlamaqui, Jean-Jacques 161; and unsocial sociability 325–6, 329

Butler, Bishop J. 40, 74, 134, 137, 163; against egoism 361–3; and Price 376

Calvin, John 102, 136, 139; and voluntarism 203, 220, 234–5

Cherbury, Lord Herbert of, originator of moral rationalism 227; against voluntarism 228, 231

Chew, Samuel 43n

Christ, as revealing morality 113–14, 116

Chrysippus, as Jewish 119, 295

Chubb, Thomas, anti-voluntarist 229

Cicero 108, 295

Clarke, John, of Hull 229

Clarke, Samuel 91, 94; and revelation 113, 114; anti-voluntarism 209–11, 226–7, 229; plurality of basic principles 211; need for revelation 232–3, 280; on freedom 371–3; and agency 373–5; and Price 376, 379

Collingwood, R. G. 106

Collins, Anthony 227

Comte, Auguste 130

Condorcet, A. N. 307–8

Cooper, John 116n 423

Craig, Edward, on Hume against religion 222

Cramer, K. 423

Crusius, Christian, and revelation 113–14; teaching 137; and voluntarism 219; and moral necessity 253–4; moral motivation 268, 280; and freedom 385–6, 388–9; and will 386–7; and desire 387–8; motives and causes 389, 394

Cudworth, Ralph 124, 125; against voluntarism 205, 226; as originator of rationalism in ethics 206, 227, 377

Cumberland, Richard, on virtue and law 180; anti-voluntarist 208; and God's freedom 209

D'Alembert, Jean 299–300; division of mental powers 343

Descartes, Rene 82, 124; and tree of knowledge 128, 132, 149, 171; reconciles Stoicism and Epicureanism 286; on activity 345–6

Dewey, John x, 10, 134

Diderot, Denis 68, 73, 124; against Hobbes and voluntarism 205

Diogenes, Laertius 117

Donagan, Alan 107

Dupleix, Scipio, on Pythagoras 111–12

DuVair, Guillaume 88, 139

Eliot, George xi, 42, 57–61

Elton, Oliver 43n

Euthyphro 124

Falk, W. D. 47n

Ficino, Marsilio 112

Foot, Philippa, on neglect of virtue theory 177

Foucault, Michel 130, 134

Frankena, W. 423, 424

Freud 336, 337–8

Gaskell, Mrs. xi, 42; and intuitionism 55, 57

Gaskin, J. C. A., on Hume 223

Gawlick, Gunter, on Hume 223

Gay, John 22, 136; associationism and defence of egoism 363–4

Gewirth, Alan 70

Glafey, Adam, and Pythagoras 117

God, will of 22, 69, 96, 203; governance by 40, 72–5, 111, 128, 171–3, 174–5, 241; and obligation 93, 101, 102, 135, 251–2; in Divine Corporation 155–56, 158, 160, 165, 168–9; Christian view against Aristotle on virtue 181–2, 190; not under law, so will untrammeled 204–5, 216, 218; need for in ethics 206, 213–14; reason alike in God and humans 207, 208, 218; not tyrannical 225; and good life 241

Grote, John 43, 44n, 45n, 46n

Grotius, Hugo xiii; and unequal moral ability 89–90; on abrogating law 96; central issue for 97–9, 199; and sanction 102; teaching 136–40, 161, 171; on perfect and imperfect rights

and duties 184; and Adam Smith 191; and unsocial sociability 322–3, 328–9

Guyau, M. J. 42n

Guyer, Paul, his reading of Kant 279–80

Hadot, Pierre 130

Haman, J. G., against Kant 308–9

Hare, R. M. 67; and equal moral ability 87n; view of ethics 412

Hartley, and associationism 364–5

Hegel 336

Herder, G. cited 286

Herdt, Jennifer 115n

Herman, Barbara, her anti-deontological reading of Kant 280–3

Hibben, John 408

Hobbes, Thomas 73; and unequal moral ability 90; on conflict 100, 114, 121, 123; and teaching 136–40; and Divine Corporation 165–6; his religion 184; and voluntarism 203, 204, 205, 218, 219, 225; and unsocial sociability 323–4, 329, 358, 374

Höffding, H. 43n

Holbach, Paul, Baron 304–6, 318

Hooker, Richard, on divine governance 99, 150 161

Houghton, Walter 43n, 48n

House, Humphrey 43n

Hume, David xiv, 68, 73, 104, 122; and teaching 134–40; and Divine Corporation 164–66; alleged neglect of virtue 176; natural and artificial virtues 186–9; and justice 189–90; knew Pufendorf's views 186; against natural law views 193–4; and Kant 198; openness to voluntarism 211; attack on rationalism aimed at religion 222; not obviously a deist 223–4; denies moral attributes to deity 234; and voluntarism 234; implications of his sentimentalism 234; and evil 235; voluntarism or nothing 235–6; atheistic moralist 243; Kant's reply on reason as motive 268; not ascetic 286; superstition 303–4; his psychology 365–9; and will 369–70, 373, 375, 379; on brevity 406

Hunter, Ian 130

Hutcheson, Francis 46n, 104, 137, 164; criticized by Price 211; virtue central 252;

on motivation 268; and sociability 327; against Mandeville 361, 363

Hutchins, R. M. 408

Irwin, Terence 107
Israel, Jonathan 298

Johnson, Samuel, on virtue and law 180
Josephus, and Pythagoras 113n

Kant, Immanuel xi, xiv; his alleged failure 67–8, 75, 81, 85; on equal moral ability 86–7, 95, 251–3, 91–2; on supremacy of morality 96, 103; 104–5; and Pythagoras story 119–20; and teaching 132, 135–9, 150, 162; turning point in history 165, 167–9, 248; and Divine Corporation 165–6; alleged neglect of virtue 176; perfect and imperfect duties and love 195–7; duties of virtue 197; and Hume 198; against his virtue theory 199; and voluntarism 215–16, 288; originality of his ethics, and influence 239, 249; autonomy 241, 242, 249–50, 254–5, 259; free will 244; rejection of naturalism 244; on importance of happiness 245–6, 275–6, 286, 263; intuitionism 246; importance of obligation 250–1; moral necessity 253, 255–6; moral worth, rightness, goodness of states of affairs 256; right prior to good 257, 283–4; formal nature of moral law 259, 263; maxims 260; hypothetical imperative and categorical imperative 260–1; how categorical imperative works 261–3; various formulations 263–5; adequacy of categorical imperative as test 266; good will 267; reason and moral motivation 267; and respect 268; objections 269–70; justifying hypothetical imperative and categorical imperative 270–4; fact of reason 273; primacy of practical reason 274; and arguments for immortality, historical progress 275; and intrinsic value 278, 279–80; and value of lawful action 281–2; motives as nonrational forces 282; desires and happiness 283, 290–1, 292; agency 283; and Stoicism 286–91; neutrality of natural world 288–90; function of moral philosophy 292; and enlightenment 299;
and prejudice 300; source of darkness within us 300; public uses of reason 308; enlightenment and individuals 309, 311; and adopting maxims 310–11; and radical evil 312–14, 316–17; and superstition and priestcraft 314–15; and enthusiasm 316; and unsocial sociability 319–20, 329–35, 338; and unintended consequences 335–6, 339; no scientific psychology 393; and predecessors 394–5; on pleasure and desire 395–7; on freedom 397–9; testing desires 399–400; limits to knowledge 400

Kelley, Donald xii
Kierkegaard, Soren 67
King, William 203, 204
King, M. L. 417
Kleist, Heinrich von 171
Kuhn, Thomas 134
Kuklick, Bruce 150

Law, William, and Socrates story 110; and voluntarism 206; against Tindal 229–31; voluntarist view 230–1; need for revelation 231

Law, Edmund, and agency 373
Lecky, W. E. H. 42n
Leibniz, G., as teachable 136; against King 203–4; against Pufendorf, Hobbes, King 204–5; anti-voluntarist theory 207, 208, 226, 287, 288; and God's freedom 209; and suffering of the damned 211; and perfection of world 212–13; and evil 235; and Stoicism 287–88; and freedom 287–8; and harmony of universe 288–90; on desires and will 291; against separate powers of mind 343f.; against Malebranche 346f. and Wolffian view 347–8; and theodicy 351f; and freedom 352, 357, 374

Leland, John, on Bolingbroke 227
Lewis, C. I. 412
Locke, John, and unequal moral ability 90; and revelation 113–14; a criticism of 133, 149; virtue as habit of obeying moral law 179–80; and voluntarism 203, 218; on motives 282; failure of reason 302–3; on mental powers 343f. 346f; on passions and will 353–4; on freedom 354–8, 374

Lowell 408
Lucretius 321
Luther, Martin, and two kingdoms 102, 136, 139; strong voluntarist 203, 220, 234–5, 242

Machiavelli, Niccolo 139–40
MacIntyre, Alasdair, xii; his position 65–71; analysis 71–2; criticism 71–2; objections to his history 76–9; and epistemological crisis 79–81; morality as "in order" 81–3, 107; and teaching 132–3
Maimon, Salomon, on unequal moral ability 91–2
Malebranche, Nicolas 91, 138; anti-voluntarist 226; as originator of moral rationalism 227; need for revelation 232; and evil 235; on active power 346
Mandelbaum, M. 419
Mandeville, Bernard de 137, 139; and voluntarism 218; and sociability 326–7, 329; and egoism 359–61
Mansel, H. L. 43, 44n
Martineau, James 43, and n, 45n, 46n, 49n, 51n, 52n
Marx, Karl 336
McCosh, James 32, 44n, 45n, 46n
Meiners, Christoph, on Pythagoras 118
Mill, John Stuart 6, 10, 22, 34, 35, 36n, 43, and n, 46n, 48, 49n, 58n; and equal moral ability 86–7; and Socrates story 108–9, 130, 144, 412–14
Monro, D. H. 7
Montaigne, Michel de, and teaching 131–2, 135, 136, 138, 150
Moore, G. E. 43n, 124, 125; neglected virtue theory 176; on instrinic value 278, 412
More, Henry, and Pythagoras 113
Morgan, Thomas 229, morality and religion of nature 233
Moses 112
Mothersill, Mary 422

Nehamas, Alexander 130
Newton, on active power 346f.
Nicole, Jean 137
Nietzsche, Friedrich 67; his importance 70, 132–3; and unsocial sociability 336–7
Noah 110

Ockham, William of, and voluntarism 242

Paley, William 22, 34, 43n
Parfit, Derek 121, 123, 422
Passmore, John 43n
Peirce, C. S. ix, x 8
Perkins, William, virtue as habit of obeying moral law 180
Plato 117, 118, 124, 125, 217
Plutarch, on soul 289
Pocock, J. G. A. 141
Price, Richard 86; on obligation and motivation 94–5, 164; anti-voluntarism 211–13; priority of right to good 213; God and morality 214, 217, 280, 373; and agency 376–8; reason and feeling 378; and morality 378–80
Prichard, H. A. 164; neglected virtue theory 176, 412
Protagoras 108
Pufendorf, Samuel xiii, xiv 90n; on abrogating law 96, 115; teaching 136–41, 161; life 170–1; *Law of Nature* 171; obligation 172; sociability 172–3; rights 173; and duties 174; love 175; centrality of law in 183; on perfect and imperfect rights and duties 184–5, 193; and voluntarism 203–4, 225, 242; and Leibniz 205; and language 218; and unsocial sociability 324–5, 329
Pythagoras, a Jew? 110, 111–14

Quine, W. 423
Quinn, Philip 421

Rachel, Samuel, defends Aristotle against Grotius 183n
Radcliffe, E. 421
Rawls, John 132, 144; and recent Kantianism 247, 411, 415, 417, 422
Reale, Giovanni, and Pythagoras story 119
Reid, Thomas xi, 86, 95, 103; and Socrates 108; and teaching, 132, 134, 135, 137, 150, 162, 164–5; Christianity a morality of duty not virtue 179, 280; and active powers 380–2; strength of motives 383–4
Rorty, Richard 422

Ross, Sir W. D. 164; neglected virtue theory 176
Rousseau, Jean-Jacques 140; and autonomy 254; and moral necessity 255–6; and sociability 328, 329

Sachs, David 423
Sade, Marquis de 132
Santinello, Giovanni 110
Sartre, Jean-Paul 67
Schlick, Moritz 130
Schmucker, Josef xi, 419
Schneewind, J. B. ix–xv, Ch. 19 passim
Schopenhauer, and porcupines 319, 401
Scotus, Duns, and voluntarism 242
Selden, John, and Pythagoras 112–13
Sellars, W. 416
Shaftesbury, Lord 137; and centrality of virtue 252; and sociability 326, 329; and self-control 359; and egoism, 360, 379
Sherlock, William, and voluntarism 226
Sidgwick, Henry x; problem of establishing a first principle 21–4; nature of moral judgments 24–7; Dependence argument, outlined 27–9; used 29–32; relation to moral judgements 32–4; Systematization argument 34–9; problem due to Egoism 39–41, 42n, 43, 44n, 50n, 61; on ancient and modern ethics 97, 121, 129–30, 144, 220; difficulty of 411–12, 413–14, 422
Skinner, Quentin 141
Smith, John, against voluntarism as teaching servility 205
Smith, John 416
Smith, Adam, admired Grotius 191; on law and perfect/imperfect duties 191–2; on virtue and justice 192; ethics, jurisprudence, casuistry 192–3; on Cudworth 206; on God in morality 214; and hidden hand 336; on passions 370
Socrates 107, 117, 120, 124
Spencer, Herbert 10
Spinoza, Benedict 60n; on unequal moral ability 91; and obligation 94; teaching 136–41; and prejudice 299; and superstition 300–1
St. Ireneus 112
St. Paul 88
St. Augustine 96, 116, 136

St. Ambrose 112
Stanley, Thomas, on Pythagoras 111, 117
Stäudlin, Carl Friedrich, as first modern historian of ethics 118–19
Stephen, Leslie 60
Stevens, Wallace 53
Stevenson, Charles 67
Stewart, Dugald 128; on Grotius 183
Suarez, Francisco, and unequal moral ability 89; and obligation 92–3, 96, 161; and voluntarism 203

Tawney, R. H. 13
Taylor, Charles 107
Tetens, and mental powers 389–90; evidence from experience 391–2; and self-activating power 392–3; and Kant 394
Thoreau 408
Tindal, Matthew, deist opposing voluntarism 228–9, 230
Toland, John 227
Toulmin, S. 412

Vattel, Emir 161
Vico, Giambattista, and Pythagoras 117
Voltaire, and voluntarism 217, 219
von Wright, G. H., virtue theory neglected 176

Wexler, J. 419
Whewell, William 32, 40, 43, 44n, 45n, 413–14
White, William Hale xi, 42; and intuitionism 55–7
Williams, Bernard 107; and Socrates 109, 120; on ancient and modern ethics 285
Wittgenstein, Ludwig 52, 409–10, 411
Wolff, Christian, on unequal moral ability 91, 101, 244, 136; moral obligation explained 252–3; on enlightenment and clouds 297; on unity of mind 348–9; on passions and desires 350–1; and theodicy 351; and freedom 352f

Xenophon 108

Yonge, C. xi, 42; and intuitionism 54–5

Zeno, as Jewish 119

Subject Index

accountability 384, 385
action for moral, not ulterior reason 284–5
active and passive powers 345–7, 381, 384
  and self-active powers 385–6
affections 325, 326, 329, 361, 378
"affects" 350–1
agency 373–4, 375, 382, 383–4, 391
aggression 337–8
  see also conflict
aims of moral philosophy 109, 120–6
American college education: preparation for
      leadership 143
angels 99
anger 354
"anomie" 14
anti-Semitism 406–8, 423
approval 252, 263, 316, 366–7, 377
  through benevolent action 363–4
association of ideas 363, 364
atheism 171, 243, 276
authorities 87, 90, 130
  not needed for moral knowledge 249–50
  secular and spiritual 101–2
  and self-governance 102, 249
autonomy 86, 105–6, 244–5, 249–59
  and respect 268–9
  social and political implications 249–50
awareness of morality 379
  as motivation 101, 333, 335, 379

basic actions 386
beliefs
  accounts of 151–2
  changing outlooks 76–7
  and changing social conditions 14–15
  as help for misfortunes of life 300
  and moral knowledge 109
  not always based on reason 301, 302, 303
  open to criticism and revision 10–11
  religious *see* Christianity; God; religion
  and world outlook 11
benevolence 29, 30, 39–40, 137, 215, 325,
      329, 363
  and autonomy 251
  and love 366

"best of all possible worlds" 349, 351
Bible 228

casuistry 89, 179, 192–3
categorical imperative 38, 198, 261–76, 279
  adequacy as moral guide 266
  domains of right and virtue 264, 265
  formulations of 263–4
  impartiality 264
  motive for compliance 279–80, 282
  need for desires 283
  prohibitions 264
  respect 268–9, 280, 290
cause and effect 222, 346, 347, 369,
      395–6
changes in moral views 76–7, 78
character 49, 50, 51, 265
charity 185
choices 58, 272, 313, 351, 352–3, 373, 398,
      399
  of God 206, 210, 213, 288, 352
Christian Fathers 116
Christianity 68, 73–4, 88–9, 94, 96, 102
  and ancient culture 123
  and Aristotelian *telos* 73–4, 179
  and moral world 157
  morality upheld by moral
      education 143–4
  role in narrative of moral
      philosophy 111–14
  and virtue ethics 179
  see also Divine Corporation; God; religion
cognitivism 104, 134, 159
common-sense morality x, 21, 27–8, 86, 380
  adequacy of 29–30
  cases and exceptions 27–8, 32–3
    consensus about exceptions 33
  genuine knowledge 122
  intuitionism 29, 30
  and need also for fundamental principle/s
      21, 32–3
  not independently valid 21
  not precise 29
  providing rules 35
  and reason 36, 214

systematized by utilitarian principle *see*
        utilitarian principle
valid and binding 24
see also utilitarian principle
communities 66, 388
    and individuals 50, 105, 139, 309
    interaction of 78
    and self-governance/control 254
    and unrecognized groups/persons 78
    see also sociability; society
competition 320, 328, 334
    and cooperation 321
confession 89
conflict 97–100, 199–200, 320, 323
    ineradicable 98, 101
    and need for cooperation 322–6
conscience 40, 57, 72, 135, 240, 362–3,
        376, 389
    need for guidance 88–9
consciousness of law 155, 159
consensus 159
contentment 397
contracts 186
cooperation 74, 76, 153–5, 160–1, 321,
        322–6
courage 286, 308, 316
cowardice 308, 309
culture
    concealing self-governing capacity
        254
    in moral collapse 79, 81
customs 29

Decalog 121
deism 223, 227–9
    and need for revelation 231
desires 253, 256, 260, 282
    arising from instinct 366
    basic 388
    capacity for 396
    given by God 387
    not reducible to single principle 380
    for pleasure 321
    as propositions 290
    rational consistency 399, 400
    selfish and unselfish 345
    social 397
    spur to action 282–3
    strength of 374
    as uneasiness 353–4, 355, 357
    and will 258, 282, 291

determinism 50, 57–60, 247, 271–2, 345,
        370, 371
    compatible with liberty 368
    and intuitionism 58, 61
    and necessity 352
    presupposed by morality 369–70
    and scientific laws 271, 272, 287, 347,
        389
    and utilitarianism 45, 46, 58–9
disagreement/debate 66–7, 69, 71, 77–8,
        98, 199–200, 323
    and consensus 73, 78–9
Divine Corporation 153–69
    ambiguity of 157–8
    analogy of cooperative endeavor 153–5,
        160–1
    and changes in Christian and moral
        thought 161–5
    individual responsibility 153–4
    laws of nature and moral laws 155–7
    and role of supervisors 154–5
    and secular theories 165–9
duties 50–1, 74, 75
    arising from laws 174
    Christian, grounded in reason 114
    moral and legal 196–7
    perfect and imperfect 184–6, 187–8, 192,
        193, 195, 199–200

edification 130
educated clergy, need for 89
education 303, 306
egoism x, 134, 137, 350, 360, 361, 362, 364–5
emotivism 65, 67, 83
empiricism 211, 215, 225, 227, 228, 305,
        307, 380
England 298
Enlightenment 68–9, 70, 76, 135–6, 151,
        296–318
    individual and communal 311–12
    maxims 309–12
    rejecting superstition and
        enthusiasm 310–11
    and source of darkness 299–318
    varieties of 297–300
    "enthusiasm" 299
envy 350, 354
Epicureans 286, 321, 322
equity 210, 211
error 133, 305
eudaimonia 291, 295

evil 212, 213, 235, 316
  and guilt 309
  of human species 313, 334–5
exemplary persons 51–2, 54–5
experts in morality 87

faculties of the mind 343, 344
faith
  and moral religion 314
  and reason 302
fall 111, 225, 241
families 173
fear 354
fear of death 323, 358
feelings 44, 48, 196, 243, 244, 269
  aroused by moral knowledge 377
  barrier to moral merit 269–70
  need to foster 332
  order, through natural interactions
    of 368
  in Stoicism 286, 289
  worthiness of 45
fitness of things 210, 228, 229, 230, 234, 372
France 298
freedom 44, 84, 95, 210, 244, 254, 271–4
  absolute value of 279–80
  as active power 386
  allowing relationship with God 386
  and choice 58, 272, 313, 351, 352–3, 373,
    398, 399
  and determinism see determinism
  empirical evidence for 389–93, 398, 401
  experienced when we act 372
  freely given by God 372
  and God's creation 386
  no proof 271–2
  power over oneself 391
  rational 244–5
  required by morality 291, 388
  source of choice 347–8
  to make use of reason 309
freedom from interference 30
freedom in society 301, 309
freedom of thought 301
future of humanity 274, 275–6

Germany 298
giving 184
God
  able to abrogate natural law 96, 114
  absolute power of 226
  as Benevolent Author of Nature 163
  choices of 206, 210, 213, 288, 352
  and common-sense morality x
  creator of "best of all possible
    worlds" 349, 351
  creator and ruler of nature 73–5, 99, 137,
    163, 172, 204
  essential to morality 206, 213–14, 243
  existence essential to human life 171
  existence known by empirical
    evidence 225
  freedom of 209, 210–11, 371–2
  giver of purpose (telos) 72–5
  giving self-evident moral principles
    243–4
  glory of, as aim of morality 158, 163
  imprinting natural truths 133
  knowledge of as basis of morality 128,
    129
  known by reason 115–16
  love of 205, 208, 225–6, 242–3
  moral community with 204, 205, 210,
    227
  morality independent of 224
  moved by awarenes of moral
    principle 207
  and necessary moral truth 209
  and need for grace 135
  not bound by obligations 172, 204–5
  not sole cause of creation 222
  omnipotence 204
  only location of real power 212, 346
  perfection of 207–8, 209
  providence 92, 163, 212, 213–14, 274
  punishing disobedience 93, 172
  rational, governed by morality 215
  reason of, and our reason 287
  sanctioning (not making) moral
    obligation 22
  source of wisdom 110
  speaking within us 40, 56–7, 72–3,
    240
  union with 241, 386
  voluntarism xiv, 96, 136–7, 153, 202–21,
    224–7, 242, 288
    and anti-foundationalism 216–19
    and deism 227–9
    political implications 202, 205, 228–9,
      288
    and rationalism 206, 207–13, 217–18,
      219

will of
    arbitrary and tyrannical 225–6, 228,
        242, 288
    as righteous 225
    wholly active 346
    see also Christianity; Divine Corporation;
        natural law
Golden Rule 166
good 123, 241
    absence of 356
    in Christianity 241
    and control over desires 245–6
    definability 124–5
    kinds of 267, 278
    knowledge of 129
    natural and moral 278
    need of self-control 393
    pursuit of 138
    and right 212, 247, 256–8
    of this life (Montaigne) 131–2
good will 278
    value of 278
government 100, 174
    despotic rule 300–1
    from consent or contract 174
    need for 173
    for security 323–4
grace 96, 135, 137, 203, 232
    and moral effort 314–15
gratitude 30, 331
Greek philosophers 121
    Jewish influence 112–13

happiness 69, 73, 74, 96, 158, 163
    aim of God 209
    depending on reason 228
    depending on virtue 241, 245, 274–5
    distributed by merit 168
    end of God's providence 212
    fluctuating 292, 397
    as satisfaction of desires 282–3, 286
    in Stoicism 284
    as union with God 241
    worthiness of 168, 197, 275–6, 286
harmony 289–90, 349
    inner 359
hatred 332
history 276, 336
history of moral philosophy
    affected by views of modern
        morality 133

and aims of moral philosophy 120–6,
    129–30
    single aim 120–2, 123, 125, 129
    variable-aim view 125–6
approaches to 293–5
changes in moral questions 123, 126
continuities and discontinuities 124,
    152
and discipline of moral philosophy 107–8
"Eastern Countries": origins of moral
        philosophy 115, 117
Greeks 109, 117, 118
    and Christianity 111–14
in historical context 133–4, 141–2, 152
as history of epistemology and
        metaphysics 149–50
influence on developments in
        philosophy 129
and intentions of past philosophers 123–4
moral systems 13
as narrative 72, 131
    religious 110–14
    secular 115–18
    shaped in different ways 132–3
needed for understanding of modern
        morality 103–4, 106, 142
past views in present terminology 121–2
progress of 107–8, 125, 126
as tool for ethical theory 65, 80–1, 107
undergraduate courses 127–45
    Descartes-to-Kant 128
    and foundationalism 129
    Montaigne to Kant 131–8
    13 week outline 134–5
history of philosophy, value of 84–5
homosexuality 138
hope for future 274
human development, theories of 321–2
human and mechanical action 391
human nature
    animality 243, 322, 324, 334, 335
    depravity of 303, 313
    development of capacities 319–20
    displaying natural law 172–5
    distinguished by reason and language
        172
    evil/sinful xv, 111, 114, 135, 136, 303,
        313, 334–5
    God-given role of 72
    in God's image 243
    prone to conflict 99, 100, 101, 320

human nature (*cont.*)
   self-directing/controlling 188
   sociability 172-5
   in "state of nature" 173
   telos (goal) of 68, 69, 72, 76
human relations
   between strangers 48-51
   families 173
   personal relationships 37, 48-51
hypothetical imperative 260-1

impartiality 37-8, 264
imperatives 260
individual and community
      responsibility 309
individualism 65
individuals and communities 50, 105, 139,
      309
instinctive desires 366, 378
intellectual perfectionism 136
intellectualists 243-4
internal auditor 359-60
international law 322, 323, 330
intuitional morality x, 23, 29
   and determinism 58
   displayed in Victorian fiction xi, 42
   emotivist 69-70
   evidence not possible 43-4
   and free will 45, 46
   knowledge and motive 46
   shortcomings 246
   and social groups 48-51
   and utilitarianism (debate) 42-51, 53, 75,
      246
   values: moral/authoritative 45
   in Victorian fiction 54-6

Jesuits 89
Jewish influence on Greek
      philosophers 112-13, 117, 119
jurisprudence 192
just world, belief in 168-9
justice 30, 37, 181, 186, 212
   artificial 187
 ʹ respect for possessions 189, 190
   as "sacred" 192

knowledge
   from sensory experience 305
   progress of 306
   see also moral knowledge

language and concepts 52, 77, 218
law *see* natural law
laws
   contingent 216-17
   formal 259
   self-imposed 250
laws of association 365
liberalism 65, 121
liberty of indifference 369
liberty of spontaneity 369
life to come 96
   to achieve moral perfection 274-5
literature 52-3
   revealing moral outlook 53, 54
   see also Victorian fiction
love 94, 175, 184, 185, 195-6, 197-8, 338
   and benevolence 366
   as desire for good of others 208, 326,
      331-2
   and moral approval 366-7
   not a motive 366
   pleasure in happiness of another 350, 366

male rule 173
manipulative moral language 72, 77
masses, unable to follow argument 301
mathematics 301, 331
maxims 260-3, 278, 282, 290, 399-400
memory 349
metaphysics 128, 285, 289
mind, three functions of 395
modern moral philosophy
   challenges
      antifoundationalist criticism 104
      communitarian/anti-individualist
         objection 105
      neglect of virtue 104-5
      unified subject objection 105-6
   emergence from predecessors 97, 99-102
   emerging from criticism of
      voluntarism 202-3
   essential and superficial 103-4
   university courses [need for] xiii
modern morality
   in disorder 65-7, 71, 76, 77, 79
      and criteria for order 81-3
   and earlier disagreements 71
   and epistemological crisis 79-80, 81
   incoherence of 70
   interminable debates 66-7, 69, 71, 77-8
   lack of rational justification 67

and moral competence 87
and sociological discussions 71, 72
transition into modernity 69–70
monotheism 303, 304
moral awareness 377
moral competence 86–92
  not all equally competent 88–9
  seventeenth century views 87–92
moral faculty 376–7
moral judgments
  and appeal to common-sense
    morality 28–9
  binding 24
  and categorical imperative 267
  disagreement on 26–7
  and exceptions 32–3
  and moral principles 8–9
  need for evidence 43–4
  objectivity of 25–7
  supported by reason 26–7, 32–4, 38
  see also intuitional morality; utilitarian
    principle
moral knowledge
  available to all adults 86–92, 169, 228,
    244, 251, 254, 292
  clouded by sin 116
  and common-sense morality 122
  dependent on classical first principles
    4–10
  dependent on metaphysics and
    epistemology 128
  empirical evidence 209, 217
  esoteric 15–16
  and ignorance 89, 293
  inferred/not inferred 8
  lying far back in antiquity 118
  and moral progress 15
  and motivation 46, 86, 168
  and necessity of moral truths 209, 211
  need for guidance 87–92, 116
  need for testing 16–17
  not final, open to revision 15
  old as mankind 109–10
  revealed 110, 112–14, 118
  see also natural law
moral necessity 251, 258
  and scientific laws 255
moral obligation 22, 24, 29
  and conflict of impulses 27
  disagreement 30–1
  founded on reason 229

free will as grounds of 273
imposed by God 93, 172, 251–2
as means to an end 92, 93, 94
and motivation 92–5, 101, 188, 189–90,
  249
necessity to act as God acts 210
need for sanctions 92–3, 93–4, 102, 213
need for superior 92, 93, 94
obedience to God 172, 173
overriding other constraints 86, 94–5, 102
self-imposed 249, 253–4
and self-motivation 249
moral philosophy
  aims of 109, 120–6, 129
  edification 130
  error in 119, 293
  independent of theology 138
  as knowledge 130
  and leadership role 143, 145
  and natural philosophy 156–7
  providing guidance 194
  three parts: ethics, jurisprudence,
    casuistry (Smith) 192–3
  use of 292–3
moral principles 89
  applicable to all agents 206
  classical first principles required for moral
    reasoning/knowledge 4–10
  and conflict of cases 6–7
  finding suitable candidates as 9
  intuitionism 7–8
  and non-cognitive views 9–10
  single first principle 6–8, 108–9, 198
  and utilitarianism 6, 10, 198
  developed from what we know 266–7
  four main features
    foundational 4
    having substantial generality 3
    no exceptions/context free 3–4, 8
    not merely formal 4, 9
  ignorance of 89
  and moral judgments 8–9
  and moral progress 15
  and moral rules 3
  need for revision 13–14
  need for testing 16–17
  and science
    science as model for morality 10–11
    scientific laws 11–12
    theories, need to revise 12–13
  self-evident 164, 165, 243

moral principles (*cont.*)
  simple: within reach of all 115, 116
  and social changes 13–14
  see also common-sense morality;
    utilitarian principle
moral progress 15
moral world 157
morality
  human creation 241
motives 92–5, 159–61
  for compliance to categorical
    imperative 279–80, 282
  concern for good of others 194, 197–8,
    265, 267–8
  desire for good 267–8
  of God 207
  influencing actions 383
  no natural motives 189
  not causal 382–3
  in personal relationships 49
  principles as 94–5
  respect 268–9, 280, 290
  reward and punishment 92–3, 188
  strength of 383
  and subordination of motives to
    non-moral desires 334–5
  as sufficient reason for action 392
  as virtue 188–9

natural law xiii–xiv, 30–1, 72, 88, 98, 132,
    155–6, 171–5, 172–5
  bringing good of society 330
  definitions 99
  and discretion of agent 182, 192
  evidence for in human nature 172–5
  as expression of God's love 243
  given by all members of a group 240
  giving rational guidance 100
  grounding for universal laws 330
  and need for guidance 89–92
  performabilty 156, 159
  possibly abrogated by God 96, 114
  promulgated through reason 89, 240
  securing peace 323–4
  status of 158–9
  supremacy of 95–6
natural order 100
natural philosophy 156–7
nature 75, 285, 288, 289
  humanity part of 365

reducible to ideas 374–5
regularity in 292, 293, 371–2, 381
remedy for prejudices 304–5
necessity 209, 211, 375
  absolute and hypothetical 352, 388

obedience 93–4, 250, 268
objectivity 25–7
  ethical and physical 25–6
oikeiosis 289
order 31
  forms of 255–6
original sin 111, 114
others
  as ends, not means 263
  neglect of 265
  rights of 265
"ought" 22, 23, 218, 258, 260, 261

pain 356
passions 181–2, 194
  characterised by kind of good 350
  conducive to order 367
  slavery to 254, 350–1
  in Stoicism 289
paternalism 251
perfection 349, 387
  basic desire for 388
  bringing about 253, 265
  of species 330
personal relations, impartiality in 264
personality, predisposition to 334
"philosophical intuitionism" 23
physical and exemplary causes 389
pleasure 131, 138, 246, 321
  and free will 387
  intuition of perfection 349–50
  and pain 349–50
  relation to desire 396
polytheism 303–4
power 323, 354, 390
predestination 203, 228
predictability of action 49–50, 369
predispositions to good in human
    nature 334–5
prejudice 300
pride 111, 133, 366
priests and ministers
  as moral leaders 116, 144, 301, 302
  power of 307–8, 315

promise-keeping 31
property rights 173, 174, 181, 184, 187,
    189–90
Protestantism 89, 220, 299
prudence 270, 376, 384
psychological egoism 327, 362
punishment see reward and punishment

rational egoism 39–41
    and rational benevolence 39
reason
    basis for morality 67–9, 75, 206, 207–13,
        217–18, 219
        Enlightenment 68–9
    and Christianity 231–2, 302
    and deism 227–9
    and desires 258, 283
    "fact of" 273
    and faith 302
    happiness depends on 228
    ignored by many 302
    and natural law 89, 90–1
    part of human nature 397
    and predisposition to humanity 334
    and predisposition to personality 334
    prudential and practical 120, 274,
        283–4
    and revelation 114, 231, 232–3, 233–4
    as revelation 228
    sinful misuse of 111
    "slave of passions" 367, 381
    source of simple ideas 377
    and thinking for oneself 308–9, 311
    and will 244–5, 256
    see also Enlightenment
reflection 119, 120, 122, 349
Reformation 144
religion
    beliefs accepted on practical grounds
        311
    and delusion of anthropomorphism
        314
    and independence of morality 169
    natural religion 227, 232, 233
    rational and moral v. mere cult 313–14,
        315
    role in narrative of moral
        philosophy 110–14, 128
    and secularization 135–6, 220–1
    as source of darkness 299–308

"superstition" and "enthusiasm"
        299–300, 315, 316
    and use of own reason 309
    views on origins of 303–4, 305–6
    wars of 135, 171, 323
    see also Christianity; God
remorse 350
representation 386, 387, 390, 395
republicanism 139
respect 268–9, 332
    and disrespect 332
revelation 302
    and deism 228, 231
    moral need for 232–3
    need for in Christianity 231–4
    need for moral test 228
    and rationalism xiv
reward and punishment 46, 86–7, 92–3,
        168, 213
    by God 93, 172, 358
    in future life 232–3
right 22, 23, 218
    and good 212, 257–8
rights 173, 174–5, 182, 323
    perfect and imperfect 184, 187–8
    and well-being 265
role models 51–2, 54–5
Roman Catholicism 88–9, 96, 220, 299,
        304

salvation 73, 96
science
    changes 76, 80
    defeating superstition 306, 307–8
    and determinism 247
    laws of 11–12, 271
    as model for morality 10–11
    and morality 10–11, 82, 331
    rise of 136, 179
    showing truth 301, 306
    theories, need to revise 12–13
    see also nature
"scientific" morality 10
scientific psychology 331, 393
Scottish Enlightenment 297
self 103, 105–6
self-activating power 385–6, 390–3
self-awareness 391
self-concern 50, 75
self-evident axioms 373, 381

self-evident moral principles 164, 165, 212, 243
  necessary features of ix
self-governance/control 86–7, 102, 137, 249, 252
  and inner harmony 259
  and self-imposition of moral requirements 86, 249
  and self-interest 344
  through seeing consequences 252–3
self-incurred tutelage 308–9, 317
self-interest 189, 190, 193, 316–17, 322, 360–2
  and care for others 322–3, 338
  and development of society 322
  overriden by moral imperatives 339
self-love 365–6
  transferred to others 360–1
sensations 348–9, 395
"sense of the world" 53
sensibility 390
sentimentalism 134, 137, 211, 214, 234, 244, 359–60
  and sociability 326–7
seventeenth and eighteenth centuries: religious/philosophical outlook 72–5
sex 173, 337
sin 225, 241
  causing moral blindness 116, 303
slave morality 337
sociability 172–5, 319–39
  and competition 320
  first law of nature 324–5
  as imperative 324
  as love 175
  natural to humans 327–8
  prime duty 325–6
  resistance to 320, 326
  supported by sentiment 326
  unsociable sociability 319–20, 329–39
    knowledge of 333
    and predispositions to good 334–5
    and social progress 335–6
    spur to social and personal improvement 330–1
social contract 105
society
  development of 321–2
  and individuals 337–8

  need for 325
  need for transformation 328
  obligations and rights 101
  see also sociability
solitariness 320, 326
soul 331, 343, 351
  one power in 348
  representative power in 351
sources of darkness 299–318
"special joys" (besondere Freuden) 280
spirit 375, 376
spontaneity 398
statecraft 300
Stoicism xv, 88, 119, 121, 207, 284–91
  happiness 284
  harmony 289–90
  importance of metaphysics 289
  infusion of divinity 287
  and Nature 292, 293
  needs 286–7
  oikeiosis 289
  passions 289, 290
strong and weak, struggle between 336–7
"superstition" 299, 300–1
supremacy of morality 86, 94–5, 96, 102
sympathy 350, 368

taste 356
teachers 92, 116, 130
teleontology and deontology 278, 281, 293, 294
temptations 258
theological utilitarianism 22, 23, 34, 163
thinking for oneself 309–10, 316

unconditional good 278
understanding 343, 387
unified self 105–6
unintended consequences of action 336
unsocial vices 332
utilitarian principle 6, 10, 21–41
  and common-sense morality 27–8
  definitional 9, 34
  dependence argument 24, 26, 27–34
  and determinism 45, 46, 58–9
  inductive evidence needed 43–4
  and intuitionism (debate) 42–51, 53, 75
  and moral competence 86–7
  and moral experience 163–4
  and moral judgments 25–7, 164

natural value 47
possibility of proof 23–4
rational egoism 39–41
and social groups 48–51
standard method for reaching
      decisions 36–8
as supreme principle 34, 39
systematization argument x, 24, 27, 34–9
value of actions shown in results 44–5
in Victorian fiction 58–9
and will of God 22, 23, 34, 74, 163

value of being moral 84
value of history of philosophy 84–5
value of motives 44–5
varieties of morality 120–1
veracity 31, 212
Victorian fiction expressing moral
      outlooks xi, 54–61
   change of outlook 55, 56
   freedom and determinism 58–60
   utilitarianism vs intuitionism 42, 43, 57–8
Victorian moral philosophy xi
virtue xiv, 22, 66, 104–5, 116–17, 176–201
   action for good of another 265
   ancient and modern views 139–40
   artificial and natural 186–7
   as benevolence 137
   concern for good of others 194, 197–8
   and control of passions 393
   desire for general happiness 364
   in disposition of agent 177, 180
   function of knowledge 287
   and happiness 241
   and insight of agent 182, 199
   law prior to 250
   and mean of passions 181–2

motives as 188–90
natural to humans 178
as reason to act 284
recent neglect of 176–7
v. rule-centered views/natural law
      178–201
and sin 111
sociable virtues 331–2
in Stoicism 284
as struggle 199, 250, 258–9
as worthiness of happiness 168, 197, 275–
      6, 286
see also duties
voluntarism xiv, 96, 136–7, 153, 202–21,
      224–7, 242, 288
   and anti-foundationalism 216–19
   and deism 227–9
   political implications 202, 205, 228–9,
      288
   and rationalism 206, 207–13, 217–18,
      219

war 98–9, 275
weakness of man 325, 326
will
   active power of the soul 343–4
   basic laws of 260–1
   bound by necessity 253–4
   causally determined 368–9
   and constraint of desires 258
   desires adopted by 282
   determinations of 382
   good will 267, 278
   motives of actions of 369–70
   and practical reason 256
   rational 278
   see also freedom